AIA

Foundation Level

MANAGEMENT ACCOUNTING
LEARNING & PRACTICE WORKBOOK

In this edition

- A **user-friendly format** for easy navigation
- **Exam-centred topic coverage**, directly linked to AIA's syllabus
- **Exam focus points** showing you what the examiner will want you to do
- Regular **fast forward** summaries emphasising the key points in each chapter
- **Questions** and **quick quizzes** to test your understanding
- **Practice question bank** containing exam-standard questions with answers
- **Exam question bank** containing recent exam questions with answers
- **2 Mock exams**
- **A full index**

FOR EXAMS FROM MAY 2025

Second edition October 2024

ISBN 9781 0355 2574 4

eISBN 9781 0355 2602 4

British Library Cataloguing-in-Publication Data
A catalogue record for this book is available from the British Library

Published by

BPP Learning Media Ltd
BPP House, Aldine Place
142-144 Uxbridge Road
London W12 8AA

www.bpp.com/learningmedia

Printed in the United Kingdom

Your learning materials, published by BPP Learning Media Ltd, are printed on paper obtained from traceable sustainable sources.

All rights reserved. No part of this publication may be reproduced, stored in a retrieval system or transmitted in any form or by any means, electronic, mechanical, photocopying, recording or otherwise, without the prior written permission of BPP Learning Media.

The contents of this book are intended as a guide and not professional advice. Although every effort has been made to ensure that the contents of this book are correct at the time of going to press, BPP Learning Media makes no warranty that the information in this book is accurate or complete and accept no liability for any loss or damage suffered by any person acting or refraining from acting as a result of the material in this book.

We are grateful to the Association of International Accountants for permission to reproduce past examination questions. The suggested solutions in the exam answer bank have been prepared by BPP Learning Media Ltd.

BPP Learning Media is grateful to the IASB for permission to reproduce extracts from the International Financial Reporting Standards including all International Accounting Standards, SIC and IFRIC Interpretations (the Standards). The Standards together with their accompanying documents are issued by:

The International Accounting Standards Board (IASB) 30 Cannon Street, London, EC4M 6XH, United Kingdom. Email: info@ifrs.org Web: www.ifrs.org

Disclaimer: The IASB, the International Financial Reporting Standards (IFRS) Foundation, the authors and the publishers do not accept responsibility for any loss caused by acting or refraining from acting in reliance on the material in this publication, whether such loss is caused by negligence or otherwise to the maximum extent permitted by law.

©
BPP Learning Media Ltd
2024

A note about copyright

Dear Customer

What does the little © mean and why does it matter?

Your market-leading BPP books, course materials and e-learning materials do not write and update themselves. People write them on their own behalf or as employees of an organisation that invests in this activity. Copyright law protects their livelihoods. It does so by creating rights over the use of the content.

Breach of copyright is a form of theft – as well as being a criminal offence in some jurisdictions, it is potentially a serious breach of professional ethics.

With current technology, things might seem a bit hazy but, basically, without the express permission of BPP Learning Media:

- Photocopying our materials is a breach of copyright
- Scanning, ripcasting or conversion of our digital materials into different file formats, uploading them to facebook or e-mailing them to your friends is a breach of copyright

You can, of course, sell your books, in the form in which you have bought them – once you have finished with them. (Is this fair to your fellow students? We update for a reason.) Please note the e-products are sold on a single user licence basis: we do not supply 'unlock' codes to people who have bought them secondhand.

And what about outside the UK? BPP Learning Media strives to make our materials available at prices students can afford by local printing arrangements, pricing policies and partnerships which are clearly listed on our website. A tiny minority ignore this and indulge in criminal activity by illegally photocopying our material or supporting organisations that do. If they act illegally and unethically in one area, can you really trust them?

Copyright © IFRS Foundation

All rights reserved. Reproduction and use rights are strictly limited. No part of this publication may be translated, reprinted or reproduced or utilised in any form either in whole or in part or by any electronic, mechanical or other means, now known or hereafter invented, including photocopying and recording, or in any information storage and retrieval system, without prior permission in writing from the IFRS Foundation. Contact the IFRS Foundation for further details.

The IFRS Foundation logo, the IASB logo, the IFRS for SMEs logo, the "Hexagon Device", "IFRS Foundation", "eIFRS", "IAS", "IASB", "IFRS for SMEs", "IASs", "IFRS", "IFRSs", "International Accounting Standards" and "International Financial Reporting Standards", "IFRIC" "SIC" and "IFRS Taxonomy" are **Trade Marks** of the IFRS Foundation.

Further details of the Trade Marks including details of countries where the Trade Marks are registered or applied for are available from the Licensor on request.

Contents

Page

Introduction

The introduction pages contain lots of valuable advice and information. They include tips on studying for and passing the exam, also the content of the syllabus and what has been examined.

How the BPP Learning Media Learning & Practice Workbook can help you pass – Help yourself study for your AIA exams – Syllabus – Command words and learning outcomes – The exam paper

C1 Introduction to the role and nature of management accounting
1 Information for management 3
2 Cost classification and behaviour 25

C2 Cost identification and measuring costs for management purposes
3 Material costs 51
4 Labour costs 87
5 Overheads and absorption costing 109
6 Marginal and absorption costing 137
7 Activity based costing 151

C3 Introduction to costing systems
8 Process costing 173
9 Process costing – joint products and by-products 205
10 Job, batch, service and contract costing 221

C4 Information for planning and performance management
11 Budgeting 259
12 Standard costing 285
13 Variance analysis 295

C5 Information for decision making
14 Cost-volume-profit (CVP) analysis 327
15 Relevant costing and decision making 347
16 Modern approaches to management accounting 367

Answers to end of chapter questions 383
Exam question bank 501
Exam answer bank 537
Mock exam 1 559
Mock exam 2 571
Index 585

How the BPP Learning Media Learning & Practice Workbook can help you pass

> It provides you with the knowledge and understanding, skills and application techniques that you need to be successful in your exams

This Learning & Practice Workbook has been targeted at the **Management Accounting** syllabus.

- It is **comprehensive**. It covers the syllabus content. No more, no less.
- It is written at the **right level**. Each chapter is written with AIA's syllabus in mind.
- It is aimed at the **exam**. We have taken account of recent exams, guidance the examiner has given and the assessment methodology.

> It allows you to study in the way that best suits your learning style and the time you have available, by following your personal Study Plan (see page vii)

You may be studying at home on your own or you may be attending a course. You may like to read every word, or you may prefer to do a fast read through and learn through doing practice questions the rest of the time. However you study, you will find the BPP Learning Media Learning & Practice Workbook meets your needs in designing and following your personal Study Plan.

Help yourself study for your AIA exams

Exams for professional bodies such as AIA are very different from those you have taken at college or university. You will be under **greater time pressure before** the exam – as you may be combining your study with work. Here are some hints and tips.

The right approach

1 **Develop the right attitude**

Believe in yourself	Yes, there is a lot to learn. But thousands have succeeded before and you can too.
Remember why you're doing it	You are studying for a good reason: to advance your career.

2 **Focus on the exam**

Read through the Syllabus	This tells you what you are expected to know and is supplemented by **Exam focus points** in the text.
Study the Exam paper section	Past papers are likely to be good guides to what you should expect in the exam.

3 **The right method**

See the whole picture	Keeping in mind how all the detail you need to know fits into the whole picture will help you understand it better. • The **Introduction** of each chapter puts the material in context. • The **Syllabus content** and **Exam focus points** show you what you need to **grasp**.
Use your own words	To absorb the information (and to practise your written communication skills), you need to **put it into your own words**. • Take **notes**. • Answer the **questions** in each chapter. • Draw **mind maps**. • Try **'teaching' a subject** to a colleague or friend.
Give yourself cues to jog your memory	The Learning & Practice Workbook uses **bold** to highlight **key points**. • Try **colour coding** with a highlighter pen. • Write **key points** on cards.

4 **The right recap**

Review, review, review	Regularly reviewing a topic in summary form can **fix it in your memory**. The Learning & Practice Workbook helps you review in many ways. • **Chapter roundups** summarise the 'Fast forward' key points in each chapter. Use them to recap each study session. • The **Quick quiz** actively tests your grasp of the essentials. • Go through the **Examples** in each chapter a second or third time.

Developing your personal Study Plan

BPP recommends that you follow a study plan. Planning and sticking to the plan are key elements of learning successfully.

There are five steps you should work through.

Step 1 **How do you learn?**

What types of intelligence do you display when learning? You might be advised to brush up on certain study skills before launching into this Learning & Practice Workbook, but refer to the 'tackling your studies' section below which will help.

Step 2 **What do you prefer to do first?**

If you prefer to get to grips with a theory before seeing how it is applied, we suggest you concentrate first on the explanations we give in each chapter before looking at the examples and case studies. If you prefer to see first how things work in practice, read through the detail in each chapter, and concentrate on the examples and case studies, before supplementing your understanding by reading the detail.

Step 3 **How much time do you have?**

Work out the time you have available per week, given the following.

- The standard you have set yourself
- The other exam(s) you are sitting
- Practical matters such as work, travel, exercise, sleep and social life

		Hours
Note your time available in box A.	A	

Step 4 **Allocate your time**

- Take the time you have available per week for this Learning & Practice Workbook shown in box A, multiply it by the number of weeks available and insert the result in box B.   B
- Divide the figure in box B by the number of chapters in this text and insert the result in box C.   C

Remember that this is only a rough guide. Some of the chapters in this book are longer and more complicated than others, and you will find some subjects easier to understand than others.

Step 5 **Implement**

Set about studying each chapter in the time shown in box C, following the key study steps in the order suggested by your particular learning style.

This is your personal **Study Plan**. You should try to combine it with the study sequence outlined below. You may want to modify the sequence to adapt it to your **personal style**.

Tackling your studies

The best way to approach this Learning & Practice Workbook is to tackle the chapters in order. Taking into account your individual learning style, you could follow this sequence for each chapter.

Key study steps	Activity
Step 1 **Topic list**	This topic list helps you navigate each chapter; each numbered topic is a numbered section in the chapter.
Step 2 **Introduction**	This sets your objectives for study by giving you the big picture in terms of the context of the chapter. The content is referenced to the syllabus, and Exam guidance shows how the topic is likely to be examined. The Introduction tells you **why** the topics covered in the chapter need to be studied.
Step 3 **Fast forward**	Fast forward boxes give you a quick summary of the content of each of the main chapter sections. They are listed together in the roundup at the end of each chapter to help you review each chapter quickly.
Step 4 **Explanations**	Proceed methodically through each chapter, particularly focusing on areas highlighted as significant in the chapter introduction, or areas that are frequently examined.
Step 5 **Key terms and Exam focus points**	• Key terms are definitions of important concepts that you really need to know and understand before the exam. • Exam focus points highlight areas or topics that may be examined.
Step 6 **Note taking**	Take brief notes, if you wish. Don't copy out too much. Remember that being able to record something yourself is a sign of being able to understand it. Your notes can be in whatever format you find most helpful; lists, diagrams, mind maps.
Step 7 **Examples**	Work through the examples very carefully as they illustrate key knowledge and techniques.
Step 8 **Case studies**	Study each one, and try to add flesh to them from your own experience. They are designed to show how the topics you are studying come alive in the real world.
Step 9 **Questions**	Attempt each one, as they will illustrate how well you have understood what you have read.
Step 10 **Answers**	Check yours against ours, and make sure you understand any discrepancies.
Step 11 **Chapter roundup**	Review it carefully, to make sure you have grasped the significance of all the important points in the chapter.
Step 12 **Quick quiz**	Use the Quick quiz to check how much you have remembered of the topics covered and to practise questions in a variety of formats.
Step 13 **Question practice**	Attempt the questions suggested at the very end of each chapter. The AIA Foundation Management Accounting exam contains multiple choice questions only, however the questions at the end of each chapter are purposely longer style questions which are designed for you to practise some of the key concepts set out in each chapter. Some of these questions are designed to cover more than one topic area to develop your ability to apply syllabus learning. Once you have completed each set of end of chapter questions, you are ready to attempt the multiple choice questions related to this chapter which are contained in the question bank at the end of this Learning & Practice Workbook.

AIA Achieve Academy

AIA provides an interactive course of study, AIA Achieve Academy, which offers students the tools, resources and learning environment to study for the exams. The study tools include a course of study e-book, marked practice questions, marked mock exam papers and feedback and technical advice via an e-Tutor. Contact the Study Support team at: Achieve@aiaworldwide.com.

Moving on...

When you are ready to start revising, you should still refer back to this Learning & Practice Workbook.

- As a source of **reference** (you should find the index particularly helpful for this)
- As a way to **review** (the Fast forwards, Exam focus points, Chapter roundups and Quick quizzes help you here)

PQ Qualification Syllabus

The assessment requirements in the AIA exams at the Foundation, Professional 1 and 2 stages reflect a progression of cognitive levels which successful students are expected to demonstrate in satisfying each stage of the qualification. The levels progress from an emphasis on 'knowledge and comprehension' at the Foundation stage, to a predominance of 'application and analysis' at the subsequent Professional 1 and 2 stages and incorporate 'synthesis and evaluation' at the Professional 2 stage.

Indicative weightings for the cognitive levels at each stage of the qualification are defined in the following table.

Stage of qualification	Cognitive levels of learning*			Associated learning outcomes
	Knowledge and comprehension	Application and Analysis	Synthesis and evaluation	
Foundation Level	90%	10%	0%	Outcomes consistent with the International Education Standards Board (IAESB) standards
Professional 1 Level	50%	50%	0%	
Professional 2 Level	10%	70%	20%	

*The cognitive levels of learning are associated with the following:

'Knowledge and comprehension' refer to
The acquisition of concepts, ideas, terms, facts, practices and techniques in accounting and related disciplines and understanding of how they relate to the conduct, management, reporting and assessment of the activities of business and other organisations.

'Application and analysis' refer to
The ability to apply knowledge and comprehension to actual circumstances and situations and to identify constituent components involved (concepts, ideas, terms, facts, practices, and techniques) and the relationship between these elements.

'Synthesis and evaluation' refer to
The ability to bring together a variety of components in order to form a coherent whole, and to form judgements about the application of and value of those components in a particular context or for a particular purpose.

INTRODUCTION

Foundation Level Syllabus

The Foundation level examination is intended to establish that students have attained the necessary knowledge of accounting in its economic context and relevant skills to be permitted to commence study for the first Professional stage examinations of the Association. It does so by assessing students in four foundational areas of knowledge and understanding relevant for prospective professional accountants; offered within the Foundation Unit.

In designing the syllabus and the related examination papers AIA has employed 'intended learning outcomes' as the means to communicate expectations to potential students and stakeholders and to inform the specification requirements to be tested in the assessment of students.

The use of learning outcomes:

- Is consistent with what is commonly acknowledged as good practice in the higher education sector; and
- Is consistent with the approach embodied in International Accounting Education Standards

At the Foundation Levels students are expected to demonstrate that they are able to achieve the following:

Intended Learning Outcomes[1] – Description of expectations	
Foundation level	At the Foundation level students are expected to demonstrate that they: • Understand basic principles and concepts underpinning accounting and related practices in organisations • Understand the role of accounting and related practices within the financial and governance context of organisations • Know and can execute basic recording and measurement techniques relevant to accounting, management and assurance • Are able to analyse financial information and interpret it for the purpose of supporting decision making

Foundation level syllabus components

The Foundation Unit is made up of four components:

- Section A: Financial Accounting
- Section B: Corporate Governance and Audit
- Section C: Management Accounting
- Section D: Business Management

Relationship to Qualification Structure

[1] The description of the levels of proficiency supports the IAESB's use of learning outcomes in its International Education Standards (IESs) 2, 3, and 4.

INTRODUCTION

This Learning & Practice Workbook covers **Section C: Management Accounting.**

Demonstrating that the learning outcomes associated with the Foundation syllabus have been met is a requirement for all students before they are permitted to proceed to Professional level studies.

Students able to demonstrate they have met the learning outcomes based on prior study and educational qualification can be granted exemption from the Foundation Examination.

For those students unable to do so, passing the Foundation Examination is a core requirement to Professional levels studies.

Aims

The aim of this paper is to develop and examine the candidate's knowledge and understanding of:

1. The theory of accounting and its application to the practical situations indicated in the syllabus.
2. The fundamental elements of corporate governance and audit and the inter-relationship between these areas.
3. The fundamentals of management and cost accounting and their application in cost ascertainment, the control of operations, and the provision of information to assist management decision making and policy formulation.
4. Business management and the role of the manager in modern business organisations.

Foundation Level learning outcomes

In order to successfully complete this paper, candidates will demonstrate that they are able to:

FINANCIAL ACCOUNTING

1. Explain and identify accounting concepts and the regulatory purpose of accounting standards and sustainability standards.
2. Describe, prepare and summarise basic accounting records.
3. Identify accounting concepts in presenting financial statements for sole traders and limited companies.
4. Describe and explain the financial position and performance of an organisation.

CORPORATE GOVERNANCE AND AUDIT

1. Identify and explain the purpose of corporate governance and auditing.
2. Explain the inter-relationship between corporate governance and auditing.
3. Relate the contribution of corporate governance and auditing to the safeguarding of capital markets.

MANAGEMENT ACCOUNTING

1. Explain the role of management and cost accounting within an organisation.
2. Describe the nature of costs and how and why they are classified in different ways for different purposes.
3. Calculate material, labour, expense and overhead costs for products, processes, services and functions.
4. Identify and discuss appropriate principles and techniques to advise managers on short-term and long-run decision making.

BUSINESS MANAGEMENT

1. Describe the major schools of management thought, their development and their implications.
2. Explain the key aspects of organisational structure and design.
3. Identify the nature and importance of managerial control, including the main elements and types of control in the business organisation and the role and importance of management information in the control process.
4. Describe the use of information technology in modern business management.

This Learning & Practice Workbook covers **Section C: Management Accounting.**

Detailed learning outcomes for Section C: Management Accounting

C1 INTRODUCTION TO THE ROLE AND NATURE OF MANAGEMENT ACCOUNTING (LEARNING OUTCOME 8)

Topic Weighting 10%

- The role of management accounting and management accountants within the overall accounting function and its contribution to the management processes of planning, controlling and decision making.
- The nature of costs, cost classifications, cost units and cost centres, cost behaviour (fixed costs, variable costs and semi-variable costs, and linear approximations).
- The need to understand business models and underlying business transactions; and the role of management accounting information in the modern business organisation.

C2 COST IDENTIFICATION AND MEASURING COSTS FOR MANAGEMENT PURPOSES (LEARNING OUTCOMES 9, 10)

Topic Weighting 20%

The process of incurring costs and the need for cost management; the cost constituents of products in both traditional and modern products.

Materials:

- Procurement (ordering procedure, purchase requisition, purchase invoice);
- Receipt (goods receiving procedure, goods received note, inspection);
- Custody (store keeping principles, centralised, decentralised and sub-stores, bin cards);
- Issue, control (two bin system, periodic review system, ABC inventory analysis);
- Inventory levels (maximum, minimum, reorder levels and quantities, just-in-time and material requirements planning);
- Utilisation, pricing receipts and issues (FIFO, LIFO, weighted average and standard prices);
- Valuation of inventories (application of IAS 2);
- Material cost control;
- Materials cost in relation to the environment.

Labour:

- Time recording analysis;
- Remuneration systems (timework, piecework, incentive schemes, premium bonus plans, measured day work, share and group schemes, techniques for incentive schemes);
- Payroll preparation;
- Wages;
- Office procedure;
- Treatment of overtime and idle time;
- Productivity;
- Labour cost control.

Overhead:

- Nature;
- Methods and purpose of charging overheads to products, services and departments;
- Traditional and activity-based costing approaches;
- Classification, allocation, apportionment and absorption;
- Treatment of under-and-over-absorbed overhead;
- Treatment of depreciation;
- Interest on capital and notional costs;
- Overhead cost control;
- Environmental and social cost allocation to products and services.

C3 INTRODUCTION TO COSTING SYSTEMS (LEARNING OUTCOMES 9 and 10)

Topic Weighting 20%

The cost information needs of the business firm today

Job costing:

- Job cost sheet;
- Direct and indirect costs;
- Reconciling job costs with profit and loss account;
- Order, batch and contract costing;

Unit costing:

- Output costing;
- Process costing;
- Normal/abnormal losses and gains;
- Equivalent units;
- Work-in-process valuation;
- Inter-process profits;
- Joint and by-products;
- Operations and service costing.

Absorption and marginal costing:

- Relative benefits and problems.

C4 INFORMATION FOR PLANNING AND PERFORMANCE MANAGEMENT (LEARNING OUTCOME 11)

Topic Weighting 25%

Cost control:

- Nature and purpose;
- Techniques;
- Uniform costing systems;
- Traditional costing system;
- Activity based costing system;
- Standard costing;
- Types of standard;
- Procedures and systems;
- Variances eg cost and sales variance;
- Investigation of variances;
- Inter-dependence of variances.

Budgetary control:

- Nature and purpose;
- Organisation and structure and responsibility accounting;
- Introduction to the behavioural aspect of budgeting;
- Usefulness of budgeting for the modern business organisation;
- Preparation of budgets;
- Limiting factors;
- Flexible budgets, rolling budgets, zero based budgeting;
- Reporting.

C5 INFORMATION FOR DECISION MAKING (LEARNING OUTCOME 11)

Topic weighting 25%

- The contribution approach, break-even and profit-volume charts;
- Relevant costs;
- Limiting factors;
- Product mix and discontinuance;
- Make or buy decisions (outsourcing);
- Quantitative and qualitative factors;
- Environmental costs and management information for decision making;
- The changing nature of costs in the modern business;
- The application of the theory of constraints and activity-based costing;
- Activity-based management and activity-based budgeting and the conditions for their success;
- The use of activity-based costing for pricing and the application of 'activity-based pricing'.

Structure of the Foundation Level exam

Assessment is by a **three-hour 15 minute examination (including 15 minutes reading time)** consisting of 100 questions. There are 25 objective test style questions in the form of multiple choice questions covering each component area of the syllabus. All questions are compulsory.

The assessment covers the learning outcomes for each of the four component areas of study in the foundation syllabus.

The coverage of questions will reflect the weighting of different areas of syllabus content as specified in the Foundation examination syllabus, but the format of questions associated with each area of study may vary between sittings of the examination.

Relationship to overall AIA syllabus

This syllabus provides a broad understanding of the foundations of cost accounting which will be developed further in the Professional Level 1 Management Accounting paper and the Professional Level 2 Business and Financial Management paper.

Ethics

Candidates are advised that the standards outlined in The Code of Ethics for Professional Accountants issued by the International Ethics Standards Board for Accountants (IESBA Code) are implicit in, and examinable throughout, the AIA syllabus. The Code can be accessed via the AIA website at www.aiaworldwide.com.

INTRODUCTION

Recommended Reading

This reading list is recommended and not essential for your studies.

You can purchase any of the books listed quickly and easily on the AIA website www.aiaworldwide.com/books.

AIA Magazine – International Accountant
ISSN: 1465 – 5144

AIA Learning and Practice Workbooks
Foundation Unit
Publisher: BPP Learning Media

Four books – one for each component:

Financial Accounting
ISBN: 9781035525737

Management Accounting
ISBN: 9781035525744

Corporate Governance and Audit
ISBN: 9781035525720

Business Management
ISBN: 9781035525713

Financial Accounting (15th Edition 2021)
Business Accounting Volume 1
Author: Wood, F, Sangster, A and Gordon, L
Publisher: Pearson Education Ltd.
ISBN: 9781292365435

Free website providing comprehensive information about IFRS: www.iasplus.com

Corporate Governance: Principles Policies and Practices (4th Edition)
Author: Bob Tricker
Publisher: Oxford University Press
ISBN: 9780198809869

Corporate Governance and Accountability (5th Edition)
Author: Jill Solomon
Publisher: Wiley
ISBN: 9781119561200

Auditing (12th Edition)
Author: Millichamp, A and Taylor, R
Publisher: Cengage Learning EMEA
ISBN: 9781473778993

Modern Auditing (3rd Edition 2009)
Author: Cosserat, G We; and Rodda, N
Publisher: Wiley
ISBN   9780470319734

The Audit Process: Principles practice and cases (7th Edition)
Author: Gray, L, Manson, S and Crawford, L
Publisher: London Thomson
ISBN: 9781473760189

Management Accounting and Business Management and Cost Accounting (7th Edition 2019)
Author: Bhimani A., Horngren C.T., Datar S.M., Rajan M.V
Publisher: Pearson
ISBN: 9781292232669

Management Accounting (UK Edition 2013)
Author: Burns, J., Quinn, M., Warren, L., Olivera, J
Publisher: McGraw-Hill Education/Europe, Middle East & Africa
ISBN: 9780077121617

Management and Cost Accounting, (11th Edition 2020)
Author: Drury, C
Publisher: Cengage Learning EMEA
ISBN: 9781473773615

Management (1st International Edition 2016)
Author: Daft, R L and Benson, A
Publisher: Cengage Learning EMA
ISBN: 9781408063859

ISE Contemporary Management (12th Edition 2021)
Author: Jones, G. and George, J
Publisher: McGraw-Hill
ISBN: 9781264972432

Organisational Behaviour in the Workplace (12th Edition 2019)
Author: Mullins, L. J
Publisher: Pearson
ISBN: 9781292245485

Management (15th Edition 2020)
Author: Robbins, S. P. and Coulter, M
Publisher: Pearson
ISBN: 9781292340883

INTRODUCTION

PART C1

Introduction to the role and nature of management accounting

Information for management

Topic list	Syllabus reference
1 Information	C1.1
2 Planning, control and decision making	C1.1
3 Financial accounting and cost and management accounting	C1.1
4 Presentation of information to management	C1.1
5 The changing business environment	C1.3

Introduction

This and the following chapter provides an introduction to **Management Accounting**. This chapter looks at **information** and introduces **cost accounting**.

In recent years there have been **significant changes in the business environment** in which both manufacturing and service organisations operate. We look at these **changes** in some detail in **Section 5**.

Chapters 2 provides basic information on how costs are classified and how they behave.

PART A INTRODUCTION TO THE ROLE AND NATURE OF MANAGEMENT ACCOUNTING

> **Exam focus point**
>
> A lot of the material in this chapter is background information which provides important context. There could be questions on the difference between financial accounting and management accounting.

1 Information

1.1 Data and information

> **FAST FORWARD**
>
> **Data** is the raw material for data processing. Data relate to facts, events and transactions and so forth.
>
> **Information** is data that has been processed in such a way as to be **meaningful** to the person who receives it. **Information** is anything that is communicated.

Information is sometimes referred to as **processed data**. The terms 'information' and 'data' are often used interchangeably. It is important to understand the difference between these two terms.

Researchers who conduct market research surveys might ask members of the public to complete questionnaires about a product or a service. These completed questionnaires are **data**; they are processed and analysed in order to prepare a report on the survey. This resulting report is **information** and may be used by management for decision-making purposes.

1.2 Qualities of good information

> **FAST FORWARD**
>
> Good information should be **relevant, complete, accurate, clear**, it should **inspire confidence**, it should be **appropriately communicated**, its **volume** should be manageable, it should be **timely** and its **cost** should be less than the benefits it provides.

Let us look at those qualities in more detail.

(a) **Relevance**. Information must be relevant to the purpose for which a manager wants to use it. In practice, far too many reports fail to 'keep to the point' and contain irrelevant paragraphs which only annoy the managers reading them.

(b) **Completeness**. An information user should have all the information he needs to do his job properly. If he does not have a complete picture of the situation, he might well make bad decisions.

(c) **Accuracy**. Information should obviously be accurate because using incorrect information could have serious and damaging consequences. However, information should only be accurate enough for its purpose and there is no need to go into unnecessary detail for pointless accuracy.

(d) **Clarity**. Information must be clear to the user. If the user does not understand it properly he cannot use it properly. Lack of clarity is one of the causes of a breakdown in communication. It is therefore important to choose the most appropriate presentation medium or channel of communication.

(e) **Confidence**. Information must be trusted by the managers who are expected to use it. However not all information is certain. Some information has to be certain, especially operating information, for example, related to a production process. Strategic information, especially relating to the environment, is uncertain. However, if the assumptions underlying it are clearly stated, this might enhance the confidence with which the information is perceived.

(f) **Communication**. Within any organisation, individuals are given the authority to do certain tasks, and they must be given the information they need to do them. An office manager might be made responsible for controlling expenditures in his office, and given a budget expenditure limit for the year. As the year progresses, he might try to keep expenditure in check but unless he is told

throughout the year what is his current total expenditure to date, he will find it difficult to judge whether he is keeping within budget or not.

(g) **Volume**. There are physical and mental limitations to what a person can read, absorb and understand properly before taking action. An enormous mountain of information, even if it is all relevant, cannot be handled. Reports to management must therefore be **clear** and **concise** and in many systems, control action works basically on the 'exception' principle.

(h) **Timing**. Information which is not available until after a decision is made will be useful only for comparisons and longer-term control, and may serve no purpose even then. Information prepared too frequently can be a serious disadvantage. If, for example, a decision is taken at a monthly meeting about a certain aspect of a company's operations, information to make the decision is only required once a month, and weekly reports would be a time-consuming waste of effort.

(i) **Channel of communication**. There are occasions when using one particular method of communication will be better than others. For example, job vacancies should be announced in a medium where they will be brought to the attention of the people most likely to be interested. The channel of communication might be the company's in-house journal, a national or local newspaper, a professional magazine, a job centre or school careers office. Some internal memoranda may be better sent by email. Some information is best communicated informally by telephone or word-of-mouth, whereas other information ought to be formally communicated in writing or figures.

(j) **Cost**. Information should have some value, otherwise it would not be worth the cost of collecting and filing it. The benefits obtainable from the information must also exceed the costs of acquiring it, and whenever management is trying to decide whether or not to produce information for a particular purpose (for example whether to computerise an operation or to build a financial planning model) a cost/benefit study ought to be made.

Question — Value of information

The value of information lies in the action taken as a result of receiving it. What questions might you ask in order to make an assessment of the value of information?

Answer

(a) What information is provided?
(b) What is it used for?
(c) Who uses it?
(d) How often is it used?
(e) Does the frequency with which it is used coincide with the frequency with which it is provided?
(f) What is achieved by using it?
(g) What other relevant information is available which could be used instead?

An assessment of the value of information can be derived in this way, and the cost of obtaining it should then be compared against this value. On the basis of this comparison, it can be decided whether certain items of information are worth having. It should be remembered that there may also be intangible benefits which may be harder to quantify.

1.3 Why is information important?

Consider the following problems and what management needs to solve these problems.

(a) A company wishes to launch a new product. The company's pricing policy is to charge cost plus 20%. What should the price of the product be?

(b) An organisation's widget-making machine has a fault. The organisation has to decide whether to repair the machine, buy a new machine or hire a machine. What does the organisation do if its aim is to control costs?

(c) A firm is considering offering a discount of 2% to those customers who pay an invoice within 7 days of the invoice date and a discount of 1% to those customers who pay an invoice within 8 to 14 days of the invoice date. How much will this discount offer cost the firm?

In solving these and a wide variety of other problems, **management need information**.

(a) In problem (a) above, management would need information about the **cost of the new product**.

(b) Faced with problem (b), management would need information on the **cost of repairing, buying and hiring the machine**.

(c) To calculate the cost of the discount offer described in (c), information would be required about **current sales settlement patterns** and **expected changes to the pattern** if discounts were offered.

The successful management of **any** organisation depends on information: non-profit making organisations such as charities, clubs and local authorities need information for decision making and for reporting the results of their activities just as multi-nationals do. For example a tennis club needs to know the cost of undertaking its various activities so that it can determine the amount of annual subscription it should charge its members.

1.4 What type of information is needed?

Most organisations require the following types of information.

- Financial
- Non-financial
- A combination of financial and non-financial information

1.4.1 Example: Financial and non-financial information

Suppose that the management of ABC Co have decided to provide a canteen for their employees.

(a) The **financial information** required by management might include canteen staff costs, costs of subsidising meals, capital costs, costs of heat and light and so on.

(b) The **non-financial information** might include management comment on the effect on employee morale of the provision of canteen facilities, details of the number of meals served each day, meter readings for gas and electricity and attendance records for canteen employees.

ABC Co could now **combine financial and non-financial information** to calculate the **average cost** to the company of each meal served, thereby enabling them to predict total costs depending on the number of employees in the work force.

1.4.2 Non-financial information

Most people probably consider that management accounting is only concerned with financial information and that people do not matter. This is, nowadays, a long way from the truth. For example, managers of business organisations need to know whether employee morale has increased due to introducing a canteen, whether the bread from particular suppliers is fresh and the reason why the canteen staff are demanding a new dishwasher. This type of non-financial information will play its part in **planning, controlling** and **decision making** and is therefore just as important to management as financial information is.

Non-financial information must therefore be **monitored** as carefully, **recorded** as accurately and **taken into account** as fully as financial information. There is little point in a careful and accurate recording of total canteen costs if the recording of the information on the number of meals eaten in the canteen is uncontrolled and therefore produces inaccurate information.

While management accounting is mainly concerned with the provision of **financial information** to aid planning, control and decision making, the management accountant cannot ignore **non-financial influences** and should qualify the information he provides with non-financial matters as appropriate.

2 Planning, control and decision making

2.1 Planning

> **FAST FORWARD**
>
> Information for management is likely to be used for **planning**, **control**, and **decision making**.

An organisation should never be surprised by developments which occur gradually over an extended period of time because the organisation should have **implemented a planning process**. Planning involves the following.

- Establishing objectives
- Selecting appropriate strategies to achieve those objectives

Planning therefore forces management to think ahead systematically in both the **short term** and the **long term**.

2.2 Objectives of organisations

> **FAST FORWARD**
>
> An **objective** is the aim or **goal** of an organisation (or an individual). Note that in practice, the terms objective, goal and aim are often used interchangeably. A **strategy** is a possible course of action that might enable an organisation (or an individual) to achieve its objectives.

The two main types of organisation that you are likely to come across in practice are as follows.

- Profit making
- Non profit making

The main objective of profit making organisations is to **maximise profits**. A secondary objective of profit making organisations might be to increase output of its goods/services.

The main objective of non profit making organisations is usually to **provide goods and services**. A secondary objective of non profit making organisations might be to minimise the costs involved in providing the goods/services.

In conclusion, the objectives of an organisation might include one or more of the following.

- Maximise profits
- Maximise shareholder value
- Minimise costs
- Maximise revenue
- Increase market share

Remember that the type of organisation concerned will have an impact on its objectives.

2.3 Strategy and organisational structure

There are two schools of thought on the link between strategy and organisational structure.

- Structure follows strategy
- Strategy follows structure

Let's consider the first idea that **structure follows strategy**. What this means is that organisations develop strategies in order that they can cope with changes in the structure of an organisation. Or do they?

The second school of thought suggests that **strategy follows structure**. This side of the argument suggests that the strategy of an organisation is determined or influenced by the structure of the organisation. The structure of the organisation therefore limits the number of strategies available.

We could explore these ideas in much more detail, but for the purposes of your **Management Accounting** studies, you really just need to be aware that there is a link between **strategy** and the **structure** of an organisation.

2.4 Long-term strategic planning

Key term

> **Long-term planning**, also known as **corporate planning**, involves selecting appropriate strategies so as to prepare a long-term plan to attain the objectives.

The time span covered by a long-term plan depends on the **organisation**, the **industry** in which it operates and the particular **environment** involved. Typical periods are two, five, seven or ten years although longer periods are frequently encountered.

Long-term strategic planning is a **detailed, lengthy process**, essentially incorporating three stages and ending with a **corporate plan**. The diagram on the next page provides an overview of the process and shows the link between short-term and long-term planning.

2.5 Short-term tactical planning

The **long-term corporate plan** serves as the **long-term framework** for the organisation as a whole but for operational purposes it is necessary to convert the corporate plan into a series of **short-term plans**, usually covering **one year**, which relate to **sections**, **functions** or **departments**. The annual process of short-term planning should be seen as stages in the progressive fulfilment of the corporate plan as each short-term plan steers the organisation towards its long-term objectives. It is therefore vital that, to obtain the maximum advantage from short-term planning, some sort of long-term plan exists.

1: INFORMATION FOR MANAGEMENT

The planning process

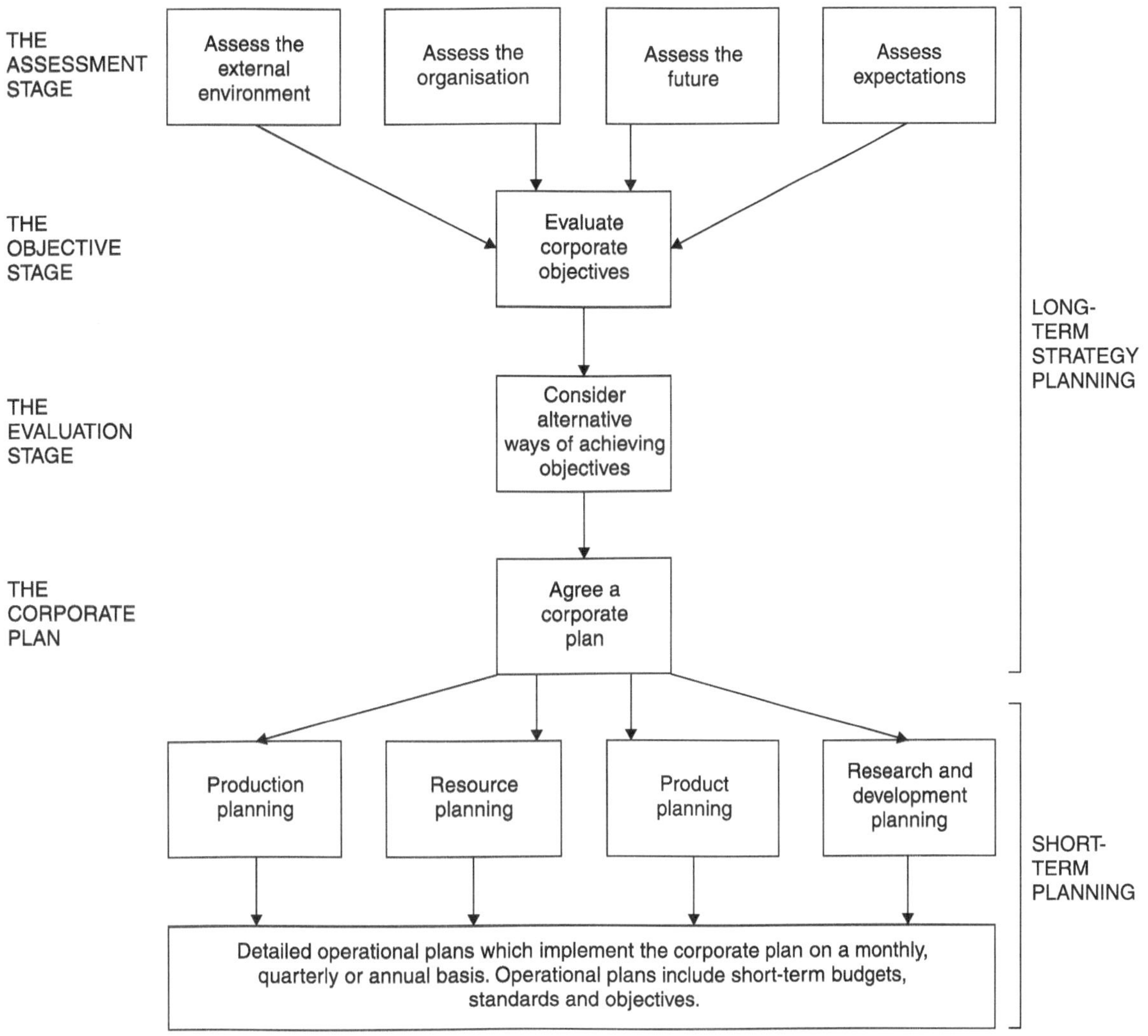

```
THE                Assess the      Assess the      Assess the      Assess
ASSESSMENT         external        organisation    future          expectations
STAGE              environment
                        │              │               │               │
                        └──────────────┼───────────────┼───────────────┘
                                       ▼               ▼
THE                                  Evaluate
OBJECTIVE                            corporate
STAGE                                objectives
                                         │
                                         ▼
THE                                  Consider                              LONG-
EVALUATION                           alternative                           TERM
STAGE                                ways of achieving                     STRATEGY
                                     objectives                            PLANNING
                                         │
                                         ▼
THE                                  Agree a
CORPORATE                            corporate
PLAN                                 plan
                    ┌────────────┬───────┴───────┬────────────┐
                    ▼            ▼               ▼            ▼
             Production    Resource        Product      Research and
             planning      planning        planning     development
                                                        planning         SHORT-
                    │            │               │            │          TERM
                    ▼            ▼               ▼            ▼          PLANNING
             Detailed operational plans which implement the corporate plan on a monthly,
             quarterly or annual basis. Operational plans include short-term budgets,
                                    standards and objectives.
```

2.6 Control

There are two stages in the **control process**.

(a) The **performance of the organisation** as set out in the detailed operational plans is compared with the actual performance of the organisation on a regular and continuous basis. Any deviations from the plans can then be identified and corrective action taken.

(b) **The corporate plan** is reviewed in the light of the comparisons made and any changes in the parameters on which the plan was based (such as new competitors, government instructions and so on) to assess whether the objectives of the plan can be achieved. The plan is modified as necessary before any serious damage to the organisation's future success occurs.

Effective control is therefore not practical without planning, and planning without control is pointless.

An established organisation should have a system of management reporting that produces control information in a specified format at regular intervals.

Smaller organisations may rely on informal information flows or ad hoc reports produced as required.

2.7 Decision making

Management is decision-taking. Managers of all levels within an organisation take decisions. Decision making always involves a **choice between alternatives** and it is the role of the management accountant to provide information so that management can reach an informed decision. It is therefore vital that the management accountant understands the decision-making process so that he can supply the appropriate type of information.

2.7.1 Decision-making process

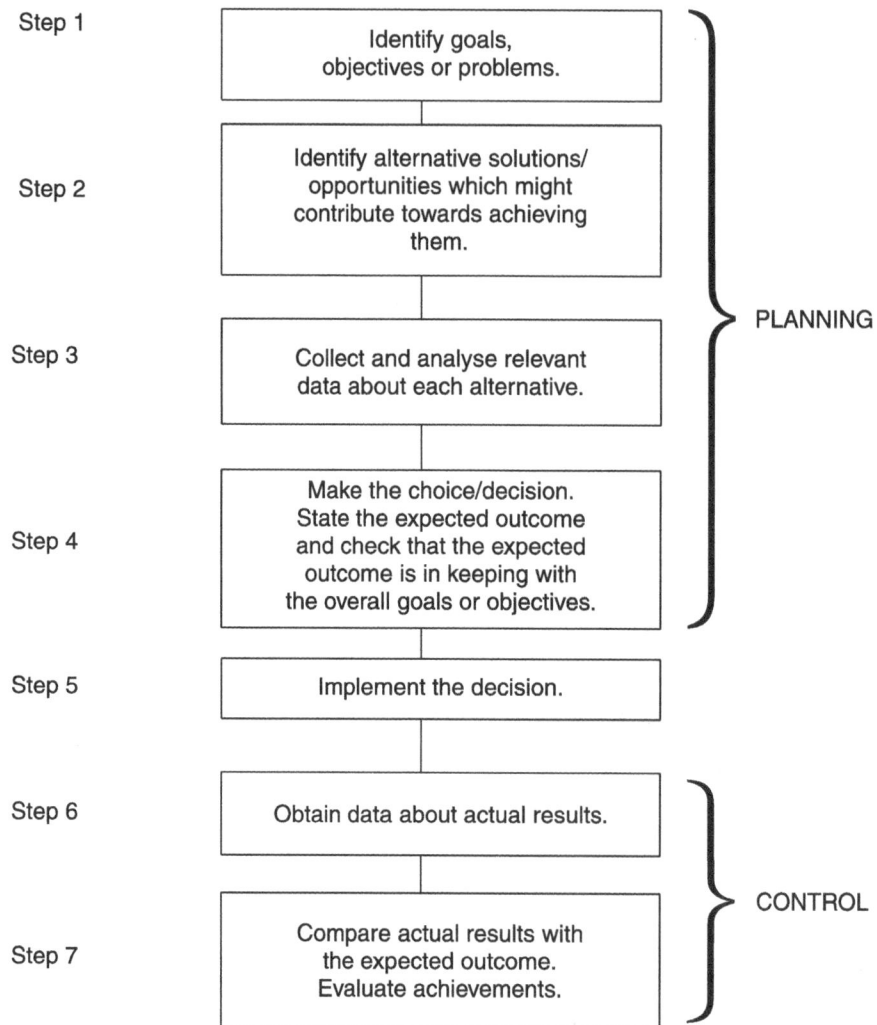

2.8 Anthony's view of management activity

FAST FORWARD

Anthony divides management activities into **strategic planning, management control** and **operational control.**

R N Anthony, a leading writer on organisational control, has suggested that the activities of **planning, control and decision making should not be separated** since all managers make planning and control decisions. He has identified three types of management activity.

(a) **Strategic planning:** 'The process of deciding on objectives of the organisation, on changes in these objectives, on the resources used to attain these objectives, and on the policies that are to govern the acquisition, use and disposition of these resources'.

(b) **Management control:** 'The process by which managers assure that resources are obtained and used effectively and efficiently in the accomplishment of the organisation's objectives'.

(c) **Operational control:** 'The process of assuring that specific tasks are carried out effectively and efficiently'.

2.8.1 Strategic planning

Strategic plans are those which **set or change the objectives**, or **strategic targets** of an organisation. They would include such matters as the selection of products and markets, the required levels of company profitability, the purchase and disposal of subsidiary companies or major fixed assets and so on.

2.8.2 Management control

Whilst strategic planning is concerned with setting objectives and strategic targets, **management control** is concerned with **decisions about the efficient and effective use of an organisation's resources** to achieve these objectives or targets.

(a) **Resources**, often referred to as the **'4 Ms'** (men, materials, machines and money).

(b) **Efficiency** in the use of resources means that optimum **output** is achieved from the **input** resources used. It relates to the combinations of men, land and capital (for example how much production work should be automated) and to the productivity of labour, or material usage.

(c) **Effectiveness** in the use of resources means that the **outputs** obtained are in line with the intended **objectives** or **targets**.

2.8.3 Operational control

The third, and lowest tier, in Anthony's hierarchy of decision making, consists of **operational control decisions**. As we have seen, operational control is the task of ensuring that **specific tasks** are carried out effectively and efficiently. Just as 'management control' plans are set within the guidelines of strategic plans, so too are 'operational control' plans set within the guidelines of both strategic planning and management control. Consider the following.

(a) Senior management may decide that the company should increase sales by 5% per annum for at least five years – **a strategic plan**.

(b) The sales director and senior sales managers will make plans to increase sales by 5% in the next year, with some provisional planning for future years. This involves planning direct sales resources, advertising, sales promotion and so on. Sales quotas are assigned to each sales territory – **a tactical plan** (management control).

(c) The manager of a sales territory specifies the weekly sales targets for each sales representative. This is **operational planning**: individuals are given tasks which they are expected to achieve.

Although we have used an example of selling tasks to describe operational control, it is important to remember that this level of planning occurs in all aspects of an organisation's activities, even when the activities cannot be scheduled nor properly estimated because they are non-standard activities (such as repair work, answering customer complaints).

The scheduling of unexpected or 'ad hoc' work must be done at short notice, which is a feature of much **operational planning**. In the repairs department, for example, routine preventive maintenance can be scheduled, but breakdowns occur unexpectedly and repair work must be scheduled and controlled 'on the spot' by a repairs department supervisor.

2.9 Management control systems

> **FAST FORWARD**
>
> A **management control system** is a system which measures and corrects the performance of activities of subordinates in order to make sure that the objectives of an organisation are being met and the plans devised to attain them are being carried out.

The management function of control is the measurement and correction of the activities of subordinates in order to make sure that the goals of the organisation, or planning targets are achieved.

The basic elements of a management control system are as follows.

- **Planning:** deciding what to do and identifying the desired results
- **Recording** the plan which should incorporate standards of efficiency or targets
- **Carrying out** the plan and measuring actual results achieved
- **Comparing** actual results against the plans
- **Evaluating** the comparison, and deciding whether further action is necessary
- Where **corrective action** is necessary, this should be implemented

2.10 Types of information

> **FAST FORWARD**
>
> Information within an organisation can be analysed into the three levels assumed in Anthony's hierarchy: **strategic**; **tactical**; and **operational**.

2.10.1 Strategic information

Strategic information is used by senior managers to plan the objectives of their organisation, and to assess whether the objectives are being met in practice. Such information includes **overall** profitability, the profitability of different segments of the business, capital equipment needs and so on.

Strategic information therefore has the following features.

- It is derived from both **internal** and **external** sources.
- It is summarised at a **high level**.
- It is relevant to the **long term**.
- It deals with the **whole organisation** (although it might go into some detail).
- It is often prepared on an **'ad hoc'** basis.
- It is both **quantitative** and **qualitative** (see below).
- It cannot provide complete certainty, given that the future cannot be predicted.

2.10.2 Tactical information

Tactical information is used by middle management to decide how the resources of the business should be employed, and to monitor how they are being and have been employed. Such information includes **productivity measurements** (output per man hour or per machine hour), **budgetary control** or **variance analysis reports**, and **cash flow forecasts** and so on.

Tactical information therefore has the following features.

- It is primarily generated internally.
- It is summarised at a lower level.
- It is relevant to the short and medium term.
- It describes or analyses activities or departments.
- It is prepared routinely and regularly.
- It is based on quantitative measures.

2.10.3 Operational information

Operational information is used by 'front-line' managers such as foremen or head clerks to ensure that specific tasks are planned and carried out properly within a factory or office and so on. In the payroll office, for example, information at this level will relate to day-rate labour and will include the hours worked each week by each employee, his rate of pay per hour, details of his deductions, and for the purpose of wages analysis, details of the time each person spent on individual jobs during the week. In this example, the information is required weekly, but more urgent operational information, such as the amount of raw materials being input to a production process, may be required daily, hourly, or in the case of automated production, second by second.

Operational information has the following features.

- It is derived almost entirely from internal sources.
- It is highly detailed, being the processing of raw data.
- It relates to the immediate term, and is prepared constantly, or very frequently.
- It is task-specific and largely quantitative.

3 Financial accounting and cost and management accounting

3.1 Financial accounts and management accounts

> **FAST FORWARD**
>
> **Financial accounting systems** ensure that the assets and liabilities of a business are properly accounted for, and provide information about profits and so on to shareholders and to other interested parties. **Management accounting systems** provide information specifically for the use of managers within an organisation.

Management information provides a common source from which is drawn information for two groups of people.

(a) **Financial accounts** are prepared for individuals **external** to an organisation: shareholders, customers, suppliers, tax authorities, employees.

(b) **Management accounts** are prepared for **internal** managers of an organisation.

The data used to prepare financial accounts and management accounts are the same. The differences between the financial accounts and the management accounts arise because the data is analysed differently.

3.2 Financial accounts versus management accounts

Financial accounts	Management accounts
Financial accounts detail the performance of an organisation over a defined period and the state of affairs at the end of that period.	Management accounts are used to aid management record, plan and control the organisation's activities and to help the decision-making process.
Limited liability companies must, by law, prepare financial accounts.	There is no legal requirement to prepare management accounts.

PART A INTRODUCTION TO THE ROLE AND NATURE OF MANAGEMENT ACCOUNTING

Financial accounts	Management accounts
The format of published financial accounts is determined by local law, by International Accounting Standards and International Financial Reporting Standards. In principle the accounts of different organisations can therefore be easily compared.	The format of management accounts is entirely at management discretion: no strict rules govern the way they are prepared or presented. Each organisation can devise its own management accounting system and format of reports.
Financial accounts concentrate on the business as a whole, aggregating revenues and costs from different operations, and are an end in themselves.	Management accounts can focus on specific areas of an organisation's activities. Information may be produced to aid a decision rather than to be an end product of a decision.
Most financial accounting information is of a monetary nature.	Management accounts incorporate non-monetary measures. Management may need to know, for example, tons of aluminium produced, monthly machine hours, or miles travelled by salesmen.
Financial accounts present an essentially historic picture of past operations.	Management accounts are both an historical record and a future planning tool.

Question — Management accounts

Which of the following statements about management accounts is/are true?

(i)   There is a legal requirement to prepare management accounts.
(ii) The format of management accounts is largely determined by law.
(iii) They serve as a future planning tool and are not used as a historical record.

A   (i) and (ii)
B   (ii) and (iii)
C   (iii) only
D   None of the statements are correct

Answer

D

Statement (i) is incorrect. Limited liability companies must, by law, prepare **financial** accounts.

The format of published financial accounts is determined by law. Statement (ii) is therefore incorrect.

Management accounts do serve as a future planning tool but they are also useful as a historical record of performance. Therefore all three statements are incorrect and D is the correct answer.

3.3 Cost accounts

FAST FORWARD

Cost accounting and management accounting are terms which are often used interchangeably. It is **not** correct to do so. **Cost accounting is part of management accounting. Cost accounting provides a bank of data for the management accountant to use.**

Cost accounting is concerned with the following.

- Preparing statements (eg budgets, costing)
- Cost data collection
- Applying costs to inventory, products and services

Management accounting is concerned with the following.

- Using financial data and communicating it as information to users

3.3.1 Aims of cost accounts

(a) The **cost** of goods produced or services provided.

(b) The **cost** of a department or work section.

(c) What **revenues** have been.

(d) The **profitability** of a product, a service, a department, or the organisation in total.

(e) **Selling prices** with some regard for the costs of sale.

(f) The **value of inventories of goods** (raw materials, work in progress, finished goods) that are still held in store at the end of a period, thereby aiding the preparation of a statement of financial position of the company's assets and liabilities.

(g) **Future costs** of goods and services (costing is an integral part of budgeting (planning) for the future).

(h) **How actual costs compare with budgeted costs.** If an organisation plans for its revenues and costs to be a certain amount, but they actually turn out differently, the differences can be measured and reported. Management can use these reports as a guide to whether corrective action (or 'control' action) is needed to sort out a problem revealed by these differences between budgeted and actual results. This system of control is often referred to as budgetary control.

(i) **What information management needs** in order to make sensible decisions about profits and costs.

It would be wrong to suppose that cost accounting systems are restricted to manufacturing operations, although they are probably more fully developed in this area of work. **Service industries**, **government departments** and **welfare activities** can all make use of cost accounting information. Within a manufacturing organisation, the cost accounting system should be applied not only to **manufacturing** but also to **administration**, **selling and distribution**, **research and development** and all other departments.

4 Presentation of information to management

4.1 Reports

FAST FORWARD

> Data and information are usually presented to management in the form of a **report**. The main features of a report are: TITLE; TO; FROM; DATE; and SUBJECT.

In small organisations it is possible, however, that information will be communicated in a less formal manner than writing a report (orally or using informal reports/memos).

Throughout this Learning & Practice Workbook, you will come across a number of techniques which allow financial information to be collected. Once it has been collected it is usually analysed and reported back to management in the form of a **report**.

4.2 Main features of a report

- **TITLE**

    Most reports are usually given a heading to show that it is a report.

- **WHO IS THE REPORT INTENDED FOR?**

  It is vital that the intended recipients of a report are clearly identified. For example, if you are writing a report for Joe Bloggs, it should be clearly stated at the head of the report.

- **WHO IS THE REPORT FROM?**

  If the recipients of the report have any comments or queries, it is important that they know who to contact.

- **DATE**

  We have already mentioned that information should be communicated at the most appropriate time. It is also important to show this timeliness by giving your report a date.

- **SUBJECT**

  What is the report about? Managers are likely to receive a great number of reports that they need to review. It is useful to know what a report is about before you read it!

- **APPENDIX**

  In general, information is summarised in a report and the more detailed calculations and data are included in an appendix at the end of the report.

5 The changing business environment

FAST FORWARD

> Changes to the **competitive environment, product life cycles** and **customer requirements** have had a significant impact on the modern business environment.

5.1 The changing competitive environment for manufacturing organisations

Modern technology and transport have overcome barriers of geographical distance which limited the extent to which overseas organisations could compete in domestic markets. In the past, cost increases could often be passed on to customers and so there were **few efforts to maximise efficiency and improve management practices**, or to reduce costs. **Now overseas competitors** access domestic markets by **establishing global networks for acquiring raw materials and distributing high-quality, low-priced goods**. To succeed, organisations have to compete against the best companies in the world.

5.2 The changing competitive environment for service organisations

In the past, many service organisations (such as the utilities, the financial services and airlines industries) were either **government-owned monopolies** or were **protected by a highly-regulated, non-competitive environment. Improvements in quality and efficiency** of operations or levels of profitability were not expected, and costs increases were often covered by increasing service prices. Cost systems to measure costs and profitability of individual services were not deemed necessary.

In many countries the competitive environment for service organisations have changed radically with **privatisation** of government-owned monopolies and **deregulation**. The resulting intense competition and increasing product range has led to the **requirement for cost management and management accounting information systems** which allow service organisations to assess the costs and profitability of services, customers and markets.

5.3 Changing product life cycles

Today's **competitive environment**, along with high levels of **technological innovation** and **increasingly discriminating and sophisticated customer demands**, constantly **threaten a product's life cycle**.

Key term

> **Product life cycle** is the 'Period which begins with the initial product specification and ends with the withdrawal from the market of both the product and its support. It is characterised by defined stages including research, development, introduction, maturity, decline and abandonment.'
>
> *CIMA Official Terminology*

Organisations can no longer rely on years of high demand for products and so, to compete effectively, they need to continually **redesign their products** and to **shorten the time it takes to get them to the market place**.

In many organisations today, **up to 90% of a product's life cycle cost is determined by decisions made** early within the cycle, **at the design stage. Management accounting systems that monitor spending and commitment to spend during the early stages of a product's life cycle** are therefore becoming **increasingly important**.

5.4 Changing customer requirements

Successful organisations in today's competitive environment make **customer satisfaction** their **priority** and concentrate on the following **key success factors**.

Key success factor	Detail
Cost efficiency	Achieving optimum output at minimum cost
Quality	Focusing on total quality management (TQM)
Time	Providing a speedier response to customer requests, ensuring 100% on-time delivery and reducing the time taken to develop and bring new products to market
Innovation	Developing a steady stream of innovative new products and having the flexibility to respond to customer requirements

They are also taking on board **new management approaches**.

Approach	Detail
Continuous improvement	A facet of TQM, being a continuous search to reduce costs, eliminate waste and improve the quality and performance of activities that increase customer satisfaction or value
Employee empowerment	Providing employees with the information to enable them to make continuous improvements without authorisation from superiors
Total value-chain analysis	Ensuring that all the factors which add value to an organisation's products – the value chain of research and development, design, production, marketing, distribution and customer service – are co-ordinated within the overall organisational framework

5.5 Changing manufacturing systems

FAST FORWARD

> Different approaches for **organising a manufacturing process** include **jobbing industries, batch processing** and **mass production**.

Traditionally, manufacturing industries have fallen into a few broad groups according to the **nature of the production process** and **materials flow**.

Type of production	Description
Jobbing industries	Industries in which **items are produced individually**, often for a specific customer order, as a 'job'. Such a business requires versatile equipment and highly skilled workers to give it the flexibility to turn its hand to a variety of jobs. The jobbing factory is typically laid out on a **functional** basis with, say, a milling department, a cutting department, finishing, assembly and so on.
Batch processing	Involves the manufacture of **standard goods in batches**. 'Batch production is often carried out using **functional** layouts but with a greater number of more **specialised machines**. With a functional layout batches move by different and complex routes through various specialised departments travelling over much of the factory floor before they are completed.' (Drury, *Management and Cost Accounting*)
Mass or flow production	Involves the **continuous production of standard items** from a sequence of continuous or repetitive operations. This sort of production often uses a **product-based** layout whereby product A moves from a milling machine to a cutting machine to a paint-spraying machine, product B moves from a sawing machine to a milling machine to an oven and then to finishing and so on. The point is that there is no separate 'milling department' or 'assembly department' to which all products must be sent to await their turn on the machines: each product has its own dedicated machine.

In recent years, however, a new type of manufacturing system known as **group technology** (or **repetitive manufacturing**) has emerged. The system involves a **flexible or cellular arrangement of machines** which **manufacture groups of products having similar manufacturing requirements.** By grouping together facilities required to produce similar products, some of the **benefits associated with flow production systems** (lower throughput times, easier scheduling, reduced set-up times and reduced work in progress) are possible to achieve. Moreover, the increase in **customer demand for product diversity can be satisfied** by such a manufacturing system.

5.5.1 Dedicated cell layout

The modern development in this sphere is to merge the flexibility of the functional layout with the speed and productivity of the product layout. **Cellular** manufacturing involves a **U-shaped flow** along which are arranged a number of different machines that are used to make products with similar machining requirements.

The machines are operated by workers who are **multi-skilled** (can operate each machine within the cell rather than being limited to one operation such as 'lathe-operator', 'grinder') and are able to perform routine preventative maintenance on the cell machines. The aim is to facilitate **just-in-time** production and obtain the associated improvements in **quality** and reductions in **costs**.

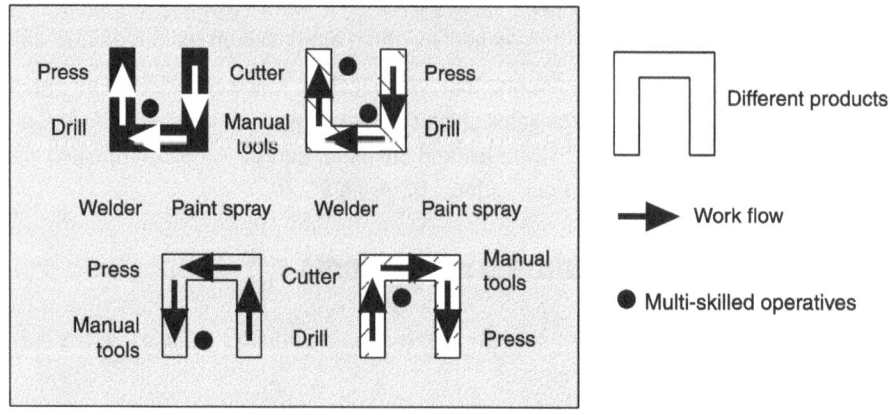

Case Study

The *Financial Times* carried a good example of this approach in an article about the Paddy Hopkirk car accessory factory in Bedfordshire.

One morning the factory was just an untidy sprawl of production lines surrounded by piles of crates holding semi-finished components. Two days later, when the workforce came to work (after Christmas), the machines has been brought together in tightly grouped 'cells'. The piles of components had disappeared, and the newly cleared floor space was neatly marked with colour-coded lines mapping out the flow of materials.

Overnight there were dramatic differences. In the first full day, productivity on some lines increased by up to 30%, the space needed for some processes had been halved, and work in progress had been cut considerably. The improved layout had allowed some jobs to be combined, freeing up operators for development elsewhere in the factory.

As we saw earlier, **to compete effectively** organisations need to **continually redesign their products** and to **shorten the time it takes to get them to the market place**. **Manufacturing processes** must therefore be **sufficiently flexible** both to accommodate new product design rapidly and to satisfy the demand for greater product diversity.

5.6 The changing role of the management accountant

Over the last two decades there have been significant changes in the management accounting environment. These include:

- Globalisation and increased competition
- Information technology changes resulting in changes in production and information flows
- Changes in organisations including reorganisations and external mergers
- The development of a knowledge-based economy with a focus on intellectual property
- Changes to corporate governance and the need to be accountable to a wide range of stakeholders

Traditional management accounting systems may be inadequate for a modern business environment. Management accountants have responded to the changes in the environment such as the development of just-in-time (JIT), TQM and lean management accounting by techniques such as target costing, lifecycle costing and Kaizen.

The role of the management accountant is to provide information to decision makers, and to provide advice based on that information. The information provided by the management accountant covers all areas of strategy and operations, and includes **information to assist** with **planning, control and other decision making** by management.

The role of the management accountant today is more concerned with providing complex analysis and information to support business management than with providing routine reports, since much routine work is now computerised. At the same time the areas covered by management accounting have extended to include strategic information and non-financial information, and information to support risk management. Developments in technology have also made it easier to provide accounting information to non-financial managers.

In some organisations, the cost and management accounting function may be organised as a functional section or department within the organisation. However, because management accountants provide information to other managers, it has become fairly common to include management accountants within cross-functional teams, or to assign them to work with non-accounting functions.

In addition to contributing their technical expertise as accounting and finance experts and their functional expertise as information providers, management accountants have a key role to play in helping maximise the potential of a cross-functional team by:

- Providing, collecting and assessing critical team information
- Helping establish goals and set priorities
- Assisting with problem solving and decision making, through the application of decision-making models and other techniques
- Ensuring the team maintains an organisation-wide perspective

In conclusion the management accountant's role is to implement processes and practices that focus on effective and efficient use of organisational resources to support managers to enhance customer and stakeholder value (IFAC).

Chapter roundup

- **Data** is the raw material for data processing. Data relate to facts, events and transactions and so forth.
- **Information** is data that has been processed in such a way as to be **meaningful** to the person who receives it. **Information** is anything that is communicated.
- Good information should be **relevant, complete, accurate, clear**, it should **inspire confidence**, it should be **appropriately communicated**, its **volume** should be manageable, it should be **timely** and its **cost** should be less than the benefits it provides.
- Information for management accounting is likely to be used for **planning, control** and **decision making**.
- An **objective** is the aim or **goal** of an organisation (or an individual). Note that in practice, the terms objective, goal and aim are often used interchangeably. A **strategy** is a possible course of action that might enable an organisation (or an individual) to achieve its objectives.
- Anthony divides management activities into **strategic planning, management control** and **operational control**.
- A **management control system** is a system which measures and corrects the performance of activities of subordinates in order to make sure that the objectives of an organisation are being met and the plans devised to attain them are being carried out.
- Information within an organisation can be analysed into the three levels assumed in Anthony's hierarchy: **strategic, tactical** and **operational**.
- **Financial accounting systems** ensure that the assets and liabilities of a business are properly accounted for, and provide information about profits and so on to shareholders and to other interested parties. **Management accounting systems** provide information specifically for the use of managers within the organisation.
- Cost accounting and management accounting are terms which are often used interchangeably. It is **not** correct to do so. **Cost accounting is part of management accounting. Cost accounting provides a bank of data for the management accountant to use**.
- Data and information are usually presented to management in the form of a report. The main features of a report are: TITLE; TO; FROM; DATE; and SUBJECT.
- Changes to the **competitive environment, product life cycles** and **customer requirements** have had a significant impact on the modern business environment.
- Different approaches for **organising a manufacturing process** include **jobbing industries, batch processing** and **mass production**.

PART A INTRODUCTION TO THE ROLE AND NATURE OF MANAGEMENT ACCOUNTING

Quick quiz

1. Define the terms **data** and **information**.

2. The four main qualities of good information are:
   - ....
   - ....
   - ....
   - ....

3. In terms of management accounting, information is most likely to be used for:

   (1) ....
   (2) ....
   (3) ....

4. A strategy is the aim or goal of an organisation.

   True ☐

   False ☐

5. **Organisation**   **Objective**

   Profit making
   Non profit making

6. What are the three types of management activity identified by R N Anthony?

   (1) ....
   (2) ....
   (3) ....

7. A management control system is:

   A A possible course of action that might enable an organisation to achieve its objectives

   B A collective term for the hardware and software used to drive a database system

   C A set up that measures and corrects the performance of activities of subordinates in order to make sure that the objectives of an organisation are being met and their associated plans are being carried out

   D A system that controls and maximises the profits of an organisation

8. List six differences between financial accounts and management accounts.

9. When preparing reports, what are the five key points to remember?
   - ....
   - ....
   - ....
   - ....
   - ....

10   Match the type of production with one of the descriptions (1) to (4).

Jobbing industries	(1)	Merges the flexibility of the functional layout with the speed and productivity of the product layout
Batch processing	(2)	Uses a product-based layout
Mass/flow production	(3)	Factory is typically laid out on a functional basis
Cellular manufacturing	(4)	Uses functional layout but with a high number of specialised machines

PART A INTRODUCTION TO THE ROLE AND NATURE OF MANAGEMENT ACCOUNTING

Answers to quick quiz

1. **Data** is the raw material for data processing. **Information** is data that has been processed in such a way as to be meaningful to the person who receives it. **Information** is anything that is communicated.

2.
   - Relevance
   - Completeness
   - Accuracy
   - Clarity

3. (1) Planning
   (2) Control
   (3) Decision making

4. False. This is the definition of an **objective**. A strategy is a possible course of action that might enable an organisation to **achieve** its objectives.

5. Profit making = maximise profits
   Non profit making = provide goods and services

6. (1) Strategic planning
   (2) Management control
   (3) Operational control

7. C

8. See Paragraph 3.2

9.
   - Title
   - Who is the report to
   - Who is the report from
   - Date
   - Subject

10. Jobbing industries — description (3)
    Batch processing — description (4)
    Mass/flow production — description (2)
    Cellular manufacturing — description (1)

Cost classification and behaviour

Topic list	Syllabus reference
1 Total product/service costs	C1.2
2 Direct costs and indirect costs	C1.2
3 Functional costs	C1.2
4 Classification of environmental costs	C1.2
5 Fixed costs and variable costs	C1.2
6 Production and non-production costs	C1.2
7 Other cost classifications	C1.2
8 Cost units, cost objects and responsibility centres	C1.2
9 Introduction to cost behaviour	C1.2
10 Cost behaviour patterns	C1.2

Introduction

The **classification of costs** as either **direct** or **indirect**, for example, is essential in the costing method used by an organisation to determine the cost of a unit of product or service.

The **fixed** and **variable cost classifications**, on the other hand, are important in **absorption** and **marginal costing**, **cost behaviour** and **cost-volume-profit analysis**.

You will meet all of these topics as we progress through the Learning & Practice Workbook.

This chapter therefore acts as a foundation stone for a number of other chapters in the text and hence an understanding of the concepts covered in it is vital before you move on.

Exam focus point

Cost classification and behaviour is one of the key areas of the syllabus. You can expect to see a few questions on this area in the exam.. It is vital to an understanding of much of the syllabus. Read, learn and apply!

1 Total product/service costs

The total cost of making a product or providing a service consists of the following.

(a) Cost of **materials**
(b) Cost of the **wages** and **salaries** (labour costs)
(c) Cost of **other expenses**

    (i) Rent and rates
    (ii) Electricity and gas bills
    (iii) Depreciation

2 Direct costs and indirect costs

2.1 Materials, labour and expenses

FAST FORWARD

A **direct cost** is a cost that can be traced in full to the product, service, or department that is being costed. An **indirect cost** (or **overhead**) is a cost that is incurred in the course of making a product, providing a service or running a department, but which cannot be traced directly and in full to the product, service or department.

Materials, labour costs and other expenses can be classified as either **direct costs** or **indirect costs**.

(a) **Direct material costs** are the costs of materials that are known to have been used in making and selling a product (or even providing a service).

(b) **Direct labour costs** are the specific costs of the workforce used to make a product or provide a service. Direct labour costs are established by measuring the time taken for a job, or the time taken in 'direct production work'.

(c) **Other direct expenses** are those expenses that have been incurred in full as a direct consequence of making a product, or providing a service, or running a department.

Examples of indirect costs include supervisors' wages, cleaning materials and buildings insurance.

2.2 Analysis of total cost

Materials	=	Direct materials	+	Indirect materials
+		+		+
Labour	=	Direct labour	+	Indirect labour
+		+		+
Expenses	=	Direct expenses	+	Indirect expenses
Total cost	=	Direct cost	+	Overhead

2.3 Direct material

Key term

Direct material is all material becoming part of the product (unless used in negligible amounts and/or having negligible cost).

Direct material costs are charged to the product as part of the **prime cost**. Examples of direct material are as follows.

(a) **Component parts**, specially purchased for a particular job, order or process

(b) **Part-finished work** which is transferred from department 1 to department 2 becomes finished work of department 1 and a direct material cost in department 2

(c) **Primary packing materials** like cartons and boxes

2.4 Direct labour

Key term

> **Direct wages** are all wages paid for labour (either as basic hours or as overtime) expended on work on the product itself.

Direct wages costs are charged to the product as part of the **prime cost**.

Examples of groups of labour receiving payment as direct wages are as follows.

(a) Workers engaged in **altering** the condition or composition of the product.
(b) Inspectors, analysts and testers **specifically required** for such production.
(c) Foremen, shop clerks and anyone else whose wages are **specifically identified**.

Two **trends** may be identified in **direct labour costs**.

- The ratio of direct labour costs to total product cost is falling as the use of machinery increases, and hence depreciation charges increase.
- Skilled labour costs and sub-contractors' costs are increasing as direct labour costs decrease.

Question — Labour costs

Classify the following labour costs as either direct or indirect.
(a) The basic pay of direct workers (cash paid, tax and other deductions)
(b) The basic pay of indirect workers
(c) Overtime premium
(d) Bonus payments
(e) Social insurance contributions
(f) Idle time of direct workers
(g) Work on installation of equipment

Answer

(a) The basic pay of direct workers is a direct cost to the unit, job or process.

(b) The basic pay of indirect workers is an indirect cost, unless a customer asks for an order to be carried out which involves the dedicated use of indirect workers' time, when the cost of this time would be a direct labour cost of the order.

(c) Overtime premium paid to both direct and indirect workers is an indirect cost, except in two particular circumstances.

   (i) If overtime is worked at the specific request of a customer to get his order completed, the overtime premium paid is a direct cost of the order.

   (ii) If overtime is worked regularly by a production department in the normal course of operations, the overtime premium paid to direct workers could be incorporated into the (average) direct labour hourly rate.

(d) Bonus payments are generally an indirect cost.
(e) Employer's National Insurance contributions (which are added to employees' total pay as a wages cost) are normally treated as an indirect labour cost.
(f) Idle time is an overhead cost, that is an indirect labour cost.
(g) The cost of work on capital equipment is incorporated into the capital cost of the equipment.

2.5 Direct expenses

Key term

> **Direct expenses** are any expenses which are incurred on a specific product other than direct material cost and direct wages.

Direct expenses are charged to the product as part of the **prime** cost. Examples of direct expenses are as follows.

- The **hire of tools** or equipment for a particular job
- **Maintenance costs** of tools, fixtures and so on

Direct expenses are also referred to as **chargeable expenses.**

2.6 Production overhead

Key term

> **Production (or factory) overhead** includes all indirect material costs, indirect wages and indirect expenses incurred in the factory from receipt of the order until its completion.

Production overhead includes the following.

(a) **Indirect materials** which cannot be traced in the finished product.

Consumable stores, eg material used in negligible amounts

(b) **Indirect wages**, meaning all wages not charged directly to a product.

Wages of non-productive personnel in the production department, eg foremen

(c) **Indirect expenses** (other than material and labour) not charged directly to production.
  (i) Rent, rates and insurance of a factory
  (ii) Depreciation, fuel, power, maintenance of plant, machinery and buildings

2.7 Administration overhead

Key term

> **Administration overhead** is all indirect material costs, wages and expenses incurred in the direction, control and administration of an undertaking.

Examples of administration overhead are as follows.

- **Depreciation** of office buildings and equipment
- **Office salaries**, including salaries of directors, secretaries and accountants
- Rent, rates, insurance, lighting, cleaning, telephone charges and so on

2.8 Selling overhead

Key term

Selling overhead is all indirect materials costs, wages and expenses incurred in promoting sales and retaining customers.

Examples of selling overhead are as follows.

- **Printing** and **stationery**, such as catalogues and price lists
- **Salaries** and **commission** of salesmen, representatives and sales department staff
- **Advertising** and **sales promotion**, market research
- Rent, rates and insurance of sales offices and showrooms, bad debts and so on

2.9 Distribution overhead

Key term

Distribution overhead is all indirect material costs, wages and expenses incurred in making the packed product ready for despatch and delivering it to the customer.

Examples of distribution overhead are as follows.

- Cost of packing cases
- Wages of packers, drivers and despatch clerks
- Insurance charges, rent, rates, depreciation of warehouses and so on

Question — Direct labour cost

A direct labour employee's wage in week 5 consists of the following.

		$
(a)	Basic pay for normal hours worked, 36 hours at $4 per hour =	144
(b)	Pay at the basic rate for overtime, 6 hours at $4 per hour =	24
(c)	Overtime shift premium, with overtime paid at time-and-a-quarter $\frac{1}{4} \times 6$ hours $\times$ $4 per hour =	6
(d)	A bonus payment under a group bonus (or 'incentive') scheme – bonus for the month =	30
	Total gross wages in week 5 for 42 hours of work	204

What is the direct labour cost for this employee in week 5?

A $144   B $168   C $198   D $204

Answer

The correct answer is B because the basic rate for overtime is a part of direct wages cost. It is only the overtime premium that is usually regarded as an overhead or indirect cost.

3 Functional costs

3.1 Classification by function

FAST FORWARD

> **Classification by function** involves classifying costs as production/manufacturing costs, administration costs or marketing/selling and distribution costs.

In a 'traditional' costing system for a manufacturing organisation, costs are classified as follows.

(a) **Production** or **manufacturing costs.** These are costs associated with the factory.

(b) **Administration costs.** These are costs associated with general office departments.

(c) **Marketing**, or **selling** and **distribution costs.** These are costs associated with sales, marketing, warehousing and transport departments.

Classification in this way is known as **classification by function**. Expenses that do not fall fully into one of these classifications might be categorised as **general overheads** or even listed as a classification on their own (for example research and development costs).

3.2 Full cost of sales

In costing a small product made by a manufacturing organisation, direct costs are usually restricted to some of the production costs. A commonly found build-up of costs is therefore as follows.

	$
Production costs	
Direct materials	A
Direct wages	B
Direct expenses	C
Prime cost	A+B+C
Production overheads	D
Full factory cost	A+B+C+D
Administration costs	E
Selling and distribution costs	F
Full cost of sales	A+B+C+D+E+F

3.3 Functional costs

(a) **Production costs** are the costs which are incurred by the sequence of operations beginning with the supply of raw materials, and ending with the completion of the product ready for warehousing as a finished goods item. Packaging costs are production costs where they relate to 'primary' packing (boxes, wrappers and so on).

(b) **Administration costs** are the costs of managing an organisation, that is, planning and controlling its operations, but only insofar as such administration costs are not related to the production, sales, distribution or research and development functions.

(c) **Selling costs**, sometimes known as marketing costs, are the costs of creating demand for products and securing firm orders from customers.

(d) **Distribution costs** are the costs of the sequence of operations with the receipt of finished goods from the production department and making them ready for despatch and ending with the reconditioning for reuse of empty containers.

(e) **Research costs** are the costs of searching for new or improved products, whereas **development costs** are the costs incurred between the decision to produce a new or improved product and the commencement of full manufacture of the product.

(f) **Financing costs** are costs incurred to finance the business such as loan interest.

Question: Cost classification

Within the costing system of a manufacturing company the following types of expense are incurred.

Reference number

1	Cost of oils used to lubricate production machinery
2	Motor vehicle licences for lorries
3	Depreciation of factory plant and equipment
4	Cost of chemicals used in the laboratory
5	Commission paid to sales representatives
6	Salary of the secretary to the finance director
7	Trade discount given to customers
8	Holiday pay of machine operatives
9	Salary of security guard in raw material warehouse
10	Fees to advertising agency
11	Rent of finished goods warehouse
12	Salary of scientist in laboratory
13	Insurance of the company's premises
14	Salary of supervisor working in the factory
15	Cost of typewriter ribbons in the general office
16	Protective clothing for machine operatives

Required

Complete the following table by placing each expense in the correct cost classification.

Cost classification	Reference number					
Production costs						
Selling and distribution costs						
Administration costs						
Research and development costs						

Each type of expense should appear only once in your answer. You may use the reference numbers in your answer.

Answer

Cost classification	Reference number					
Production costs	1	3	8	9	14	16
Selling and distribution costs	2	5	7	10	11	
Administration costs	6	13	15			
Research and development costs	4	12				

4 Classification of environmental costs

FAST FORWARD

The **classification of environmental costs** involves categorising costs to better understand the expenses associated with both conformance and non-conformance. Conformance costs include prevention and appraisal costs, while non-conformance costs encompass internal and external failure costs.

4.1 Introduction

Environmental issues are becoming **increasingly important** in the business world. Firms have become responsible for the environmental impacts of their operations and, therefore, they are now more aware of problems such as carbon emissions. The growth of **environmental legislation and regulations** has also affected business operations and reporting. **Environmental costs**, like any other costs, need to be considered with regard to **planning, control** and **decision making**. The main difference between environmental costs and other costs is that they may be more difficult to identify and to quantify. For example, businesses may suffer a loss of reputation if problems arise.

4.2 Direct and indirect environmental costs

- Waste management
- Remediation costs or expenses
- Compliance costs
- Environmental certification and labelling
- Environmentally driven research and development
- Legal costs and fines
- Permit fees
- Record keeping and reporting
- Environmental training

4.3 Contingent or intangible environmental costs

- Uncertain future remediation or compensation costs
- Risk posed by future regulatory changes
- Sustainability of raw material inputs
- Product quality
- Employee health and safety
- Public/customer perception

4.4 Environmental cost classification

Simply collecting environmental costs provides very little insight. By classifying these costs, it becomes clearer **which costs** represent **investments in sustainability** and which are the **costs of not investing in preventive measures**. This classification helps organisations understand the **financial impact** of their environmental strategies and make **informed decisions** to enhance their **environmental performance** and **reduce overall costs**. Environmental costs can be classified into one of four categories: prevention, appraisal, internal failure and external failure costs. Conformance costs include prevention and appraisal costs, while non-conformance costs encompass internal and external failure costs.

Classification	Definition	Examples
Environmental prevention costs	Costs incurred to **avoid** environmental impacts **before they occur**	Staff training Enhancing production processes to reduce resource use and waste Developing environmental management plans Choosing suppliers based on their environmental performance

2: COST CLASSIFICATION AND BEHAVIOUR

Classification	Definition	Examples
Environmental appraisal costs	Costs associated with evaluating and auditing products and processes to ensure they **meet** environmental **standards**	Conducting inspections and tests Evaluating suppliers' adherence to environmental criteria Maintaining environmental monitoring equipment
Environmental internal failure costs	Costs that arise when environmental issues are **detected** within the organisation **before they affect** the external environment	Handling and processing waste materials Correcting processes that do not meet environmental standards Implementing measures to control emissions and discharges Recycling materials
Environmental external failure costs	Costs that occur when environmental issues **impact the external environment**	Fines and penalties for non-compliance with environmental regulations Cleaning up environmental damage Managing the organisation's reputation following environmental incidents

Question

Environmental costs

A manufacturing company is assessing its annual environmental costs. The following information is available for the year:

Environmental costs $
Training and process improvements   50,000
Inspections and testing   75,000
Recycling waste materials   100,000
Fines   150,000

What percentage of the total cost is attributable to conformance costs (to 1 decimal place)?

[   ] %

Answer

[33.3] %

Conformance costs (costs related to preventing environmental issues and ensuring standards are met):

- Training and process improvement costs are prevention costs because they relate to steps taken to avoid environmental impacts from happening.
- Inspections and testing costs are appraisal costs because they relate to ensuring that environmental standards are met.

Non-conformance costs (failure costs that occur when the product does not meet standards):

- Recycling waste materials is an internal failure cost because it relates to environmental issues detected within the organisation before they affect the external environment.
- Fines are external failure costs because they arise after environmental issues have had an impact on the external environment.

Total cost = $50,000 + $75,000 + $100,000 + $150,000 = $375,000

Conformance costs = $50,000 (prevention) + $75,000 (appraisal) = $125,000

Percentage of conformance costs = ($125,000 / $375,000) × 100 = 33.3%

5 Fixed costs and variable costs

FAST FORWARD

A different way of analysing and classifying costs is into **fixed costs** and **variable costs**. Many items of expenditure are part-fixed and part-variable and hence are termed **semi-fixed** or **semi-variable costs**.

Key terms

A **fixed cost** is a cost which is incurred for a particular period of time and which, within certain activity levels, is unaffected by changes in the level of activity.

A **variable cost** is a cost which tends to vary with the level of activity.

5.1 Examples of fixed and variable costs

(a) Direct material costs are **variable costs** because they rise as more units of a product are manufactured.

(b) Sales commission is often a fixed percentage of sales turnover, and so is a **variable cost** that varies with the level of sales.

(c) Telephone call charges are likely to increase if the volume of business expands, but there is also a fixed element of line rental, and so they are a **semi-fixed** or **semi-variable overhead cost**.

(d) The rental cost of business premises is a constant amount, at least within a stated time period, and so it is a **fixed cost.**

6 Production and non-production costs

FAST FORWARD

For the preparation of financial statements, costs are often classified as **production costs** and **non-production costs**. Production costs are costs identified with goods produced for resale. Non-production costs are cost deducted as expenses during the current period.

Production costs are all the costs involved in the manufacture of goods. In the case of manufactured goods, these costs consist of direct material, direct labour and manufacturing overhead.

Non-production costs are taken directly to the profit and loss account as expenses in the period in which they are incurred; such costs consist of selling and administrative expenses.

6.1 Production and non-production costs

The distinction between production and non-production costs is the basis of valuing inventory.

6.2 Example

A business has the following costs for a period:

	$
Materials	600
Labour	1,000
Production overheads	500
Administration overheads	700
	2,800

During the period 100 units are produced. If all of these costs were allocated to production units, each unit would be valued at $28.

This would be incorrect. Only **production** costs are allocated to units of inventory. Administrative overheads are **non-production** costs.

So each unit of inventory should be valued at $21((600 + 1,000 + 500)/100).

This affects both gross profit and the valuation of closing inventory. If during the period 80 units are sold at $40 each, the gross profit will be:

	$
Sales (80 × 40)	3,200
Cost of sales (80 × 21)	(1,680)
Gross profit	1,520

The value of closing (unsold) inventory will be $420 (20 × 21).

7 Other cost classifications

Key terms

> **Avoidable costs** are specific costs of an activity or business which would be avoided if the activity or business did not exist.
>
> **Unavoidable costs** are costs which would be incurred whether or not an activity or sector existed.
>
> A **controllable cost** is a cost which can be influenced by management decisions and actions.
>
> An **uncontrollable cost** is any cost that cannot be affected by management within a given time span.
>
> **Discretionary costs** are costs which are likely to arise from decisions made during the budgeting process. They are likely to be fixed amounts of money over fixed periods of time.

Examples of discretionary costs are as follows.

- Advertising
- Research and development
- Training

8 Cost units, cost objects and responsibility centres

8.1 Cost centres

> **Cost centres** are collecting places for costs before they are further analysed. Costs are further analysed into cost units once they have been traced to cost centres.

Costs consist of the costs of the following.

- Direct materials
- Direct labour
- Direct expenses
- Production overheads
- Administration overheads
- General overheads

When costs are incurred, they are generally allocated to a **cost centre**. Cost centres may include the following.

- A department
- A machine, or group of machines
- A project (eg the installation of a new computer system)
- Overhead costs eg rent, rates, electricity (which may then be allocated to departments or projects)

Cost centres are an essential 'building block' of a costing system. They are the starting point for the following.

(a) The classification of actual costs incurred
(b) The preparation of budgets of planned costs
(c) The comparison of actual costs and budgeted costs (management control)

8.2 Cost units

> A **cost unit** is a unit of product or service to which costs can be related. The cost unit is the basic control unit for costing purposes.

Once costs have been traced to cost centres, they can be further analysed in order to establish a **cost per cost unit**. Alternatively, some items of cost may be charged directly to a cost unit, for example direct materials and direct labour costs.

Examples of cost units include the following.

- Patient episode (in a hospital)
- Barrel (in the brewing industry)
- Room (in a hotel)

Question — Cost units

Suggest suitable cost units which could be used to aid control within the following organisations.

(a) A hotel with 50 double rooms and 10 single rooms
(b) A hospital
(c) A road haulage business

Answer

(a) Guest/night
    Bed occupied/night
    Meal supplied

(b) Patient/night
    Operation
    Outpatient visit

(c) Tonne/mile
    Mile

8.3 Cost objects

FAST FORWARD A **cost object** is any activity for which a separate measurement of costs is desired.

If the users of management information wish to know the cost of something, this something is called a **cost object**. Examples include the following.

- The cost of a product
- The cost of a service
- The cost of operating a department

8.4 Profit centres

FAST FORWARD **Profit centres** are similar to cost centres but are accountable for **costs and revenues**.

We have seen that a cost centre is where costs are collected. Some organisations, however, work on a profit centre basis.

Profit centre managers should normally have control over how revenue is raised and how costs are incurred. Often, several cost centres will comprise one profit centre. The profit centre manager will be able to make decisions about both purchasing and selling and will be expected to do both as profitably as possible.

A profit centre manager will want information regarding both revenues and costs. He will be judged on the profit margin achieved by his division. In practice, it may be that there are fixed costs which he cannot control, so he should be judged on contribution, which is revenue less variable costs. In this case he will want information about which products yield the highest contribution.

8.5 Revenue centres

FAST FORWARD **Revenue centres** are similar to cost centres and profit centres but are accountable for **revenues only**. Revenue centre managers should normally have control over how revenues are raised.

A revenue centre manager is not accountable for costs. He will be aiming purely to maximise sales revenue. He will want information on markets and new products and he will look closely at pricing and the sales performance of competitors – in addition to monitoring revenue figures.

8.6 Investment centres

FAST FORWARD An **investment centre** is a profit centre with additional responsibilities for capital investment and possibly for financing, and whose performance is measured by its return on investment.

An investment centre manager will take the same decisions as a profit centre manager but he also has additional responsibility for investment. So he will be judged additionally on his handling of cash surpluses and he will seek to make only those investments which yield a higher percentage than the company's notional cost of capital. So the investment centre manager will want the same information as the profit centre manager and in addition he will require quite detailed appraisals of possible investments and information regarding the results of investments already undertaken. He will have to make decisions regarding the purchase or lease of non-current assets and the investment of cash surpluses. Most of these decisions involve large sums of money.

8.7 Responsibility centres

> A **responsibility centre** is a department or organisational function whose performance is the direct responsibility of a specific manager.

Cost centres, revenue centres, profit centres and investment centres are also known as **responsibility centres**.

Question — Investment centre

Which of the following is a characteristic of an investment centre?

A Managers have control over marketing.
B Management have a sales team.
C Management have a sales team and are given a credit control function.
D Managers can purchase capital assets.

Answer

The correct answer is D.

9 Introduction to cost behaviour

9.1 Cost behaviour and decision making

> **Cost behaviour** is the way in which costs are affected by changes in the volume of output.

Management decisions will often be based on how costs and revenues vary at different activity levels. Examples of such decisions are as follows.

- What should the **planned activity level** be for the next period?
- Should the **selling price** be reduced in order to sell more units?
- Should a particular component be **manufactured internally** or **bought in**?
- Should a **contract** be undertaken?

9.2 Cost behaviour and cost control

If the accountant does not know the level of costs which should have been incurred as a result of an organisation's activities, how can he or she hope to control costs?

9.3 Cost behaviour and budgeting

Knowledge of cost behaviour is obviously essential for the tasks of **budgeting**, **decision making** and **control accounting**.

Exam focus point

Remember that the behavioural analysis of costs is important for planning, control and decision making.

9.4 Cost behaviour and levels of activity

There are many factors which may influence costs. The major influence is **volume of output**, or the **level of activity**. The level of activity may refer to one of the following.

- Number of units produced
- Value of items sold
- Number of items sold
- Number of invoices issued
- Number of units of electricity consumed

9.5 Cost behaviour principles

FAST FORWARD

The basic principle of cost behaviour is that **as the level of activity rises, costs will usually rise**. It will cost more to produce 2,000 units of output than it will cost to produce 1,000 units.

This principle is common sense. The problem for the accountant, however, is to determine, for each item of cost, the way in which costs rise and by how much as the level of activity increases. For our purposes here, the level of activity for measuring cost will generally be taken to be the **volume of production**.

9.6 Example: cost behaviour and activity level

Hans Bratch has a fleet of company cars for sales representatives. Running costs have been estimated as follows.

(a) Cars cost $12,000 when new, and have a guaranteed trade-in value of $6,000 at the end of two years. Depreciation is charged on a straight-line basis.

(b) Petrol and oil cost 15 cents per mile.

(c) Tyres cost $300 per set to replace; replacement occurs after 30,000 miles.

(d) Routine maintenance costs $200 per car (on average) in the first year and $450 in the second year.

(e) Repairs average $400 per car over two years and are thought to vary with mileage. The average car travels 25,000 miles per annum.

(f) Tax, insurance, membership of motoring organisations and so on cost $400 per annum per car.

Required

Calculate the average cost per annum of cars which travel 15,000 miles per annum and 30,000 miles per annum.

Solution

Costs may be analysed into fixed, variable and stepped cost items, a stepped cost being a cost which is fixed in nature but only within certain levels of activity.

(a) **Fixed costs**

	$ per annum
Depreciation $(12,000 − 6,000) ÷ 2	3,000
Routine maintenance $(200 + 450) ÷ 2	325
Tax, insurance etc	400
	3,725

(b) **Variable costs**

	Cents per mile
Petrol and oil	15.0
Repairs ($400 ÷ 50,000 miles)*	0.8
	15.8

* If the average car travels 25,000 miles per annum, it will be expected to travel 50,000 miles over 2 years (this will correspond with the repair bill of $400 over 2 years).

(c) Step costs are tyre replacement costs, which are $300 at the end of every 30,000 miles.

(i) If the car travels less than or exactly 30,000 miles in 2 years, the tyres will not be changed. Average cost of tyres per annum = $0.

(ii) If a car travels more than 30,000 miles and up to (and including) 60,000 miles in 2 years, there will be 1 change of tyres in the period. Average cost of tyres per annum = $150 ($300 ÷ 2).

(iii) If a car exceeds 60,000 miles in 2 years (up to 90,000 miles) there will be 2 tyre changes. Average cost of tyres per annum = $300 ($600 ÷ 2).

The estimated costs per annum of cars travelling 15,000 miles per annum and 30,000 miles per annum would therefore be as follows.

	15,000 miles per annum $	30,000 miles per annum $
Fixed costs	3,725	3,725
Variable costs (15.8c per mile)	2,370	4,740
Tyres	–	150
Cost per annum	6,095	8,615

10 Cost behaviour patterns

10.1 Fixed costs

FAST FORWARD

A **fixed cost** is a cost which tends to be unaffected by increases or decreases in the volume of output.

Fixed costs are a **period charge**, in that they relate to a span of time; as the time span increases, so too will the fixed costs (which are sometimes referred to as period costs for this reason). It is important to understand that **fixed costs always have a variable element**, since an increase or decrease in production may also bring about an increase or decrease in fixed costs.

A sketch graph of fixed cost would look like this.

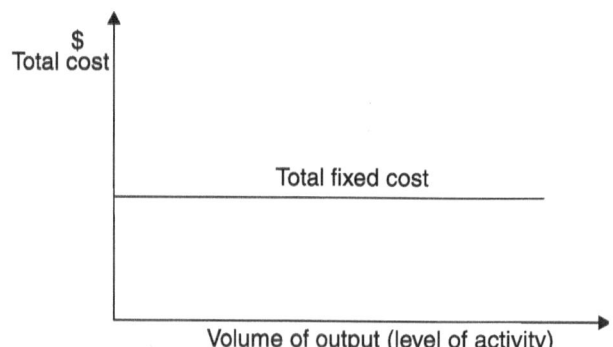

Examples of a fixed cost would be as follows.

- The salary of the managing director (per month or per annum)
- The rent of a single factory building (per month or per annum)
- Straight line depreciation of a single machine (per month or per annum)

10.2 Step costs

FAST FORWARD A **step cost** is a cost which is fixed in nature but only within certain levels of activity.

Consider the depreciation of a machine which may be fixed if production remains below 1,000 units per month. If production exceeds 1,000 units, a second machine may be required, and the cost of depreciation (on two machines) would go up a step. A sketch graph of a step cost could look like this.

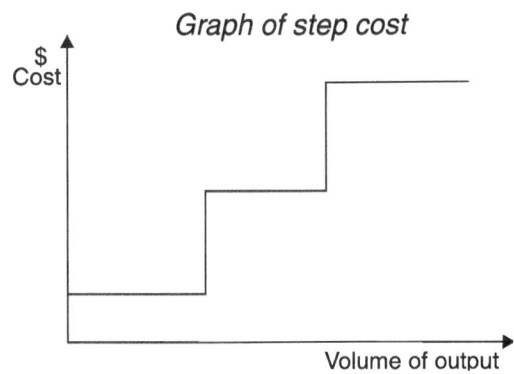

Graph of step cost

Other examples of step costs are as follows.

(a) Rent is a step cost in situations where accommodation requirements increase as output levels get higher.
(b) Basic pay of employees is nowadays usually fixed, but as output rises, more employees (direct workers, supervisors, managers and so on) are required.
(c) Royalties.

10.3 Variable costs

FAST FORWARD A **variable cost** is a cost which tends to vary directly with the volume of output. The variable cost per unit is the same amount for each unit produced.

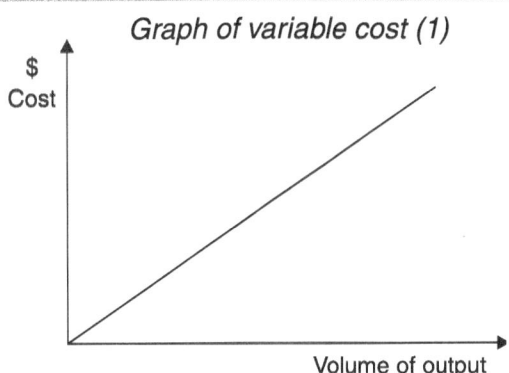

Graph of variable cost (1)

A constant variable cost per unit implies that the price per unit of say, material purchased is constant, and that the rate of material usage is also constant.

(a) The most important variable cost is the **cost of raw materials** (where there is no discount for bulk purchasing since bulk purchase discounts reduce the cost of purchases).
(b) **Direct labour costs** are, for very important reasons, classed as a variable cost even though basic wages are usually fixed.
(c) **Sales commission** is variable in relation to the volume or value of sales.
(d) **Bonus payments** for productivity to employees might be variable once a certain level of output is achieved, as the following diagram illustrates.

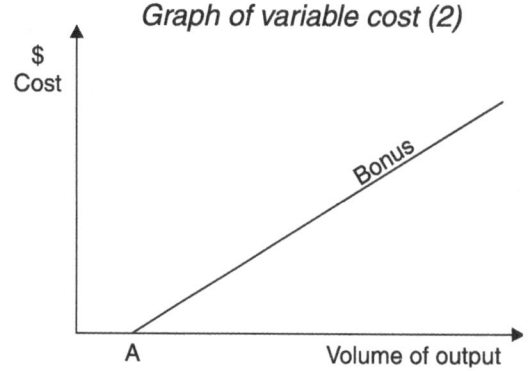

Up to output A, no bonus is earned.

10.4 Non-linear or curvilinear variable costs

FAST FORWARD

If the relationship between total variable cost and volume of output can be shown as a curved line on a graph, the relationship is said to be **curvilinear**.

Two typical relationships are as follows.

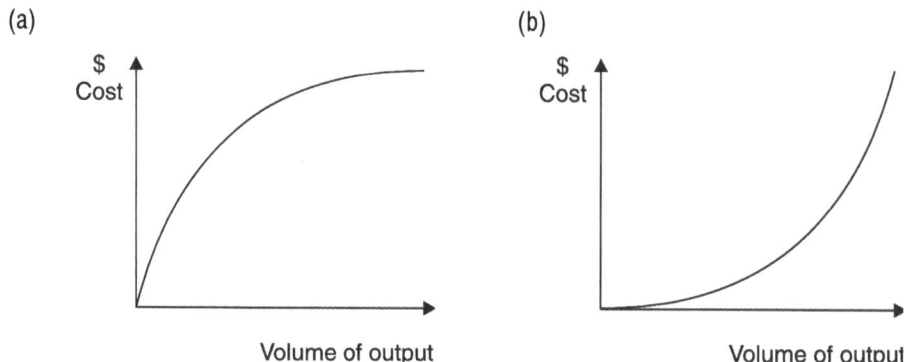

Each extra unit of output in graph (a) causes a **less than proportionate** increase in cost whereas in graph (b), each extra unit of output causes **a more than proportionate** increase in cost.

The cost of a piecework scheme for individual workers with differential rates could behave in a **curvilinear** fashion if the rates increase by small amounts at progressively higher output levels.

10.5 Semi-variable costs (or semi-fixed costs or mixed costs)

FAST FORWARD

A **semi-variable/semi-fixed/mixed cost** is a cost which contains both fixed and variable components and so is partly affected by changes in the level of activity.

Examples of these costs include the following.

(a) **Electricity and gas bills**

　　(i) Fixed cost = standing charge
　　(ii) Variable cost = charge per unit of electricity used

(b) **Salesman's salary**

　　(i) Fixed cost = basic salary
　　(ii) Variable cost = commission on sales made

(c) **Costs of running a car**

   (i) Fixed cost = road tax, insurance
   (ii) Variable costs = petrol, oil, repairs (which vary with miles travelled)

10.6 Other cost behaviour patterns

Other cost behaviour patterns may be appropriate to certain cost items. Examples of two other cost behaviour patterns are shown below.

(a) *Cost behaviour pattern (1)*   (b) *Cost behaviour pattern (2)*

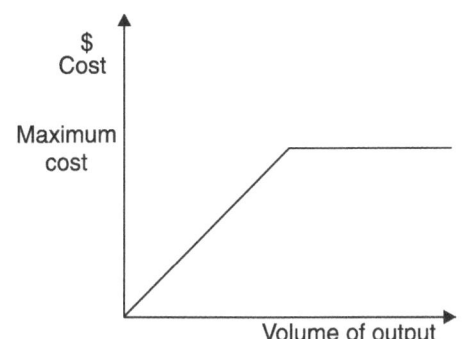
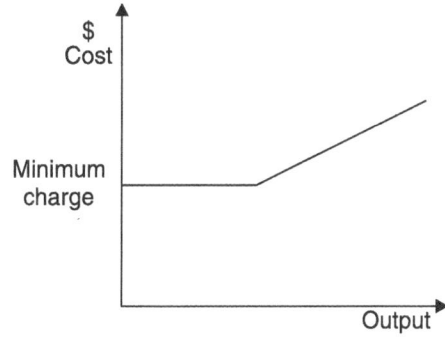

- Graph (a) represents an item of cost which is variable with output up to a certain maximum level of cost.
- Graph (b) represents a cost which is variable with output, subject to a minimum (fixed) charge.

10.7 Cost behaviour and total and unit costs

The following table relates to different levels of production of the zed. The variable cost of producing a zed is $5. Fixed costs are $5,000.

PART A INTRODUCTION TO THE ROLE AND NATURE OF MANAGEMENT ACCOUNTING

	1 zed $	10 zeds $	50 zeds $
Total variable cost	5	50	250
Variable cost per unit	5	5	5
Total fixed cost	5,000	5,000	5,000
Fixed cost per unit	5,000	500	100
Total cost (fixed and variable)	5,005	5,050	5,250
Total cost per unit	5,005	505	105

What happens when activity levels rise can be summarised as follows.

- The variable cost per unit remains constant
- The fixed cost per unit falls
- The total cost per unit falls

This may be illustrated graphically as follows.

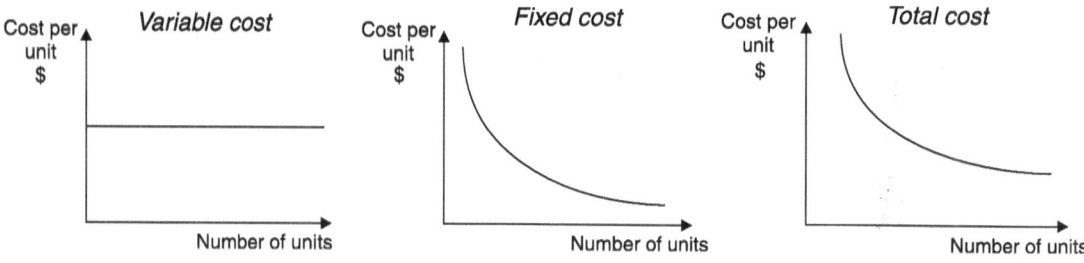

Question
Fixed, variable, mixed costs

Are the following likely to be fixed, variable or mixed costs?

(a) Telephone bill
(b) Annual salary of the chief accountant
(c) The accountant's annual membership fee to AIA (paid by the company)
(d) Cost of materials used to pack 20 units of product X into a box
(e) Wages of warehousemen

Answer

(a) Mixed
(b) Fixed
(c) Fixed
(d) Variable
(e) Variable

Exam focus point An exam question may give you a graph and require you to extract information from it.

10.8 Assumptions about cost behaviour

Assumptions about cost behaviour include the following.

(a) Within the normal or **relevant range** of output, costs are often assumed to be either **fixed, variable** or **semi-variable** (mixed).

(b) Departmental costs within an organisation are assumed to be **mixed costs**, with a **fixed** and a **variable** element.

(c) Departmental costs are assumed to rise in a straight line as the volume of activity increases. In other words, these costs are said to be **linear**.

Chapter roundup

- A **direct cost** is a cost that can be traced in full to the product, service or department being costed. An **indirect cost** (or overhead) is a cost that is incurred in the course of making a product, providing a service or running a department, but which cannot be traced directly and in full to the product, service or department.
- **Classification by function** involves classifying costs as production/manufacturing costs, administration costs or marketing/selling and distribution costs.
- The **classification of environmental costs** involves categorising costs to better understand the expenses associated with both conformance and non-conformance. Conformance costs include prevention and appraisal costs, while non-conformance costs encompass internal and external failure costs.
- A different way of analysing and classifying costs is into **fixed costs** and **variable costs**. Many items of expenditure are part-fixed and part-variable and hence are termed **semi-fixed** or **semi-variable costs**.
- For the preparation of financial statements, costs are often classified as **production costs** and **non-production costs**. Production costs are costs identified with goods produced or purchased for resale. Non-production costs are costs deducted as expenses during the current period.
- **Cost centres** are collecting places for costs before they are further analysed. Costs are further analysed into cost units once they have been traced to cost centres.
- A **cost unit** is a unit of product or service to which costs can be related. The cost unit is the basic control unit for costing purposes.
- A **cost object** is any activity for which a separate measurement of costs is desired.
- **Profit centres** are similar to cost centres but are accountable for both **costs and revenues**.
- **Revenue centres** are similar to cost centres and profit centres but are accountable for **revenues only**. Revenue centre managers should normally have control over how revenues are raised.
- An **investment centre** is a profit centre with additional responsibilities for capital investment and possibly financing, and whose performance is measured by its return on investment.
- A **responsibility centre** is a department or organisational function whose performance is the direct responsibility of a specific manager.
- **Cost behaviour** is the way in which costs are affected by changes in the volume of output.
- The basic principle of cost behaviour is that **as the level of activity rises, costs will usually rise**. It will cost more to produce 2,000 units of output than it will to produce 1,000 units.
- A **fixed cost** is a cost which tends to be unaffected by increases or decreases in the volume of output.
- A **step cost** is a cost which is fixed in nature but only within certain levels of activity.
- A **variable cost** is a cost which tends to vary directly with the volume of output. The variable cost per unit is the same amount for each unit produced.
- If the relationship between total variable cost and volume of output can be shown as a curved line on a graph, the relationship is said to be **curvilinear**.
- A **semi-variable/semi-fixed/mixed cost** is a cost which contains both fixed and variable components and so is partly affected by changes in the level of activity.

Quick quiz

1. Give two examples of direct expenses; and an example of an administration overhead, a selling overhead and a distribution overhead.
2. What are functional costs?
3. What is the distinction between fixed and variable costs; and between production costs and non-production costs?
4. What is a cost centre, a cost unit and a profit centre?
5. Cost behaviour is ....
6. The basic principle of cost behaviour is that as the level of activity rises, costs will usually rise/fall.
7. Fill in the gaps for each of the graph titles below.

(a)

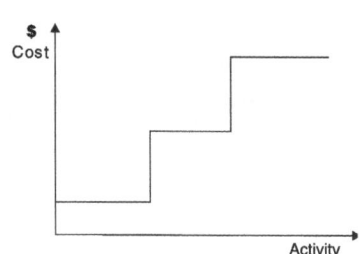

Graph of a ....cost

Example:

(b)

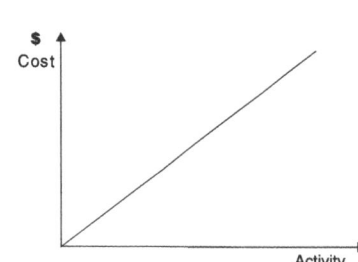

Graph of a ....cost

Example:

(c)

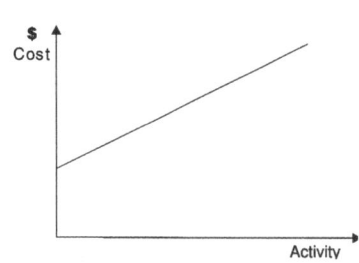

Graph of a ....cost

Example:

(d)

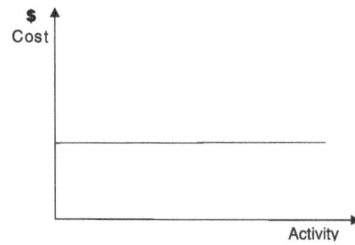

Graph of a ....cost

Example:

8   Costs are assumed to be either fixed, variable or semi-variable within the normal or relevant range of output.

   True   ☐

   False   ☐

Answers to quick quiz

1. - The hire of tools or equipment for a particular job
   - Maintenance costs of tools, fixtures and so on
   - **Administration overhead** = Depreciation of office buildings and equipment
   - **Selling overhead** = Printing and stationery (catalogues, price lists)
   - **Distribution overhead** = Wages of packers, drivers and despatch clerks

2. Functional costs are classified as follows.
   - **Production** or **manufacturing costs**
   - **Administration costs**
   - **Marketing** or **selling and distribution costs**

3. A **fixed cost** is a cost which is incurred for a particular period of time and which, within certain activity levels, is unaffected by changes in the level of activity.

   A **variable cost** is a cost which tends to vary with the level of activity.

   Production costs are costs identified with a finished product. Such costs are initially identified as part of the value of inventory. They become expenses only when the inventory is sold.

   Non-production costs are costs that are deducted as expenses during the current period without ever being included in the value of inventory held.

4. A **cost centre** acts as a collecting place for certain costs before they are analysed further.

   A **cost unit** is a unit of product or service to which costs can be related. The cost unit is the basic control unit for costing purposes.

   A **profit centre** is similar to a cost centre but is accountable for **costs** and **revenues**.

5. The variability of input costs with activity undertaken

6. Rise

7. (a) Step cost. Example: rent, supervisors' salaries
   (b) Variable cost. Example: raw materials, direct labour
   (c) Semi-variable cost. Example: electricity and telephone
   (d) Fixed. Example: rent, depreciation (straight-line)

8. True

PART C2

Cost identification and measuring costs for management purposes

Material costs

Topic list	Syllabus reference
1 What is inventory control?	C2.1
2 The ordering, receipt and issue of raw materials	C2.1
3 The storage of raw materials	C2.1
4 Inventory control levels	C2.1
5 The environmental impact of inventory	C2.1
6 Inventory valuation	C2.1
7 FIFO (first in, first out)	C2.1
8 LIFO (last in, first out)	C2.1
9 AVCO (cumulative weighted average pricing)	C2.1
10 IAS 2 Inventories	C2.1
11 Inventory valuation and profitability	C2.1

Introduction

The investment in inventory is a very important one for most businesses, both in terms of monetary value and relationships with customers (no inventory, no sale, loss of customer goodwill). It is therefore vital that management establish and maintain an **effective inventory control system**.

This chapter begins by concentrating on an **inventory control system** for materials, but similar problems and considerations apply to all forms of inventory.

Management should be are aware of the major costing problem relating to materials, that of pricing materials issues and valuing inventory at the end of each period.

In this chapter we will therefore conclude by considering the methods for **pricing materials issues/valuing inventory**. We will look at the various methods, their advantages and disadvantages and their impact on profitability.

PART B COST IDENTIFICATION AND MEASURING COSTS FOR MANAGEMENT PURPOSES

Exam focus point

Material costs could be examined in a number of ways in multiple choice questions. There could be calculation questions, for example requiring the calculation of the economic order quantity or valuation under FIFO for example. There could also be qualitative MCQs, for example, asking you to identify different documents or reasons for holding inventory.

1 What is inventory control?

1.1 Introduction

FAST FORWARD

Inventory control includes the functions of inventory ordering and purchasing, receiving goods into store, storing and issuing inventory and controlling levels of inventory.

Classifications of inventories

- Raw materials
- Work in progress
- Spare parts/consumables
- Finished goods

This chapter will concentrate on an **inventory control system** for materials, but similar problems and considerations apply to all forms of inventory. Controls should cover the following functions.

- The **ordering** of inventory
- The **purchase** of inventory
- The **receipt** of goods into store
- **Storage**
- The **issue** of inventory and maintenance of inventory at the most appropriate level

1.2 Qualitative aspects of inventory control

We may wish to **control inventory** for the following reasons.

- Holding costs of inventory may be expensive.
- Production will be disrupted if we run out of raw materials.
- Unused inventory with a short shelf life may incur unnecessary expenses.

If manufactured goods are made out of low quality materials, the end product will be of low quality also. It may therefore be necessary to control the quality of inventory, in order to maintain a good reputation with consumers.

2 The ordering, receipt and issue of raw materials

2.1 Ordering and receiving materials

FAST FORWARD

Every movement of a material in a business should be documented using the following as appropriate: purchase requisition; purchase order; GRN; materials requisition note; materials transfer note; and materials returned note.

Proper records must be kept of the physical procedures for ordering and receiving a consignment of materials to ensure the following.

- That enough inventory is held
- That there is no duplication of ordering
- That quality is maintained
- That there is adequate record keeping for accounts purposes

2.2 Purchase requisition

Current inventories run down to the level where a reorder is required. The stores department issues a **purchase requisition** which is sent to the purchasing department, authorising the department to order further inventory. An example of a purchase requisition is shown below.

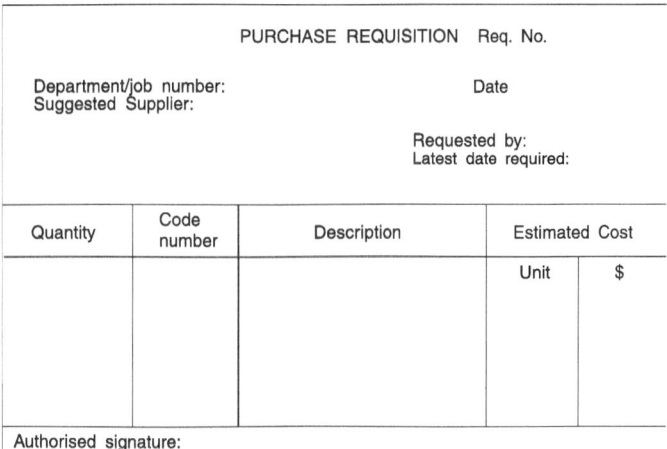

2.3 Purchase order

The purchasing department draws up a **purchase order** which is sent to the supplier. (The supplier may be asked to return an acknowledgement copy as confirmation of his acceptance of the order.) Copies of the purchase order must be sent to the accounts department and the storekeeper (or receiving department).

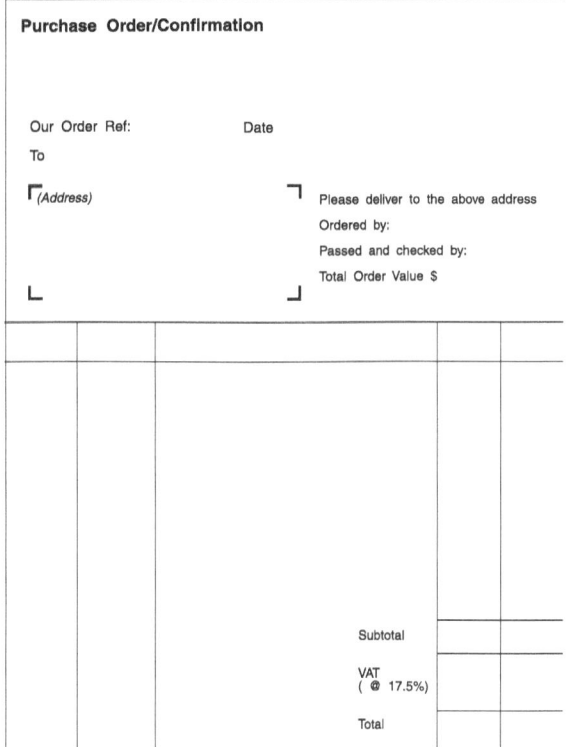

2.4 Quotations

The purchasing department may have to obtain a number of quotations if either a new inventory line is required, the existing supplier's costs are too high or the existing supplier no longer stocks the goods needed. Trade discounts (reduction in the price per unit given to some customers) should be negotiated where possible.

2.5 Delivery note

The supplier delivers the consignment of materials, and the storekeeper signs a **delivery note** for the carrier. The packages must then be checked against the copy of the purchase order, to ensure that the supplier has delivered the types and quantities of materials which were ordered. (Discrepancies would be referred to the purchasing department.)

2.6 Goods received note

If the delivery is acceptable, the storekeeper prepares a **goods received note (GRN)**, an example of which is shown below.

GOODS RECEIVED NOTE	WAREHOUSE COPY NO 5565
DATE: _____ TIME: _____	
OUR ORDER NO: _____	WAREHOUSE A
SUPPLIER AND SUPPLIER'S ADVICE NOTE NO: _____	

QUANTITY	CAT NO	DESCRIPTION

RECEIVED IN GOOD CONDITION: _____ (INITIALS)

A copy of the GRN can be sent to the purchasing department so that it can be matched with the purchase order. This is to make sure that the correct number and specification of items have been received. Any discrepancies would be taken up with the supplier.

A copy of the GRN would also be sent to the accounts department so that it can be matched with the **purchase invoice** when it is received. The payment of the invoice is the end of the transaction (unless there is a mistake on the invoice or there was some problem with the delivery, in which case a **credit note** may later be received from the supplier).

Question — Ordering materials

What are the possible consequences of a failure of control over ordering and receipt of materials?

Answer

(a) Incorrect materials being delivered, disrupting operations
(b) Incorrect prices being paid
(c) Deliveries other than at the specified time (causing disruption)
(d) Insufficient control over quality
(e) Invoiced amounts differing from quantities of goods actually received or prices agreed

You may, of course, have thought of equally valid consequences.

2.7 Materials requisition note

Materials can only be issued against a **materials/stores requisition**. This document must record not only the quantity of goods issued, but also the cost centre or the job number for which the requisition is being made. The materials requisition note may also have a column, to be filled in by the cost department, for recording the cost or value of the materials issued to the cost centre or job.

Materials requisition note			
Date required _____		Cost centre No/ Job No _____	
Quantity	Item code	Description	$
Signature of requisitioning Manager/ Foreman _____			Date _____

2.8 Materials transfers and returns

Where materials, having been issued to one job or cost centre, are later transferred to a different job or cost centre, without first being returned to stores, a **materials transfer note** should be raised. Such a note must show not only the job receiving the transfer, but also the job from which it is transferred. This enables the appropriate charges to be made to jobs or cost centres.

Material returns must also be documented on a **materials returned note**. This document is the 'reverse' of a requisition note, and must contain similar information. In fact it will often be almost identical to a requisition note. It will simply have a different title and perhaps be a distinctive colour, such as red, to highlight the fact that materials are being returned.

2.9 Computerised inventory control systems

Many inventory control systems these days are computerised. Computerised inventory control systems vary greatly, but most will have the features outlined below.

(a) **Data must be input into the system**. For example, details of goods received may simply be written on to a GRN for later entry into the computer system. Alternatively, this information may be keyed in directly to the computer: a GRN will be printed and then signed as evidence of the transaction, so that both the warehouse and the supplier can have a hard copy record in case of dispute. Some systems may incorporate the use of devices such as bar code readers.

   Other types of transaction which will need to be recorded include the following.

   (i) **Transfers** between different categories of inventory (for example from work in progress to finished goods).

   (ii) **Despatch**, resulting from a sale, of items of finished goods to customers.

   (iii) **Adjustments** to inventory records if the amount of inventory revealed in a physical inventory count differs from the amount appearing on the inventory records.

(b) **An inventory master file is maintained**. This file will contain details for every category of inventory and will be updated for new inventory lines. A database file may be maintained.

Question — Inventory master file

What type of information do you think should be held on an inventory master file?

Answer

Here are some examples.

(a)	Inventory code number, for reference	(e)	Cost per unit
(b)	Brief description of inventory item	(f)	Selling price per unit (if finished goods)
(c)	Reorder level	(g)	Amount in inventory
(d)	Reorder quantity	(h)	Frequency of usage

The file may also hold details of inventory movements over a period, but this will depend on the type of system in operation. In a **batch system**, transactions will be grouped and input in one operation and details of the movements may be held in a separate transactions file, the master file updated in total only. In an **online system**, transactions may be input directly to the master file, where the record of movements is thus likely to be found. Such a system will mean that the inventory records are constantly up to date, which will help in monitoring and controlling inventory.

The system may generate orders automatically once the amount in inventory has fallen to the reorder level.

(c) **The system will generate outputs**. These may include, depending on the type of system, any of the following.

   (i) **Hard copy** records, for example a printed GRN, of transactions entered into the system.

   (ii) Output on a **VDU** screen in response to an enquiry (for example the current level of a particular line of inventory, or details of a particular transaction).

   (iii) Various **printed reports**, devised to fit in with the needs of the organisation. These may include inventory movement reports, detailing over a period the movements on all inventory lines, listings of GRNs, despatch notes and so forth.

A computerised inventory control system is usually able to give more up to date information and more flexible reporting than a manual system but remember that both manual and computer based inventory control systems need the same types of data to function properly.

3 The storage of raw materials

3.1 Objectives of storing materials

- Speedy **issue** and **receipt** of materials
- Full **identification** of all materials at all times
- Correct **location** of all materials at all times
- **Protection** of materials from damage and deterioration
- Provision of **secure stores** to avoid pilferage, theft and fire
- **Efficient** use of storage space
- **Maintenance** of correct inventory levels
- Keeping correct and up-to-date **records** of receipts, issues and inventory levels

3.2 Recording inventory levels

One of the objectives of storekeeping is to maintain accurate records of current inventory levels. This involves the accurate recording of inventory movements (issues from and receipts into stores). The most frequently encountered system for recording inventory movements is the use of bin cards and stores ledger accounts.

3.2.1 Bin cards

A **bin card** shows the level of inventory of an item at a particular stores location. It is kept with the actual inventory and is updated by the storekeeper as inventories are received and issued. A typical bin card is shown below.

Bin card

Part code no _____			Location _____		
Bin number _____			Stores ledger no _____		
Receipts			Issues		Inventory balance
Date	Quantity	G.R.N. No.	Date	Quantity Req. No.	

The use of bin cards is decreasing, partly due to the difficulty in keeping them updated and partly due to the merging of inventory recording and control procedures, frequently using computers.

3.2.2 Stores ledger accounts

A typical stores ledger account is shown below. Note that it shows the value of inventory.

Stores ledger account

Material _____				Maximum Quantity _____					
Code _____				Minimum Quantity _____					
Date	Receipts				Issues			Inventory		
	G.R.N No.	Quantity	Unit price $	Amount $	Stores Req. No	Quantity	Unit price $	Amount $	Quantity	Unit price $	Amount $

The above illustration shows a card for a manual system, but even when the inventory records are computerised, the same type of information is normally included in the computer file. The running balance on the stores ledger account allows inventory levels and valuation to be monitored.

3.2.3 Free inventory

Managers need to know the **free inventory balance** in order to obtain a full picture of the current inventory position of an item. Free inventory represents what is really **available for future use** and is calculated as follows.

	Materials in inventory	X
+	Materials on order from suppliers	X
–	Materials requisitioned, not yet issued	(X)
	Free inventory balance	X

Knowledge of the level of physical inventory assists inventory issuing, inventory counting and controlling maximum and minimum inventory levels: knowledge of the level of free inventory assists ordering.

Question — Units on order

A wholesaler has 8,450 units outstanding for Part X100 on existing customers' orders; there are 3,925 units in inventory and the calculated free inventory is 5,525 units.

How many units does the wholesaler have on order with his supplier?

A 9,450   B 10,050   C 13,975   D 17,900

Answer

Free inventory balance = units in inventory + units on order – units ordered, but not yet issued
5,525 = 3,925 + units on order – 8,450
Units on order = 10,050

The correct answer is B.

3.3 Identification of materials: inventory codes (materials codes)

Materials held in stores are **coded** and **classified**. Advantages of using code numbers to identify materials are as follows.

(a) Ambiguity is avoided.

(b) Time is saved. Descriptions can be lengthy and time-consuming.

(c) Production efficiency is improved. The correct material can be accurately identified from a code number.

(d) Computerised processing is made easier.

(e) Numbered code systems can be designed to be flexible, and can be expanded to include more inventory items as necessary.

The digits in a code can stand for the type of inventory, supplier, department and so forth.

3.4 The inventory count (stocktake)

FAST FORWARD

The **inventory count (stocktake)** involves counting the physical inventory on hand at a certain date, and then checking this against the balance shown in the inventory records. The count can be carried out on a **continuous** or **periodic** basis.

Key terms

Periodic stocktaking is a process whereby all inventory items are physically counted and valued at a set point in time, usually at the end of an accounting period.

Continuous stocktaking is counting and valuing selected items at different times on a rotating basis. This involves a specialist team counting and checking a number of inventory items each day, so that each item is checked at least once a year. Valuable items or items with a high turnover could be checked more frequently.

3.4.1 Advantages of continuous stocktaking compared to periodic stocktaking

(a) The annual stocktaking is unnecessary and the disruption it causes is avoided.

(b) Regular skilled stocktakers can be employed, reducing likely errors.

(c) More time is available, reducing errors and allowing investigation.

(d) Deficiencies and losses are revealed sooner than they would be if stocktaking were limited to an annual check.

(e) Production hold-ups are eliminated because the stores staff are at no time so busy as to be unable to deal with material issues to production departments.

(f) Staff morale is improved and standards raised.

(g) Control over inventory levels is improved, and there is less likelihood of overstocking or running out of inventory.

3.4.2 Inventory discrepancies

There will be occasions when inventory checks disclose discrepancies between the physical amount of an item in inventory and the amount shown in the inventory records. When this occurs, the cause of the discrepancy should be investigated, and appropriate action taken to ensure that it does not happen again.

3.4.3 Perpetual inventory

> **FAST FORWARD**
>
> **Perpetual inventory** refers to an inventory recording system whereby the records (bin cards and stores ledger accounts) are updated for each receipt and issue of inventory as it occurs.

This means that there is a continuous record of the balance of each item of inventory. The balance on the stores ledger account therefore represents the inventory on hand and this balance is used in the calculation of closing inventory in monthly and annual accounts. In practice, physical inventories may not agree with recorded inventories and therefore continuous stocktaking is necessary to ensure that the perpetual inventory system is functioning correctly and that minor inventory discrepancies are corrected.

3.4.4 Obsolete, deteriorating and slow-moving inventories and wastage

> **FAST FORWARD**
>
> **Obsolete inventories** are those items which have become out of date and are no longer required. Obsolete items are written off and disposed of.

Inventory items may be wasted because, for example, they get broken. All **wastage** should be noted on the inventory records immediately so that physical inventory equals the inventory balance on records and the cost of the wastage written off.

Slow-moving inventories are inventory items which are likely to take a long time to be used up. For example, 5,000 units are in inventory, and only 20 are being used each year. This is often caused by overstocking. Managers should investigate such inventory items and, if it is felt that the usage rate is unlikely to increase, excess inventory should be written off as for obsolete inventory, leaving perhaps four or five years' supply in inventory.

4 Inventory control levels

4.1 Inventory costs

> **FAST FORWARD**
>
> **Inventory costs** include purchase costs, holding costs, ordering costs and costs of running out inventory.

The costs of purchasing inventory are usually one of the largest costs faced by an organisation and, once obtained, inventory has to be carefully controlled and checked.

4.1.1 Reasons for holding inventories

- To ensure sufficient goods are available to meet expected demand
- To provide a buffer between processes
- To meet any future shortages
- To take advantage of bulk purchasing discounts
- To absorb seasonal fluctuations and any variations in usage and demand
- To allow production processes to flow smoothly and efficiently
- As a necessary part of the production process (such as when maturing cheese)
- As a deliberate investment policy, especially in times of inflation or possible shortages

4.1.2 Holding costs

If inventories are too high, **holding costs** will be incurred unnecessarily. Such costs occur for a number of reasons.

(a) **Costs of storage and stores operations.** Larger inventories require more storage space and possibly extra staff and equipment to control and handle them.

(b) **Interest charges**. Holding inventories involves the tying up of capital (cash) on which interest must be paid.

(c) **Insurance costs**. The larger the value of inventories held, the greater insurance premiums are likely to be.

(d) **Risk of obsolescence**. The longer an inventory item is held, the greater is the risk of obsolescence.

(e) **Deterioration**. When materials in store deteriorate to the extent that they are unusable, they must be thrown away with the likelihood that disposal costs would be incurred.

4.1.3 Costs of obtaining inventory

On the other hand, if inventories are kept low, small quantities of inventory will have to be ordered more frequently, thereby increasing the following **ordering or procurement costs**.

(a) **Clerical and administrative costs** associated with purchasing, accounting for and receiving goods

(b) **Transport costs**

(c) **Production run costs**, for inventory which is manufactured internally rather than purchased from external sources

4.1.4 Stockout costs (running out of inventory)

An additional type of cost which may arise if inventory are kept too low is the type associated with running out of inventory. There are a number of causes of **stockout costs**.

- Lost contribution from lost sales
- Loss of future sales due to disgruntled customers

3: MATERIAL COSTS

- Loss of customer goodwill
- Cost of production stoppages
- Labour frustration over stoppages
- Extra costs of urgent, small quantity, replenishment orders

4.1.5 Objective of inventory control

The overall objective of inventory control is, therefore, to maintain inventory levels so that the total of the following costs is minimised.

- Holding costs
- Ordering costs
- Stockout costs

4.2 Inventory control levels

FAST FORWARD

Inventory control levels can be calculated in order to maintain inventories at the optimum level. The three critical control levels are reorder level, minimum level and maximum level.

Based on an analysis of past inventory usage and delivery times, inventory control levels can be calculated and used to maintain inventory at their optimum level (in other words, a level which minimises costs). These levels will determine 'when to order' and 'how many to order'.

4.2.1 Reorder level

When inventories reach this level, an order should be placed to replenish inventories. The reorder level is determined by consideration of the following.

- The maximum rate of consumption
- The maximum lead time

The maximum lead time is the time between placing an order with a supplier, and the inventory becoming available for use.

Formula to learn

Reorder level = maximum usage × maximum lead time

4.2.2 Minimum level

This is a warning level to draw management attention to the fact that inventories are approaching a dangerously low level and that stockouts are possible.

Formula to learn

Minimum level = reorder level − (average usage × average lead time)

4.2.3 Maximum level

This also acts as a warning level to signal to management that inventories are reaching a potentially wasteful level.

Formula to learn

Maximum level = reorder level + reorder quantity − (minimum usage × minimum lead time)

Question — Maximum inventory level

A large retailer with multiple outlets maintains a central warehouse from which the outlets are supplied. The following information is available for Part Number SF525.

Average usage	350 per day
Minimum usage	180 per day
Maximum usage	420 per day
Lead time for replenishment	11–15 days
Re-order quantity	6,500 units
Re-order level	6,300 units

(a) Based on the data above, what is the maximum level of inventory?

    A 5,250   B 6,500   C 10,820   D 12,800

(b) Based on the data above, what is the approximate number of Part Number SF525 carried as buffer inventory?

    A 200   B 720   C 1,680   D 1,750

Answer

(a) Maximum inventory level = reorder level + reorder quantity − (min usage × min lead time)
= 6,300 + 6,500 − (180 × 11)
= 10,820

The correct answer is C.

Using good MCQ technique, if you were resorting to a guess you should have eliminated option A. The maximum inventory level cannot be less than the reorder quantity.

(b) Buffer inventory = minimum level

Minimum level = reorder level − (average usage × average lead time)
= 6,300 − (350 × 13) = 1,750

The correct answer is D.

Option A could again be easily eliminated. With minimum usage of 180 per day, a buffer inventory of only 200 would not be much of a buffer!

4.2.4 Reorder quantity

This is the quantity of inventory which is to be ordered when inventory reaches the reorder level. If it is set so as to minimise the total costs associated with holding and ordering inventory, then it is known as the economic order quantity.

4.2.5 Average inventory

The formula for the average inventory level assumes that inventory levels fluctuate evenly between the minimum (or safety) inventory level and the highest possible inventory level (the amount of inventory immediately after an order is received, ie safety inventory + reorder quantity).

Formula to learn

Average inventory = safety inventory + ½ reorder quantity

Question — Average inventory

A component has a safety inventory of 500, a re-order quantity of 3,000 and a rate of demand which varies between 200 and 700 per week. The average inventory is approximately:

A 2,000　　　　　　B 2,300　　　　　　C 2,500　　　　　　D 3,500

Answer

Average inventory = safety inventory + ½ reorder quantity
= 500 + (0.5 × 3,000)
= 2,000

The correct answer is A.

4.3 Economic order quantity (EOQ)

FAST FORWARD

The **economic order quantity (EOQ)** is the order quantity which minimises inventory costs. The EOQ can be calculated using a table, graph or formula.

Economic order theory assumes that the average inventory held is equal to one half of the reorder quantity (although as we saw in the last section, if an organisation maintains some sort of buffer or safety inventory then average inventory = buffer inventory + half of the reorder quantity). We have seen that there are certain costs associated with holding inventory. These costs tend to increase with the level of inventories, and so could be reduced by ordering smaller amounts from suppliers each time.

On the other hand, as we have seen, there are costs associated with ordering from suppliers: documentation, telephone calls, payment of invoices, receiving goods into stores and so on. These costs tend to increase if small orders are placed, because a larger number of orders would then be needed for a given annual demand.

4.3.1 Example: Economic order quantity

Suppose a company purchases raw material at a cost of $16 per unit. The annual demand for the raw material is 25,000 units. The holding cost per unit is $6.40 and the cost of placing an order is $32.

We can tabulate the annual relevant costs for various order quantities as follows.

Order quantity (units)		100	200	300	400	500	600	800	1,000
Average inventory (units)	(a)	50	100	150	200	250	300	400	500
Number of orders	(b)	250	125	83	63	50	42	31	25
		$	$	$	$	$	$	$	$
Annual holding cost	(c)	320	640	960	1,280	1,600	1,920	2,560	3,200
Annual order cost	(d)	8,000	4,000	2,656	2,016	1,600	1,344	992	800
Total relevant cost		8,320	4,640	3,616	3,296	3,200	3,264	3,552	4,000

Notes

(a) Average inventory = Order quantity ÷ 2 (ie assuming no safety inventory)
(b) Number of orders = annual demand ÷ order quantity
(c) Annual holding cost = Average inventory × $6.40
(d) Annual order cost = Number of orders × $32

You will see that the economic order quantity is 500 units. At this point the total annual relevant costs are at a minimum.

4.3.2 Example: Economic order quantity graph

We can present the information tabulated in Paragraph 4.3.1 in graphical form. The vertical axis represents the relevant annual costs for the investment in inventories, and the horizontal axis can be used to represent either the various order quantities or the average inventory levels; two scales are actually shown on the horizontal axis so that both items can be incorporated. The graph shows that, as the average inventory level and order quantity increase, the holding cost increases. On the other hand, the ordering costs decline as inventory levels and order quantities increase. The total cost line represents the sum of both the holding and the ordering costs.

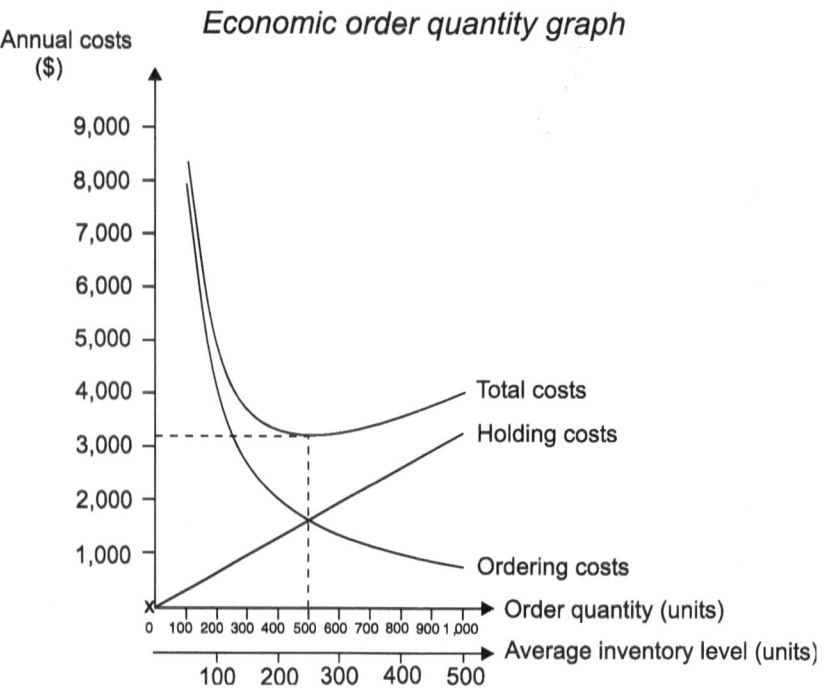

Economic order quantity graph

Note that the total cost line is at a minimum for an order quantity of 500 units and occurs at the point where the ordering cost curve and holding cost curve intersect. **The EOQ is therefore found at the point where holding costs equal ordering costs.**

4.3.3 EOQ formula

The formula for the EOQ will be provided in your examination.

Exam formula

$$EOQ = \sqrt{\frac{2C_o D}{C_H}}$$

where C_H = cost of holding one unit of inventory for one time period
C_O = cost of ordering a consignment from a supplier
D = demand during the time period

Question — EOQ

Calculate the EOQ using the formula and the information in Paragraph 4.3.1.

Answer

$$EOQ = \sqrt{\frac{2 \times \$32 \times 25{,}000}{\$6.40}}$$

$$= \sqrt{250{,}000}$$

$$= 500 \text{ units}$$

Question — EOQ and holding costs

A manufacturing company uses 25,000 components at an even rate during a year. Each order placed with the supplier of the components is for 2,000 components, which is the economic order quantity. The company holds a buffer inventory of 500 components. The annual cost of holding one component in inventory is $2.

What is the total annual cost of holding inventory of the component?

A $2,000   B $2,500   C $3,000   D $4,000

Answer

The correct answer is C.

[Buffer inventory + (EOQ/2)] × Annual holding cost per component

= [500 + (2,000/2)] × $2

= $3,000

Exam focus point: Economic Order Quantity questions are likely to appear regularly in exams.

4.4 Other systems of stores control and reordering

4.4.1 Order cycling method

Under the order cycling method, quantities on hand of each stores item are reviewed periodically (every 1, 2 or 3 months). For low-cost items, a technique called the 90-60-30 day technique can be used, so that when inventories fall to 60 days' supply, a fresh order is placed for a 30 days' supply so as to boost inventories to 90 days' supply. For high-cost items, a more stringent stores control procedure is advisable so as to keep down the costs of inventory holding.

4.4.2 Two-bin system

The two-bin system of stores control (or visual method of control) is one whereby each stores item is kept in two storage bins. When the first bin is emptied, an order must be placed for re-supply; the second bin will contain sufficient quantities to last until the fresh delivery is received. This is a simple system which is not costly to operate but it is not based on any formal analysis of inventory usage and may result in the holding of too much or too little inventory.

4.4.3 Classification of materials

Materials items may be classified as expensive, inexpensive or in a middle-cost range. Because of the practical advantages of simplifying stores control procedures without incurring unnecessary high costs, it may be possible to segregate materials for selective stores control.

(a) Expensive and medium-cost materials are subject to careful stores control procedures to minimise cost.

(b) Inexpensive materials can be stored in large quantities because the cost savings from careful stores control do not justify the administrative effort required to implement the control.

This selective approach to stores control is sometimes called the **ABC method** whereby materials are classified A, B or C according to their expense-group A being the expensive, group B the medium-cost and group C the inexpensive materials.

4.4.4 Pareto (80/20) distribution

A similar selective approach to stores control is the **Pareto (80/20) distribution, which** which is based on the finding that in many stores, 80% of the value of stores is accounted for by only 20% of the stores items, and inventories of these more expensive items should be controlled more closely.

4.4.5 Just-in-time (JIT) systems

> **FAST FORWARD**
>
> JIT aims for zero inventory and perfect quality and operates by demand-pull. It consists of **JIT purchasing** and **JIT production** and results in lower investment requirements, space savings, greater customer satisfaction and increased flexibility.

'Traditional' responses to the problems of improving manufacturing capacity and reducing unit costs of production might be described as follows.

- Longer production runs
- Economic batch quantities
- Fewer products in the product range
- More overtime
- Reduced time on preventive maintenance, to keep production flowing

In general terms, longer production runs and large batch sizes should mean less disruption, better capacity utilisation and lower unit costs.

Just-in-time systems challenge such 'traditional' views of manufacture.

Key terms

> **Just-in-time (JIT)** is a 'System whose objective is to produce or to procure products or components as they are required by a customer or for use, rather than for stock. A JIT system is a **pull** system, which responds to demand, in contrast to a **push** system, in which stocks act as buffers between the different elements of the system, such as purchasing, production and sales.'
>
> **Just-in-time production** is a 'Production system which is driven by demand for finished products whereby each component on a production line is produced only when needed for the next stage.'
>
> **Just-in-time purchasing** is a 'Purchasing system in which material purchases are contracted so that the receipt and usage of material, to the maximum extent possible, coincide.' *CIMA Official Terminology*

Although described as a technique in the *Official Terminology*, JIT is more of a **philosophy or approach to management** since it encompasses a **commitment to continuous improvement** and the **search for excellence** in the design and operation of the production management system.

4.4.6 Material requirements planning (MRP)

Key term

> **Material requirements planning (MRP)** is a 'System that converts a production schedule into a listing of the materials and components required to meet that schedule, so that adequate stock levels are maintained and items are available when needed.'
> *CIMA Official Terminology*

MRP is a computerised information, planning and control system that can be used in a traditional manufacturing environment as well as with AMT. MRP uses information from a master production schedule which details how many finished goods items are needed, and when, and works back from this to determine the requirements for parts and materials in the earlier stages of the production process. MRP systems are chiefly used in a batch manufacturing environment.

4.5 The aims of MRP

- Minimising inventory levels
- Avoiding the high costs of rush orders
- Minimum disruption to production

MRP is therefore concerned with **maximising efficiency in the timing of orders for raw materials or parts that are placed with external suppliers** and **efficient scheduling of the manufacturing and assembly of the end product**.

5 The environmental impact of inventory

FAST FORWARD

> The environmental costs associated with materials include resource utilisation, energy consumption, waste disposal, compliance costs and sustainability investments.

Considering environmental impact costs has become increasingly relevant in inventory management. These costs are associated with the **ecological footprint of managing and storing inventory** and they can influence both operational and financial outcomes.

(a) **Resource utilisation.** Excessive inventory often results in inefficient use of resources. Overproduction can lead to waste and increased consumption of raw materials. Managing inventory levels more precisely can reduce resource wastage and support sustainability efforts.

(b) **Energy consumption.** Larger inventories require more storage facilities, which typically consume more energy for climate control and lighting. Minimising inventory levels can lead to lower energy usage and reduced carbon emissions.

(c) **Waste disposal costs.** Obsolete or deteriorated inventory must be disposed of, which can incur additional costs and environmental impacts. Proper inventory management can reduce the frequency of waste and therefore associated disposal costs.

(d) **Compliance costs.** Adhering to environmental regulations related to inventory, such as those governing emissions or waste management, can result in additional costs. Efficient inventory practices can help mitigate these compliance expenses.

(e) **Sustainability investments.** Investing in sustainable practices, such as eco-friendly packaging or energy-efficient storage systems, can initially increase costs but may lead to long-term savings and improved brand reputation.

PART B COST IDENTIFICATION AND MEASURING COSTS FOR MANAGEMENT PURPOSES

Question — Inventory and the environment

Enviromad Ltd uses 25,000 kg of material H every year. The costs associated with material H are as follows:

	$ per kg
Resource utilisation	4.00
Energy consumption	3.00
Waste disposal	1.00
Compliance costs	0.60
Sustainability investments	1.40

What are the total environmental costs for material H for the year?

$ ☐

Answer

$ 250,000

Workings

	$ per kg
Resource utilisation	4.00
Energy consumption	3.00
Waste disposal	1.00
Compliance costs	0.60
Sustainability investments	1.40
	10.00

10.00 × 25,000 kgs = $250,000

6 Inventory valuation

FAST FORWARD

The correct **pricing of issues and valuation of inventory** are of the utmost importance because they have a direct effect on the calculation of profit. Several different methods can be used in practice.

6.1 Valuing inventory in financial accounts

You may be aware from your studies for the Fundamentals of Financial Accounting paper that, for financial accounting purposes, inventories are valued at the **lower of cost and net realisable value**. In practice, inventories will probably be valued at cost in the stores records throughout the course of an accounting period. Only when the period ends will the value of the inventory in hand be reconsidered so that items with a net realisable value below their original cost will be revalued downwards, and the inventory records altered accordingly.

6.2 Charging units of inventory to cost of production or cost of sales

It is important to be able to distinguish between the ways in which the physical items in inventory are actually issued. In practice a storekeeper may issue goods in the following way.

- The oldest goods first
- The latest goods received first
- Randomly
- Those which are easiest to reach

By comparison the cost of the goods issued must be determined on a **consistently applied basis**, and must ignore the likelihood that the materials issued will be costed at a price different to the amount paid for them.

This may seem a little confusing at first, and it may be helpful to explain the point further by looking at an example.

6.3 Example: Inventory valuation

Suppose that there are three units of a particular material in inventory.

Units	Date received	Purchase cost
A	June 20X1	$100
B	July 20X1	$106
C	August 20X1	$109

In September, one unit is issued to production. As it happened, the physical unit actually issued was B. The accounting department must put a value or cost on the material issued, but the value would not be the cost of B, $106. The principles used to value the materials issued are not concerned with the actual unit issued, A, B, or C. Nevertheless, the accountant may choose to make one of the following assumptions.

(a) The unit issued is valued as though it were the earliest unit in inventory, ie at the purchase cost of A, $100. This valuation principle is called **FIFO**, or **first in, first out**.

(b) The unit issued is valued as though it were the most recent unit received into inventory, ie at the purchase cost of C, $109. This method of valuation is **LIFO**, or **last in, first out**.

(c) The unit issued is valued at an **average** price of A, B and C, ie $105.

(It may be that each item of inventory is marked with the purchase cost, as it is received. This method is known as the specific price method. In the majority of cases this method is not practical.)

6.4 A chapter example

In the following sections we will consider each of the pricing methods detailed above, using the following transactions to illustrate the principles in each case.

TRANSACTIONS DURING MAY 20X6

	Quantity Units	Unit cost $	Total cost $	Market value per unit on date of transaction $
Opening balance, 1 May	100	2.00	200	
Receipts, 3 May	400	2.10	840	2.11
Issues, 4 May	200			2.11
Receipts, 9 May	300	2.12	636	2.15
Issues, 11 May	400			2.20
Receipts, 18 May	100	2.40	240	2.35
Issues, 20 May	100			2.35
Closing balance, 31 May	200			2.38
			1,916	

7 FIFO (first in, first out)

FIFO assumes that materials are issued out of inventory in the order in which they were delivered into inventory: issues are priced at the cost of the earliest delivery remaining in inventory.

Key term

FIFO (first in, first out) is 'used to price issues of goods or materials based on the cost of the oldest units held, irrespective of the sequence in which the actual issue of units held takes place. Closing stock is, therefore, valued at the cost of the most recent purchases.'

CIMA Official Terminology

7.1 Example: FIFO

Using **FIFO**, the cost of issues and the closing inventory value in the transactions in Section 5.4 would be as follows.

Date of issue	Quantity issued Units	Value	$	$
4 May	200	100 o/s at $2	200	
		100 at $2.10	210	
				410
11 May	400	300 at $2.10	630	
		100 at $2.12	212	
				842
20 May	100	100 at $2.12		212
Cost of issues				1,464
Closing inventory value	200	100 at $2.12	212	
		100 at $2.40	240	
				452
				1,916

Notes

1. The cost of materials issued plus the value of closing inventory equals the cost of purchases plus the value of opening inventory ($1,916).

2. The market price of purchased materials is rising dramatically. In a period of inflation, there is a tendency with FIFO for materials to be issued at a cost lower than the current market value, although closing inventories tend to be valued at a cost approximating to current market value. FIFO is therefore essentially a **historical cost method**, materials included in cost of production being valued at historical cost.

7.2 Advantages and disadvantages of the FIFO method

Advantages	Disadvantages
It is a logical pricing method which probably represents what is physically happening: in practice the oldest inventory is likely to be used first.	FIFO can be cumbersome to operate because of the need to identify each batch of material separately.
It is easy to understand and explain to managers.	Managers may find it difficult to compare costs and make decisions when they are charged with varying prices for the same materials.
The inventory valuation can be near to a valuation based on replacement cost.	In a period of high inflation, inventory issue prices will lag behind current market value.

Question

FIFO

Complete the table below in as much detail as possible using the information in Sections 5.4 and 6.1.

Date	Receipts			Issues			Inventory		
	Quantity	Unit price $	Amount $	Quantity	Unit price $	Amount $	Quantity	Unit price $	Amount $

Answer

Date	Receipts			Issues			Inventory		
	Quantity	Unit price $	Amount $	Quantity	Unit price $	Amount $	Quantity	Unit price $	Amount $
1.5.X3							100	2.00	200.00
3.5.X3	400	2.10	840.00				100	2.00	200.00
							400	2.10	840.00
							500		1,040.00
4.5.X3				100	2.00	200.00			
				100	2.10	210.00	300	2.10	630.00
9.5.X3	300	2.12	636.00				300	2.10	630.00
							300	2.12	636.00
							600		1,266.00
11.5.X3				300	2.10	630.00			
				100	2.12	212.00	200	2.12	424.00
18.5.X3	100	2.40	240.00				200	2.12	424.00
							100	2.40	240.00
							300		664.00
20.5.X3				100	2.12	212.00	100	2.12	212.00
							100	2.40	240.00
31.5.X3							200		452.00

Note that this type of record is called a **perpetual inventory system** as it shows each receipt and issue of inventory as it occurs.

8 LIFO (last in, first out)

FAST FORWARD

LIFO assumes that materials are issued out of inventory in the reverse order to which they were delivered: the most recent deliveries are issued before earlier ones, and issues are priced accordingly.

Key term

LIFO (last in, first out) is 'used to price issues of goods or materials based on the cost of the most recently received units. Cost of sales in the statement of profit or loss is, therefore, valued at the cost of the most recent purchases.'

8.1 Example: LIFO

Using LIFO, the cost of issues and the closing inventory value in the example above would be as follows.

Date of issue	Quantity issued Units	Valuation	$	$
4 May	200	200 at $2.10		420
11 May	400	300 at $2.12	636	
		100 at $2.10	210	
				846
20 May	100	100 at $2.40		240
Cost of issues				1,506
Closing inventory value	200	100 at $2.10	210	
		100 at $2.00	200	
				410
				1,916

Notes

1 The cost of materials issued plus the value of closing inventory equals the cost of purchases plus the value of opening inventory ($1,916).

2 In a period of inflation there is a tendency with **LIFO** for the following to occur.

- Materials are issued at a price which approximates to current market value (or **economic cost**).
- Closing inventories become undervalued when compared to market value.

8.2 Advantages and disadvantages of the LIFO method

Advantages	Disadvantages
Inventories are issued at a price which is close to current market value.	The method can be cumbersome to operate because it sometimes results in several batches being only part-used in the inventory records before another batch is received.
Managers are continually aware of recent costs when making decisions, because the costs being charged to their department or products will be current costs.	LIFO is often the opposite to what is physically happening and can therefore be difficult to explain to managers.

	As with FIFO, decision making can be difficult because of the variations in prices.

9 AVCO (cumulative weighted average pricing)

FAST FORWARD

The cumulative weighted average pricing method (or AVCO) calculates a **weighted average price** for all units in inventory. Issues are priced at this average cost, and the balance of inventory remaining would have the same unit valuation. The average price is determined by dividing the total cost by the total number of units.

A new weighted average price is calculated whenever a new delivery of materials is received into store. This is the key feature of cumulative weighted average pricing.

Key terms

Average cost is 'used to price issues of goods or materials at the weighted average cost of all units held'.
CIMA *Official Terminology*

9.1 Example: AVCO

In our example, issue costs and closing inventory values would be as follows.

Date	Received Units	Issued Units	Balance Units	Total inventory value $	Unit cost $	$
Opening inventory			100	200	2.00	
3 May	400			840	2.10	
			* 500	1,040	2.08	
4 May		200		(416)	2.08	416
			300	624	2.08	
9 May	300			636	2.12	
			* 600	1,260	2.10	
11 May		400		(840)	2.10	840
			200	420	2.10	
18 May	100			240	2.40	
			* 300	660	2.20	
20 May		100		(220)	2.20	220
						1,476
Closing inventory value			200	440	2.20	440
						1,916

* A new inventory value per unit is calculated whenever a new receipt of materials occurs.

Notes

1   The cost of materials issued plus the value of closing inventory equals the cost of purchases plus the value of opening inventory ($1,916).

2   In a period of inflation, using the cumulative weighted average pricing system, the value of material issues will rise gradually, but will tend to lag a little behind the current market value at the date of issue. Closing inventory values will also be a little below current market value.

9.2 Advantages and disadvantages of AVCO

Advantages	Disadvantages
Fluctuations in prices are smoothed out, making it easier to use the data for decision making.	The resulting issue price is rarely an actual price that has been paid, and can run to several decimal places.
It is easier to administer than FIFO and LIFO, because there is no need to identify each batch separately.	Prices tend to lag a little behind current market values when there is gradual inflation.

Question — Inventory valuation methods

Shown below is an extract from records for inventory code no. 988988.

Date	Qty	Receipts Value $	Total $	Qty	Issues Value $	Total $	Qty	Balance Value $	Total $
5 June							30	2.50	75
8 June	20	3.00	60						
10 June				10	A				
14 June				20	B				
18 June	40	2.40	96						
20 June				6	C				D

(a) The values that would be entered on the stores ledger card for A, B, C and D in a cumulative weighted average pricing system would be:

A $ ☐
B $ ☐
C $ ☐
D $ ☐

(b) The values that would be entered on the stores ledger card for A, B, C and D in a LIFO system would be:

A $ ☐
B $ ☐
C $ ☐
D $ ☐

Answer

(a) A $ 27

B $ 54

C $ 15

D $ 135

Workings

				$
8 June	Inventory balance	30	units @ $2.50	75
		20	units @ $3.00	60
		50		135

Weighted average price = $135/50 = $2.70

				$
10 June	Issues	10	units × $2.70	27
14 June	Issues	20	units × $2.70	54
18 June	Inventory balance	20	units @ $2.70	54
	Remaining receipts	40	units @ $2.40	96
		60		150

Weighted average price = $150/60 = $2.50

20 June	Issues	6	units × $2.50	15
	Inventory balance	54	units × $2.50	135

(b) A $ 30
B $ 55
C $ 14.40
D $ 131.60

Workings

				$
10 June		10	units × $3.00	30
14 June	Remaining	10	units × $3.00	30
		10	units × $2.50	25
				55
20 June	Issues:	6	units × $2.40	14.40
	Balance:	34	units × $2.40	81.60
		20	units × $2.50	50.00
		54		131.60

9.3 Periodic weighted average

The periodic weighted average pricing method calculates an average price at the end of the period, based on the total purchases in that period.

$$\text{Periodic weighted average} = \frac{\text{Cost of opening inventory} + \text{total cost of receipts}}{\text{Units of opening inventory} + \text{total units received}}$$

9.3.1 Example: Periodic weighted average

A wholesaler had the following receipts and issues during May.

	Receipts units	Issues units	$/unit
4 May	800		30
6 May		400	
13 May	600		35
14 May		400	
23 May	600		40
25 May		400	
29 May		400	
	2,000	1,600	

Calculate the value of closing inventory at the end of May using the periodic weighted average.

$$\text{Periodic weighted average} = \frac{(800 \times \$30) + (600 \times \$35) + (600 \times \$40)}{800 + 600 + 600}$$

$$= \$34.50 \text{ per unit}$$

Value of closing inventory = 400 units × $34.50

= $13,800

10 IAS 2 Inventories

FAST FORWARD

Inventory should be valued at the lower of cost and net realisable value.

IAS 2 lays out the required accounting treatment for under the historical cost system. The major area of contention is the cost **value of inventory** to be recorded. This is recognised as an asset of the enterprise until the related revenues are recognised (ie the item is sold) at which point the inventory is recognised as an expense (ie cost of sales). Part or all of the cost of inventories may also be expensed if a write-down to **net realisable value** is necessary.

In other words, the fundamental accounting assumption of **accrual** requires costs to be matched with associated revenues. In order to achieve this, costs incurred for goods which remain unsold at the year end must be carried forward in the statement of financial position and matched against future revenues.

10.1 Scope

The following items are **excluded** from the scope of the standard.

- Work in progress under **construction contracts**
- **Financial instruments** (ie shares, bonds)
- **Livestock**, agricultural and forest products and mineral ores

10.2 Definitions

The standard gives the following important definitions.

Key terms

> - **Inventories** are assets:
>   - held for sale in the ordinary course of business;
>   - in the process of production for such sale; or
>   - in the form of materials or supplies to be consumed in the production process or in the rendering of services.
> - **Net realisable value** is the estimated selling price in the ordinary course of business less the estimated costs of completion and the estimated costs necessary to make the sale. *(IAS 2)*

Inventories can **include** any of the following.

- **Goods purchased and held for resale**, eg goods held for sale by a retailer, or land and buildings held for resale
- **Finished goods** produced
- **Work in progress** being produced
- Materials and supplies awaiting use in the production process (**raw materials**)

10.3 Measurement of inventories

The standard states that '**Inventories should be measured at the lower of cost and net realisable value.**'

10.4 Cost of inventories

The cost of inventories will consist of all the following costs.

(a) **Purchase**
(b) **Costs of conversion**
(c) Other costs incurred in bringing the inventories to their **present location and condition**

10.4.1 Costs of purchase

The standard lists the following as comprising the costs of purchase of inventories.

(a) **Purchase price**; plus
(b) **Import duties** and other taxes; plus
(c) Transport, handling and any other cost **directly attributable** to the acquisition of finished goods, services and materials; less
(d) **Trade discounts**, rebates and other similar amounts.

10.4.2 Costs of conversion

Costs of conversion of inventories consist of two main parts.

(a) Costs **directly related** to the units of production, eg direct materials, direct labour
(b) Fixed and variable **production overheads** that are incurred in converting materials into finished goods, allocated on a systematic basis

10.4.3 Other costs

Any other costs should only be recognised if they are incurred in bringing the inventories to their **present location and condition**.

The standard lists types of cost which **would not be included** in cost of inventories. Instead, they should be recognised as an **expense** in the period they are incurred.

- **Abnormal amounts** of wasted materials, labour or other production costs
- **Storage costs** (except costs which are necessary in the production process before a further production stage)
- **Administrative overheads** not incurred to bring inventories to their present location and conditions
- **Selling costs**

10.4.4 Techniques for the measurement of cost

Two techniques are mentioned by the standard, both of which produce results which **approximate to cost**, and so both of which may be used for convenience.

(a) **Standard costs** are set up to take account of normal production values: amount of raw materials used, labour time etc. They are reviewed and revised on a regular basis.

(b) **Retail method**: this is often used in the retail industry where there is a large turnover of inventory items, which nevertheless have similar profit margins. The only practical method of inventory valuation may be to take the total selling price of inventories and deduct an overall average profit margin, thus reducing the value to an approximation of cost. The percentage will take account of reduced price lines. Sometimes different percentages are applied on a department basis.

10.5 Cost formulas

Cost of inventories should be assigned by **specific identification** of their individual costs.

(a) Items that are **not ordinarily interchangeable**
(b) Goods or services produced and segregated for **specific projects**

Specific costs should be attributed to individual items of inventory when they are segregated for a specific project, but not where inventories consist of a large number of interchangeable (ie identical or very similar) items. In the latter circumstances, one of **two approaches** may be taken.

The cost formula is that the cost of inventories should be assigned by using the **first-in, first-out (FIFO)** or **weighted average** cost formulas.

Under the weighted average cost method, a recalculation can be made after each purchase (as we calculated), **or alternatively only at the period end**.

LIFO is no longer permitted under IAS 2.

Question — Inventory valuation

You are the accountant at Water Pumps Co, and you have been asked to calculate the valuation of the company's inventory at cost at its year end of 30 April 20X5.

Water Pumps manufactures a range of pumps. The pumps are assembled from components bought by Water Pumps (the company does not manufacture any parts).

The company does not use a standard costing system, and work in progress and finished goods are valued as follows.

(a) Material costs are determined from the product specification, which lists the components required to make a pump.

(b) The company produces a range of pumps. Employees record the hours spent on assembling each type of pump, this information is input into the payroll system which prints the total hours spent each week assembling each type of pump. All employees assembling pumps are paid at the same rate and there is no overtime.

(c) Overheads are added to the inventory value in accordance with IAS 2 *Inventories*. The financial accounting records are used to determine the overhead cost, and this is applied as a percentage based on the direct labour cost.

For direct labour costs, you have agreed that the labour expended for a unit in work in progress is half that of a completed unit.

The draft accounts show the following materials and direct labour costs in inventory.

	Raw materials	Work in progress	Finished goods
Materials ($)	74,786	85,692	152,693
Direct labour ($)		13,072	46,584

The costs incurred in April, as recorded in the financial accounting records, were as follows.

	$
Direct labour	61,320
Selling costs	43,550
Depreciation and finance costs of production machines	4,490
Distribution costs	6,570
Factory manager's wage	2,560
Other production overheads	24,820
Purchasing and accounting costs relating to production	5,450
Other accounting costs	7,130
Other administration overheads	24,770

For your calculations assume that all work in progress and finished goods were produced in April 20X5 and that the company was operating at a normal level of activity.

Required

Calculate the value of overheads which should be added to work in progress and finished goods in accordance with IAS 2 *Inventories*.

Note. You should include details and a description of your workings and all figures should be calculated to the nearest $.

Answer

Calculation of overheads for inventory

Production overheads are as follows.

	$
Depreciation/finance costs	4,490
Factory manager's wage	2,560
Other production overheads	24,820
Accounting/purchase costs	5,450
	37,320

Direct labour = $61,320

∴ Production overhead rate = $\frac{37,320}{61,320}$ = 60.86%

PART B COST IDENTIFICATION AND MEASURING COSTS FOR MANAGEMENT PURPOSES

Inventory valuation

	Raw materials $	WIP $	Finished goods $	Total $
Materials	74,786	85,692	152,693	313,171
Direct labour	–	13,072	46,584	59,656
Production overhead (at 60.86% of labour)	–	7,956	28,351	36,307
	74,786	106,720	227,628	409,134

Variable overheads will be included in the cost of inventory.

10.6 Net realisable value (NRV)

As a general rule assets should not be carried at amounts greater than those expected to be realised from their sale or use. In the case of inventories this amount could fall below cost when items are **damaged or become obsolete**, or where the **costs to completion have increased** in order to make the sale.

In fact we can identify the principal situations in which **NRV is likely to be less than cost**.

(a) An **increase in costs** or a **fall in selling price**
(b) A **physical deterioration** in the condition of inventory
(c) **Obsolescence** of products
(d) A decision as part of the company's marketing strategy to manufacture and sell products at a **loss**
(e) **Errors in production or purchasing**

A write down of inventories would normally take place on an item by item basis, but similar or related items may be **grouped together**. This grouping together is acceptable for, say, items in the same product line, but it is not acceptable to write down inventories based on a whole classification (eg finished goods) or a whole business.

The assessment of NRV should take place **at the same time** as estimates are made of selling price, using the most reliable information available. Fluctuations of price or cost should be taken into account if they relate directly to **events after the reporting period,** which confirm conditions existing at the end of the period.

The reasons why inventory is held must also be taken into account. Some inventory, for example, may be held to satisfy a firm contract and its NRV will therefore be the **contract price**. Any additional inventory of the same type held at the period end will, in contrast, be assessed according to general sales prices when NRV is estimated.

Net realisable value must be reassessed at the end of each period and compared again with cost. If the NRV has risen for inventories held over the end of more than one period, then the previous write down must be **reversed** to the extent that the inventory is then valued at the lower of cost and the new NRV. This may be possible when selling prices have fallen in the past and then risen again.

On occasion a write down to NRV may be of such size, incidence or nature that it must be **disclosed separately**.

10.7 Recognition as an expense

The following treatment is required **when inventories are sold**.

(a) The **carrying amount** is recognised as an expense in the period in which the related revenue is recognised.

(b) The amount of any **write-down of inventories** to NRV and all losses of inventories are recognised as an expense in the period the write-down or loss occurs.

(c) The amount of any **reversal of any write-down of inventories**, arising from an increase in NRV, is recognised as a reduction in the amount of inventories recognised as an expense in the period in which the reversal occurs.

11 Inventory valuation and profitability

FAST FORWARD

> Each method of inventory valuation (usually) produces different figures for both the value of closing inventories and also the cost of material issues. Since materials costs affect the cost of production, and the cost of production works through eventually into the cost of sales (which is also affected by the value of closing inventories), it follows that **different methods of inventory valuation will provide different profit figures**.

The following example will help to illustrate the point.

11.1 Example: inventory valuation and profitability

On 1 November 20X2, Delilah's Dresses Ltd held 3 pink satin dresses with orange sashes, designed by Freda Swoggs. These were valued at $120 each. During November 20X2, 12 more of the dresses were delivered as follows.

Date	Units received	Purchase cost per dress
10 November	4	$125
20 November	4	$140
25 November	4	$150

A number of the pink satin dresses with orange sashes were sold during November as follows.

Date	Dresses sold	Sales price per dress
14 November	5	$200
21 November	5	$200
28 November	1	$200

Required

Calculate the gross profit (sales – (opening inventory + purchases – closing inventory)) from selling the pink satin dresses with orange sashes in November 20X2, applying the following principles of inventory valuation.

(a) FIFO
(b) LIFO
(c) AVCO

Solution

(a) **FIFO**

Date	Cost of sales	Total $	Closing inventory $
14 November	3 units × $120 + 2 units × $125	610	
21 November	2 units × $125 + 3 units × $140	670	
28 November	1 unit × $140	140	
Closing inventory	4 units × $150		600
		1,420	600

(b) **LIFO**

Date	Cost of sales	Total $	Closing inventory $
14 November	4 units × $125 + 1 unit × $120	620	
21 November	4 units × $140 + 1 unit × $120	680	
28 November	1 unit × $150	150	
Closing inventory	3 units × $150 + 1 unit × $120		570
		1,450	570

(c) **AVCO**

	Units	Unit cost $	Balance in inventory $	Cost of sales $	Closing inventory $
1 November	3	120.00	360		
10 November	4	125.00	500		
	7	122.86	860		
14 November	5	122.86	614	614	
	2		246		
20 November	4	140.00	560		
	6	134.33	806		
21 November	5	134.33	672	672	
	1		134		
25 November	4	150.00	600		
	5	146.80	734		
28 November	1	146.80	147	147	
30 November	4	146.80	587	1,433	587

Profitability

	FIFO $	LIFO $	Weighted average $
Opening inventory	360	360	360
Purchases	1,660	1,660	1,660
	2,020	2,020	2,020
Closing inventory	600	570	587
Cost of sales	1,420	1,450	1,433
Sales (11 × $200)	2,200	2,200	2,200
Gross profit	780	750	767

11.2 Profit differences

In the example above, **different inventory valuation methods produced different costs of sale and hence different gross profits. As opening inventory values and purchase costs are the same for each method, the different costs of sale are due to different closing inventory valuations. The differences in gross profits therefore equal the differences in closing inventory valuations.**

The profit differences are only **temporary**. In the example, the opening inventory in December 20X2 will be $600, $570 or $587, depending on the inventory valuation method used. Different opening inventory values will affect the cost of sales and profits in December, so that in the long run, inequalities in costs of sales each month will even themselves out.

Chapter roundup

- **Inventory control** includes the functions of inventory ordering and purchasing, receiving goods into store, storing and issuing inventory and controlling levels of inventory.

- Every movement of material in a business should be documented using the following as appropriate: purchase requisition; purchase order; GRN; materials requisition note; materials transfer note and materials returned note.

- The **inventory count (stocktake)** involves counting the physical inventory on hand at a certain date, and then checking this against the balance shown in the inventory records. The inventory count can be carried out on a **continuous** or **periodic** basis.

- **Perpetual inventory** refers to an inventory recording system whereby the records (bin cards and stores ledger accounts) are updated for each receipt and issue of inventory as it occurs.

- **Obsolete inventories** are those items which have become out of date and are no longer required. Obsolete items are written off and disposed of.

- **Inventory costs** include purchase costs, holding costs, ordering costs and costs of running out of inventory.

- **Inventory control levels** can be calculated in order to maintain inventories at the optimum level. The three critical control levels are reorder level, minimum level and maximum level.

- The **economic order quantity (EOQ)** is the order quantity which minimises inventory costs. The EOQ can be calculated using a table, graph or formula.

- **JIT** aims for zero inventory and perfect quality and operates by demand-pull. It consists of **JIT purchasing** and **JIT production** and results in lower investment requirements, space savings, greater customer satisfaction and increased flexibility.

- The environmental costs associated with materials include resource utilisation, energy consumption, waste disposal, compliance costs and sustainability investments.

- The correct **pricing of issues and valuation of inventory** are of the utmost importance because they have a direct effect on the calculation of profit. Several different methods can be used in practice.

- **FIFO** assumes that materials are issued out of inventory in the order in which they were delivered into inventory: issues are priced at the cost of the earliest delivery remaining in inventory.

- **LIFO** assumes that materials are issued out of inventory in the reverse order to which they were delivered: the most recent deliveries are issued before earlier ones, and issues are priced accordingly.

- The cumulative weighted average pricing method (or AVCO) calculates a **weighted average price** for all units in inventory. Issues are priced at this average cost, and the balance of inventory remaining would have the same unit valuation. The average price is determined by dividing the total cost by the total number of units.

- A new weighted average price is calculated whenever a new delivery of materials is received into store. This is the key feature of cumulative weighted average pricing.

- Inventory should be valued at the lower of cost and net realisable value.

- Each method of inventory valuation (usually) produces different figures for both the value of closing inventories and also the cost of material issues. Since materials costs affect the cost of production, and the cost of production works through eventually into the cost of sales (which is also affected by the value of closing inventories), it follows that **different methods of inventory valuation will provide different profit figures**.

PART B COST IDENTIFICATION AND MEASURING COSTS FOR MANAGEMENT PURPOSES

Quick quiz

1 List six objectives of storekeeping.

   * ....   * ....
   * ....   * ....
   * ....   * ....

2 Free inventory represents..

3 Free inventory is calculated as follows. (Delete as appropriate)

   (a) + – Materials in inventory   X
   (b) + – Materials in order   X
   (c) + – Materials requisitioned (not yet issued)   X
           Free Inventory balance   X

4 How does periodic inventory counting differ from continuous inventory counting?

5 Match up the following.

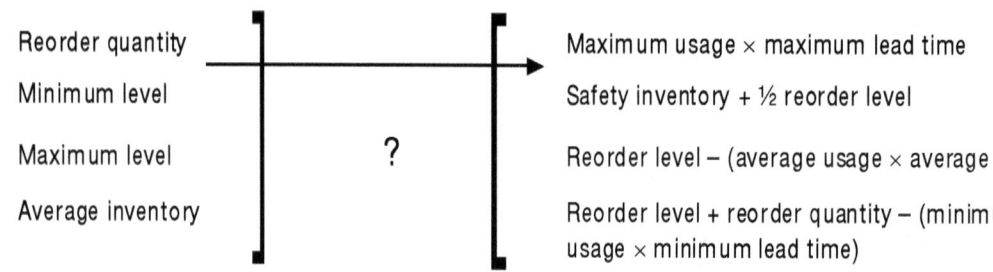

   Reorder quantity   Maximum usage × maximum lead time
   Minimum level   Safety inventory + ½ reorder level
   Maximum level   ?   Reorder level – (average usage × average lead time)
   Average inventory   Reorder level + reorder quantity – (minimum usage × minimum lead time)

6 $EOQ = \sqrt{\dfrac{2C_o D}{C_H}}$

   Where

   (a) C_H = ...
   (b) C_o = ...
   (c) D = ...

7 Name three environmental costs associated with inventory.

Answers to quick quiz

1. - Speedy **issue** and **receipt** of materials
   - Full **identification** of all materials at all times
   - Correct **location** of all materials at all times
   - **Protection** of materials from damage and deterioration
   - Provision of **secure stores** to avoid pilferage, theft and fire
   - **Efficient** use of storage space
   - **Maintenance** of correct inventory levels
   - Keeping correct and up-to-date **records** of receipts, issues and inventory levels

2. Inventory that is readily available for future use

3. (a) +
   (b) +
   (c) −

4. **Periodic inventory counting.** All inventory items physically counted and valued, usually annually.

   Continuous inventory counting. Counting and valuing selected items at different times of the year (at least once a year).

5.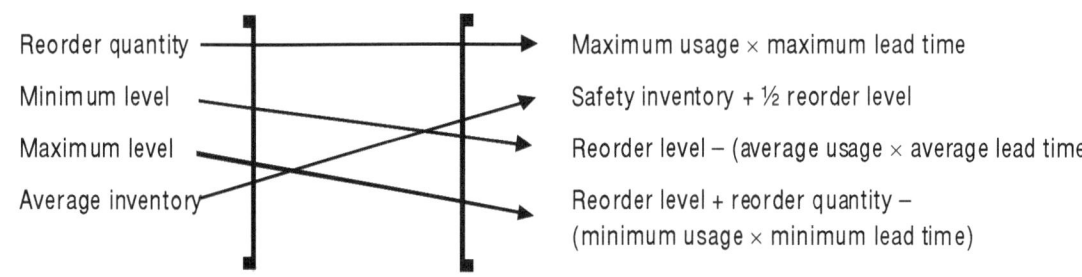

6. (a) Cost of holding one unit of inventory for one time period
   (b) Cost of ordering a consignment from a supplier
   (c) Demand during the time period

7. Any three from: resource utilisation, energy consumption, waste disposal, compliance costs and sustainability investments.

PART B COST IDENTIFICATION AND MEASURING COSTS FOR MANAGEMENT PURPOSES

End of chapter question

Midtec Ltd

Midtec Ltd manufactures specialist lubricants for use in industrial processes. Two key materials used in the process are Kitain and Jensten. Kitain costs $2 per litre to purchase and Jensten $1 per litre. Annual usage of Kitain and Jensten is 30,000 and 85,000 litres respectively. Holding costs for Kitain are 8c per litre per year and 11c per year for Jensten. Buying costs for Kitain are $85 per order and $55 per order for Jensten. At present, the Economic Order Quantity for Kitain is 7,984 litres and for Jensten 9,220 litres.

The suppliers of materials Kitain and Jensten have offered Midtec Ltd a discount of 2% off the buying price for orders of 15,000 litres of Kitain and 20,000 litres of Jensten. If this policy is adopted, the management estimate that there will be an effect on the amounts of materials that the company is able to store. More storage space will have to be rented and managed at an estimated total cost of £1,750 per annum.

Required

(a) For each material, using the EOQ, calculate the re-order costs, holding costs and total costs per annum. **(6 marks)**

(b) Evaluate the proposal from the supplier to determine whether it is financially worthwhile ordering larger quantities instead of ordering the EOQ. **(10 marks)**

(c) What practical problems may arise when pursuing an EOQ policy within a company? **(4 marks)**

(Total = 20 marks)

Labour costs

Topic list	Syllabus reference
1 Measuring labour activity	C2.2
2 Remuneration systems	C2.2
3 Recording labour costs	C2.2
4 Accounting for labour costs	C2.2

Introduction

Just as management need to control inventories and operate an appropriate valuation policy in an attempt to control material costs, so too must they be aware of the most suitable **remuneration policy** for their organisation. We will be looking at a number of methods of remuneration and will consider the various types of **incentive scheme** that exist. We will also examine the procedures and documents required for the accurate **recording of labour costs**.

1 Measuring labour activity

Production and productivity are common methods of measuring labour activity.

1.1 Production and productivity

FAST FORWARD

Production is the quantity or volume of output produced. **Productivity** is a measure of the efficiency with which output has been produced. An increase in production without an increase in productivity will not reduce unit costs.

1.2 Example: Production and productivity

Suppose that an employee is expected to produce three units in every hour that he works. The standard rate of productivity is three units per hour, and one unit is valued at $1/3$ of a standard hour of output. If, during one week, the employee makes 126 units in 40 hours of work the following comments can be made.

(a) **Production** in the week is 126 units.

(b) **Productivity** is a relative measure of the hours actually taken and the hours that should have been taken to make the output.

   (i) **Either**, 126 units should take   42 hours
       But did take   40 hours
       Productivity ratio = 42/40 × 100% =   105%

   (ii) **Or alternatively**, in 40 hours, he should make (× 3)   120 units
        But did make   126 units
        Productivity ratio = 126/120 × 100% =   105%

A productivity ratio greater than 100% indicates that actual efficiency is better than the expected or 'standard' level of efficiency.

Key term

Standard hour of production is a concept used in standard costing, and means the number of units that can be produced by one worker working in the standard way at the standard rate for one hour.

1.3 Planning and controlling production and productivity

Management will wish to **plan** and **control** both production levels and labour productivity.

(a) **Production levels can be raised** as follows.

   (i)   Working overtime
   (ii) Hiring extra staff
   (iii) Sub-contracting some work to an outside firm
   (iv) Managing the work force so as to achieve more output

(b) **Production levels can be reduced** as follows.

   (i) Cancelling overtime
   (ii) Laying off staff

(c) **Productivity**, if improved, will enable a company to achieve its production targets in fewer hours of work, and therefore at a lower cost.

1.4 Productivity and its effect on cost

Improved productivity is an important means of reducing total unit costs. In order to make this point clear, a simple example will be used.

1.4.1 Example: Productivity and its effect on cost

Clooney Co has a production department in its factory consisting of a work team of just two men, Doug and George. Doug and George each work a 40 hour week and refuse to do any overtime. They are each paid $100 per week and production overheads of $400 per week are charged to their work.

(a) In week one, they produce 160 units of output between them. Productivity is measured in units of output per man hour.

Production	160 units
Productivity (80 man hours)	2 units per man hour
Total cost	$600 (labour plus overhead)
Cost per man hour	$7.50
Cost per unit	$3.75

(b) In week two, management pressure is exerted on Doug and George to increase output and they produce 200 units in normal time.

Production	200 units (up by 25%)
Productivity	2.5 units per man hour (up by 25%)
Total cost	$600
Cost per man hour	$7.50 (no change)
Cost per unit	$3.00 (a saving of 20% on the previous cost; 25% on the new cost)

(c) In week three, Doug and George agree to work a total of 20 hours of overtime for an additional $50 wages. Output is again 200 units and overhead charges are increased by $100.

Production	200 units (up 25% on week one)
Productivity (100 man hours)	2 units per hour (no change on week one)
Total cost ($600 + $50 + $100)	$750
Cost per unit	$3.75

(d) Conclusions

(i) An increase in production without an increase in productivity will not reduce unit costs (week one compared with week three).

(ii) An **increase in productivity will reduce unit costs** (week one compared with week two).

1.4.2 Automation

Labour cost control is largely concerned with **productivity**. Rising wage rates have increased automation, which in turn has improved productivity and reduced costs.

Where **automation** is introduced, productivity is often, but misleadingly, measured in terms of **output per man-hour**.

1.4.3 Example: Automation

Suppose, for example, that a work-team of 6 men (240 hours per week) is replaced by 1 machine (40 hours per week) and a team of 4 men (160 hours per week), and as a result output is increased from 1,200 units per week to 1,600 units.

	Production	Man hours	Productivity
Before the machine	1,200 units	240	5 units per man hour
After the machine	1,600 units	160	10 units per man hour

Labour productivity has doubled because of the machine, and employees would probably expect extra pay for this success. For control purposes, however, it is likely that a new measure of productivity is required, **output per machine hour**, which may then be measured against a standard output for performance reporting.

1.5 Efficiency, capacity and production volume ratios

Other measures of labour activity include the following.

- Production volume ratio, or activity ratio
- Efficiency ratio (or productivity ratio)
- Capacity ratio

$$\text{Efficiency ratio} \times \text{Capacity ratio} = \text{Production volume ratio}$$

$$\frac{\text{Expected hours to make output}}{\text{Actual hours taken}} \times \frac{\text{Actual hours worked}}{\text{Hours budgeted}} = \frac{\text{Output measured in expected or standard hours}}{\text{Hours budgeted}}$$

These ratios are usually expressed as percentages.

1.5.1 Example: Labour activity ratios

Rush and Fluster Co budgets to make 25,000 standard units of output (in four hours each) during a budget period of 100,000 hours.

Actual output during the period was 27,000 units which took 120,000 hours to make.

Required

Calculate the efficiency, capacity and production volume ratios.

Solution

(a) Efficiency ratio $\quad \dfrac{(27,000 \times 4) \text{ hours}}{120,000} \times 100\% = 90\%$

(b) Capacity ratio $\quad \dfrac{120,000 \text{ hours}}{100,000 \text{ hours}} \times 100\% = 120\%$

(c) Production volume ratio $\quad \dfrac{(27,000 \times 4) \text{ hours}}{100,000} \times 100\% = 108\%$

(d) The production volume ratio of 108% (more output than budgeted) is explained by the 120% capacity working, offset to a certain extent by the poor efficiency (90% × 120% = 108%).

Where efficiency standards are associated with remuneration schemes they generally allow 'normal time' (that is, time required by the average person to do the work under normal conditions) plus an allowance for rest periods and possible delays. There should therefore be a readily achievable standard of efficiency (otherwise any remuneration scheme will fail to motivate employees), but without being so lax that it makes no difference to the rate at which work is done.

4: LABOUR COSTS

2 Remuneration systems

FAST FORWARD

There are three basic groups of **remuneration** systems: **time work**; **piecework schemes**; and **bonus/incentive schemes**.

Labour remuneration systems have an effect on the following.

- The cost of finished products and services
- The morale and efficiency of employees

2.1 Time work

Formula to learn

The most common form of **time work** is a **day-rate system** in which wages are calculated by the following formula.

Wages = Hours worked × rate of pay per hour

2.1.1 Overtime premiums

If an employee works for more hours than the basic daily requirement he may be entitled to an **overtime payment**. Hours of overtime are usually paid at a **premium rate**. For instance, if the basic day-rate is $4 per hour and overtime is paid at time-and-a-quarter, eight hours of overtime would be paid the following amount.

	$
Basic pay (8 × $4)	32
Overtime premium (8 × $1)	8
Total (8 × $5)	40

The **overtime premium** is the extra rate per hour which is paid, not the whole of the payment for the overtime hours.

If employees work unsocial hours, for instance overnight, they may be entitled to a **shift premium**. The extra amount paid per hour, above the basic hourly rate, is the **shift premium**.

2.1.2 Summary of day-rate systems

(a) They are easy to understand.
(b) They do not lead to very complex negotiations when they are being revised.
(c) They are most appropriate when the quality of output is more important than the quantity, or where there is no basis for payment by performance.
(d) There is no incentive for employees who are paid on a day-rate basis to improve their performance.

2.2 Piecework schemes

Formula to learn

In a **piecework scheme**, wages are calculated by the following formula.

Wages = Units produced × Rate of pay per unit

Suppose for example, an employee is paid $1 for each unit produced and works a 40 hour week. Production overhead is added at the rate of $2 per direct labour hour.

PART B COST IDENTIFICATION AND MEASURING COSTS FOR MANAGEMENT PURPOSES

Weekly production Units	Pay (40 hours) $	Overhead $	Conversion cost $	Conversion cost per unit $
40	40	80	120	3.00
50	50	80	130	2.60
60	60	80	140	2.33
70	70	80	150	2.14

As his output increases, his wage increases and at the same time unit costs of output are reduced.

It is normal for pieceworkers to be offered a **guaranteed minimum wage**, so that they do not suffer loss of earnings when production is low through no fault of their own.

If an employee makes several different types of product, it may not be possible to add up the units for payment purposes. Instead, a **standard time allowance** is given for each unit to arrive at a total of piecework hours for payment.

Question
Weekly pay

Penny Pincher is paid 50c for each towel she weaves, but she is guaranteed a minimum wage of $60 for a 40 hour week. In a series of four weeks, she makes 100, 120, 140 and 160 towels.

Required

Calculate her pay each week, and the conversion cost per towel if production overhead is added at the rate of $2.50 per direct labour hour.

Answer

Week	Output Units		Pay $	Production overhead $	Conversion cost $	Unit conversion cost $
1	100	(minimum)	60	100	160	1.60
2	120		60	100	160	1.33
3	140		70	100	170	1.21
4	160		80	100	180	1.13

There is no incentive to Penny Pincher to produce more output unless she can exceed 120 units in a week. The guaranteed minimum wage in this case is too high to provide an incentive.

2.2.1 Example: Piecework

An employee is paid $5 per piecework hour produced. In a 35 hour week he produces the following output.

	Piecework time allowed per unit
3 units of product A	2.5 hours
5 units of product B	8.0 hours

Required

Calculate the employee's pay for the week.

Solution

Piecework hours produced are as follows.

Product A	3 × 2.5 hours	7.5 hours
Product B	5 × 8 hours	40.0 hours
Total piecework hours		47.5 hours

Therefore employee's pay = 47.5 × $5 = $237.50 for the week.

2.2.2 Differential piecework scheme

Differential piecework schemes offer an incentive to employees to increase their output by paying higher rates for increased levels of production. For example:

up to 80 units per week, rate of pay per unit	=	$1.00
80 to 90 units per week, rate of pay per unit	=	$1.20
above 90 units per week, rate of pay per unit	=	$1.30

Employers should obviously be careful to make it clear whether they intend to pay the increased rate on all units produced, or on the extra output only.

2.2.3 Summary of piecework schemes

- They enjoy fluctuating popularity.
- They are occasionally used by employers as a means of increasing pay levels.
- They are often seen to drive employees to work too hard to earn a satisfactory wage.

Careful inspection of output is necessary to ensure that quality doesn't fall as production increases.

2.3 Bonus/incentive schemes

2.3.1 Introduction

In general, **bonus schemes** were introduced to compensate workers paid under a time-based system for their inability to increase earnings by working more efficiently. Various types of incentive and bonus schemes have been devised which encourage greater productivity. The characteristics of such schemes are as follows.

(a) Employees are paid more for their efficiency.
(b) The profits arising from productivity improvements are shared between employer and employee.
(c) Morale of employees is likely to improve since they are seen to receive extra reward for extra effort.

A bonus scheme must satisfy certain conditions to operate successfully.

(a) Its **objectives** should be **clearly stated** and **attainable** by the employees.
(b) The **rules** and conditions of the scheme should be **easy to understand**.
(c) It must **win** the full **acceptance** of everyone concerned.
(d) It should be seen to be **fair to employees and employers**.
(e) The bonus should ideally be **paid soon after the extra effort has been made** by the employees.
(f) **Allowances** should be made for external factors outside the employees' control which reduce their productivity (machine breakdowns, material shortages).
(g) Only those employees who make the extra effort should be rewarded.
(h) The scheme must be **properly communicated** to employees.

To align bonus schemes with modern values and environmental goals, additional sustainability considerations such as the following can be incorporated.

(a) The scheme could encourage practices that promote environmental sustainability, such as reducing waste or improving energy efficiency.
(b) Incentives could reward efforts that contribute to the long-term health of the company and the environment, not just short-term productivity gains.
(c) The scheme could support and recognise initiatives that reduce the company's carbon footprint or enhance social responsibility.
(d) Any scheme should be designed to balance economic benefits with ecological and social impacts, ensuring that improvements do not come at the expense of environmental or community well-being.

We shall be looking at the following types of incentive schemes in detail.

- High day rate system
- Individual bonus schemes
- Group bonus schemes
- Profit sharing schemes
- Incentive schemes involving shares
- Value added incentive schemes

Some organisations employ a variety of incentive schemes. These schemes may be regularly reviewed, and altered as circumstances dictate.

2.4 High day-rate system

Key term

A **high day-rate system** is a system where employees are paid a high hourly wage rate in the expectation that they will work more efficiently than similar employees on a lower hourly rate in a different company.

2.4.1 Example: High day-rate system

For example if an employee would make 100 units in a 40 hour week if he were paid $2 per hour, but 120 units if he were paid $2.50 per hour, and if production overhead is added to cost at the rate of $2 per direct labour hour, costs per unit of output would be as follows.

(a) Costs per unit of output on the low day-rate scheme would be:

$$\frac{(40 \times \$4)}{100} = \$1.60 \text{ per unit}$$

(b) Costs per unit of output on the high day-rate scheme would be:

$$\frac{(40 \times \$4.50)}{120} = \$1.50 \text{ per unit}$$

(c) Note that in this example the labour cost per unit is lower in the first scheme (80c) than in the second (83.3c), but the unit conversion cost (labour plus production overhead) is higher because overhead costs per unit are higher at 80c than with the high day-rate scheme (66.7c).

(d) In this example, the high day-rate scheme would reward both employer (a lower unit cost by 10c) and employee (an extra 50c earned per hour).

2.4.2 Advantages and disadvantages of high day rate schemes

There are two **advantages** of a high day-rate scheme over other incentive schemes.

(a) It is **simple** to calculate and **easy** to understand.
(b) It **guarantees** the employee a consistently **high wage**.

The **disadvantages** of such schemes are as follows.

(a) **Employees cannot earn more than the fixed hourly rate for their extra effort**. In the previous example, if the employee makes 180 units instead of 120 units in a 40 hour week on a high day-rate pay scheme, the cost per unit would fall to $1 but his wage would be the same – 40 hours at $4.50. All the savings would go to benefit the company and none would go to the employee.

(b) **There is no guarantee that the scheme will work consistently**. The high wages may become the accepted level of pay for normal working, and supervision may be necessary to ensure that a high level of productivity is maintained. Unit costs would rise.

(c) **Employees may prefer to work at a normal rate of output**, even if this entails accepting the lower wage paid by comparable employers.

2.5 Individual bonus schemes

Key term

An **individual bonus scheme** is a remuneration scheme whereby **individual** employees qualify for a bonus on top of their basic wage, with each person's bonus being calculated separately.

(a) The bonus is **unique** to the individual. It is not a share of a group bonus.

(b) The individual can earn a bonus by working at an **above-target** standard of efficiency.

(c) The individual earns a **bigger bonus the greater his efficiency**, although the bonus scheme might incorporate quality safeguards, to prevent individuals from sacrificing quality standards for the sake of speed and more pay.

To be successful, however, an **individual bonus scheme** must take account of the following factors.

(a) Each individual should be rewarded for the **work done by that individual**. This means that each person's output and time must be measured separately. Each person must therefore work without the assistance of anyone else.

(b) Work should be **fairly routine**, so that standard times can be set for jobs.

(c) The bonus should be **paid soon after the work is done**, to provide the individual with the incentive to try harder.

2.6 Group bonus schemes

Key term

A **group bonus scheme** is an incentive plan which is related to the output performance of an entire group of workers, a department, or even the whole factory.

Where individual effort cannot be measured, and employees work as a team, an individual incentive scheme is impracticable but a **group bonus scheme** would be feasible.

The other **advantages** of group bonus schemes are as follows.

(a) They are **easier to administer** because they reduce the clerical effort required to measure output and calculate individual bonuses.

(b) They **increase co-operation** between fellow workers.

(c) They have been found to **reduce** accidents, spoilage, waste and absenteeism.

Serious **disadvantages** would occur in the following circumstances.

(a) The employee groups demand **low efficiency standards** as a condition of accepting the scheme.

(b) Individual employees are browbeaten by their fellow workers for working too slowly.

2.7 Profit-sharing schemes

Key term

A **profit sharing scheme** is a scheme in which employees receive a certain proportion of their company's year-end profits (the size of their bonus being related to their position in the company and the length of their employment to date).

The advantage of these schemes is that the company will only pay what it can afford out of actual profits and the bonus can be paid also to non-production staff.

The disadvantages of profit sharing are as follows.

(a) Employees must **wait until the year end** for a bonus. The company is therefore expecting a long-term commitment to greater efforts and productivity from its workers without the incentive of immediate reward.

(b) **Factors** affecting profit may be **outside the control** of employees, in spite of their greater efforts.

(c) **Too many employees** are involved in a single scheme for the scheme to have a great motivating effect on individuals.

2.7.1 Incentive schemes involving shares

It is becoming increasingly common for companies to use their shares, or the right to acquire them, as a form of incentive.

Key terms

A **share option scheme** is a scheme which gives its members the right to buy shares in the company for which they work at a set date in the future and at a price usually determined when the scheme is set up.

An **employee share ownership plan** is a scheme which acquires shares on behalf of a number of employees, and it must distribute these shares within a certain number of years of acquisition.

Some governments have encouraged companies to set up schemes of this nature in the hope that workers will feel they have a stake in the company which employs them. The **disadvantages** of these schemes are as follows.

(a) The benefits are not certain, as the market value of shares at a future date cannot realistically be predicted in advance.

(b) The benefits are not immediate, as a scheme must be in existence for a number of years before members can exercise their rights.

2.7.2 Value added incentive schemes

Value added is an alternative to profit as a business performance measure and it can be used as the basis of an incentive scheme. It is calculated as follows.

Key term

Value added = sales − cost of bought-in materials and services

The advantage of value added over profit as the basis for an incentive scheme is that it excludes any bought-in costs, and is affected only by costs incurred internally, such as labour.

A basic value added figure would be agreed as the target for a business, and some of any excess value added earned would be paid out as a bonus. For example, it could be agreed that value added should be, say, treble the payroll costs and a proportion of any excess earned, say one third, would be paid as bonus.

	$
Payroll costs for month	40,000
Therefore, value added target (× 3)	120,000
Value added achieved	150,000
Therefore, excess value added	30,000
Employee share to be paid as bonus	10,000

2.7.3 Example: incentive schemes

Swetton Tyres Co manufactures a single product. Its work force consists of 10 employees, who work a 36-hour week exclusive of lunch and tea breaks. The standard time required to make one unit of the product is two hours, but the current efficiency (or productivity) ratio being achieved is 80%. No overtime is worked, and the work force is paid $4 per attendance hour.

Because of agreements with the work force about work procedures, there is some unavoidable idle time due to bottlenecks in production, and about four hours per week per person are lost in this way.

The company can sell all the output it manufactures, and makes a 'cash profit' of $20 per unit sold, deducting currently achievable costs of production but **before** deducting labour costs.

An incentive scheme is proposed whereby the work force would be paid $5 per hour in exchange for agreeing to new work procedures that would reduce idle time per employee per week to two hours and also raise the efficiency ratio to 90%.

Required

Evaluate the incentive scheme from the point of view of profitability.

Solution

The current situation

Hours in attendance	10 × 36	= 360 hours
Hours spent working	10 × 32	= 320 hours
Units produced, at 80% efficiency	$\frac{320}{2} \times \frac{80}{100}$	= 128 units

	$
Cash profits before deducting labour costs (128 × $20)	2,560
Less labour costs ($4 × 360 hours)	1,440
Net profit	1,120

The incentive scheme

Hours spent working	10 × 34	= 340 hours
Units produced, at 90% efficiency	$\frac{340}{2} \times \frac{90}{100}$	= 153 units

	$
Cash profits before deducting labour costs (153 × $20)	3,060
Less labour costs ($5 × 360)	1,800
Net profit	1,260

In spite of a 25% increase in labour costs, profits would rise by $140 per week. The company and the workforce would both benefit provided, of course, that management can hold the work force to their promise of work reorganisation and improved productivity.

PART B COST IDENTIFICATION AND MEASURING COSTS FOR MANAGEMENT PURPOSES

Question — Labour cost

The following data relate to work at a certain factory.

Normal working day	8 hours
Basic rate of pay per hour	$6
Standard time allowed to produce 1 unit	2 minutes
Premium bonus	75% of time saved at basic rate

What will be the labour cost in a day when 340 units are made?

A $48   B $51   C $63   D $68

Answer

Standard time for 340 units (× 2 minutes)	680 minutes
Actual time (8 hours per day)	480 minutes
Time saved	200 minutes

	$
Bonus = 75% × 200 minutes × $6 per hour	15
Basic pay = 8 hours × $6	48
Total labour cost	63

Therefore the correct answer is C.

Using basic MCQ technique you can eliminate option A because this is simply the basic pay without consideration of any bonus. You can also eliminate option D, which is based on the standard time allowance without considering the basic pay for the eight-hour day. Hopefully your were not forced to guess, but had you been you would have had a 50% chance of selecting the correct answer (B or C) instead of a 25% chance because you were able to eliminate two of the options straightaway.

3 Recording labour costs

FAST FORWARD

Labour attendance time is recorded on, for example, an attendance record or clock card. Job time may be recorded on daily time sheets, weekly time sheets or job cards depending on the circumstances. The manual recording of times on time sheets or job cards is, however, liable to error or even deliberate deception and may be unreliable. The labour cost of pieceworkers is recorded on a piecework ticket/operation card.

3.1 Organisation for controlling and measuring labour costs

Several departments and management groups are involved in the collection, recording and costing of labour. These include the following.

- Human resources (HR)
- Production planning
- Timekeeping
- Wages
- Cost accounting

3.2 Human resources department

The **human resources (HR) department** is responsible for the following:

- Engagement, transfer and discharge of employees
- Classification and method of remuneration

The department is headed by a **professional HR officer** trained in **HR** management, labour laws, company **HR** policy and industry conditions who should have an understanding of the needs and problems of the employees.

When a person is engaged a **HR record card** should be prepared showing full personal particulars, previous employment, medical category and wage rate. Other details to be included are social security number, address, telephone number, transfers, promotions, changes in wage rates, sickness and accidents and, when an employee leaves, the reason for leaving.

HR departments sometimes **maintain records of overtime and shift working**. Overtime has to be sanctioned by the works manager or **HR** office who advise the time-keepers who control the time booked.

The **HR** department is responsible for issuing **reports to management** on normal and overtime hours worked, absenteeism and sickness, lateness, labour turnover and disciplinary action.

3.3 Production planning department

This department is responsible for the following.

- Scheduling work
- Issuing job orders to production departments
- Chasing up jobs when they run late

3.4 Timekeeping department

The **timekeeping department** is responsible for recording the attendance time and job time of the following.

- The time spent in the factory by each worker
- The time spent by each worker on each job

Such timekeeping provides basic data for statutory records, payroll preparation, labour costs of an operation or overhead distribution (where based on wages or labour hours) and statistical analysis of labour records for determining productivity and control of labour costs.

3.5 Attendance time

The bare minimum record of employees' time is a simple **attendance record** showing days absent because of holiday, sickness or other reason. A typical record of attendance is shown as follows.

It is also necessary to have a record of the following.

- Time of arrival
- Time of breaks
- Time of departure

These may be recorded as follows.

- In a signing-in book
- By using a time recording clock which stamps the time on a clock card
- By using swipe cards (which make a computer record)

An example of a clock card is shown as follows.

No				Ending	
Name					
	HOURS	RATE	AMOUNT	DEDUCTIONS	
Basic				Tax	
O/T				Insurance	
Others				Other	
				Total deduction	
Total					
Less deductions					
Net due					
Time		Day		Basic time	Overtime
1230 T					
0803 T					
1700 M					
1305 M					
1234 M					
0750 M					
Signature _ _ _ _ _ _ _ _ _ _ _					

3.6 Job time

Continuous production. Where **routine, repetitive** work is carried out it might not be practical to record the precise details. For example if a worker stands at a conveyor belt for seven hours his work can be measured by keeping a note of the number of units that pass through his part of the process during that time.

Job costing. When the work is not of a repetitive nature the records required might be one or several of the following.

(a) **Daily time sheets.** A time sheet is filled in by the employee as a record of how their time has been spent. The total time on the time sheet should correspond with time shown on the attendance record.

(b) **Weekly time sheets.** These are similar to daily time sheets but are passed to the cost office at the end of the week. An example of a weekly timesheet is shown below.

	Time Sheet No. _____						
Employee Name _____		Clock Code _____			Dept _____		
Date _____		Week No. _____					
Job No.	Start Time	Finish Time	Qty	Checker	Hrs	Rate	Extension

(c) **Job cards**. Cards are prepared for each job or batch. When an employee works on a job he or she records on the job card the time spent on that job. Job cards are therefore likely to contain entries relating to numerous employees. On completion of the job it will contain a full record of the times and quantities involved in the job or batch. A typical job card is shown as follows.

JOB CARD

Department _____			Job no _____		
Date _____			Operation no. _____		
Time allowance _____			Time started _____		
			Time finished _____		
			Hours on the job _____		
Description of job			Hours	Rate	Cost
Employee no_____			Certified by _____		
Signature_____					

A job card will be given to the employee, showing the work to be done and the expected time it should take. The employee will record the time started and time finished for each job. Breaks for tea and lunch may be noted on the card, as standard times, by the production planning department. The hours actually taken and the cost of those hours will be calculated by the accounting department.

Piecework. The wages of pieceworkers and the labour cost of work done by them is determined from what is known as a **piecework ticket** or an **operation card**. The card records the total number of items (or 'pieces') produced and the number of rejects. Payment is only made for 'good' production.

```
┌─────────────────────────────────────────────────────────────────────┐
│                         OPERATION CARD                              │
├─────────────────────────────────────────────────────────────────────┤
│  Operator's Name _____      Total Batch Quantity _____  │
│  Clock No _____       Start Time _____   │
│  Pay week No _____ Date ____       Stop Time _____   │
│                                                                     │
│  Part No _____       Works Order No _____   │
│  Operation _____       Special Instructions _____   │
├──────────────────┬──────────────┬──────────────────┬────────┬──────┤
│ Quantity Produced│ No Rejected  │ Good Production  │  Rate  │  $   │
│                  │              │                  │        │      │
│                  │              │                  │        │      │
│                  │              │                  │        │      │
│                  │              │                  │        │      │
├──────────────────┴──────────────┴──────────────────┴────────┴──────┤
│  Inspector _____       Operative _____    │
│  Foreman _____       Date _____    │
├─────────────────────────────────────────────────────────────────────┤
│   PRODUCTION CANNOT BE CLAIMED WITHOUT A PROPERLY SIGNED CARD       │
└─────────────────────────────────────────────────────────────────────┘
```

Note that the attendance record of a pieceworker is required for calculations of holidays, sick pay and so on.

Other types of work. Casual workers are paid from job cards or time sheets. Time sheets are also used where outworkers are concerned.

Office work can be measured in a similar way, provided that the work can be divided into distinct jobs. Firms of accountants and advertising agencies, for example, book their staff time to individual clients and so make use of time sheets for salaried staff.

3.7 Salaried labour

Even though salaried staff are paid a flat rate monthly, they may be required to prepare timesheets. The reasons are as follows.

(a) Timesheets provide management with information (eg product costs).

(b) Timesheet information may provide a basis for billing for services provided (eg service firms where clients are billed based on the number of hours work done).

(c) Timesheets are used to record hours spent and so support claims for overtime payments by salaried staff.

An example of a timesheet (as used in the service sector) is shown as follows.

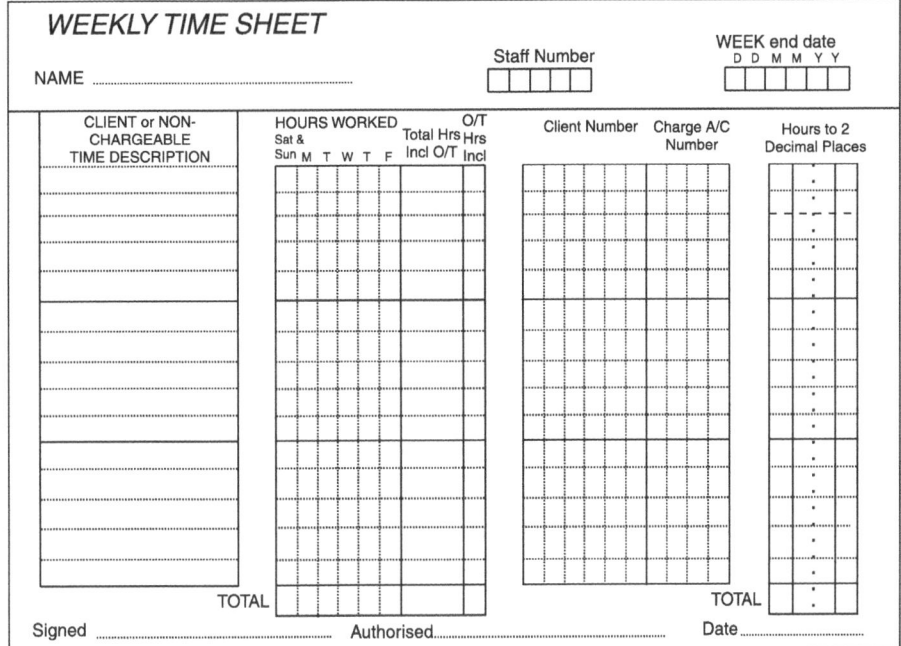

3.8 Idle time

FAST FORWARD

> **Idle time** has a cost because employees will still be paid their basic wage or salary for these unproductive hours and so there should be a record of idle time.

Idle time occurs when employees cannot get on with their work, through no fault of their own. Examples are as follows.

- Machine breakdowns
- Shortage of work

A record of idle time may simply comprise an entry on time sheets coded to 'idle time' generally, or separate idle time cards may be prepared. A supervisor might enter the time of a stoppage, its cause, its duration and the employees made idle on an idle time record card. Each stoppage should have a reference number which can be entered on time sheets or job cards.

3.9 Wages department

Responsibilities of the payroll department include the following.

- Preparation of the payroll and payment of wages
- Maintenance of employee records
- Summarising wages cost for each cost centre
- Summarising the hours worked for each cost centre
- Summarising other payroll information eg bonus payment, pensions
- Providing an internal check for the preparation and payout of wages

Attendance cards are the basis for payroll preparation. For **time workers**, the gross wage is the product of time attended and rate of pay. To this is added any overtime premium or bonus. For **piece workers**, gross wages are normally obtained by the product of the number of good units produced and the unit rate, with any premiums, bonuses and allowances for incomplete jobs added.

After calculation of net pay, a pay slip is prepared showing all details of earnings and deductions. The wage envelope or the attendance card may be used for this purpose.

When the payroll is complete, a coin and note analysis is made and a cheque drawn to cover the total amount. On receipt of the cash, the pay envelopes are made up and sealed. A receipt is usually obtained on payout (the attendance card can be used). Wages of absentees are retained until claimed by an authorised person.

Internal checks are necessary to prevent fraud. One method is to distribute the payroll work so that no person deals completely with any transaction. All calculations should be checked on an adding machine where possible. Makeup of envelopes should not be done by persons who prepare the payroll. The cashier should reconcile his analysis with the payroll summary.

3.10 Cost accounting department

The cost accounting department has the following responsibilities.

- The accumulation and classification of all cost data (which includes labour costs)
- Preparation of cost data reports for management
- Analysing labour information on time cards and payroll

In order to establish the labour cost involved in products, operations, jobs and cost centres, the following documents are used.

- Clock cards
- Job cards
- Idle time cards
- Payroll

Analyses of labour costs are used for the following.

(a) Charging wages directly attributable to production to the appropriate job or operation.

(b) Charging wages which are not directly attributable to production as follows.

　(i)　Idle time of production workers is charged to indirect costs as part of the overheads.

　(ii)　Wages costs of supervisors, or store assistants are charged to the overhead costs of the relevant department.

(c) Producing idle time reports which show a summary of the hours lost through idle time, and the cause of the idle time. Idle time may be analysed as follows.

　(i)　Controllable eg lack of materials
　(ii)　Uncontrollable eg power failure

3.11 Idle time ratio

Formula to learn

$$\text{Idle time ratio} = \frac{\text{Idle hours}}{\text{Total hours}} \times 100\%$$

The idle time ratio is useful because it shows the proportion of available hours which were lost as a result of idle time.

Exam focus point

Make sure you understand the distinction between direct and indirect labour costs and the classification of overtime premium.

4 Accounting for labour costs

We will use an example to briefly review the principal bookkeeping entries for wages.

4.1 Example: The wages control account

The following details were extracted from a weekly payroll for 750 employees at a factory.

Analysis of gross pay

	Direct workers $	Indirect workers $	Total $
Ordinary time	36,000	22,000	58,000
Overtime: basic wage	8,700	5,430	14,130
premium	4,350	2,715	7,065
Shift allowance	3,465	1,830	5,295
Sick pay	950	500	1,450
Idle time	3,200	–	3,200
	56,665	32,475	89,140
Net wages paid to employees	$45,605	$24,220	$69,825

Required

Prepare the wages control account for the week.

Solution

(a) **The wages control account** acts as a sort of 'collecting place' for net wages paid and deductions made from gross pay. The gross pay is then analysed between direct and indirect wages.

(b) The first step is to determine which wage costs are **direct** and which are **indirect**. The direct wages will be debited to the work in progress account and the indirect wages will be debited to the production overhead account.

(c) There are in fact only two items of direct wages cost in this example, the ordinary time ($36,000) and the basic overtime wage ($8,700) paid to direct workers. All other payments (including the overtime premium) are indirect wages.

(d) The net wages paid are debited to the control account, and the balance then represents the deductions which have been made for tax, social insurance, and so on.

WAGES CONTROL ACCOUNT

	$		$
Bank: net wages paid	69,825	Work in progress – direct labour	44,700
Deductions control accounts*		Production overhead control:	
($89,140 – $69,825)	19,315	Indirect labour	27,430
		Overtime premium	7,065
		Shift allowance	5,295
		Sick pay	1,450
		Idle time	3,200
	89,140		89,140

* In practice there would be a separate deductions control account for each type of deduction made (for example, tax and social insurance).

Chapter roundup

- **Production** is the quantity or volume of output produced. **Productivity** is a measure of the efficiency with which output has been produced. An increase in production without an increase in productivity will not reduce unit costs.

- There are three basic groups of **remuneration** method: **time work, piecework schemes** and **bonus/incentive schemes**.

- Labour attendance time is recorded on, for example, an attendance record or clock card. Job time may be recorded on daily time sheets, weekly time sheets or job cards depending on the circumstances. The manual recording of times on time sheets or job cards, is however, liable to error or even deliberate deception and may be unreliable. The labour cost of pieceworkers is recorded on a piecework ticket/operation card.

- **Idle time** has a cost because employees will still be paid their basic wage or salary for these unproductive hours and so there should be a record of idle time.

Quick quiz

1. Match the terms with their definition:

    Terms: Production

    Productivity

    Definitions: A measure of the efficiency with which output has been produced
    The quantity or volume of output produced

2. List five types of incentive scheme.

3. Which of the following is **not** a requirement for a successful individual bonus scheme:

    (a) Each individual should be rewarded for the work done by that individual.
    (b) Workers should be aware of other people's bonuses.
    (c) Work should be fairly routine, so that standard times can be set for jobs.
    (d) The bonus should be paid soon after the work is done.

4. **Value added** is an alternative to profit as a business performance measure and it can be used as the basis of an incentive scheme.

    Complete the formula below:

    Value added = ... less ....

5. When does idle time occur?

6. What are the responsibilities of a typical wages department?

7. The idle time ratio = $\dfrac{\text{Total hours}}{\text{Idle hours}} \times 100\%$. True or false?

Answers to quick quiz

1. - **Production** is the quantity or volume of output produced.
   - **Productivity** is a measure of the efficiency with which output has been produced.

2. Any five from:
   - High day rate system
   - Individual bonus schemes
   - Group bonus schemes
   - Profit sharing schemes
   - Incentive schemes involving shares
   - Value added incentive schemes

3. (b) it is not necessary to know other's bonuses. Indeed this is an area that can often cause problems!

4. Value added = Sales − cost of bought-in materials and services

5. **Idle time** occurs when employees cannot get on with their work, through no fault of their own, for example when machines break down or there is a shortage of work.

6. - Preparation of the payroll and payment of wages
   - Maintenance of employee records
   - Summarising wages cost for each cost centre
   - Summarising the hours worked for each cost centre
   - Summarising other payroll information, eg bonus payment, pensions etc
   - Providing an internal check for the preparation and payout of wages

7. False. The idle time ratio = $\dfrac{\text{Idle hours}}{\text{Total hours}} \times 100\%$

PART B COST IDENTIFICATION AND MEASURING COSTS FOR MANAGEMENT PURPOSES

Overheads and absorption costing

Topic list	Syllabus reference
1 Overheads	C2.3
2 Absorption costing: an introduction	C2.3
3 Overhead allocation	C2.3
4 Overhead apportionment	C2.3
5 Overhead absorption	C2.3
6 Blanket absorption rates and departmental absorption rates	C2.3
7 Over and under absorption of overheads	C2.3
8 Ledger entries relating to overheads	C2.3
9 Non-manufacturing overheads	C2.3

Introduction

This is the first of three chapters on overheads. The first of which deals with absorption costing.

Absorption costing is a method of accounting for overheads. It is basically a method of sharing out overheads incurred amongst units produced.

This chapter begins by explaining why absorption costing might be necessary and then provides an overview of how the cost of a unit of product is built up under a system of absorption costing. A detailed analysis of this costing method is then provided, covering the three stages of absorption costing: **allocation**, **apportionment** and **absorption**.

PART B   COST IDENTIFICATION AND MEASURING COSTS FOR MANAGEMENT PURPOSES

Exam focus point

Overhead apportionment and absorption is one of the most important topics in your Management Accounting studies and is almost certain to appear in the exam. Make sure that you study the contents of this and the next two chapters and work through the calculations very carefully.

1 Overheads

FAST FORWARD

Overhead is the cost incurred in the course of making a product, providing a service or running a department, but which cannot be traced directly and in full to the product, service or department.

Overhead is actually the total of the following.

- Indirect materials
- Indirect labour
- Indirect expenses

The total of these indirect costs is usually split into the following categories.

- **Production**
- **Administration**
- **Selling and distribution**

In cost accounting there are two schools of thought as to the correct method of dealing with overheads.

- Absorption costing
- Marginal costing

2 Absorption costing: an introduction

FAST FORWARD

The objective of absorption costing is to include in the total cost of a product an appropriate share of the organisation's total overhead. An appropriate share is generally taken to mean an amount which reflects the amount of time and effort that has gone into producing a unit or completing a job.

An organisation with one production department that produces identical units will divide the total overheads among the total units produced. **Absorption costing is a method for sharing overheads between different products on a fair basis**.

2.1 Is absorption costing necessary?

Suppose that a company makes and sells 100 units of a product each week. The prime cost per unit is $6 and the unit sales price is $10. Production overhead costs $200 per week and administration, selling and distribution overhead costs $150 per week. The weekly profit could be calculated as follows.

	$	$
Sales (100 units × $10)		1,000
Prime costs (100 × $6)	600	
Production overheads	200	
Administration, selling and distribution costs	150	
		950
Profit		50

In absorption costing, overhead costs will be added to each unit of product manufactured and sold.

	$ per unit
Prime cost per unit	6
Production overhead ($200 per week for 100 units)	2
Full factory cost	8

110

The weekly profit would be calculated as follows.

	$
Sales	1,000
Less factory cost of sales	800
Gross profit	200
Less administration, selling and distribution costs	150
Net profit	50

Sometimes, but not always, the overhead costs of administration, selling and distribution are also added to unit costs, to obtain a full cost of sales.

	$ per unit
Prime cost per unit	6.00
Factory overhead cost per unit	2.00
Administration etc costs per unit	1.50
Full cost of sales	9.50

The weekly profit would be calculated as follows.

	$
Sales	1,000
Less full cost of sales	950
Profit	50

It may already be apparent that the weekly profit is $50 no matter how the figures have been presented. So, how does absorption costing serve any useful purpose in accounting?

The **theoretical justification** for using absorption costing is that all production overheads are incurred in the production of the organisation's output and so each unit of the product receives some benefit from these costs. Each unit of output should therefore be charged with some of the overhead costs.

2.2 Practical reasons for using absorption costing

FAST FORWARD

> The main reasons for using absorption costing are for **inventory valuations**, **pricing decisions**, and **establishing the profitability of different products**.

(a) **Inventory valuations**. Inventory in hand must be valued for two reasons:

  (i) For the closing inventory figure in the statement of financial position

  (ii) For the cost of sales figure in the statement of comprehensive income

  The valuation of inventory will affect profitability during a period because of the way in which the cost of sales is calculated.

  ```
      The cost of goods produced
  +   the value of opening inventories
  −   the value of closing inventories
  =   the cost of goods sold
  ```

  In our example, closing inventories might be valued at prime cost ($6), but in absorption costing, they would be valued at a fully absorbed factory cost, $8 per unit. (They would not be valued at $9.50, the full cost of sales, because the only costs incurred in producing goods for finished inventory are factory costs.)

(b) **Pricing decisions**. Many companies attempt to fix selling prices by calculating the full cost of production or sales of each product, and then adding a margin for profit. In our example, the company might have fixed a gross profit margin at 25% on factory cost, or 20% of the sales price, in order to establish the unit sales price of $10. 'Full cost plus pricing' can be particularly useful for companies which do jobbing or contract work, where each job or contract is different, so that a standard unit sales price cannot be fixed. Without using absorption costing, a full cost is difficult to ascertain.

(c) **Establishing the profitability of different products**. This argument in favour of absorption costing is more contentious, but is worthy of mention here. If a company sells more than one product, it will be difficult to judge how profitable each individual product is, unless overhead costs are shared on a fair basis and charged to the cost of sales of each product.

2.3 IAS 2 *Inventories*

Absorption costing is recommended in financial accounting by International Accounting Standard (IAS 2) *Inventories*. IAS 2 deals with **financial accounting systems**. The cost accountant is (in theory) free to value inventories by whatever method seems best, but where companies integrate their financial accounting and cost accounting systems into a single system of accounting records, the valuation of closing inventories will be determined by IAS 2.

IAS 2 states that costs of all inventories should comprise those costs which have been incurred in the normal course of business in **bringing the inventories to their 'present location and condition'**. These costs incurred will include all related production overheads, even though these overheads may accrue on a time basis. In other words, in financial accounting, closing inventories should be valued at full factory cost, and it may therefore be convenient and appropriate to value inventories by the same method in the cost accounting system.

2.4 Absorption costing stages

> **FAST FORWARD**
>
> The three stages of absorption costing are:
> - Allocation
> - Apportionment
> - Absorption

We shall now begin our study of absorption costing by looking at the process of **overhead allocation**.

3 Overhead allocation

3.1 Introduction

> **FAST FORWARD**
>
> **Allocation** is the process by which whole cost items are charged direct to a cost unit or cost centre.

Cost centres may be one of the following types.

(a) A **production department**, to which production overheads are charged.

(b) A **production area service department**, to which production overheads are charged.

(c) An **administrative department**, to which administration overheads are charged.

(d) A **selling** or a **distribution department**, to which sales and distribution overheads are charged.

(e) An **overhead cost centre**, to which items of expense which are shared by a number of departments, such as rent and rates, heat and light and the canteen, are charged.

The following costs would therefore be charged to the following cost centres via the process of allocation.

- Direct labour will be charged to a production cost centre.
- The cost of a warehouse security guard will be charged to the warehouse cost centre.
- Paper (recording computer output) will be charged to the computer department.
- Costs such as the canteen are charged direct to various overhead cost centres.

3.2 Example: Overhead allocation

Consider the following costs of a company.

Wages of the foreman of department A	$200
Wages of the foreman of department B	$150
Indirect materials consumed in department A	$50
Rent of the premises shared by departments A and B	$300

The cost accounting system might include three overhead cost centres.

Cost centre: 101   Department A
               102   Department B
               201   Rent

Overhead costs would be allocated directly to each cost centre, ie $200 + $50 to cost centre 101, $150 to cost centre 102 and $300 to cost centre 201. The rent of the factory will be subsequently shared between the two production departments, but for the purpose of day to day cost recording, the rent will first of all be charged in full to a separate cost centre.

4 Overhead apportionment

FAST FORWARD

Apportionment is a procedure whereby indirect costs are spread fairly between cost centres. Service cost centre costs may be apportioned to production cost centres by using the reciprocal method.

The following question will be used to illustrate the overhead apportionment process.

4.1 Example: Overhead apportionment – Swotathon

Swotathon Inc has two production departments (A and B) and two service departments (maintenance and stores). Details of next year's budgeted overheads are shown below.

	Total
	$
Heat and light	19,200
Repair costs	9,600
Machinery depreciation	54,000
Rent and rates	38,400
Canteen	9,000
Machinery insurance	25,000

Details of each department are as follows.

	A	B	Maintenance	Stores	Total
Floor area (m²)	6,000	4,000	3,000	2,000	15,000
Machinery carrying amount ($'000)	48	20	8	4	80
Number of employees	50	40	20	10	120
Allocated overheads ($'000)	15	20	12	5	50

Service departments' services were used as follows.

	A	B	Maintenance	Stores	Total
Maintenance hours worked	5,000	4,000	----	1,000	10,000
Number of stores requisitions	3,000	1,000	----	----	4,000

4.2 Stage 1: Apportioning general overheads

Overhead apportionment follows on from overhead allocation. The first stage of overhead apportionment is to identify all overhead costs as production department, production service department, administration or selling and distribution overhead. The costs for heat and light, rent and rates, the canteen and so on (ie costs allocated to general overhead cost centres) must therefore be shared out between the other cost centres.

4.2.1 Bases of apportionment

It is considered important that overhead costs should be shared out on a **fair basis**. You will appreciate that because of the complexity of items of cost it is rarely possible to use only one method of apportioning costs to the various departments of an organisation. The bases of apportionment for the most usual cases are given below.

Overhead to which the basis applies	Basis
Rent, rates, heating and light, repairs and depreciation of buildings	Floor area occupied by each cost centre
Depreciation, insurance of equipment	Cost or carrying amount of equipment
HR office, canteen, welfare, wages and cost offices, first aid	Number of employees, or labour hours worked in each cost centre

Note that heating and lighting may also be apportioned using volume of space occupied by each cost centre.

4.2.2 Example: Swotathon

Using the Swotathon question above, show how overheads should be apportioned between the four departments.

Solution

Item of cost	Basis of apportionment	Department			
		A	B	Maintenance	Stores
		$	$	$	$
Heat and light	Floor area	7,680	5,120	3,840	2,560
Repair costs	Floor area	3,840	2,560	1,920	1,280
Machine dep^n	Machinery value	32,400	13,500	5,400	2,700
Rent and rates	Floor area	15,360	10,240	7,680	5,120
Canteen	No. of employees	3,750	3,000	1,500	750
Machine insurance	Machinery value	15,000	6,250	2,500	1,250
Total		78,030	40,670	22,840	13,660

Workings

1 Overhead apportioned by floor area

$$\text{Overhead apportioned to department} = \frac{\text{Floor area occupied by department}}{\text{Total floor area}} \times \text{total overhead}$$

For example:

Heat and light apportioned to Dept A $= \frac{6,000}{15,000} \times 19,200 = \$7,680$

2   *Overheads apportioned by machinery value*

Overheads apportioned to department = $\dfrac{\text{Value of department's machinery}}{\text{Total value of machinery}} \times$ total overhead

3   *Overheads apportioned by number of employees*

Overheads apportioned to department = $\dfrac{\text{No of employees in department}}{\text{Total no of employees}} \times$ total overhead

4.3 Stage 2 – Apportion service department costs

Only production departments produce goods that will ultimately be sold. In order to calculate a correct price for these goods, we must determine the **total cost** of producing each unit – that is, not just the cost of the labour and materials that are directly used in production, but also the **indirect** costs of services provided by such departments as maintenance, stores and canteen.

Our aim is to apportion all the **service** department costs to the **production** departments, in one of three ways.

(a)   The **direct** method, where the service centre costs are apportioned to production departments only.

(b)   The **step-down** method, where each service centre's costs are not only apportioned to production departments but to some (but not all) of the other service centres that make use of the services provided.

(c)   The **repeated distribution** (or **reciprocal**) method, where service centre costs are apportioned to both the production departments and service departments that use the services. The service centre costs are then gradually apportioned to the production departments. This method is used only when service departments work for each other – that is, **service departments use each other's services** (for example, the maintenance department will use the canteen, whilst the canteen may rely on the maintenance department to ensure its equipment is functioning properly or to replace bulbs, plugs, etc).

The **direct** and **step-down** methods are **not examinable**.

Exam focus point

Remember that **all** service department costs must be allocated – that is, both **general overheads** that were apportioned and those overheads that are **specific** to the individual departments.

4.3.1 Basis of apportionment

Whichever method is used to apportion service cost centre costs, **the basis of apportionment must be fair**. A different apportionment basis may be applied for each service cost centre. This is demonstrated in the following table.

Service cost centre	Possible basis of apportionment
Stores	Number or cost value of material requisitions
Maintenance	Hours of maintenance work done for each cost centre
Production planning	Direct labour hours worked in each production cost centre

Although both the **direct** and **step-down** methods are **not in your syllabus**, the following illustration will give you an idea of how to carry out simple apportionments before we move onto the more complex reciprocal method.

4.3.2 Example: Swotathon with simple apportionment

Using the information contained in the Swotathon question and the results of the calculations in Section 4.2.2 above, apportion the Maintenance and Stores departments' overheads to production departments A and B and calculate the total overheads for each of these production departments.

Solution

(1) Decide how the **service departments'** overheads will be apportioned. The table above tells us that maintenance overheads can be apportioned according to the **hours of maintenance work done**, whilst we can use the number or cost value of stores/material requisitions for apportioning stores.

The question gives us information about maintenance hours worked and the number of stores requisitions.

(2) **Apportion the overheads** of the **service** department whose services are also used by another service department (in this case, maintenance). This allows us to obtain a total overhead cost for stores.

Total overheads for maintenance department

	$	
General overheads	22,840	(see Section 4.2.2 above)
Allocated overheads	12,000	(from information given in Section 4.1)
	34,840	

Apportioned as follows:

$$\frac{\text{Maintenance hours worked in department}}{\text{Total maintenance hours worked}} \times \$34,840$$

Production department A = $\frac{5,000}{10,000} \times \$34,840 = \$17,420$

Production department B = $\frac{4,000}{10,000} \times \$34,840 = \$13,936$

Stores department = $\frac{1,000}{10,000} \times \$34,840 = \$3,484$

(3) Apportion **Stores department's** overheads.

Total overheads for stores

	$	
General overheads	13,660	(see Section 4.2.2 above)
Allocated overheads	5,000	(from information given in Section 4.1)
Apportioned from maintenance	3,484	(see above)
	22,144	

Apportioned as follows:

$$\frac{\text{Number of stores requisitions for department}}{\text{Total number of stores requisitions}} \times \$22,144$$

Production department A = $\frac{3,000}{4,000} \times \$22,144 = \$16,608$

Production department B = $\frac{1,000}{4,000} \times \$22,144 = \$5,536$

(4) **Total overheads** for each production department

	A	B	
	$	$	
General overheads	78,030	40,670	(see Section 4.2.2)
Allocated overheads	15,000	20,000	(from information in Section 4.1)
Maintenance	17,420	13,936	
Stores	16,608	5,536	
	127,058	80,142	

4.4 The reciprocal (repeated distribution) method of apportionment

Now that we have looked at the 'simple' scenario of only one service department making use of the other service department's services, we can move onto the more complicated situation of **'reciprocal' servicing**. This is where each service department makes use of the other service department (in the Swotathon example, stores would use maintenance and maintenance would use stores).

4.4.1 Example: Swotathon using repeated distribution method

Suppose the usage of Swotathon's service departments' services were amended to be as follows:

	A	B	Maintenance	Stores	Total
Maintenance hours used	5,000	4,000	–	1,000	10,000
Number of stores requisitions	3,000	1,000	1,000	–	5,000

Show how the Maintenance and Stores departments' overheads would be apportioned to the two production departments and calculate total overheads for each of the production departments.

Solution

Remember to apportion both the general and allocated overheads (see Section 4.2.2). The bases of apportionment for Maintenance and Stores are the same as for the example in Section 4.2.2 (that is, maintenance hours worked and number of stores requisitions).

	A	B	Maintenance	Stores
	$	$	$	$
Total overheads (general and allocated)	93,030	60,670	34,840	18,660
Apportion maintenance (note (a))	17,420	13,936	(34,840)	3,484
			NIL	22,144
Apportion stores (note (b))	13,286	4,429	4,429	(22,144)
			4,429	NIL
Apportion maintenance	2,215	1,772	(4,429)	442
			NIL	442
Apportion stores (note (c))	332	110	NIL	(442)
Total overheads	126,283	80,917	NIL	NIL

Notes

(a) It does not matter which department you choose to apportion first. Maintenance overheads were apportioned using the calculations illustrated in Section 4.3.2.

(b) Stores overheads are apportioned using the same formula as used in Section 4.3.2 but with the amended number of stores requisitions given above.

(c) The problem with the repeated distribution method is that you can keep performing the same calculations many times. When you are dealing with a small number (such as $442 above) you can take the decision to apportion the figure between the production departments only. In this case, we ignore the stores requisitions for Maintenance and base the apportionment on the total stores requisitions for the production departments (that is, 4,000). The amount apportioned to production department A was calculated as follows.

$$\frac{\text{Stores requisitions for A}}{\text{Total stores requisitions (A+B)}} \times \text{Stores overheads} = \frac{3,000}{4,000} \times \$442 = \$332$$

4.5 The reciprocal (algebraic) method of apportionment

FAST FORWARD

The results of the reciprocal method of apportionment may also be obtained using **algebra** and **simultaneous equations**.

If you are unsure about how to solve simultaneous equations, look at Section 9 of the basic maths chapter at the beginning of this Learning & Practice Workbook.

4.5.1 Example: Swotathon using the algebraic method of apportionment

Whenever you are using equations you must define each variable.

Let   M = total overheads for the Maintenance department
      S = total overheads for the Stores department

Remember that total overheads for the Maintenance department consist of general overheads apportioned, allocated overheads and the share of Stores overheads (20%).

Similarly, total overheads for Stores will be the total of general overheads apportioned, allocated overheads and the 10% share of Maintenance overheads.

| M = 0.2S + $34,840 | (1) | ($34,840 was calculated in Section 4.3.2) |
| S = 0.1M + $18,660 | (2) | ($18,660 was calculated in Section 4.3.2) |

We now solve the equations.

Multiply equation (1) by 5 to give us

| 5M = S + 174,200 | (3), which can be rearranged as |
| S = 5M − 174,200 | (4) |

Subtract equation (2) from equation (4)

| S = 5M − 174,200 | (4) |
| S = 0.1M + 18,660 | (2) |

0 = 4.9M − 192,860

4.9M = 192,860

$$M = \frac{192,860}{4.9} = \$39,359$$

Substitute M = 39,359 into equation (2)

S = 0.1 × 39,359 + 18,660
S = 3,936 + 18,660 = 22,596

These overheads can now be apportioned to the production departments using the proportions in Section 4.3.1 above.

	A $	B $	Maintenance $	Stores $
Overhead costs	93,030	60,670	34,840	18,660
Apportion maintenance	19,680	15,743	(39,359)	3,936
Apportion stores	13,558	4,519	4,519	(22,596)
Total	126,268	80,932	Nil	Nil

You will notice that the total overheads for production departments A and B are the same regardless of the method used (difference is due to rounding).

Exam focus point

You must never ignore the existence of reciprocal services unless a question specifically instructs you to do so.

4.6 A full example for you to try

Now that we have worked through the various stages of overhead apportionment, you should try this question to ensure you understand the techniques.

Question — Reapportionment

Sandstorm is a jobbing engineering concern which has three production departments (forming, machines and assembly) and two service departments (maintenance and general).

The following analysis of overhead costs has been made for the year just ended.

	$	$
Rent and rates		8,000
Power		750
Light, heat		5,000
Repairs, maintenance:		
Forming	800	
Machines	1,800	
Assembly	300	
Maintenance	200	
General	100	
		3,200
Departmental expenses:		
Forming	1,500	
Machines	2,300	
Assembly	1,100	
Maintenance	900	
General	1,500	
		7,300
Depreciation:		
Plant		10,000
Fixtures and fittings		250
Insurance:		
Plant		2,000
Buildings		500
Indirect labour:		
Forming	3,000	
Machines	5,000	
Assembly	1,500	
Maintenance	4,000	
General	2,000	
		15,500
		52,500

PART B COST IDENTIFICATION AND MEASURING COSTS FOR MANAGEMENT PURPOSES

Other available data are as follows.

	Floor area sq. ft	Plant value $	Fixtures & fittings $	Effective horse-power	Direct cost for year $	Labour hours worked	Machine hours worked
Forming	2,000	25,000	1,000	40	20,500	14,400	12,000
Machines	4,000	60,000	500	90	30,300	20,500	21,600
Assembly	3,000	7,500	2,000	15	24,200	20,200	2,000
Maintenance	500	7,500	1,000	5			
General	500	–	500	–	–	–	–
	10,000	100,000	5,000	150	75,000	55,100	35,600

Service department costs are apportioned as follows.

	Maintenance %	General %
Forming	20	20
Machines	50	60
Assembly	20	10
General	10	–
Maintenance	–	10
	100	100

Required

Using the data provided prepare an analysis showing the distribution of overhead costs to departments. Reapportion service cost centre costs using the reciprocal method.

Answer

Analysis of distribution of actual overhead costs

	Basis	Forming $	Machines $	Assembly $	Maint. $	General $	Total $
Directly allocated overheads:							
Repairs, maintenance		800	1,800	300	200	100	3,200
Departmental expenses		1,500	2,300	1,100	900	1,500	7,300
Indirect labour		3,000	5,000	1,500	4,000	2,000	15,500
Apportionment of other overheads:							
Rent, rates	1	1,600	3,200	2,400	400	400	8,000
Power	2	200	450	75	25	0	750
Light, heat	1	1,000	2,000	1,500	250	250	5,000
Depreciation of plant	3	2,500	6,000	750	750	0	10,000
Depreciation of F and F	4	50	25	100	50	25	250
Insurance of plant	3	500	1,200	150	150	0	2,000
Insurance of buildings	1	100	200	150	25	25	500
		11,250	22,175	8,025	6,750	4,300	52,500

Basis of apportionment:

1 Floor area
2 Effective horsepower
3 Plant value
4 Fixtures and fittings value

Apportionment of service department overheads to production departments, using the reciprocal method.

5: OVERHEADS AND ABSORPTION COSTING

	Forming $	Machines $	Assembly $	Maintenance $	General $	Total $
Overheads	11,250	22,175	8,025	6,750	4,300	52,500
	1,350	3,375	1,350	(6,750)	675	
					4,975	
	995	2,985	498	497	(4,975)	
	99	249	99	(497)	50	
	10	30	5	5	(50)	
	1	3	1	(5)		
	13,705	28,817	9,978	0	0	52,500

Question — Apportioning service department overheads

Spaced Out Co has two production departments (F and G) and two service departments (Canteen and Maintenance). Total allocated and apportioned general overheads for each department are as follows.

F	G	Canteen	Maintenance
$125,000	$80,000	$20,000	$40,000

Canteen and Maintenance perform services for both production departments and Canteen also provides services for Maintenance in the following proportions.

	F	G	Canteen	Maintenance
% of Canteen to	60	25	–	15
% of Maintenance to	65	35	–	–

What would be the total overheads for production department G once the service department costs have been apportioned?

A $90,763 B $100,500 C $99,000 D $100,050

Answer

The correct answer is D.

Total Maintenance overheads = $40,000 + 15% of Canteen overheads
= $40,000 + 15% of $20,000
= $43,000

Of which 35% are apportioned to G = $15,050

Canteen costs apportioned to G = 25% of $20,000 = $5,000

Total overheads for G = $80,000 + 15,050 + 5,000 = $100,050

5 Overhead absorption

5.1 Introduction

> **FAST FORWARD**
>
> **Overhead absorption** is the process whereby overhead costs allocated and apportioned to production cost centres are added to unit, job or batch costs. Overhead absorption is sometimes called **overhead recovery**.

Having allocated and/or apportioned all overheads, the next stage in the costing treatment of overheads is to add them to, or **absorb them into, cost units.**

Overheads are usually added to cost units using a **predetermined overhead absorption rate**, which is calculated using figures from the budget.

5.2 Calculation of overhead absorption rates

Step 1 Estimate the overhead likely to be incurred during the coming period.

Step 2 Estimate the activity level for the period. This could be total hours, units, or direct costs or whatever it is upon which the overhead absorption rates are to be based.

Step 3 Divide the estimated overhead by the budgeted activity level. This produces the overhead absorption rate.

Step 4 Absorb the overhead into the cost unit by applying the calculated absorption rate.

5.3 Example: The basics of absorption costing

Athena Co makes two products, the Greek and the Roman. Greeks take two labour hours each to make and Romans take five labour hours. What is the overhead cost per unit for Greeks and Romans respectively if overheads are absorbed on the basis of labour hours?

Solution

Step 1 Estimate the overhead likely to be incurred during the coming period

Athena Co estimates that the total overhead will be $50,000.

Step 2 Estimate the activity level for the period

Athena Co estimates that a total of 100,000 direct labour hours will be worked.

Step 3 Divide the estimated overhead by the budgeted activity level

$$\text{Absorption rate} = \frac{\$50,000}{100,000 \text{ hrs}} = \$0.50 \text{ per direct labour hour}$$

Step 4 Absorb the overhead into the cost unit by applying the calculated absorption rate

	Greek	Roman
Labour hours per unit	2	5
Absorption rate per labour hour	$0.50	$0.50
Overhead absorbed per unit	$1	$2.50

It should be obvious to you that, even if a company is trying to be 'fair', there is a great lack of precision about the way an absorption base is chosen.

This arbitrariness is one of the main criticisms of absorption costing, and if absorption costing is to be used (because of its other virtues) then it is important that **the methods used are kept under regular review.** Changes in working conditions should, if necessary, lead to changes in the way in which work is accounted for.

For example, a labour intensive department may become mechanised. If a direct labour hour rate of absorption had been used previous to the mechanisation, it would probably now be more appropriate to change to the use of a machine hour rate.

5.4 Choosing the appropriate absorption base

The different **bases of absorption** (or 'overhead recovery rates') are as follows.

- A percentage of direct materials cost
- A percentage of direct labour cost
- A percentage of prime cost
- A rate per machine hour
- A rate per direct labour hour
- A rate per unit
- A percentage of factory cost (for administration overhead)
- A percentage of sales or factory cost (for selling and distribution overhead)

The choice of an absorption basis is a matter of judgement and common sense, what is required is an **absorption basis** which realistically reflects the characteristics of a given cost centre and which avoids undue anomalies.

Many factories use a **direct labour hour rate** or **machine hour rate** in preference to a rate based on a percentage of direct materials cost, wages or prime cost.

(a) A **direct labour** hour basis is most appropriate in a **labour intensive** environment.

(b) A **machine hour** rate would be used in departments where production is controlled or dictated by machines.

(c) A **rate per unit** would be effective only if all units were identical.

5.5 Example: Overhead absorption

The budgeted production overheads and other budget data of Bridge Cottage Co are as follows.

Budget	Production dept A	Production dept B
Overhead cost	$36,000	$5,000
Direct materials cost	$32,000	
Direct labour cost	$40,000	
Machine hours	10,000	
Direct labour hours	18,000	
Units of production		1,000

Required

Calculate the absorption rate using the various bases of apportionment.

Solution

Department A

(i) Percentage of direct materials cost $\quad \dfrac{\$36,000}{\$32,000} \times 100\% = 112.5\%$

(ii) Percentage of direct labour cost $\quad \dfrac{\$36,000}{\$40,000} \times 100\% = 90\%$

(iii) Percentage of prime cost $\quad \dfrac{\$36,000}{\$72,000} \times 100\% = 50\%$

(iv) Rate per machine hour $\quad \dfrac{\$36,000}{10,000 \text{ hrs}} = \$3.60$ per machine hour (v)　Rate per direct labour hour　　$\dfrac{\$36{,}000}{18{,}000\,\text{hrs}}$ = $2 per direct labour hour

The department B absorption rate will be based on units of output.

$\dfrac{\$5{,}000}{1{,}000\,\text{units}}$ = $5 per unit produced

5.6 Bases of absorption

The choice of the basis of absorption is significant in determining the cost of individual units, or jobs, produced. Using the previous example, suppose that an individual product has a material cost of $80, a labour cost of $85, and requires 36 labour hours and 23 machine hours to complete. The overhead cost of the product would vary, depending on the basis of absorption used by the company for overhead recovery.

(a) As a percentage of direct material cost, the overhead cost would be

112.5% × $80　　　　　　　　　　　　　　　　　　　　　　　= $90.00

(b) As a percentage of direct labour cost, the overhead cost would be

90% × $85　　　　　　　　　　　　　　　　　　　　　　　　= $76.50

(c) As a percentage of prime cost, the overhead cost would be 50% × $165　　= $82.50

(d) Using a machine hour basis of absorption, the overhead cost would be

23 hrs × $3.60　　　　　　　　　　　　　　　　　　　　　　= $82.80

(e) Using a labour hour basis, the overhead cost would be 36 hrs × $2　　　= $72.00

In theory, each basis of absorption would be possible, but the company should choose a basis for its own costs which seems to be **'fairest'**.

6 Blanket absorption rates and departmental absorption rates

6.1 Introduction

FAST FORWARD

A **blanket overhead absorption rate** is an absorption rate used throughout a factory and for all jobs and units of output irrespective of the department in which they were produced.

For example, if total overheads were $500,000 and there were 250,000 direct machine hours during the period, the **blanket overhead rate** would be $2 per direct machine hour and all jobs passing through the factory would be charged at that rate.

Blanket overhead rates are not appropriate in the following circumstances.

- There is more than one department.
- Jobs do not spend an equal amount of time in each department.

If a single factory overhead absorption rate is used, some products will receive a higher overhead charge than they ought 'fairly' to bear, whereas other products will be under-charged.

If **a separate absorption rate** is used for each department, charging of overheads will be fair and the full cost of production of items will represent the amount of the effort and resources put into making them.

6.2 Example: Separate absorption rates

The Old Grammar School has two production departments, for which the following budgeted information is available.

	Department A	Department B	Total
Budgeted overheads	$360,000	$200,000	$560,000
Budgeted direct labour hours	200,000 hrs	40,000 hrs	240,000 hrs

If a single factory overhead absorption rate is applied, the rate of overhead recovery would be:

$$\frac{\$560,000}{240,000 \text{ hours}} = \$2.33 \text{ per direct labour hour}$$

If separate departmental rates are applied, these would be:

$$\text{Department A} = \frac{\$360,000}{200,000 \text{ hours}} = \$1.80 \text{ per direct labour hour}$$

$$\text{Department B} = \frac{\$200,000}{40,000 \text{ hours}} = \$5 \text{ per direct labour hour}$$

Department B has a higher overhead rate of cost per hour worked than department A.

Now let's consider two separate jobs.

Job X has a prime cost of $100, takes 30 hours in department B and does not involve any work in department A.

Job Y has a prime cost of $100, takes 28 hours in department A and 2 hours in department B.

What would be the factory cost of each job, using the following rates of overhead recovery?

(a) A single factory rate of overhead recovery
(b) Separate departmental rates of overhead recovery

Solution

		Job X	Job Y
(a)	**Single factory rate**	$	$
	Prime cost	100	100
	Factory overhead (30 × $2.33)	70	70
	Factory cost	170	170
(b)	**Separate departmental rates**	$	$
	Prime cost	100	100.00
	Factory overhead: department A	0	(28 × $1.80) 50.40
	department B (30 × $5)	150	(2 × $5) 10.00
	Factory cost	250	160.40

Using a single factory overhead absorption rate, both jobs would cost the same. However, since job X is done entirely within department B where overhead costs are relatively higher, whereas job Y is done mostly within department A, where overhead costs are relatively lower, it is arguable that job X should cost more than job Y. This will occur if separate departmental overhead recovery rates are used to reflect the work done on each job in each department separately.

If all jobs do not spend approximately the same time in each department then, to ensure that all jobs are charged with their fair share of overheads, it is necessary to establish **separate overhead rates for each department**.

PART B COST IDENTIFICATION AND MEASURING COSTS FOR MANAGEMENT PURPOSES

Question — Machine hour absorption rate

The following data relate to one year in department A.

Budgeted machine hours	25,000
Actual machine hours	21,875
Budgeted overheads	$350,000
Actual overheads	$350,000

Based on the data above, what is the machine hour absorption rate as conventionally calculated?

A $12 B $14 C $16 D $18

Answer

Don't forget, if your calculations produce a solution which does not correspond with any of the options available, then eliminate the unlikely options and make a guess from the remainder. Never leave out a multiple choice question.

A common pitfall is to think 'we haven't had answer A for a while, so I'll guess that'. The examiner is **not** required to produce an even spread of A, B, C and D answers in the examination. There is no reason why the answer to **every** question cannot be D!

The correct answer in this case is B.

$$\text{Overhead absorption rate} = \frac{\text{Budgeted overheads}}{\text{Budgeted machine hours}} = \frac{\$350,000}{25,000} = \$14 \text{ per machine hour}$$

7 Over and under absorption of overheads

7.1 Introduction

FAST FORWARD

Over and **under absorption** of overheads occurs because the predetermined overhead absorption rates are based on estimates.

The rate of overhead absorption is based on estimates (of both numerator and denominator) and it is quite likely that either one or both of the estimates will not agree with what actually occurs.

(a) **Over absorption** means that the overheads charged to the cost of sales are greater then the overheads actually incurred.

(b) **Under absorption** means that insufficient overheads have been included in the cost of sales.

It is almost inevitable that at the end of the accounting year there will have been an over absorption or under absorption of the overhead actually incurred.

7.2 Example: Over and under absorption

Suppose that the budgeted overhead in a production department is $80,000 and the budgeted activity is 40,000 direct labour hours. The overhead recovery rate (using a direct labour hour basis) would be $2 per direct labour hour.

Actual overheads in the period are, say $84,000 and 45,000 direct labour hours are worked.

	$
Overhead incurred (actual)	84,000
Overhead absorbed (45,000 × $2)	90,000
Over absorption of overhead	6,000

In this example, the cost of produced units or jobs has been charged with $6,000 more than was actually spent. An adjustment to reconcile the overheads charged to the actual overhead is necessary and the over-absorbed overhead will be credited to the profit and loss account at the end of the accounting period.

7.3 The reasons for under-/over-absorbed overhead

The overhead absorption rate is predetermined from budget estimates of overhead cost and the expected volume of activity. Under- or over-recovery of overhead will occur in the following circumstances.

- Actual overhead costs are different from budgeted overheads.
- The actual activity level is different from the budgeted activity level.
- Actual overhead costs **and** actual activity level differ from the budgeted costs and level.

7.4 Example: Reasons for under-/over-absorbed overhead

Pembridge Co has a budgeted production overhead of $50,000 and a budgeted activity of 25,000 direct labour hours and therefore a recovery rate of $2 per direct labour hour.

Required

Calculate the under-/over-absorbed overhead, and the reasons for the under-/over-absorption, in the following circumstances.

(a) Actual overheads cost $47,000 and 25,000 direct labour hours are worked.
(b) Actual overheads cost $50,000 and 21,500 direct labour hours are worked.
(c) Actual overheads cost $47,000 and 21,500 direct labour hours are worked.

Solution

(a)

	$
Actual overhead	47,000
Absorbed overhead (25,000 × $2)	50,000
Over-absorbed overhead	3,000

The reason for the over absorption is that although the actual and budgeted direct labour hours are the same, actual overheads cost less than expected.

(b)

	$
Actual overhead	50,000
Absorbed overhead (21,500 × $2)	43,000
Under-absorbed overhead	7,000

The reason for the under absorption is that although budgeted and actual overhead costs were the same, fewer direct labour hours were worked than expected.

(c)

	$
Actual overhead	47,000
Absorbed overhead (21,500 × $2)	43,000
Under-absorbed overhead	4,000

The reason for the under absorption is a combination of the reasons in (a) and (b).

The distinction between **overheads incurred** (actual overheads) and **overheads absorbed** is an important one which you must learn and understand. The difference between them is known as under- or over-absorbed overheads.

PART B COST IDENTIFICATION AND MEASURING COSTS FOR MANAGEMENT PURPOSES

Question — Under-/over-absorbed overhead

The budgeted and actual data for River Arrow Products Co for the year to 31 March 20X5 are as follows.

	Budgeted	Actual
Direct labour hours	9,000	9,900
Direct wages	$34,000	$35,500
Machine hours	10,100	9,750
Direct materials	$55,000	$53,900
Units produced	120,000	122,970
Overheads	$63,000	$61,500

The cost accountant of River Arrow Products Co has decided that overheads should be absorbed on the basis of labour hours.

Required

Calculate the amount of under- or over-absorbed overheads for River Arrow Products Co for the year to 31 March 20X5.

Answer

Overhead absorption rate = $\dfrac{\$63,000}{9,000}$ = $7 per hour

Overheads absorbed by production = 9,900 × $7 = $69,300

	$
Actual overheads	61,500
Overheads absorbed	69,300
Over-absorbed overheads	7,800

Exam focus point

You can always work out whether overheads are under- or over-absorbed by using the following rule.

- If Actual overhead incurred − Absorbed overhead = NEGATIVE (N), then overheads are over-absorbed (O) (NO).
- If Actual overhead incurred − Absorbed overhead = POSITIVE (P), then overheads are under-absorbed (U) (PU).

So, remember the NOPU rule when you go into your examination and you won't have any trouble in deciding whether overheads are under- or over-absorbed!

Question — Budgeted overhead absorption rate

A management consultancy recovers overheads on chargeable consulting hours. Budgeted overheads were $615,000 and actual consulting hours were 32,150. Overheads were under-recovered by $35,000.

If actual overheads were $694,075 what was the budgeted overhead absorption rate per hour?

A $19.13   B $20.50   C $21.59   D $22.68

Answer

	$
Actual overheads	694,075
Under-recoverable overheads	35,000
Overheads recovered for 32,150 hours at budgeted overhead absorption rate (x)	659,075

32,150 × = 659,075

$$x = \frac{659{,}075}{32{,}150} = \$20.50$$

The correct option is B.

8 Ledger entries relating to overheads

8.1 Introduction

The bookkeeping entries for overheads are not as straightforward as those for materials and labour. We shall now consider the way in which overheads are dealt with in a cost accounting system.

When an absorption costing system is in use we now know that the amount of overhead included in the cost of an item is absorbed at a predetermined rate. The entries made in the cash book and the nominal ledger, however, are the actual amounts.

You will remember that it is highly unlikely that the actual amount and the predetermined amount will be the same. The difference is called **under- or over-absorbed overhead**. To deal with this in the cost accounting books, therefore, we need to have an account to collect under- or over-absorbed amounts for each type of overhead.

8.2 Example: The under-/over-absorbed overhead account

Mariott's Motorcycles absorbs production overheads at the rate of $0.50 per operating hour and administration overheads at 20% of the production cost of sales. Actual data for one month was as follows.

Administration overheads	$32,000
Production overheads	$46,500
Operating hours	90,000
Production cost of sales	$180,000

What entries need to be made for overheads in the ledgers?

Solution

PRODUCTION OVERHEADS

	DR $		CR $
Cash	46,500	Absorbed into WIP (90,000 × $0.50)	45,000
		Under absorbed overhead	1,500
	46,500		46,500

ADMINISTRATION OVERHEADS

	DR $		CR $
Cash	32,000	To cost of sales (180,000 × 0.2)	36,000
Over-absorbed overhead	4,000		
	36,000		36,000

UNDER-/OVER-ABSORBED OVERHEADS

	DR $		CR $
Production overhead	1,500	Administration overhead	4,000
Balance to profit and loss account	2,500		
	4,000		4,000

Less production overhead has been absorbed than has been spent so there is **under-absorbed overhead** of $1,500. More administration overhead has been absorbed (into cost of sales, note, not into WIP) and so there is **over-absorbed overhead** of $4,000. The net over-absorbed overhead of $2,500 is a credit in the statement of profit or loss.

9 Non-manufacturing overheads

9.1 Introduction

FAST FORWARD

> **Non-manufacturing overheads** may be allocated by choosing a basis for the overhead absorption rate which most closely matches the non-production overhead, or on the basis of a product's ability to bear the costs.

For **external reporting** (eg statutory accounts) it is not necessary to allocate non-manufacturing overheads to products. This is because many of the overheads are non-manufacturing, and are regarded as **period costs**.

For **internal reporting** purposes and for a number of industries which base the selling price of their product on estimates of **total** cost or even actual cost, a **total cost per unit of output** may be required.

Builders, law firms and garages often charge for their services by adding a **percentage profit margin** to actual cost. For product pricing purposes and for internal management reports it may therefore be appropriate to allocate non-manufacturing overheads to units of output.

9.2 Bases for apportioning non-manufacturing overheads

A number of non-manufacturing overheads such as delivery costs or salespersons' salaries are clearly identified with particular products and can therefore be classified as direct costs. The majority of non-manufacturing overheads, however cannot be directly allocated to particular units of output. Two possible methods of allocating such non-manufacturing overheads are as follows.

Method 1: Choose a basis for the overhead absorption rate which most closely matches the non-manufacturing overhead such as direct labour hours, direct machine hours and so on. The problem with such a method is that most non-manufacturing overheads are unaffected in the short term by changes in the level of output and tend to be fixed costs.

Method 2: Allocate non-manufacturing overheads on the ability of the products to bear such costs. One possible approach is to use the manufacturing cost as the basis for allocating non-manufacturing costs to products.

Formula to learn

The **overhead absorption rate** is calculated as follows.

$$\text{Overhead absorption rate} = \frac{\text{Estimated non-manufacturing overheads}}{\text{Estimated manufacturing costs}}$$

If, for example, budgeted distribution overheads are $200,000 and budgeted manufacturing costs are $800,000, the predetermined distribution overhead absorption rate will be 25% of manufacturing cost. Other bases for absorbing overheads are as follows.

Type of overhead	Possible absorption base
Selling and marketing	Sales value
Research and development	Consumer cost (= production cost minus cost of direct materials) or added value (= sales value of product minus cost of bought in materials and services)
Distribution	Sales values
Administration	Consumer cost or added value

9.3 Administration overheads

The administration overhead usually consists of the following.

- Executive salaries
- Office rent and rates
- Lighting
- Heating and cleaning the offices

In cost accounting, administration overheads are regarded as periodic charges which are charged against the gross costing profit for the year (as in financial accounting).

9.4 Selling and distribution overheads

Selling and distribution overheads are often considered collectively as one type of overhead but they are actually quite different forms of expense.

(a) **Selling costs** are incurred in order to obtain sales.

(b) **Distribution costs** begin as soon as the finished goods are put into the warehouse and continue until the goods are despatched or delivered to the customer.

Selling overhead is therefore often absorbed on the basis of sales value so that the more profitable product lines take a large proportion of overhead. The normal cost accounting entry for selling overhead is as follows.

    DR   Cost of goods sold
    CR   Selling overhead control account

Distribution overhead is more closely linked to production than sales and from one point of view could be regarded as an extra cost of production. It is, however, more usual to regard production cost as ending on the factory floor and to deal with distribution overhead separately. It is generally absorbed on a percentage of production cost but special circumstances, such as size and weight of products affecting the delivery charges, may cause a different basis of absorption to be used. The cost accounting entry is as follows.

    DR   Cost of goods sold
    CR   Distribution overhead control account

9.5 Interest on loans

Although interest on loans used to finance a business is a genuine business expense, interest is not usually included in the absorption or activity based cost per unit. Instead it is treated as a period cost, and expensed in the statement of profit or loss in the period to which it relates.

An exception to this is where a company is developing assets that take a substantial period of time to make. Typically this would mean the manufacture of property, plant and equipment, and intangible assets, such as development of new drugs. Part of the interest cost may be included in the cost of constructing such assets if the interest relates to loans used to finance the construction of the asset.

While cost accountants are not obliged to follow IFRS, the principles of IAS 23, Borrowing Costs, illustrate how interest costs can be apportioned to qualifying assets:

- Only interest costs incurred during the period of actively constructing the assets should be added to the value of the asset.

- Where funds are borrowed specifically for the asset being constructed, all of the interest on the loan would be allocated to the asset, during the period of construction. Where funds are borrowed as part of a general pool, interest would need to be apportioned, based on the amount of funds used for the specific asset as a % of all assets of the company.

Interest costs are not normally absorbed into the manufacture of inventories that are produced regularly, and in large quantities. Interest costs on loans to finance such activities are usually treated as period costs.

Notional interest is sometimes charged by head office to responsibility centres, particularly investment centres, based on the value of the assets under the control of the investment centre. Such notional interest is used as a method of assessing the performance of the investment centre manager, who is encouraged to earn a profit in excess of this notional interest. Such notional interest is not absorbed into the cost of production.

Chapter roundup

- **Overhead** is the cost incurred in the course of making a product, providing a service or running a department, but which cannot be traced directly and in full to the product, service or department.

- The **objective of absorption costing** is to include in the total cost of a product an appropriate share of the organisation's total overhead. An appropriate share is generally taken to mean an amount which reflects the amount of time and effort that has gone into producing a unit or completing a job.

- The main reasons for using absorption costing are for **stock valuations, pricing decisions** and **establishing the profitability of different products**.

- The three stages of absorption costing are:
  - Allocation
  - Apportionment
  - Absorption

- **Allocation** is the process by which whole cost items are charged direct to a cost unit or cost centre.

- **Apportionment** is a procedure whereby indirect costs are spread fairly between cost centres. Service cost centre costs may be apportioned to production cost centres by using the reciprocal method.

- The results of the reciprocal method of apportionment may also be obtained by using **algebra** and **simultaneous equations**.

- **Overhead absorption** is the process whereby overhead costs allocated and apportioned to production cost centres are added to unit, job or batch costs. Overhead absorption is sometimes called **overhead recovery**.

- A **blanket overhead absorption rate** is an absorption rate used throughout a factory and for all jobs and units of output irrespective of the department in which they were produced.

- **Over** and **under absorption** of overheads occurs because the predetermined overhead absorption rates are based on estimates.

- **Non-manufacturing overheads** may be allocated by choosing a basis for the overhead absorption rate which most closely matches the non-production overhead, or on the basis of a product's ability to bear the costs.

PART B COST IDENTIFICATION AND MEASURING COSTS FOR MANAGEMENT PURPOSES

Quick quiz

1   Name the three stages in charging overheads to units of output.

2   Match the following overheads with the most appropriate basis of apportionment.

    Overhead
    (a) Depreciation of equipment
    (b) Heat and light costs
    (c) Canteen
    (d) Insurance of equipment

    Basis of apportionment
    (1) Direct machine hours
    (2) Number of employees
    (3) Carrying amount of equipment
    (4) Floor area

3   A direct labour hour basis is most appropriate in which of the following environments?

    A   Machine-intensive
    B   Labour-intensive
    C   When all units produced are identical
    D   None of the above

4   What is the problem with using a single factory overhead absorption rate?

5   How is under-/over-absorbed overhead accounted for?

6   Which of the following is **not** a reason why under- or over-absorption of overheads occur?

    (a) Suppliers were late invoicing for the year.
    (b) Actual overhead costs are different from budgeted overheads.
    (c) The actual activity level is different from the budgeted activity level.
    (d) Actual overhead costs **and** actual activity level differ from the budgeted costs and level.

Answers to quick quiz

1. - Allocation
   - Apportionment
   - Absorption

2. (a) (3)
   (b) (4)
   (c) (2)
   (d) (3)

3. B

4. Because some products will receive a higher overhead charge than they ought 'fairly' to bear and other products will be undercharged

5. Under-/over-absorbed overhead is written as an adjustment to the statement of profit or loss at the end of an accounting period.

   - Over-absorbed overhead → credit in statement of profit or loss
   - Under-absorbed overhead → debit in statement of profit or loss

6. Suppliers were late invoicing for the year is **not** a reason why under- or over-absorption of overheads occur.

PART B COST IDENTIFICATION AND MEASURING COSTS FOR MANAGEMENT PURPOSES

End of chapter question

Damex

Damex medical centre which operates three clinics is in the process of preparing its budget for the coming financial year. Budgeted information for the coming year is as follows:

General unallocated costs:	$
Staff pension	50,000
Depreciation – Equipment	36,000
– Motor Vehicles	48,000

The following additional information is available on each clinic for the same period:

	South Clinic	North Clinic	Central Clinic
Direct Allocated Overheads:			
Insurance	$20,000	$24,000	$12,000
Heating and Lighting	$20,000	$30,000	$10,000
Fixed Assets:			
Equipment	$120,000	$160,000	$80,000
Motor Vehicles	$160,000	$200,000	$120,000
Patients and Income Levels:			
Number of patients treated	2,000	3,000	1,000
Income	$500,000	$550,000	$220,000
Number of Employees:			
Doctors	4	4	2
Nurses	3	4	2
Medical assistants	2	3	1

Additional information:

(i) Each doctor is paid a salary of $50,000 per annum; each nurse is paid $25,000 per annum and each medical assistant is paid $15,000 per annum.

(ii) The unallocated costs should be apportioned as follows:

- Staff pension should be based on the number of employees.
- Depreciation of Equipment should be based on the value of equipment.
- Depreciation of Motor Vehicles should be based on the value of motor vehicles.

Required

(a) Produce a report for management showing:

(i) The total cost of operating each clinic
(ii) The profit or loss made by each clinic
(iii) The profit per patient for each clinic

(15 marks)

(b) Comment on the importance of the report you have presented above. Your comments should highlight any weaknesses in your report.

(5 marks)

(Total = 20 marks)

Marginal and absorption costing

Topic list	Syllabus reference
1 Marginal cost and marginal costing	C3.3
2 The principles of marginal costing	C3.3
3 Marginal costing and absorption costing and the calculation of profit	C3.3
4 Reconciling profits	C3.3
5 Marginal costing versus absorption costing	C3.3

Introduction

This chapter defines **marginal costing** and compares it with absorption costing. Whereas absorption costing recognises fixed costs (usually fixed production costs) as part of the cost of a unit of output and hence as product costs, marginal costing treats all fixed costs as period costs. Two such different costing methods obviously each have their supporters and so we will be looking at the arguments both in favour of and against each method. Each costing method, because of the different inventory valuation used, produces a different profit figure and we will be looking at this particular point in detail.

1 Marginal cost and marginal costing

1.1 Introduction

FAST FORWARD

> **Marginal cost** is the variable cost of one unit of product or service.

Key term

> **Marginal costing** is an alternative method of costing to absorption costing. In marginal costing, only variable costs are charged as a cost of sale and a contribution is calculated (sales revenue minus variable cost of sales). Closing inventories of work in progress or finished goods are valued at marginal (variable) production cost. Fixed costs are treated as a period cost, and are charged in full to the profit and loss account of the accounting period in which they are incurred.

The **marginal production cost** per unit of an item usually consists of the following.

- Direct materials
- Direct labour
- Variable production overheads

Direct labour costs might be excluded from marginal costs when the work force is a given number of employees on a fixed wage or salary. Even so, it is not uncommon for direct labour to be treated as a variable cost, even when employees are paid a basic wage for a fixed working week. If in doubt, you should treat direct labour as a variable cost unless given clear indications to the contrary. Direct labour is often a step cost, with sufficiently short steps to make labour costs act in a variable fashion.

The **marginal cost of sales** usually consists of the marginal cost of production adjusted for inventory movements plus the variable selling costs, which would include items such as sales commission, and possibly some variable distribution costs.

1.2 Contribution

FAST FORWARD

> **Contribution** is an important measure in marginal costing, and it is calculated as the difference between sales value and marginal or variable cost of sales.

Contribution is of fundamental importance in marginal costing, and the term 'contribution' is really short for 'contribution towards covering fixed overheads and making a profit'.

2 The principles of marginal costing

The principles of marginal costing are as follows.

(a) **Period fixed costs are the same, for any volume of sales and production** (provided that the level of activity is within the 'relevant range'). Therefore, by selling an extra item of product or service the following will happen.

   (i) Revenue will increase by the sales value of the item sold.
   (ii) Costs will increase by the variable cost per unit.
   (iii) Profit will increase by the amount of contribution earned from the extra item.

(b) Similarly, if the volume of sales falls by one item, the profit will fall by the amount of contribution earned from the item.

(c) **Profit measurement should therefore be based on an analysis of total contribution**. Since fixed costs relate to a period of time, and do not change with increases or decreases in sales volume, it is misleading to charge units of sale with a share of fixed costs. Absorption costing is therefore misleading, and it is more appropriate to deduct fixed costs from total contribution for the period to derive a profit figure.

(d) When a unit of product is made, the extra costs incurred in its manufacture are the **variable production costs**. Fixed costs are unaffected, and no extra fixed costs are incurred when output is increased. It is therefore argued that **the valuation of closing inventories should be at variable production cost** (direct materials, direct labour, direct expenses (if any) and variable production overhead) because these are the only costs properly attributable to the product.

2.1 Example: Marginal costing principles

Rain Until September Co makes a product, the Splash, which has a variable production cost of $6 per unit and a sales price of $10 per unit. At the beginning of September 20X0, there were no opening inventories and production during the month was 20,000 units. Fixed costs for the month were $45,000 (production, administration, sales and distribution). There were no variable marketing costs.

Required

Calculate the contribution and profit for September 20X0, using marginal costing principles, if sales were as follows.

(a) 10,000 Splashes
(b) 15,000 Splashes
(c) 20,000 Splashes

Solution

The stages in the profit calculation are as follows.

- To **identify the variable cost of sales, and then the contribution**.
- Deduct fixed costs from the total contribution to derive the profit.
- Value all closing inventories at marginal production cost ($6 per unit).

	10,000 Splashes		15,000 Splashes		20,000 Splashes	
	$	$	$	$	$	$
Sales (at $10)		100,000		150,000		200,000
Opening inventory	0		0		0	
Variable production cost	120,000		120,000		120,000	
	120,000		120,000		120,000	
Less value of closing inventory (at marginal cost)	60,000		30,000		–	
Variable cost of sales		60,000		90,000		120,000
Contribution		40,000		60,000		80,000
Less fixed costs		45,000		45,000		45,000
Profit/(loss)		(5,000)		15,000		35,000
Profit (loss) per unit		$(0.50)		$1		$1.75
Contribution per unit		$4		$4		$4

The conclusions which may be drawn from this example are as follows.

(a) The **profit per unit varies** at differing levels of sales, because the average fixed overhead cost per unit changes with the volume of output and sales.

(b) The **contribution per unit is constant** at all levels of output and sales. Total contribution, which is the contribution per unit multiplied by the number of units sold, increases in direct proportion to the volume of sales.

(c) Since the **contribution per unit does not change**, the most effective way of calculating the expected profit at any level of output and sales would be as follows.

   (i) First calculate the total contribution
   (ii) Then deduct fixed costs as a period charge in order to find the profit

(d) In our example the expected profit from the sale of 17,000 Splashes would be as follows.

	$
Total contribution (17,000 × $4)	68,000
Less fixed costs	45,000
Profit	23,000

(i) If total contribution **exceeds fixed costs**, a profit is made.
(ii) If total contribution **exactly equals fixed costs**, no profit or loss is made.
(iii) If total contribution is **less than fixed costs**, there will be a loss.

Question — Marginal costing principles

Mill Stream makes two products, the Mill and the Stream. Information relating to each of these products for April 20X1 is as follows.

	Mill	Stream
Opening inventory	nil	nil
Production (units)	15,000	6,000
Sales (units)	10,000	5,000
Sales price per unit	$20	$30
Unit costs	$	$
Direct materials	8	14
Direct labour	4	2
Variable production overhead	2	1
Variable sales overhead	2	3

Fixed costs for the month	$
Production costs	40,000
Administration costs	15,000
Sales and distribution costs	25,000

Required

(a) Using marginal costing principles and the method in 2.1(d) above, calculate the profit in April 20X1.

(b) Calculate the profit if sales had been 15,000 units of Mill and 6,000 units of Stream.

Answer

(a)

	$
Contribution from Mills (unit contribution = $20 − $16 = $4 × 10,000)	40,000
Contribution from Streams (unit contribution = $30 − $20 = $10 × 5,000)	50,000
Total contribution	90,000
Fixed costs for the period	80,000
Profit	10,000

(b) At a higher volume of sales, profit would be as follows.

	$
Contribution from sales of 15,000 Mills (× $4)	60,000
Contribution from sales of 6,000 Streams (× $10)	60,000
Total contribution	120,000
Less fixed costs	80,000
Profit	40,000

2.2 Profit or contribution information

The main advantage of **contribution information** (rather than profit information) is that it allows an easy calculation of profit if sales increase or decrease from a certain level. By comparing total contribution with fixed overheads, it is possible to determine whether profits or losses will be made at certain sales levels. **Profit information**, on the other hand, does not lend itself to easy manipulation but note how easy it was to calculate profits using contribution information in the question entitled *Marginal costing principles*. **Contribution information** is more useful for **decision making** than profit information, as we shall see when we go on to study information for decision making in Section F of this Learning & Practice Workbook.

3 Marginal costing and absorption costing and the calculation of profit

3.1 Introduction

> **FAST FORWARD**
>
> In **marginal costing**, fixed production costs are treated as **period costs** and are written off as they are incurred. In **absorption costing**, fixed production costs are absorbed into the cost of units and are carried forward in inventory to be charged against sales for the next period. Inventory values using absorption costing are therefore greater than those calculated using marginal costing.

Marginal costing as a cost accounting system is significantly different from absorption costing. It is an **alternative method** of accounting for costs and profit, which rejects the principles of absorbing fixed overheads into unit costs.

Marginal costing	Absorption costing
Closing inventories are valued at marginal production cost	Closing inventories are valued at full production cost
Fixed costs are period costs	Fixed costs are absorbed into unit costs
Cost of sales does not include a share of fixed overheads	Cost of sales does include a share of fixed overheads (see note below)

Note. The share of fixed overheads included in cost of sales are from the previous period (in opening inventory values). Some of the fixed overheads from the current period will be excluded by being carried forward in closing inventory values.

In **marginal costing**, it is necessary to identify the following.

- Variable costs
- Fixed costs
- Contribution

In **absorption costing** (sometimes known as **full costing**), it is not necessary to distinguish variable costs from fixed costs.

3.2 Example: Marginal and absorption costing compared

The following example will be used to lead you through the various steps in calculating marginal and absorption costing profits, and will highlight the differences between the two techniques.

Big Woof Co manufactures a single product, the Bark, details of which are as follows.

Per unit	$
Selling price	180.00
Direct materials	40.00
Direct labour	16.00
Variable overheads	10.00

Annual fixed production overheads are budgeted to be $1.6 million and Big Woof expects to produce 1,280,000 units of the Bark each year. Overheads are absorbed on a per unit basis. Actual overheads are $1.6 million for the year.

Budgeted fixed selling costs are $320,000 per quarter.

Actual sales and production units for the first quarter of 20X8 are given below.

	January–March
Sales	240,000
Production	280,000

There is no opening inventory at the beginning of January.

Prepare statements of profit or loss for the quarter, using:

(a) Marginal costing
(b) Absorption costing

Solution

Step 1 Calculate the overhead absorption rate per unit

Remember that overhead absorption rate is based only on budgeted figures.

$$\text{Overhead absorption rate} = \frac{\text{Budgeted fixed overheads}}{\text{Budgeted units}}$$

Also be careful with your calculations. You are dealing with a three month period but the figures in the question are for a whole year. You will have to convert these to quarterly figures.

$$\text{Budgeted overheads (quarterly)} = \frac{\$1.6 \text{ million}}{4} = \$400,000$$

$$\text{Budgeted production (quarterly)} = \frac{1,280,000}{4} = 320,000 \text{ units}$$

$$\text{Overhead absorption rate per unit} = \frac{\$400,000}{320,000} = \$1.25 \text{ per unit}$$

Step 2 Calculate total cost per unit

Total cost per unit (absorption costing) = Variable cost + fixed production cost
= (40 + 16 + 10) + 1.25
= $67.25

Total cost per unit (marginal costing) = Variable cost per unit = $66

Step 3 Calculate closing inventory in units

Closing inventory = Opening inventory + production – sales
Closing inventory = 0 + 280,000 – 240,000 = 40,000 units

Step 4 Calculate under/over absorption of overheads

This is based on the difference between actual production and budgeted production.

Actual production = 280,000 units

Budgeted production = 320,000 units (see step 1 above)

Under-production = 40,000 units

As Big Woof produced 40,000 fewer units than expected, there will be an **under-absorption** of overheads of 40,000 × $1.25 (see step 1 above) = $50,000. This will be added to production costs in the statement of profit or loss.

Step 5 Produce statements of profit or loss

	Marginal costing		Absorption costing	
	$'000	$'000	$'000	$'000
Sales (240,000 × $180)		43,200		43,200
Less cost of sales				
Opening inventory	0		0	
Add production cost				
280,000 × $66	18,480			
280,000 × $67.25			18,830	
Less closing inventory				
40,000 × $66	(2,640)			
40,000 × $67.25			(2,690)	
		(15,840)	16,140	
Add under absorbed O/H			50	
				(16,190)
Contribution		27,360		
Gross profit				27,010
Less				
Fixed production O/H	400		Nil	
Fixed selling O/H	320		320	
		(720)		(320)
Net profit		26,640		26,690

3.3 No changes in inventory

You will notice from the above calculations that there are **differences** between marginal and absorption costing profits. Before we go on to reconcile the profits, how would the profits for the two different techniques differ if there were **no changes** between opening and closing inventory (that is, if production = sales)?

For the first quarter we will now assume that sales were 280,000 units.

PART B COST IDENTIFICATION AND MEASURING COSTS FOR MANAGEMENT PURPOSES

	Marginal costing		Absorption costing	
	$'000	$'000	$'000	$'000
Sales (280,000 × $180)		50,400		50,400
Less cost of sales				
Opening inventory	0			
Add production cost				
280,000 × $66	18,480			
280,000 × $67.25			18,830	
Less closing inventory	NIL		NIL	
		(18,480)	18,830	
Add under absorbed O/H			50	
				(18,880)
Contribution		31,920		
Gross profit				31,520
Less				
Fixed production O/H	400			
Fixed selling O/H	320		320	
		(720)		(320)
Net profit		31,200		31,200

You will notice that there are now no differences between the two profits. The difference in profits is due to changes in inventory levels during the period.

Question
AC versus MC

The overhead absorption rate for product X is $10 per machine hour. Each unit of product X requires five machine hours. Inventory of product X on 1.1.X1 was 150 units and on 31.12.X1 it was 100 units. What is the difference in profit between results reported using absorption costing and results reported using marginal costing?

- A The absorption costing profit would be $2,500 less
- B The absorption costing profit would be $2,500 greater
- C The absorption costing profit would be $5,000 less
- D The absorption costing profit would be $5,000 greater

Answer

Difference in profit = **change** in inventory levels × fixed overhead absorption per unit = (150 – 100) × $10 × 5 = $2,500 **lower** profit, because inventory levels **decreased**. The correct answer is therefore option A.

The key is the change in the volume of inventory. Inventory levels have **decreased** therefore absorption costing will report a **lower** profit. This eliminates options B and D.

Option C is incorrect because it is based on the closing inventory only (100 units × $10 × 5 hours).

4 Reconciling profits

4.1 Introduction

FAST FORWARD

Reported profit figures using marginal costing or absorption costing will differ if there is any change in the level of inventories in the period. If production is equal to sales, there will be no difference in calculated profits using the costing methods.

The difference in profits reported under the two costing systems is due to the different inventory valuation methods used.

If inventory levels increase between the beginning and end of a period, absorption costing will report the higher profit. This is because some of the fixed production overhead incurred during the period will be carried forward in closing inventory (which reduces cost of sales) to be set against sales revenue in the following period instead of being written off in full against profit in the period concerned.

If inventory levels decrease, absorption costing will report the lower profit because as well as the fixed overhead incurred, fixed production overhead which had been carried forward in opening inventory is released and is also included in cost of sales.

4.2 Example: Reconciling profits

The profits reported under absorption costing and marginal costing for January to March in the Big Woof question above can be reconciled as follows.

	$'000
Marginal costing profit	26,640
Adjust for fixed overhead included in inventory:	
Inventory increase of 40,000 units × $1.25	50
Absorption costing profit	26,690

4.3 Reconciling profits – a shortcut

A quick way to establish the difference in profits without going through the whole process of drawing up the statements of profit or loss is as follows.

Difference in profits = change in inventory level × overhead absorption rate per unit

If inventory levels have **gone up** (that is, closing inventory > opening inventory) then **absorption costing** profit will be **greater** than **marginal costing** profit.

If inventory levels have **gone down** (that is, closing inventory < opening inventory) then **absorption costing** profit will be **less** than **marginal costing** profit.

In the Big Woof example above

Change in inventory = 40,000 units (an increase)

Overhead absorption rate = $1.25 per unit

We would expect absorption costing profit to be **greater** than marginal costing profit by 40,000 × $1.25 = **$50,000**. If you check back to the answer, you will find that this is the case.

PART B COST IDENTIFICATION AND MEASURING COSTS FOR MANAGEMENT PURPOSES

Question — Absorption costing profit

When opening inventories were 8,500 litres and closing inventories 6,750 litres, a firm had a profit of $62,100 using marginal costing.

Assuming that the fixed overhead absorption rate was $3 per litre, what would be the profit using absorption costing?

A $41,850 B $56,850 C $67,350 D $82,350

Answer

Difference in profit = (8,500 – 6,750) × $3 = $5,250

Absorption costing profit = $62,100 – $5,250 = $56,850

The correct answer is B.

Since inventory levels reduced, the absorption costing profit will be lower than the marginal costing profit. You can therefore eliminate options C and D.

Question — Absorption versus marginal costing profits

Last month a manufacturing company's profit was $2,000, calculated using absorption costing principles. If marginal costing principles has been used, a loss of $3,000 would have occurred. The company's fixed production cost is $2 per unit. Sales last month were 10,000 units.

What was last month's production (in units)?

A 7,500 B 9,500 C 10,500 D 12,500

Answer

The correct answer is D.

Any difference between marginal and absorption costing profit is due to changes in inventory.

	$
Absorption costing profit	2,000
Marginal costing loss	(3,000)
Difference	5,000

Change in inventory = Difference in profit/fixed product cost per unit

= $5,000/$2 = 2,500 units

Marginal costing loss is lower than absorption costing profit therefore inventory has gone up – that is, production was greater than sales by 2,500 units.

Production = 10,000 units (sales) + 2,500 units = 12,500 units

6: MARGINAL AND ABSORPTION COSTING

5 Marginal costing versus absorption costing

FAST FORWARD

Absorption costing is most often used for routine profit reporting and must be used for financial accounting purposes. **Marginal costing** provides better management information for planning and decision making. There are a number of arguments both for and against each of the costing systems.

The following diagram summarises the arguments in favour of both marginal and absorption costing.

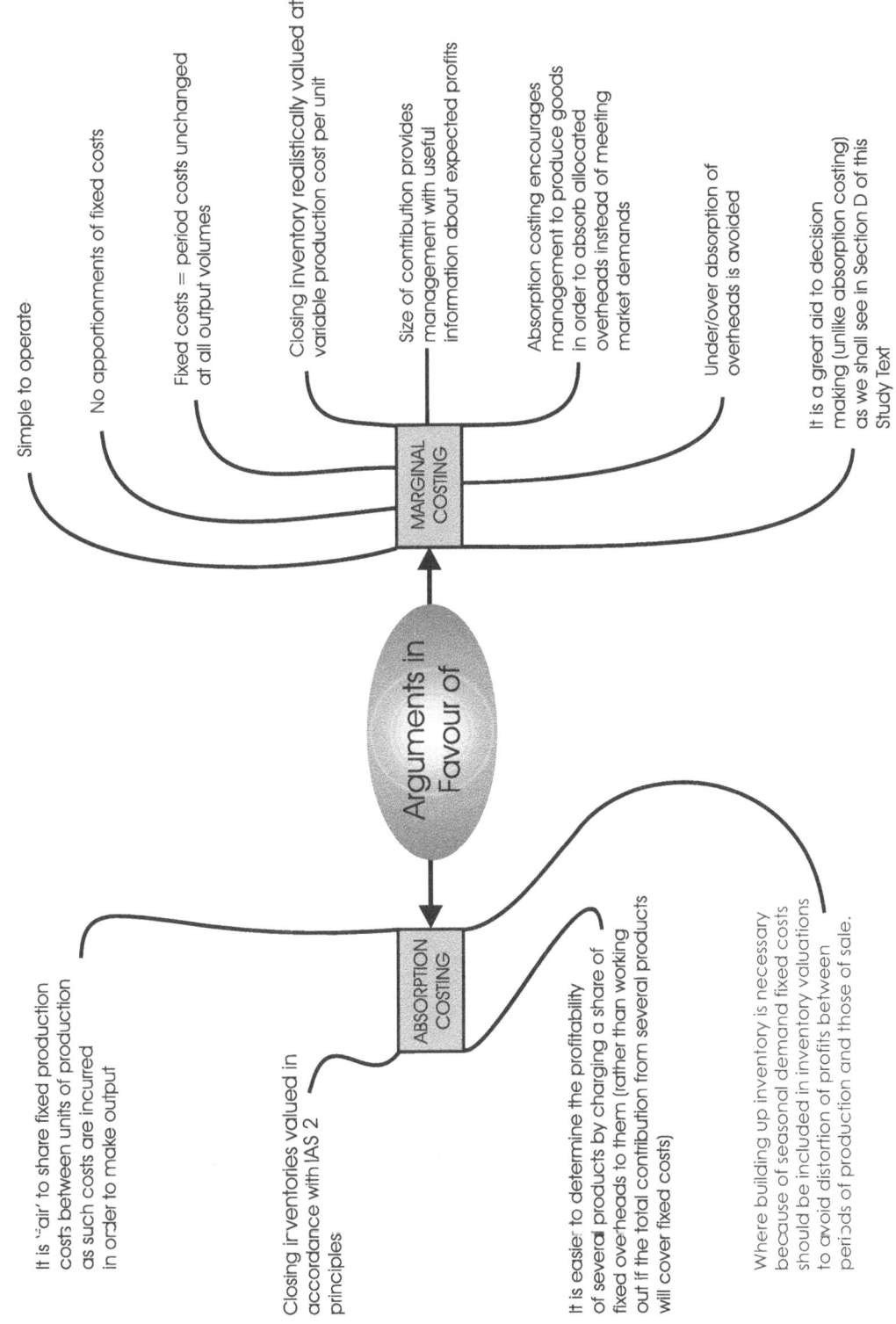

Arguments in Favour of

MARGINAL COSTING
- Simple to operate
- No apportionments of fixed costs
- Fixed costs = period costs unchanged at all output volumes
- Closing inventory realistically valued at variable production cost per unit
- Size of contribution provides management with useful information about expected profits
- Absorption costing encourages management to produce goods in order to absorb allocated overheads instead of meeting market demands
- Under/over absorption of overheads is avoided
- It is a great aid to decision making (unlike absorption costing) as we shall see in Section D of this Study Text

ABSORPTION COSTING
- It is 'fair' to share fixed production costs between units of production as such costs are incurred in order to make output
- Closing inventories valued in accordance with IAS 2 principles
- It is easier to determine the profitability of several products by charging a share of fixed overheads to them (rather than working out if the total contribution from several products will cover fixed costs)
- Where building up inventory is necessary because of seasonal demand fixed costs should be included in inventory valuations to avoid distortion of profits between periods of production and those of sale.

PART B COST IDENTIFICATION AND MEASURING COSTS FOR MANAGEMENT PURPOSES

Exam focus point

> There may be some questions requiring calculations in the exam, so it is important to be able to do these. However, don't ignore the discussion parts, as there will often be relatively easy questions of a qualitative nature too.

Chapter roundup

- **Marginal cost** is the variable cost of one unit of product or service.
- **Contribution** is an important measure in marginal costing, and it is calculated as the difference between sales value and marginal or variable cost of sales.
- In **marginal costing**, fixed production costs are treated as **period costs** and are written off as they are incurred. In **absorption costing**, fixed production costs are absorbed into the cost of units and are carried forward in inventory to be charged against sales for the next period. Inventory values using absorption costing are therefore greater than those calculated using marginal costing.
- **Reported profit figures using marginal costing or absorption costing will differ if there is any change in the level of inventories in the period.** If production is equal to sales, there will be no difference in calculated profits using these costing methods.
- **Absorption costing** is most often used for routine profit reporting and must be used for financial accounting purposes. **Marginal costing** provides better management information for planning and decision making. There are a number of arguments both for and against each of the costing systems.

Quick quiz

1. What is marginal costing?
2. What is a period cost in marginal costing?
3. Sales value – marginal cost of sales = ...
4. What is a breakeven point?
5. Marginal costing and absorption costing are different techniques for assessing profit in a period. If there are changes in inventory during a period, marginal costing and absorption costing give different results for profit obtained.

    Which of the following statements are true?

    | I | If inventory levels increase, marginal costing will report the higher profit. |
    | II | If inventory levels decrease, marginal costing will report the lower profit. |
    | III | If inventory levels decrease, marginal costing will report the higher profit. |
    | IV | If the opening and closing inventory volumes are the same, marginal costing and absorption costing will give the same profit figure. |

    A   All of the above   C   I and IV
    B   I, II and IV   D   III and IV

6. Which of the following are arguments in favour of marginal costing?

    (a) Closing stock (inventory) is valued in accordance with IAS 2.
    (b) It is simple to operate.
    (c) There is no under or over absorption of overheads.
    (d) Fixed costs are the same regardless of activity levels.
    (e) The information from this costing method may be used for decision making.

Answers to quick quiz

1. Marginal costing is an alternative method of costing to absorption costing. In marginal costing, only variable costs are charged as a cost of sale and a contribution is calculated (sales revenue – variable cost of sales).

2. A fixed cost

3. Contribution

4. The point at which total contribution exactly equals fixed costs (no profit or loss is made).

5. D

6. (b), (c), (d), (e)

End of chapter question

Overheads and marginal costing

(a) Explain the advantages of using marginal costing as the basis of providing managers with information for decision making. **(5 marks)**

(b) Explain why absorption costing is usually considered to be unsuitable for decision making. Justify your answer. **(5 marks)**

(c) Y plc has two production departments, the Assembly and Painting and two service departments, Stores and Maintenance. Maintenance provides the following service to the production and service departments: 40% to Assembly, 45% to Painting and 15% to Stores.

Stores provides: 60% to Assembly and 40% to Painting.

The budgeted fixed production overheads for the period are as follows:

Assembly	$200,000
Painting	$300,000
Stores	$100,000
Maintenance	$80,000

The budgeted output is 100,000 units.

At the end of the year after apportioning the service department overheads, the total overheads debited to the Assembly department's fixed production overhead control were $360,000.

The actual output achieved was 120,000 units.

Calculate the over/under absorption of fixed overheads for the Assembly department. **(5 marks)**

(d) Explain the terms overhead allocation and overhead apportionment. **(5 marks)**

(e) Explain the term overhead absorption rate and briefly discuss how an entity may select a suitable absorption rate. **(5 marks)**

(Total = 25 marks)

Activity based costing

Topic list	Syllabus reference
1 The reasons for the development of ABC	C2.3
2 Outline of an ABC system	C2.3
3 Absorption costing versus ABC	C2.3
4 Marginal costing versus ABC	C2.3
5 Introducing an ABC system	C2.3
6 Merits and criticisms of ABC	C2.3
7 Pricing and ABC	C2.3
8 Environmental management accounting	C2.3

Introduction

In this chapter we look at a costing system that has been developed to suit modern practices: **activity based costing**.

Basically, activity based costing (ABC) is the **modern alternative to traditional absorption costing**.

Exam questions could ask you to **calculate activity-based costs**, and we show you how to do this in **Section 3**. Or you could get a **qualitative question** on the topic, testing your understanding of the reasoning behind activity based costing and the advantages and disadvantages of it.

PART B COST IDENTIFICATION AND MEASURING COSTS FOR MANAGEMENT PURPOSES

Exam focus point

> Activity based costing is a key area of management accounting so it is likely that there will be one or two questions in your exam about this topic. Questions may be numeric or qualitative in nature.

1 The reasons for the development of ABC

FAST FORWARD

> **Traditional costing systems**, which assume that all products consume all resources in proportion to their production volumes, tend to **allocate too great a proportion of overheads to high volume products** (which cause relatively little diversity and hence use fewer support services) and **too small a proportion of overheads to low volume products** (which cause greater diversity and therefore use more support services). **Activity based costing (ABC) attempts to overcome this problem**.

The traditional cost accumulation system of **absorption costing** was developed in a time when most organisations produced only a **narrow range of products** and when **overhead costs were only a very small fraction of total costs**. Direct labour and direct material costs accounted for the largest proportion of the costs. Errors made in attributing overheads to products were not too significant.

Nowadays, however, with the advent of **advanced manufacturing technology (AMT)**, **overheads** are likely to be far **more important** and in fact direct labour may account for as little as five per cent of a product's cost. It therefore now appears difficult to justify the use of direct labour or direct material as the basis for absorbing overheads or to believe that errors made in attributing overheads will not be significant.

Many resources are used in **non-volume related support activities**, (which have increased due to AMT) such as setting-up, production scheduling, inspection and data processing. These support activities assist the efficient manufacture of a wide range of products (necessary if businesses are to compete effectively) and are **not, in general, affected by changes in production volume**. They tend to **vary in the long term according to the range and complexity** of the products manufactured rather than the volume of output.

The wider the range and the more complex the products, the more support services will be required. Consider, for example, factory X which produces 10,000 units of one product, the Alpha, and factory Y which produces 1,000 units each of ten slightly different versions of the Alpha. Support activity costs in the factory Y are likely to be a lot higher than in factory X but the factories produce an identical number of units. For example, factory X will only need to set-up once whereas Factory Y will have to set-up the production run at least ten times for the ten different products. Factory Y will therefore incur more set-up costs for the same volume of production.

2 Outline of an ABC system

FAST FORWARD

> An alternative to the traditional method of accounting for costs – absorption costing – is **activity based costing (ABC)**. ABC involves the identification of the factors (**cost drivers**) which cause the costs of an organisation's major activities. Support overheads are charged to products on the basis of their usage of an activity.

2.1 The definition of ABC

Key term

> **Activity based costing (ABC)** is an approach to the costing and monitoring of activities which involves tracing resource consumption and costing final outputs. Resources are assigned to activities and activities to cost objects based on consumption estimates. The latter utilise cost drivers to attach activity costs to outputs.

The **major ideas** behind activity based costing are as follows.

(a) **Activities cause costs**. Activities include ordering, materials handling, machining, assembly, production scheduling and despatching.

(b) Producing products creates demand for the activities.

(c) Costs are assigned to a product on the basis of the product's consumption of the activities.

2.2 The operation of an ABC system

An ABC system operates as follows.

Step 1 Identify an organisation's major activities.

Step 2 Identify the **factors which determine the size of the costs of an activity/cause the costs of an activity**. These are known as **cost drivers**.

Key term

> A **cost driver** is a factor influencing the level of cost. Often used in the context of ABC to denote the factor which links activity resource consumption to product outputs, for example the number of purchase orders would be a cost driver for procurement cost.

Look at the following examples.

Costs	Possible cost driver
Ordering costs	Number of orders
Materials handling costs	Number of production runs
Production scheduling costs	Number of production runs
Despatching costs	Number of despatches

For those **costs that vary with production levels in the short term**, ABC uses **volume-related cost drivers** such as labour or machine hours. The cost of oil used as a lubricant on the machines would therefore be added to products on the basis of the number of machine hours, since oil would have to be used for each hour the machine ran.

Step 3 Collect the costs associated with each cost driver into what are known as cost pools.

Key term

> A **cost pool** is a grouping of costs relating to a particular activity in an activity-based costing system.

Step 4 Charge the costs of each cost pool to products on the basis of their usage of the activity (measured by the number of the activity's cost driver a product generates) using a cost driver rate (total costs in cost pool/number of cost drivers).

Question

Cost drivers

Which of the following definitions best describes a cost driver?

A Any activity which causes an increase in costs
B A collection of costs associated with a particular activity
C A cost that varies with production levels
D Any factor which causes a change in the cost of an activity

Answer

The correct answer is D.

2.3 Transactions analysis

FAST FORWARD

When using ABC, for costs that vary with production levels in the short term, the cost driver will be volume related (labour or machine hours). Overheads that vary with some other activity (and not volume of production) should be traced to products using transaction-based cost drivers such as production runs or number of orders received. One way of classifying these transactions is **logistical, balancing, quality** and **change**.

ABC recognises that factors other than volume can explain the level of overhead. Miller and Vollman (1985, The Hidden Factory. *Harvard Business Review*) provided a useful system for analysing the different types of transactions which cause overheads to be incurred.

Types of transaction	Detail
Logistical transactions	Those activities concerned with organising the flow of resources throughout the manufacturing process.
Balancing transactions	Those activities which ensure that demand for and supply of resources are matched.
Quality transactions	Those activities which relate to ensuring that production is at the required level of quality.
Change transactions	Those activities associated with ensuring that customers' requirements (delivery date, changed design and so on) are met.

Note that the primary driver of these transactions is not usually production volume. For example, the level of change transactions might be determined by the number of customers and the number of different product types, rather than by production volume.

Such an analysis provides a better understanding of long-term cost behaviour and allows for the costs associated with particular transactions to be assigned to only those products causing the transactions.

3 Absorption costing versus ABC

FAST FORWARD

Although ABC has obvious merits, a number of criticisms have been raised.

The following example illustrates the point that traditional cost accounting techniques result in a misleading and inequitable division of costs between low-volume and high-volume products, and that ABC can provide a more meaningful allocation of costs.

3.1 Example: Activity based costing

Suppose that Cooplan manufactures four products, W, X, Y and Z. Output and cost data for the period just ended are as follows.

	Output units	Number of production runs in the period	Material cost per unit $	Direct labour hours per unit	Machine hours per unit
W	10	2	20	1	1
X	10	2	80	3	3
Y	100	5	20	1	1
Z	100	5	80	3	3
		14			

7: ACTIVITY BASED COSTING

Direct labour cost per hour $5

	$
Overhead costs	
Short run variable costs	3,080
Set-up costs	10,920
Expediting and scheduling costs	9,100
Materials handling costs	7,700
	30,800

Required

Prepare unit costs for each product using conventional costing and ABC.

Solution

Using a **conventional absorption costing approach** and an absorption rate for overheads based on either direct labour hours or machine hours, the product costs would be as follows.

	W	X	Y	Z	Total
	$	$	$	$	$
Direct material	200	800	2,000	8,000	
Direct labour	50	150	500	1,500	
Overheads *	700	2,100	7,000	21,000	
	950	3,050	9,500	30,500	44,000
Units produced	10	10	100	100	
Cost per unit	$95	$305	$95	$305	

* $30,800 ÷ 440 hours = $70 per direct labour or machine hour.

Using **activity based costing** and assuming that the number of production runs is the cost driver for set-up costs, expediting and scheduling costs and materials handling costs and that machine hours are the cost driver for short-run variable costs, unit costs would be as follows.

	W	X	Y	Z	Total
	$	$	$	$	$
Direct material	200	800	2,000	8,000	
Direct labour	50	150	500	1,500	
Short-run variable overheads (W1)	70	210	700	2,100	
Set-up costs (W2)	1,560	1,560	3,900	3,900	
Expediting, scheduling costs (W3)	1,300	1,300	3,250	3,250	
Materials handling costs (W4)	1,100	1,100	2,750	2,750	
	4,280	5,120	13,100	21,500	44,000
Units produced	10	10	100	100	
Cost per unit	$428	$512	$131	$215	

Workings

1	$3,080 ÷ 440 machine hours =	$7 per machine hour
2	$10,920 ÷ 14 production runs =	$780 per run
3	$9,100 ÷ 14 production runs =	$650 per run
4	$7,700 ÷ 14 production runs =	$550 per run

Summary

Product	Conventional costing unit cost	ABC unit cost	Difference per unit	Difference in total
	$	$	$	$
W	95	428	+ 333	+3,330
X	305	512	+ 207	+2,070
Y	95	131	+ 36	+3,600
Z	305	215	−90	−9,000

The figures suggest that the **traditional volume-based absorption costing system is flawed**.

(a) It under-allocates overhead costs to low-volume products (here, W and X) and over-allocates overheads to higher-volume products (here Z in particular).

(b) It under-allocates overhead costs to smaller-sized products (here W and Y with just one hour of work needed per unit) and over-allocates overheads to larger products (here X and particularly Z).

3.2 ABC versus traditional costing methods

Both traditional absorption costing and ABC systems adopt the two stage allocation process.

3.2.1 Allocation of overheads

ABC establishes **separate cost pools for support activities** such as despatching. As the costs of these activities are assigned directly to products through cost driver rates, **reapportionment of service department costs is avoided**.

3.2.2 Absorption of overheads

The principal difference between the two systems is the way in which overheads are absorbed into products.

(a) **Absorption costing** most commonly uses two **absorption bases** (labour hours and/or machine hours) to charge overheads to products.

(b) **ABC** uses **many cost drivers** as absorption bases (number of orders, number of despatches and so on).

Absorption rates under **ABC** should therefore be **more closely linked to the causes of overhead costs.**

3.3 Cost drivers

The **principal idea** of ABC is to **focus attention on what causes costs to increase,** ie the **cost drivers**.

(a) Those **costs that do vary with production volume**, such as power costs, should be traced to products using production **volume-related cost drivers** as appropriate, such as direct labour hours or direct machine hours. Such costs tend to be **short-term variable overheads** such as power costs.

Overheads which do not **vary** with output but **with some other activity** should be traced to products using **transaction-based cost drivers**, such as number of production runs and number of orders received. Such costs tend to be **long-term variable overheads** (overheads that traditional accounting would classify as fixed).

(b) Traditional costing systems allow overheads to be related to products in rather more arbitrary ways producing, it is claimed, less accurate product costs.

Question — ABC versus traditional costing

A company manufactures two products, L and M, using the same equipment and similar processes. An extract of the production data for these products in one period is shown below.

	L	M
Quantity produced (units)	5,000	7,000
Direct labour hours per unit	1	2
Machine hours per unit	3	1
Set-ups in the period	10	40
Orders handled in the period	15	60

7: ACTIVITY BASED COSTING

Overhead costs	$
Relating to machine activity	220,000
Relating to production run set-ups	20,000
Relating to handling of orders	45,000
	285,000

Required

Calculate the production overheads to be absorbed by one unit of each of the products using the following costing methods.

(a) A traditional absorption costing approach using a direct labour hour rate to absorb overheads
(b) An activity based costing approach, using suitable cost drivers to trace overheads to products

Answer

(a) **Traditional absorption costing approach**

	Direct labour hours
Product L = 5,000 units × 1 hour	5,000
Product M = 7,000 units × 2 hours	14,000
	19,000

$$\therefore \text{Overhead absorption rate} = \frac{\$285,000}{19,000}$$

$$= \$15 \text{ per hour}$$

Overhead absorbed would be as follows.

Product L	1 hour × $15	=	$15 per unit
Product M	2 hours × $15	=	$30 per unit

(b) **ABC approach**

		Machine hours
Product L	= 5,000 units × 3 hours	15,000
Product M	= 7,000 units × 1 hour	7,000
		22,000

Using ABC the overhead costs are absorbed according to the **cost drivers**.

	$	
Machine-hour driven costs	220,000 ÷ 22,000 m/c hours	= $10 per m/c hour
Set-up driven costs	20,000 ÷ 50 set-ups	= $400 per set-up
Order driven costs	45,000 ÷ 75 orders	= $600 per order

Overhead costs are therefore as follows.

	Product L		Product M	
		$		$
Machine-driven costs	(15,000 hrs × $10)	150,000	(7,000 hrs × $10)	70,000
Set-up costs	(10 × $400)	4,000	(40 × $400)	16,000
Order handling costs	(15 × $600)	9,000	(60 × $600)	36,000
		163,000		122,000
Units produced		5,000		7,000
Overhead cost per unit		$32.60		$17.43

These figures suggest that product M absorbs an unrealistic amount of overhead using a direct labour hour basis. Overhead absorption should be based on the activities which drive the costs, in this case machine hours, the number of production run set-ups and the number of orders handled for each product.

4 Marginal costing versus ABC

FAST FORWARD

The main criticism of marginal costing decision making information is that marginal costing analyses cost behaviour patterns according to the volume of production. However, although certain costs may be fixed in relation to the volume of production, they **may in fact be variable in relation to some other cost driver.**

Some commentators argue that only marginal costing provides suitable information for decision making but this is not true. Marginal costing provides a crude method of differentiating between different types of cost behaviour by splitting costs into their variable and fixed elements. However, such an analysis can be used only for **short-term decisions** and usually even these have longer-term implications which ought to be considered.

The problem with marginal costing is that it analyses cost behaviour patterns according to the volume of production. However, although certain costs may be fixed in relation to the volume of production, they **may in fact be variable in relation to some other cost driver.** A failure to allocate such costs to individual products could result in incorrect decisions concerning the future management of the products.

The advantage of ABC is that **it spreads costs across products according to a number of different bases.** For example an ABC analysis may show that one particular activity which is carried out primarily for one or two products is expensive. A correct allocation of the costs of this activity may reveal that these particular products are not profitable. If these costs are fixed in relation to the volume of production then they would be treated as **period costs** in a marginal costing system and **written off against the marginal costing contribution for the period.**

The marginal costing system would therefore make no attempt to allocate these 'fixed' costs to individual products and a false impression would be given of the long run average cost of the products.

Thus, marginal costing may provide incorrect decision making information, **particularly in a situation where 'fixed' costs are vary large compared with 'variable' costs.**

5 Introducing an ABC system

FAST FORWARD

ABC should only be introduced if the additional information it provides will result in action that will increase the organisation's overall profitability.

5.1 When should ABC be introduced?

ABC should only be introduced if the **additional information** it provides will **result in action that will increase** the organisation's overall **profitability**. This is most likely to **occur** in situations such as the following, when the **ABC analysis differs significantly from the traditional absorption costing analysis**.

- Production overheads are high in relation to direct costs, especially direct labour.
- Overhead resource consumption is not just driven by production volume.
- There is wide variety in the product range.
- The overhead resource input varies significantly across the product range.

5.2 Analysis of activities

FAST FORWARD

ABC identifies four levels of activities: product level, batch level, product sustaining level and facility sustaining level.

ABC attempts to **relate the incidence of costs to the level of activities undertaken**. A **hierarchy of activities** has been suggested.

Key term

The **hierarchy of activities** is a classification of activities by level of organisation, for example unit, batch, product sustaining and facility sustaining.

Type of activities	Costs are dependent on ...	Examples
Product level	Volume of production	Machine power
Batch level	Number of batches	Set-up costs
Product sustaining	Existence of a product group/line	Product management
Facility sustaining	Organisation simply being in business	Rent and rates

Key terms

Product-sustaining activities are 'Activities undertaken to develop or sustain a product (or service). Product sustaining costs are linked to the number of products or services not to the number of units produced.'

Facility-sustaining activities are 'Activities undertaken to support the organisation as a whole, and which cannot be logically linked to individual units of output.'

The difference between a unit product cost determined using traditional absorption costing and one determined using ABC will depend on the proportion of overhead cost which falls into each of the categories above.

(a) If most overheads are related to unit level and facility level activities, the costs will be similar.

(b) If the overheads tend to be associated with batch or product level activities they will be significantly different.

Consider the following example.

5.3 Example: Batch-level activities

XYZ produces a number of products including product D and product E and produces 500 units of each of products D and E every period at a rate of ten of each every hour. The overhead cost is $500,000 and a total of 40,000 direct labour hours are worked on all products. A traditional overhead absorption rate would be $12.50 per direct labour hour and the overhead cost per product would be $1.25.

Production of D requires five production runs per period, while production of E requires 20. An investigation has revealed that the overhead costs relate mainly to 'batch-level' activities associated with setting-up machinery and handling materials for production runs.

There are 1,000 production runs per period and so overheads could be attributed to XYZ's products at a rate of $500 per run.

- Overhead cost per D = ($500 × 5 runs)/500 = $5
- Overhead cost per E = ($500 × 20 runs)/500 = $20

These overhead costs are activity based and recognise that overhead costs are incurred due to batch level activities. The fact that E has to be made in frequent small batches, perhaps because it is perishable, means that it uses more resources than D. This is recognised by the ABC overhead costs, not the traditional absorption costing overhead costs.

Such an analysis of costs gives management an **indication of the decision level at which costs can be influenced**. For example, a decision to reduce production costs will not simply depend on making a general reduction in output volumes: production may need to be organised to reduce **batch** volumes; a **process** may need to be modified or eliminated; **product lines** may need to be merged or cut out; **facility** capacity may need to be altered.

5.4 ABC in service and retail organisations

ABC was **first introduced in manufacturing organisations** but it can equally well be used in **other types of organisation**. For example, the management of the Post Office in the US introduced ABC. They analysed the activities associated with cash processing as follows.

Activities	Examples	Possible cost driver
Unit level	Accept cash	Number of transactions
	Processing of cash by bank	Number of transactions
Batch level	'Close out' and supervisor review of clerk	Number of 'close outs'
	Deposits	Number of deposits
	Review and transfer of funds	Number of accounts
Product level	Maintenance charges for bank accounts	Number of accounts
	Reconciling bank accounts	Number of accounts

Question

ABC and retail organisations

List five activities that might be identified in a retail organisation and state one possible cost driver for each of the activities you have identified.

Answer

Activities	Possible cost driver
Procure goods	Number of orders
Receive goods	Number of orders or pallets
Store goods	Volume of goods
Pick goods	Number of packs
Handle returnables/recyclables	Volume of goods

6 Merits and criticisms of ABC

ABC has a range of uses and has many advantages over more traditional costing methods. However, the system does have its critics and it is not used as a panacea for all costing problems.

6.1 Merits of ABC

As you will have discovered when you attempted the question above, there is nothing difficult about ABC. Once the necessary information has been obtained it is similar to traditional absorption costing. This simplicity is part of its appeal. Further merits of ABC are as follows.

(a) The **complexity of manufacturing has increased**, with wider product ranges, shorter product life cycles and more complex production processes. **ABC recognises this complexity with its multiple cost drivers.**

(b) In a more competitive environment, companies must be able to assess product profitability realistically. **ABC facilitates a good understanding of what drives overhead costs**.

(c) In modern manufacturing systems, overhead functions include a lot of non-factory-floor activities such as product design, quality control, production planning and customer services. **ABC is concerned with all overhead costs** and so it takes management accounting beyond its 'traditional' factory floor boundaries.

(d) By controlling the incidence of the cost driver, the level of the **cost** can be **controlled**.

(e) The costs of activities not included in the costs of the products an organisation makes or the services it provides can be considered to be **not contributing to the value of the product/service**. The following questions can then be asked.
- What is the purpose of this activity?
- How does the organisation benefit from this activity?
- Could the number of staff involved in the activity be reduced?

(f) ABC can help with **cost management**. For example, suppose there is a fall in the number of orders placed by a purchasing department. This fall would not impact on the amount of overhead absorbed in a traditional absorption costing system as the cost of ordering would be part of the general overhead absorption rate (assuming no direct link between the overhead absorption basis of, say, direct labour hours, and the number of orders placed). The reduction in the workload of the purchasing department might therefore go unnoticed and the same level of resources would continue to be provided, despite the drop in number of orders. In an ABC system, however, this drop would be immediately apparent because the cost driver rate would be applied to fewer orders.

(g) Many costs are driven by customers (delivery costs, discounts, after-sales service and so on), but traditional absorption costing systems do not account for this. Organisations may be trading with certain customers at a loss but may not realise it because costs are not analysed in a way that reveals the true situation. ABC can be **used in conjunction with customer profitability analysis (CPA)** to determine more accurately the profit earned by servicing particular customers.

Key term

> **Customer profitability analysis (CPA)** is an analysis of the revenue streams and service costs associated with specific customers or customer groups.

(h) Many **service businesses** have characteristics similar to those required for the successful application of ABC.
- A highly **competitive** market
- **Diversity** of products, processes and customers
- **Significant overhead costs** not easily assigned to individual 'products'
- Demands placed on overhead resources by individual 'products' and customers, which are not proportional to volume

If ABC were to be used in a hotel, for example, attempts could be made to identify the activities required to support each guest by category and the cost drivers of these activities. The cost of a

6.2 Criticisms of ABC

one-night stay midweek by a businessman could then be distinguished from the cost of a one-night stay by a teenager at the weekend. Such information could prove invaluable for **CPA**.

It has been suggested by critics that **activity based costing has some serious flaws.**

(a) Some measure of (arbitrary) cost apportionment may still be required at the cost pooling stage for items like rent, rates and building depreciation.

(b) Can a single cost driver explain the cost behaviour of all items in its associated pool?

(c) On the other hand, the number of cost pools and cost drivers cannot be excessive otherwise an ABC system would be too complex and too expensive.

(d) Unless costs are caused by an activity that is measurable in quantitative terms and which can be related to production output, cost drivers will not be usable. What drives the cost of the annual external audit, for example?

(e) ABC is sometimes introduced because it is fashionable, not because it will be used by management to provide meaningful product costs or extra information. If management is not going to use ABC information, an absorption costing system may be simpler to operate.

(f) The costs of ABC may outweigh the benefits.

7 Pricing and ABC

FAST FORWARD

> **Activity-based costing** provides an opportunity for organisations that use cost-based pricing to gain a greater understanding of their costs and so correct pricing anomalies that derive from the distorted view given by conventional volume-related costing.

As you know, under the ABC approach overheads are allocated to products on the basis of the activities that cause them to be incurred, rather than according to some arbitrary base like labour hours. The implication for pricing is that the **full cost** on which prices are based may be **radically different** if ABC is used.

7.1 Example: Activity-based costing and pricing

ABP Co makes two products, X and Y, with the following cost patterns.

	Product X $	Product Y $
Direct materials	27	24
Direct labour at $5 per hour	20	25
Variable production overheads at $6 per hour	3	6
	50	55

Production fixed overheads total $300,000 per month and these are absorbed on the basis of direct labour hours. Budgeted direct labour hours are 25,000 per month. However, the company has carried out an analysis of its production support activities and found that its 'fixed costs' actually vary in accordance with non volume related factors.

Activity	Cost driver	Product X	Product Y	Total cost $
Set-ups	Production runs	30	20	40,000
Materials handling	Production runs	30	20	150,000
Inspection	Inspections	880	3,520	110,000
				300,000

Budgeted production is 1,250 units of product X and 4,000 units of product Y.

Required

Given that the company wishes to make a profit of 20% on full production cost, calculate the prices that should be charged for products X and Y using the following.

(a) Full cost pricing
(b) Activity-based cost pricing

Solution

(a) The **full cost and mark-up** will be calculated as follows.

	Product X $	Product Y $
Variable costs	50.00	55.00
Fixed prod o/hds ($300,000/25,000 = $12 per direct labour hr)	48.00	60.00
	98.00	115.00
Profit mark-up (20%)	19.60	23.00
Selling price	117.60	138.00

(b) Using **activity-based costing**, overheads will be allocated on the basis of cost drivers.

	X	Y	Total
Set ups (30:20)	24,000	16,000	40,000
Materials handling (30:20)	90,000	60,000	150,000
Inspections (880:3,520)	22,000	88,000	110,000
	136,000	164,000	300,000
Budgeted units	1,250	4,000	
Overheads per unit	$108.80	$41.00	

The price is then calculated as before.

	Product X $	Product Y $
Variable costs	50.00	55.00
Production overheads	108.80	41.00
	158.80	96.00
Profit mark-up (20%)	31.76	19.20
	190.56	115.20

(c) **Commentary**

The results in (b) are radically different from those in (a). On this basis it appears that the company has **previously been making a huge loss** on every unit of product X sold for $117.60. If the market will not accept a price increase, it may be worth considering ceasing production of product X entirely. It also appears that there is scope for a reduction in the price of product Y, and this would certainly be worthwhile if demand for the product is elastic.

7.2 The pricing implications of activity-based costing

Consider a business that produces a **large volume** standard product and a number of **variants** which are more refined versions of the basic product and sell in low volumes at a higher price. Such companies are common in practice in the modern business environment. In practice, also, such companies absorb fixed overheads on a conventional basis such as direct labour hours, and price their products by adding a mark up to full cost.

In the situation described, the **majority of the overheads** would be allocated to the **standard** range, and only a small percentage to the up-market products. The result would be that the profit margin achieved on the standard range would be much lower than that on the up-market range.

Thus the traditional costing and pricing system indicates that the firm might be wise to concentrate on its high margin, up-market products and drop its standard range. This is **absurd**, however. Much of the overhead cost incurred in such an organisation is the cost of support activities like production scheduling: the more different **varieties** of product there are, the higher the level of such activities will become. The cost of marketing and distribution also increases disproportionately to the volume of products being made.

The bulk of the overheads in such an organisation are actually the '**costs of complexity**'. Their arbitrary allocation on the basis of labour hours gives an entirely **distorted** view of production line profitability; many products that appear to be highly profitable actually make a loss if costs are allocated on the basis of what activities cause them.

The problem arises with **marginal cost-plus** approaches as well as with absorption cost based approaches, particularly in a modern manufacturing environment, where a relatively small proportion of the total cost is variable. The implication in both cases is that conventional costing should be abandoned in favour of ABC.

8 Environmental management accounting

> **FAST FORWARD**
>
> More companies are now identifying and measuring direct environmental costs by revising allocation bases so as to separate out **indirect environmental costs using ABC**.

In **traditional** cost accounting, **environmental costs** might be lumped together with **general overhead** costs, making it difficult to determine the exact environmental cost associated with each product or service. With **ABC**, these **environmental costs** are **separated from general overheads** and traced directly to the **activities that cause them**.

For example, if a specific production **process generates waste** or requires pollution control measures, the costs associated with these activities are **directly allocated to the products involved in that process**.

By **isolating environmental costs** and linking them to the specific products or services that generate them, ABC helps in achieving a more **accurate product costing**. This precision reduces distortions that can occur when environmental costs are spread evenly across all products. For example, if one product is significantly more resource-intensive and environmentally impactful than another, ABC helps in capturing this difference accurately.

Furthermore, this detailed **allocation provides valuable information** for environmental management. Companies can identify which products or processes are more environmentally costly and make more **informed decisions** on how to manage and reduce these costs. This can lead to better strategies for **reducing environmental impact, improving sustainability practices** and potentially **reducing costs** associated with environmental compliance.

8.1 Example: Using ABC to apportion environmental costs

Fantasia, a glass manufacturer, has identified the following activities and cost drivers relating to environmental costs:

	$'000	Cost drivers	'000
Preventing water pollution	3,520	Waste water output m^3	1,600
General waste recycling & disposal	2,520	Kg of general waste	3.0
Hazardous waste recycling & disposal	3,680	Kg of recycled waste	1.6
Research & development (R&D) related to environment	7,420	R&D hours	140
Total	17,140		

Fantasia makes two products – Products A and B.

Currently, environmental costs are a part of Fantasia's general overhead pool and apportioned per unit. Fantasia produces 82,000 units of Product A and 8,000 units of Product B.

An ABC analysis of this environmental data has been prepared by a junior member of staff who has now been transferred to another department. Her workings are correct but incomplete.

	Product A			Product B		
	Activity '000	Cost $'000	Cost/unit $	Activity '000	Cost $'000	Cost/unit $
Water pollution	1,120			480		
General waste	2.7			0.3		
Hazardous waste	0.8			0.8		
R&D	90			50		
Total						

Required

Prepare an ABC analysis of the environmental costs including a calculation of the environmental cost per unit. Comment on how this differs from the allocation of cost under traditional absorption costing and the implications this has for performance management.

Solution

Cost driver charge out rates	Working	
Waste water output m^3	$3,520/1,600	$2.20 per m^3
Kg of general waste	$2,520/3	$840 per kg
Kg of recycled waste	$3,680/1.6	$2,300 per kg
R&D hours	$7,420/140	$53 per hour

	Product A			Product B		
	Activity '000 × rate	Cost $'000	Cost/unit $ (÷82)	Activity '000 × rate	Cost $'000	Cost/unit $ (÷8)
Water pollution	1,120 × $2.20	2,464	30.05	480 × $2.20	1,056	132.00
General waste	2.7 × $840	2,268	27.66	0.3 × $840	252	31.50
Hazardous waste	0.8 × $2,300	1,840	22.44	0.8 × $2,300	1,840	230.00
R&D	90 × $53	4,770	58.17	50 × $53	2,650	331.25
Total cost/unit			138.32			724.75

Implications for performance management

Under the existing costing system, the environmental cost per unit is $17,140,000/90,000 = $190.44 per unit.

Under the revised costing, Product B will see a significant cost increase and, as a result, will be correctly seen as a less profitable product.

This may affect the R&D spending being targeted at Product B.

It may also affect B's pricing, which may need to increase.

Finally, it provides clear visibility of the environmental impact of Product B, which can be used to control the activities that are driving these costs. For example, it may be sensible from an environmental and a costing viewpoint to amend the formulation of Product B to reduce its use of hazardous chemicals.

Chapter roundup

- **Traditional costing systems**, which assume that all products consume all resources in proportion to their production volumes, tend to **allocate too great a proportion of overheads to high volume products** (which cause relatively little diversity and hence use fewer support services) and **too small a proportion of overheads** to low volume products (which cause greater diversity and therefore use more support services). **Activity based costing (ABC) attempts to overcome this problem.**

- An alternative to the traditional method of accounting for costs – absorption costing – is **activity based costing (ABC)**. ABC involves the identification of the factors (**cost drivers**) which cause the costs of an organisation's major activities. Support overheads are charged to products on the basis of their usage of an activity.

- When using ABC, for costs that vary with production levels in the short term, the cost driver will be volume related (labour or machine hours). Overheads that vary with some other activity (and not volume of production) should be traced to products using transaction-based cost drivers such as production runs or number of orders received. One way of classifying these transactions is **logistical, balancing, quality and change**.

- Although ABC has obvious merits, a number of criticisms have been raised.

- The main criticism of marginal costing decision making information is that marginal costing analyses cost behaviour patterns according to the volume of production. However, although certain costs may be fixed in relation to the volume of production, they **may in fact be variable in relation to some other cost driver.**

- ABC should only be introduced if the additional information it provides will result in action that will increase the organisation's overall profitability.

- ABC identifies four levels of activities: product level, batch level, product sustaining level and facility sustaining level.

- ABC has a range of uses and has many advantages over more traditional costing methods. However, the system does have its critics and it is not used as a panacea for all costing problems.

- **Activity-based costing** provides an opportunity for organisations that use cost-based pricing to gain a greater understanding of their costs and so correct pricing anomalies that derive from the distorted view given by conventional volume-related costing.

- More companies are now identifying and measuring direct environmental costs by revising allocation bases so as to separate out **indirect environmental costs using ABC**.

Quick Quiz

1 Choose the correct words from those highlighted.

Traditional costing systems tend to allocate **too great/too small** a proportion of overheads to high volume products and **too great/too small** a proportion of overheads to low volume products.

2 Fill in the blanks.

The major ideas behind ABC are as follows.
(a) Activities cause ....
(b) Producing products creates demand for the ....
(c) Costs are assigned to a product on the basis of the product's consumption of the
 ....

3 Match the most appropriate cost driver to each cost.

Costs		Cost driver
(a)	Set-up costs	Number of machine hours
(b)	Short-run variable costs	Number of production runs
(c)	Materials handling and despatch	Number of orders executed

4 ABC recognises the complexity of modern manufacturing by the use of multiple cost pools. True or false?

5 The use of direct labour hours or direct machine hours to trace costs to products occurs with the use of absorption costing but not with the use of ABC. True or false?

6 The cost driver for quality inspection is likely to be batch size. True or false?

7 ABC is not a system that is suitable for use by service organisations. True or false?

Answers to Quick Quiz

1. Too great
   Too small

2. (a) Costs
   (b) Activities
   (c) Activities

3. (a) Number of production runs
   (b) Number of machine hours
   (c) Number of orders executed

4. False. Complexity is recognised by the use of multiple cost drivers.

5. False. The use of volume-related cost drivers should be used for costs that do vary with production volume.

6. False

7. False. It is highly suitable.

End of chapter question

TQG Ltd

TQG Ltd manufacturers top quality granite work tops for industrial and commercial kitchens. The company uses three types of granite and cost their products based upon a labour hour absorption rate. TQG Ltd has invested heavily in new computer controlled cutting and polishing machinery. Despite this, in recent months the company has lost several orders for their standard brand, 'Jet Black' granite, to competitors and the management is considering changing the costing method to an activity-based costing system.

Information relating to last month's production of the three types of granite is as follows:

		Granite Type	
	Gold Pearl	Sapphire Blue	Jet Black
Direct materials (£)	103,680	165,730	209,420
Direct labour (£)	48,300	36,550	68,800
Labour hours	6,900	7,310	8,600
Worktops produced	207	285	525

Absorption of production overheads using labour hours is based on the following monthly budget:

	$
Machine maintenance	6,350
Machine production running costs	128,750
Machine set-up costs	29,860
Inventory and purchasing costs	61,020
	225,980

PART B COST IDENTIFICATION AND MEASURING COSTS FOR MANAGEMENT PURPOSES

In anticipation of changing to an activity-based costing system, TQG Ltd has recorded the following cost drivers for the three types of granite over the month's production.

		Granite Type		
Activity	Cost Driver	Gold Pearl	Sapphire Blue	Jet Black
Machine maintenance	Hours maintenance	65	45	30
Machine production running costs	Machine hours	5,450	3,250	2,500
Machine set-up costs	No. of set-ups	207	285	525
Inventory and purchasing costs	No. of requisitions	780	456	325

Required

(a) Briefly explain what is meant by a cost driver, and why it is important in activity-based costing.

(3 marks)

(b) Using the labour hour as the overhead absorption base, calculate the unit cost for each type of granite worktop.

(4 marks)

(c) Using activity-based costing, calculate the unit cost for each type of granite worktop.   **(8 marks)**

(d) Compare the results in overhead absorbed given by each costing method per granite type and suggest how this may help solve the company's problem relating to loss of orders for Jet Black.

(5 marks)

(Total = 20 marks)

PART C3

Introduction to costing systems

Process costing

Topic list	Syllabus reference
1 The basics of process costing	C3.2
2 Losses in process costing	C3.2
3 Losses with scrap value	C3.2
4 Losses with a disposal cost	C3.2
5 Valuing closing work in progress	C3.2
6 Valuing opening work in progress: FIFO method	C3.2
7 Valuing opening work in progress: weighted average cost method	C3.2

Introduction

In this chapter we will consider **process costing**. The chapter will consider the topic from basics, looking at how to account for the most simple of processes. We then move on to how to account for any **losses** which might occur, as well as what to do with any **scrapped units** which are sold. We also consider how to deal with any **closing work in progress** and then look at two methods of valuing **opening work in progress**. Valuation of both opening and closing work in progress hinges on the concept of **equivalent units**, which will be explained in detail.

PART C INTRODUCTION TO COSTING SYSTEMS

1 The basics of process costing

1.1 Introduction to process costing

FAST FORWARD

> **Process costing** is a costing method used where it is not possible to identify separate units of production, or jobs, usually because of the continuous nature of the production processes involved.

It is common to identify process costing with **continuous production** such as the following.

- Oil refining
- Paper
- Foods and drinks
- Chemicals

Process costing may also be associated with the continuous production of large volumes of low-cost items, such as **cans** or **tins**.

1.2 Features of process costing

(a) The **output** of one process becomes the **input** to the next until the finished product is made in the final process.

(b) The continuous nature of production in many processes means that there will usually be **closing work in progress which must be valued**. In process costing it is not possible to build up cost records of the cost per unit of output or the cost per unit of closing inventory because production in progress is an **indistinguishable homogeneous mass**.

(c) There is often a **loss in process** due to spoilage, wastage, evaporation and so on.

(d) Output from production may be a single product, but there may also be a **by-product** (or by-products) and/or **joint products.**

The aim of this chapter is to describe how cost accountants keep a set of accounts to record the costs of production in a processing industry. The aim of the set of accounts is to derive a cost, or valuation, for output and closing inventory.

1.3 Process accounts

Where a series of separate processes is required to manufacture the finished product, the output of one process becomes the input to the next until the final output is made in the final process. If two processes are required the accounts would look like this.

PROCESS 1 ACCOUNT

	Units	$		Units	$
Direct materials	1,000	50,000	Output to process 2	1,000	90,000
Direct labour		20,000			
Production overhead		20,000			
	1,000	90,000		1,000	90,000

PROCESS 2 ACCOUNT

	Units	$		Units	$
Materials from process 1	1,000	90,000	Output to finished goods	1,000	150,000
Added materials		30,000			
Direct labour		15,000			
Production overhead		15,000			
	1,000	150,000		1,000	150,000

Note that direct labour and production overhead may be treated together in an examination question as **conversion cost**.

Added materials, labour and overhead in process 2 are added gradually throughout the process. Materials from process 1, in contrast, will often be introduced in full at the start of process 2.

The 'units' columns in the process accounts are for **memorandum purposes** only and help you to ensure that you do not miss out any entries.

1.4 Framework for dealing with process costing

> **FAST FORWARD**
>
> Process costing is centred around **four key steps**. The exact work done at each step will depend on whether there are normal losses, scrap, opening and closing work in progress.
>
> **Step 1** Determine output and losses
> **Step 2** Calculate cost per unit of output, losses and WIP
> **Step 3** Calculate total cost of output, losses and WIP
> **Step 4** Complete accounts

Let's look at these steps in more detail.

Step 1 **Determine output and losses.** This step involves the following.

- Determining expected output
- Calculating normal loss and abnormal loss and gain
- Calculating equivalent units if there is closing or opening work in progress

Step 2 **Calculate cost per unit of output, losses and WIP.** This step involves calculating cost per unit or cost per equivalent unit.

Step 3 **Calculate total cost of output, losses and WIP.** In some examples this will be straightforward; however in cases where there is closing and/or opening work-in-progress a **statement of evaluation** will have to be prepared.

Step 4 **Complete accounts.** This step involves the following.

- Completing the process account
- Writing up the other accounts required by the question

Exam focus point

Many students find process costing rather daunting at first. The best way to learn process costing is by learning the steps involved and then having plenty of practice working through the steps.

2 Losses in process costing

2.1 Introduction

> **FAST FORWARD**
>
> **Losses** may occur in process. If a certain level of loss is expected, this is known as **normal loss**. If losses are greater than expected, the extra loss is **abnormal loss**. If losses are less than expected, the difference is known as **abnormal gain**.

Key terms

Normal loss is the loss expected during a process. It is not given a cost.

Abnormal loss is the extra loss resulting when actual loss is greater than normal or expected loss, and it is given a cost.

Abnormal gain is the gain resulting when actual loss is less than the normal or expected loss, and it is given a 'negative cost'.

Since normal loss is not given a cost, the cost of producing these units is borne by the 'good' units of output.

Abnormal loss and gain units are valued at the same unit rate as 'good' units. Abnormal events do not therefore affect the cost of good production. Their costs are **analysed separately** in an **abnormal loss or abnormal gain account**.

2.2 Example: Abnormal losses and gains

Suppose that input to a process is 1,000 units at a cost of $4,500. Normal loss is 10% and there are no opening or closing stocks. Determine the accounting entries for the cost of output and the cost of the loss if actual output were as follows.

(a) 860 units (so that actual loss is 140 units)
(b) 920 units (so that actual loss is 80 units)

Solution

Before we demonstrate the use of the 'four-step framework' we will summarise the way that the losses are dealt with.

(a) Normal loss is given no share of cost.

(b) The cost of output is therefore based on the **expected** units of output, which in our example amount to 90% of 1,000 = 900 units.

(c) Abnormal loss is given a cost, which is written off to the profit and loss account via an abnormal loss/gain account.

(d) Abnormal gain is treated in the same way, except that being a gain rather than a loss, it appears as a **debit** entry in the process account (whereas a loss appears as a **credit** entry in this account).

(a) **Output is 860 units**

Step 1 Determine output and losses

If actual output is 860 units and the actual loss is 140 units:

	Units
Actual loss	140
Normal loss (10% of 1,000)	100
Abnormal loss	40

Step 2 Calculate cost per unit of output and losses

The cost per unit of output and the cost per unit of abnormal loss are based on expected output.

$$\frac{\text{Costs incurred}}{\text{Expected output}} = \frac{\$4,500}{900 \text{ units}} = \$5 \text{ per unit}$$

Step 3 Calculate total cost of output and losses

Normal loss is not assigned any cost.

	$
Cost of output (860 × $5)	4,300
Normal loss	0
Abnormal loss (40 × $5)	200
	4,500

Step 4 Complete accounts

PROCESS ACCOUNT

	Units	$		Units		$
Cost incurred	1,000	4,500	Normal loss	100		0
			Output (finished goods a/c)	860	(× $5)	4,300
			Abnormal loss	40	(× $5)	200
	1,000	4,500		1,000		4,500

ABNORMAL LOSS ACCOUNT

	Units	$		Units	$
Process a/c	40	200	Statement of profit or loss	40	200

(b) **Output is 920 units**

Step 1 Determine output and losses

If actual output is 920 units and the actual loss is 80 units:

	Units
Actual loss	80
Normal loss (10% of 1,000)	100
Abnormal gain	20

Step 2 Calculate cost per unit of output and losses

The cost per unit of output and the cost per unit of abnormal gain are based on **expected** output.

$$\frac{\text{Costs incurred}}{\text{Expected output}} = \frac{\$4,500}{900 \text{ units}} = \$5 \text{ per unit}$$

(Whether there is abnormal loss or gain does not affect the valuation of units of output. The figure of $5 per unit is exactly the same as in the previous paragraph, when there were 40 units of abnormal loss.)

Step 3 Calculate total cost of output and losses

	$
Cost of output (920 × $5)	4,600
Normal loss	0
Abnormal gain (20 × $5)	(100)
	4,500

Step 4 Complete accounts

PROCESS ACCOUNT

	Units		$		Units		$
Cost incurred	1,000		4,500	Normal loss	100		0
Abnormal gain a/c	20	(× $5)	100	Output (finished goods a/c)	920	(× $5)	4,600
	1,020		4,600		1,020		4,600

ABNORMAL GAIN

	Units	$		Units	$
Statement of profit or loss	20	100	Process a/c	20	100

PART C INTRODUCTION TO COSTING SYSTEMS

Question — Abnormal losses and gains

Shiny Co has two processes, Y and Z. There is an expected loss of 5% of input in process Y and 7% of input in process Z. Activity during a four week period is as follows.

	Y	Z
Material input (kg)	20,000	28,000
Output (kg)	18,500	26,100

Is there an abnormal gain or abnormal loss for each process?

	Y	Z
A	Abnormal loss	Abnormal loss
B	Abnormal gain	Abnormal loss
C	Abnormal loss	Abnormal gain
D	Abnormal gain	Abnormal gain

Answer

The correct answer is C.

	Y	Z
Input (kg)	20,000	28,000
Normal loss (kg)	1,000 (5% of 20,000)	1,960 (7% of 28,000)
Expected output	19,000	26,040
Actual output	18,500	26,100
Abnormal loss/gain	500 (loss)	60 (gain)

2.3 Example: Abnormal losses and gains again

During a four-week period, period 3, costs of input to a process were $29,070. Input was 1,000 units, output was 850 units and normal loss is 10%.

During the next period, period 4, costs of input were again $29,070. Input was again 1,000 units, but output was 950 units.

There were no units of opening or closing inventory.

Required

Prepare the process account and abnormal loss or gain account for each period.

Solution

Step 1 Determine output and losses

Period 3

	Units
Actual output	850
Normal loss (10% × 1,000)	100
Abnormal loss	50
Input	1,000

Period 4

	Units
Actual output	950
Normal loss (10% × 1,000)	100
Abnormal gain	(50)
Input	1,000

Step 2 Calculate cost per unit of output and losses

For each period the cost per unit is based on expected output.

$$\frac{\text{Cost of input}}{\text{Expected units of output}} = \frac{\$29,070}{900} = \$32.30 \text{ per unit}$$

Step 3 Calculate total cost of output and losses

Period 3

	$
Cost of output (850 × $32.30)	27,455
Normal loss	0
Abnormal loss (50 × $32.30)	1,615
	29,070

Period 4

	$
Cost of output (950 × $32.30)	30,685
Normal loss	0
Abnormal gain (50 × $32.30)	1,615
	29,070

Step 4 Complete accounts

PROCESS ACCOUNT

	Units	$		Units	$
Period 3					
Cost of input	1,000	29,070	Normal loss	100	0
			Finished goods a/c (× $32.30)	850	27,455
			Abnormal loss a/c (× $32.30)	50	1,615
	1,000	29,070		1,000	29,070
Period 4					
Cost of input	1,000	29,070	Normal loss	100	0
Abnormal gain a/c (× $32.30)	50	1,615	Finished goods a/c (× $32.30)	950	30,685
	1,050	30,685		1,050	30,685

ABNORMAL LOSS OR GAIN ACCOUNT

	$		$
Period 3		*Period 4*	
Abnormal loss in process a/c	1,615	Abnormal gain in process a/c	1,615

A nil balance on this account will be carried forward into period 5.

If there is a closing balance in the abnormal loss or gain account when the profit for the period is calculated, this balance is taken to the statement of profit or loss: an abnormal gain will be a credit to the statement of profit or loss and an abnormal loss will be a debit to the statement of profit or loss.

PART C INTRODUCTION TO COSTING SYSTEMS

Question
Process account

3,000 units of material are input to a process. Process costs are as follows.

Material $11,700
Conversion costs $6,300

Output is 2,000 units. Normal loss is 20% of input.

Required

Prepare a process account and the appropriate abnormal loss/gain account.

Answer

Step 1 **Determine output and losses**

We are told that output is 2,000 units.
Normal loss = 20% × 3,000 = 600 units
Abnormal loss = (3,000 − 600) − 2,000 = 400 units

Step 2 **Calculate cost per unit of output and losses**

$$\text{Cost per unit} = \frac{\$(11{,}700 + 6{,}300)}{2{,}400} = \$7.50$$

Step 3 **Calculate total cost of output and losses**

		$
Output	(2,000 × $7.50)	15,000
Normal loss		0
Abnormal loss	(400 × $7.50)	3,000
		18,000

Step 4 **Complete accounts**

PROCESS ACCOUNT

	Units	$		Units	$
Material	3,000	11,700	Output	2,000	15,000
Conversion costs		6,300	Normal loss	600	
			Abnormal loss	400	3,000
	3,000	18,000		3,000	18,000

ABNORMAL LOSS ACCOUNT

	$		$
Process a/c	3,000	Statement of profit or loss	3,000

Question
Finished output

Charlton Co manufactures a product in a single process operation. Normal loss is 10% of input. Loss occurs at the end of the process. Data for June are as follows.

Opening and closing inventories of work in progress	Nil
Cost of input materials (3,300 units)	$59,100
Direct labour and production overhead	$30,000
Output to finished goods	2,750 units

The full cost of finished output in June was:

A $74,250   B $81,000   C $82,500   D $89,100

Answer

Step 1 **Determine output and losses**

	Units
Actual output	2,750
Normal loss (10% × 3,300)	330
Abnormal loss	220
	3,300

Step 2 **Calculate cost per unit of output and losses**

$$\frac{\text{Cost of input}}{\text{Expected units of output}} = \frac{\$89,100}{3,300 - 330} = \$30 \text{ per unit}$$

Step 3 **Calculate total cost of output and losses**

	$
Cost of output (2,750 × $30)	82,500 **(The correct answer is C)**
Normal loss	0
Abnormal loss (220 × $30)	6,600
	89,100

If you were reduced to making a calculated guess, you could have eliminated option D. This is simply the total input cost, with no attempt to apportion some of the cost to the abnormal loss.

Option A is incorrect because it results from allocating a full unit cost to the normal loss: remember that normal loss does not carry any of the process cost.

Option B is incorrect because it results from calculating a 10% normal loss based on **output** of 2,750 units (275 units normal loss), rather than on **input** of 3,300 units.

3 Losses with scrap value

Key term

Scrap is 'Discarded material having some value'.

Loss or spoilage may have scrap value.

FAST FORWARD

The **scrap value** of normal loss is usually deducted from the cost of materials.

The **scrap value** of abnormal loss (or abnormal gain) is usually set off against its cost, in an abnormal loss (abnormal gain) account.

As the questions that follow will show, the three steps to remember are these.

Step 1 Separate the **scrap value** of **normal loss** from the **scrap value** of **abnormal loss** or **gain**.

Step 2 In effect, subtract the scrap value of normal loss from the cost of the process, by crediting it to the process account (as a 'value' for normal loss).

Step 3 **Either** subtract the value of abnormal loss scrap from the cost of abnormal loss, by crediting the abnormal loss account; or

Subtract the cost of the abnormal gain scrap from the value of abnormal gain, by debiting the abnormal gain account.

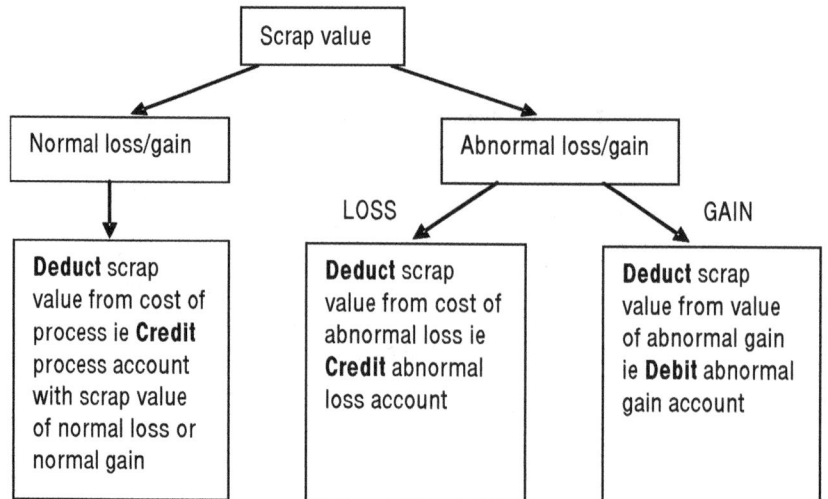

Question
Losses and scrap

3,000 units of material are input to a process. Process costs are as follows.

Material	$11,700
Conversion costs	$6,300

Output is 2,000 units. Normal loss is 20% of input.

The units of loss could be sold for $1 each. Prepare appropriate accounts.

Answer

Step 1 **Determine output and losses**

Input	3,000 units
Normal loss (20% of 3,000)	600 units
Expected output	2,400 units
Actual output	2,000 units
Abnormal loss	400 units

Step 2 **Calculate cost per unit of output and losses**

	$
Scrap value of normal loss	600
Scrap value of abnormal loss	400
Total scrap (1,000 units × $1)	1,000

$$\text{Cost per expected unit} = \frac{\$((11{,}700 - 600) + 6{,}300)}{2{,}400} = \$7.25$$

Step 3 **Calculate total cost of output and losses**

		$
Output	(2,000 × $7.25)	14,500
Normal loss	(600 × $1.00)	600
Abnormal loss	(400 × $7.25)	2,900
		18,000

Step 4 Complete accounts

PROCESS ACCOUNT

	Units	$		Units	$
Material	3,000	11,700	Output	2,000	14,500
Conversion costs		6,300	Normal loss	600	600
			Abnormal loss	400	2,900
	3,000	18,000		3,000	18,000

ABNORMAL LOSS ACCOUNT

	$		$
Process a/c	2,900	Scrap a/c	400
		P&L a/c	2,500
	2,900		2,900

SCRAP ACCOUNT

	$		$
Normal loss	600	Cash	1,000
Abnormal loss	400		
	1,000		1,000

Question — Two processes, losses and scrap

JJ has a factory which operates two production processes, cutting and pasting. Normal loss in each process is 10%. Scrapped units out of the cutting process sell for $3 per unit whereas scrapped units out of the pasting process sell for $5. Output from the cutting process is transferred to the pasting process: output from the pasting process is finished output ready for sale.

Relevant information about costs for control period 7 are as follows.

	Cutting process		Pasting process	
	Units	$	Units	$
Input materials	18,000	54,000		
Transferred to pasting process	16,000			
Materials from cutting process			16,000	
Added materials			14,000	70,000
Labour and overheads		32,400		135,000
Output to finished goods			28,000	

Required

Prepare accounts for the cutting process, the pasting process, abnormal loss, abnormal gain and scrap.

Answer

(a) Cutting process

Step 1 Determine output and losses

The normal loss is 10% of 18,000 units = 1,800 units, and the actual loss is (18,000 − 16,000) = 2,000 units. This means that there is abnormal loss of 200 units.

Actual output	16,000 units
Abnormal loss	200 units
Expected output (90% of 18,000)	16,200 units

Step 2 Calculate cost per unit of output and losses

(i) The total value of scrap is 2,000 units at $3 per unit = $6,000. We must split this between the scrap value of normal loss and the scrap value of abnormal loss.

	$
Normal loss (1,800 × $3)	5,400
Abnormal loss (200 × $3)	600
Total scrap (2,000 units × $3)	6,000

(ii) The scrap value of normal loss is first deducted from the materials cost in the process, in order to calculate the output cost per unit and then credited to the process account as a 'value' for normal loss. The cost per unit in the cutting process is calculated as follows.

	Total cost $		Cost per expected unit of output $
Materials	54,000		
Less normal loss scrap value*	5,400		
	48,600	(÷ 16,200)	3.00
Labour and overhead	32,400	(÷ 16,200)	2.00
Total	81,000	(÷ 16,200)	5.00

* It is usual to set this scrap value of normal loss against the cost of materials.

Step 3 Calculate total cost of output and losses

		$
Output	(16,000 units × $5)	80,000
Normal loss	(1,800 units × $3)	5,400
Abnormal loss	(200 units × $5)	1,000
		86,400

Step 4 Complete accounts

PROCESS 1 ACCOUNT

	Units	$		Units	$
Materials	18,000	54,000	Output to pasting process *	16,000	80,000
Labour and			Normal loss (scrap a/c) **	1,800	5,400
overhead		32,400	Abnormal loss a/c *	200	1,000
	18,000	86,400		18,000	86,400

* At $5 per unit ** At $3 per unit

(b) Pasting process

Step 1 Determine output and losses

The normal loss is 10% of the units processed = 10% of (16,000 + 14,000) = 3,000 units. The actual loss is (30,000 – 28,000) = 2,000 units, so that there is abnormal gain of 1,000 units. These are **deducted** from actual output to determine expected output.

	Units
Actual output	28,000
Abnormal gain	(1,000)
Expected output (90% of 30,000)	27,000

8: PROCESS COSTING

Step 2 **Calculate cost per unit of output and losses**

(i) The total value of scrap is 2,000 units at $5 per unit = $10,000. We must split this between the scrap value of normal loss and the scrap value of abnormal gain. Abnormal gain's scrap value is 'negative'.

		$
Normal loss scrap value	3,000 units × $5	15,000
Abnormal gain scrap value	1,000 units × $5	(5,000)
Scrap value of actual loss	2,000 units × $5	10,000

(ii) The scrap value of normal loss is first deducted from the cost of materials in the process, in order to calculate a cost per unit of output, and then credited to the process account as a 'value' for normal loss. The cost per unit in the pasting process is calculated as follows.

	Total cost $		Cost per expected unit of output $
Materials:			
Transfer from cutting process	80,000		
Added in pasting process	70,000		
	150,000		
Less scrap value of normal loss	15,000		
	135,000	(÷ 27,000)	5
Labour and overhead	135,000	(÷ 27,000)	5
	270,000	(÷ 27,000)	10

Step 3 **Calculate total cost of output and losses**

		$
Output	(28,000 units × $10)	280,000
Normal loss	(3,000 units × $5)	15,000
		295,000
Abnormal gain	(1,000 units × $10)	(10,000)
		285,000

Step 4 **Complete accounts**

PASTING PROCESS ACCOUNT

	Units	$		Units	$
From cutting process	16,000	80,000	Finished output *	28,000	280,000
Added materials	14,000	70,000			
Labour and overhead		135,000	Normal loss	3,000	15,000
	30,000	285,000	(scrap a/c)		
Abnormal gain a/c	1,000*	10,000			
	31,000	295,000		31,000	295,000

* At $10 per unit

(c) and (d)

Abnormal loss and abnormal gain accounts

For each process, one or the other of these accounts will record three items.

(i) The cost/value of the abnormal loss/gain (corresponding entry to that in the process account).

(ii) The scrap value of the abnormal loss or gain, to set off against it.

(iii) A balancing figure, which is written to the statement of profit or loss as an adjustment to the profit figure.

ABNORMAL LOSS ACCOUNT

	Units	$		$
Cutting process	200	1,000	Scrap a/c (scrap value of ab. loss)	600
			Statement of profit or loss (balance)	400
		1,000		1,000

ABNORMAL GAIN ACCOUNT

	$		Units	$
Scrap a/c (scrap value of abnormal gain units)	5,000	Pasting process	1,000	10,000
Statement of profit or loss (balance)	5,000			
	10,000			10,000

(e) **Scrap account**

This is credited with the cash value of actual units scrapped. The other entries in the account should all be identifiable as corresponding entries to those in the process accounts, and abnormal loss and abnormal gain accounts.

SCRAP ACCOUNT

	$		$
Normal loss:		Cash:	
Cutting process (1,800 × $3)	5,400	Sale of cutting process scrap (2,000 × $3)	6,000
Pasting process (3,000 × $5)	15,000	Sale of pasting process scrap (2,000 × $5)	10,000
Abnormal loss a/c	600	Abnormal gain a/c	5,000
	21,000		21,000

Abnormal losses and gains never affect the cost of good units of production. The scrap value of abnormal losses is **not** credited to the process account, and abnormal loss and gain units carry the same **full cost** as a good unit of production.

4 Losses with a disposal cost

4.1 Introduction

You must also be able to deal with losses which have a **disposal cost**.

The basic calculations required in such circumstances are as follows.

(a) Increase the process costs by the cost of disposing of the units of normal loss and use the resulting cost per unit to value good output and abnormal loss/gain.

(b) The normal loss is given no value in the process account.

(c) Include the disposal costs of normal loss on the debit side of the process account.

(d) Include the disposal costs of abnormal loss in the abnormal loss account and hence in the transfer of the cost of abnormal loss to the statement of profit or loss.

4.2 Example: Losses with a disposal cost

Suppose that input to a process was 1,000 units at a cost of $4,500. Normal loss is 10% and there are no opening and closing inventories. Actual output was 860 units and loss units had to be disposed of at a cost of $0.90 per unit.

Normal loss = 10% × 1,000 = 100 units. ∴ Abnormal loss = 900 − 860 = 40 units

$$\text{Cost per unit} = \frac{\$4,500 + (100 \times \$0.90)}{900} = \$5.10$$

The relevant accounts would be as follows.

PROCESS ACCOUNT

	Units	$		Units	$
Cost of input	1,000	4,500	Output	860	4,386
Disposal cost of			Normal loss	100	
normal loss		90	Abnormal loss	40	204
	1,000	4,590		1,000	4,590

ABNORMAL LOSS ACCOUNT

	$		$
Process a/c	204	Statement of profit or loss	240
Disposal cost (40 × $0.90)	36		
	240		240

5 Valuing closing work in progress

5.1 Introduction

FAST FORWARD

> When units are partly completed at the end of a period (and hence there is closing work in progress), it is necessary to calculate the **equivalent units of production** in order to determine the cost of a completed unit.

In the examples we have looked at so far we have assumed that opening and closing inventories of work in process have been nil. We must now look at more realistic examples and consider how to allocate the costs incurred in a period between completed output (that is, finished units) and partly completed closing inventory.

Some examples will help to illustrate the problem, and the techniques used to share out (apportion) costs between finished output and closing inventories.

Suppose that we have the following account for Process 2 for period 9.

PROCESS ACCOUNT

	Units	$		Units	$
Materials	1,000	6,200	Finished goods	800	?
Labour and overhead		2,850	Closing WIP	200	?
	1,000	9,050		1,000	9,050

How do we value the finished goods and closing work in process?

With any form of process costing involving closing WIP, we have to apportion costs between output and closing WIP. To apportion costs 'fairly' we make use of the concept of **equivalent units of production**.

5.2 Equivalent units

Key term

> **Equivalent units** are notional whole units which represent incomplete work, and which are used to apportion costs between work in process and completed output.

PART C INTRODUCTION TO COSTING SYSTEMS

We will assume that in the example above the degree of completion is as follows.

(a) **Direct materials.** These are added in full at the start of processing, and so any closing WIP will have 100% of their direct material content. (This is not always the case in practice. Materials might be added gradually throughout the process, in which case closing inventory will only be a certain percentage complete as to material content. We will look at this later in the chapter.)

(b) **Direct labour and production overhead.** These are usually assumed to be incurred at an even rate through the production process, so that when we refer to a unit that is 50% complete, we mean that it is half complete for labour and overhead, although it might be 100% complete for materials.

Let us also assume that the closing WIP is 100% complete for materials and 25% complete for labour and overhead.

How would we now put a value to the finished output and the closing WIP?

In **Step 1** of our framework, we have been told what output and losses are. However we also need to calculate **equivalent units**.

STATEMENT OF EQUIVALENT UNITS

	Total units	Materials Degree of completion	Equivalent units	Labour and overhead Degree of completion	Equivalent units
Finished output	800	100%	800	100%	800
Closing WIP	200	100%	200	25%	50
	1,000		1,000		850

In **Step 2** the important figure is **average cost per equivalent unit**. This can be calculated as follows.

STATEMENT OF COSTS PER EQUIVALENT UNIT

	Materials	Labour and overhead
Costs incurred in the period	$6,200	$2,850
Equivalent units of work done	1,000	850
Cost per equivalent unit (approx)	$6.20	$3.3529

To calculate total costs for **Step 3**, we prepare a statement of evaluation to show how the costs should be apportioned between finished output and closing WIP.

STATEMENT OF EVALUATION

Item	Equivalent units	Materials Cost per equivalent units $	Cost $	Equivalent units	Labour and overheads Cost per equivalent units $	Cost $	Total cost $
Finished output	800	6.20	4,960	800	3.3529	2,682	7,642
Closing WIP	200	6.20	1,240	50	3.3529	168	1,408
	1,000		6,200	850		2,850	9,050

The process account (work in progress, or work in process account) would be shown as follows.

PROCESS ACCOUNT

	Units	$		Units	$
Materials	1,000	6,200	Finished goods	800	7,642
Labour overhead		2,850	Closing WIP	200	1,408
	1,000	9,050		1,000	9,050

Question — Equivalent units for closing WIP

Ally Co has the following information available on Process 9.

PROCESS 9 ACCOUNT

		$			$
Input	10,000 kg	59,150	Finished goods	8,000 kg	52,000
			Closing WIP	2,000 kg	7,150
		59,150			59,150

How many equivalent units were there for Closing WIP?

A 1,000
B 1,100
C 2,000

Answer

The correct answer is B.

This question requires you to **work backwards**. You can calculate the cost per unit using the Finished Goods figures.

$$\text{Cost per unit} = \frac{\text{Cost of finished goods}}{\text{Number of kg}} = \frac{52,000}{8,000} = \$6.50$$

If 2,000 kg (Closing WIP figure) were fully complete total cost would be

2,000 × $6.50 = $13,000

Actual cost of Closing WIP = $7,150

$$\text{Degree of completion} = \frac{7,150}{13,000} = 55\%$$

Therefore equivalent units = 55% of 2,000 = 1,100 kg

Question — Equivalent units

Ashley Co operates a process costing system. The following details are available for Process 2.

Materials input at beginning of process   12,000 kg, costing $18,000
Labour and overheads added $28,000

10,000 kg were completed and transferred to the Finished Goods account. The remaining units were 60% complete with regard to labour and overheads. There were no losses in the period.

What is the value of Closing WIP in the process account?

A $4,800
B $6,000
C $7,667
D $8,000

Answer

The correct answer is B.

STATEMENT OF EQUIVALENT UNITS

	Units completion	Material Degree of units	Equivalent	Units completion	Labour Degree of units	Equivalent
Finished goods	10,000	100%	10,000	10,000	100%	10,000
Closing WIP	2,000	100%	2,000	2,000	60%	1,200
	12,000		12,000	12,000		11,200

COSTS PER EQUIVALENT UNIT

	Material	Labour
Total cost	$18,000	$28,000
Equivalent units	12,000	11,200
Cost per unit	$1.50	$2.50

Total cost per unit = $4.00

Value of Closing WIP = ($1.50 × 2,000) + ($2.50 × 1,200) = $6,000

5.3 Different rates of input

In many industries, materials, labour and overhead may be **added at different rates** during the course of production.

(a) Output from a previous process (for example the output from process 1 to process 2) may be introduced into the subsequent process all at once, so that closing inventory is 100% complete in respect of these materials.

(b) Further materials may be added gradually during the process, so that closing inventory is only partially complete in respect of these added materials.

(c) Labour and overhead may be 'added' at yet another different rate. When production overhead is absorbed on a labour hour basis, however, we should expect the degree of completion on overhead to be the same as the degree of completion on labour.

When this situation occurs, **equivalent units**, and a **cost per equivalent unit**, should be calculated separately for each type of material, and also for conversion costs.

5.4 Example: Equivalent units and different degrees of completion

Suppose that Columbine Co is a manufacturer of processed goods, and that results in process 2 for April 20X3 were as follows.

Opening inventory	NIL
Material input from process 1	4,000 units

Costs of input:

	$
Material from process 1	6,000
Added materials in process 2	1,080
Conversion costs	1,720

Output is transferred into the next process, process 3.

8: PROCESS COSTING

Closing work in process amounted to 800 units, complete as to:

Process 1 material	100%
Added materials	50%
Conversion costs	30%

Required

Prepare the account for process 2 for April 20X3.

Solution

(a) STATEMENT OF EQUIVALENT UNITS (OF PRODUCTION IN THE PERIOD)

			Equivalent units of production					
			Process 1 material		Added materials		Labour and overhead	
Input Units	Output	Total Units	Units	%	Units	%	Units	%
4,000	Completed production	3,200	3,200	100	3,200	100	3,200	100
	Closing inventory	800	800	100	400	50	240	30
4,000		4,000	4,000		3,600		3,440	

(b) STATEMENT OF COST (PER EQUIVALENT UNIT)

Input	Cost $	Equivalent production in units	Cost per unit $
Process 1 material	6,000	4,000	1.50
Added materials	1,080	3,600	0.30
Labour and overhead	1,720	3,440	0.50
	8,800		2.30

(c) STATEMENT OF EVALUATION (OF FINISHED WORK AND CLOSING INVENTORIES)

Production	Cost element	Number of equivalent units	Cost per equivalent unit $	Total $	Cost $
Completed production		3,200	2.30		7,360
Closing inventory:	process 1 material	800	1.50	1,200	
	added material	400	0.30	120	
	labour and overhead	240	0.50	120	
					1,440
					8,800

(d) PROCESS ACCOUNT

	Units	$		Units	$
Process 1 material	4,000	6,000	Process 3 a/c	3,200	7,360
Added material		1,080			
Conversion costs		1,720	Closing inventory c/f	800	1,440
	4,000	8,800		4,000	8,800

6 Valuing opening work in progress: FIFO method

6.1 Introduction

FAST FORWARD

Account can be taken of opening work in progress using either the **FIFO** method or the **weighted average cost method**.

Opening work in progress is partly complete at the beginning of a period and is valued at the cost incurred to date. In the example in Paragraph 4.4, closing work in progress of 800 units at the end of April 20X3 would be carried forward as opening inventory, value $1,440, at the beginning of May 20X3.

It therefore follows that the work required to complete units of opening inventory is 100% minus the work in progress done in the previous period. For example, if 100 units of opening inventory are 70% complete at the beginning of June 20X2, the equivalent units of production would be as follows.

Equivalent units in previous period	(May 20X2) (70%)	=	70
Equivalent units to complete work in current period	(June 20X2) (30%)	=	30
Total work done			100

The FIFO method of valuation deals with production on a first in, first out basis. The assumption is that the first units completed in any period are the units of opening inventory that were held at the beginning of the period.

6.2 Example: WIP and FIFO

Suppose that information relating to process 1 of a two-stage production process is as follows, for August 20X2.

Opening inventory 500 units: degree of completion	60%
Cost to date	$2,800

Costs incurred in August 20X2	$
Direct materials (2,500 units introduced)	13,200
Direct labour	6,600
Production overhead	6,600
	26,400

Closing inventory 300 units: degree of completion	80%

There was no loss in the process.

Required

Prepare the process 1 account for August 20X2.

Solution

As the term implies, first in, first out means that in August 20X2 the first units completed were the units of opening inventory.

Opening inventories: work done to date =	60%
plus work done in August 20X2 =	40%

The cost of the work done up to 1 August 20X2 is known to be $2,800, so that the cost of the units completed will be $2,800 plus the cost of completing the final 40% of the work on the units in August 20X2.

Once the opening inventory has been completed, all other finished output in August 20X2 will be work started as well as finished in the month.

8: PROCESS COSTING

	Units
Total output in August 20X2 *	2,700
Less opening inventory, completed first	500
Work started and finished in August 20X2	2,200

(* Opening inventory plus units introduced minus closing inventory = 500 + 2,500 – 300)

What we are doing here is taking the total output of 2,700 units, and saying that we must divide it into two parts as follows.

(a) The opening inventory, which was first in and so must be first out
(b) The rest of the units, which were 100% worked in the period

Dividing finished output into two parts in this way is a necessary feature of the FIFO valuation method.

Continuing the example, closing inventory of 300 units will be started in August 20X2, but not yet completed.

The total cost of output to process 2 during 20X2 will be as follows.

		$
Opening stock	cost brought forward	2,800 (60%)
	plus cost incurred during August 20X2, to complete	x (40%)
		2,800 + x
Fully worked 2,200 units		y
Total cost of output to process 2, FIFO basis		2,800 + x + y

Equivalent units will again be used as the basis for apportioning **costs incurred during August 20X2**. Be sure that you understand the treatment of 'opening inventory units completed', and can relate the calculations to the principles of FIFO valuation.

Step 1 Determine output and losses

STATEMENT OF EQUIVALENT UNITS

	Total units		Equivalent units of production in August 20X2
Opening inventory units completed	500	(40%)	200
Fully worked units	2,200	(100%)	2,200
Output to process 2	2,700		2,400
Closing inventory	300	(80%)	240
	3,000		2,640

Step 2 Calculate cost per unit of output and losses

The cost per equivalent unit in August 20X2 can now be calculated.

STATEMENT OF COST PER EQUIVALENT UNIT

$$\frac{\text{Cost incurred}}{\text{Equivalent units}} = \frac{\$26,400}{2,640}$$

Cost per equivalent unit = $10

Step 3 Calculate total costs of output, losses and WIP

STATEMENT OF EVALUATION

	Equivalent units	Valuation $
Opening inventory, work done in August 20X2	200	2,000
Fully worked units	2,200	22,000
Closing inventory	240	2,400
	2,640	26,400

The total value of the completed opening inventory will be $2,800 (brought forward) plus $2,000 added in August before completion = $4,800.

Step 4 Complete accounts

PROCESS 1 ACCOUNT

	Units	$		Units	$
Opening inventory	500	2,800	Output to process 2:		
Direct materials	2,500	13,200	Opening inventory completed	500	4,800
Direct labour		6,600	Fully worked units	2,200	22,000
Production o'hd		6,600		2,700	26,800
			Closing inventory	300	2,400
	3,000	29,200		3,000	29,200

We now know that the value of x is $(4,800 – 2,800) = $2,000 and the value of y is $22,000.

Question   FIFO and equivalent units

Walter Co uses the FIFO method of process costing. At the end of a four week period, the following information was available for process P.

Opening WIP   2,000 units (60% complete) costing $3,000 to date
Closing WIP   1,500 units (40% complete)
Transferred to next process   7,000 units

How many units were started and completed during the period?

A   5,500 units   C   8,400 units
B   7,000 units   D   9,000 units

Answer

The correct answer is A.

As we are dealing with the FIFO method, Opening WIP must be completed first.

Total output *	7,500 units
Less Opening WIP (completed first)	2,000 units
Units started and completed during the period	5,500 units

* Opening WIP + units introduced – Closing WIP

= 2,000 + 7,000 – 1,500
= 7,500 units

Question   Closing WIP – FIFO

The following information relates to process 3 of a three-stage production process for the month of January 20X4.

Opening inventory

300 units complete as to:

		$
materials from process 2	100%	4,400
added materials	90%	1,150
labour	80%	540
production overhead	80%	810
		6,900

8: PROCESS COSTING

In January 20X4, a further 1,800 units were transferred from process 2 at a valuation of $27,000. Added materials amounted to $6,600 and direct labour to $3,270. Production overhead is absorbed at the rate of 150% of direct labour cost. Closing inventory at 31 January 20X4 amounted to 450 units, complete as to:

process 2 materials	100%
added materials	60%
labour and overhead	50%

Required

Prepare the process 3 account for January 20X4 using FIFO valuation principles.

Answer

Step 1 Statement of equivalent units

	Total units	Process 2 materials		Added materials		Conversion costs
Opening inventory	300	0	(10%)	30	(20%)	60
Fully worked units *	1,350	1,350		1,350		1,350
Output to finished goods	1,650	1,350		1,380		1,410
Closing inventory	450	450	(60%)	270	(50%)	225
	2,100	1,800		1,650		1,635

* Transfers from process 2, minus closing inventory.

Step 2 Statement of costs per equivalent unit

	Total cost $	Equivalent units	Cost per equivalent unit $
Process 2 materials	27,000	1,800	15.00
Added materials	6,600	1,650	4.00
Direct labour	3,270	1,635	2.00
Production overhead (150% of $3,270)	4,905	1,635	3.00
			24.00

Step 3 Statement of evaluation

	Process 2 materials $		Additional materials $		Labour $		Overhead $	Total $
Opening inventory cost b/f	4,400		1,150		540		810	6,900
Added in Jan 20X4	–	(30x$4)	120	(60x$2)	120	(60x$3)	180	420
	4,400		1,270		660		990	7,320
Fully worked units	20,250		5,400		2,700		4,050	32,400
Output to finished Goods	24,650		6,670		3,360		5,040	39,720
Closing inventory (450x$15)	6,750	(270x$4)	1,080	(225x$2)	450	(225x$3)	675	8,955
	31,400		7,750		3,810		5,715	48,675

Step 4 Complete accounts

PROCESS 3 ACCOUNT

	Units	$		Units	$
Opening inventory b/f	300	6,900	Finished goods a/c	1,650	39,720
Process 2 a/c	1,800	27,000			
Stores a/c		6,600			
Wages a/c		3,270			
Production o'hd a/c		4,905	Closing inventory c/f	450	8,955
	2,100	48,675		2,100	48,675

Question — Equivalent units and FIFO

Cheryl Co operates a FIFO process costing system. The following information is available for last month.

Opening work in progress	2,000 units valued at	$3,000
Input	60,000 units costing	$30,000
Conversion costs		$20,000
Units transferred to next process	52,000 units	
Closing work in progress	10,000 units	

Opening work in progress was 100% complete with regard to input materials and 70% complete as to conversion. Closing work in progress was complete with regard to input materials and 80% complete as to conversion.

What was the number of equivalent units with regard to conversion costs?

- A 44,000
- B 50,600
- C 52,000
- D 58,600

Answer

The correct answer is D.

		Units
Opening work in progress	30% of 2,000 units still to be completed	600
Closing work in progress	80% of 10,000 units completed	8,000
Units started and completed	(Opening WIP + input − closing WIP) − opening WIP	50,000
		58,600

7 Valuing opening work in progress: weighted average cost method

7.1 Introduction

An alternative to FIFO is the **weighted average cost method of inventory valuation** which calculates a weighted average cost of units produced from both opening inventory and units introduced in the current period.

8: PROCESS COSTING

By this method **no distinction is made between units of opening inventory and new units introduced** to the process during the accounting period. The cost of opening inventory is added to costs incurred during the period, and completed units of opening inventory are each given a value of one full equivalent unit of production.

7.2 Example: Weighted average cost method

Magpie produces an item which is manufactured in two consecutive processes. Information relating to process 2 during September 20X3 is as follows.

Opening inventory 800 units
Degree of completion:

		$
process 1 materials	100%	4,700
added materials	40%	600
conversion costs	30%	1,000
		6,300

During September 20X3, 3,000 units were transferred from process 1 at a valuation of $18,100. Added materials cost $9,600 and conversion costs were $11,800.

Closing inventory at 30 September 20X3 amounted to 1,000 units which were 100% complete with respect to process 1 materials and 60% complete with respect to added materials. Conversion cost work was 40% complete.

Magpie uses a weighted average cost system for the valuation of output and closing inventory.

Required

Prepare the process 2 account for September 20X3.

Solution

Step 1 Opening inventory units count as a full equivalent unit of production when the weighted average cost system is applied. Closing inventory equivalent units are assessed in the usual way.

STATEMENT OF EQUIVALENT UNITS

					Equivalent units			
	Total units		Process 1 material		Added material		Conversion costs	
Opening inventory	800	(100%)	800		800		800	
Fully worked units*	2,000	(100%)	2,000		2,000		2,000	
Output to finished goods	2,800		2,800		2,800		2,800	
Closing inventory	1,000	(100%)	1,000	(60%)	600	(40%)	400	
	3,800		3,800		3,400		3,200	

(*3,000 units from process 1 minus closing inventory of 1,000 units)

Step 2 The cost of opening inventory is added to costs incurred in September 20X3, and a cost per equivalent unit is then calculated.

STATEMENT OF COSTS PER EQUIVALENT UNIT

	Process 1 material	Added materials	Conversion costs
	$	$	$
Opening inventory	4,700	600	1,000
Added in September 20X3	18,100	9,600	11,800
Total cost	22,800	10,200	12,800
Equivalent units	3,800 units	3,400 units	3,200 units
Cost per equivalent unit	$6	$3	$4

Step 3 STATEMENT OF EVALUATION

	Process 1 material $	Added materials $	Conversion costs $	Total cost $
Output to finished goods (2,800 units)	16,800	8,400	11,200	36,400
Closing inventory	6,000	1,800	1,600	9,400
				45,800

Step 4 PROCESS 2 ACCOUNT

	Units	$		Units	$
Opening inventory b/f	800	6,300	Finished goods a/c	2,800	36,400
Process 1 a/c	3,000	18,100			
Added materials		9,600			
Conversion costs		11,800	Closing inventory c/f	1,000	9,400
	3,800	45,800		3,800	45,800

7.3 Which method should be used?

FIFO inventory valuation is more common than the weighted average method, and should be used unless an indication is given to the contrary. You may find that you are presented with limited information about the opening inventory, which forces you to use either the FIFO or the weighted average method. The rules are as follows.

(a) If you are told the degree of completion of each element in opening inventory, but not the value of each cost element, then you must use the **FIFO method**.

(b) If you are not given the degree of completion of each cost element in opening inventory, but you are given the value of each cost element, then you must use the **weighted average method.**

Question   Equivalent units

During August, a factory commenced work on 20,000 units. At the start of the month there were no partly finished units but at the end of the month there were 2,000 units which were only 40% complete. Costs in the month were $3,722,400.

(a) How many equivalent units of closing WIP were there in the month?

    A   20,000   C   18,000

    B   2,000   D   800

(b) What is the total value of fully completed output which would show in the process account?

    A $3,960,000   C $3,722,400

    B $3,564,000   D $3,350,160

Answer

(a) **D**   Equivalent units of WIP = 40% × 2,000 = 800

(b) **B**

Total finished output	18,000	units
Total equivalent units =		
18,000 × 100%	18,000	
2,000 × 40%	800	
	18,800	
Cost per equivalent unit = 3,722,400/18,800 =	$198	
∴ Value of fully completed output:		
18,000 × 198 =	$3,564,000	

PART C INTRODUCTION TO COSTING SYSTEMS

Chapter roundup

- **Process costing** is a costing method used where it is not possible to identify separate units of production or jobs, usually because of the continuous nature of the production processes involved.

- Process costing is centred around **four key steps**. The exact work done at each step will depend on whether there are normal losses, scrap, opening and closing work in progress.

    Step 1   Determine output and losses
    Step 2   Calculate cost per unit of output, losses and WIP
    Step 3   Calculate total cost of output, losses and WIP
    Step 4   Complete accounts

- **Losses** may occur in process. If a certain level of loss is expected, this is known as **normal loss**. If losses are greater than expected, the extra loss is **abnormal loss**. If losses are less than expected, the difference is known as **abnormal gain**.

- The **scrap value** of normal loss is usually deducted from the cost of materials.

- The **scrap value** of abnormal loss (or abnormal gain) is usually set off against its cost, in an abnormal loss (abnormal gain) account.

- Abnormal losses and gains never affect the cost of good units of production. The scrap value of abnormal loss is **not** credited to the process account, and abnormal loss and gain units carry the same **full cost** as a good unit of production.

- When units are partly completed at the end of a period (and hence there is closing work in progress), it is necessary to calculate the **equivalent units of production** in order to determine the cost of a completed unit.

- Account can be taken of opening work in progress using either the **FIFO** method or the **weighted average cost method**.

Quick quiz

1. Define process costing.

2. Process costing is centred around four key steps.

   Step 1 ....

   Step 2 ....

   Step 3 ....

   Step 4 ....

3. Abnormal gains result when actual loss is less than normal or expected loss.

   True ☐

   False ☐

4.
Normal loss (no scrap value)		Same value as good output (positive cost)
Abnormal loss	?	No value
Abnormal gain		Same value as good output (negative cost)

5. How is revenue from scrap treated?

   A   As an addition to sales revenue   C   As a bonus to employees
   B   As a reduction in costs of processing   D   Any of the above

6. What is an equivalent unit?

7. When there is closing WIP at the end of a process, what is the first step in the four-step approach to process costing questions and why must it be done?

8. What is the weighted average cost method of inventory valuation?

9. Unless given an indication to the contrary, the weighted average cost method of inventory valuation should be used to value opening WIP.

   True ☐

   False ☐

Answers to quick quiz

1 **Process costing** is a costing method used where it is not possible to identify separate units of production, or jobs, usually because of the continuous nature of the production processes involved.

2 **Step 1** Determine output and losses
 Step 2 Calculate cost per unit of output, losses and WIP
 Step 3 Calculate total cost of output, losses and WIP
 Step 4 Complete accounts

3 True

4
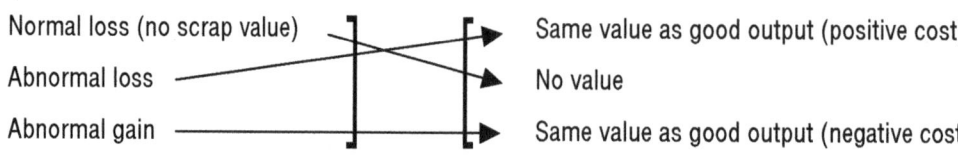

5 B

6 An **equivalent unit** is a notional whole unit which represents incomplete work, and which is used to apportion costs between work in process and completed output.

7 **Step 1.** It is necessary to calculate the equivalent units of production (by drawing up a statement of equivalent units). Equivalent units of production are notional whole units which represent incomplete work and which are used to apportion costs between work in progress and completed output.

8 A method where no distinction is made between units of opening inventory and new units introduced to the process during the current period.

9 False. FIFO inventory valuation is more common than the weighted average method and should be used unless an indication is given to the contrary.

End of chapter question

B Ltd

B Ltd produces chemical A using a four-stage production process.

During control period 5, 1,200 units were transferred from process 2 to process 3. These units were valued at $4.135 per unit. Material valued at $12,880 was added to process 3 during the period and conversion cost for the process was $9,160.

There were 50 units in work in progress (WIP) in process 3 at the beginning of control period 5, and 150 units in progress at the end of the period. The degree of completion of these units was as follows.

	Opening WIP % completion	$	Closing WIP % completion
Material from process 2	100	96	100
Material added	50	402	70
Conversion cost	60	710	90
		1,208	

The expected level of loss in the process is 5% of material input from process 2 during the period. 150 units were actually scrapped during the period. Any units of loss can be sold for scrap for $1 per unit.

Required

(a) Prepare the process account and the abnormal loss account for process 3 in period 5, using the FIFO method of stock valuation. **(10 marks)**

(b) Prepare the process account again, but this time using the weighted average method of stock valuation. **(10 marks)**

(Total = 20 marks)

PART C INTRODUCTION TO COSTING SYSTEMS

Process costing – joint products and by-products

Topic list	Syllabus reference
1 Joint products and by-products	C3.2
2 Dealing with common costs	C3.2
3 Joint products in process accounts	C3.2
4 Accounting for by-products	C3.2

Introduction

You should now be aware of the most simple and the more complex areas of process costing. In this chapter we are going to turn our attention to the methods of accounting for **joint products** and **by-products** which arise as a result of a **continuous process**.

1 Joint products and by-products

1.1 Introduction

FAST FORWARD

Joint products are two or more products separated in a process, each of which has a **significant value** compared to the other. A **by-product** is an incidental product from a process which has an **insignificant value** compared to the main product.

Key terms

Joint products are two or more products which are output from the same processing operation, but which are indistinguishable from each other up to their point of separation.

A **by-product** is a supplementary or secondary product (arising as the result of a process) whose value is small relative to that of the principal product.

(a) Joint products have a **substantial sales value**. Often they require further processing before they are ready for sale. Joint products arise, for example, in the oil refining industry where diesel fuel, petrol, paraffin and lubricants are all produced from the same process.

(b) The distinguishing feature of a by-product is its **relatively low sales value** in comparison to the main product. In the timber industry, for example, by-products include sawdust, small offcuts and bark.

What exactly separates a joint product from a by-product?

(a) A **joint product** is regarded as an important saleable item, and so it should be **separately costed**. The profitability of each joint product should be assessed in the cost accounts.

(b) A **by-product** is not important as a saleable item, and whatever revenue it earns is a 'bonus' for the organisation. Because of their relative insignificance, by-products are **not separately costed**.

1.2 Problems in accounting for joint products

FAST FORWARD

The point at which **joint products** and **by-products** become separately identifiable is known as the **split-off point** or **separation point**. Costs incurred up to this point are called **common costs** or **joint costs**.

Costs incurred prior to this point of separation are **common** or **joint costs**, and these need to be allocated (apportioned) in some manner to each of the joint products. In the following sketched example, there are two different split-off points.

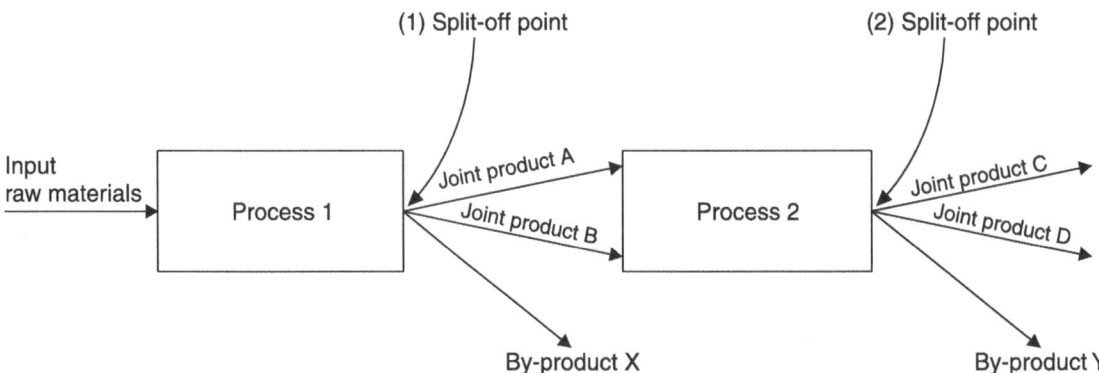

Problems in accounting for joint products are basically of two different sorts.

(a) How common costs should be apportioned between products, in order to put a value to closing inventories and to the cost of sale (and profit) for each product.

(b) Whether it is more profitable to sell a joint product at one stage of processing, or to process the product further and sell it at a later stage.

2 Dealing with common costs

2.1 Introduction

> **FAST FORWARD**
>
> The main methods of apportioning joint costs, each of which can produce significantly different results, are as follows: physical measurement; relative sales value apportionment method; sales value at split-off point.

The problem of costing for joint products concerns **common costs**, that is those common processing costs shared between the units of eventual output up to their 'split-off point'. Some method needs to be devised for sharing the common costs between the individual joint products for the following reasons.

(a) To put a value to closing inventories of each joint product.
(b) To record the costs and therefore the profit from each joint product.
(c) Perhaps to assist in pricing decisions.

Here are some examples of the common costs problem.

(a) How to spread the common costs of oil refining between the joint products made (petrol, naphtha, kerosene and so on).

(b) How to spread the common costs of running the telephone network between telephone calls in peak and cheap rate times, or between local and long distance calls.

Various methods that might be used to establish a basis for apportioning or allocating common costs to each product are as follows.

- Physical measurement
- Relative sales value apportionment method; sales value at split-off point

2.2 Dealing with common costs: physical measurement

With physical measurement, **the common cost is apportioned to the joint products on the basis of the proportion that the output of each product bears by weight or volume to the total output.** An example of this would be the case where two products, product 1 and product 2, incur common costs to the point of separation of $3,000 and the output of each product is 600 tons and 1,200 tons respectively.

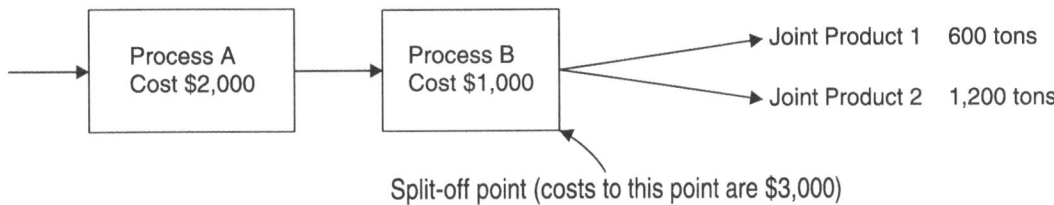

Split-off point (costs to this point are $3,000)

Product 1 sells for $4 per ton and product 2 for $2 per ton.

The division of the common costs ($3,000) between product 1 and product 2 could be based on the tonnage of output.

	Product 1		Product 2	Total
Output	600 tons	+	1,200 tons	1,800 tons
Proportion of common cost	$\dfrac{600}{1,800}$	+	$\dfrac{1,200}{1,800}$	

PART C INTRODUCTION TO COSTING SYSTEMS

	$	$	$
Apportioned cost	1,000	2,000	3,000
Sales	2,400	2,400	4,800
Profit	1,400	400	1,800
Profit/sales ratio	58.3%	16.7%	37.5%

Physical measurement has the following limitations.

(a) Where the products separate during the processes into different states, for example where one product is a gas and another is a liquid, this method is unsuitable.

(b) This method does not take into account the relative income-earning potentials of the individual products, with the result that one product might appear very profitable and another appear to be incurring losses.

2.3 Dealing with common costs: sales value at split-off point

FAST FORWARD

The **relative sales value method** is the most widely used method of apportioning joint costs because (ignoring the effect of further processing costs) it assumes that all products achieve the same profit margin.

With relative sales value apportionment of common costs, **the cost is allocated according to the product's ability to produce income**. This method is most widely used because the assumption that some profit margin should be attained for all products under normal marketing conditions is satisfied. The common cost is apportioned to each product in the proportion that the sales (market) value of that product bears to the sales value of the total output from the particular processes concerned. Using the previous example where the sales price per unit is $4 for product 1 and $2 for product 2.

(a) Common costs of processes to split-off point $3,000
(b) Sales value of product 1 at $4 per ton $2,400
(c) Sales value of product 2 at $2 per ton $2,400

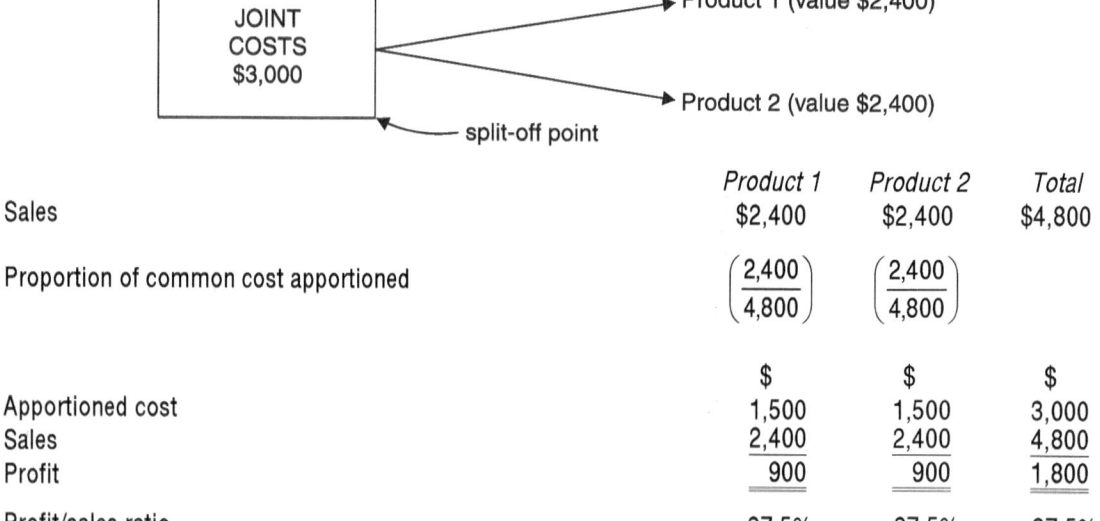

	Product 1	Product 2	Total
Sales	$2,400	$2,400	$4,800
Proportion of common cost apportioned	(2,400/4,800)	(2,400/4,800)	
	$	$	$
Apportioned cost	1,500	1,500	3,000
Sales	2,400	2,400	4,800
Profit	900	900	1,800
Profit/sales ratio	37.5%	37.5%	37.5%

A comparison of the gross profit margin resulting from the application of the above methods for allocating common costs will illustrate the greater acceptability of the relative sales value apportionment method. Physical measurement gives a higher profit margin to product 1, not necessarily because product 1 is highly profitable, but because it has been given a smaller share of common costs.

9: PROCESS COSTING - JOINT PRODUCTS AND BY-PRODUCTS

Question — Joint products

In process costing, a joint product is:

A   A product which is produced simultaneously with other products but which is of lesser value than at least one of the other products.

B   A product which is produced simultaneously with other products and is of similar value to at least one of the other products.

C   A product which is produced simultaneously with other products but which is of greater value than any of the other products.

D   A product produced jointly with another organisation.

Answer

The correct answer is B, a product which is of similar value to at least one of the other products.

Question — Sales value method

Two products (W and X) are created from a joint process. Both products can be sold immediately after split-off. There are no opening inventories or work in progress. The following information is available for last period.

Total joint production costs $776,160

Product	Production units	Sales units	Selling price per unit
W	12,000	10,000	$10
X	10,000	8,000	$12

Using the sales value method of apportioning joint production costs, what was the value of the closing inventory of product X for last period?

A $68,992
B $70,560
C $76,032
D $77,616

Answer

The correct answer is D.

Sales value of production:

Product W	(12,000 × $10)	$120,000
Product X	(10,000 × $12)	$120,000

Therefore joint costs are apportioned in the ratio 1:1.

Amount apportioned to product X   (776,160/2) $388,080

20% of X's production is in closing inventory = 20% of $388,080 = $77,616

Exam focus point

The above question is one many students will struggle with. Make sure you split the joint costs according to **sales value of production** rather than individual selling prices or sales value of sales.

PART C INTRODUCTION TO COSTING SYSTEMS

3 Joint products in process accounts

This example illustrates how joint products are incorporated into process accounts.

3.1 Example: Joint products and process accounts

Three joint products are manufactured in a common process, which consists of two consecutive stages. Output from process 1 is transferred to process 2, and output from process 2 consists of the three joint products, Hans, Nils and Bumpsydaisies. All joint products are sold as soon as they are produced.

Data for period 2 of 20X6 are as follows.

	Process 1	Process 2
Opening and closing inventory	None	None
Direct material		
(30,000 units at $2 per unit)	$60,000	–
Conversion costs	$76,500	$226,200
Normal loss	10% of input	10% of input
Scrap value of normal loss	$0.50 per unit	$2 per unit
Output	26,000 units	10,000 units of Han
		7,000 units of Nil
		6,000 units of Bumpsydaisy

Selling prices are $18 per unit of Han, $20 per unit of Nil and $30 per unit of Bumpsydaisy.

Required

(a) Prepare the Process 1 account.
(b) Prepare the Process 2 account using the sales value method of apportionment.
(c) Prepare a profit statement for the joint products.

Solution

(a) **Process 1 equivalent units**

	Total Units	Equivalent Units
Output to process 2	26,000	26,000
Normal loss	3,000	0
Abnormal loss (balance)	1,000	1,000
	30,000	27,000

Costs of process 1

	$
Direct materials	60,000
Conversion costs	76,500
	136,500
Less scrap value of normal loss (3,000 × $0.50)	1,500
	135,000

Cost per equivalent unit = $\dfrac{\$135,000}{27,000}$ = $5

PROCESS 1 ACCOUNT

	$		$
Direct materials	60,000	Output to process 2 (26,000 × $5)	130,000
Conversion costs	76,500	Normal loss (scrap value)	1,500
		Abnormal loss a/c (1,000 × $5)	5,000
	136,500		136,500

(b) Process 2 equivalent units

	Total Units	Equivalent Units
Units of Hans produced	10,000	10,000
Units of Nils produced	7,000	7,000
Units of Bumpsydaisies produced	6,000	6,000
Normal loss (10% of 26,000)	2,600	0
Abnormal loss (balance)	400	400
	26,000	23,400

Costs of process 2

	$
Material costs – from process 1	130,000
Conversion costs	226,200
	356,200
Less scrap value of normal loss (2,600 × $2)	5,200
	351,000

Cost per equivalent unit $\dfrac{\$351{,}000}{23{,}400} = \$15$

Cost of good output (10,000 + 7,000 + 6,000) = 23,000 units × $15 = $345,000

The sales value of joint products, and the apportionment of the output costs of $345,000, is as follows.

	Sales value $	%	Costs (process 2) $
Hans (10,000 × $18)	180,000	36	124,200
Nils (7,000 × $20)	140,000	28	96,600
Bumpsydaisy (6,000 × $30)	180,000	36	124,200
	500,000	100	345,000

PROCESS 2 ACCOUNT

	$		$
Process 1 materials	130,000	Finished goods accounts	
Conversion costs	226,200	– Hans	124,200
		– Nils	96,600
		– Bumpsydaisies	124,200
		Normal loss (scrap value)	5,200
		Abnormal loss a/c	6,000
	356,200		356,200

(c) PROFIT STATEMENT

	Hans $'000	Nils $'000	Bumpsydaisies $'000
Sales	180.0	140.0	180.0
Costs	124.2	96.6	124.2
Profit	55.8	43.4	55.8
Profit/ sales ratio	31%	31%	31%

Question — Unit basis of apportionment

Prepare the Process 2 account and a profit statement for the joint products in the above example using the units basis of apportionment.

Answer

PROCESS 2 ACCOUNT

	$		$
Process 1 materials	130,000	Finished goods accounts	
Conversion costs	226,200	– Hans (10,000 × $15)	150,000
		– Nils (7,000 × $15)	105,000
		– Bumpsydaisies (6,000 × $15)	90,000
		Normal loss (scrap value)	5,200
		Abnormal loss a/c	6,000
	356,200		356,200

PROFIT STATEMENT

	Hans $'000	Nils $'000	Bumpsydaisies $'000
Sales	180	140	180
Costs	150	105	90
Profit	30	35	90
Profit/ sales ratio	16.7%	25%	50%

Question — Joint costs and process costing

Polly Co operates a process costing system, the final output from which is three different products: Bolly, Dolly and Folly. Details of the three products for March are as follows.

	Bolly	Dolly	Folly
Selling price per unit	$25	$18	$32
Output for March	6,000 units	10,000 units	4,000 units

22,000 units of material were input to the process, costing $242,000. Conversion costs were $121,000. No losses were expected and there were no opening or closing inventories.

Using the units basis of apportioning joint costs, what was the profit or loss on sales of Dolly for March?

- A $(1,500)
- B $30,000
- C $50,306
- D $15,000

Answer

The correct answer is D.

Total output	20,000	units (6,000 + 10,000 + 4,000)
Total input	22,000	units
Abnormal loss	2,000	units

Total cost = $363,000

Cost per unit = $\dfrac{\$363,000}{22,000}$ = $16.50

Cost of 'good' output = 20,000 units × $16.50 = $330,000

$$\text{Amount apportioned to Dolly} = \frac{\text{Units of Dolly}}{\text{Total 'good' units}} \times \$330,000$$

$$= (10,000/20,000) \times \$330,000$$

$$= \$165,000$$

Profit for Dolly = Sales Revenue – apportioned costs

$$= (10,000 \times \$18) - \$165,000$$
$$= \$15,000$$

4 Accounting for by-products

4.1 Introduction

FAST FORWARD

The most common method of accounting for by-products is to deduct the **net realisable value** of the by-product from the cost of the main products.

A by-product has some commercial value and any income generated from it may be treated as follows.

(a) Income (minus any post-separation further processing or selling costs) from the sale of the by-product may be **added to sales of the main product**, thereby increasing sales turnover for the period.

(b) The sales of the by-product may be **treated as a separate, incidental source of income** against which are set only post-separation costs (if any) of the by-product. The revenue would be recorded in the statement of profit or loss as 'other income'.

(c) The sales income of the by-product may be **deducted from the cost of production** or cost of sales of the main product.

(d) The **net realisable value of the by-product may be deducted from the cost of production of the main product**. The net realisable value is the final saleable value of the by-product minus any post-separation costs. Any closing inventory valuation of the main product or joint products would therefore be reduced.

The choice of method (a), (b), (c) or (d) will be influenced by the circumstances of production and ease of calculation, as much as by conceptual correctness. The method you are most likely to come across in examinations is method (d). An example will help to clarify the distinction between the different methods.

4.2 Example: Methods of accounting for by-products

During November 20X3, Splatter Co recorded the following results.

Opening inventory	main product P, nil
	by-product Z, nil
Cost of production	$120,000

Sales of the main product amounted to 90% of output during the period, and 10% of production was held as closing inventory at 30 November.

Sales revenue from the main product during November 20X2 was $150,000.

A by-product Z is produced, and output had a net sales value of $1,000. Of this output, $700 was sold during the month, and $300 was still in inventory at 30 November.

Required

Calculate the profit for November using the four methods of accounting for by-products.

Solution

The four methods of accounting for by-products are shown below.

(a) **Income from by-product added to sales of the main product**

	$	$
Sales of main product ($150,000 + $700)		150,700
Opening inventory	0	
Cost of production	120,000	
	120,000	
Less closing inventory (10%)	12,000	
Cost of sales		108,000
Profit, main product		42,700

The closing inventory of the by-product has no recorded value in the cost accounts.

(b) **By-product income treated as a separate source of income**

	$	$
Sales, main product		150,000
Opening inventory	0	
Cost of production	120,000	
	120,000	
Closing inventory (10%)	12,000	
Cost of sales, main product		108,000
Profit, main product		42,000
Other income		700
Total profit		42,700

The closing inventory of the by-product again has no value in the cost accounts.

(c) **Sales income of the by-product deducted from the cost of production in the period**

	$	$
Sales, main product		150,000
Opening inventory	0	
Cost of production (120,000 – 700)	119,300	
	119,300	
Less closing inventory (10%)	11,930	
Cost of sales		107,370
Profit, main product		42,630

Although the profit is different from the figure in (a) and (b), the by-product closing inventory again has no value.

(d) **Net realisable value of the by-product deducted from the cost of production in the period**

	$	$
Sales, main product		150,000
Opening inventory	0	
Cost of production (120,000 – 1,000)	119,000	
	119,000	
Less closing inventory (10%)	11,900	
Cost of sales		107,100
Profit, main product		42,900

As with the other three methods, closing inventory of the by-product has no value in the books of accounting, but the value of the closing inventory ($300) has been used to reduce the cost of

9: PROCESS COSTING - JOINT PRODUCTS AND BY-PRODUCTS

production, and in this respect it has been allowed for in deriving the cost of sales and the profit for the period.

Question

Profits

Randolph manufactures two joint products, J and K, in a common process. A by-product X is also produced. Data for the month of December 20X2 were as follows.

Opening inventories	nil	
Costs of processing	direct materials	$25,500
	direct labour	$10,000

Production overheads are absorbed at the rate of 300% of direct labour costs.

		Production Units	Sales Units
Output and sales consisted of:	product J	8,000	7,000
	product K	8,000	6,000
	by-product X	1,000	1,000

The sales value per unit of J, K and X is $4, $6 and $0.50 respectively. The saleable value of the by-product is deducted from process costs before apportioning costs to each joint product. Costs of the common processing are apportioned between product J and product K on the basis of sales value of production.

The individual profits for December 20X2 are:

	Product J	Product K
	$	$
A	5,250	6,750
B	6,750	5,250
C	22,750	29,250
D	29,250	22,750

Answer

The sales value of production was $80,000.

	$	
Product J (8,000 × $4)	32,000	(40%)
Product K (8,000 × $6)	48,000	(60%)
	80,000	

The costs of production were as follows.

	$
Direct materials	25,500
Direct labour	10,000
Overhead (300% of $10,000)	30,000
	65,500
Less sales value of by-product (1,000 × 50c)	500
Net production costs	65,000

The profit statement would appear as follows (nil opening inventories).

		Product J			Product K	Total
		$			$	$
Production costs	(40%)	26,000	(60%)		39,000	65,000
Less closing inventory (see working below)	(1,000 units)	3,250	(2,000 units)		9,750	13,000
Cost of sales		22,750			29,250	52,000
Sales	(7,000 units)	28,000	(6,000 units)		36,000	64,000
Profit		5,250			6,750	12,000

Working

Closing inventory = (Production units − sales units) × (production costs/production units)

For J, closing inventory = (8,000 − 7,000) × ($26,000/8,000) = $3,250

For K, closing inventory = (8,000 − 6,000) × ($39,000/8,000) = $9,750

The correct answer is therefore A.

If you selected option B, you got the profits for each product mixed up.

If you selected option C or D, you calculated the cost of sales instead of the profit.

Chapter roundup

- **Joint products** are two or more products separated in a process, each of which has a **significant value** compared to the other. A **by-product** is an incidental product from a process which has an **insignificant value** compared to the main product.
- The point at which **joint products** and **by-products** become separately identifiable is known as the **split-off point** or **separation point**. Costs incurred up to this point are called **common costs** or **joint costs**.
- The main methods of apportioning joint costs, each of which can produce significantly different results, are as follows: physical measurement; relative sales value apportionment method; sales value at split-off point.
- The **relative sales value method** is the most widely used method of apportioning joint costs because (ignoring the effect of further processing costs) it assumes that all products achieve the same profit margin.
- The most common method of accounting for by-products is to deduct the **net realisable value** of the by-product from the cost of the main products.

Quick quiz

1. A **joint product** is regarded as an important saleable item whereas a **by-product** is not.

    True ☐

    False ☐

2. The **split-off point** is the point at which joint products become separately identifiable in a processing operation. Which of the following is another term for the split-off point:

    A   The divorce point
    B   Decoupling
    C   The separation point
    D   TTFN

3. The point at which joint products and by-products become separately identifiable is known as the split-off point Costs incurred up to this point are called common costs.

    Which of the following is another term for common costs:

    A   Average costs
    B   Union costs
    C   Pot costs
    D   Joint costs

4. Name two methods of apportioning common costs to joint products.

5. Describe the four methods of accounting for by-products.

PART C INTRODUCTION TO COSTING SYSTEMS

Answers to quick quiz

1. True. A **joint product** is regarded as an important saleable item whereas a **by-product** is not.
2. C The **split-off point** (or the **separation point**) is the point at which joint products become separately identifiable in a processing operation.
3. D The point at which joint products and by-products become separately identifiable is known as the split-off point or separation point. Costs incurred up to this point are called **common costs** or **joint costs**.
4. Physical measurement and sales value at split-off point
5. See Paragraph 4.1

End of chapter question

ABC Ltd

ABC Ltd has a financial year which ends on 30 September. It operates in a processing industry in which a single product is produced by passing inputs through two sequential processes. A normal loss of 10% of input is expected in each process.

The following account balances have been extracted from its ledger at 31 August 20X8.

	Debit $	Credit $
Process 1 (Materials $4,400; Conversion costs $3,744)	8,144	
Process 2 (Process 1 $4,431; Conversion costs $5,250)	9,681	
Abnormal loss	1,400	
Abnormal gain		300
Overhead control account		250
Sales		585,000
Cost of sales	442,500	
Finished goods stock	65,000	

ABC Ltd uses the weighted average method of accounting for work in process.

During September 20X8 the following transactions occurred.

Process 1	Materials input	4,000 kg costing	$22,000
	Labour cost		$12,000
	Transfer to process 2	2,400 kg	
Process 2	Transfer from process 1	2,400 kg	
	Labour cost		$15,000
	Transfer to finished goods	2,500 kg	
Overhead costs incurred		£54,000	
Sales to customers		£52,000	

Overhead costs are absorbed into process costs on the basis of 150% of labour cost.

The losses which arise in process 1 have no scrap value: those arising in process 2 can be sold for $2 per kg.

Details of opening and closing work in process for the month of September 20X8 are as follows.

	Opening kg	Closing kg
Process 1	3,000	3,400
Process 2	2,250	2,600

In both processes closing work in process is fully complete as to material cost and 40% complete as to conversion cost.

Stocks of finished goods at 30 September 20X8 were valued at cost of $60,000.

Required

(a) Prepare the statement of profit or loss of ABC Ltd for the year to 30 September 20X8. **(20 marks)**

(b) Discuss the problems associated with joint cost apportionments in relation to:

    (i) Planning
    (ii) Control
    (iii) Decision making **(10 marks)**

(Total = 30 marks)

PART C INTRODUCTION TO COSTING SYSTEMS

Job, batch, service and contract costing

Topic list	Syllabus reference
1 Costing methods	C3.1
2 Job costing	C3.1
3 Batch costing	C3.1
4 Service costing	C3.1
5 Contract costs	C3.1
6 Progress payments and retentions	C3.1
7 Profits on contracts	C3.1
8 Losses on incomplete contracts	C3.1

Introduction

The first costing method that we shall be looking at is **job costing**. We will see the circumstances in which job costing should be used and how the costs of jobs are calculated. We will look at how the **costing of individual jobs** fits in with the recording of total costs in control accounts and then we will move on to **batch costing**, the procedure for which is similar to job costing.

Service costing deals with **specialist services** supplied to third parties or an **internal service** supplied within an organisation.

The final costing method considered in this chapter is **contract costing**. Contract costing is similar to job costing but the job is of such importance that a formal contract is made between the supplier and the customer. We will see how to record contract costs, and how to account for any profits and losses arising on contracts at the end of an accounting period.

1 Costing methods

> **FAST FORWARD**
>
> A **costing method** is designed to suit the way goods are processed or manufactured or the way services are provided.

Each organisation's costing method will therefore have unique features but costing methods of firms in the same line of business will more than likely have common aspects. Organisations involved in completely different activities, such as hospitals and car part manufacturers, will use very different methods.

We will be considering these important costing methods in this chapter.

- Job
- Batch
- Service

2 Job costing

2.1 Introduction

> **FAST FORWARD**
>
> **Job costing** is a costing method applied where work is undertaken to customers' special requirements and each order is of comparatively short duration.

Key term

A **job** is a cost unit which consists of a single order or contract.

The work relating to a job moves through processes and operations as a **continuously identifiable unit**. Job costing is most commonly applied within a factory or workshop, but may also be applied to property repairs and internal capital expenditure.

2.2 Procedure for the performance of jobs

The normal procedure in jobbing concerns involves:

(a) The prospective customer approaches the supplier and indicates the **requirements** of the job.

(b) A representative sees the prospective customer and agrees with him the **precise details** of the items to be supplied. For example the quantity, quality, size and colour of the goods, the date of delivery and any special requirements.

(c) The estimating department of the organisation then **prepares an estimate for the job**. This will be based on the cost of the materials to be used, the labour expense expected, the cost overheads, the cost of any additional equipment needed specially for the job, and finally the supplier's **profit margin**. The total of these items will represent the **quoted selling price**.

(d) If the estimate is accepted the job can be **scheduled**. All materials, labour and equipment required will be 'booked' for the job. In an efficient organisation, the start of the job will be timed to ensure that while it will be ready for the customer by the promised date of delivery it will not be loaded too early, otherwise storage space will have to be found for the product until the date it is required by (and was promised to) the customer.

2.3 Job cost sheets/cards

> **FAST FORWARD**
>
> Costs for each job are collected on a **job cost sheet** or **job card**.

With other methods of costing, it is usual to produce for inventory; this means that management must decide in advance how many units of each type, size, colour, quality and so on will be produced during the coming year, regardless of the identity of the customers who will eventually buy the product. In job costing, because production is usually carried out in accordance with the **special requirements of each customer**, it is **usual for each job to differ in one or more respects from another job.**

A separate record must therefore be maintained to show the details of individual jobs. Such records are often known as **job cost sheets** or **job cost cards**. An example is shown on the next page.

Either the **detail of relatively small jobs** or a **summary** of direct materials, direct labour and so on **for larger jobs** will be shown on a job cost sheet.

2.4 Job cost information

> **FAST FORWARD**
>
> **Material costs** for each job are determined from **material requisition notes**. **Labour times** on each job are recorded on a **job ticket**, which is then costed and recorded on the job cost sheet. Some labour costs, such as overtime premium or the cost of rectifying sub-standard output, might be charged either directly to a job or else as an overhead cost, depending on the circumstances in which the costs have arisen. **Overhead** is absorbed into the cost of jobs using the predetermined overhead absorption rates.

Information for the direct and indirect costs will be gathered as follows.

2.4.1 Direct material cost

(a) The estimated cost will be calculated by valuing all items on the **bill of materials**. Materials that have to be specially purchased for the job in question will need to be priced by the purchasing department.

(b) The actual cost of materials used will be calculated by valuing materials issues notes for those issues from store for the job and/or from invoices for materials specially purchased. All documentation should indicate the job number to which it relates.

2.4.2 Direct labour cost

(a) The estimated **labour time requirement** will be calculated from past experience of similar types of work or work study engineers may prepare estimates following detailed specifications. Labour rates will need to take account of any increases, overtime and bonuses.

(b) The actual labour hours will be available from either time sheets or job tickets/cards, using job numbers where appropriate to indicate the time spent on each job. The actual labour cost will be calculated using the hours information and current labour rates (plus bonuses, overtime payments and so on).

2.4.3 Direct expenses

(a) The estimated cost of **any expenses likely** to be incurred can be obtained from a supplier.
(b) The details of actual direct expenses incurred can be taken from invoices.

PART C INTRODUCTION TO COSTING SYSTEMS

JOB COST CARD

Job No.	B641
Customer	Mr J White
Job Description	Repair damage to offside front door
Estimate Ref.	2599
Quoted price	$338.68
Customer's Order No.	
Invoice No.	
Invoice price	$355.05
Vehicle make	Peugot 205 GTE
Vehicle reg. no.	G 614 SOX
Date to collect	14.6.00

Material

Date	Req. No.	Qty.	Price	Cost $	c
12.6	36815	1	75.49	75	49
12.6	36816	1	33.19	33	19
12.6	36842	5	6.01	30	05
13.6	36881	5	3.99	19	95
Total C/F				158	68

Labour

Date	Employee	Cost Ctre	Hrs.	Rate	Bonus	Cost $	c
12.6	018	B	1.98	6.50	-	12	87
13.6	018	B	5.92	6.50	-	38	48
					13.65	13	65
Total C/F						65	00

Overheads

Hrs	OAR	Cost $	c
7.9	2.50	19	75
Total C/F		19	75

Expenses

Date	Ref.	Description	Cost $	c
12.6	-	N. Jolley Panel-beating	50	-
Total C/F			50	-

Job Cost Summary

	Actual $	c	Estimate $	c
Direct Materials B/F	158	68	158	68
Direct Expenses B/F	50	00		
Direct Labour B/F	65	00	180	00
Direct Cost	273	68		
Overheads B/F	19	75		
	293	43		
Admin overhead (add 10%)	29	34		
= Total Cost	322	77	338	68
Invoice Price	355	05		
Job Profit/Loss	32	28		

Comments

Job Cost Card Completed by _____

2.4.4 Production overheads

(a) The **estimated production overheads** to be included in the job cost will be calculated from **overhead absorption rates** in operation and the estimate of the basis of the absorption rate (for example, direct labour hours). This assumes the job estimate is to include overheads (in a competitive environment management may feel that if overheads are to be incurred irrespective of whether or not the job is taken on, the minimum estimated quotation price should be based on variable costs only).

(b) The actual production overhead to be included in the job cost will be calculated from the overhead absorption rate and the actual results (such as labour hours coded to the job in question).

Inaccurate overhead absorption rates can seriously harm an organisation; if jobs are over priced, customers will go elsewhere and if jobs are under priced revenue will fail to cover costs.

2.4.5 Administration, selling and distribution overheads

The organisation may absorb **non-production overheads** using any one of a variety of methods (percentage on full production cost, for example) and estimates of these costs and the actual costs should be included in the estimated and actual job cost.

2.5 Rectification costs

If the finished output is found to be sub-standard, it may be possible to rectify the fault. The sub-standard output will then be returned to the department or cost centre where the fault arose.

Rectification costs can be treated in two ways.

(a) If rectification work is not a frequent occurrence, but arises on occasions with specific jobs to which it can be traced directly, then the rectification costs should be **charged as a direct cost to the jobs concerned.**

(b) If rectification is regarded as a normal part of the work carried out generally in the department, then the rectification costs should be **treated as production overheads**. This means that they would be included in the total of production overheads for the department and absorbed into the cost of all jobs for the period, using the overhead absorption rate.

2.6 Work in progress

At the year end, the **value of work in progress** is simply the **sum of the costs incurred on incomplete jobs** (provided that the costs are lower than the net realisable value of the customer order).

2.7 Pricing the job

> **FAST FORWARD**
>
> The usual method of fixing prices in a jobbing concern is **cost plus pricing**.

Cost plus pricing means that a desired profit margin is added to total costs to arrive at the selling price.

The estimated profit will depend on the particular circumstance of the job and organisation in question. In competitive situations the profit may be small but if the organisation is sure of securing the job the margin may be greater. In general terms, the profit earned on each job should **conform to the requirements of the organisation's overall business plan**.

The final price quoted will, of course, be affected by what competitors charge and what the customer will be willing to pay.

2.8 Job costing and computerisation

Job cost sheets exist in manual systems, but it is **increasingly likely** that in large organisations the **job costing system will be computerised**, using accounting software specifically designed to deal with job costing requirements. A computerised job accounting system is likely to contain the following features.

(a) Every job will be given a **job code number**, which will determine how the data relating to the job is stored.

(b) A separate set of **codes will be given for the type of costs** that any job is likely to incur. Thus, 'direct wages', say, will have the same code whichever job they are allocated to.

PART C INTRODUCTION TO COSTING SYSTEMS

(c) In a sophisticated system, **costs can be analysed both by job** (for example all costs related to Job 456), **but also by type** (for example direct wages incurred on all jobs). It is thus easy to perform control analysis and to make comparisons between jobs.

(d) A job costing system might have facilities built into it which incorporate other factors relating to the performance of the job. In complex jobs, sophisticated planning techniques might be employed to ensure that the job is performed in the minimum time possible: time management features may be incorporated into job costing software.

2.9 Example: Job costing

Fateful Morn is a jobbing company. On 1 June 20X2, there was one uncompleted job in the factory. The job card for this work is summarised as follows.

Job Card, Job No. 6832

	$
Costs to date	
Direct materials	630
Direct labour (120 hours)	350
Factory overhead ($2 per direct labour hour)	240
Factory cost to date	1,220

During June, three new jobs were started in the factory, and costs of production were as follows.

Direct materials		$
Issued to:	Job 6832	2,390
	Job 6833	1,680
	Job 6834	3,950
	Job 6835	4,420
Damaged inventory written off from stores		2,300

Material transfers	$
Job 6834 to Job 6833	250
Job 6832 to 6834	620

Materials returned to store	$
From Job 6832	870
From Job 6835	170

Direct labour hours recorded

Job 6832	430 hrs
Job 6833	650 hrs
Job 6834	280 hrs
Job 6835	410 hrs

The cost of labour hours during June 20X2 was $3 per hour, and production overhead is absorbed at the rate of $2 per direct labour hour. Production overheads incurred during the month amounted to $3,800. Completed jobs were delivered to customers as soon as they were completed, and the invoiced amounts were as follows.

Job 6832	$5,500
Job 6834	$8,000
Job 6835	$7,500

Administration and marketing overheads are added to the cost of sales at the rate of 20% of factory cost. Actual costs incurred during June 20X2 amounted to $3,200.

Required

(a) Prepare the job accounts for each individual job during June 20X2 (the accounts should only show the cost of production, and not the full cost of sale).

10: JOB, BATCH, SERVICE AND CONTRACT COSTING

(b) Prepare the summarised job cost cards for each job, and calculate the profit on each completed job.

Solution

(a) **Job accounts**

JOB 6832

	$		$
Balance b/f	1,220	Job 6834 a/c	620
Materials (stores a/c)	2,390	(materials transfer)	
Labour (wages a/c)	1,290	Stores a/c (materials returned)	870
Production overhead (o'hd a/c)	860	Cost of sales a/c (balance)	4,270
	5,760		5,760

JOB 6833

	$		$
Materials (stores a/c)	1,680	Balance c/f	5,180
Labour (wages a/c)	1,950		
Production overhead (o'hd a/c)	1,300		
Job 6834 a/c (materials transfer)	250		
	5,180		5,180

JOB 6834

	$		$
Materials (stores a/c)	3,950	Job 6833 a/c (materials transfer)	250
Labour (wages a/c)	840		
Production overhead (o'hd a/c)	560	Cost of sales a/c (balance)	5,720
Job 6832 a/c (materials transfer)	620		
	5,970		5,970

JOB 6835

	$		$
Materials (stores a/c)	4,420	Stores a/c (materials returned)	170
Labour (wages a/c)	1,230		
Production overhead (o'hd a/c)	820	Cost of sales a/c (balance)	6,300
	6,470		6,470

(b) **Job cards, summarised**

	Job 6832	Job 6833	Job 6834	Job 6835
	$	$	$	$
Materials	1,530*	1,930	4,320**	4,250
Labour	1,640	1,950	840	1,230
Production overhead	1,100	1,300	560	820
Factory cost	4,270	5,180 (c/f)	5,720	6,300
Admin & marketing o'hd (20%)	854		1,144	1,260
Cost of sale	5,124		6,864	7,560
Invoice value	5,500		8,000	7,500
Profit/(loss) on job	376		1,136	(60)

*$(630 + 2,390 – 620 – 870)
**$(3,950 + 620 – 250)

2.10 Job costing for internal services

FAST FORWARD

It is possible to use a job costing system **to control the costs of an internal service department**, such as the maintenance department or the printing department.

If a job costing system is used it is possible to **charge the user departments for the cost of specific jobs carried out, rather than apportioning the total costs of these service departments** to the user departments using an arbitrarily determined apportionment basis.

An internal job costing system for service departments will have the following advantages.

Advantages	Comment
Realistic apportionment	The identification of expenses with jobs and the subsequent charging of these to the department(s) responsible means that costs are borne by those who incurred them.
Increased responsibility and awareness	User departments will be aware that they are charged for the specific services used and may be more careful to use the facility more efficiently. They will also appreciate the true cost of the facilities that they are using and can take decisions accordingly.
Control of service department costs	The service department may be restricted to charging a standard cost to user departments for specific jobs carried out or time spent. It will then be possible to measure the efficiency or inefficiency of the service department by recording the difference between the standard charges and the actual expenditure.
Planning information	This information will ease the planning process, as the purpose and cost of service department expenditure can be separately identified.

Question — Total job cost

A furniture-making business manufactures quality furniture to customers' orders. It has three production departments (A, B and C) which have overhead absorption rates (per direct labour hour) of $12.86, $12.40 and $14.03 respectively.

Two pieces of furniture are to be manufactured for customers. Direct costs are as follows.

	Job XYZ	Job MNO
Direct material	$154	$108
Direct labour	20 hours dept A	16 hours dept A
	12 hours dept B	10 hours dept B
	10 hours dept C	14 hours dept C

Labour rates are as follows: $3.80(A); $3.50 (B); $3.40 (C)

Calculate the total cost of each job.

Answer

			Job XYZ $		Job MNO $
Direct material			154.00		108.00
Direct labour:	dept A	(20 × 3.80)	76.00	(16 × 3.80)	60.80
	dept B	(12 × 3.50)	42.00	(10 × 3.50)	35.00
	dept C	(10 × 3.40)	34.00	(14 × 3.40)	47.60
Total direct cost			306.00		251.40
Overhead:	dept A	(20 × 12.86)	257.20	(16 × 12.86)	205.76
	dept B	(12 × 12.40)	148.80	(10 × 12.40)	124.00
	dept C	(10 × 14.03)	140.30	(14 × 14.03)	196.42
Total cost			852.30		777.58

Question — Closing work in progress

A firm uses job costing and recovers overheads on direct labour.

Three jobs were worked on during a period, the details of which are as follows.

	Job 1 $	Job 2 $	Job 3 $
Opening work in progress	8,500	0	46,000
Material in period	17,150	29,025	0
Labour for period	12,500	23,000	4,500

The overheads for the period were exactly as budgeted, $140,000.

Jobs 1 and 2 were the only incomplete jobs.

What was the value of closing work in progress?

A $81,900   B $90,175   C $140,675   D $214,425

Answer

Total labour cost = $12,500 + $23,000 + $4,500 = $40,000

Overhead absorption rate = $\frac{\$140,000}{\$40,000}$ × 100% = 350% of direct labour cost

Closing work in progress valuation

		Job 1 $		Job 2 $	Total $
Costs given in question		38,150		52,025	90,175
Overhead absorbed	(12,500 × 350%)	43,750	(23,000 × 350%)	80,500	124,250
					214,425

Option D is correct.

We can eliminate option B because $90,175 is simply the total of the costs allocated to Jobs 1 and 2, with no absorption of overheads. Option A is an even lower cost figure, therefore it can also be eliminated.

Option C is wrong because it is a simple total of all allocated costs, including Job 3 which is not incomplete.

PART C INTRODUCTION TO COSTING SYSTEMS

> **Exam focus point**
>
> You may be asked to compare the accuracy of job costing with, say, process costing.

3 Batch costing

3.1 Introduction

> **FAST FORWARD**
>
> **Batch costing** is similar to job costing in that each batch of similar articles is separately identifiable. The **cost per unit** manufactured in a batch is the total batch cost divided by the number of units in the batch.

> **Key term**
>
> A **batch** is a group of similar articles which maintains its identity during one or more stages of production and is treated as a cost unit.

In general, the **procedures for costing batches are very similar to those for costing jobs**.

(a) The **batch is treated as a job during production** and the costs are collected in the manner already described in this chapter.

(b) Once the batch has been completed, the **cost per unit can be calculated as the total batch cost divided into the number of units in the batch**.

3.2 Example: Batch costing

Rio manufactures Brazils to order and has the following budgeted overheads for the year, based on normal activity levels.

Production departments	Budgeted overheads $	Budgeted activity
Welding	12,000	3,000 labour hours
Assembly	20,000	2,000 labour hours

Selling and administrative overheads are 25% of factory cost. An order for 500 Brazils, made as Batch 38, incurred the following costs.

Materials $24,000

Labour 200 hours in the Welding Department at $5 per hour
400 hours in the Assembly Department at $10 per hour

$1,000 was paid for the hire of x-ray equipment for testing the accuracy of the welds.

Required

Calculate the cost per unit for Batch 38.

Solution

The first step is to calculate the overhead absorption rate for the production departments.

Welding = $\dfrac{\$12,000}{3,000}$ = $4 per labour hour

Assembly = $\dfrac{\$20,000}{2,000}$ = $10 per labour hour

Total cost – Batch 38

		$	$
Direct material			24,000
Direct expense			1,000
Direct labour	200 × $5 =	1,000	
	400 × $10 =	4,000	
			5,000
Prime cost			30,000
Overheads	200 × $4 =	800	
	400 × $10 =	4,000	
			4,800
Factory cost			34,800
Selling and administrative cost (25% of factory cost)			8,700
Total cost			43,500

Cost per unit = $\dfrac{\$43,500}{500}$ = $87

4 Service costing

4.1 What is service costing?

FAST FORWARD

> Service costing can be used by companies operating in a service industry or by companies wishing to establish the cost of services carried out by some of their departments. Service organisations do not make or sell tangible goods.

Key term

> **Service costing** (or **function costing**) is a costing method concerned with establishing the costs, not of items of production, but of services rendered.

Service costing is used in the following circumstances.

(a) A company operating in a service industry will cost its services, for which sales revenue will be earned; examples are electricians, car hire services, road, rail or air transport services and hotels.

(b) A company may wish to establish the cost of services carried out by some of its departments; for example the costs of the vans or lorries used in distribution, the costs of the computer department, or the staff canteen.

4.2 Service costing versus product costing (such as job or process costing)

(a) With many services, the cost of direct materials consumed will be relatively small compared to the labour, direct expenses and overheads cost. In product costing the direct materials are often a greater proportion of the total cost.

(b) Although many services are revenue-earning, others are not (such as the distribution facility or the staff canteen). This means that the purpose of service costing may not be to establish a profit or loss (nor to value closing inventories for the statement of financial position) but may rather be to provide management information about the comparative costs or efficiency of the services, with a view to helping managers to budget for their costs using historical data as a basis for estimating costs in the future and to control the costs in the service departments.

(c) The procedures for recording material costs, labour hours and other expenses will vary according to the nature of the service.

PART C INTRODUCTION TO COSTING SYSTEMS

4.3 Specific characteristics of services

FAST FORWARD

Specific characteristics of services
- Simultaneity
- Heterogeneity
- Intangibility
- Perishability

Consider the service of providing a haircut.

(a) The production and consumption of a haircut are **simultaneous,** and therefore it cannot be inspected for quality in advance, nor can it be returned if it is not what was required.

(b) A haircut is **heterogeneous** and so the exact service received will vary each time: not only will two hairdressers cut hair differently, but a hairdresser will not consistently deliver the same standard of haircut.

(c) A haircut is **intangible** in itself, and the performance of the service comprises many other intangible factors, like the music in the salon, the personality of the hairdresser, the quality of the coffee.

(d) Haircuts are **perishable,** that is, they cannot be stored. You cannot buy them in bulk, and the hairdresser cannot do them in advance and keep them stocked away in case of heavy demand. The incidence of work in progress in service organisations is less frequent than in other types of organisation.

Note the mnemonic **SHIP** for remembering the specific characteristics of services.

4.4 Unit cost measures

FAST FORWARD

The main problem with service costing is the **difficulty in defining a realistic cost unit** that represents a suitable measure of the service provided. Frequently, a composite cost unit may be deemed more appropriate. Hotels, for example, may use the 'occupied bed-night' as an appropriate unit for cost ascertainment and control.

Typical cost units used by companies operating in a service industry are shown below.

Service	Cost unit
Road, rail and air transport services	Passenger/mile or kilometre, ton/mile, tonne/kilometre
Hotels	Occupied bed-night
Education	Full-time student
Hospitals	Patient
Catering establishment	Meal served

Question   Internal services

Can you think of examples of cost units for internal services such as canteens, distribution and maintenance?

Answer

Service	Cost unit
Canteen	Meal served
Vans and lorries used in distribution	Mile or kilometre, ton/mile, tonne/kilometre
Maintenance	Labour hour

Each organisation will need to ascertain the **cost unit** most appropriate to its activities. If a number of organisations within an industry use a common cost unit, then valuable comparisons can be made between similar establishments. This is particularly applicable to hospitals, educational establishments and local authorities. Whatever cost unit is decided upon, the calculation of a cost per unit is as follows.

Formula to learn

$$\text{Cost per service unit} = \frac{\text{Total costs for period}}{\text{Number of service units in the period}}$$

4.5 Service cost analysis

Service cost analysis should be performed in a manner which ensures that the following objectives are attained.

(a) Planned costs should be compared with actual costs.

Differences should be investigated and corrective action taken as necessary.

(b) A cost per unit of service should be calculated.

If each service has a number of variations (such as maintenance services provided by plumbers, electricians and carpenters) then the calculation of a cost per unit of each service may be necessary.

(c) The cost per unit of service should be used as part of the control function.

For example, costs per unit of service can be compared, month by month, period by period, year by year and so on and any unusual trends can be investigated.

(d) Prices should be calculated for services being sold to third parties.

The procedure is similar to job costing. A mark-up is added to the cost per unit of service to arrive at a selling price.

(e) Costs should be analysed into fixed, variable and semi-variable costs to help assist management with planning, control and decision making.

4.6 Service cost analysis in internal service situations

FAST FORWARD

Service department costing is also used to establish a specific cost for an internal service which is a service provided by one department for another, rather than sold externally to customers eg canteen, maintenance.

4.6.1 Transport costs

'**Transport costs**' is a term used here to refer to the costs of the transport services used by a company, rather than the costs of a transport organisation, such as a rail network.

PART C INTRODUCTION TO COSTING SYSTEMS

If a company has a fleet of lorries or vans which it uses to distribute its goods, it is useful to know how much the department is costing for a number of reasons.

(a) Management should be able to budget for expected costs, and to control actual expenditure on transport by comparing actual costs with budgeted costs.

(b) The company may charge customers for delivery or 'carriage outwards' costs, and a charge based on the cost of the transport service might be appropriate.

(c) If management knows how much its own transport is costing, a comparison can be made with alternative forms of transport to decide whether a cheaper or better method of delivery can be found.

(d) Similarly, if a company uses, say, a fleet of lorries, knowledge of how much transport by lorry costs should help management to decide whether another type of vehicle, say vans, would be cheaper to use.

Transport costs may be analysed to provide the cost of operating one van or lorry each year, but it is more informative to analyse costs as follows.

(a) The cost per mile or kilometre travelled

(b) The cost per ton/mile or tonne/kilometre (the cost of carrying one tonne of goods for one kilometre distance) or the cost per kilogram/metre

For example, suppose that a company lorry makes five deliveries in a week.

Delivery	Tonnes carried	Distance (one way) Kilometres	Tonne/kilometres carried
1	0.4	180	72
2	0.3	360	108
3	1.2	100	120
4	0.8	250	200
5	1.0	60	60
			560

If the costs of operating the lorry during the week are known to be $840, the cost per tonne/kilometre would be:

$$\frac{\$840}{560 \text{ tonne/kilometre}} = \$1.50 \text{ per tonne/kilometre}$$

Transport costs might be collected under five broad headings.

(a) **Running costs** such as petrol, oil, drivers' wages
(b) **Loading costs** (the labour costs of loading the lorries with goods for delivery)
(c) **Servicing, repairs**, spare parts and tyre usage
(d) **Annual direct expenses** such as road tax, insurance and depreciation
(e) **Indirect costs of the distribution department** such as the wages of managers

The role of the cost accountant is to provide a system for **recording and analysing costs**. Just as production costs are recorded by means of material requisition notes, labour time sheets and so on, so too must transport costs be recorded by means of log sheets or time sheets, and material supply notes.

The purpose of a lorry driver's log sheet is to record distance travelled, or the number of tonne/kilometres and the drivers' time.

4.6.2 Canteen costs

Another example of service costing is the cost of a company's **canteen services**. A feature of canteen costing is that some revenue is earned when employees pay for their meals, but the prices paid will be insufficient to cover the costs of the canteen service. The company will subsidise the canteen and a major purpose of canteen costing is to establish the size of the subsidy.

If the costs of the canteen service are recorded by a system of service cost accounting, the likely headings of expense would be as follows.

(a) **Food and drink**: separate canteen stores records may be kept, and the consumption of food and drink recorded by means of 'materials issues' notes.

(b) **Labour costs of the canteen staff**: hourly paid staff will record their time at work on a time card or time sheet. Salaried staff will be a 'fixed' cost each month.

(c) **Consumable stores** such as crockery, cutlery, glassware, table linen and cleaning materials will also be recorded in some form of inventory control system.

(d) **The cost of gas and electricity** may be separately metered; otherwise an apportionment of the total cost of such utilities for the building as a whole will be made to the canteen department.

(e) Asset records will be kept and **depreciation charges** made for major items of equipment like ovens and furniture.

(f) An apportionment of other **overhead costs** of the building (rent and rates, building insurance and maintenance and so on) may be charged against the canteen.

Cash income from canteen sales will also be recorded.

4.6.3 Example: Service cost analysis

Suppose that a canteen recorded the following costs and revenue during the month.

	$
Food and drink	11,250
Labour	11,250
Heating and lighting	1,875
Repairs and consumable stores	1,125
Financing costs	1,000
Depreciation	750
Other apportioned costs	875
Revenue	22,500

The canteen served 37,500 meals in the month.

The size of the subsidy could be easily identified as follows:

	$
The total costs of the canteen	28,125
Revenue	22,500
Loss, to be covered by the company	5,625

The cost per meal averages 75c and the revenue per meal 60c. If the company decided that the canteen should pay its own way, without a subsidy, the average price of a meal would have to be raised by 15 cents.

4.7 The usefulness of costing services that do not earn revenue

4.7.1 Purposes of service costing

The techniques for costing services are similar to the techniques for costing products, but why should we want to establish a cost for 'internal' services, services that are provided by one department for another, rather than sold externally to customers? In other words, what is the purpose of service costing for non revenue earning services?

Service costing has two basic purposes.

(a) **To control the costs in the service department.** If we establish a distribution cost per tonne kilometre, a canteen cost per employee, or job costs of repairs, we can establish control measures in the following ways.

 (i) Comparing actual costs against a target or standard
 (ii) Comparing current actual costs against actual costs in previous periods

(b) **To control the costs of the user departments**, and prevent the unnecessary use of services. If the costs of services are charged to the user departments in such a way that the charges reflect the use actually made by each department of the service department's services then the following will occur.

 (i) The overhead costs of user departments will be established more accurately; indeed some service department variable costs might be identified as directly attributable costs of the user department.

 (ii) If the service department's charges for a user department are high, the user department might be encouraged to consider whether it is making an excessively costly and wasteful use of the service department's service.

 (iii) The user department might decide that it can obtain a similar service at a lower cost from an external service company.

4.7.2 Example: Costing internal services

(a) If maintenance costs in a factory are costed as jobs (that is, if each bit of repair work is given a job number and costed accordingly) repair costs can be charged to the departments on the basis of repair jobs actually undertaken, instead of on a more generalised basis, such as apportionment according to machine hour capacity in each department. Departments with high repair costs could then consider their high incidence of repairs, the age and reliability of their machines, or the skills of the machine operatives.

(b) If IT costs are charged to a user department on the basis of a cost per hour, the user department would assess whether it was getting good value from its use of the IT department and whether it might be better to outsource some of its IT work.

4.8 Service cost analysis in service industry situations

4.8.1 Distribution costs

Example: service cost analysis in the service industry

This example shows how a rate per tonne/kilometre can be calculated for a distribution service.

Rick Shaw operates a small fleet of delivery vehicles. Standard costs have been established as follows.

Loading	1 hour per tonne loaded
Loading costs:	
Labour (casual)	$2 per hour

Equipment depreciation $80 per week
Supervision $80 per week
Drivers' wages (fixed) $100 per person per week
Petrol   10c per kilometre
Repairs   5c per kilometre
Depreciation $80 per week per vehicle
Supervision $120 per week
Other general expenses (fixed) $200 per week

There are two drivers and two vehicles in the fleet.

During a slack week, only six journeys were made.

Journey	Tonnes carried (one way)	One-way distance of journey Kilometres
1	5	100
2	8	20
3	2	60
4	4	50
5	6	200
6	5	300

Required

Calculate the expected average full cost per tonne/kilometre for the week.

Solution

Variable costs	Journey	1	2	3	4	5	6
		$	$	$	$	$	$
Loading labour		10	16	4	8	12	10
Petrol (both ways)		20	4	12	10	40	60
Repairs (both ways)		10	2	6	5	20	30
		40	22	22	23	72	100

Total costs

	$
Variable costs (total for journeys 1 to 6)	279
Loading equipment depreciation	80
Loading supervision	80
Drivers' wages	200
Vehicles depreciation	160
Drivers' supervision	120
Other costs	200
	1,119

Journey	Tonnes	One way distance Kilometres	Tonne/kilometres
1	5	100	500
2	8	20	160
3	2	60	120
4	4	50	200
5	6	200	1,200
6	5	300	1,500
			3,680

Cost per tonne/kilometre $\frac{\$1,119}{3,680} = \$0.304$

Note that the large element of fixed costs may distort this measure but that a variable cost per tonne/kilometre of $279/3,680 = $0.076 may be useful for budgetary control.

4.8.2 Education

The techniques described in the preceding paragraphs can be applied, in general, to any service industry situation. Attempt the following question about education.

Question — Suitable cost unit

A university with annual running costs of $3 million has the following students.

Classification	Number	Attendance weeks per annum	Hours per week
3 year	2,700	30	28
4 year	1,500	30	25
Sandwich	1,900	35	20

Required

Calculate a cost per suitable cost unit for the university to the nearest cent.

Answer

We need to begin by establishing a cost unit for the university. Since there are three different categories of students we cannot use 'a student' as the cost unit. Attendance hours would seem to be the most appropriate cost unit. The next step is to calculate the number of units.

Number of students	Weeks	Hours	Total hours per annum
2,700	× 30	× 28	= 2,268,000
1,500	× 30	× 25	= 1,125,000
1,900	× 35	× 20	= 1,330,000
			4,723,000

The cost per unit is calculated as follows.

$$\text{Cost per unit} = \frac{\text{Total cost}}{\text{Number of units}} = \$\left(\frac{3,000,000}{4,723,000}\right) = \underline{\$0.64}$$

Question — Service costing

State which of the following are characteristics of service costing.

(i) High levels of indirect costs as a proportion of total costs
(ii) Use of composite cost units
(iii) Use of equivalent units

A (i) only
B (i) and (ii) only
C (ii) only
D (ii) and (iii) only

Answer

B   In service costing it is difficult to identify many attributable direct costs. Many costs must be shared over several cost units, therefore characteristic (i) does apply. Composite cost units such as tonne-mile or room-night are often used, therefore characteristic (ii) does apply. Equivalent units are more often used in costing for tangible products, therefore characteristic (iii) does not apply. The correct answer is therefore B.

5 Contract costs

5.1 Contract accounts

FAST FORWARD Contract costs are collected in **contract accounts**.

Guess what contract accounts are similar to? Yes, that's right, the process accounts and job accounts we have covered already. Inputs are recorded on the left hand side, outputs on the right.

5.2 Direct materials

The direct materials used on a contract may be obtained in two ways.

5.2.1 Materials obtained from the company's central stores

(a) A material requisition note must be sent to the store keeper from the contract site. The requisition note provides a record of the cost of the materials issued to the contract.

Contract managers prefer to have too much material, rather than run out. This means that they will often requisition more material than actually needed and the surplus material will need to be returned to stores. As with job costing, the **material returned** is classified as an output and **recorded on the right hand side of the account**.

(b) **Materials on site which** relate to an **incomplete contract** should be **carried forward** as '**closing inventory of materials on site**'.

5.2.2 Materials obtained from the company's suppliers (direct)

The entire invoice cost will be charged directly to the contract.

5.3 Direct labour

It is usual for direct labour on a contract site to be **paid on an hourly basis**. Employees who work on several contracts at the same time will have to record the time spent on each contract on time sheets. Each contract will then be charged with the cost of these recorded hours.

5.4 The cost of supervision and subcontractors

The **cost of supervision**, which is usually a production overhead in unit costing, job costing and so on, will be a **direct cost** of a contract.

On large contracts, much work may be done by **subcontractors**. The invoices of subcontractors will be treated as a **direct expense** to the contract.

5.5 The cost of plant

A feature of most contract work is the amount of plant used. Plant used on a contract may be **owned** by the company, or **hired** from a plant hire firm.

(a) If the plant is **hired**, the cost will be a **direct expense** of the contract.
(b) If the plant is **owned**, a **variety of accounting methods** may be employed.

5.5.1 Method one: Charging depreciation

The contract may be charged depreciation on the plant, on a straight line or reducing balance basis. For example if a company has some plant which cost $10,000 and is depreciated at 10% per annum straight line (to a residual value of nil) and a contract makes use of the plant for six months, a depreciation charge of $500 would be made against the contract. The disadvantage of this method of costing for plant is that the contract site manager is not made directly responsible and accountable for the actual plant in his charge. The contract manager must be responsible for receipt of the plant, returning the plant after it has been used and proper care of the plant while it is being used.

5.5.2 Method two: Charging the contract with current carrying amount

A **more common method** of costing for plant is to **charge the contract with the change in carrying amount of the plant during the period**.

For example, suppose contract number 123 obtained some plant and loose tools from central store on 1 January 20X2. The carrying amount of the plant was $100,000 and the carrying amount of the loose tools was $8,000. On 1 October 20X2, some plant was removed from the site: this plant had a carrying amount on 1 October of $20,000. At 31 December 20X2, the plant remaining on site had a carrying amount of $60,000 and the loose tools had a carrying amount of $5,000.

CONTRACT 123 ACCOUNT

	$		$
1 January 20X2		1 October 20X2	
Plant issued to site	100,000	Plant transferred	20,000
Loose tools issued to site	8,000	31 December 20X2	
		Plant value c/f	60,000
		Loose tools value c/f	5,000
		Depreciation (bal fig)	23,000
	108,000		108,000

The difference between the values on the debit and the credit sides of the account ($20,000 for plant and $3,000 for loose tools) is the depreciation cost of the equipment for the year.

5.5.3 Method three: Using a plant account

A third method of accounting for plant costs is to **open a plant account, which is charged with the depreciation costs and the running costs** (repairs, fuel and so on) **of the equipment**. A notional hire charge is then made to contracts using the plant. For example suppose that a company owns some equipment which is depreciated at the rate of $100 per month. Running costs in May 20X3 are $300. The plant is used on 20 days in the month, 12 days on Contract X and 8 days on Contract Y. The accounting entries would be as follows.

PLANT ACCOUNT

	$		$
Depreciation	100	Contract X (hire for 12 days)	240
Running costs (wages a/c, stores a/c)	300	Contract Y (hire for 8 days)	160
	400		400

CONTRACT X

	$	$
Plant account (notional hire)	240	

CONTRACT Y

	$	$
Plant account (notional hire)	160	

Question — Contract AB3

Contract number AB3 commenced on 1 April and plant with a carrying amount of $300,000 was delivered to the site from central stores. On 1 September further plant was delivered with a carrying amount of $24,000.

Company policy is to depreciate plant at a rate of 20% of the carrying amount each year.

The carrying amount of the plant on site as at 31 December is:

A $200,000
B $250,000
C $257,400
D $277,400

Answer

D

	$
Carrying amount of plant delivered to site	324,000
Depreciation on plant delivered	
1 April $300,000 × 20% × 9/12	(45,000)
1 September $24,000 × 20% × 4/12	(1,600)
Carrying amount of plant on site as at 31 December	277,400

5.6 Overhead costs

Overhead costs are **added periodically** (for example at the end of an accounting period) and are **based on predetermined overhead absorption rates for the period**. You may come across examples where a share of head office general costs is absorbed as an overhead cost to the contract, but this should not happen if the contract is unfinished at the end of the period, because only production overheads should be included in the value of any closing work in progress.

5.7 Recording contract costs

If we ignore, for the moment, profits on a part-finished contract (we'll come to this in a minute), a typical contract account might appear as shown below. Check the items in the account carefully, and notice how the cost (or value) of the work done emerges as work in progress. On an unfinished contract, where no profits are taken mid-way through the contract, this cost of work in progress is carried forward as a closing inventory balance. Here's an example.

PART C INTRODUCTION TO COSTING SYSTEMS

CONTRACT 794

	$		$
Materials requisition from stores	15,247	Materials returned to stores or transferred to other sites	2,100
Materials and equipment purchased	36,300	Proceeds from sale of materials on site and jobbing work for other customers	600
Maintenance and operating costs of plant and vehicles	14,444	Carrying amount of plant transferred	4,800
Hire charges for plant and vehicles not owned	6,500	Materials on site c/d	7,194
Tools and consumables	8,570	Carrying amount of plant on site c/d	6,640
Carrying amount of plant on site b/d	14,300		21,334
Direct wages	23,890	Cost of work done c/d (balancing item)	139,917
Supervisors' and engineers' salaries (proportion relating to time spent on the contract)	13,000		
Other site expenses	12,000		
Overheads (apportioned perhaps on the basis of direct labour hours)	17,000		
	161,251		161,251
Materials on site b/d	7,194		
Carrying amount of plant on site b/d	6,640		
Cost of work done b/d	139,917		

6 Progress payments and retentions

FAST FORWARD

A customer is likely to be required under the terms of the contract to make **progress payments** which are calculated as the **value of work done** and certified by the architect or engineer minus a **retention** minus the payments made to date.

6.1 Progress payment due

       The value of work done and certified by the architect or engineer
minus   **a retention (commonly 10%)**
minus   **the payments made to date**
equals **payment due.**

Thus, if an architect's certificate assesses the value of work done on a contract to be $125,000 and if the retention is 10%, and if $92,000 has already been paid in progress payments the current payment = $125,000 − $12,500 − $92,000 = $20,500.

6.2 Retention monies

Retention monies are released either when the contract is completed and accepted by the customer or within an agreed period after this date.

7 Profits on contracts

You may have noticed that the progress payments do not necessarily give rise to profit immediately because of **retentions**. So how are profits calculated on contracts?

7.1 Example: Profits on contracts completed in one accounting period

If a contract is started and completed in the same accounting period, the calculation of the profit is straightforward, sales minus the cost of the contract. Suppose that a contract, No. 6548, has the following costs.

	$
Direct materials (less returns)	40,000
Direct labour	35,000
Direct expenses	8,000
Plant costs	6,000
Overhead	11,000
	100,000

The work began on 1 February 20X3 and was completed on 15 November 20X3 in the contractor's same accounting year.

The contract price was $120,000 and on 20 November the inspecting engineer issued the final certificate of work done. At that date the customer had already paid $90,000 and the remaining $30,000 was still outstanding at the end of the contractor's accounting period. The contract account would appear as follows.

CONTRACT 6548 ACCOUNT

	$		$
Materials less returns	40,000	Cost of sales (Income statement)	100,000
Labour	35,000		
Expenses	8,000		
Plant cost	6,000		
Overhead	11,000		
	100,000		100,000

The profit on the contract will be treated in the statement of profit or loss as follows.

	$
Revenue	120,000
Cost of sales	(100,000)
	20,000

Here's how we account for the contract revenue (the price is $120,000) and for amount of $30,000 outstanding from the customer (contractee).

WORK CERTIFIED ACCOUNT

	$		$
Revenue (statement of profit or loss)	120,000	Contractee account	120,000
	120,000		120,000

CONTRACTEE (CUSTOMER) ACCOUNT

	$		$
Work certified a/c – value of work certified	120,000	Cash	90,000
		Balance c/f (account receivable in statement of financial position)	30,000
	120,000		120,000

7.2 Taking profits on incomplete contracts

FAST FORWARD

The long duration of a contract usually means that an **estimate** must be made of the profit earned on each **incomplete contract** at the end of the accounting period. This avoids excessive fluctuations in reported profits.

A more difficult problem emerges when a contract is **incomplete** at the end of an accounting period. The contractor may have spent considerable sums of money on the work, and received substantial progress payments, and even if the work is not finished, the contractor will want to claim some profit on the work done so far.

Suppose that a company starts four new contracts in its accounting year to 31 December 20X1, but at the end of the year, none of them has been completed. All of the contracts are eventually completed in the first few months of 20X2 and they make profits of $40,000, $50,000, $60,000 and $70,000 respectively, $220,000 in total. If profits are not taken until the contracts are finished, the company would make no profits at all in 20X1, when most of the work was done, and $220,000 in 20X2. Such violent fluctuations in profitability would be confusing not only to the company's management, but also to shareholders and the investing public at large.

The problem arises because **contracts are for long-term work**, and it is a well-established practice that some profits should be taken in an accounting period, even if the contract is incomplete.

7.2.1 Example: Profits on incomplete contracts

Suppose that contract 246 is started on 1 July 20X2. Costs to 31 December 20X2, when the company's accounting year ends, are derived from the following information.

	$
Direct materials issued from store	18,000
Materials returned to store	400
Direct labour	15,500
Plant issued, at carrying amount 1 July 20X2	32,000
Written-down value of plant 31 December 20X2	24,000
Materials on site, 31 December 20X2	1,600
Overhead costs	2,000

As at 31 December, certificates had been issued for work valued at $50,000 and the contractee had made progress payments of $45,000. The company has calculated that more work has been done since the last certificates were issued, and that the cost of work done but not yet certified is $8,000.

Solution

The contract account would be prepared as follows.

CONTRACT 246 ACCOUNT

	$	$		$
Materials	18,000		Value of plant c/d	24,000
Less returns	400		Materials on site c/d	1,600
		17,600	Cost of work done not certified c/d	8,000
Labour		15,500		
Plant issued at carrying amount		32,000	Cost of sales (statement of profit or loss)	33,500
Overheads		2,000		
		67,100		67,100

10: JOB, BATCH, SERVICE AND CONTRACT COSTING

Points to note

(a) **The work done, but not yet certified, must be valued at cost,** and not at the value of the unissued certificates. It would be imprudent to suppose that the work has been done to the complete satisfaction of the architect or engineer, who may not issue certificates until further work is done.

(b) It would appear that $50,000 should be recognised as revenue and $33,500 as cost of sales leaving $16,500 as net profit. However it is often considered imprudent to claim this full amount of profit, and it is commonly argued that the profit taken should be a more conservative figure (in our example, less than $16,500, so that amounts taken to revenue and cost of sales relating to the contract should be less than $50,000 and $33,500 respectively).

(c) We have ignored retentions here.

Question — Cost bookkeeping and contract costing

Complete the following work certified and contractee accounts.

WORK CERTIFIED ACCOUNT

	$		$
Revenue	☐	Contractee account	☐
	☐		☐

CONTRACTEE ACCOUNT

	$		$
Work certified account	☐	Cash	☐
		Balance c/f	☐
	☐		☐

Answer

WORK CERTIFIED ACCOUNT

	$		$
Revenue	50,000	Contractee account	50,000
	50,000		50,000

CONTRACTEE ACCOUNT

	$		$
Work certified account	50,000	Cash (progress payment)	45,000
		Balance c/f	5,000
	50,000		50,000

7.3 Estimating the size of the profit

FAST FORWARD

There are several different ways of calculating contract profits, but the overriding consideration must be the application of the prudence concept. **If a loss is expected on a contract, the total expected loss should be taken into account as soon as it is recognised, even if the contract is not complete.**

Exam focus

The method of calculating profit on an incomplete contract may vary and you should follow the instructions carefully in any question on contract costing.

The **concept of prudence** should be applied when estimating the size of the profit on an incomplete contract and the guidelines in the following paragraphs should be noted.

7.4 Guidelines for estimating profits

(a) **If the contract is in its early stages, no profit should be taken.** Profit should only be taken when the outcome of the contract can be assessed with reasonable accuracy.

(b) **For a contract on which substantial costs have been incurred, but which is not yet near completion** (that is, it is in the region of 30% to 85% complete) a formula which has often been used in the past is as follows.

> Profit taken = $^2/_3$ (or $^3/_4$) of the notional profit

where notional profit = (the value of work certified to date) – (the cost of the work certified).

In the example above, the notional profit for contract 246 is $16,500 ($(50,000 – 33,500)) and the profit taken for the period using the above formula would be calculated as follows.

$^2/_3$ of $16,500 = $11,000 (or $^3/_4$ of $16,500 = $12,375)

(c) **Where the contractee withholds a retention, or where progress payments are not made as soon as work certificates are issued**, it would be more prudent to reduce the profit taken by the proportion of retentions to the value of work certified.

> Profit taken = $^2/_3$ (or $^3/_4$) × notional profit × $\dfrac{\text{cash received on account}}{\text{value of work certified}}$

In our example of contract 246, this would be:

$^2/_3 \times \$16{,}500 \times \dfrac{\$45{,}000}{\$50{,}000} = \$9{,}900$

(d) **If the contract is nearing completion, the size of the eventual profit should be foreseeable with reasonable certainty and there is no need to be excessively prudent.** The profit taken may be calculated by one of three methods.

   (i) **Work certified to date minus the cost of work certified**. In our example, this would be the full $16,500.

   (ii) Profit taken = $\dfrac{\text{cost of work done}}{\text{estimated total cost of contract}}$ × estimated total profit

   In our example, if the estimated total cost of the contract 246 is $64,000 and the estimated total profit on the contract is $18,000, the profit taken would be:

$$\frac{\$(33,500 + 8,000)}{\$64,000} \times \$18,000 = \$11,672$$

(iii) $$\boxed{\text{Profit taken} = \frac{\text{value of work certified}}{\text{contract price}} \times \text{estimated total profit}}$$

This is perhaps the most-favoured of the three methods. In our example of contract 246, if the final contract price is $82,000 and the estimated total profit is $18,000 the profit taken would be:

$$\frac{\$50,000}{\$82,000} \times \$18,000 = \$10,976$$

Some companies may feel that it is prudent to reduce the profit attributed to the current accounting period still further, to allow for retentions of cash by the contractee. In our example, the profit taken would now be:

$$\frac{\$50,000}{\$82,000} \times \$18,000 \times \frac{\$45,000}{\$50,000} = \$9,878$$

This formula simplifies to:

$$\boxed{\frac{\text{cash received to date}}{\text{contract price}} \times \text{estimated total profit from the contract}}$$

(e) **A loss on the contract may be foreseen.** The method of dealing with losses is covered in the next section.

It should be apparent from these different formulae that the profit taken on an incomplete contract will depend on two things.

- The degree of completion
- The choice of formula

Question — Profits on contracts

LS Company is a construction company. Data relating to one of its contracts, XYZ, for the year to 31 December 20X2, are as follows.

	$'000
Value of work certified to 31 December 20X1	500
Cost of work certified to 31 December 20X1	360
Plant on site b/f at 1 January 20X2	30
Materials on site b/f at 1 January 20X2	10
Cost of contract to 1 January 20X2 b/f	370
Materials issued from store	190
Sub-contractors' costs	200
Wages and salaries	200
Overheads absorbed by contract in 20X2	100
Plant on site c/f at 31 December 20X2	15
Materials on site c/f at 31 December 20X2	5
Value of work certified to 31 December 20X2	1,200
Cost of work certified to 31 December 20X2	950

No profit has been taken on the contract prior to 20X2. There are no retentions.

(a) The total cumulative cost of contract XYZ to the end of December 20X2 is $ ☐.

(b) Revenue on the contract is taken as the value of work certified. The gross profit for the contract for the year to 31 December 20X2 is $ ☐.

Answer

(a) **The cost is $ 1,080,000**.

Workings

CONTRACT ACCOUNT

	$'000		$'000
Cost of contract b/f	370	Plant on site c/f	15
Plant on site b/f	30	Materials on site c/f	5
Materials on site b/f	10	Cost of contract c/f (balance)	1,080
Materials from stores	190		
Sub-contractors' costs	200		
Wages and salaries	200		
Overheads	100		
	1,100		1,100

(b) **The profit is $ 250,000**.

Workings

No profit had been taken on the contract prior to 20X2, and so profit is quite simply calculated as follows.

	$'000
Value of work certified to 31.12.X2	1,200
Cost of work certified to 31.12.X2	950
Gross profit to 31.12.X2	250

8 Losses on incomplete contracts

FAST FORWARD

Any **loss** on a contract should be deducted from the amounts for long-term contracts included under inventories in the statement of financial position. If the resulting balance is a credit, it should be disclosed separately under accounts payable or allowance for liabilities and charges.

At the end of an accounting period, it may be that instead of finding that the contract is profitable, a loss is expected. When this occurs, the **total expected loss should be taken into account as soon as it is recognised, even though the contract is not yet complete.** The contract account should be debited with the **anticipated future loss** (final cost of contract – full contract price – (cost of work at present – value of work certified at present)) and the statement of profit or loss debited with the total expected loss (final cost of contract – full contract price).

The same accounting procedure would be followed on completed contracts, as well as incomplete contracts, but it is essential that the full amount of the loss on the total contract, if foreseeable, should be charged against company profits at the earliest opportunity, even if a contract is incomplete. This means that in the next accounting period, the contract should break even, making neither a profit nor a loss, because the full loss has already been charged to the statement of profit or loss.

8.1 Example: Loss on contract

Contract 257 was begun on 22 March 20X3. By 31 December 20X3, the end of the contractor's accounting year, costs incurred were as follows.

	$
Materials issued	24,000
Materials on site, 31 December	2,000
Labour	36,000
Plant issued to site 22 March	40,000
Written-down value of plant, 31 December	28,000
Overheads	6,000

The contract is expected to end in February 20X4 and at 31 December 20X3, the cost accountant estimated that the final cost of the contract would be $95,000. The full contract price is $90,000. Work certified at 31 December was valued at $72,000. The contractee has made progress payments up to 31 December of $63,000.

Required

Prepare the contract account.

Solution

CONTRACT 257 ACCOUNT

	$		$
Materials issued	24,000	Materials on site c/f	2,000
Labour	36,000	Plant at written-down value, c/f	28,000
Plant issued, written-down value	40,000	Cost of work done c/d (balancing figure)	76,000
Overheads	6,000		
	106,000		106,000
Cost of work done, b/d	76,000	Cost of sales (statement of profit or loss)	77,000
Anticipated future loss*	1,000		
	77,000		77,000

* The total estimated loss on the contract is $5,000 ($90,000 – $95,000). Of this amount $4,000 has been lost in the current period ($76,000 – $72,000) and so $1,000 is anticipated as arising in the future: the company will invoice $18,000 ($90,000 – $72,000) and will incur costs of $19,000 ($95,000 – $76,000). This is taken as a loss in the current period.

The loss is posted $72,000 to revenue and $77,000 to cost of sales ($5,000 net).

Question   Contract account

Jibby Co's year end is 30 April. At 30 April 20X4 costs of $43,750 have been incurred on contract N53. The value of work certified at the period end is $38,615. The contract price is $57,500 but it is anticipated that the final costs at 30 September 20X4, when the contract is expected to end, will be $63,111.

(a) The anticipated future loss on the contract is $ ☐.

(b) The revenue figure for the period to 30 April 20X4 is $ ☐.

(c) The cost of sales figure for the period to 30 April 20X4 is $ ☐.

Answer

(a) The anticipated future loss on the contract is $ 476 .

(b) The revenue figure for the period to 30 April 20X4 is $ 36,615 .

(c) The cost of sales figure for the period to 30 April 20X4 is $ 44,226 .

Workings

CONTRACT N53

	$		$
Cost of work done b/d	43,750	Cost of sales	44,226
Anticipated future loss*	476		
	44,226		44,226

*$[(63,111 − 57,500) − (43,750 − 38,615)] = $476

Chapter roundup

- A **costing method** is designed to suit the way goods are processed or manufactured or the way services are provided.
- **Job costing** is a costing method applied where work is undertaken to customers' special requirements and each order is of comparatively short duration.
- Costs for each job are collected on a **job cost sheet** or **job card**.
- **Material costs** for each job are determined from **material requisition notes**. **Labour times** on each job are recorded on a **job ticket**, which is then costed and recorded on the job cost sheet. Some labour costs, such as overtime premium or the cost of rectifying sub-standard output, might be charged either directly to a job or else as an overhead cost, depending on the circumstances in which the costs have arisen. **Overhead** is absorbed into the cost of jobs using the predetermined overhead absorption rates.
- The usual method of fixing prices within a jobbing concern is **cost plus pricing**.
- It is possible to use a job costing system **to control the costs of an internal service department**, such as the maintenance department or the printing department.
- **Batch costing** is similar to job costing in that each batch of similar articles is separately identifiable. The **cost per unit** manufactured in a batch is the total batch cost divided by the number of units in the batch.
- Service costing can be used by companies operating in a service industry or by companies wishing to establish the cost of services carried out by some of their departments. Service organisations do not make or sell tangible goods.
- Specific characteristics of services
    - Simultaneity
    - Heterogeneity
    - Intangibility
    - Perishability
- The main problem with service costing is the difficulty in **defining a realistic cost unit** that represents a suitable measure of the service provided. Frequently, a composite cost unit may be deemed more appropriate. Hotels, for example, may use the 'occupied bed-night' as an appropriate cost unit for ascertainment and control.
- Service department costing is also used to establish a specific cost for an internal service which is a service provided by one department for another, rather than sold externally to customers eg canteen, maintenance.
- Contract costs are collected in **contract accounts**.
- A customer is likely to be required under the terms of the contract to make **progress payments** which are calculated as the **value of work done** and certified by the architect or engineer minus a **retention** minus the payments made to date.
- The long duration of a contract usually means that an **estimate** must be made of the profit earned on each **incomplete contract** at the end of the accounting period. This avoids excessive fluctuations in reported profits.

PART C INTRODUCTION TO COSTING SYSTEMS

- There are several different ways of calculating contract profits, but the overriding consideration must be the application of the prudence concept. **If a loss is expected on a contract, the total expected loss should be taken into account as soon as it is recognised, even if the contract is not complete.**

- Any **loss** on a contract should be deducted from the amounts for long-term contracts included under inventories in the statement of financial position. If the resulting balance is a credit, it should be disclosed separately under accounts payable or allowances for liabilities and charges.

Quick quiz

1 How are the material costs for each job determined?

2 Which of the following are not characteristics of job costing?

    I   Customer driven production
    II   Complete production possible within a single accounting period
    III Homogeneous products

    A   I and II only   C   II and III only
    B   I and III only   D   III only

3 The cost of a job is $100,000

    (a)   If profit is 25% of the job cost, the price of the job = $..................
    (b)   If there is a 25% margin, the price of the job = $.....................

4 What is a batch?

5 How would you calculate the cost per unit of a completed batch?

6 Define service costing.

7 Match up the following services with their typical cost units.

Service	Cost unit
Hotels	Patient-day
Education	Meal served
Hospitals	Full-time student
Catering organisations	Occupied bed-night

8 What is the advantage of organisations within an industry using a common cost unit?

9 Cost per service unit = ...

10 Service department costing is used to establish a specific cost for an 'internal service' which is a service provided by one department for another.

    True   ☐

    False ☐

11 List six features of contract costing.

- ....
- ....
- ....
- ....
- ....
- ....

12 What are the three methods of calculating profit on a contract which is nearing completion?

(a) .... minus ....

(b) $\dfrac{\text{........................}}{\text{........................}}$ × ....

(c) $\dfrac{\text{........................}}{\text{........................}}$ × ....

13 How would you account for a loss on an incomplete contract?

Answers to quick quiz

1. From materials requisition notes, or from suppliers' invoices if materials are purchased specifically for a particular job.

2. D

3. (a) $100,000 + (25\% \times \$100,000) = \$100,000 + \$25,000 = \$125,000$

   (b) Let price of job = x

   $$\therefore \text{Profit} = 25\% \times x \text{ (selling price)}$$
   $$\text{If profit} = 0.25x$$
   $$x - 0.25x = \text{cost of job}$$
   $$0.75x = \$100,000$$
   $$x = \frac{\$100,000}{0.75}$$
   $$= \$133,333$$

4. A group of similar articles which maintains its identity during one or more stages of production and is treated as a cost unit

5. $\dfrac{\text{Total batch cost}}{\text{Number of units in the batch}}$

6. Cost accounting for services or functions eg canteens, maintenance, personnel (service centres/functions)

7.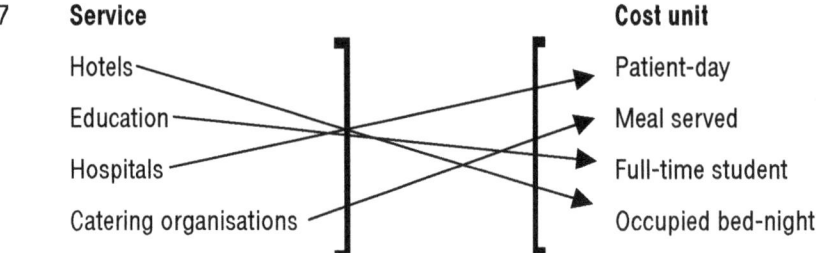

8. It is easier to make comparisons.

9. Cost per service unit = $\dfrac{\text{Total costs for period}}{\text{Number of service units in the period}}$

10. True

11. - A formal contract is made between customer and supplier.
    - Work is undertaken to customers' special requirements.
    - The work is for a relatively long duration.
    - The work is frequently constructional in nature.
    - The method of costing is similar to job costing.
    - The work is frequently based on site.

12. (a) Work certified to date – cost of work certified

    (b) $\dfrac{\text{Cost of work done}}{\text{Estimated total cost of contract}} \times$ estimated total profit on contract

    (c) $\dfrac{\text{Value of work certified}}{\text{Contract price}} \times$ estimated total profit on contract

13. If a loss is expected on an incomplete contract, the total expected loss should be taken into account as soon as it is recognised, even though the contract is not yet complete.

End of chapter question

Job costing

A company which uses a job-costing system is in the process of preparing its accounts for the year 20X9. Stocks of finished goods at the beginning of the year amounted to $250,000. In addition the company had opening stocks of materials of $50,000 and work-in-progress of $30,000.

You have been provided with the following information for the year 20X9.

(i) During the year, $400,000 of materials (direct and indirect) were purchased and paid for.

(ii) $355,000 materials were issued to production as direct materials and another $50,000 issued to production as indirect materials.

(iii) Total labour cost incurred during the period amounted to $110,000. Out of this $65,000 was classified as direct labour. The balance is indirect labour.

(iv) Repairs to machinery during the period amounted to $47,000.

(v) Selling and administration costs were $108,000.

(vi) Completed production during the period amounted to $206,000.

(vii) Goods costing $201,000 were sold for $400,000 during the period.

(viii) Manufacturing overhead is absorbed on the basis of 200% of direct labour costs. Any over- or under-absorbed overheads are charged to cost of goods sold.

Required

(a) Prepare journal entries to record the above transactions for 20X9. **(14 marks)**
(b) Prepare a statement of profit or loss for the period. **(3 marks)**
(c) Comment on the suggestion that job costing is more accurate than process costing. **(3 marks)**

(Total = 20 marks)

PART C INTRODUCTION TO COSTING SYSTEMS

Information for planning and performance management

Budgeting

Topic list	Syllabus reference
1 Budgetary planning and control systems	C4.1
2 The preparation of budgets	C4.2
3 The sales budget	C4.2
4 Production and related budgets	C4.2
5 Fixed and flexible budgets	C4.2
6 Preparing flexible budgets	C4.2
7 Flexible budgets and budgetary control	C4.2
8 Budgeting, performance and motivation	C4.2
9 Further budgeting techniques	C4.2

Introduction

This chapter covers the topic, **budgeting**. You will meet the topic at all stages of your future examination studies and so it is vital that you get a firm grasp of it now.

The first seven topic areas deal with the process of budgeting, you could see it as the mechanics of budgeting.

The final topics examines the human aspect of budgeting and further budgeting techniques.

PART C4 INFORMATION FOR PLANNING AND PERFORMANCE MANAGEMENT

1 Budgetary planning and control systems

FAST FORWARD

A **budget** is a quantified plan of action for a forthcoming accounting period. A **budget** is a plan of what the organisation is aiming to achieve and what is has set as a target whereas a **forecast** is an estimate of what is likely to occur in the future.

Key term

The **budget** is 'a quantitative statement for a defined period of time, which may include planned revenues, expenses, assets, liabilities and cash flows. A budget facilitates planning'.

There is, however, little point in an organisation simply preparing a budget for the sake of preparing a budget. A beautifully laid out budgeted statement of profit or loss filed in the cost accountant's file and never looked at again is worthless. The organisation should gain from both the actual preparation process and from the budget once it has been prepared.

FAST FORWARD

The **objectives** of a budgetary planning and control system are as follows.

- To ensure the achievement of the organisation's objectives
- To compel planning
- To communicate ideas and plans
- To co-ordinate activities
- To provide a framework for responsibility accounting
- To establish a system of control
- To motivate employees to improve their performance

Budgets are therefore not prepared in isolation and then filed away but are the fundamental components of what is known as the **budgetary planning and control system**. A budgetary planning and control system is essentially a system for ensuring **communication**, **coordination** and **control** within an organisation. Communication, coordination and control are general objectives: more information is provided by an inspection of the specific objectives of a budgetary planning and control system.

Objective	Comment
Ensure the achievement of the organisation's objectives	Objectives are set for the organisation as a whole, and for individual departments and operations within the organisation. Quantified expressions of these objectives are then drawn up as targets to be achieved within the timescale of the budget plan.
Compel planning	This is probably the most important feature of a budgetary planning and control system. Planning forces management to look ahead, to set out detailed plans for achieving the targets for each department, operation and (ideally) each manager and to anticipate problems. It thus prevents management from relying on ad hoc or uncoordinated planning which may be detrimental to the performance of the organisation. It also helps managers to **foresee potential threats or opportunities**, so that they may **take action now** to avoid or minimise the effect of the threats and to take full advantage of the opportunities.
Communicate ideas and plans	A formal system is necessary to ensure that each person affected by the plans is aware of what he or she is supposed to be doing. Communication might be one-way, with managers giving orders to subordinates, or there might be a two-way dialogue and exchange of ideas.

Objective	Comment
Coordinate activities	The activities of different departments or sub-units of the organisation need to be coordinated to ensure maximum integration of effort towards common goals. This concept of coordination implies, for example, that the purchasing department should base its budget on production requirements and that the production budget should in turn be based on sales expectations. Although straightforward in concept, coordination is remarkably difficult to achieve, and there is often **'sub-optimality'** and conflict between departmental plans in the budget so that the efforts of each department are not fully integrated into a combined plan to achieve the company's best targets.
Provide a framework for responsibility accounting	Budgetary planning and control systems require that managers of **budget centres** are made responsible for the achievement of budget targets for the operations under their personal control.
Establish a system of control	A budget is a **yardstick** against which actual performance is monitored and assessed. Control over actual performance is provided by the comparisons of actual results against the budget plan. Departures from budget can then be investigated and the reasons for the departures can be divided into **controllable** and **uncontrollable** factors.
Motivate employees to improve their performance	The interest and commitment of employees can be retained via a system of feedback of actual results, which lets them know how well or badly they are performing. The identification of controllable reasons for departures from budget with managers responsible provides an incentive for improving future performance.
Provide a framework for authorisation	Once the budget has been agreed by the directors and senior managers it acts as an authorisation for each budget holder to incur the costs included in the budget centre's budget. **As long as the expenditure is included in the formalised budget** the budget holder can carry out day to day operations without needing to seek separate authorisation for each item of expenditure.
Provide a basis for performance evaluation	As well as providing a yardstick for control by comparison, the monitoring of actual results compared with the budget can provide a basis for **evaluating the performance of the budget holder.** As a result of this evaluation the manager might be rewarded, perhaps with a financial bonus or promotion. Alternatively the evaluation process might highlight the need for more investment in staff development and training.

2 The preparation of budgets

Having seen why organisations prepare budgets, we will now turn our attention to the mechanics of budget preparation. We will begin by defining and explaining a number of terms.

PART C4 INFORMATION FOR PLANNING AND PERFORMANCE MANAGEMENT

2.1 Planning

Key term

Planning is the establishment of objectives, and the formulation of the policies, strategies and tactics required to achieve them. Planning comprises long-term/strategic planning, and short-term operation planning.

2.1.1 The value of long-term planning

A **budgetary planning and control system** operating in **isolation** without any form of long-term planning as a framework is **unlikely to produce maximum potential benefits** for an organisation.

(a) **Without stated long-term objectives**, managers **do not know what they should be trying to achieve** and so there are **no criteria against which to assess possible courses of action**.

(b) Without long-term planning, budgets may simply be based on a sales forecast. Performance can therefore only be judged in terms of previous years' results, **no analysis of the organisation's potential** having been carried out.

(c) Many business **decisions need to be taken on a long-term basis**. For instance, **new products** cannot simply be introduced when sales of existing products begin to decline. Likewise, **capital equipment** cannot necessarily be purchased and installed in the short term if production volumes start to increase.

(d) With long-term planning, **limiting factors** (other than sales) which might arise can possibly be anticipated, and avoided or overcome.

2.2 The budget period

Except for capital expenditure budgets, the budget period is commonly the accounting year (sub-divided into 12 or 13 control periods).

2.3 The budget manual

Key term

The **budget manual** is a collection of instructions governing the responsibilities of persons and the procedures, forms and records relating to the preparation and use of budgetary data.

Likely contents of a budget manual	Examples
An explanation of the objectives of the budgetary process	• The purpose of budgetary planning and control • The objectives of the various stages of the budgetary process • The importance of budgets in the long-term planning and administration of the enterprise
Organisational structures	• An organisation chart • A list of individuals holding budget responsibilities
Principal budgets	• An outline of each • The relationship between them
Administrative details of budget preparation	• Membership and terms of reference of the budget committee • The sequence in which budgets are to be prepared • A timetable
Procedural matters	• Specimen forms and instructions for their completion • Specimen reports • Account codes (or a chart of accounts) • The name of the budget officer to whom enquiries must be sent

2.4 The responsibility for preparing budgets

The initial responsibility for preparing the budget will normally be with the managers (and their subordinates) who will be carrying out the budget, selling goods or services and authorising expenditure. However, the budget is normally set as part of a longer process, involving the authorisation of set targets by senior management and the negotiation process with the budget holders. Depending on the size of the organisation there may be a large number of **budget centres** and a separate **budget holder** would be responsible for setting and achieving the budget for the centre.

Examples of the functional budgets that would be prepared and **the managers responsible for their preparation** are as follows.

(a) The **sales manager** should draft the **sales budget** and **selling overhead** cost centre budgets.

(b) The **purchasing manager** should draft the **material purchases** budget.

(c) The **production manager** should draft the **direct production** cost budgets.

(d) Various **cost centre managers** should prepare the individual production, administration and distribution cost centre budgets for their own cost centre.

(e) The **cost accountant** will **analyse** the budgeted overheads to determine the overhead absorption rates for the next budget period.

2.5 Budget committee

> **FAST FORWARD**
>
> The **budget committee** is the co-ordinating body in the preparation and administration of budgets.

The **co-ordination** and **administration** of budgets is usually the responsibility of a **budget committee** (with the managing director as chair).

(a) The budget committee is assisted by a **budget officer** who is usually an accountant. Every part of the organisation should be represented on the committee, so there should be a representative from sales, production, marketing and so on.

(b) **Functions of the budget committee**

   (i) **Co-ordination** of the preparation of budgets, which includes the issue of the budget manual.

   (ii) **Issuing of timetables** for the preparation of functional budgets.

   (iii) **Allocation of responsibilities** for the preparation of functional budgets.

   (iv) **Provision of information** to assist in the preparation of budgets.

   (v) **Communication of final budgets** to the appropriate managers.

   (vi) **Comparison** of actual results with budget and the investigation of variances.

   (vii) **Continuous assessment** of the budgeting and planning process, in order to improve the planning and control function.

2.6 Budget preparation

Let us now look at the steps involved in the preparation of a budget. The procedures will differ from organisation to organisation, but the step-by-step approach described in this chapter is indicative of the steps followed by many organisations. The preparation of a budget may take weeks or months, and the budget committee may meet several times before the functional budgets are co-ordinated and the master budget is finally agreed.

2.7 The principal budget factor

FAST FORWARD

The **principal budget factor** should be identified at the beginning of the budgetary process, and the budget for this is prepared before all the others.

After determining the company's long-term objectives, the first task in the budgetary process is to identify the **principal budget factor**. This is also known as the **key** budget factor or **limiting** budget factor.

Key term

The **principal budget factor** is the factor which limits the activities of an organisation.

Likely principal budget factors

(a) The **principal budget factor** is usually **sales demand**: a company is usually restricted from making and selling more of its products because there would be no sales demand for the increased output at a price which would be acceptable/profitable to the company.

(b) Other possible factors

    (i)   Machine capacity   (iii)   The availability of key raw materials
    (ii)   Distribution and selling resources   (iv)   The availability of cash

Once this factor is defined then the remainder of the budgets can be prepared. For example, if sales are the principal budget factor then the production manager can only prepare his budget after the sales budget is complete.

Management may not know what the limiting budget factor is until a draft budget has been attempted. The first draft budget will therefore usually begin with the preparation of a draft sales budget.

Question — Budgets

A company that manufactures and sells a range of products, with sales potential limited by market share, is considering introducing a system of budgeting.

Required

(a) List (in order of preparation) the functional budgets that need to be prepared.

(b) State which budgets will comprise the master budget.

(c) Consider how the work outlined in (a) and (b) can be co-ordinated in order for the budgeting process to be successful.

Answer

(a) The **sequence of budget preparation** will be roughly as follows.

    (i)   Sales budget (The market share limits demand and so sales is the principal budget factor. All other activities will depend upon this forecast.)

    (ii)   Finished goods inventory budget (in units)

    (iii) Production budget (in units)

    (iv) Production resources budgets (materials, machine hours, labour)

    (v)   Overhead budgets for production, administration, selling and distribution, research and development and so on

Other budgets required will be the capital expenditure budget, the working capital budget (receivables and payables) and, very importantly, the cash budget.

(b) The **master budget** is the summary of all the functional budgets. It often includes a summary statement of profit or loss and statement of financial position.

(c) Procedures for preparing budgets can be contained in a **budget manual** which shows which budgets must be prepared when and by whom, what each functional budget should contain and detailed directions on how to prepare budgets including, for example, expected price increases, rates of interest, rates of depreciation and so on.

The formulation of budgets can be co-ordinated by a **budget committee** comprising the senior executives of the departments responsible for carrying out the budgets: sales, production, purchasing, personnel and so on.

The budgeting process may also be assisted by the use of a **spreadsheet/computer budgeting package**.

3 The sales budget

We have already established that, for many organisations, the principal budget factor is sales volume. The sales budget is therefore **often the primary budget** from which the majority of the other budgets are derived.

Before the sales budget can be prepared a sales forecast has to be made. A **forecast** is an estimate of what is likely to occur in the future. A budget, in contrast, is a plan of what the organisation is aiming to achieve and what it has set as a target.

On the basis of the sales forecast and the production capacity of the organisation, a sales budget will be prepared. This may be subdivided, possible subdivisions being by product, by sales area, by management responsibility and so on.

Once the sales budget has been agreed, related budgets can be prepared.

4 Production and related budgets

If the principal budget factor was production capacity then the production budget would be the first to be prepared. To assess whether production is the principal budget factor, the **production capacity available** must be determined, taking account of a number of factors.

- **Available labour**, including idle time, overtime and standard output rates per hour.
- **Availability of raw materials** including allowances for losses during production.
- **Maximum machine hours available**, including expected idle time and expected output rates per machine hour.

It is, however, normally sales volume that is the constraint and therefore the production budget is usually prepared after the sales budget and the finished goods inventory budget.

The production budget will show the quantities and costs for each product and product group and will tie in with the sales and inventory budgets. This co-ordinating process is likely to show any shortfalls or excesses in capacity at various times over the budget period.

If there is likely to be a **shortfall** then consideration should be given to how this can be avoided. Possible **options** include the following.

- Overtime working
- Subcontracting
- Machine hire
- New sources of raw materials

A significant shortfall means that production capacity is, in fact, the limiting factor.

PART C4 INFORMATION FOR PLANNING AND PERFORMANCE MANAGEMENT

If **capacity exceeds sales volume** for a length of time then consideration should be given to **product diversification**, a **reduction in selling price** (if demand is price elastic) and so on.

Once the production budget has been finalised, the labour, materials and machine budgets can be drawn up. These budgets will be based on budgeted activity levels, planned inventory positions and projected labour and material costs.

4.1 Example: The production budget and direct labour budget

Landy manufactures two products, A and B, and is preparing its budget for 20X3. Both products are made by the same grade of labour, grade Q. The company currently holds 800 units of A and 1,200 units of B in inventory, but 250 of these units of B have just been discovered to have deteriorated in quality, and must therefore be scrapped. Budgeted sales of A are 3,000 units and of B 4,000 units, provided that the company maintains finished goods inventories at a level equal to three months' sales.

Grade Q labour was originally expected to produce one unit of A in two hours and one unit of B in three hours, at an hourly rate of $2.50 per hour. In discussions with trade union negotiators, however, it has been agreed that the hourly wage rate should be raised by 50c per hour, provided that the times to produce A and B are reduced by 20%.

Required

Prepare the production budget and direct labour budget for 20X3.

Solution

The expected time to produce a unit of A will now be 80% of 2 hours = 1.6 hours, and the time for a unit of B will be 2.4 hours. The hourly wage rate will be $3, so that the direct labour cost will be $4.80 for A and $7.20 for B (thus achieving a saving for the company of 20c per unit of A produced and 30c per unit of B).

(a) **Production budget**

	Product A		Product B	
	Units	Units	Units	Units
Budgeted sales		3,000		4,000
Closing inventories ($^3/_{12}$ of 3,000)	750	($^3/_{12}$ of 4,000)	1,000	
Opening inventories (minus inventories scrapped)	800		950	
(Decrease)/increase in inventories		(50)		50
Production		2,950		4,050

(b) **Direct labour budget**

	Grade Q Hours	Cost $
2,950 units of product A	4,720	14,160
4,050 units of product B	9,720	29,160
Total	14,440	43,320

It is assumed that there will be no idle time among grade Q labour which, if it existed, would have to be paid for at the rate of $3 per hour.

4.2 The standard hour

Key term

A **standard hour** or standard minute is the amount of work achievable at standard efficiency levels in that time period.

This is a useful concept in budgeting for labour requirements. For example, budgeted **output of different products or jobs** in a period could be converted into standard hours of production, and a labour budget constructed accordingly.

Standard hours are particularly useful when management wants to monitor the production levels of a variety of dissimilar units. For example product A may take five hours to produce and product B, seven hours. If four units of each product are produced, instead of saying that total output is eight units, we could state the production level as (4 × 5) + (4 × 7) standard hours = 48 standard hours.

4.3 Example: Direct labour budget based on standard hours

Truro manufactures a single product, Q, with a single grade of labour. Its sales budget and finished goods inventory budget for period 3 are as follows.

Sales	700 units
Opening inventories, finished goods	50 units
Closing inventories, finished goods	70 units

The goods are inspected only when production work is completed, and it is budgeted that 10% of finished work will be scrapped.

The standard direct labour hour content of product Q is three hours. The budgeted productivity ratio for direct labour is only 80% (which means that labour is only working at 80% efficiency).

The company employs 18 direct operatives, who are expected to average 144 working hours each in period 3.

Required

(a) Prepare a production budget.

(b) Prepare a direct labour budget.

(c) Comment on the problem that your direct labour budget reveals, and suggest how this problem might be overcome.

Solution

(a) **Production budget**

	Units
Sales	700
Add closing inventory	70
	770
Less opening inventory	50
Production required of 'good' output	720
Wastage rate	10%

Total production required $720 \times \dfrac{100^*}{90} = 800$ units

(* Note that the required adjustment is 100/90, not 110/100, since the waste is assumed to be 10% of total production, not 10% of good production.)

(b) Now we can prepare the **direct labour budget**.

Standard hours per unit	3
Total standard hours required = 800 units × 3 hours	2,400 hours
Productivity ratio	80%

Actual hours required $2,400 \times \dfrac{100}{80} = 3,000$ hours

(c) If we look at the **direct labour budget** against the information provided, we can identify the problem.

	Hours
Budgeted hours available (18 operatives × 144 hours)	2,592
Actual hours required	3,000
Shortfall in labour hours	408

The (draft) budget indicates that there will not be enough direct labour hours to meet the production requirements.

(d) **Overcoming insufficient labour hours**

(i) **Reduce the closing inventory** requirement below 70 units. This would reduce the number of production units required.

(ii) Persuade the workforce to do some **overtime** working.

(iii) Perhaps **recruit** more direct labour if long-term prospects are for higher production volumes.

(iv) **Improve** the **productivity** ratio, and so reduce the number of hours required to produce the output.

(v) If possible, **reduce** the **wastage** rate below 10%.

4.4 Example: The material purchases budget

Tremor manufactures two products, S and T, which use the same raw materials, D and E. One unit of S uses 3 litres of D and 4 kilograms of E. One unit of T uses 5 litres of D and 2 kilograms of E. A litre of D is expected to cost $3 and a kilogram of E $7.

Budgeted sales for 20X2 are 8,000 units of S and 6,000 units of T; finished goods in inventory at 1 January 20X2 are 1,500 units of S and 300 units of T, and the company plans to hold inventories of 600 units of each product at 31 December 20X2.

Inventories of raw material are 6,000 litres of D and 2,800 kilograms of E at 1 January, and the company plans to hold 5,000 litres and 3,500 kilograms respectively at 31 December 20X2.

The warehouse and stores managers have suggested that a provision should be made for damages and deterioration of items held in store, as follows.

Product S:	loss of 50 units	Material D:	loss of 500 litres
Product T:	loss of 100 units	Material E:	loss of 200 kilograms

Required

Prepare a material purchases budget for the year 20X2.

Solution

To calculate material purchase requirements, it is first of all necessary to calculate the budgeted production volumes and material usage requirements.

	Product S		Product T	
	Units	Units	Units	Units
Sales		8,000		6,000
Provision for losses		50		100
Closing inventory	600		600	
Opening inventory	1,500		300	
(Decrease)/increase in inventory		(900)		300
Production budget		7,150		6,400

	Material D		Material E	
	Litres	Litres	Kg	Kg
Usage requirements				
To produce 7,150 units of S		21,450		28,600
To produce 6,400 units of T		32,000		12,800
Usage budget		53,450		41,400
Provision for losses		500		200
		53,950		41,600
Closing inventory	5,000		3,500	
Opening inventory	6,000		2,800	
(Decrease)/increase in inventory		(1,000)		700
Material purchases budget		52,950		42,300
	Material D		Material E	
Cost per unit	$3 per litre		$7 per kg	
Cost of material purchases	$158,850		$296,100	
Total purchases cost		$454,950		

Question — Material purchases budget

J purchases a basic commodity and then refines it for resale. Budgeted sales of the refined product are as follows.

	April	May	June
Sales in kg	9,000	8,000	7,000

- The basic raw material costs $3 per kg.
- Material losses are 10% of finished output.
- The target month-end raw material inventory level is 5,000 kg plus 25% of the raw material required for next month's budgeted production.
- The target month-end inventory level for finished goods is 6,000 kg plus 25% of next month's budgeted sales.

What are the budgeted raw material purchases for April?

A   8,500 kg   C   9,447 kg
B   9,350 kg   D   9,722 kg

PART C4 INFORMATION FOR PLANNING AND PERFORMANCE MANAGEMENT

Answer

The correct answer is C.

	March kg	April kg	May kg
Required finished inventory:			
Base inventory	6,000	6,000	6,000
+ 25% of next month's sales	2,250	2,000	1,750
= Required inventory	8,250	8,000	7,750
Sales for month		9,000	8,000
		17,000	15,750
Less opening inventory		8,250	8,000
Required finished production		8,750	7,750
Wastage rate as % of finished output		10%	10%
Raw material required		$8{,}750 \times \dfrac{100}{90}$ = 9,722 kg	$7{,}750 \times \dfrac{100}{90}$ = 8,611 kg
25% required for closing inventory		2,430.5 kg	2,152.75 kg
Required material inventory:			
Base inventory	5,000.00	5,000.00	
+ 25% of material for next month's production	2,430.50	2,152.75	
= Required closing material inventory	7,430.50	7,152.75	
Production requirements		9,722.00	
		16,874.75	
Less opening inventory		7,430.50	
Required material purchases		9,444.25	

4.5 Non-production overheads

In the modern business environment, an increasing proportion of overheads are not directly related to the volume of production, such as administration overheads and research and development costs.

4.6 Key decisions in the budgeting process for non-production overheads

Deciding which fixed costs are committed (will be incurred no matter what) and which fixed costs will depend on management decisions.

Deciding what factors will influence the level of variable costs. Administration costs for example may be partly governed by the number of orders received.

5 Fixed and flexible budgets

FAST FORWARD

> **Fixed budgets** remain unchanged regardless of the level of activity; **flexible budgets** are designed to flex with the level of activity.
>
> **Flexible budgets** are prepared using marginal costing and so mixed costs must be split into their fixed and variable components (possibly using the **high/low method**).

5.1 Fixed budgets

The master budget prepared before the beginning of the budget period is known as the **fixed** budget. By the term 'fixed', we do not mean that the budget is kept unchanged. Revisions to a fixed master budget will be made if the situation so demands. The term 'fixed' means the following.

(a) The budget is prepared on the basis of an estimated volume of production and an estimated volume of sales, but no plans are made for the event that actual volumes of production and sales may differ from budgeted volumes.

(b) When actual volumes of production and sales during a control period (month or four weeks or quarter) are achieved, a fixed budget is not adjusted (in retrospect) to represent a new target for the new levels of activity.

The major purpose of a fixed budget lies in its use at the planning stage, when it seeks to define the broad objectives of the organisation.

Key term

> A **fixed budget** is a budget which is normally set prior to the start of an accounting period, and which is not changed in response to changes in activity or costs/revenues.

Fixed budgets (in terms of a **pre-set expenditure limit**) are also useful for **controlling any fixed cost**, and **particularly non-production fixed costs** such as advertising, because such costs should be unaffected by changes in activity level (within a certain range).

5.2 Flexible budgets

FAST FORWARD

> Comparison of a fixed budget with the actual results for a different level of activity is of little use for **budgetary control purposes**. Flexible budgets should be used to show what cost and revenues should have been for the actual level of activity. Differences between the flexible budget figures and actual results are **variances**.

Key term

> A **flexible budget** is a budget which is designed to change as volume of activity changes.

Two uses of flexible budgets

(a) **At the planning stage**. For example, suppose that a company expects to sell 10,000 units of output during the next year. A master budget (the fixed budget) would be prepared on the basis of these expected volumes. However, if the company thinks that output and sales might be as low as 8,000 units or as high as 12,000 units, it may prepare **contingency** flexible budgets, at volumes of, say 8,000, 9,000, 11,000 and 12,000 units, and then assess the possible outcomes.

(b) **Retrospectively**. At the end of each control period, flexible budgets can be used to compare actual results achieved with what results should have been under the circumstances. Flexible budgets are an essential factor in budgetary control.

   (i) Management needs to know about how good or bad actual performance has been. To provide a measure of performance, there must be a yardstick (budget/ standard) against which actual performance can be measured.

   (ii) Every business is dynamic, and actual volumes of output cannot be expected to conform exactly to the fixed budget. Comparing actual costs directly with the fixed budget costs is meaningless.

   (iii) For useful control information, it is necessary to compare actual results at the actual level of activity achieved against the results that should have been expected at this level of activity, which are shown by the flexible budget.

6 Preparing flexible budgets

6.1 Example: Fixed and flexible budgets

Suppose that Gemma expects production and sales during the next year to be 90% of the company's output capacity, that is, 9,000 units of a single product. Cost estimates will be made using the high-low method and the following historical records of cost.

Units of output/sales	Cost of sales
	$
9,800	44,400
7,700	38,100

The company's management is not certain that the estimate of sales is correct, and has asked for flexible budgets to be prepared at output and sales levels of 8,000 and 10,000 units. The sales price per unit has been fixed at $5.

Required

Prepare appropriate budgets.

Solution

If we assume that within the range 8,000 to 10,000 units of sales, all costs are fixed, variable or mixed (in other words there are no stepped costs, material discounts, overtime premiums, bonus payments and so on) the fixed and flexible budgets would be based on the estimate of fixed and variable cost.

		$
Total cost of 9,800 units	=	44,400
Total cost of 7,700 units	=	38,100
Variable cost of 2,100 units	=	6,300

The variable cost per unit is $3.

		$
Total cost of 9,800 units	=	44,400
Variable cost of 9,800 units (9,800 × $3)	=	29,400
Fixed costs (all levels of output and sales)	=	15,000

The fixed budgets and flexible budgets can now be prepared as follows.

	Flexible budget 8,000 units	Fixed budget 9,000 units	Flexible budget 10,000 units
	$	$	$
Sales (× $5)	40,000	45,000	50,000
Variable costs (× $3)	24,000	27,000	30,000
Contribution	16,000	18,000	20,000
Fixed costs	15,000	15,000	15,000
Profit	1,000	3,000	5,000

6.2 The need for flexible budgets

We have seen that flexible budgets may be prepared in order to plan for variations in the level of activity above or below the level set in the fixed budget. It has been suggested, however, that since many cost items in modern industry are fixed costs, the value of flexible budgets in planning is dwindling.

(a) In many manufacturing industries, plant costs (depreciation, rent and so on) are a very large proportion of total costs, and these tend to be fixed costs.

(b) Wage costs also tend to be fixed, because employees are generally guaranteed a basic wage for a working week of an agreed number of hours.

(c) With the growth of service industries, labour (wages or fixed salaries) and overheads will account for most of the costs of a business, and direct materials will be a relatively small proportion of total costs.

Flexible budgets are nevertheless necessary, and even if they are not used at the planning stage, they must be used for budgetary control variance analysis.

7 Flexible budgets and budgetary control

> **FAST FORWARD**
>
> Budgetary control is based around a system of **budget centres**. Each centre has its own budget which is the responsibility of the **budget holder**.

In other words, individual managers are held responsible for investigating differences between budgeted and actual results, and are then expected to take corrective action or amend the plan in the light of actual events.

It is therefore vital to ensure that valid comparisons are being made. Consider the following example.

7.1 Example

Penny manufactures a single product, the Darcy. Budgeted results and actual results for May are as follows.

	Budget	Actual	Variance
Production and sales of the Darcy (units)	7,500	8,200	
	$	$	$
Sales revenue	75,000	81,000	6,000 (F)
Direct materials	22,500	23,500	1,000 (A)
Direct labour	15,000	15,500	500 (A)
Production overhead	22,500	22,800	300 (A)
Administration overhead	10,000	11,000	1,000 (A)
	70,000	72,800	2,800 (A)
Profit	5,000	8,200	3,200 (F)

Note. (F) denotes a favourable variance and (A) an unfavourable or adverse variance.

In this example, the variances are meaningless for the purposes of control. All costs were higher than budgeted but the volume of output was also higher; it is to be expected that actual variable costs would be greater those included in the fixed budget. However, it is not possible to tell how much of the increase is due to **poor cost control** and how much is due to the **increase in activity**.

Similarly it is not possible to tell how much of the increase in sales revenue is due to the increase in activity. Some of the difference may be due to a difference between budgeted and actual selling price but we are unable to tell from the analysis above.

For control purposes we need to know the answers to questions such as the following.

- Were actual costs higher than they should have been to produce and sell 8,200 Darcys?
- Was actual revenue satisfactory from the sale of 8,200 Darcys?

Instead of comparing actual results with a fixed budget which is based on a different level of activity to that actually achieved, the correct approach to budgetary control is to compare actual results with a budget which has been **flexed** to the actual activity level achieved.

Suppose that we have the following estimates of the behaviour of Penny's costs.

(a) Direct materials and direct labour are variable costs.

(b) Production overhead is a semi-variable cost, the budgeted cost for an activity level of 10,000 units being $25,000.

(c) Administration overhead is a fixed cost.

(d) Selling prices are constant at all levels of sales.

Solution

The **budgetary control analysis** should therefore be as follows.

	Fixed budget	Flexible budget	Actual results	Variance
Production and sales (units)	7,500	8,200	8,200	
	$	$	$	$
Sales revenue	75,000	82,000 (W1)	81,000	1,000 (A)
Direct materials	22,500	24,600 (W2)	23,500	1,100 (F)
Direct labour	15,000	16,400 (W3)	15,500	900 (F)
Production overhead	22,500	23,200 (W4)	22,800	400 (F)
Administration overhead	10,000	10,000 (W5)	11,000	1,000 (A)
	70,000	74,200	72,800	1,400 (F)
Profit	5,000	7,800	8,200	400 (F)

Workings

1. Selling price per unit = $75,000 ÷ 7,500 = $10 per unit
   Flexible budget sales revenue = $10 × 8,200 = $82,000

2. Direct materials cost per unit = $22,500 ÷ 7,500 = $3
   Budget cost allowance = $3 × 8,200 = $24,600

3. Direct labour cost per unit = $15,000 ÷ 7,500 = $2
   Budget cost allowance = $2 × 8,200 = $16,400

4. Variable production overhead cost per unit = $(25,000 − 22,500)/(10,000 − 7,500)
   = $2,500/2,500 = $1 per unit

   ∴ Fixed production overhead cost = $22,500 − (7,500 × $1) = $15,000
   ∴ Budget cost allowance = $15,000 + (8,200 × $1) = $23,200

5. Administration overhead is a fixed cost and hence budget cost allowance = $10,000

Comment

(a) In selling 8,200 units, the expected profit should have been, not the fixed budget profit of $5,000, but the flexible budget profit of $7,800. Instead actual profit was $8,200 ie $400 more than we should have expected.

One of the reasons for this improvement is that, given output and sales of 8,200 units, the cost of resources (material, labour etc) was $1,400 lower than expected. (A comparison of the fixed budget and the actual costs in Example 7.1 appeared to indicate that costs were not being controlled since all of the variances were adverse).

Total cost variances can be analysed to reveal how much of the variance is due to lower resource prices and how much is due to efficient resource usage.

(b) The sales revenue was, however, $1,000 less than expected because a lower price was charged than budgeted.

We know this because flexing the budget has eliminated the effect of changes in the volume sold, which is the only other factor that can affect sales revenue. You have probably already realised that this variance of $1,000 (A) is a **selling price variance**.

The lower selling price could have been caused by the increase in the volume sold (to sell the additional 700 units the selling price had to fall below $10 per unit). We do not know if this is the case but without flexing the budget we could not know that a different selling price to that budgeted had been charged. Our initial analysis above had appeared to indicate that sales revenue was ahead of budget.

The difference of $400 between the flexible budget profit of $7,800 at a production level of 8,200 units and the actual profit of $8,200 is due to the net effect of cost savings of $1,400 and lower than expected sales revenue (by $1,000).

The difference between the original budgeted profit of $5,000 and the actual profit of $8,200 is the total of the following.

(a) The savings in resource costs/lower than expected sales revenue (a net total of $400 as indicated by the difference between the flexible budget and the actual results).

(b) The effect of producing and selling 8,200 units instead of 7,500 units (a gain of $2,800 as indicated by the difference between the fixed budget and the flexible budget). This is the **sales volume contribution variance**.

A **full variance analysis statement** would be as follows.

	$	$
Fixed budget profit		5,000
Variances		
Sales volume	2,800 (F)	
Selling price	1,000 (A)	
Direct materials cost	1,100 (F)	
Direct labour cost	900 (F)	
Production overhead cost	400 (F)	
Administration overhead cost	1,000 (A)	
		3,200 (F)
Actual profit		8,200

If management believes that any of the variances are large enough to justify it, they will investigate the reasons for their occurrence to see whether any corrective action is necessary.

Question — Flexible budget

Flower budgeted to sell 200 units and produced the following budget.

	$	$
Sales		71,400
Variable costs		
Labour	31,600	
Material	12,600	
		44,200
Contribution		27,200
Fixed costs		18,900
Profit		8,300

Actual sales turned out to be 230 units, which were sold for $69,000. Actual expenditure on labour was $27,000 and on material $24,000. Fixed costs totalled $10,000.

Required

Prepare a flexible budget that will be useful for management control purposes.

Answer

	Budget 200 units $	Budget per unit $	Flexed budget 230 units $	Actual 230 units $	Variance $
Sales	71,400	357	82,110	69,000	13,110 (A)
Variable costs					
Labour	31,600	158	36,340	27,000	9,340 (F)
Material	12,600	63	14,490	24,000	9,510 (A)
	44,200	221	50,830	51,000	
Contribution	27,200	136	31,280	18,000	13,280 (A)
Fixed costs	18,900		18,900	10,000	8,900 (F)
Profit	8,300		12,380	8,000	4,380 (A)

7.2 Flexible budgets, control and computers

The production of flexible budget control reports is an area in which computers can provide invaluable assistance to the cost accountant, calculating flexed budget figures using fixed budget and actual results data and hence providing detailed variance analysis. For control information to be of any value it must be produced quickly: speed is one of the many advantages of computers.

7.3 The link between standard costing and budget flexing

The calculation of standard cost variances and the use of a flexed budget to control costs and revenues are **very similar in concept**.

For example, a direct material total variance in a standard costing system is calculated by **comparing the material cost that should have been incurred for the output achieved, with the actual cost that was incurred**.

Exactly the same process is undertaken when a budget is flexed to provide a basis for comparison with the actual cost: **the flexible budget cost allowance for material cost is the same as the cost that should have been incurred for the activity level achieved**. In the same way as for standard costing, this is then compared with the actual cost incurred in order to practice control by comparison.

However, there are differences between the two techniques.

(a) **Standard costing variance analysis is more detailed**. The total material cost variance is analysed further to determine how much of the total variance is caused by a difference in the price paid for materials (the material price variance) and how much is caused by the usage of material being different from the standard (the material usage variance). In flexible budget comparisons only total cost variances are derived.

(b) **For a standard costing system to operate it is necessary to determine a standard unit cost for all items of output**. All that is required to operate a flexible budgeting system is an understanding of the cost behaviour patterns and a measure of activity to use to flex the budget cost allowance for each cost element.

Exam focus point

Make sure you understand the **principal budget factor** and the difference between **fixed** and **flexible** budgets.

8 Budgeting, performance and motivation

8.1 Introduction

FAST FORWARD

Human behaviour affects the budgeting process, the resulting budgets and the performance of managers and employees alike.

An important aspect of the budgeting process is the human behavioural aspect, the effect that the budgeting process and resulting budgets has on the performance of managers and employees alike.

8.2 Budgets and motivation

Much has been written about the motivational effect of the budgeting process on managers in a business and there are many conflicting views. However it is well recognised that the budgetary process has the potential to be a powerful motivating tool, but conversely can also quite easily have a demotivating effect on managers.

The effect of the eventual budgets on the motivation of managers will largely be due to the level of difficulty of the targets set by the budget, and the manner in which the budgets are set – are these imposed budgets or have the managers taken part in the budgeting process?

8.3 Budgets and standards as targets

Once decided, budgets become targets. But **how difficult** should the targets be? And how might people react to targets which are easy to achieve, or difficult to achieve?

The **quantity of material and labour time included in the budget** will **depend on the level of performance** required by management. Four types of performance standard might be set.

Ideal standards are based on **perfect operating conditions**: no wastage, no spoilage, no inefficiencies, no idle time, no breakdowns. Employees will often feel that the goals are unattainable, become demotivated and not work so hard.

Attainable standards are based on the hope that a standard amount of work will be carried out efficiently, machines properly operated or materials properly used. **Some allowance is made for wastage and inefficiencies**. If well-set they provide a useful psychological incentive by giving employees a realistic, but challenging target of efficiency.

Current standards are based on **current working conditions** (current wastage, current inefficiencies). They do not attempt to improve on current levels of efficiency.

Basic standards are kept unaltered over a long period of time, and may be out of date. They are used to show change in efficiency or performance over a long period of time. They are perhaps the least useful and least common type of standard in use.

The impact on employee behaviour of budgets based on these different standards is summarised in the table below.

Type of standard	Impact
Ideal standards:	Some say that they provide employees with an incentive to be more efficient even though it is highly unlikely that the standard will be achieved. Others argue that they are likely to have an unfavourable effect on employee motivation because the differences between standards and actual results will always be adverse. The employees may feel that the goals are unattainable and so they will not work so hard.

Type of standard	Impact
Attainable standards:	Might be an incentive to work harder as they provide a realistic but challenging target of efficiency.
Current standards:	Will not motivate employees to do anything more than they are currently doing.
Basic standards:	May have an unfavourable impact on the motivation of employees. Over time they will discover that they are easily able to achieve the standards. They may become bored and lose interest in what they are doing if they have nothing to aim for.

Similar comments apply to budgets.

Budgets and standards are **more likely to motivate** employees if employees accept that the budget or standard is **achievable**. If it can be achieved too easily, it will not provide sufficient motivation. If it is too difficult, employees will not accept it because they will believe it to be unachievable. In extreme circumstances, if employees believe a budget is impossible to achieve, they might be so demotivated that they attempt to prove that the budget is wrong. This is obviously the completely opposite effect to that intended.

The various **research** projects into the behavioural effects of budgeting have given **conflicting views** on certain points. However, there appears to be **general agreement** that a **target must fulfil certain conditions** if it is to motivate employees to work towards it.

(a) It must be sufficiently difficult to be a challenging target.
(b) It must **not be so difficult** that it is not achievable.
(c) It must be **accepted** by the employees as their personal goal.

8.4 Participation

There are basically two ways in which a budget can be set: from the **top down** (**imposed** budget) or from the **bottom up** (**participatory** budget).

8.5 Imposed style of budgeting

In this approach to budgeting, **top management prepare a budget with little or no input from operating personnel.** This budget is then **imposed** upon the employees who have to work to the budgeted figures. The times when imposed budgets are **effective** are as follows.

(a) In newly formed organisations, because of employees' lack of knowledge
(b) In very small businesses, because the owner/manager has a complete overview of the business
(c) When operational managers lack budgeting skills
(d) When the organisation's different units require precise co-ordination
(e) When budgets need to be set quickly

There are, of course, advantages and disadvantages to this style of setting budgets.

Advantages

(a) The aims of long-term plans are more likely to be incorporated into short-term plans.
(b) They improve the co-ordination between the plans and objectives of divisions.
(c) They use senior management's overall awareness of the organisation.
(d) There is less likelihood of input from inexperienced or uninformed lower-level employees.
(e) Budgets can be drawn up in a shorter period of time because a consultation process is not required.

Disadvantages

(a) Dissatisfaction, defensiveness and low morale amongst employees who have to work to meet the targets. It is hard for people to be motivated to achieve targets set by somebody else. Employees might put in only just enough effort to achieve targets, without trying to beat them.

(b) The feeling of team spirit may disappear.

(c) Organisational goals and objectives might not be accepted so readily and/or employees will not be aware of them.

(d) Employees might see the budget as part of a system of trying to find fault with their work: if they cannot achieve a target that has been imposed on them they will be punished.

(e) If consideration is not given to local operating and political environments, unachievable budgets for overseas divisions could be produced.

(f) Lower-level management initiative may be stifled if they are not invited to participate.

8.6 Participative style of budgeting

In this approach to budgeting, **budgets are developed by lower-level managers who then submit the budgets to their superiors**. The budgets are based on the lower-level managers' perceptions of what is achievable and the associated necessary resources.

The **advantages** of participative budgets are as follows:

(a) They are based on information from employees most familiar with the department. Budgets should therefore be more realistic.

(b) Knowledge spread among several levels of management is pulled together, again producing more realistic budgets.

(c) Because employees are more aware of organisational goals, they should be more committed to achieving them.

(d) Co-ordination and cooperation between those involved in budget preparation should improve.

(e) Senior managers' overview of the business can be combined with operational-level details to produce better budgets.

(f) Managers should feel that they 'own' the budget and will therefore be more committed to the targets and more motivated to achieve them.

Participation will broaden the experience of those involved and enable them to develop new skills.

Overall, participation in budget setting should give those involved a more positive attitude towards the organisation, which should lead to better performance.

There are, on the other hand, a number of **disadvantages** of participative budgets:

(a) They consume more time.

(b) Any changes made by senior management to the budgets submitted by lower-level management may cause dissatisfaction.

(c) Budgets may be unachievable if managers are not qualified to participate.

(d) Managers may not co-ordinate their own plans with those of other departments.

(e) Managers may include budgetary slack (padding the budget) in their budgets. This means they have over-estimated costs or under-estimated income. Actual results are then more likely to be better than the budgeted target results.

(f) An earlier start to the budgeting process could be required.

The research projects do not appear to provide definite conclusions about the motivational effects of budgeting. The **attitudes of the individuals** involved have an impact.

8.7 Negotiated style of budgeting

At the two extremes, budgets can be dictated from above or simply emerge from below but, in practice, different levels of management often agree budgets by a process of negotiation.

In the imposed budget approach, operational managers will try to negotiate with senior managers the budget targets which they consider to be unreasonable or unrealistic. Likewise senior management usually review and revise budgets presented to them under a participative approach through a process of negotiation with lower level managers. **Final budgets are therefore most likely to lie between what top management would really like and what junior managers believe is feasible**.

8.8 Creative budgets

In the process of preparing budgets, managers might **deliberately overestimate costs and underestimate sales**, so that they will not be blamed in the future for overspending and poor results.

In controlling actual operations, managers must then **ensure that their spending rises to meet their budget**, otherwise they will be 'blamed' for careless budgeting.

A typical situation is for a manager to **pad the budget** and waste money on non-essential expenses so that he uses all his budget allowances. The reason behind his action is the fear that unless the allowance is fully spent it will be reduced in future periods thus making his job more difficult as the future reduced budgets will not be so easy to attain. Because inefficiency and slack are allowed for in budgets, achieving a budget target means only that costs have remained within the accepted levels of inefficient spending.

Budget bias can **work in the other direction** too. It has been noted that, after a run of mediocre results, some managers **deliberately overstate revenues and understate cost estimates**, no doubt feeling the need to make an immediate favourable impact by promising better performance in the future. They may merely delay problems, however, as the managers may well be censured when they fail to hit these optimistic targets.

8.9 Goal congruence and dysfunctional decision making

Individuals are motivated by personal desires and interests. These desires and interests may tie in with the objectives of the organisation – after all, some people 'live for their jobs'. Other individuals see their job as a chore, and their motivations will have nothing to do with achieving the objectives of the organisation for which they work.

It is therefore important that **some of the desires, interests and goals motivating employees correspond with the goals of the organisation as a whole.** This is known as **goal congruence**. Such a state would exist, for example, if the manager of department A worked to achieve a 10% increase in sales for the department, this 10% increase being part of the organisation's overall plan to increase organisational sales by 20% over the next three years.

On the other hand, **dysfunctional behaviour** can occur if a **manager's goals are not in line with those of the organisation as a whole.** Attempts to enhance his or her own situation or performance (typically **'empire building'** – employing more staff, cutting costs to achieve favourable variances but causing quality problems in other departments) will be at the expense of the best interests of the organisation as a whole. **Participation is not necessarily the answer**. Goal congruence does not necessarily result from allowing managers to develop their own budgets.

A well designed standard costing and budgetary control system can help to ensure goal congruence: continuous feedback prompting appropriate control action should steer the organisation in the right direction.

9 Further budgeting techniques

9.1 Zero based budgeting and incremental budgeting

ZBB is a technique used to allocate resources more efficiently thus reducing waste and increasing efficiency. The process of ZBB starts from the basic premise that next year's budget is zero; every process or item of expenditure or intended activity (referred to as a 'decision package') has to be justified in its entirety before it can be included in the budget.

Incremental budgeting is where the budget is based on current year's budget (or results) plus an extra amount for estimated growth or inflation. It is administratively fairly easy to prepare but can be inefficient. It also tends to encourage budgetary slack/wasteful spending to creep into the budget. This method will be sufficient if current operations are as efficient, effective and economical as they can be, without any alternative courses of action available to the organisation.

9.2 Rolling budgets

Rolling budgets are also called continuous budgets. They are particularly useful when an organisation is facing a period of uncertainty so that it is difficult to prepare accurate forecasts. For example it may be difficult to estimate the level of inflation for the forthcoming period.

Rolling budgets are an attempt to prepare targets and plans which are more realistic and certain, particularly with a regard to price levels, by shortening the period between preparing budgets.

Instead of preparing a periodic budget annually for the full budget period, budgets would be prepared, say, every 1, 2 or 3 months (4, 6, or even 12 budgets each year). Each of these budgets would plan for the next 12 months so that the current budget is extended by an extra period as the current period ends: hence the name rolling budgets. Cash budgets are usually prepared on a rolling basis.

9.3 Activity based budgeting

Activity based budgeting is the use of activity based costing (ABC) when setting budgets. ABC was developed to improve the cost allocation process as traditional techniques assumed that costs were only driven by volume. Production overheads are not necessarily driven by volume therefore allocation using traditional methods is not necessarily meaningful. With ABC, multiple overhead absorption rates are calculated based on the different activities that cause the costs to change.

Chapter roundup

- A **budget** is a quantified plan of action for a forthcoming accounting period. A **budget** is a plan of what the organisation is aiming to achieve and what is has set as a target, whereas a **forecast** is an estimate of what is likely to occur in the future.

- The **objectives** of a budgetary planning and control system are as follows.
    - To ensure the achievement of the organisation's objectives
    - To compel planning
    - To communicate ideas and plans
    - To co-ordinate activities
    - To provide a framework for responsibility accounting
    - To establish a system of control
    - To motivate employees to improve their performance

- The **budget committee** is the co-ordinating body in the preparation and administration of budgets.

- The **principal budget factor** should be identified at the beginning of the budgetary process, and the budget for this is prepared before all the others.

- **Fixed budgets** remain unchanged regardless of the level of activity; **flexible budgets** are designed to flex with the level of activity.

- **Flexible budgets** are prepared using marginal costing and so mixed costs must be split into their fixed and variable components (possibly using the **high/low method**).

- Comparison of a fixed budget with the actual results for a different level of activity is of little use for **budgeting control purposes**. Flexible budgets should be used to show what cost and revenues should have been for the actual level of activity. Differences between the flexible budget figures and actual results are **variances**.

- Budgetary control is based around a system of **budget centres**. Each centre has its own budget which is the responsibility of the **budget holder**.

- Human behaviour affects the budgeting process, the resulting budgets and the performance of managers and employees alike.

Quick quiz

1. Which of the following is not an objective of a system of budgetary planning and control?

    A   To establish a system of control
    B   To co-ordinate activities
    C   To compel planning
    D   To motivate employees to maintain current performance levels

2. Sales is always the principal budget factor and so it is always the first budget to be prepared. True or false?

3. Choose the appropriate words from those highlighted.

    A **forecast/budget** is an **estimate/guarantee** of what is **likely to occur in the future/has happened in the past**.

    A **forecast/budget** is a **quantified plan/unquantified plan/guess** of what the organisation is aiming to **achieve/spend**.

4. Fill in the blanks.

    When preparing a production budget, the quantity to be produced is equal to sales ……………….. opening inventory ……………….. closing inventory.

5. Match the descriptions to the budgeting style.

    Description

    (a) Budget allowances are set without the involvement of the budget holder.

    (b) All budget holders are involved in setting their own budgets.

    (c) Budget allowances are set on the basis of discussions between budget holders and those to whom they report.

    Budgeting style

    Negotiated budgeting

    Participative budgeting

    Imposed budgeting

6. Budgetary slack is necessary to ensure that managers are able to meet their targets. True or false?

Answers to quick quiz

1. D. The objective is to motivate employees to **improve** their performance.
2. False. The budget for the principal budget factor must be prepared first, but sales is not always the principal budget factor.
3. A forecast is an estimate of what is likely to occur in the future.

   A budget is a quantified plan of what the organisation is aiming to achieve.
4. When preparing a production budget, the quantity to be produced is equal to sales minus opening inventory plus closing inventory.
5. (a) Imposed budgeting
   (b) Participative budgeting
   (c) Negotiated budgeting
6. False. Budgets should be reviewed to ensure that operational managers have not included slack.

End of chapter question

Utilities Company Ltd

Utilities Company Limited operates a supermarket chain throughout the UK. The company is currently in the process of preparing its budget for the five month period to April 20X1. The following information has been provided for the period December 20X0 through to April 20X1.

	December $	January $	February $	March $	April $
Sales	400,000	600,000	320,000	550,000	500,000
Purchases	240,000	350,000	175,000	250,000	245,000
Salaries	45,000	50,000	40,000	60,000	55,000
Advertising	130,000	145,000	80,000	100,000	75,000
Administration	19,000	19,000	19,000	19,000	19,000
Rent	60,000	40,000	55,000	62,500	70,000
Insurance	30,000	-	-	-	-

Additional information:

(i) Sales for October and November 20X0 are expected to be $250,000 and $500,000 respectively. Past experience shows that 25% of the sales in any particular month are collected in the month of sale, 70% in the month following sale and 3% in the second month following sale. Any balance uncollected after this should be written off as bad debts.

(ii) Purchases for November 20X0 are estimated at $180,000. Purchases are paid for in the month following purchase.

(iii) A motor car costing $40,000 will be bought and paid for in December 20X0.

(iv) The monthly administration costs above include $10,000 depreciation.

(v) Equipment costing $10,000 will be purchased and paid for in December 20X0.

(vi) The cash balance at the beginning of December 20X0 will be $50,000.

Required

(a) Prepare a month by month cash budget for the company for the period December 20X0 to April 20X1. **(15 marks)**

(b) Comment on the cash flow position of the company and suggest what measures the company could take to improve its cash flow position. **(5 marks)**

(Total = 20 marks)

Standard costing

Topic list	Syllabus reference
1 What is standard costing?	C4.1
2 Setting standards	C4.1

Introduction

Just as there are **standards** for most things in our daily lives (cleanliness in hamburger restaurants, educational achievement of nine year olds, number of trains running on time), there are standards for the costs of products and services. Moreover, just as the standards in our daily lives are not always met, the standards for the costs of products and services are not always met. We will not, however, be considering the standards of cleanlinesss of hamburger restaurants in this chapter but we will be looking at standards for **costs**, what they are used for and how they are set. We also consider how activity based costing can be used to set standards.

In the next chapter we will see how **standard costing** forms the basis of a process called **variance analysis**, a vital management control tool.

Exam focus point

Standard costing can be applied under both absorption and marginal costing and is important in calculating variances, which we look at in the next chapter. Questions will not only be numerical in nature so it is important that you understand the purposes of standards and are familiar with the different types of standard.

1 What is standard costing?

1.1 Introduction

FAST FORWARD

A **standard cost** is a **predetermined estimated unit cost**, used for inventory valuation and control.

The building blocks of standard costing are standard costs and so before we look at standard costing in any detail you really need to know what a standard cost is.

1.2 Standard cost card

FAST FORWARD

A **standard cost card** shows full details of the standard cost of each product.

The standard cost card of product 1234 is set out below.

STANDARD COST CARD – PRODUCT 1234

	$	$
Direct materials		
Material X – 3 kg at $4 per kg	12	
Material Y – 9 litres at $2 per litre	18	
		30
Direct labour		
Grade A – 6 hours at $1.50 per hour	9	
Grade B – 8 hours at $2 per hour	16	
		25
Standard direct cost		55
Variable production overhead – 14 hours at $0.50 per hour		7
Standard variable cost of production		62
Fixed production overhead – 14 hours at $4.50 per hour		63
Standard full production cost		125
Administration and marketing overhead		15
Standard cost of sale		140
Standard profit		20
Standard sales price		160

Notice how the total standard cost is built up from standards for each cost element: standard quantities of materials at standard prices, standard quantities of labour time at standard rates and so on. It is therefore determined by management's estimates of the following.

- The expected prices of materials, labour and expenses
- Efficiency levels in the use of materials and labour
- Budgeted overhead costs and budgeted volumes of activity

We will see how management arrives at these estimates in Section 2.

But why should management want to prepare standard costs? Obviously to assist with standard costing, but what is the point of standard costing?

1.3 The uses of standard costing

Standard costing has a variety of uses but its two principal ones are as follows.

(a) To **value inventories** and **cost production** for cost accounting purposes.

(b) To act as a **control device** by establishing standards (planned costs), highlighting (via **variance analysis** which we will cover in the next chapter) activities that are not conforming to plan and thus **alerting management** to areas which may be out of control and in need of corrective action.

Question — Standard cost card

Bloggs makes one product, the joe. Two types of labour are involved in the preparation of a joe, skilled and semi-skilled. Skilled labour is paid $10 per hour and semi-skilled $5 per hour. Twice as many skilled labour hours as semi-skilled labour hours are needed to produce a joe, four semi-skilled labour hours being needed.

A joe is made up of three different direct materials. Seven kilograms of direct material A, four litres of direct material B and three metres of direct material C are needed. Direct material A costs $1 per kilogram, direct material B $2 per litre and direct material C $3 per metre.

Variable production overheads are incurred at Bloggs Co at the rate of $2.50 per direct labour (skilled) hour.

A system of absorption costing is in operation at Bloggs Co. The basis of absorption is direct labour (skilled) hours. For the forthcoming accounting period, budgeted fixed production overheads are $250,000 and budgeted production of the joe is 5,000 units.

Administration, selling and distribution overheads are added to products at the rate of $10 per unit.

A mark-up of 25% is made on the joe.

Required

Using the above information draw up a standard cost card for the joe.

Answer

STANDARD COST CARD – PRODUCT JOE

	$	$
Direct materials		
A – 7 kgs × $1	7	
B – 4 litres × $2	8	
C – 3 m × $3	9	
		24
Direct labour		
Skilled – 8 × $10	80	
Semi-skilled – 4 × $5	20	
		100
Standard direct cost		124
Variable production overhead – 8 × $2.50		20
Standard variable cost of production		144
Fixed production overhead – 8 × $6.25 (W)		50
Standard full production cost		194
Administration, selling and distribution overhead		10
Standard cost of sale		204
Standard profit (25% × 204)		51
Standard sales price		255

Working

Overhead absorption rate = $\dfrac{\$250{,}000}{5{,}000 \times 8}$ = $6.25 per skilled labour hour

Question — Marginal costing system

What would a standard cost card for product joe show under a marginal system?

Answer

STANDARD COST CARD – PRODUCT JOE

	$
Direct materials	24
Direct labour	100
Standard direct cost	124
Variable production overhead	20
Standard variable production cost	144
Standard sales price	255
Standard contribution	111

Although the use of standard costs to simplify the keeping of cost accounting records should not be overlooked, we will be concentrating on the **control** and **variance analysis** aspect of standard costing.

Key term

> **Standard costing** is a control technique which compares standard costs and revenues with actual results to obtain variances which are used to improve performance.

Notice that the above definition highlights the control aspects of standard costing.

1.4 Standard costing as a control technique

FAST FORWARD

> Differences between actual and standard costs are called **variances**.

Standard costing therefore involves the following.

- The establishment of predetermined estimates of the costs of products or services
- The collection of actual costs
- The comparison of the actual costs with the predetermined estimates

The predetermined costs are known as **standard costs** and the difference between standard and actual cost is known as **a variance**. The process by which the total difference between standard and actual results is analysed is known as **variance analysis**.

Although standard costing can be used in a variety of costing situations (batch and mass production, process manufacture, jobbing manufacture (where there is standardisation of parts) and service industries (if a realistic cost unit can be established)), the greatest benefit from its use can be gained if there is a **degree of repetition** in the production process. It is therefore most suited to **mass production** and **repetitive assembly work**.

2 Setting standards

2.1 Introduction

Standard costs may be used in both absorption costing and in marginal costing systems. We shall, however, confine our description to standard costs in absorption costing systems.

As we noted earlier, the standard cost of a product (or service) is made up of a number of different standards, one for each cost element, each of which has to be set by management. We have divided this section into two: the first part looks at setting the monetary part of each standard, whereas the second part looks at setting the resources requirement part of each standard.

2.2 Types of performance standard

FAST FORWARD

Performance standards are used to set efficiency targets. There are four types: ideal, attainable, current and basic.

The setting of standards raises the problem of how demanding the standard should be. Should the standard represent a perfect performance or an easily attainable performance? The type of performance standard used can have behavioural implications. There are four types of standard.

Type of standard	Description
Ideal	These are based on **perfect operating conditions**: no wastage, no spoilage, no inefficiencies, no idle time, no breakdowns. Variances from ideal standards are useful for pinpointing areas where a close examination may result in large savings in order to maximise efficiency and minimise waste. However ideal standards are likely to have an unfavourable motivational impact because reported variances will always be adverse. Employees will often feel that the goals are unattainable and not work so hard.
Attainable	These are based on the hope that a standard amount of work will be carried out efficiently, machines properly operated or materials properly used. **Some allowance is made for wastage and inefficiencies**. If well-set they provide a useful psychological incentive by giving employees a realistic, but challenging target of efficiency. The consent and co-operation of employees involved in improving the standard are required.
Current	These are based on **current working conditions** (current wastage, current inefficiencies). The disadvantage of current standards is that they do not attempt to improve on current levels of efficiency.
Basic	These are **kept unaltered over a long period of time**, and may be out of date. They are used to show changes in efficiency or performance over a long period of time. Basic standards are perhaps the least useful and least common type of standard in use.

Ideal standards, attainable standards and current standards each have their supporters and it is by **no means clear which of them is preferable**.

Question
Performance standards

Which of the following statements is not true?

A   Variances from ideal standards are useful for pinpointing areas where a close examination might result in large cost savings.

B   Basic standards may provide an incentive to greater efficiency even though the standard cannot be achieved.

C   Ideal standards cannot be achieved and so there will always be adverse variances. If the standards are used for budgeting, an allowance will have to be included for these 'inefficiencies'.

D   Current standards or attainable standards are a better basis for budgeting, because they represent the level of productivity which management will wish to plan for.

Answer

The correct answer is B.

Statement B is describing ideal standards, not basic standards.

2.3 Direct material prices

Direct material prices will be estimated by the purchasing department from their knowledge of the following.

- Purchase contracts already agreed
- Pricing discussions with regular suppliers
- The forecast movement of prices in the market
- The availability of bulk purchase discounts

Price inflation can cause difficulties in setting realistic standard prices. Suppose that a material costs $10 per kilogram at the moment and during the course of the next 12 months it is expected to go up in price by 20% to $12 per kilogram. What standard price should be selected?

- The current price of $10 per kilogram
- The average expected price for the year, say $11 per kilogram

Either would be possible, but neither would be entirely satisfactory.

(a) If the **current price** were used in the standard, the reported price variance will become adverse as soon as prices go up, which might be very early in the year. If prices go up gradually rather than in one big jump, it would be difficult to select an appropriate time for revising the standard.

(b) If an **estimated mid-year price** were used, price variances should be favourable in the first half of the year and adverse in the second half of the year, again assuming that prices go up gradually throughout the year. Management could only really check that in any month, the price variance did not become excessively adverse (or favourable) and that the price variance switched from being favourable to adverse around month six or seven and not sooner.

2.4 Direct labour rates

Direct labour rates per hour will be set by discussion with the personnel department and by reference to the payroll and to any agreements on pay rises with trade union representatives of the employees.

(a) A separate hourly rate or weekly wage will be set for each different labour grade/type of employee.

(b) An average hourly rate will be applied for each grade (even though individual rates of pay may vary according to age and experience).

Similar problems when dealing with inflation to those described for material prices can be met when setting labour standards.

2.5 Overhead absorption rates

When standard costs are fully absorbed costs, the **absorption rate** of fixed production overheads will be **predetermined**, usually each year when the budget is prepared, and based in the usual manner on budgeted fixed production overhead expenditure and budgeted production.

For selling and distribution costs, standard costs might be absorbed as a percentage of the standard selling price.

Standard costs under marginal costing are likely to include a standard for variable production overhead but will, of course, not include any element of absorbed fixed overheads.

2.6 Activity based costing and standard costs

As an alternative to using a traditional costing approach, activity-based costing (ABC) can be used to create standard costs for overheads.

ABC focuses on identifying activities that give rise to costs, forming cost pools for each activity, and allocating overhead costs to products based on the products' use of each activity.

Using traditional costing, we would normally establish a single standard variable overhead rate and standard quantity, based on the labour or machine hours required to make a unit of product.

Instead ABC establishes several standard variable overhead rates and quantities, for each activity that has its own cost driver.

For example under ABC the total variable overhead incurred in manufacturing a product might be broken down into the cost of product testing, the cost of the energy used for the machines and the cost of machine repairs.

The standard cost card would then include standard costs for:

- Product testing (based on the time spent testing the product)
- Machine power (based on the machine hours used)
- Machine repairs (based on the number of callouts)

Regardless of whether a company uses the traditional costing approach or an activity-based costing approach, the process of performing variance analysis (comparing the actual cost with the pre-determined estimate) would remain the same. However as ABC typically breaks the costs down further, and links them to the factors that cause the costs, it may provide more useful feedback to management.

2.7 Standard resource requirements

To estimate the materials required to make each product (**material usage**) and also the labour hours required (**labour efficiency**), **technical specifications** must be prepared for each product by production experts (either in the production department or the work study department).

(a) The **'standard product specification'** for materials must list the quantities required per unit of each material in the product. These standard input quantities must be made known to the operators in the production department so that control action by management to deal with **excess material wastage** will be understood by them.

(b) The **'standard operation sheet'** for labour will specify the expected hours required by each grade of labour in each department to make one unit of product. These standard times must be carefully set (for example by work study) and must be understood by the labour force. Where necessary, **standard procedures** or **operating methods** should be stated.

Exam focus point

An exam question may give you actual costs and variances and require you to calculate the standard cost.

Chapter roundup

- A **standard cost** is a **predetermined estimated unit cost**, used for inventory valuation and control.
- A **standard cost card** shows full details of the standard cost of each product.
- Differences between actual and standard cost are called **variances**.
- **Performance standards** are used to set efficiency targets. There are four types: ideal, attainable, current and basic.

Quick quiz

1. A standard cost is ………………………………………………… .

2. What are two main uses of standard costing?

3. A control technique which compares standard costs and revenues with actual results to obtain variances which are used to stimulate improved performance is known as:

    A Standard costing
    B Variance analysis
    C Budgetary control
    D Budgeting

4. Standard costs may only be used in absorption costing.

    True ☐
    False ☐

5. Two types of performance standard are:

    (a) ……………………………..
    (b) ……………………………..

Answers to quick quiz

1. A planned unit cost
2. (a) To value inventories and cost production for cost accounting purposes
   (b) To act as a control device by establishing standards and highlighting activities that are not conforming to plan and bringing these to the attention of management
3. A
4. False. They may be used in a marginal costing system as well.
5. (a) Attainable
   (b) Ideal

End of chapter question

Standard costing

(a) Explain the term standard costing and briefly discuss how you would set standards for material costs. **(5 marks)**

(b) State and briefly explain the four types of standards and their behavioural implications. **(5 marks)**

(c) Discuss the similarities and differences between budgets and standards. **(5 marks)**

(d) Distinguish between the use of budgetary control and standard costing as a means of cost control in service-based organisations. Explain clearly the arguments in favour of using both of these methods simultaneously. **(5 marks)**

(Total = 20 marks)

PART C4 INFORMATION FOR PLANNING AND PERFORMANCE MANAGEMENT

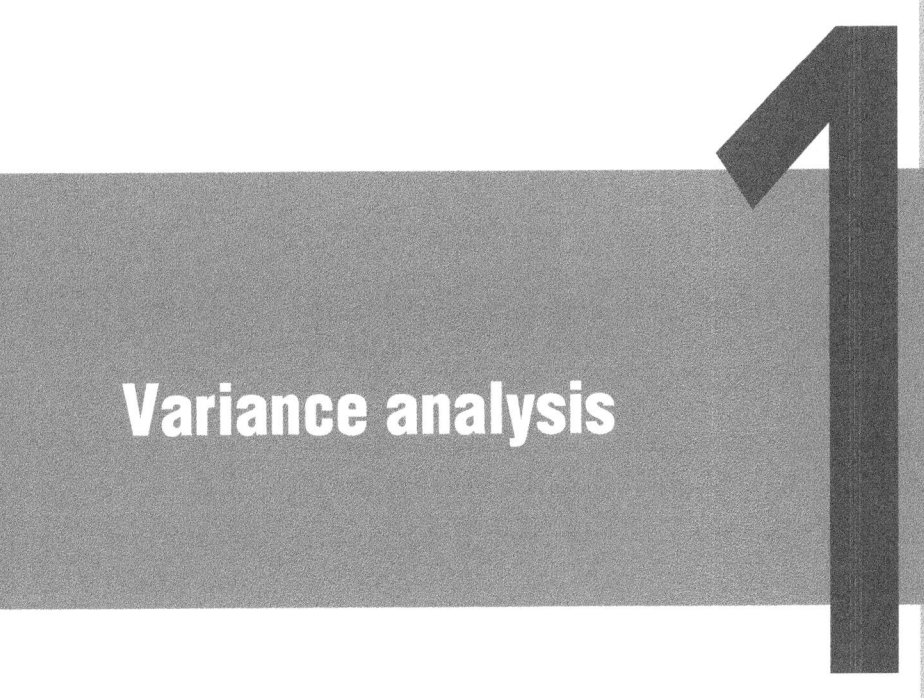

Variance analysis

Topic list	Syllabus reference
1 Variances	C4.1
2 Direct material cost variances	C4.1
3 Direct labour cost variances	C4.1
4 Variable production overhead variances	C4.1
5 Fixed production overhead variances	C4.1
6 The reasons for cost variances	C4.1
7 The significance of cost variances	C4.1
8 Sales variances	C4.1
9 Operating statements	C4.1
10 Variances in a standard marginal costing system	C4.1

Introduction

The actual results achieved by an organisation during a reporting period (week, month, quarter, year) will, more than likely, be different from the expected results. Such differences may occur between individual items, such as the cost of labour and the volume of sales, and between the total expected profit/contribution and the total actual profit/contribution.

Management will have spent considerable time and trouble setting standards. Actual results have differed from the standards. The wise manager will consider the differences that have occurred and use the results of these considerations to assist in attempts to attain the standards. The wise manager will use **variance analysis** as a method of **control**.

The objective of cost variance analysis is to assist management in the **control of costs**. Costs are, however, only one factor which contribute to the achievement of planned profit. **Sales** are another important factor and sales variances can be calculated to aid management's control of their business. We will therefore examine **sales variances**.

Having discussed the variances you need to know about, we will then look at the **ways in which variances should be presented to management** to aid their control of the organisation.

Finally we consider how **marginal cost variances** differ from absorption cost variances and how marginal costing information should be presented.

> **Exam focus point**
> Variance calculation is a very important part of your Management Accounting studies and it is vital that you are able to calculate all of the different types of variance included in the syllabus. It is an area that has appeared regularly in past exams.

1 Variances

> **FAST FORWARD**
> A **variance** is the difference between a planned, budgeted, or standard cost and the actual cost incurred. The same comparisons may be made for revenues. The process by which the **total** difference between standard and actual results is analysed is known as **variance analysis**.

When actual results are better than expected results, we have a **favourable variance** (F). If, on the other hand, actual results are worse than expected results, we have an **adverse variance** (A).

Variances can be divided into three main groups.

- Variable cost variances
- Sales variances
- Fixed production overhead variances

In the remainder of this chapter we will consider, in detail, variable cost variances and fixed production overhead variances.

2 Direct material cost variances

2.1 Introduction

> **FAST FORWARD**
> The direct material total variance can be subdivided into the **direct material price** variance and the **direct material usage** variance.

> **Key terms**
> The **direct material total variance** is the difference between what the output actually cost and what it should have cost, in terms of material.
>
> The **direct material price variance.** This is the **difference between the standard cost and the actual cost for the actual quantity of material used or purchased.** In other words, it is the difference between what the material did cost and what it should have cost.
>
> The **direct material usage variance.** This is the **difference between the standard quantity of materials that should have been used for the number of units actually produced, and the actual quantity of materials used, valued at the standard cost per unit of material.** In other words, it is the difference between how much material should have been used and how much material was used, valued at standard cost.

2.2 Example: Direct material variances

Product X has a standard direct material cost as follows.

    10 kilograms of material Y at $10 per kilogram = $100 per unit of X.

During period 4, 1,000 units of X were manufactured, using 11,700 kilograms of material Y which cost $98,600.

Required

Calculate the following variances.

(a) The direct material total variance
(b) The direct material price variance
(c) The direct material usage variance

Solution

(a) **The direct material total variance**

This is the difference between what 1,000 units should have cost and what they did cost.

	$
1,000 units should have cost (× $100)	100,000
but did cost	98,600
Direct material total variance	1,400 (F)

The variance is **favourable** because the units cost less than they should have cost.

Now we can break down the direct material total variance into its two constituent parts: the direct material **price** variance and the direct material **usage** variance.

(b) **The direct material price variance**

This is the difference between what 11,700 kg should have cost and what 11,700 kg did cost.

	$
11,700 kg of Y should have cost (× $10)	117,000
but did cost	98,600
Material Y price variance	18,400 (F)

The variance is **favourable** because the material cost less than it should have.

(c) **The direct material usage variance**

This is the difference between how many kilograms of Y should have been used to produce 1,000 units of X and how many kilograms were used, valued at the standard cost per kilogram.

1,000 units should have used (× 10 kg)	10,000 kg
but did use	11,700 kg
Usage variance in kg	1,700 kg (A)
× standard cost per kilogram	× $10
Usage variance in $	$17,000 (A)

The variance is **adverse** because more material than should have been used was used.

(d) **Summary**

	$
Price variance	18,400 (F)
Usage variance	17,000 (A)
Total variance	1,400 (F)

2.3 Materials variances and opening and closing inventory

> **FAST FORWARD**
>
> Direct material price variances are usually extracted at the time of the **receipt** of the materials rather than at the time of usage.

Suppose that a company uses raw material P in production, and that this raw material has a standard price of $3 per metre. During one month 6,000 metres are bought for $18,600, and 5,000 metres are used in production. At the end of the month, inventory will have been increased by 1,000 metres. In variance analysis, the problem is to decide the **material price variance**. Should it be calculated on the basis of **materials purchased** (6,000 metres) or on the basis of **materials used** (5,000 metres)?

The answer to this problem depends on how **closing inventories** of the raw materials will be valued.

(a) If they are valued at **standard cost** (1,000 units at $3 per unit) the price variance is calculated on material **purchases** in the period.

(b) If they are valued at **actual cost** (FIFO) (1,000 units at $3.10 per unit) the price variance is calculated on materials **used in production** in the period.

A **full standard costing system** is usually in operation and therefore the price variance is usually calculated on **purchases** in the period. The variance on the full 6,000 metres will be written off to the costing profit and loss account, even though only 5,000 metres are included in the cost of production.

There are two main advantages in extracting the material price variance at the time of **receipt**.

(a) If variances are extracted at the time of receipt they will be **brought to the attention of managers earlier** than if they are extracted as the material is used. If it is necessary to correct any variances then management action can be more timely.

(b) Since variances are extracted at the time of receipt, **all inventories will be valued at standard price**. This is administratively easier and it means that all issues from inventory can be made at standard price. If inventories are held at actual cost it is necessary to calculate a separate price variance on each batch as it is issued. Since issues are usually made in a number of small batches this can be a time-consuming task, especially with a manual system.

The price variance would be calculated as follows.

	$
6,000 metres of material P purchased should cost (× $3)	18,000
but did cost	18,600
Price variance	600 (A)

3 Direct labour cost variances

3.1 Introduction

> **FAST FORWARD**
>
> The direct labour total variance can be subdivided into the **direct labour rate** variance and the **direct labour efficiency** variance.

Key terms

The **direct labour total variance** is the difference between what the output should have cost and what it did cost, in terms of labour.

The **direct labour rate variance**. This is similar to the direct material price variance. It is the **difference between the standard cost and the actual cost for the actual number of hours paid for.**

In other words, it is the difference between what the labour did cost and what it should have cost.

> The **direct labour efficiency variance** is similar to the direct material usage variance. It is the **difference between the hours that should have been worked for the number of units actually produced, and the actual number of hours worked, valued at the standard rate per hour.**
>
> In other words, it is the difference between how many hours should have been worked and how many hours were worked, valued at the standard rate per hour.

The calculation of **direct labour variances** is very similar to the calculation of direct material variances.

3.2 Example: Direct labour variances

The standard direct labour cost of product X is as follows.

  2 hours of grade Z labour at $5 per hour = $10 per unit of product X.

During period 4, 1,000 units of product X were made, and the direct labour cost of grade Z labour was $8,900 for 2,300 hours of work.

Required

Calculate the following variances.

(a) The direct labour total variance
(b) The direct labour rate variance
(c) The direct labour efficiency (productivity) variance

Solution

(a) **The direct labour total variance**

This is the difference between what 1,000 units should have cost and what they did cost.

	$
1,000 units should have cost (× $10)	10,000
but did cost	8,900
Direct labour total variance	1,100 (F)

The variance is **favourable** because the units cost less than they should have done.

Again we can analyse this total variance into its two constituent parts.

(b) **The direct labour rate variance**

This is the difference between what 2,300 hours should have cost and what 2,300 hours did cost.

	$
2,300 hours of work should have cost (× $5 per hr)	11,500
but did cost	8,900
Direct labour rate variance	2,600 (F)

The variance is **favourable** because the labour cost less than it should have cost.

(c) **The direct labour efficiency variance**

1,000 units of X should have taken (× 2 hrs)	2,000 hrs
but did take	2,300 hrs
Efficiency variance in hours	300 hrs (A)
× standard rate per hour	× $5
Efficiency variance in $	$1,500 (A)

The variance is **adverse** because more hours were worked than should have been worked.

(d) **Summary**

	$
Rate variance	2,600 (F)
Efficiency variance	1,500 (A)
Total variance	1,100 (F)

4 Variable production overhead variances

FAST FORWARD

The variable production overhead total variance can be subdivided into the variable production overhead **expenditure** variance and the variable production overhead **efficiency** variance (**based on actual hours**).

4.1 Example: Variable production overhead variances

Suppose that the variable production overhead cost of product X is as follows.

    2 hours at $1.50 = $3 per unit

During period 6, 400 units of product X were made. The labour force worked 820 hours, of which 60 hours were recorded as idle time. The variable overhead cost was $1,230.

Calculate the following variances.

(a) The variable overhead total variance
(b) The variable production overhead expenditure variance
(c) The variable production overhead efficiency variance

Since this example relates to variable production costs, the total variance is based on actual units of production. (If the overhead had been a variable selling cost, the variance would be based on sales volumes.)

	$
400 units of product X should cost (× $3)	1,200
but did cost	1,230
Variable production overhead total variance	30 (A)

In many variance reporting systems, the variance analysis goes no further, and expenditure and efficiency variances are not calculated. However, the adverse variance of $30 may be explained as the sum of two factors.

(a) The hourly rate of spending on variable production overheads was higher than it should have been, that is there is an expenditure variance.

(b) The labour force worked inefficiently, and took longer to make the output than it should have done. This means that spending on variable production overhead was higher than it should have been, in other words there is an efficiency (productivity) variance. The variable production overhead efficiency variance is exactly the same, in hours, as the direct labour efficiency variance, and occurs for the same reasons.

It is usually assumed that **variable overheads are incurred during active working hours**, but are not incurred during idle time (for example the machines are not running, therefore power is not being consumed, and no indirect materials are being used). This means in our example that although the labour force was paid for 820 hours, they were actively working for only 760 of those hours and so variable production overhead spending occurred during 760 hours.

Key term

> The **variable production overhead expenditure variance** is the difference between the amount of variable production overhead that should have been incurred in the actual hours actively worked, and the actual amount of variable production overhead incurred.

(a)

		$
760 hours of variable production overhead should cost (× $1.50)		1,140
but did cost		1,230
Variable production overhead expenditure variance		90 (A)

Key term

The **variable production overhead efficiency variance**. If you already know the direct labour efficiency variance, the variable production overhead efficiency variance is exactly the same in hours, but priced at the variable production overhead rate per hour.

(b) In our example, the efficiency variance would be as follows.

400 units of product X should take (× 2 hrs)	800 hrs
but did take (active hours)	760 hrs
Variable production overhead efficiency variance in hours	40 hrs (F)
× standard rate per hour	× $1.50
Variable production overhead efficiency variance in $	$60 (F)

(c) **Summary**

	$
Variable production overhead expenditure variance	90 (A)
Variable production overhead efficiency variance	60 (F)
Variable production overhead total variance	30 (A)

5 Fixed production overhead variances

Exam focus point

Fixed production overhead variances (particularly the capacity variance) are an area where students perform poorly. Make sure you study this section carefully and attempt all the questions to ensure you will not be one of these students!

5.1 Introduction

FAST FORWARD

The fixed production overhead total variance can be subdivided into an **expenditure** variance and a **volume** variance. The fixed production overhead volume variance can be further subdivided into an **efficiency** and **capacity** variance.

You may have noticed that the method of calculating cost variances for variable cost items is essentially the same for labour, materials and variable overheads. Fixed production overhead variances are very different. In an **absorption costing system**, they are an attempt to explain the **under– or over-absorption of fixed production overheads** in production costs. We looked at under/over absorption of fixed overheads in Part B.

The fixed production overhead total variance (ie the under– or over-absorbed fixed production overhead) may be broken down into two parts as usual.

- An **expenditure** variance
- A **volume** variance. This in turn may be split into two parts.
  - A **volume efficiency variance**
  - A **volume capacity variance**

You will find it easier to calculate and understand **fixed overhead variances**, if you keep in mind the whole time that you are trying to 'explain' (put a name and value to) any under– or over-absorbed overhead.

PART C4 INFORMATION FOR PLANNING AND PERFORMANCE MANAGEMENT

Exam focus point

> You may need to be able to distinguish between marginal and absorption costing. The variances introduced above and discussed below relate to an absorption costing system. Marginal costing is dealt with in the final section of this chapter. In the marginal costing system the only fixed overhead variance is an expenditure variance.

5.2 Under/over absorption

Remember that the **absorption rate** is calculated as follows.

$$\text{Overhead absorption rate} = \frac{\text{Budgeted fixed overhead}}{\text{Budgeted activity level}}$$

Remember that the budgeted fixed overhead is the **planned** or **expected** fixed overhead and the budgeted activity level is the **planned** or **expected** activity level.

If either of the following are incorrect, then we will have an under- or over-absorption of overhead.

- The numerator (number on top) = Budgeted fixed overhead
- The denominator (number on bottom) = Budgeted activity level

5.3 The fixed overhead expenditure variance

The fixed overhead expenditure variance occurs if the numerator is incorrect. It measures the under- or over-absorbed overhead caused by the **actual total overhead** being different from the budgeted total overhead.

Therefore, fixed overhead expenditure variance = **Budgeted (planned) expenditure – Actual Expenditure**.

5.4 The fixed overhead volume variance

As we have already stated, the fixed overhead volume variance is made up of the following sub-variances.

- Fixed overhead efficiency variance
- Fixed overhead capacity variance

These variances arise if the denominator (ie the budgeted activity level) is incorrect.

The fixed overhead efficiency and capacity variances measure the under– or over-absorbed overhead caused by the **actual activity level** being different from the budgeted activity level used in calculating the absorption rate.

There are two reasons why the **actual activity** level may be different from the **budgeted activity level** used in calculating the absorption rate.

(a) The workforce may have worked more or less efficiently than the standard set. This deviation is measured by the **fixed overhead efficiency variance**.

(b) The hours worked by the workforce could have been different to the budgeted hours (regardless of the level of efficiency of the workforce) because of overtime and strikes etc. This deviation from the standard is measured by the **fixed overhead capacity variance**.

5.5 How to calculate the variances

In order to clarify the overhead variances which we have encountered in this section, consider the following definitions which are expressed in terms of how each overhead variance should be calculated.

13: VARIANCE ANALYSIS

Key terms

> **Fixed overhead total variance** is the difference between fixed overhead incurred and fixed overhead absorbed. In other words, it is the under– or over-absorbed fixed overhead.
>
> **Fixed overhead expenditure variance** is the difference between the budgeted fixed overhead expenditure and actual fixed overhead expenditure.
>
> **Fixed overhead volume variance** is the difference between actual and budgeted (planned) volume multiplied by the standard absorption rate per **unit**.
>
> **Fixed overhead volume efficiency variance** is the difference between the number of hours that actual production should have taken, and the number of hours actually taken (that is, worked) multiplied by the standard absorption rate per **hour**.
>
> **Fixed overhead volume capacity variance** is the difference between budgeted (planned) hours of work and the actual hours worked, multiplied by the standard absorption rate per **hour**.

You should now be ready to work through an example to demonstrate all of the fixed overhead variances.

5.6 Example: Fixed overhead variances

Suppose that a company plans to produce 1,000 units of product E during August 20X3. The expected time to produce a unit of E is five hours, and the budgeted fixed overhead is $20,000. The standard fixed overhead cost per unit of product E will therefore be as follows.

    5 hours at $4 per hour = $20 per unit

Actual fixed overhead expenditure in August 20X3 turns out to be $20,450. The labour force manages to produce 1,100 units of product E in 5,400 hours of work.

Required

Calculate the following variances.

(a) The fixed overhead total variance
(b) The fixed overhead expenditure variance
(c) The fixed overhead volume variance
(d) The fixed overhead volume efficiency variance
(e) The fixed overhead volume capacity variance

Solution

All of the variances help to assess the under- or over-absorption of fixed overheads, some in greater detail than others.

(a) **Fixed overhead total variance**

	$
Fixed overhead incurred	20,450
Fixed overhead absorbed (1,100 units × $20 per unit)	22,000
Fixed overhead total variance	1,550 (F)
(= under-/over-absorbed overhead)	

The variance is favourable because more overheads were absorbed than budgeted.

(b) **Fixed overhead expenditure variance**

	$
Budgeted fixed overhead expenditure	20,000
Actual fixed overhead expenditure	20,450
Fixed overhead expenditure variance	450 (A)

The variance is adverse because actual expenditure was greater than budgeted expenditure.

PART C4 INFORMATION FOR PLANNING AND PERFORMANCE MANAGEMENT

(c) **Fixed overhead volume variance**

The production volume achieved was greater than expected. The fixed overhead volume variance measures the difference at the standard rate.

	$
Actual production at standard rate (1,100 × $20 per unit)	22,000
Budgeted production at standard rate (1,000 × $20 per unit)	20,000
Fixed overhead volume variance	2,000 (F)

The variance is **favourable** because output was greater than expected.

(i) The labour force may have worked efficiently, and produced output at a faster rate than expected. Since overheads are absorbed at the rate of $20 per unit, more will be absorbed if units are produced more quickly. This **efficiency variance** is exactly the same in hours as the direct labour efficiency variance, but is valued in $ at the standard absorption rate for fixed overhead.

(ii) The labour force may have worked longer hours than budgeted, and therefore produced more output, so there may be a **capacity variance**.

(d) **Fixed overhead volume efficiency variance**

The volume efficiency variance is calculated in the same way as the labour efficiency variance.

1,100 units of product E should take (× 5 hrs)	5,500 hrs
but did take	5,400 hrs
Fixed overhead volume efficiency variance in hours	100 hrs (F)
× standard fixed overhead absorption rate per hour	× $4
Fixed overhead volume efficiency variance in $	$400 (F)

The labour force has produced 5,500 standard hours of work in 5,400 actual hours and so output is 100 standard hours (or 20 units of product E) higher than budgeted for this reason and the variance is **favourable**.

(e) **Fixed overhead volume capacity variance**

The volume capacity variance is the difference between the budgeted hours of work and the actual active hours of work (excluding any idle time).

Budgeted hours of work	5,000 hrs
Actual hours of work	5,400 hrs
Fixed overhead volume capacity variance	400 hrs (F)
× standard fixed overhead absorption rate per hour	× $4
Fixed overhead volume capacity variance in $	$1,600 (F)

Since the labour force worked 400 hours longer than planned, we should expect output to be 400 standard hours (or 80 units of product E) higher than budgeted and hence the variance is **favourable**.

The variances may be summarised as follows.

	$
Expenditure variance	450 (A)
Efficiency variance	400 (F)
Capacity variance	1,600 (F)
Over-absorbed overhead (total variance)	$1,550 (F)

Exam focus point

> In general, a favourable cost variance will arise if actual results are less than expected results. Be aware, however, of the **fixed overhead volume variance** and the **fixed overhead volume capacity variance** which give rise to favourable and adverse variances in the following situations.
>
> - A favourable fixed overhead volume variance occurs when actual production is **greater than** budgeted (planned) production.
>
> - An adverse fixed overhead volume variance occurs when actual production is **less than budgeted** (planned) production.
>
> - A favourable fixed overhead volume capacity variance occurs when actual hours of work are **greater than** budgeted (planned) hours of work.
>
> - An adverse fixed overhead volume capacity variance occurs when actual hours of work are **less than** budgeted (planned) hours of work.

Do not worry if you find fixed production overhead variances more difficult to grasp than the other variances we have covered. Most students do. Read over this section again and then try the following practice questions.

Question — Capacity variance

A manufacturing company operates a standard absorption costing system. Last month 25,000 production hours were budgeted and the budgeted fixed production overhead cost was $125,000. Last month the actual hours worked were 24,000 and the standard hours for actual production were 27,000.

What was the fixed production overhead capacity variance for last month?

- A $5,000 Adverse
- B $5,000 Favourable
- C $10,000 Adverse
- D $10,000 Favourable

Answer

The correct answer is A.

Standard fixed overhead absorption rate per hour = $125,000/25,000 = $5 per hour.

Fixed overhead volume capacity variance

Budgeted hours of work	25,000 hrs
Actual hours of work	24,000 hrs
Fixed overhead volume capacity variance	1,000 hrs (A)
× standard fixed overhead absorption rate per hour	× $5
Fixed overhead volume capacity variance in $	$5,000 (A)

Refer to the exam focus point above for the rules on how to identify an adverse fixed overhead volume capacity variance. Remember that the capacity variance represents part of the over/under absorption of overheads. As the company worked less hours than budgeted (and the standard fixed overhead absorption rate is calculated using budgeted hours) this will result in an under-absorption of overheads.

PART C4 INFORMATION FOR PLANNING AND PERFORMANCE MANAGEMENT

The following information relates to the questions shown below.

Barbados has prepared the following standard cost information for one unit of Product Zeta.

Direct materials	4 kg @ $10/kg	$40.00
Direct labour	2 hours @ $4/hour	$8.00
Fixed overheads	3 hours @ $2.50	$7.50

The fixed overheads are based on a budgeted expenditure of $75,000 and budgeted activity of 30,000 hours.

Actual results for the period were recorded as follows.

Production	9,000 units
Materials – 33,600 kg	$336,000
Labour – 16,500 hours	$68,500
Fixed overheads	$70,000

Question   Material variances

The direct material price and usage variances are:

	Material price $	Material usage $
A	–	24,000 (F)
B	–	24,000 (A)
C	24,000 (F)	–
D	24,000 (A)	–

Answer

Material price variance

	$
33,600 kg should have cost (× $10/kg)	336,000
and did cost	336,000
	–

Material usage variance

9,000 units should have used (× 4kg)	36,000 kg
but did use	33,600 kg
	2,400 kg (F)
× standard cost per kg	× $10
	24,000 (F)

The correct answer is therefore A.

Question   Labour variances

The direct labour rate and efficiency variances are:

	Labour rate $	Labour efficiency $
A	6,000 (F)	2,500 (A)
B	6,000 (A)	2,500 (F)
C	2,500 (A)	6,000 (F)
D	2,500 (F)	6,000 (A)

Answer

Direct labour rate variance

	$
16,500 hrs should have cost (× $4)	66,000
but did cost	68,500
	2,500 (A)

Direct labour efficiency variance

9,000 units should have taken (× 2 hrs)	18,000 hrs
but did take	16,500 hrs
	1,500 (F)
× standard rate per hour (× $4)	× $4
	6,000 (F)

The correct answer is therefore C.

Question — Overhead variances

The total fixed production overhead variance is:

A $5,000 (A)
B $5,000 (F)
C $2,500 (A)
D $2,500 (F)

Answer

	$
Fixed production overhead absorbed ($7.50 × 9,000)	67,500
Fixed production overhead incurred	70,000
	2,500 (A)

The correct answer is therefore C.

6 The reasons for cost variances

There are many possible reasons for cost variances arising, as you will see from the following list of possible causes.

Exam focus point: This is not an exhaustive list and in an examination question you should review the information given and use your imagination and common sense in analysing possible reasons for variances.

Variance	Favourable	Adverse
(a) Material price	Unforeseen discounts received More care taken in purchasing Change in material standard	Price increase Careless purchasing Change in material standard
(b) Material usage	Material used of higher quality than standard More effective use made of material Errors in allocating material to jobs	Defective material Excessive waste Theft Stricter quality control Errors in allocating material to jobs
(c) Labour rate	Use of apprentices or other workers at a rate of pay lower than standard	Wage rate increase Use of higher grade labour
(d) Idle time	The idle time variance is always adverse	Machine breakdown Non-availability of material Illness or injury to worker
(e) Labour efficiency	Output produced more quickly than expected because of work motivation, better quality of equipment or materials, or better methods. Errors in allocating time to jobs	Lost time in excess of standard allowed Output lower than standard set because of deliberate restriction, lack of training, or sub-standard material used Errors in allocating time to jobs
(f) Overhead expenditure	Savings in costs incurred More economical use of services	Increase in cost of services used Excessive use of services Change in type of services used
(g) Overhead volume efficiency	Labour force working more efficiently (favourable labour efficiency variance)	Labour force working less efficiently (adverse labour efficiency variance)
(h) Overhead volume capacity	Labour force working overtime	Machine breakdown, strikes, labour shortages

7 The significance of cost variances

7.1 Introduction

FAST FORWARD

Materiality, controllability, the type of standard being used, the interdependence of variances and the cost of an investigation should be taken into account when deciding whether to investigate reported variances.

Once variances have been calculated, management have to decide whether or not to investigate their causes. It would be extremely time consuming and expensive to investigate every variance therefore managers have to decide which variances are worthy of investigation.

There are a number of factors which can be taken into account when deciding whether or not a variance should be investigated.

(a) **Materiality.** A standard cost is really only an **average** expected cost and is not a rigid specification. Small variations either side of this average are therefore bound to occur. The problem is to decide whether a variation from standard should be considered **significant** and worthy of investigation. **Tolerance limits** can be set and only variances which exceed such limits would require investigating.

(b) **Controllability.** Some types of variance may not be controllable even once their cause is discovered. For example, if there is a general worldwide increase in the price of a raw material there is nothing that can be done internally to control the effect of this. If a central decision is made to award all employees a 10% increase in salary, staff costs in division A will increase by this amount and the variance is not controllable by division A's manager. Uncontrollable variances call for a change in the plan, not an investigation into the past.

(c) **The type of standard being used.**

 (i) The efficiency variance reported in any control period, whether for materials or labour, will depend on the **efficiency level** set. If, for example, an **ideal standard** is used, variances will always be **adverse**.

 (ii) A similar problem arises if **average price levels** are used as standards. If inflation exists, favourable price variances are likely to be reported at the beginning of a period, to be offset by adverse price variances later in the period as inflation pushes prices up.

(d) **Interdependence between variances.** Quite possibly, individual variances should not be looked at in isolation. One variance might be inter-related with another, and much of it might have occurred only because the other, inter-related, variance occurred too. We will investigate this issue further in a moment.

(e) **Costs of investigation.** The costs of an investigation should be weighed against the benefits of correcting the cause of a variance.

7.2 Interdependence between variances

When two variances are interdependent (interrelated) one will usually be adverse and the other one favourable.

7.3 Interdependence – materials price and usage variances

It may be decided to purchase cheaper materials for a job in order to obtain a favourable **price variance**. This may lead to higher materials wastage than expected and therefore, **adverse usage variances occur**. If the cheaper materials are more difficult to handle, there might be some **adverse labour efficiency variance** too.

If a decision is made to purchase more expensive materials, which perhaps have a longer service life, the price variance will be adverse but the usage variance might be favourable.

7.4 Interdependence – labour rate and efficiency variances

If employees in a workforce are paid higher rates for experience and skill, using a highly skilled team should incur an **adverse rate variance** at the same time as a **favourable efficiency variance**. In contrast, a **favourable rate variance** might indicate a high proportion of inexperienced workers in the workforce, which could result in an **adverse labour efficiency variance** and possibly an **adverse materials usage variance** (due to high rates of rejects).

8 Sales variances

8.1 Selling price variance

> The **selling price variance** is a measure of the effect on expected profit of a different selling price to standard selling price. It is calculated as the difference between what the sales revenue should have been for the actual quantity sold, and what it was.

8.2 Example: Selling price variance

Suppose that the standard selling price of product X is $15. Actual sales in 20X3 were 2,000 units at $15.30 per unit. The selling price variance is calculated as follows.

	$
Sales revenue from 2,000 units should have been (× $15)	30,000
but was (× $15.30)	30,600
Selling price variance	600 (F)

The variance calculated is **favourable** because the price was higher than expected.

8.3 Sales volume profit variance

> The **sales volume profit variance** is the difference between the actual units sold and the budgeted (planned) quantity, valued at the standard profit per unit. In other words, it measures the increase or decrease in standard profit as a result of the sales volume being higher or lower than budgeted (planned).

8.4 Example: Sales volume profit variance

Suppose that a company budgets to sell 8,000 units of product J for $12 per unit. The standard full cost per unit is $7. Actual sales were 7,700 units, at $12.50 per unit.

The **sales volume profit variance** is calculated as follows.

Budgeted sales volume	8,000 units
Actual sales volume	7,700 units
Sales volume variance in units	300 units (A)
× standard profit per unit ($(12 – 7))	× $5
Sales volume variance	$1,500 (A)

The variance calculated above is **adverse** because actual sales were less than budgeted (planned).

Question — Selling price variance

Jasper Co has the following budget and actual figures for 20X4.

	Budget	Actual
Sales units	600	620
Selling price per unit	$30	$29

Standard full cost of production = $28 per unit.

Required

Calculate the selling price variance and the sales volume profit variance.

Answer

Sales revenue for 620 units should have been (× $30)	18,600
but was (× $29)	17,980
Selling price variance	620 (A)
Budgeted sales volume	600 units
Actual sales volume	620 units
Sales volume variance in units	20 units (F)
× standard profit per unit ($(30 – 28))	× $2
Sales volume profit variance	$40 (F)

8.5 The significance of sales variances

The possible **interdependence** between sales price and sales volume variances should be obvious to you. A reduction in the sales price might stimulate bigger sales demand, so that an adverse sales price variance might be counterbalanced by a favourable sales volume variance. Similarly, a price rise would give a favourable price variance, but possibly at the cost of a fall in demand and an adverse sales volume variance.

It is therefore important in analysing an unfavourable sales variance that the overall consequence should be considered, that is, has there been a counterbalancing favourable variance as a direct result of the unfavourable one?

9 Operating statements

9.1 Introduction

FAST FORWARD

Operating statements show how the combination of variances reconcile budgeted profit and actual profit.

So far, we have considered how variances are calculated without considering how they combine to reconcile the difference between budgeted profit and actual profit during a period. This reconciliation is usually presented as a report to senior management at the end of each control period. The report is called an **operating statement** or **statement of variances**.

Key term

> An **operating statement** is a regular report for management of actual costs and revenues, usually showing variances from budget.

An extensive example will now be introduced, both to revise the variance calculations already described, and also to show how to combine them into an operating statement.

9.2 Example: Variances and operating statements

Sydney manufactures one product, and the entire product is sold as soon as it is produced. There are no opening or closing inventories and work in progress is negligible. The company operates a standard costing system and analysis of variances is made every month. The standard cost card for the product, a boomerang, is as follows.

PART C4 INFORMATION FOR PLANNING AND PERFORMANCE MANAGEMENT

STANDARD COST CARD – BOOMERANG

		$
Direct materials	0.5 kilos at $4 per kilo	2.00
Direct wages	2 hours at $2.00 per hour	4.00
Variable overheads	2 hours at $0.30 per hour	0.60
Fixed overhead	2 hours at $3.70 per hour	7.40
Standard cost		14.00
Standard profit		6.00
Standing selling price		20.00

Selling and administration expenses are not included in the standard cost, and are deducted from profit as a period charge.

Budgeted (planned) output for the month of June 20X7 was 5,100 units. Actual results for June 20X7 were as follows.

Production of 4,850 units was sold for $95,600.
Materials consumed in production amounted to 2,300 kg at a total cost of $9,800.
Labour hours paid for amounted to 8,500 hours at a cost of $16,800.
Actual operating hours amounted to 8,000 hours.
Variable overheads amounted to $2,600.
Fixed overheads amounted to $42,300.
Selling and administration expenses amounted to $18,000.

Required

Calculate all variances and prepare an operating statement for the month ended 30 June 20X7.

Solution

(a)

	$
2,300 kg of material should cost (× $4)	9,200
but did cost	9,800
Material price variance	600 (A)

(b)

4,850 boomerangs should use (× 0.5 kg)	2,425 kg
but did use	2,300 kg
Material usage variance in kg	125 kg (F)
× standard cost per kg	× $4
Material usage variance in $	$ 500 (F)

(c)

	$
8,500 hours of labour should cost (× $2)	17,000
but did cost	16,800
Labour rate variance	200 (F)

(d)

4,850 boomerangs should take (× 2 hrs)	9,700 hrs
but did take (active hours)	8,000 hrs
Labour efficiency variance in hours	1,700 hrs (F)
× standard cost per hour	× $2
Labour efficiency variance in $	$3,400 (F)

(e) **Idle time variance** 500 hours (A) × $2 $1,000 (A)

(f)

	$
8,000 hours incurring variable o/hd expenditure should cost (× $0.30)	2,400
but did cost	2,600
Variable overhead expenditure variance	200 (A)

(g) **Variable overhead efficiency variance** in hours is the same as the labour efficiency variance:
1,700 hours (F) × $0.30 per hour $510 (F)

(h)
	$
Budgeted fixed overhead (5,100 units × 2 hrs × $3.70)	37,740
Actual fixed overhead	42,300
Fixed overhead expenditure variance	4,560 (A)

(i)
	$
4,850 boomerangs should take (× 2 hrs)	9,700 hrs
but did take (active hours)	8,000 hrs
Fixed overhead volume efficiency variance in hrs	1,700 hrs (F)
× standard fixed overhead absorption rate per hour	× $3.70
Fixed overhead volume efficiency variance in $	6,290 (F)

(j)
	$
Budgeted hours of work (5,100 × 2 hrs)	10,200 hrs
Actual hours of work	8,000 hrs
Fixed overhead volume capacity variance in hrs	2,200 hrs (A)
× standard fixed overhead absorption rate per hour	× $3.70
Fixed overhead volume capacity variance in $	8,140 (A)

(k)
	$
Revenue from 4,850 boomerangs should be (× $20)	97,000
but was	95,600
Selling price variance	1,400 (A)

(l)
Budgeted sales volume	5,100 units
Actual sales volume	4,850 units
Sales volume profit variance in units	250 units
× standard profit per unit	× $6 (A)
Sales volume profit variance in $	$1,500 (A)

There are several ways in which an operating statement may be presented. Perhaps the most common format is one which **reconciles budgeted profit to actual profit**. In this example, sales and administration costs will be introduced at the end of the statement, so that we shall begin with 'budgeted profit before sales and administration costs'.

Sales variances are reported first, and the total of the budgeted profit and the two sales variances results in a figure for 'actual sales minus the standard cost of sales'. The cost variances are then reported, and an actual profit (before sales and administration costs) calculated. Sales and administration costs are then deducted to reach the actual profit for June 20X7.

SYDNEY – OPERATING STATEMENT JUNE 20X7

		$	$
Budgeted (planned) profit before sales and administration costs			30,600
Sales variances:	price	1,400 (A)	
	volume	1,500 (A)	
			2,900 (A)
Actual sales minus the standard cost of sales			27,700

	(F)	(A)	
Cost variances	$	$	
Material price		600	
Material usage	500		
Labour rate	200		
Labour efficiency	3,400		
Labour idle time		1,000	
Variable overhead expenditure		200	
Variable overhead efficiency	510		
Fixed overhead expenditure		4,560	
Fixed overhead volume efficiency	6,290		
Fixed overhead volume capacity		8,140	
	10,900	14,500	3,600 (A)
Actual profit before sales and administration costs			24,100
Sales and administration costs			18,000
Actual profit, June 20X7			6,100

		$	$
Check			
Sales			95,600
Materials		9,800	
Labour		16,800	
Variable overhead		2,600	
Fixed overhead		42,300	
Sales and administration		18,000	
			89,500
Actual profit			6,100

10 Variances in a standard marginal costing system

10.1 Introduction

FAST FORWARD

There are two main differences between the variances calculated in an absorption costing system and the variances calculated in a marginal costing system.

- In the marginal costing system **the only fixed overhead variance is an expenditure variance**.
- The sales volume variance is **valued at standard contribution margin**, not standard profit margin.

In all of the examples we have worked through so far, a system of standard absorption costing has been in operation. If an organisation uses **standard marginal costing** instead of standard absorption costing, there will be two differences in the way the variances are calculated.

(a) In marginal costing, fixed costs are not absorbed into product costs and so there are no fixed cost variances to explain any under or over absorption of overheads. There will, therefore, be **no fixed overhead volume variance**. There will be a fixed overhead expenditure variance which is calculated in exactly the same way as for absorption costing systems.

(b) The **sales volume variance** will be valued at **standard contribution margin** (sales price per unit minus variable costs of sale per unit), **not** standard **profit** margin.

10.2 Preparing a marginal costing operating statement

Returning once again to the example of Sydney, the variances in a system of standard marginal costing would be as follows.

(a) There is **no fixed overhead volume variance** (and therefore no fixed overhead volume efficiency and volume capacity variances).

(b) The standard contribution per unit of boomerang is $(20 – 6.60) = $13.40, therefore the **sales volume contribution variance** of 250 units (A) is valued at (× $13.40) = $3,350 (A).

The other variances are unchanged. However, this operating statement differs from an absorption costing operating statement in the following ways.

(a) It begins with the budgeted **contribution** ($30,600 + budgeted fixed production costs $37,740 = $68,340).

(b) The subtotal before the analysis of cost variances is actual sales ($95,600) less the standard **variable** cost of sales ($4,850 × $6.60) = $63,590.

(c) **Actual contribution** is highlighted in the statement.

(d) Budgeted (planned) fixed production overhead is adjusted by the fixed overhead expenditure variance to show the **actual** fixed production overhead expenditure.

Therefore a marginal costing operating statement might look like this.

SYDNEY – OPERATING STATEMENT JUNE 20X7

	$	$	$
Budgeted (planned) contribution			68,340
Sales variances: volume		3,350 (A)	
price		1,400 (A)	
			4,750 (A)
Actual sales minus the standard variable cost of sales			63,590
	(F)	(A)	
Variable cost variances			
Material price		600	
Material usage	500		
Labour rate	200		
Labour efficiency	3,400		
Labour idle time		1,000	
Variable overhead expenditure		200	
Variable overhead efficiency	510		
	4,610	1,800	
			2,810 (F)
Actual contribution			66,400
Budgeted (planned) fixed production overhead		37,740	
Expenditure variance		4,560 (A)	
Actual fixed production overhead			42,300
Actual profit before sales and administration costs			24,100
Sales and administration costs			18,000
Actual profit			6,100

Notice that the actual profit is the same as the profit calculated by standard absorption costing because there were no changes in inventory levels. Absorption costing and marginal costing do not always produce an identical profit figure.

Question

Variances

Piglet, a manufacturing firm, operates a standard marginal costing system. It makes a single product, PIG, using a single raw material LET.

Standard costs relating to PIG have been calculated as follows.

Standard cost schedule – PIG

	Per unit $
Direct material, LET, 100 kg at $5 per kg	500
Direct labour, 10 hours at $8 per hour	80
Variable production overhead, 10 hours at $2 per hour	20
	600

The standard selling price of a PIG is $900 and Piglet Co produce 1,020 units a month.

During December 20X0, 1,000 units of PIG were produced. Relevant details of this production are as follows.

Direct material LET

90,000 kgs costing $720,000 were bought and used.

Direct labour

8,200 hours were worked during the month and total wages were $63,000.

Variable production overhead

The actual cost for the month was $25,000.

Inventories of the direct material LET are valued at the standard price of $5 per kg.

Each PIG was sold for $975.

Required

Calculate the following for the month of December 20X0.

(a) Variable production cost variance
(b) Direct labour cost variance, analysed into rate and efficiency variances
(c) Direct material cost variance, analysed into price and usage variances
(d) Variable production overhead variance, analysed into expenditure and efficiency variances
(e) Selling price variance
(f) Sales volume contribution variance

Answer

(a) This is simply a 'total' variance.

	$
1,000 units should have cost (× $600)	600,000
but did cost (see working)	808,000
Variable production cost variance	208,000 (A)

(b) **Direct labour cost variances**

	$
8,200 hours should cost (× $8)	65,600
but did cost	63,000
Direct labour rate variance	2,600 (F)

1,000 units should take (× 10 hours)		10,000 hrs
but did take		8,200 hrs
Direct labour efficiency variance in hrs		1,800 hrs (F)
× standard rate per hour		× $8
Direct labour efficiency variance in $		$14,400 (F)

Summary

	$
Rate	2,600 (F)
Efficiency	14,400 (F)
Total	17,000 (F)

(c) **Direct material cost variances**

	$
90,000 kg should cost (× $5)	450,000
but did cost	720,000
Direct material price variance	270,000 (A)

1,000 units should use (× 100 kg)	100,000 kg
but did use	90,000 kg
Direct material usage variance in kgs	10,000 kg (F)
× standard cost per kg	× $5
Direct material usage variance in $	$50,000 (F)

Summary

	$
Price	270,000 (A)
Usage	50,000 (F)
Total	220,000 (A)

(d) **Variable production overhead variances**

	$
8,200 hours incurring o/hd should cost (× $2)	16,400
but did cost	25,000
Variable production overhead expenditure variance	8,600 (A)

Efficiency variance in hrs (from (b))	1,800 hrs (F)
× standard rate per hour	× $2
Variable production overhead efficiency variance	$3,600 (F)

Summary

	$
Expenditure	8,600 (A)
Efficiency	3,600 (F)
Total	5,000 (A)

(e) **Selling price variance**

	$
Revenue from 1,000 units should have been (× $900)	900,000
but was (× $975)	975,000
Selling price variance	75,000 (F)

PART C4 INFORMATION FOR PLANNING AND PERFORMANCE MANAGEMENT

(f) **Sales volume contribution variance**

Budgeted sales	1,020 units
Actual sales	1,000 units
Sales volume variance in units	20 units (A)
× standard contribution margin ($(900 – 600))	× $300
Sales volume contribution variance in $	$6,000 (A)

Workings

	$
Direct material	720,000
Total wages	63,000
Variable production overhead	25,000
	808,000

Question — Reconciling contributions

A company uses standard marginal costing. Last month the standard contribution on actual sales was $10,000 and the following variances arose.

	$
Total variable costs variance	2,000 (A)
Sales price variance	500 (F)
Sales volume contribution variance	1,000 (A)

What was the actual contribution for last month?

A $7,000
B $7,500
C $8,000
D $8,500

Answer

The correct answer is D.

	$
Standard contribution on actual sales	10,000
Add favourable sales price variance	500
Less adverse total variable costs variance	(2,000)
Actual contribution	**8,500**

Question — Calculating actual contribution from variances

A company uses standard marginal costing. Last month, when all sales were at the standard selling price, the standard contribution from actual sales was $50,000 and the following variances arose:

	$
Total variable costs variance	3,500 (A)
Total fixed costs variance	1,000 (F)
Sales volume contribution variance	2,000 (F)

What was the actual contribution for last month?

A $46,500
B $47,500
C $48,500
D $49,500

Answer

The correct answer is A.

	$
Standard contribution on actual sales	50,000
Less: Adverse total variable costs variance	(3,500)
Actual contribution	46,500

Chapter roundup

- A **variance** is the difference between a planned, budgeted, or standard cost and the actual cost incurred. The same comparisons can be made for revenues. The process by which the **total** difference between standard and actual results is analysed is known as the **variance analysis**.

- The direct material total variance can be subdivided into the **direct material price** variance and the **direct material usage** variance.

- Direct material price variances are usually extracted at the time of **receipt** of the materials rather than at the time of usage.

- The direct labour total variance can be subdivided into the **direct labour rate** variance and the **direct labour efficiency** variance.

- The variable production overhead total variance can be subdivided into the variable production overhead **expenditure** variance and the variable production overhead **efficiency** variance **(based on active hours)**.

- The fixed production overhead total variance can be subdivided into an **expenditure** variance and a **volume** variance. The fixed production overhead volume variance can be further subdivided into an **efficiency** and **capacity** variance.

- Materiality, controllability, the type of standard being used, the interdependence of variances and the cost of an investigation should be taken into account when deciding whether to investigate reported variances.

- The **selling price variance** is a measure of the effect on expected profit of a different selling price to standard selling price. It is calculated as the difference between what the sales revenue should have been for the actual quantity sold, and what it was.

- The **sales volume profit variance** is the difference between the actual units sold and the budgeted (planned) quantity, valued at the standard profit per unit. In other words, it measures the increase or decrease in standard profit as a result of the sales volume being higher or lower than budgeted (planned).

- **Operating statements** show how the combination of variances reconcile budgeted profit and actual profit.

- There are two main differences between the variances calculated in an absorption costing system and the variances calculated in a marginal costing system.
    - In a marginal costing system **the only fixed overhead variance is an expenditure variance.**
    - The sales volume variance is **valued at standard contribution margin**, not standard profit margin.

Quick quiz

1. Subdivide the following variances.

    (a) Direct materials cost variance

    (b) Direct labour cost variance

    (c) Variable production overhead variance

2. What are the two main advantages in calculating the material price variance at the time of receipt of materials?

3. Idle time variances are always adverse.

    True ☐

    False ☐

4. Adverse material usage variances might occur for the following reasons.

    I   Defective material
    II   Excessive waste
    III Theft
    IV Unforeseen discounts received

    A   I
    B   I and II
    C   I, II and III
    D   I, II, III and IV

5. List the factors which should be taken into account when deciding whether or not a variance should be investigated.

6. What is the sales volume profit variance?

7. A regular report for management of actual cost, and revenue, and usually comparing actual results with budgeted (planned) results (and showing variances) is known as:

    A   Bank statement
    B   Variance statement
    C   Budget statement
    D   Operating statement

8. If an organisation uses standard marginal costing instead of standard absorption costing, which two variances are calculated differently?

Answers to quick quiz

1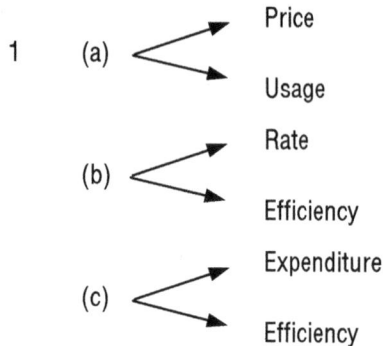
   (a) Price / Usage
   (b) Rate / Efficiency
   (c) Expenditure / Efficiency

2 (a) The earlier variances are extracted, the sooner they will be brought to the attention of managers.
   (b) All inventories will be valued at standard price which requires less administration effort.

3 True

4 C

5 - Materiality
   - Controllability
   - Type of standard being used
   - Interdependence between variances
   - Costs of investigation

6 It is a measure of the increase or decrease in standard profit as a result of the sales volume being higher or lower than budgeted (planned).

7 D

8 (a) In marginal costing there is no fixed overhead volume variance (because fixed costs are not absorbed into product costs).

   (b) In marginal costing, the sales volume variance will be valued at standard contribution margin and not standard profit margin.

End of chapter question

Sminko Ltd

Sminko Ltd manufactures and sells a single product, the Gizmo. The standard budget for the month ending 30 September 20X8 is as follows:

Sales of 1,200 Gizmos at $20 each; 380 kg of direct materials at a cost of $7.50 per kg; 950 hours of direct labour at $6.00 per hour and overheads of $8,500.

The actual results for the month were:

Sales of 1,050 Gizmos at $16 each; use of 350 kg of materials at $9.40 per kg; 900 hours of direct labour at $6.50 per hour and overheads of $9,700.

Required

Using the above information:

(a) Calculate detailed variances for sales, materials, labour and overheads. **(9 marks)**

(b) Prepare a standard cost operating statement that reconciles the standard and actual net profit for September 20X8. **(6 marks)**

(c) Comment briefly on why the variances may have arisen and suggest possible courses of action that the company could take. **(5 marks)**

(Total = 20 marks)

Information for decision making

Cost-volume-profit (CVP) analysis

Topic list	Syllabus reference
1 CVP analysis and breakeven point	C5.1
2 The contribution to sales (C/S) ratio	C5.1
3 The margin of safety	C5.1
4 Breakeven arithmetic and profit targets	C5.1
5 Breakeven charts, contribution charts and profit/volume charts	C5.1
6 Limitations of CVP analysis	C5.1

Introduction

You should by now realise that the cost accountant needs estimates of **fixed** and **variable costs**, and **revenues**, at various output levels. The cost accountant, must also be fully aware of **cost behaviour** because, to be able to estimate costs, he must know what a particular cost will do given particular conditions.

An understanding of cost behaviour is not all that you may need to know, however. The application of **cost-volume-profit analysis**, which is based on the cost behaviour principles and marginal costing ideas, is sometimes necessary so that the appropriate decision-making information can be provided. As you may have guessed, this chapter is going to look at that very topic, **cost-volume-profit analysis** or **breakeven analysis**.

1 CVP analysis and breakeven point

1.1 Introduction

> **Cost-volume-profit (CVP)/breakeven analysis** is the study of the interrelationships between costs, volume and profit at various levels of activity.

The management of an organisation usually wishes to know the profit likely to be made if the aimed-for production and sales for the year are achieved. Management may also be interested to know the following.

(a) The **breakeven** point which is the activity level at which there is neither profit nor loss
(b) The **amount** by which actual **sales can fall** below anticipated sales, **without** a **loss** being incurred

1.2 Breakeven point

> $$\text{Breakeven point} = \frac{\text{Total fixed costs}}{\text{Contribution per unit}} = \frac{\text{Contribution required to break even}}{\text{Contribution per unit}}$$
> = Number of units of sale required to break even.

1.3 Example: Breakeven point

Expected sales   10,000 units at $8 = $80,000
Variable cost $5 per unit
Fixed costs $21,000

Required

Compute the breakeven point.

Solution

The contribution per unit is $(8 – 5)   = $3
Contribution required to break even   =   fixed costs = $21,000
Breakeven point (BEP)   =   21,000 ÷ 3
                                      =   7,000 units
In revenue, BEP   =   (7,000 × $8) = $56,000

Sales above $56,000 will result in profit of $3 per unit of additional sales and sales below $56,000 will mean a loss of $3 per unit for each unit by which sales fall short of 7,000 units. In other words, profit will improve or worsen by the amount of contribution per unit.

	7,000 units $	7,001 units $
Revenue	56,000	56,008
Less variable costs	35,000	35,005
Contribution	21,000	21,003
Less fixed costs	21,000	21,000
Profit	0 (= breakeven)	3

2 The contribution to sales (C/S) ratio

> $$\frac{\text{Contribution required to breakeven}}{\text{C/S ratio}} = \frac{\text{Fixed costs}}{\text{C/S ratio}} = \text{Breakeven point in terms of sales revenue}$$
> (The contribution/sales (C/S) ratio is also sometimes called a **profit/volume** or **P/V ratio**).

An alternative way of calculating the breakeven point to give an answer in terms of sales revenue.

In the example in Paragraph 1.3 the C/S ratio is $\frac{\$3}{\$8} = 37.5\%$

Breakeven is where sales revenue equals $\frac{\$21,000}{37.5\%} = \$56,000$

At a price of $8 per unit, this represents 7,000 units of sales.

FAST FORWARD

The **C/S ratio** (or **P/V ratio**) is a measure of how much contribution is earned from each $1 of sales.

The C/S ratio of 37.5% in the above example means that for every $1 of sales, a contribution of 37.5c is earned. Thus, in order to earn a total contribution of $21,000 and if contribution increases by 37.5c per $1 of sales, sales must be:

$\frac{\$1}{37.5c} \times \$21,000 = \$56,000$

Question
Breakeven point

The C/S ratio of product W is 20%. IB, the manufacturer of product W, wishes to make a contribution of $50,000 towards fixed costs. How many units of product W must be sold if the selling price is $10 per unit?

Answer

$\frac{\text{Required contribution}}{\text{C/S ratio}} = \frac{\$50,000}{20\%} = \$250,000$

∴ Number of units = $250,000 ÷ $10 = 25,000.

Question
C/S ratio

A company manufactures a single product with a variable cost of $44. The contribution to sales ratio is 45%. Monthly fixed costs are $396,000. What is the breakeven point in units?

Answer

Contribution per unit = $44/0.55 × 0.45
 = $36

Breakeven point = Fixed costs/contribution per unit
 = –$396,000/$36
 = 11,000 units

3 The margin of safety

FAST FORWARD

The **margin of safety** is the difference in units between the **budgeted sales volume** and the **breakeven sales volume**. It is sometimes expressed as a percentage of the budgeted sales volume. The margin of safety may also be expressed as the difference between the **budgeted sales revenue** and **breakeven sales revenue** expressed as a percentage of the budgeted sales revenue.

3.1 Example: Margin of safety

Mal de Mer makes and sells a product which has a variable cost of $30 and which sells for $40. Budgeted fixed costs are $70,000 and budgeted sales are 8,000 units.

Required

Calculate the breakeven point and the margin of safety.

Solution

(a) Breakeven point $= \dfrac{\text{Total fixed costs}}{\text{Contribution per unit}} = \dfrac{\$70,000}{\$(40-30)}$

$= 7,000$ units

(b) Margin of safety $= 8,000 - 7,000$ units $= 1,000$ units

which may be expressed as $\dfrac{1,000 \text{ units}}{8,000 \text{ units}} \times 100\% \times 100\% = 12\frac{1}{2}\%$ of budget

(c) The margin of safety indicates to management that actual sales can fall short of budget by 1,000 units or 12½% before the breakeven point is reached and no profit at all is made.

4 Breakeven arithmetic and profit targets

FAST FORWARD

At the **breakeven point**, sales revenue equals total costs and there is no profit. At the breakeven point **total contribution = fixed costs**.

Formula to learn

S = V + F

where S = Sales revenue
       V = Total variable costs
       F = Total fixed costs

Subtracting V from each side of the equation, we get:

S – V = F, that is, **total contribution = fixed costs**

4.1 Example: Breakeven arithmetic

Butterfingers makes a product which has a variable cost of $7 per unit.

Required

If fixed costs are $63,000 per annum, calculate the selling price per unit if the company wishes to break even with a sales volume of 12,000 units.

Solution

			$
Contribution required to break even (= Fixed costs)	=	$63,000	
Volume of sales	=	12,000 units	
Required contribution per unit (S – V)	=	$63,000 ÷ 12,000 =	5.25
Variable cost per unit (V)	=		7.00
Required sales price per unit (S)	=		12.25

330

4.2 Target profits

FAST FORWARD

The **target profit** is achieved when S = V + F + P. Therefore the total contribution required for a target profit = **fixed costs + required profit.**

A similar formula may be applied where a company wishes to achieve a certain profit during a period. To achieve this profit, sales must cover all costs and leave the required profit.

Formula to learn

The **target profit** is achieved when: S = V + F + P,

where   P = required profit

Subtracting V from each side of the equation, we get:

S − V   = F + P, so

Total contribution required   = F + P

4.3 Example: Target profits

Riding Breeches makes and sells a single product, for which variable costs are as follows.

	$
Direct materials	10
Direct labour	8
Variable production overhead	6
	24

The sales price is $30 per unit, and fixed costs per annum are $68,000. The company wishes to make a profit of $16,000 per annum.

Required

Determine the sales required to achieve this profit.

Solution

Required contribution = fixed costs + profit = $68,000 + $16,000 = $84,000

Required sales can be calculated in one of two ways.

(a) $\dfrac{\text{Required contribution}}{\text{Contribution per unit}} = \dfrac{\$84,000}{\$(30-24)} = 14{,}000$ units, or $420,000 in revenue

(b) $\dfrac{\text{Required contribution}}{\text{C/S ratio}} = \dfrac{\$84{,}000}{20\%*} = \$420{,}000$ of revenue, or 14,000 units.

* C/S ratio = $\dfrac{\$30 - \$24}{\$30} = \dfrac{\$6}{\$30} = 0.2 = 20\%$.

Question   Target profits

Seven League Boots wishes to sell 14,000 units of its product, which has a variable cost of $15 to make and sell. Fixed costs are $47,000 and the required profit is $23,000.

Required

Calculate the sales price per unit.

PART C5 INFORMATION FOR DECISION MAKING

Answer

Required contribution	=	fixed costs plus profit
	=	$47,000 + $23,000
	=	$70,000
Required sales		14,000 units

	$
Required contribution per unit sold	5
Variable cost per unit	15
Required sales price per unit	20

4.4 Decisions to change sales price or costs

You may come across a problem in which you have to work out the effect of altering the selling price, variable cost per unit or fixed cost. Such problems are slight variations on basic breakeven arithmetic.

4.5 Example: Change in selling price

Stomer Cakes bake and sell a single type of cake. The variable cost of production is 15c and the current sales price is 25c. Fixed costs are $2,600 per month, and the annual profit for the company at current sales volume is $36,000. The volume of sales demand is constant throughout the year.

The sales manager, Ian Digestion, wishes to raise the sales price to 29c per cake, but considers that a price rise will result in some loss of sales.

Required

Ascertain the minimum volume of sales required each month to raise the price to 29c.

Solution

The minimum volume of demand which would justify a price of 29c is one which would leave total profit at least the same as before, ie $3,000 per month. Required profit should be converted into required contribution, as follows.

	$
Monthly fixed costs	2,600
Monthly profit, minimum required	3,000
Current monthly contribution	5,600
Contribution per unit (25c – 15c)	10c
Current monthly sales	56,000 cakes

The minimum volume of sales required after the price rise will be an amount which earns a contribution of $5,600 per month, no worse than at the moment. The contribution per cake at a sales price of 29c would be 14c.

$$\text{Required sales} = \frac{\text{required contribution}}{\text{contribution per unit}} = \frac{\$5,600}{14c} = 40,000 \text{ cakes per month.}$$

4.6 Example: Change in production costs

Close Brickett makes a product which has a variable production cost of $8 and a variable sales cost of $2 per unit. Fixed costs are $40,000 per annum, the sales price per unit is $18, and the current volume of output and sales is 6,000 units.

The company is considering whether to have an improved machine for production. Annual hire costs would be $10,000 and it is expected that the variable cost of production would fall to $6 per unit.

Required

(a) Determine the number of units that must be produced and sold to achieve the same profit as is currently earned, if the machine is hired.

(b) Calculate the annual profit with the machine if output and sales remain at 6,000 units per annum.

Solution

The current unit contribution is $(18 − (8 + 2)) = 8

(a)

	$
Current contribution (6,000 × $8)	48,000
Less current fixed costs	40,000
Current profit	8,000

With the new machine fixed costs will go up by $10,000 to $50,000 per annum. The variable cost per unit will fall to $(6 + 2) = 8, and the contribution per unit will be $10.

	$
Required profit (as currently earned)	8,000
Fixed costs	50,000
Required contribution	58,000
Contribution per unit	$10
Sales required to earn $8,000 profit	5,800 units

(b) **If sales are 6,000 units**

	$	$
Sales (6,000 × $18)		108,000
Variable costs: production (6,000 × $6)	36,000	
sales (6,000 × $2)	12,000	
		48,000
Contribution (6,000 × $10)		60,000
Less fixed costs		50,000
Profit		10,000

Alternative calculation

	$
Profit at 5,800 units of sale (see (a))	8,000
Contribution from sale of extra 200 units (× $10)	2,000
Profit at 6,000 units of sale	10,000

4.7 Sales price and sales volume

It may be clear by now that, given no change in fixed costs, **total profit is maximised when the total contribution is at its maximum**. Total contribution in turn depends on the unit contribution and on the sales volume.

An increase in the sales price will increase unit contribution, but sales volume is likely to fall because fewer customers will be prepared to pay the higher price. A decrease in sales price will reduce the unit contribution, but sales volume may increase because the goods on offer are now cheaper. The **optimum combination** of sales price and sales volume is arguably the one which **maximises total contribution**.

4.8 Example: Profit maximisation

C has developed a new product which is about to be launched on to the market. The variable cost of selling the product is $12 per unit. The marketing department has estimated that at a sales price of $20, annual demand would be 10,000 units.

However, if the sales price is set above $20, sales demand would fall by 500 units for each 50c increase above $20. Similarly, if the price is set below $20, demand would increase by 500 units for each 50c stepped reduction in price below $20.

Required

Determine the price which would maximise C's profit in the next year.

Solution

At a price of $20 per unit, the unit contribution would be $(20 – 12) = $8. Each 50c increase (or decrease) in price would raise (or lower) the unit contribution by 50c. The total contribution is calculated at each sales price by multiplying the unit contribution by the expected sales volume.

	Unit price $	Unit contribution $	Sales volume Units	Total contribution $
	20.00	8.00	10,000	80,000
(a) Reduce price				
	19.50	7.50	10,500	78,750
	19.00	7.00	11,000	77,000
(b) Increase price				
	20.50	8.50	9,500	80,750
	21.00	9.00	9,000	81,000
	21.50	9.50	8,500	80,750
	22.00	10.00	8,000	80,000
	22.50	10.50	7,500	78,750

The total contribution would be maximised, and therefore profit maximised, at a sales price of $21 per unit, and sales demand of 9,000 units.

Question — Breakeven output level

Betty Battle manufactures a product which has a selling price of $20 and a variable cost of $10 per unit. The company incurs annual fixed costs of $29,000. Annual sales demand is 9,000 units.

New production methods are under consideration, which would cause a $1,000 increase in fixed costs and a reduction in variable cost to $9 per unit. The new production methods would result in a superior product and would enable sales to be increased to 9,750 units per annum at a price of $21 each.

If the change in production methods were to take place, the breakeven output level would be:

A   400 units higher
B   400 units lower
C   100 units higher
D   100 units lower

Answer

	Current $	Revised $	Difference
Selling price	20	21	
Variable costs	10	9	
Contribution per unit	10	12	
Fixed costs	$29,000	$30,000	
Breakeven point (units)	2,900	2,500	**400 lower**

$$\text{Breakeven point} = \frac{\text{Total fixed costs}}{\text{Contribution per unit}}$$

$$\text{Current BEP} = \frac{\$29,000}{\$10} = 2,900 \text{ units}$$

$$\text{Revised BEP} = \frac{\$30,000}{\$12} = 2,500 \text{ units}$$

The correct answer is therefore B.

5 Breakeven charts, contribution charts and profit/volume charts

5.1 Breakeven charts

FAST FORWARD

The breakeven point can also be determined graphically using a **breakeven chart** or a **contribution breakeven chart**. These charts show approximate levels of profit or loss at different sales volume levels within a limited range.

A breakeven chart has the following axes.

- A **horizontal** axis showing the **sales/output** (in value or units)
- A **vertical axis** showing $ for **sales revenues** and **costs**

The following lines are drawn on the breakeven chart.

(a) The **sales line**

　　(i)　Starts at the origin
　　(ii)　Ends at the point signifying expected sales

(b) The **fixed costs line**

　　(i)　Runs parallel to the horizontal axis
　　(ii)　Meets the vertical axis at a point which represents total fixed costs

(c) The **total costs line**

　　(i)　Starts where the fixed costs line meets the vertical axis
　　(ii)　Ends at the point which represents anticipated sales on the horizontal axis and total costs of anticipated sales on the vertical axis

The **breakeven point** is the **intersection** of the **sales line** and the **total costs line**.

The distance between the **breakeven point** and the **expected (or budgeted) sales**, in units, indicates the **margin of safety**.

5.2 Example: A breakeven chart

The budgeted annual output of a factory is 120,000 units. The fixed overheads amount to $40,000 and the variable costs are 50c per unit. The sales price is $1 per unit.

Required

Construct a breakeven chart showing the current breakeven point and profit earned up to the present maximum capacity.

Solution

We begin by calculating the profit at the budgeted annual output.

	$
Sales (120,000 units)	120,000
Variable costs	60,000
Contribution	60,000
Fixed costs	40,000
Profit	20,000

Breakeven chart (1) is shown on the following page.

The chart is drawn as follows.

(a) The **vertical axis** represents **money** (costs and revenue) and the **horizontal axis** represents the **level of activity** (production and sales).

(b) The fixed costs are represented by a **straight line parallel to the horizontal axis** (in our example, at $40,000).

(c) The **variable costs** are added 'on top of' fixed costs, to give **total costs**. It is assumed that fixed costs are the same in total and variable costs are the same per unit at all levels of output.

The line of costs is therefore a straight line and only two points need to be plotted and joined up. Perhaps the two most convenient points to plot are total costs at zero output, and total costs at the budgeted output and sales.

- At zero output, costs are equal to the amount of fixed costs only, $40,000, since there are no variable costs.

- At the budgeted output of 120,000 units, costs are $100,000.

	$
Fixed costs	40,000
Variable costs 120,000 × 50c	60,000
Total costs	100,000

(d) The sales line is also drawn by plotting two points and joining them up.

   (i) At zero sales, revenue is nil.
   (ii) At the budgeted output and sales of 120,000 units, revenue is $120,000.

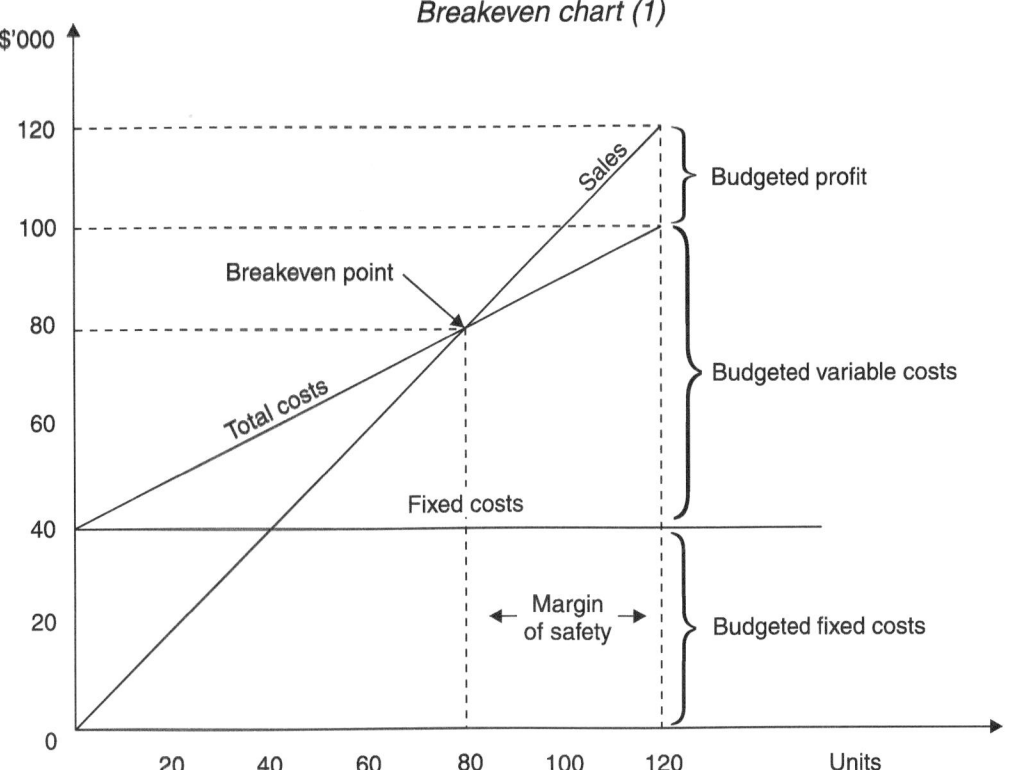

Breakeven chart (1)

The breakeven point is where total costs are matched exactly by total revenue. From the chart, this can be seen to occur at output and sales of 80,000 units, when revenue and costs are both $80,000. This breakeven point can be proved mathematically as:

$$\frac{\text{Required contribution (= fixed costs)}}{\text{Contribution per unit}} = \frac{\$40{,}000}{50\text{c per unit}} = 80{,}000 \text{ units}$$

The margin of safety can be seen on the chart as the difference between the budgeted level of activity and the breakeven level.

5.3 The value of breakeven charts

Breakeven charts are used as follows.

- To **plan** the production of a company's products
- To **market** a company's products
- To give a **visual display** of breakeven arithmetic

5.4 Example: Variations in the use of breakeven charts

Breakeven charts can be used to **show variations** in the possible **sales price**, **variable costs** or **fixed costs**. Suppose that a company sells a product which has a variable cost of $2 per unit. Fixed costs are $15,000. It has been estimated that if the sales price is set at $4.40 per unit, the expected sales volume would be 7,500 units; whereas if the sales price is lower, at $4 per unit, the expected sales volume would be 10,000 units.

Required

Draw a breakeven chart to show the budgeted profit, the breakeven point and the margin of safety at each of the possible sales prices.

Solution

Workings

	Sales price $4.40 per unit		Sales price $4 per unit
	$		$
Fixed costs	15,000		15,000
Variable costs (7,500 × $2.00)	15,000	(10,000 × $2.00)	20,000
Total costs	30,000		35,000
Budgeted revenue (7,500 × $4.40)	33,000	(10,000 × $4.00)	40,000

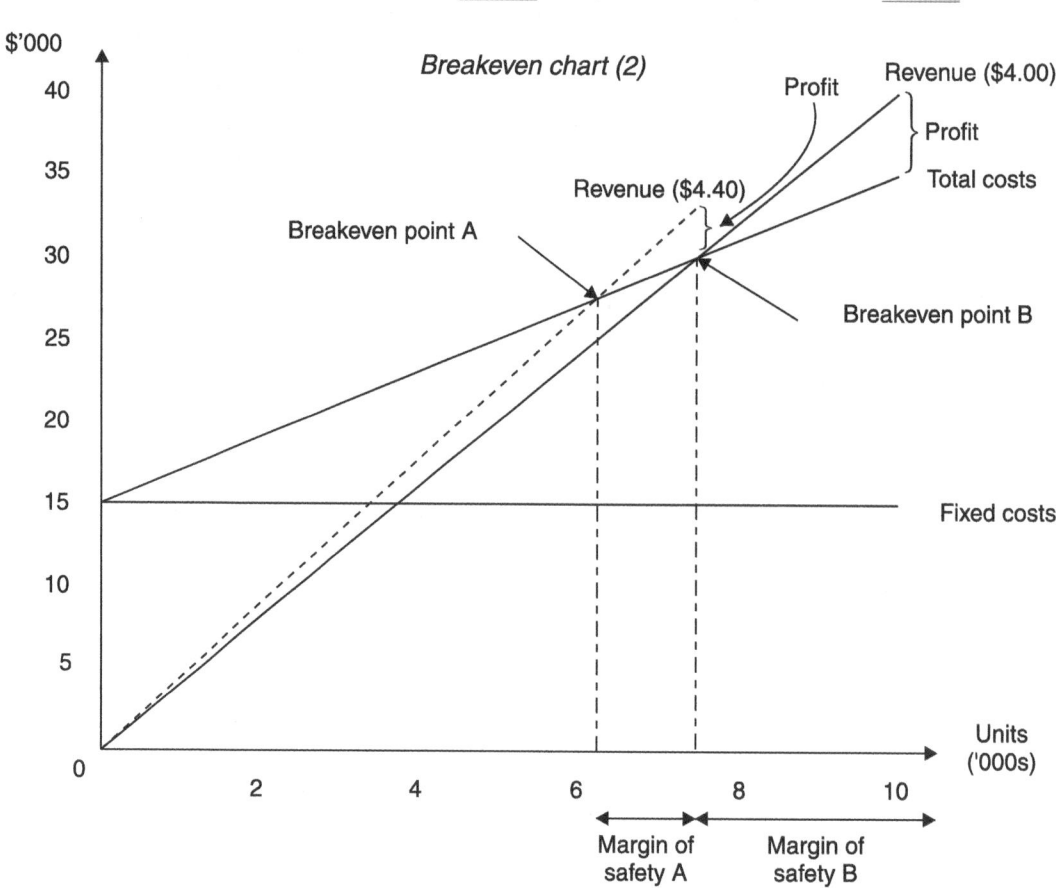

Breakeven chart (2)

(a) **Breakeven point A** is the breakeven point at a sales price of $4.40 per unit, which is 6,250 units or $27,500 in costs and revenues.

(check: $\dfrac{\text{Required contribution to breakeven}}{\text{Contribution per unit}}$ $\dfrac{\$15,000}{\$2.40 \text{ per unit}}$ = 6,250 units)

The margin of safety (A) is 7,500 units − 6,250 units = 1,250 units or 16.7% of expected sales.

(b) **Breakeven point B** is the breakeven point at a sales price of $4 per unit which is 7,500 units or $30,000 in costs and revenues.

(check: $\dfrac{\text{Required contribution to breakeven}}{\text{Contribution per unit}}$ $\dfrac{\$15,000}{\$2 \text{ per unit}}$ = 7,500 units)

The margin of safety (B) = 10,000 units − 7,500 units = 2,500 units or 25% of expected sales.

Since a price of $4 per unit gives a higher expected profit and a wider margin of safety, this price will probably be preferred even though the breakeven point is higher than at a sales price of $4.40 per unit.

Contribution (or contribution breakeven) charts

As an alternative to drawing the fixed cost line first, it is possible to start with that for variable costs. This is known as a **contribution chart**. An example is shown below using the example in Paragraphs 5.2 and 5.4.

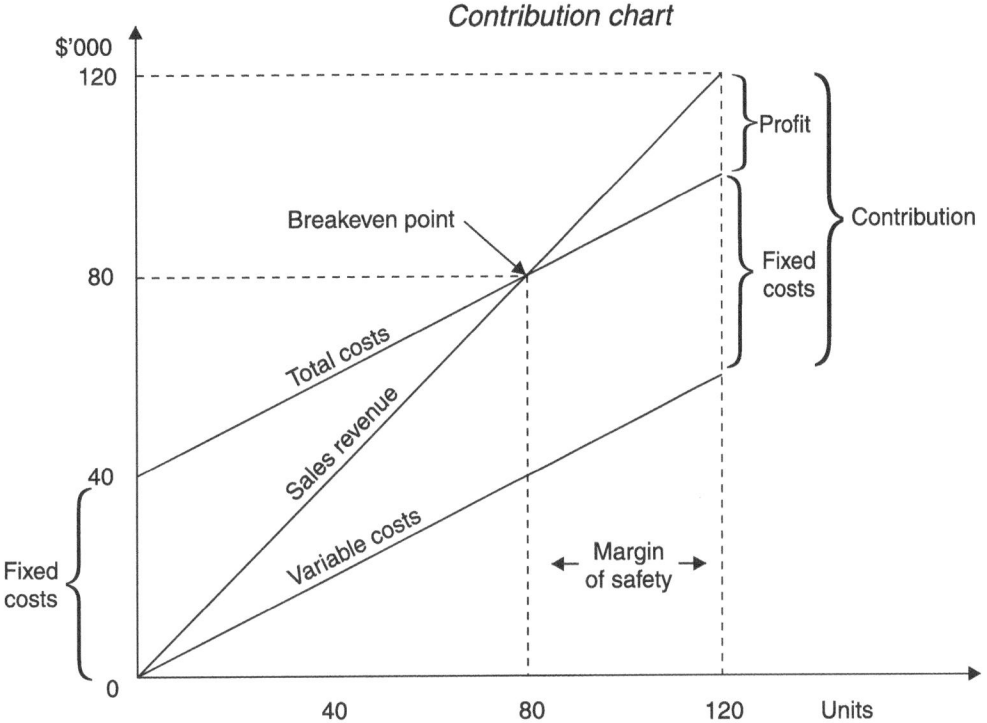

One of the **advantages** of the contribution chart is that is shows clearly the **contribution** for **different levels of production** (indicated here at 120,000 units, the budgeted level of output) as the 'wedge' shape between the sales revenue line and the variable costs line. At the **breakeven point**, the **contribution equals fixed costs** exactly. At levels of output **above** the **breakeven** point, the **contribution** is **larger**, and not only covers fixed costs, but also leaves a profit. **Below** the **breakeven** point, the **loss** is the amount by which contribution fails to cover fixed costs.

5.5 The profit/volume (P/V) chart

FAST FORWARD

The **profit/volume (P/V) chart** is a variation of the breakeven chart which illustrates the relationship of costs and profits to sales and the margin of safety.

A P/V chart is constructed as follows (look at the chart in the example that follows as you read the explanation).

(a) 'P' is on the y axis and actually comprises not only 'profit' but contribution to profit (in monetary value), extending above and below the x axis with a zero point at the intersection of the two axes, and the negative section below the x axis representing fixed costs. This means that at zero production, the firm is incurring a loss equal to the fixed costs.

(b) 'V' is on the x axis and comprises either volume of sales or value of sales (revenue).

(c) The profit-volume line is a straight line drawn with its starting point (at zero production) at the intercept on the y axis representing the level of fixed costs, and with a gradient of contribution/unit (or the P/V ratio if sales value is used rather than units). The P/V line will cut the x axis at the breakeven point of sales volume. Any point on the P/V line above the x axis represents the profit to the firm (as measured on the vertical axis) for that particular level of sales.

5.6 Example: P/V chart

Let us draw a P/V chart for our example. At sales of 120,000 units, total contribution will be 120,000 × $(1 − 0.5) = $60,000 and total profit will be $20,000.

PART C5 INFORMATION FOR DECISION MAKING

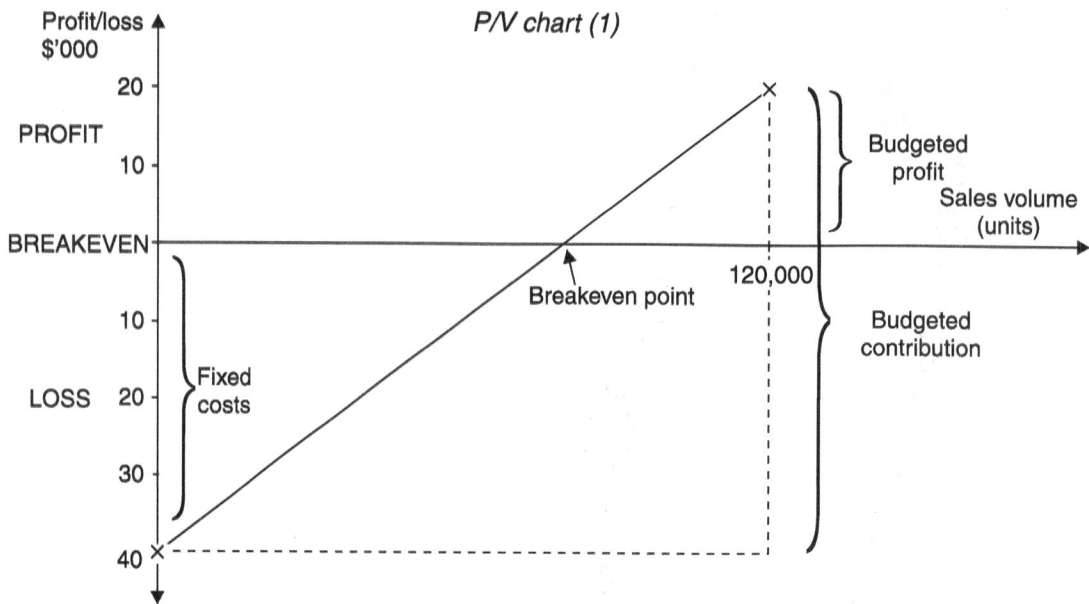

5.7 The advantage of the P/V chart

FAST FORWARD

The **P/V chart** shows clearly the effect on profit and breakeven point of any changes in selling price, variable cost, fixed cost and/or sales demand.

If the budgeted selling price of the product in our example is increased to $1.20, with the result that demand drops to 105,000 units despite additional fixed costs of $10,000 being spent on advertising, we could add a line representing this situation to our P/V chart.

At sales of 105,000 units, contribution will be 105,000 × $(1.20 − 0.50) = $73,500 and total profit will be $23,500 (fixed costs being $50,000).

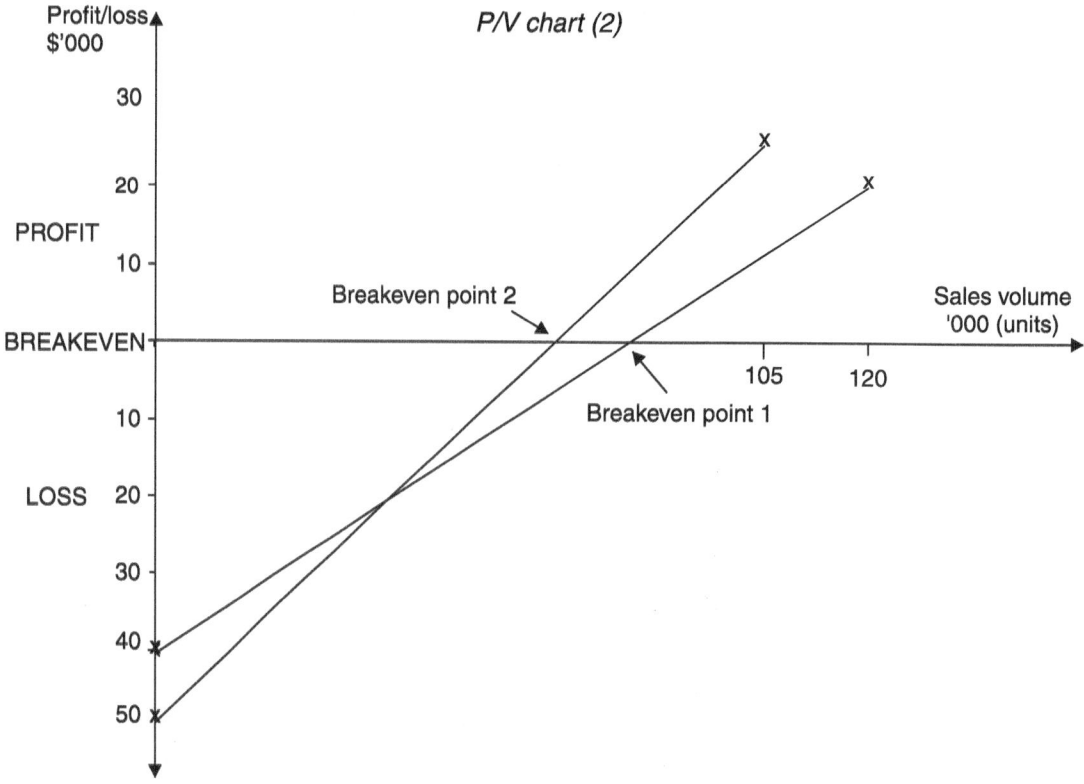

The diagram shows that if the selling price is increased, the breakeven point occurs at a lower level of sales revenue (71,429 units instead of 80,000 units), although this is not a particularly large increase when viewed in the context of the projected sales volume. It is also possible to see that for sales above 50,000 units, the profit achieved will be higher (and the loss achieved lower) if the price is $1.20. For sales volumes below 50,000 units the first option will yield lower losses.

The P/V chart is the clearest way of presenting such information; two conventional breakeven charts on one set of axes would be very confusing.

Changes in the variable cost per unit or in fixed costs at certain activity levels can also be easily incorporated into a P/V chart. The profit or loss at each point where the cost structure changes should be calculated and plotted on the graph so that the profit/volume line becomes a series of straight lines.

For example, suppose that in our example, at sales levels in excess of 120,000 units the variable cost per unit increases to $0.60 (perhaps because of overtime premiums that are incurred when production exceeds a certain level). At sales of 130,000 units, contribution would therefore be 130,000 × $(1 − 0.60) = $52,000 and total profit would be $12,000.

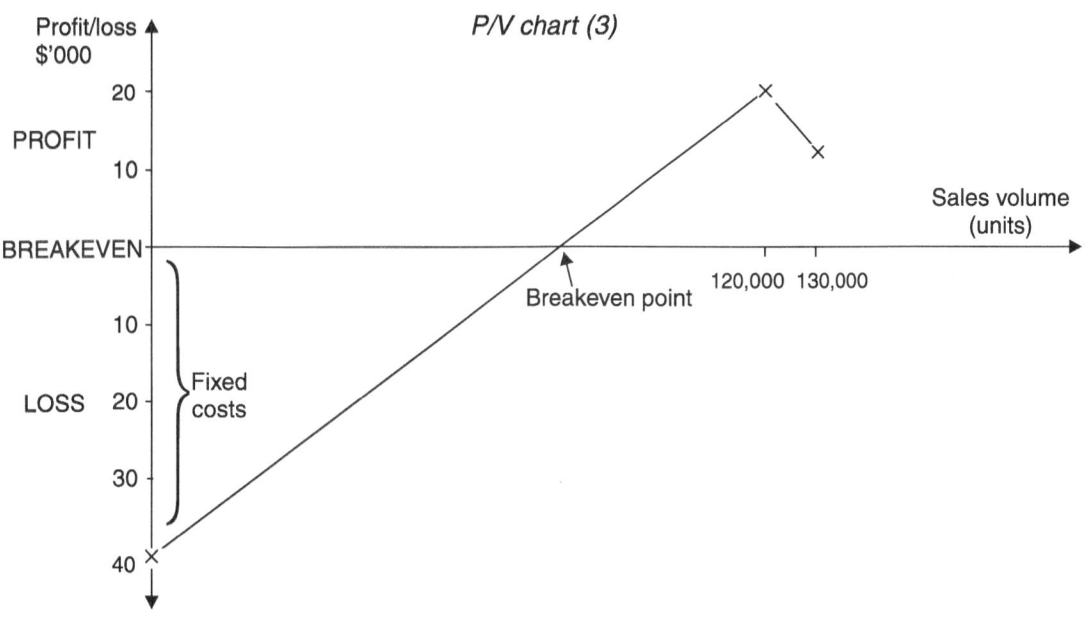

P/V chart (3)

Exam focus point

You may be given a breakeven or PV chart and required to extract the information from it. Alternatively, as in the May 2010 exam you may be asked to draw a break-even chart.

 Question   Profit/volume chart

The profit/volume chart for a single product company is as follows:

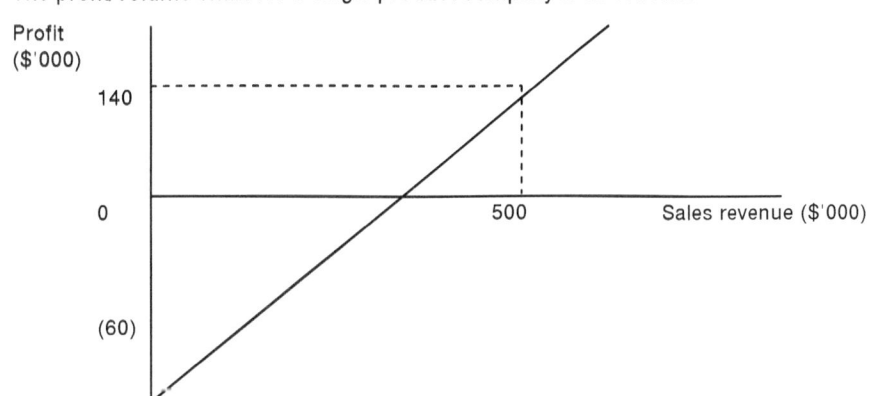

What is the product's contribution to sales ratio (expressed as a %)?

A 16%
B 28%
C 40%
D 72%

Answer

The correct answer is C.

The profit/volume graph shows levels of profit at different levels of sales. In order to answer the question, you must determine **contribution** for $500,000 sales revenue.

Remember that **profit = contribution – fixed costs**.

When sales revenue = 0, contribution = 0 and the graph shows a loss of $60,000 at zero sales revenue. This means that fixed costs must be $60,000.

Contribution at $500,000 sales revenue = $140,000 (profit) + $60,000 (fixed costs)

= $200,000

Contribution to sales ratio = contribution/sales revenue = ($200,000/$500,000) = 0.4 or 40%

6 Limitations of CVP analysis

> **FAST FORWARD**
>
> **Breakeven analysis** is a useful technique for managers as it can provide simple and quick estimates. **Breakeven charts** provide a graphical representation of breakeven arithmetic. Breakeven analysis does, however, have a number of **limitations**.

- It **can only apply to a single product** or a single mix of a group of products.
- A breakeven chart may be **time-consuming** to prepare.
- It **assumes** fixed costs are constant at all levels of output.
- It **assumes** that **variable costs** are the **same** per unit at all levels of output.
- It **assumes** that **sales prices** are **constant** at all levels of output.
- It **assumes production** and **sales** are the **same** (inventory levels are ignored).
- It **ignores** the **uncertainty** in the estimates of fixed costs and variable cost per unit.

Chapter roundup

- **Cost-volume-profit (CVP)/breakeven analysis** is the study of the interrelationships between costs, volume and profits at various levels of activity.

- **Breakeven point** $= \dfrac{\text{Total fixed costs}}{\text{Contribution per unit}} = \dfrac{\text{Contribution required to break even}}{\text{Contribution per unit}}$

  = Number of units of sale required to break even.

- $\dfrac{\text{Contribution required to breakeven}}{\text{C/S ratio}} = \dfrac{\text{Fixed costs}}{\text{C/S ratio}} =$ Breakeven point in terms of sales revenue

  (The contribution/sales (C/S) ratio is also sometimes called a **profit/volume** or **P/V ratio**.)

- The **C/S ratio** (or **P/V ratio**) is a measure of how much contribution is earned from each $1 of sales.

- The **margin of safety** is the difference in units between the **budgeted sales volume** and the **breakeven sales volume**. It is sometimes expressed as a percentage of the budgeted sales volume. The **margin of safety** may also be expressed as the difference between the **budgeted sales revenue** and the **breakeven sales revenue** expressed as a percentage of the budgeted sales revenue.

- At the **breakeven point**, sales revenue equals total costs and there is no profit. At the breakeven point **total contribution = fixed costs.**

- The **target profit** is achieved when S = V + F + P. Therefore the **total contribution required** for a target profit = **fixed costs + required profit.**

- The breakeven point can also be determined graphically using a **breakeven chart** or a **contribution breakeven chart**. These charts show approximate levels of profit or loss at different sales volume levels within a limited range.

- The **profit/volume (P/V) chart** is a variation of the breakeven chart which illustrates the relationship of costs and profits to sales and the margin of safety.

- The **P/V chart** shows clearly the effect on profit and breakeven point of any changes in selling price, variable cost, fixed cost and/or sales demand.

- **Breakeven analysis** is a useful technique for managers as it can provide simple and quick estimates. **Breakeven charts** provide a graphical representation of breakeven arithmetic. Breakeven analysis does, however, have a number of **limitations.**

PART C5 INFORMATION FOR DECISION MAKING

Quick quiz

1 What does CVP analysis study?

2 The **breakeven point** is the ....
or.. .

3 Use the following to make up three formulae which can be used to calculate the breakeven point.

Contribution per unit
Contribution per unit
Fixed costs
Fixed costs
Contribution required to breakeven
Contribution required to breakeven
C/S ratio
C/S ratio

(a) Breakeven point (sales units) = _____

or _____

(b) Breakeven point (sales revenue) = _____

or _____

4 The C/S ratio is a measure of how much profit is earned from each $1 of sales.

True ☐

False ☐

5 The **margin of safety** is the difference in units between the budgeted sales volume and the breakeven sales volume. How is it sometimes expressed?

6 Profits are maximised at the breakeven point.

True ☐

False ☐

7 At the breakeven point, total contribution = ...

8 The total contribution required for a **target profit** = ...

9 Give three uses of breakeven charts.

10 Breakeven charts show approximate levels of profit or loss at different sales volume levels within a limited range. Which of the following are true?

    I   The sales line starts at the origin.
    II   The fixed costs line runs parallel to the vertical axis.
    III   Breakeven charts have a horizontal axis showing the sales/output (in value or units).
    IV   Breakeven charts have a vertical axis showing $ for revenues and costs.
    V   The breakeven point is the intersection of the sales line and the fixed cost line.

    A   I and II
    B   I and III
    C   I, III and IV
    D   I, III, IV, and V

11 On a breakeven chart, the distance between the breakeven point and the expected (or budgeted) sales, in units, indicates the ....

12 Give seven limitations of CVP analysis.

- ....
- ....
- ....
- ....
- ....
- ....
- ....

PART C5 INFORMATION FOR DECISION MAKING

Answers to quick quiz

1 The interrelations between **costs, volume** and **profits** of a product at various activity levels

2 The **breakeven point** is the number of units of sale required to breakeven or the sales revenue required to break even.

3 (a) Breakeven point (sales units) = $\dfrac{\text{Fixed costs}}{\text{Contribution per unit}}$

　　or $\dfrac{\text{Contribution required to breakeven}}{\text{Contribution per unit}}$

　(b) Breakeven point (sales revenue) = $\dfrac{\text{Fixed costs}}{\text{C/S ratio}}$

　　or $\dfrac{\text{Contribution required to breakeven}}{\text{C/S ratio}}$

4 False. The C/S ratio is a measure of how much **contribution** is earned from each $1 of sales.

5 As a **percentage** of the budgeted sales volume

6 False. At the breakeven point there is no profit.

7 At the breakeven point, total contribution = fixed costs

8 Fixed costs + required profit

9
- To plan the production of a company's products
- To market a company's products
- To give a visual display of breakeven arithmetic

10 C

11 Margin of safety

12
- It **can only apply to a single product** or a single mix of a group of products.
- A breakeven chart may be **time-consuming** to prepare.
- It **assumes** fixed costs are constant at all levels of output.
- It **assumes** that **variable costs** are the **same** per unit at all levels of output.
- It **assumes** that **sales prices** are **constant** at all levels of output.
- It assumes **production** and **sales** are the **same** (inventory levels are ignored).
- It **ignores** the **uncertainty** in the estimates of fixed costs and variable cost per unit.

Relevant costing and decision making

Topic list	Syllabus reference
1 Relevant costs	C5.2
2 Choice of product (product mix) decisions	C5.3, C5.4
3 Make or buy decisions	C5.5
4 Shutdown problems	C5.4, C5.6

Introduction

Management at all levels within an organisation take decisions. The overriding requirement of the information that should be supplied by the cost accountant to aid decision making is that of **relevance**. This chapter therefore begins by looking at the costing technique required in decision-making situations, that of **relevant costing**, and explains how to decide which costs need taking into account when a decision is being made and which costs do not.

We then go on to see how to apply relevant costing to product mix, make or buy (outsourcing) and shut down decisions.

1 Relevant costs

1.1 Relevant costs

FAST FORWARD

Relevant costs are future cash flows arising as a direct consequence of a decision.

- Relevant costs are **future costs**.
- Relevant costs are **cash flows**.
- Relevant costs are **incremental costs**.

Decision making should be based on relevant costs.

(a) **Relevant costs are future costs**. A decision is about the future and it cannot alter what has been done already. Costs that have been incurred in the past are totally irrelevant to any decision that is being made 'now'. Such costs are **past costs** or **sunk costs**.

Costs that have been incurred include not only costs that have already been paid, but also costs that have been committed. A **committed cost** is a future cash flow that will be incurred anyway, regardless of the decision taken now.

(b) **Relevant costs are cash flows**. Only cash flow information is required. This means that costs or charges which do not reflect **additional cash spending** (such as depreciation and notional costs) should be ignored for the purpose of decision making.

(c) **Relevant costs are incremental costs**. For example, if an employee is expected to have no other work to do during the next week, but will be paid his basic wage (of, say, $100 per week) for attending work and doing nothing, his manager might decide to give him a job which earns the organisation $40. The net gain is $40 and the $100 is irrelevant to the decision because although it is a future cash flow, it will be incurred anyway whether the employee is given work or not.

1.2 Avoidable costs

Key term

Avoidable costs are costs which would not be incurred if the activity to which they relate did not exist.

One of the situations in which it is necessary to identify the avoidable costs is in deciding whether or not to **discontinue a product**. The only costs which would be saved are the **avoidable costs** which are usually the variable costs and sometimes some specific costs. Costs which would be incurred whether or not the product is discontinued are known as **unavoidable costs**.

1.3 Differential costs and opportunity costs

FAST FORWARD

Relevant costs are also **differential costs** and **opportunity costs**.

- **Differential cost** is the difference in total cost between alternatives.
- An **opportunity cost** is the value of the benefit sacrificed when one course of action is chosen in preference to an alternative.

For example, if decision option A costs $300 and decision option B costs $360, the **differential cost** is $60.

1.3.1 Example: Differential costs and opportunity costs

Suppose for example that there are three options, A, B and C, only one of which can be chosen. The net profit from each would be $80, $100 and $70 respectively.

Since only one option can be selected option B would be chosen because it offers the biggest benefit.

	$
Profit from option B	100
Less opportunity cost (ie the benefit from the most profitable alternative, A)	80
Differential benefit of option B	20

The decision to choose option B would not be taken simply because it offers a profit of $100, but because it offers a differential profit of $20 in excess of the next best alternative.

1.4 Controllable and uncontrollable costs

We came across the term **controllable costs** at the beginning of this Learning & Practice Workbook. **Controllable costs** are items of expenditure which can be directly influenced by a given manager within a given time span.

As a general rule, **committed fixed costs** such as those costs arising from the possession of plant, equipment and buildings (giving rise to depreciation and rent) are largely **uncontrollable** in the short term because they have been committed by longer-term decisions.

Discretionary fixed costs, for example, advertising and research and development costs can be thought of as being **controllable** because they are incurred as a result of decisions made by management and can be raised or lowered at fairly short notice.

1.5 Sunk cost

> **FAST FORWARD**
>
> A **sunk cost** is a past cost which is not directly relevant in decision making.

The principle underlying decision accounting is that management decisions can only affect the future. In decision making, managers therefore require information about **future costs and revenues** which would be affected by the decision under review. They must not be misled by events, costs and revenues in the past, about which they can do nothing.

Sunk costs, which have been charged already as a cost of sales in a previous accounting period or will be charged in a future accounting period although the expenditure has already been incurred, are irrelevant to decision making.

1.5.1 Example: Sunk costs

An example of a sunk cost is development costs which have already been incurred. Suppose that a company has spent $250,000 in developing a new service for customers, but the marketing department's most recent findings are that the service might not gain customer acceptance and could be a commercial failure. The decision whether or not to abandon the development of the new service would have to be taken, but the $250,000 spent so far should be ignored by the decision makers because it is a **sunk cost**.

1.6 Fixed and variable costs

> **FAST FORWARD**
>
> In general, variable costs will be relevant costs and fixed costs will be irrelevant to a decision.

PART C5 INFORMATION FOR DECISION MAKING

Exam focus point

> Unless you are given an indication to the contrary, you should assume the following.
> - Variable costs will be relevant costs.
> - Fixed costs are irrelevant to a decision.
>
> This need not be the case, however, and you should analyse variable and fixed cost data carefully. Do not forget that 'fixed' costs may only be fixed in the short term.

1.6.1 Non-relevant variable costs

There might be occasions when a variable cost is in fact a sunk cost (and therefore a **non-relevant variable cost**). For example, suppose that a company has some units of raw material in inventory. They have been paid for already, and originally cost $2,000. They are now obsolete and are no longer used in regular production, and they have no scrap value. However, they could be used in a special job which the company is trying to decide whether to undertake. The special job is a 'one-off' customer order, and would use up all these materials in inventory.

(a) In deciding whether the job should be undertaken, the relevant cost of the materials to the special job is nil. Their original cost of $2,000 is a **sunk cost**, and should be ignored in the decision.

(b) However, if the materials did have a scrap value of, say, $300, then their relevant cost to the job would be the **opportunity cost** of being unable to sell them for scrap, ie $300.

1.6.2 Attributable fixed costs

There might be occasions when a fixed cost is a relevant cost, and you must be aware of the distinction between **'specific'** or **'directly attributable' fixed costs**, and general fixed overheads.

Directly attributable fixed costs are those costs which, although fixed within a relevant range of activity level are relevant to a decision for either of the following reasons.

(a) They could increase if certain extra activities were undertaken. For example, it may be necessary to employ an extra supervisor if a particular order is accepted. The extra salary would be an **attributable fixed cost**.

(b) They would decrease or be eliminated entirely if a decision were taken either to reduce the scale of operations or shut down entirely.

General fixed overheads are those fixed overheads which will be unaffected by decisions to increase or decrease the scale of operations, perhaps because they are an apportioned share of the fixed costs of items which would be completely unaffected by the decisions. General fixed overheads are not relevant in decision making.

1.6.3 Absorbed overhead

Absorbed overhead is a **notional** accounting cost and hence should be ignored for decision-making purposes. **It is overhead incurred which may be relevant to a decision.**

1.7 The relevant cost of materials

The relevant cost of raw materials is generally their **current replacement cost**, **unless** the materials have already been purchased and would not be replaced once used. In this case the relevant cost of using them is the **higher** of the following.

- Their current resale value
- The value they would obtain if they were put to an alternative use

If the materials have no resale value and no other possible use, then the relevant cost of using them for the opportunity under consideration would be nil.

Question — Relevant cost of materials

O'Reilly has been approached by a customer who would like a special job to be done for him, and who is willing to pay $22,000 for it. The job would require the following materials.

Material	Total units required	Units already in inventory	Carrying amount of units in inventory $/unit	Realisable value $/unit	Replacement cost $/unit
A	1,000	0	–	–	6
B	1,000	600	2	2.50	5
C	1,000	700	3	2.50	4
D	200	200	4	6.00	9

Material B is used regularly by O'Reilly, and if units of B are required for this job, they would need to be replaced to meet other production demand.

Materials C and D are in inventory as the result of previous over-buying, and they have a restricted use. No other use could be found for material C, but the units of material D could be used in another job as substitute for 300 units of material E, which currently costs $5 per unit (of which the company has no units in inventory at the moment).

Required

Calculate the relevant costs of material for deciding whether or not to accept the contract.

Answer

(a) **Material A** is not yet owned. It would have to be bought in full at the replacement cost of $6 per unit.

(b) **Material B** is used regularly by the company. There are existing inventories (600 units) but if these are used on the contract under review a further 600 units would be bought to replace them. Relevant costs are therefore 1,000 units at the replacement cost of $5 per unit.

(c) 1,000 units of **material C** are needed and 700 are already in inventory. If used for the contract, a further 300 units must be bought at $4 each. The existing inventories of 700 will not be replaced. If they are used for the contract, they could not be sold at $2.50 each. The realisable value of these 700 units is an opportunity cost of sales revenue forgone.

(d) The required units of **material D** are already in inventory and will not be replaced. There is an opportunity cost of using D in the contract because there are alternative opportunities either to sell the existing inventories for $6 per unit ($1,200 in total) or avoid other purchases (of material E), which would cost 300 × $5 = $1,500. Since substitution for E is more beneficial, $1,500 is the opportunity cost.

(e) **Summary of relevant costs**

	$
Material A (1,000 × $6)	6,000
Material B (1,000 × $5)	5,000
Material C (300 × $4) plus (700 × $2.50)	2,950
Material D	1,500
Total	15,450

Question
Relevant material costs

A company regularly uses a material. It currently has 100 kg in inventory for which it paid $200. If it were sold it could be sold for $3 per kg. The market price is now $4 per kg. A customer has placed an order that will use 200 kg of the material. The relevant cost of the 200 kg is:

A $500
B $600
C $700
D $800

Answer

The material is in regular use and so 200 kg will be purchased. The relevant cost is therefore 200 × $4 = $800. Answer D.

1.8 The relevant cost of labour

The relevant cost of labour, in different situations, is best explained by means of an example.

1.8.1 Example: Relevant cost of labour

LW is currently deciding whether to undertake a new contract. 15 hours of labour will be required for the contract. LW currently produces product L, the standard cost details of which are shown below.

STANDARD COST CARD
PRODUCT L

	$/unit
Direct materials (10 kg @ $2)	20
Direct labour (5 hrs @ $6)	30
	50
Selling price	72
Contribution	22

(a) What is the relevant cost of labour if the labour must be hired from outside the organisation?
(b) What is the relevant cost of labour if LW expects to have 5 hours spare capacity?
(c) What is the relevant cost of labour if labour is in short supply?

Solution

(a) Where labour must be hired from outside the organisation, the relevant cost of labour will be the variable costs incurred.

Relevant cost of labour on new contract = 15 hours @ $6 = $90

(b) It is assumed that the 5 hours spare capacity will be paid anyway, and so if these 5 hours are used on another contract, there is no additional cost to LW.

Relevant cost of labour on new contract

	$
Direct labour (10 hours @ $6)	60
Spare capacity (5 hours @ $0)	0
	60

(c) Contribution earned per unit of Product L produced = $22

If it requires 5 hours of labour to make one unit of product L, the contribution earned per labour hour = $22/5 = $4.40.

Relevant cost of labour on new contract

	$
Direct labour (15 hours @ $6)	90
Contribution lost by not making product L ($4.40 × 15 hours)	66
	156

It is important that you should be able to identify the relevant costs which are appropriate to a decision. In many cases, this is a fairly straightforward problem, but there are cases where great care should be taken. Attempt the following question.

Question
Customer order

A company has been making a machine to order for a customer, but the customer has since gone into liquidation, and there is no prospect that any money will be obtained from the winding up of the company.

Costs incurred to date in manufacturing the machine are $50,000 and progress payments of $15,000 had been received from the customer prior to the liquidation.

The sales department has found another company willing to buy the machine for $34,000 once it has been completed.

To complete the work, the following costs would be incurred.

(a) Materials: these have been bought at a cost of $6,000. They have no other use, and if the machine is not finished, they would be sold for scrap for $2,000.

(b) Further labour costs would be $8,000. Labour is in short supply, and if the machine is not finished, the work force would be switched to another job, which would earn $30,000 in revenue, and incur direct costs of $12,000 and absorbed (fixed) overhead of $8,000.

(c) Consultancy fees $4,000. If the work is not completed, the consultant's contract would be cancelled at a cost of $1,500.

(d) General overheads of $8,000 would be added to the cost of the additional work.

Required

Assess whether the new customer's offer should be accepted.

Answer

(a) Costs incurred in the past, or revenue received in the past are not relevant because they cannot affect a decision about what is best for the future. Costs incurred to date of $50,000 and revenue received of $15,000 are 'water under the bridge' and should be ignored.

(b) Similarly, the price paid in the past for the materials is **irrelevant**. The only relevant cost of materials affecting the decision is the opportunity cost of the revenue from scrap which would be forgone – $2,000.

(c) **Labour costs**

	$
Labour costs required to complete work	8,000
Opportunity costs: contribution forgone by losing other work $(30,000 – 12,000)	18,000
Relevant cost of labour	26,000

(d) The **incremental cost** of consultancy from completing the work is $2,500.

	$
Cost of completing work	4,000
Cost of cancelling contract	1,500
Incremental cost of completing work	2,500

(e) **Absorbed overhead is a notional accounting cost** and should be ignored. Actual overhead incurred is the only overhead cost to consider. General overhead costs (and the absorbed overhead of the alternative work for the labour force) should be ignored.

(f) **Relevant costs may be summarised as follows.**

	$	$
Revenue from completing work		34,000
Relevant costs		
Materials: opportunity cost	2,000	
Labour: basic pay	8,000	
opportunity cost	18,000	
Incremental cost of consultant	2,500	
		30,500
Extra profit to be earned by accepting the order		3,500

> **Exam focus point**
>
> The key point in decision-making questions is that you let the marker see what you are doing. This is simply a matter of layout and labelling. Every examiner, in every subject, for every professional body, always complains about the layout and labelling of students' answers. Get wise to this!

1.9 The relevant cost of an asset

FAST FORWARD

> The **relevant cost** of an asset represents the amount of money that a company would have to receive if it were deprived of an asset in order to be no worse off than it already is. We can call this the **deprival value**.

The deprival value of an asset is best demonstrated by means of an example.

1.9.1 Example: Deprival value of an asset

A machine cost $14,000 ten years ago. It is expected that the machine will generate future revenues of $10,000. Alternatively, the machine could be scrapped for $8,000. An equivalent machine in the same condition would cost $9,000 to buy now. What is the deprival value of the machine?

Solution

Firstly, let us think about the relevance of the costs given to us in the question.

Cost of machine = $14,000 = past/sunk cost
Future revenues = $10,000 = revenue expected to be generated
Net realisable value = $8,000 = scrap proceeds
Replacement cost = $9,000

When calculating the **deprival value** of an asset, use the following diagram.

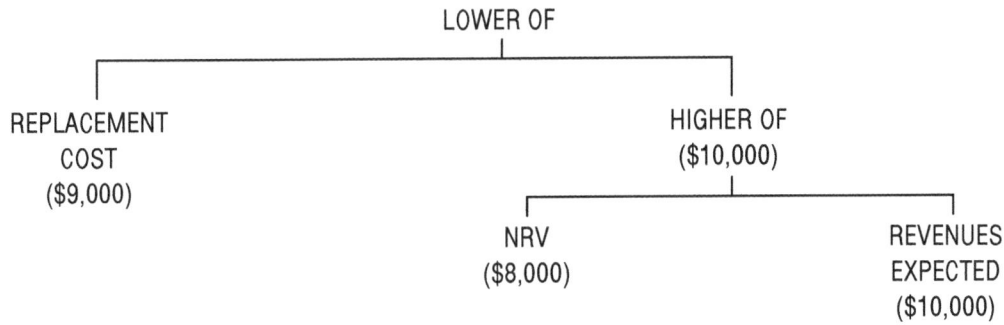

Therefore, the deprival value of the machine is the lower of the replacement cost and $10,000. The deprival value is therefore $9,000.

2 Choice of product (product mix) decisions

2.1 The limiting factor

FAST FORWARD

A **limiting factor** is a factor which limits the organisation's activities. In a **limiting factor situation**, contribution will be maximised by earning the biggest possible contribution per unit of limiting factor.

A limiting factor is anything which limits the activity of the entity. This could be the level of demand for its product or it could be one or more scarce resources which limit production to below that level.

Possible limiting factors are:

(a) **Sales**. There may be a limit to sales demand.

(b) **Labour**. There may be a limit to total quantity of labour available or to labour having particular skills.

(c) **Materials**. There may be insufficient available materials to produce enough units to satisfy sales demand.

(d) **Manufacturing capacity**. There may not be sufficient machine capacity for the production required to meet sales demand.

One of the more common decision-making problems is a situation where there are not enough resources to meet the potential sales demand, and so a decision has to be made about what mix of products to produce, using what resources there are as effectively as possible.

A **limiting factor** could be sales if there is a limit to sales demand but any one of the organisation's resources (labour, materials and so on) may be insufficient to meet the level of production demanded.

It is assumed in limiting factor accounting that management wishes to maximise profit and that **profit will be maximised when contribution is maximised** (given no change in fixed cost expenditure incurred). In other words, **marginal costing ideas are applied**.

Contribution will be maximised by earning the biggest possible contribution from each unit of limiting factor. For example if grade A labour is the limiting factor, contribution will be maximised by earning the biggest contribution from each hour of grade A labour worked.

The limiting factor decision therefore involves the determination of the contribution earned by each different product from each unit of the limiting factor.

2.2 Example: Limiting factor

AB makes two products, the Ay and the Be. Unit variable costs are as follows.

	Ay $	Be $
Direct materials	1	3
Direct labour ($3 per hour)	6	3
Variable overhead	1	1
	8	7

The sales price per unit is $14 per Ay and $11 per Be. During July 20X2 the available direct labour is limited to 8,000 hours. Sales demand in July is expected to be 3,000 units for Ays and 5,000 units for Bes.

Required

Determine the profit-maximising production mix, assuming that monthly fixed costs are $20,000, and that opening inventories of finished goods and work in progress are nil.

Solution

Step 1 Confirm that the limiting factor is something other than sales demand.

	Ays	Bes	Total
Labour hours per unit	2 hrs	1 hr	
Sales demand	3,000 units	5,000 units	
Labour hours needed	6,000 hrs	5,000 hrs	11,000 hrs
Labour hours available			8,000 hrs
Shortfall			3,000 hrs

Labour is the limiting factor on production.

Step 2 Identify the contribution earned by each product per unit of limiting factor, that is per labour hour worked.

	Ays $	Bes $
Sales price	14	11
Variable cost	8	7
Unit contribution	6	4
Labour hours per unit	2 hrs	1 hr
Contribution per labour hour (= unit of limiting factor)	$3	$4

Although Ays have a higher unit contribution than Bes, two Bes can be made in the time it takes to make one Ay. Because labour is in short supply it is more profitable to make Bes than Ays.

Step 3 Determine the **optimum production plan**. Sufficient Bes will be made to meet the full sales demand, and the remaining labour hours available will then be used to make Ays.

(a)

Product	Demand	Hours required	Hours available	Priority of manufacture
Bes	5,000	5,000	5,000	1st
Ays	3,000	6,000	3,000 (bal)	2nd
		11,000	8,000	

(b)

Product	Units	Hours needed	Contribution per unit $	Total $
Bes	5,000	5,000	4	20,000
Ays	1,500	3,000	6	9,000
		8,000		29,000
Less fixed costs				20,000
Profit				9,000

In conclusion:

(a) Unit contribution is **not** the correct way to decide priorities.

(b) Labour hours are the scarce resource, and therefore contribution **per labour hour** is the correct way to decide priorities.

(c) The Be earns $4 contribution per labour hour, and the Ay earns $3 contribution per labour hour. Bes therefore make more profitable use of the scarce resource, and should be manufactured first.

Question — Limiting factor 1

The following details relate to three products made by DSF Co.

	V $ per unit	A $ per unit	L $ per unit
Selling price	120	170	176
Direct materials	30	40	60
Direct labour	20	30	20
Variable overhead	10	16	20
Fixed overhead	20	32	40
	80	118	140
Profit	40	52	36

All three products use the same direct labour and direct materials, but in different quantities.

In a period when the labour used on these products is in short supply, the most and least profitable use of the labour is:

	Most profitable	Least profitable
A	L	V
B	L	A
C	V	A
D	A	L

Answer

The correct answer is B.

	V $	A $	L $
Selling price per unit	120	170	176
Variable cost per unit	60	86	100
Contribution per unit	60	84	76
Labour cost per unit	$20	$30	$20
Contribution per $ of labour	$3	$2.80	$3.80
Ranking	2	3	1

Question — Limiting factor 2

Jam Co makes two products, the K and the L. The K sells for $50 per unit, the L for $70 per unit. The variable cost per unit of the K is $35, that of the L $40. Each unit of K uses 2 kg of raw material. Each unit of L uses 3 kg of material.

In the forthcoming period the availability of raw material is limited to 2,000 kg. Jam Co is contracted to supply 500 units of K. Maximum demand for the L is 250 units. Demand for the K is unlimited.

What is the profit-maximising product mix?

	K	L
A	250 units	625 units
B	1,250 units	750 units
C	625 units	250 units
D	750 units	1,250 units

Answer

The correct answer is C.

	K	L
Contribution per unit	$15	$30
Contribution per unit of limiting factor	$15/2 = $7.50	$30/3 = $10
Ranking	2	1

Production plan	Raw material used kg
Contracted supply of K (500 x 2 kg)	1,000
Meet demand for L (250 x 3 kg)	750
Remainder of resource for K (125 x 2 kg)	250
	2,000

3 Make or buy decisions

A make or buy problem involves a decision by an organisation about whether it should make a product or carry out an activity with its own internal resources, or whether it should pay another organisation to make the product or carry out the activity. This is known as outsourcing. Examples include whether a company should manufacture its own components, or else buy the components from an outside supplier.

The **'make' option** should give management **more direct control** over the work, but the **'buy' option** often has the benefit that the external organisation has a **specialist skill and expertise** in the work. Make or buy decisions should certainly not be based exclusively on cost considerations. There may be other qualitative factors that influence the outsourcing decision:

(a) How can spare capacity freed up by outsourcing/subcontracting be used most profitably?

(b) Could the decision to use an outside supplier cause an industrial dispute?

(c) Would the subcontractor be reliable with delivery times and product quality?

(d) Does the company wish to be flexible and maintain better control over operations by making everything itself?

(e) Does the subcontractor have more specialist expertise or access to better technology?

(f) Will the decision to outsource have any impact on the image and reputation of the company eg adverse publicity if a factory closes or there are redundancies?

(g) Have all the additional costs of outsourcing been taken into account eg there may be redundancy costs if production ceases.

Having taken a decision to outsource, it may then be hard to go back to producing in-house at a later stage.

15: RELEVANT COSTING AND DECISION MAKING

> If an organisation has the freedom of choice about whether to **make internally or buy externally and has no scarce resources** that put a restriction on what it can do itself, the relevant costs for the decision will be the differential costs between the two options.

The **variable cost of buying** is likely to be **higher than the variable cost of making in-house**, but **savings in directly attributable fixed costs by using an outside supplier also need to be considered**.

3.1 Example: Make or buy

An organisation makes four components, W, X, Y and Z, for which costs in the forthcoming year are expected to be as follows.

	W	X	Y	Z
Production (units)	1,000	2,000	4,000	3,000
	$	$	$	$
Unit marginal costs				
Direct materials	4	5	2	4
Direct labour	8	9	4	6
Variable production overheads	2	3	1	2
	14	17	7	12

Directly attributable fixed costs per annum and committed fixed costs are as follows.

	$
Incurred as a direct consequence of making W	1,000
Incurred as a direct consequence of making X	5,000
Incurred as a direct consequence of making Y	6,000
Incurred as a direct consequence of making Z	8,000
Other fixed costs (committed)	30,000
	50,000

A subcontractor can supply units of W, X, Y and Z for $12, $21, $10 and $14 respectively.

Required

Decide whether the organisation should make or buy the components.

Solution and discussion

(a) The relevant costs are the differential costs between making and buying, and they consist of differences in unit variable costs plus differences in directly attributable fixed costs. Subcontracting will result in some fixed cost savings.

	W	X	Y	Z
	$	$	$	$
Unit variable cost of making	14	17	7	12
Unit variable cost of buying	12	21	10	14
	$(2)	$4	$3	$2
Annual requirements (units)	1,000	2,000	4,000	3,000
Extra variable cost of buying (per annum)	(2,000)	8,000	12,000	6,000
Fixed costs saved by buying	1,000	5,000	6,000	8,000
Extra total cost of buying	(3,000)	3,000	6,000	(2,000)

(b) The company would save $3,000 pa by subcontracting component W (where the purchase cost would be less than the marginal cost per unit to make internally) and would save $2,000 pa by subcontracting component Z (because of the saving in fixed costs of $8,000).

(c) Important **further considerations** would be as follows.

  (i) If components W and Z are subcontracted, the company will have spare capacity. How should that **spare capacity be profitably used**? Are there **hidden benefits** to be obtained from subcontracting? Would the company's workforce resent the loss of work to an outside subcontractor, and might such a decision cause an **industrial dispute**?

  (ii) Would the subcontractor be **reliable with delivery times**, and would he supply components of the same **quality** as those manufactured internally?

  (iii) Does the company wish to be **flexible** and **maintain better control** over operations by making everything itself?

  (iv) Are the **estimates** of fixed cost savings **reliable**? In the case of product W, buying is clearly cheaper than making in-house. In the case of product Z, the decision to buy rather than make would only be financially beneficial if the fixed cost savings of $8,000 could really be 'delivered' by management.

4 Shutdown problems

FAST FORWARD

Non-quantifiable factors in shutdown problems include the impact on employees, customers, competitors and suppliers.

Decisions to be made in shutdown or discontinuance problems

- Whether or not to close down a product line, department or other activity
- If the decision is to shut down, whether the closure should be permanent or temporary
- If there is a choice about the timing of the closure, when should it take place

Read our four step guide method in 4.1 when you come to work through these decisions.

4.1 Financial considerations

The basic method is to use short-run relevant costs to calculate contributions and profits or losses.

(1) Calculate what is earned by the process at present (perhaps in comparison with others).

(2) Calculate what will be the financial consequences of closing down (selling machines, redundancy costs etc).

(3) Compare the results and act accordingly.

(4) Bear in mind that some fixed costs may no longer be incurred if the decision is to shut down and they are therefore relevant to the decision.

Bear these in mind as you read through the example below.

4.2 Example: Adding or deleting products

An organisation manufactures three products, Pawns, Rooks and Bishops. The present net annual income from these is:

	Pawns	Rooks	Bishops	Total
	$	$	$	$
Sales	50,000	40,000	60,000	150,000
Variable costs	30,000	25,000	35,000	90,000
Contribution	20,000	15,000	25,000	60,000
Fixed costs	17,000	18,000	20,000	55,000
Profit/loss	3,000	(3,000)	5,000	5,000

The organisation is concerned about its poor profit performance, and is considering whether or not to cease selling Rooks. It is felt that selling prices cannot be raised or reduced without adversely affecting net income. $5,000 of the fixed costs of Rooks are direct fixed costs which would be saved if production ceased. All other fixed costs, it is considered, would remain the same.

Solution

By stopping production of Rooks, the consequences would be a $10,000 fall in profits:

	$
Loss of contribution	(15,000)
Savings in fixed costs	5,000
Incremental loss	(10,000)

Suppose, however, it were possible to use the resources realised by stopping production of Rooks and switch to producing a new item, Crowners, which would sell for $50,000 and incur variable costs of $30,000 and extra direct fixed costs of $6,000. A new decision is now required:

	Rooks	Crowners
	$	$
Sales	40,000	50,000
Less variable costs	25,000	30,000
	15,000	20,000
Less direct fixed costs	5,000	6,000
Contribution to shared fixed costs and profit	10,000	14,000

It would be more profitable to shut down production of Rooks and switch resources to making Crowners, in order to boost profits by $4,000 to $9,000.

4.3 Non-quantifiable considerations

As usual the decision is not merely a matter of choosing the best financial option.

(a) A product may be retained if it is providing a contribution, albeit a small one. Retaining a wide range of **low volume/low contribution products** would add to the **complexity** and hence costs of manufacture, however, but very little to overall profit. Low volume/low contribution products should therefore be examined on a regular basis.

(b) The **effect on demand for other products** if a particular product is no longer produced should be taken into account.

(c) The extent to which demand for **other products** (existing or new) can expand to **use** the **capacity** vacated by the product being deleted is an issue.

(d) **Pricing policy.** Is the product a **loss leader?** Is the product in the introductory stage of its **life cycle** and consequently priced low to help it to become accepted and hence maximise its long-term market share (**penetration pricing**). (These are issues are covered in Chapter 9.)

(e) In today's context, **environmental and social costs** are increasingly relevant for decision-making. For example, the environmental impact of the product, such as its carbon footprint and waste generation. Decisions on continuing or discontinuing a product should **align with the company's sustainability goals and regulatory compliance**. Additionally, social implications, including labour practices, community impact and ethical considerations should be evaluated. Products with **high environmental or social costs may influence the company's reputation and long-term viability**, making these factors critical in the decision-making process.

Question — Deleting products

A company's product range includes product F, on which the following data (relating to a year's production) are available.

	$
Revenue	200,000
Materials cost	157,000
Machine power cost	14,000
Overheads: type A	28,000
type B	56,000

Type A overheads would be avoided if production of product F ceased, but type B overheads would not be. Both types of overheads are absorbed in direct proportion to machine power cost, and that cost is a purely variable cost.

Production of product F should be ended. True or false?

Answer

Production of product F should continue and so the statement is false.

	$	$
Revenue		200,000
Less: materials cost	157,000	
machine power cost	14,000	
type A overheads	28,000	
		199,000
Contribution		1,000

Production of product F should be continued, because it makes a contribution of $1,000 a year.

Chapter roundup

- **Relevant costs** are future cash flows arising as a direct consequence of a decision.
    - Relevant costs are **future costs**.
    - Relevant costs are **cash flows**.
    - Relevant costs are **incremental costs**.
- Relevant costs are also **differential costs** and **opportunity costs**.
    - **Differential cost** is the difference in total cost between alternatives.
    - An **opportunity cost** is the value of the benefit sacrificed when one course of action is chosen in preference to an alternative.
- A **sunk cost** is a past cost which is not directly relevant in decision making.
- **In general**, variable costs will be relevant costs and fixed costs will be irrelevant to a decision.
- The **relevant cost** of an asset represents the amount of money that a company would have to receive if it were deprived of an asset in order to be no worse off than it already is. We can call this the **deprival value**.
- A **limiting factor** is a factor which limits the organisation's activities. In a **limiting factor situation**, contribution will be maximised by earning the biggest possible contribution per unit of limiting factor.
- If an organisation has the freedom of choice about whether to **make internally or buy externally and has no scarce resources** that put a restriction on what it can do itself, the relevant costs for the decision will be the differential costs between the two options.
- **Non-quantifiable factors in shutdown problems** include the impact on employees, customers, competitors and suppliers.

Quick quiz

1. Relevant costs are:

   (a)
   (b)
   (c)
   (d)
   (e)

2. Sunk costs are directly relevant in decision making.

   True ☐

   False ☐

3. The following information relates to machine Z.

   Purchase price = $7,000

   Expected future revenues = $5,000

   Scrap value = $4,000

   Replacement cost = $4,500

   Complete the following diagram in order to calculate the relevant cost of machine Z.

   LOWER OF [ ]
   - REPLACEMENT COST [ ]
   - HIGHER OF [ ]
     - NRV [ ]
     - REVENUES [ ]

   The relevant cost of machine Z is ....

4. A limiting factor is a factor which ....

5. A sunk cost is:

   A   A cost committed to be spent in the current period
   B   A cost which is irrelevant for decision making
   C   A cost connected with oil exploration in the North Sea
   D   A cost unaffected by fluctuations in the level of activity

6. Choose the correct words from those highlighted.
   In a situation where a company must sub-contract work to make up a shortfall in its own in-house capabilities, its total costs will be minimised if those units bought have the **lowest/highest** extra **variable/fixed** cost of **buying/making** per unit of scarce resource.

7. Sunny plc manufactures both work and leisure clothing. The company is considering whether to cease production of leisure clothing. List the **costs, which are relevant** to the decision to cease production.

Answers to quick quiz

1. (a) Future costs
   (b) Cash flows
   (c) Incremental costs
   (d) Differential costs
   (e) Opportunity costs

2. False

3.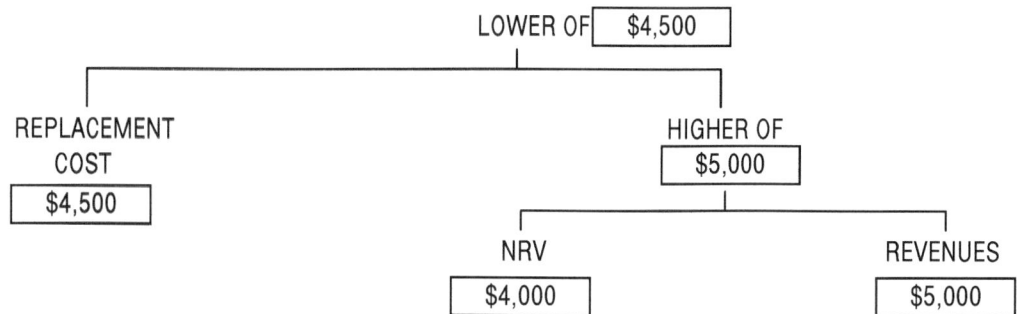

   The relevant cost of machine Z is **$4,500**.

4. Limits the organisation's activities.

5. B

6. lowest, variable, buying

7. Those costs which will be saved if production of leisure clothing ceases (that is, all variable costs plus any fixed costs which are specific to producing and selling leisure clothing (such as advertising))

   - Any closure costs such as the cost of equipment disposal and staff redundancies.

   - **Opportunity costs** such as the loss of any contribution which would have been earned from the continued manufacture and sale of leisure clothing.

   - The **opportunity costs** of continuing to produce leisure clothing such as the potential contribution which could be earned from using the capacity released to produce work clothing (although these costs will only occur if work clothing production has capacity constraints).

   Any fixed costs, which will continue whether or not leisure clothing ceases are not relevant.

End of chapter question

South-West Company Ltd

South-West Company Limited manufactures and distributes a special type of digital watch.

The current activity level is 100,000 watches per year. The company is considering whether to outsource the production of the watches to an outside manufacturer in China or to continue to produce the watches internally.

The watches are currently being produced internally at a direct material cost per unit of $15 and other variable cost per unit of $22.50. Of the company's annual fixed overheads of $625,000, 30% is general overheads, 20% is depreciation, and 50% is avoidable departmental overheads.

The outside manufacturer from China has offered to supply the company with the watches at a unit price of $40.

Required

(a) Prepare a statement comparing the two alternatives of producing the watches internally vs. outsourcing. Comment on the results of your analysis clearly stating any assumptions you have made. **(15 marks)**

(b) Discuss other factors likely to influence the decision to produce the watches internally or outsource it. **(5 marks)**

(Total = 20 marks)

Modern approaches to management accounting

Topic list	Syllabus reference
1 Nature of costs in the modern business	C5.5
2 Activity-based approaches	C5.9
3 Activity-based management	C5.9
4 Activity-based budgeting	C5.9
5 Budgeting in the modern business organisation	C4.4

Introduction

This chapter provides you with detail about changes in management accounting.

The principles of activity based costing have been applied beyond costing to managing the organisation by focussing on the activities that the organisation performs.

Some management writers have pointed out the importance of bottlenecks, which limit the output of organisations, and the theory of constraints aims to enable managers to focus on reducing the impact of bottlenecks.

Finally, many organisations believe that traditional budgeting is not appropriate in the modern business world, and alternative approaches have been adopted.

1 Nature of costs in the modern business world

1.1 Traditional manufacturing

Many of the techniques covered in this Learning & Practice Workbook were developed in the late nineteenth century, during the industrial revolution. The focus was on control of costs in the manufacturing industry. Industry was labour intensive and accounted for a large portion of total manufacturing costs. Thus management accounting focussed on efficiency, with the use of budgets, standard costing and variance analysis in particular.

1.2 Modern business world

The modern business world has changed compared to the traditional in the following ways:

(i) The greater use of technology and machinery has reduced the need for labour, but increased the overhead costs of production. In many car manufacturing plants, many of the operations are now performed by robots, for example. Traditional absorption costing is a very crude way of apportioning overhead costs to products, and while this did not matter when overhead costs were not so significant, in the modern world, a more accurate method of apportioning overhead costs is required.

(ii) There is greater flexibility in production. Manufacturers aim to meet the needs of customers rather than producing one standard product in large quantities. This makes the setting of standards more difficult since there may no longer be a standard product.

(iii) The growth of service industries. Service industries account for a much larger portion of economic activity than they did previously. Service industries use less materials but have more labour.

2 Activity-based approaches

FAST FORWARD — A focus on the **activities** that a business carries out lies behind much modern thinking.

2.1 Activities versus functions

A focus on the **activities** that a business carries out, as opposed to how its activities have traditionally been organised into separate **functions,** lies behind much modern thinking. For instance it has been found to be more fruitful to think of what may have once been called the **warehousing** department (function) in terms what that department **does**, such as **inspection of goods**, **stock control** and **materials movement** (activities).

Depending what subject you are studying or who wrote the article you are reading you might find that this modern development has different names.

(a) **Business Process Re-engineering** might be the term used, for instance, if you are looking at how **information technology** can help to eliminate non-value added activities or co-ordinate two previously separate activities, or replace one way of doing things with a completely new, quicker and cheaper way.

(b) **Activity-based** analysis might be the term used if you are looking, say, at how **costs** can be calculated in a more meaningful way.

The key point, whatever terminology is used, is that this modern development entails finding new and better ways of doing existing things so as to give greater satisfaction to customers at less cost to the business. This in turn means that **new and better information** is needed.

For instance, **activity-based costing (ABC)** was developed because it was realised that older methods such as absorption costing using labour hours as the basis for absorbing overheads, did not provide useful information about what was causing the overheads to be incurred in the first place: the **cost drivers**.

> **ABC**
>
> New technology means that overheads are now likely to represent a far larger proportion of overall costs than in the past.
>
> The proponents of ABC argue that traditional cost accounting techniques result in a misleading and inequitable division of cost between low value and high value products, and that ABC provides a more meaningful allocation of costs which make unit costs more accurate. This in turn is part of a shift in emphasis away from costing merely for stock valuation towards costing of products made to meet actual customer demand.
>
> Most overhead costs can be analysed between short-term variable costs, that vary with the volume of production, and long-term variable costs, that do not vary with the volume of production, but do vary with a different measure of activity.
>
> The ABC approach is to relate overhead costs to the activities that cause or 'drive' them to be incurred in the first place and to change subsequently.

2.2 Merits of activity-based approaches

(a) The **complexity** of many businesses has increased, with wider product ranges, shorter product life cycles, the greater importance of quality and more complex production processes. Activity-based analysis recognises this complexity with its **multiple cost drivers**, many of them **transaction-based** rather than volume-based.

(b) In a more **competitive** environment, companies must be able to assess **product profitability** realistically. To do this, they must have a good understanding of what drives overhead costs. Activity-based analysis gives a meaningful analysis of costs which should provide a better basis for pricing decisions, product mix decisions, design decisions and production decisions.

(c) In modern manufacturing systems, **overhead** functions include a lot of **non-factory-floor activities** such as product design, quality control, production planning, sales order planning and customer service. Activity-based analysis is concerned with all overhead costs, including the costs of these functions, and so it takes cost accounting beyond its 'traditional' factory floor boundaries.

(d) **Service** businesses have characteristics very similar to those required for the successful application of activity-based analysis in modern manufacturing industry.

  (i) A highly **competitive** market
  (ii) **Diversity** of products, processes and customers
  (iii) **Significant overhead costs** not easily assigned to individual products
  (iv) Demands on overhead resources related to products/customers, **not volume**

(e) Cost **control** may be improved because the **causes of increases** in costs can be more readily identified (poor use of storage space, for example) and means of reducing costs can be investigated (extra shelving, perhaps, or automated packing procedures). We look at this in more detail in Section 5.

(f) ABC techniques can be used in **customer profitability analysis** (see Chapter 7).

Case Study

As a result of an ABC study, a FMCG manufacturer discovered that three of its top five customers in terms of gross profit using traditional techniques were in the bottom five and loss making when ABC was used.

2.3 Criticisms of activity-based approaches

(a) The **costs** of obtaining and interpreting the **new information** may be considerable. Activity based analysis should not be introduced unless it can provide additional information for management to use in planning or control decisions.

(b) Many overheads relate neither to volume nor to complexity and diversity. The ability of a **single cost driver** to fully explain the cost behaviour of all items in its associated pool is **questionable**. What drives the cost of the external annual audit? What cost pool could it be placed in?

(c) Some measure of **arbitrary** cost apportionment may still be required at the cost pooling stage for items like building depreciation. If an activity based system has many cost pools the amount of apportionment needed may be greater than ever.

(d) Some people have questioned the fundamental assumption that activity **causes** cost, suggesting that it could be argued that **decisions** cause cost or the passage of **time** causes cost or that there may be **no one clear cause** of cost.

Question — Criticisms of ABC

One of the directors of the company that employs you as a management accountant observes wryly that the thing that drives sales administration costs is customers ringing up and ordering things, and that if only they did this less often sales administration costs could be dramatically reduced!

How would you respond to this implied criticism of ABC?

Answer

The director is correct after a fashion, but what this really means is that the company needs to find more cost-effective ways of taking orders, not that it needs to take fewer orders. Activity analysis, if properly directed, is likely to identify the customers who take up the most time and encourage investigation of alternatives such as EDI links.

Exam focus point

Questions requiring a knowledge of activity based approaches have appeared in some of the recent exam sittings.

2.4 Theory of constraints

The theory of constraints focusses the attention of management on bottlenecks in production. A bottleneck is a process that is working at a slower pace than the processes preceding it. It therefore slows down the whole production in the factory.

Thus, the role of a management accountant is to:

(1) Identify the weakest activity or process (called a bottleneck or constraint by some writers) which is slowing down or limiting production.

(2) Decide how to increase efficiency and remove the problem, by for example, retraining workers or increasing investment in technology or machinery or even restructuring the rest of the organisation.

(3) Implement the best solution identified at step 2.

(4) Measure the resulting increase in performance.

(5) Return to step 1 and identify what was the second weakest link, but is now the new weakest link.

3 Activity-based management

FAST FORWARD

Activity-based management (ABM) includes performing activities more efficiently, eliminating the need to perform certain activities that do not add value for customers, improving the design of products and developing better relationships with customers and suppliers. The goal of ABM is to enable customer needs to be satisfied while making fewer demands on organisational resources.

3.1 Definitions of activity based management

Recently the emphasis has switched away from using activity-based approaches for product costing to using it to improve cost management. The terms **activity based management (ABM)** and **activity-based cost management (ABCM)** are used to describe the **cost management applications of ABC**.

There are a great many different **definitions** of activity based management.

Here is Drury's (from *Management and Cost Accounting*), with BPP's emphasis.

> 'ABM views the business as a set of linked activities that ultimately add value to the customer. It focuses on managing the business on the basis of the activities that make up the organisation. ABM is based on the premise that activities consume costs. Therefore **by managing activities costs will be managed in the long term**. The **goal of ABM is to enable customer needs to be satisfied while making fewer demands on organisation resources**. The measurement of activities is a key role of the management accounting function. In particular, activity cost information is useful for prioritising those activities that need to be studied closely so that they can be eliminated or improved.
>
> ' In recent years ABM information has been used for a variety of business applications. They include cost reduction, activity-based budgeting, performance measurement, benchmarking and business process re-engineering.'

Horngren, Foster and Datar in *Cost Accounting: A Managerial Emphasis* 'define it broadly to **include pricing and product-mix decisions, cost reduction and process improvement decisions**, and **product design decisions**'.

In *Managerial Accounting*, Raiborn, Barfield and Kinney include **activity analysis, cost driver analysis, continuous improvement, operational control and performance evaluation** as the concepts covered by activity based management. 'These concepts help companies to produce more efficiently, determine costs more accurately, and control and evaluate performance more effectively.'

Clark and Baxter (*Management Accounting*, June 1992) provide a description which appears to include every management accounting buzzword.

> 'The aim of activity-based management (ABM) is to provide management with a method of introducing and managing 'process and organisational change'.
>
> It focuses on activities within a process, decision making and planning relative to those activities and the need for continuous improvement of all organisational activity. Management and staff must

determine which activities are critical to success and decide how these are to be clearly defined across all functions.

Everyone must co-operate in defining:

- Cost pools
- Cost drivers
- Key performance indicators

They must be trained and empowered to act; all must be fairly treated and success recognised.

Clearly, ABM and employee empowerment take a critical step forward beyond ABC by recognising the contribution that people make as the key resource in any organisation's success.

- It nurtures good communication and team work
- It develops quality decision making
- It leads to quality control and continuous improvement

Some accountants do not appear to understand that ABM provides an essential link to total quality management (TQM) and its concepts of 'continuous improvement'.

ABM helps deliver:

- Improved quality
- Increased customer satisfaction
- Lower costs
- Increased profitability

It provides accountants and other technical managers with a meaningful path into the business management team.'

Perhaps the clearest and most concise definition is offered by Kaplan *et al* in *Management Accounting*.

Key term

> **Activity-based management (ABM)** is '...the management processes that use the information provided by an activity-based cost analysis to improve organisational profitability. Activity-based management (ABM) includes performing activities more efficiently, eliminating the need to perform certain activities that do not add value for customers, improving the design of products, and developing better relationships with customers and suppliers. The goal of ABM is to enable customer needs to be satisfied while making fewer demands on organisational resources.'

In the following sections we examine some of the aspects of ABM mentioned in the definitions above.

3.2 Cost reduction and process improvement

Traditional cost analysis analyses costs by types of expense for each responsibility centre. ABM, on the other hand, analyses costs on the basis of cross-departmental activities and therefore provides management information on why costs are incurred and on the output of the activity in terms of cost drivers. **By controlling or reducing the incidence of the cost driver, the associated cost can be controlled or reduced**.

This difference is illustrated in the example below of a customer order processing activity.

Traditional analysis

	$
Salaries	5,700
Stationery	350
Travel	1,290
Telephone	980
Equipment depreciation	680
	9,000

ABC analysis

	$
Preparation of quotations	4,200
Receipt of customer orders	900
Assessment of customer creditworthiness	1,100
Expedition of orders	1,300
Resolution of customer problems	1,500
	9,000

Suppose that the analysis above showed that it cost $250 to process a customer's order. This would indicate to sales staff that it may not be worthwhile chasing orders with a low sales value. By eliminating lots of small orders and focusing on those with a larger value, demand for the activities associated with customer order processing should fall, with spending decreasing as a consequence.

3.2.1 Problems associated with cost reduction and ABM

(a) The extent to which activity based approaches can be applied is very dependent on an organisation's ability to identify its main activities and their associated cost drivers.

(b) If a system of 'conventional' responsibility centres has been carefully designed, this may already be a reflection of the key organisational activities. For example, a despatch department might be a cost centre, but despatch might also be a key activity.

(c) In some circumstances, the 'pooling' of activity based costs and the identification of a single cost driver for every cost pool may even hamper effective control if the cost driver is not completely applicable to every cost within that cost pool. For example, suppose the cost of materials handling was allocated to a cost pool for which the cost driver was the number of production runs. Logically, to control the cost of materials handling the number of production runs should be controlled. If the cost is actually driven by the weight of materials being handled, however, it can only be controlled if efforts are made to use lighter materials where possible.

3.3 Activity analysis

The activity based analysis above provides information not available from a traditional cost analysis. Why was $1,500 spent on resolving customer orders, for example? An **activity analysis** usually **surprises managers** who had not realised the amount being spent on certain activities. This leads to **questions** about the **necessity for particular activities** and, if an activity is required, whether it can be carried out more effectively and efficiently.

Such questions can be answered by classifying activities as value added or non value added (or as core/primary, support or diversionary/discretionary).

3.3.1 Value-added and non value added activities

Key term

> An activity may increase the worth of a product or service to the customer; in this case the customer is willing to pay for that activity and it is considered **value-added.** Some activities, though, simply increase the time spent on a product or service but do not increase its worth to the customer; these activities are **non value added**. (Raiborn, Barfield and Kinney, *Managerial Accounting*)

As an example, **getting luggage on the proper flight is a value-added activity** for airlines, **dealing with the complaints from customers whose luggage gets lost is not**.

The **time spent** on **non value added activities** creates additional costs that are unnecessary. If such activities were **eliminated, costs** would **decrease without affecting the market value or quality of the product or service**.

The processing **time** of an organisation is made up of four types.

(a) **Production** or **performance time** is the actual time that it takes to perform the functions necessary to manufacture the product or perform the service.

(b) Performing quality control results in **inspection time**.

(c) Moving products or components from one place to another is **transfer time**.

(d) Storage time and time spent waiting at the production operation for processing are **idle time**.

Production time is value added. The other three are not. The time from receipt of an order to completion of a product or performance of a service equals production time plus non value added time.

JIT would of course eliminate a significant proportion of the idle time occurring from storage and wait processes but it is important to realise that **very few organisations can completely eliminate all quality control functions and all transfer time**. If managers understand the non value added nature of these functions, however, they should be able to **minimise** such activities as much as possible.

Sometimes non value added activities arise because of inadequacies in existing processes and so they cannot be eliminated unless these inadequacies are addressed.

(a) The National Health Service (NHS) is a classic example of this. Some heart patients on the NHS wait up to four months for critical heart surgery. During this time they are likely to be severely ill on a number of occasions and have to be taken to hospital where they spend the day receiving treatment that will temporarily relieve the problem. This non value added activity is totally unnecessary and is dependent on an inadequate process: that of providing operations when required.

(b) Customer complaints services can be viewed in the same way: eliminate the source of complaints and the need for the department greatly reduces.

(c) Setting up machinery for a new production run is a non value added cost. If the number of components per product can be reduced the number of different components made will reduce and therefore set-up time will also reduce.

One of the **costliest** things an organisation can do is to **invest in equipment and people to make non value added activities more efficient**. The objective is to eliminate them altogether or subject them to a major overhaul, not make them more efficient. For example, if a supplier of raw materials makes a commitment to supply high-quality materials, inspection is no longer required, and buying testing equipment and hiring more staff to inspect incoming raw material would waste time and money. **Non value added activities are not necessary for an organisation to stay in business.**

3.3.2 Core/primary, support and diversionary/discretionary activities

This is an alternative classification of activities.

Key terms

A **core activity** or **primary activity** is one that adds value to a product, for example cutting and drilling materials and assembling them.

A **secondary activity** is one that supports a core activity, but does not add value in itself. For example setting up a machine so that it drills holes of a certain size is a secondary activity.

Diversionary activities or **discretionary activities** do not add value and are symptoms of failure within an organisation. For instance repairing faulty production work is such an activity because the production should not have been faulty in the first place.

The aim of ABM is to try to eliminate as far as possible the diversionary activities but, as with non value added activities, experience has shown that it is usually impossible to eliminate them all, although the time and cost associated with them can be greatly reduced.

3.4 Design decisions

In many organisations today, roughly 80% of a product's costs are committed at the product design stage, well before production begins. By **providing product designers with cost driver information** they can be encouraged to **design low cost products that still meet customer requirements**.

The identification of appropriate cost drivers and tracing costs to products on the basis of these cost drivers has the potential to **influence behaviour to support the cost management strategies of the organisation**.

For example, suppose product costs depend on the number and type of components. A product which is designed so that it uses fewer components will be cheaper to produce. A product using standard components will also be cheaper to produce. Management can influence the action of designers through overhead absorption rates if overheads are related to products on the basis of the number of component parts they contain. Hitachi's refrigeration plant uses this method to influence the behaviour of their product designers and ultimately the cost of manufacture.

3.5 Cost driver analysis

To reflect today's more **complex business environment**, recognition must be given to the fact that **costs are created and incurred because their cost drivers occur at different levels. Cost driver analysis investigates, quantifies and explains the relationships between cost drivers and their related costs**.

Classification level	Cause of cost	Types of cost	Necessity of cost
Unit level costs	Production/acquisition of a single unit of product or delivery of single unit of service	Direct materials Direct labour	Once for each unit produced
Batch level costs	A group of things being made, handled or processed	Purchase orders Set-ups Inspection	Once for each batch produced
Product/process level costs	Development, production or acquisition of different items	Equipment maintenance Product development	Supports a product type or a process
Organisational/ facility costs		Building depreciation Organisational advertising	Supports the overall production or service process

(Adapted from Raiborn *et al*)

Traditionally it has been assumed that if costs did not vary with changes in production at the unit level, they were fixed rather than variable. The analysis above shows this assumption to be false, and that costs vary for reasons other than production volume. To determine an accurate estimate of product or service cost, **costs should be accumulated at each successively higher level of costs**.

Unit level costs are allocated over number of units produced, batch level costs over the number of units in the batch, product level costs over the number of units produced by the product line. These costs are all related to units of product (merely at different levels) and so can be gathered together at the product level to match with revenue. Organisational level costs are not product related, however, and so should simply be deducted from net revenue.

Such an approach gives a far greater insight into product profitability.

3.6 Continuous improvement

Continuous improvement **recognises the concept of eliminating non-value-added activities** to reduce lead time, make products or perform services with zero defects, reduce product costs on an ongoing basis and simplify products and processes. It focuses on including employees in the process as they are often the best source of ideas.

3.7 Operational control

'**To control costs, managers must understand where costs are being incurred and for what purpose**. Some of this understanding will come from differentiating between value-added and non-value-added activities. Some will come from the better information generated by more appropriate tracing of overhead costs to products and services. Some will come from viewing fixed costs as long-term variable overheads and recognising that certain activities will cause those costs to change. Understanding costs allows manager to visualise what needs to be done to controls those costs, to implement cost reduction activities, and to plan resource utilisation.

......By better understanding the underlying cost of making a product or performing a service, managers obtain **new insight into product or service profitability**. Such insight could **result in management decisions** about expanding or contracting product variety, raising or reducing prices, and entering or leaving a market. For example, managers may decide to raise selling prices or discontinue production of low-volume speciality output, since that output consumes more resources than does high-volume output. Managers may decide to discontinue manufacturing products that require complex operations. Or, managers may reap the benefits from low-volume or complex production through implementing high-technology processes.'

(Raiborn *et al*, with BPP emphasis)

Innes and Mitchell (*'Activity Based Costing'*) report (with BPP emphasis) that in some organisations:

'ABCM has also been used in **make-or-buy decisions** and has led to the sub-contracting of certain activities. In another engineering company the ABCM information on purchasing **concentrated** managers' **attention** on problems such as **late deliveries, short deliveries and poor-quality raw materials**. This information enabled this engineering company to identify twenty problem suppliers and take the necessary corrective action, which varied from changing suppliers to working with others to overcome the existing problems.'

3.8 Performance evaluation

ABM encourages and rewards employees for developing new skills, accepting greater responsibilities, and making suggestions for improvements in plant layout, product design, and staff utilisation. Each of these improvements reduces non value added time and cost. In addition, by focusing on activities and costs, ABM is better able to provide more appropriate measures of performance than are found in more traditional systems.

To monitor the effectiveness and efficiency of activities, performance measures relating to volume, time, quality and costs are needed.

(a) Activity **volume** measures provide an indication of the throughput and capacity utilisation of activities. For example reporting the number of times an activity such as setting-up is undertaken focuses attention on the need to investigate ways of reducing the volume of the activity and hence future costs.

(b) To increase customer satisfaction, organisations must provide a speedy response to customer requests and reduce the time taken to develop and bring a new product to the market. Organisations must therefore focus on the **time** taken to complete an activity or sequence of

activities. This time can be reduced by eliminating (as far as is possible) the time spent on non value added activities.

(c) A focus on value chain analysis is a means of enhancing customer satisfaction. The value chain is the linked set of activities from basic raw material acquisition all the way through to the end-use product or service delivered to the customer. By viewing each of the activities in the value chain as a supplier-customer relationship, the opinions of the customers can be used to provide useful feedback on the **quality** of the service provided by the supplying activity. For example, the quality of the service provided by the processing of purchase orders activity can be evaluated by users of the activity in terms of the speed of processing orders and the quality of the service provided by the supplier chosen by the purchasing activity. Such qualitative evaluations can be supported by quantitative measures such as percentage of deliveries that are late.

(d) **Cost driver rates** (such as cost per set-up) can be communicated in a format that is easily understood by all staff and can be used to motivate managers to reduce the cost of performing activities (given that cost driver rate × activity level = cost of activity). Their use as a measure of performance can induce dysfunctional behaviour, however. By splitting production runs and therefore having more set-ups, the cost per set-up can be reduced. Workload will be increased, however, and so in the long run costs could increase.

3.9 Problems with ABM

ABM is not a panacea, however.

(a) The **amount of work** in setting up the system and in data collection must be considered.

(b) **Organisational and behavioural consequences**. Selected activity cost pools may not correspond to the formal structure of cost responsibilities within the organisation (the purchasing activity may spread across purchasing, production, stores, administrative and finance departments) and so determining 'ownership' of the activity and its costs may be problematic. We have already mentioned the behavioural impact of some performance measures.

4 Activity-based budgeting

Implementing ABC leads to the realisation that the **business as a whole** needs to be **managed** with far more reference to the behaviour of activities and cost drivers identified. For example, traditional budgeting may make managers 'responsible' for activities which are driven by factors beyond their control: the **personnel department** cost of setting up new employee records is driven by the number of new employees required by managers **other than the personnel manager**.

> **FAST FORWARD**
>
> Activity-based budgeting (ABB) involves defining the activities that underlie the financial figures in each function and using the **level of activity** to decide how much resource should be **allocated**, how well it is being **managed** and to **explain variances** from budget.

ABB is therefore based on the following **principles**.

(a) It is activities which drive costs and the aim is to control the causes (drivers) of costs rather than the costs themselves, with the result that in the long term, costs will be better managed and better understood.

(b) Not all activities are value adding and so activities must be examined and split up according to their ability to add value.

(c) Most departmental activities are driven by demands and decisions beyond the immediate control of the manager responsible for the department's budget.

(d) Traditional financial measures of performance are unable to fulfil the objective of continuous improvement. Additional measures which focus on drivers of costs, the quality of activities undertaken, the responsiveness to change and so on are needed.

4.1 Example: ABB

A stores department has two main activities, receiving deliveries of raw materials from suppliers into stores and issuing raw materials to production departments. Two major cost drivers, the number of deliveries of raw materials and the number of production runs, have been identified. Although the majority of the costs of the department can be attributed to the activities, there is a small balance, termed 'department running costs', which includes general administration costs, part of the department manager's salary and so on.

Based on activity levels expected in the next control period, the following cost driver volumes have been budgeted:

- 250 deliveries of raw materials
- 120 production runs

On the basis of budgeted departmental costs and the cost analysis, the following budget has been drawn up for the next control period.

Cost	Total $'000	Costs attributable to receiving deliveries $'000	Costs attributable to issuing materials $'000	Dept running costs $'000
Salaries – management	25	8	12	5
Salaries – store workers	27	13	12	2
Salaries – administration	15	4	5	6
Consumables	11	3	5	3
Information technology costs	14	5	8	1
Other costs	19	10	6	3
	111	43	48	20
Activity volumes		250	120	
Cost per unit of cost driver		$172	$400	$20,000

Points to note

(a) The apportionment of cost will be subjective to a certain extent. The objective of the exercise is that the resource has to be justified as supporting one or more of the activities. Costs cannot be hidden.

(b) The cost driver rates of $172 and $400 can be used to calculate product costs using ABC.

(c) Identifying activities and their costs helps to focus attention on those activities which add value and those that do not.

(d) The budget has highlighted the cost of the two activities.

4.2 Benefits of ABB

Some writers treat ABB as a complete **philosophy** in itself and attribute to it all the good features of strategic management accounting, zero base budgeting, total quality management, and other ideas. For example, the following claims have been made.

(a) Different **activity levels** will provide a foundation for the 'base' package and incremental packages of **ZBB**.

(b) It will ensure that the organisation's overall **strategy** and any actual or likely changes in that strategy will be taken into account, because it attempts to manage the business as the **sum of its interrelated parts**.

(c) **Critical success factors** will be identified and performance measures devised to monitor progress towards them. (A critical success factor is an activity in which a business **must** perform well if it is to succeed.)

(d) Because concentration is focused on the **whole of an activity**, not just its separate parts, there is more likelihood of **getting it right first time**. For example what is the use of being able to **produce** goods in time for their despatch date if the budget provides insufficient resources for the distribution manager who has to **deliver** them?

5 Budgeting in the modern business world

Traditional budgeting has been criticised by some writers for being "out of kilter" with the modern business world. Hope & Fraser in particular suggest the following problems with the traditional approaches to budgeting:

(i) Budgeting does not provide sufficient value to an organisation to justify the amount of time that senior managers spend on budget related issues.

(ii) In the competitive modern business environment, managers must react quickly to changes in the environment. Traditional budgets slow this reaction down, as new ideas cannot be implemented if they are not in the budget.

(iii) The use of budgets to assess the performance of managers leads to extensive "gaming" whereby managers take whatever action is necessary to achieve their budget targets, even if this is not in the interests of the organisation. Examples of gaming include adding budgetary slack to budgets, manipulation of results to ensure targets are met, and never beating the targets by too much.

5.1 Beyond budget approach

Hope and Fraser suggest a beyond budgeting model for the modern business world:

(i) Replace financial targets with key performance indicators that reflect more accurately the objectives of the company.

(ii) Rewards should not be based on whether plans are achieved. Plans should reflect what an organisation can achieve, to push the organisation forward. If rewards are based on achieving the plan, managers will try to make plans easy.

(iii) Use "stretch goals" to reward managers rather than fixed targets. A stretch goal means that the rewards will increase with the managers performance, rather than using a single target that is either met or not met.

(iv) Planning should be devolved from the centre. This means that managers prepare their own budgets.

(v) Use of rolling budgets that can be continually updated to adapt to changes in the external environment.

Chapter roundup

- A focus on the **activities** that a business carries out lies behind much modern thinking.
- **Activity-based management** (ABM) includes performing activities more efficiently, eliminating the need to perform certain activities that do not add value for customers, improving the design of products and developing better relationships with customers and suppliers. The goal of ABM is to enable customer needs to be satisfied while making fewer demands on organisational resources.
- Activity-based budgeting (ABB) involves defining the activities that underlie the financial figures in each function and using the **level of activity** to decide how much resource should be **allocated**, how well it is being **managed** and to **explain variances** from budget.

Quick Quiz

1. Inspection time is value added. True or false?
2. Choose the appropriate term from those highlighted.

    A **diversionary / secondary / core / primary / discretionary** activity supports a core activity, but does not add value in itself.

3. Activities occur at different levels. The first level is unit level. What are the other three levels?
4. What is the name of the new approaches to replace budgeting in the modern world?

Answers to Quick Quiz

1. False
2. Secondary
3. Batch level, product/process level, organisational/facility
4. Beyond budgeting

End of Chapter Question

ABC and ABB (AIA May 2008)

Although activity based costing (ABC) and activity based budgeting (ABB) have been widely publicised as better costing and budgeting systems, there are problems with their implementation.

Required

Discuss the above statement, identifying the problems associated with implementing ABC and ABB and recommend how organisations can overcome these problems. **(17 marks)**

Answers to end of chapter questions

Chapter 3 – Midtec Ltd

This question examines the ability of candidates to calculate costs in relation to stock ordering and holding policies and assess the consequences of changes in those policies in the light of bulk order discounts. It also asks for a discussion regarding an EOQ stock policy. (Syllabus reference 3.2)

(a) Evaluation of policy at the EOQ

Re-order costs $\dfrac{cd}{Q}$ where: c = Cost to place an order
d = Annual Demand
Q = Order Quantity

Kitain **Jensten**

$\dfrac{\$85 \times 30{,}000}{7{,}984} = \$319.39$ $\dfrac{\$55 \times 85{,}000}{9{,}220} = \$507.05$

Holding costs $\dfrac{Qh}{2}$ where: h = Cost of holding one unit of stock for one year

$\dfrac{7{,}984 \times 0.08}{2} = \$319.36$ $\dfrac{9{,}220 \times 0.11}{2} = \$507.10$

Total costs Re-order costs + holding costs

$319.39 + $319.36 = **$638.75** $507.05 + $507.10 = **$1,014.15**

(b) Evaluation of proposal from supplier

Re-order costs $\dfrac{cd}{Q}$ where: c = Cost to place an order
d = Annual Demand
Q = Order Quantity

Kitain **Jensten**

$\dfrac{\$85 \times 30{,}000}{15{,}000} = \$170$ $\dfrac{\$55 \times 85{,}000}{20{,}000} = \$233.75$

Holding costs $\dfrac{Qh}{2}$ where: h = Cost of holding one unit of stock for one year

$\dfrac{15{,}000 \times 0.08}{2} = \$600$ $\dfrac{20{,}000 \times 0.11}{2} = \$1{,}100$

Total costs Re-order costs + holding costs

$170 + $600 = **$770** $233.75 + $1,100 = **$1,333.75**

Increase in stock charges if supplier discount accepted:

    Kitain $770 – $638.75 = $131.25

    Jensten $1,333.75 – $1,014.15 = $319.60

Increase cost in storage space rental $1,750

Total **$2,200.85**

Savings to stock due to supplier discount

    Kitain $2 × 30,000 Litres × 2% = $1,200

    Jensten $1 × 85,000 Litres × 2% = $1,700

Total   **$2,900**

Total saving overall by adopting the policy $2,900 − $2,200.85 = **$699.15**

(c) Costs involved with holding stock are optimised at the EOQ. Companies may face problems in that the EOQ need not be a convenient or round number, therefore ordering their EOQ may be difficult in reality. It may also mean that the company misses out on supplier offers and discounts, but this needs to be balanced against a business ability to store any extra stock that may have been bought.

Chapter 5 – Damex

This question tests candidates' ability to undertake overhead analysis. It requires candidates to analyse and apportion overheads and then to calculate the costs and profitability of different operations. The question further requires candidates to understand the weaknesses of overhead analysis. (Syllabus references 3.2 and 3.3).

(a) (i) Analysis of cost

	Basis	Total cost $	South $	North $	Central $
Insurance	Given	56,000	20,000	24,000	12,000
Heating & Lighting	Given	60,000	20,000	30,000	10,000
Depreciation: Equip	Equip	36,000	12,000	16,000	8,000
– Motor vehicle	Motor veh	48,000	16,000	20,000	12,000
Staff pension	No of emp	50,000	18,000	22,000	10,000
Total Indirect Costs		250,000	86,000	112,000	52,000
Salaries – Doctors		500,000	200,000	200,000	100,000
– Nurses		250,000	100,000	100,000	50,000
– Assistants		90,000	30,000	45,000	15,000
Total cost		**1,090,000**	**416,000**	**457,000**	**217,000**
Income		1,270,000	500,000	550,000	220,000
(ii) **Profit**		**180,000**	**84,000**	**93,000**	**3,000**
Number of patients		6,000	2,000	3,000	1,000
(iii) **Profit per patient**		**$30**	**$42**	**$31**	**$3**

(b) Comments

Candidates should comment on the results of their analysis.

- The areas of concern that need highlighting are the low profit of the Central clinic. Also, in general the profit per patient appears to be very low.
- Salaries costs are very high and management may need addressing.
- Candidates should comment on the weaknesses of their analysis. Some of the comments would include the arbitrary basis used in apportioning the overheads. The staff pensions cost was apportioned on the basis of number of employees but there are different grades of employees (doctors, nurses and assistants). This has not been taken into consideration.

Chapter 6 – Overheads and marginal costing

(a) The **advantages** of using **marginal costing** are as follows.

(i) Marginal costing is **based on cost behaviour patterns**, the key principle being that contribution will vary in proportion to the units sold. Hence marginal costing demonstrates clearly how **cash flows and profits** will be **affected** by **changes in sales volume**.

(ii) Using marginal costing means that **fixed costs** that relate to a period of time are **matched** against the period by being charged against the period's **revenues**.

(iii) Marginal costing situations can be shown easily and clearly on graphs.

(iv) Use of marginal costing will help in **short-term pricing decisions** concerning incremental profits. It will also help in **setting a buffer stock level**. Buffer stock must be valued at marginal cost, since fixed costs have not been incurred to produce a marginal quantity of finished goods that are unsold at the end of the period.

(b) **Absorption costing purpose**

The **aim of absorption costing is to produce a product cost which ensures that overheads incurred during a period are recovered** via the inclusion of a share of overhead in each unit of output. Its principal aim is not, therefore, to produce accurate product costs.

Subjective judgement

The determination of absorption costing product costs **depends on a great deal of subjective judgement and hence, due to the requirement of accurate product costs for decision making, it is totally unsuitable for decision making.**

Due to the high degree of subjectivity involved in its operation, absorption costing can result in inaccurate and hence misleading information for decision making and should not therefore be used for that purpose.

Marginal spare capacity

It is not just the inaccuracy of the resulting product cost which makes absorption costing information unsuitable for decision making, however. Consider the following example.

Suppose that a sales manager has an item of product which he is having difficulty in selling. Its historical full cost is $80, made up of variable costs of $50 and fixed costs of $30. A customer offers $60 for it.

(i) **If there is no other customer** for the product, $60 would be better than nothing and the **product should be sold to improve income and profit** by this amount.

(ii) If the company has **spare production capacity** which would otherwise not be used, it would be **profitable to continue making more** of the same product, if customers are willing to pay $60 for each extra unit made. This is because the additional costs are only $50 so that the profit would be increased marginally by $10 per unit produced.

Thus, for **once-only decisions or decisions affecting the use of marginal spare capacity, absorption costing information about unit profits is *irrelevant*.** On the other hand, since total contribution must be sufficient to cover the fixed costs of the business, **marginal costing would be unsuitable as a basis for establishing *long-term* prices for all output.**

(c)

	Assembly $	Painting $	Stores $	Maintenance $
Overheads	200,000	300,000	100,000	80,000
Apportionment				
Maintenance	32,000	36,000	12,000	(80,000)
Stores	67,200	44,800	(112,000)	-
	299,200	380,800	-	-

Standard overhead absorption rate = $\dfrac{299,200}{100,000}$ = $2.992 per unit

	$
Overheads absorbed 120,000 × $2.992	359,040
Actual overheads incurred by Assembly department	360,000
Under absorbed	960

(d) **Overhead allocation** is the **process of assigning a whole item of cost** to a single cost unit, centre, account or time period.

An example of a cost allocation would be assigning the salary of a catering manager to the works canteen.

Overhead apportionment is the **spreading of revenues or costs** over two or more cost units, centres accounts or time periods. Apportionment may also be referred to as 'indirect allocation'.

(*CIMA Official Terminology*)

The overhead costs that have been allocated to cost centres will need to be apportioned to production departments.

An example of overhead apportionment would be the indirect allocation of the costs of the works canteen to the production department.

(e) An **overhead absorption rate** is a means of **attributing overheads to a product or service**, based for example on direct labour hours, direct labour cost or machine hours.

(*CIMA Official Terminology*)

An overhead absorption rate may be based on:
(i) Direct labour cost percentage rate
(ii) Direct labour hour rate
(iii) Machine hour rate
(iv) Volume of production

The choice is made with the objective of obtaining accurate costs. It is a matter of judgement and common sense. There are no strict rules involved but what is required is an absorption basis which realistically reflects the characteristics of a given cost centre and which avoids undue anomalies.

Chapter 7 – TQG Ltd

This question assesses a candidate's ability to apportion overheads and determine unit costs using both OAR and ABC systems. It also tests a candidate's application of knowledge in a decision making scenario involving both methods. (Syllabus reference 3.2)

(a) A cost driver is the cause of, or reason for the cost associated with the activity that has given rise to the cost. It is important because it is the basis for absorbing the cost in the cost pool. In some instances it may be difficult to determine what the cost driver is for a particular cost object.

(b)

	Gold Pearl	Granite Type Sapphire Blue	Jet Black
	$	$	$
Direct materials	103,680	165,730	209,420
Direct labour	48,300	36,550	68,800
Overheads	68,359	72,420	85,201
Total cost	220,339	274,700	363,421
OAR cost per worktop	1,064.44	963.86	692.23

Labour hour OAR $225,980 / 22,810 hours = $9.91/hr

(c) Machine maintenance $6,350/140 = $45.36/hr

Machine production running costs $128,750/11,200 = $11.50/hr

Machine set-up costs $29,860/1,017 = $29.36 per set-up

Inventory and purchasing costs $61,020/1,561 = $39.09/requisition

	Gold Pearl	Granite Type Sapphire Blue	Jet Black
	$	$	$
Direct materials	103,680	165,730	209,420
Direct labour	48,300	36,550	68,800
Overheads			
Machine maintenance	2,948	2,041	1,361
Machine production running costs	62,651	37,360	28,739
Machine set-up costs	6,078	8,368	15,414
Inventory and purchasing costs	30,490	17,825	12,705
	102,167	65,594	58,219
Total cost	254,147	267,874	336,439

(d)

	Gold Pearl $	Granite Type Sapphire Blue $	Jet Black $
Difference in cost per worktop			
ABC cost per worktop	1,227.76	939.91	640.84
OAR cost per worktop	1,064.44	963.86	692.23
Difference	–163.32	23.95	51.39
Difference in overhead absorbed			
OAR	68,359	72,420	85,201
ABC	102,167	65,594	58,219
Difference	–33,808	6,826	26,982

The ABC method gives a higher proportion of overheads for 'Gold Pearl' granite. This is because the ABC method of costing places emphasis upon levels of activity as indicated by the cost drivers.

It can be argued that in the case of TQG Ltd, that the reliance upon labour has diminished as more modern computerised machinery has been purchased. Therefore, continued use of OAR based upon labour hours is no longer a true reflection of the production process and a more appropriate method ought to be employed.

The effect is that overheads are moved away from 'Jet Black', thus making its price more competitive and ought to lead to fewer orders being lost to competitors (the same may be true for Sapphire Blue). However, this may lead to another problem in that 'Gold Pearl' granite may now become uncompetitive because it is now supporting higher overhead absorption to the amount of $33,808. TQG Ltd ought to control costs in the long term rather than merely attempt to move them around their product lines.

Chapter 8 – B Ltd

(a) **Step 1**   **Determine output and losses and equivalent units of production**

	Units
Input	
Opening WIP	50
Input material	1,200
	1,250
Output	
Opening WIP completed	50
Normal loss (5% × 1,200)	60
Abnormal loss (150 – 60)	90
Closing WIP	150
	350
Units started and finished in period 5	900

Calculate equivalent units of production

	Total units	Process 2 material	Added material	Conversion cost
		Equivalent units		
Normal loss	60	0	0	0
Abnormal loss	90	90 (100%)	90 (100%)	90 (100%)
Opening WIP completed	50	0 (0%)	25 (50%)	20 (40%)
Fully worked units	900	900 (100%)	900 (100%)	900 (100%)
Closing WIP	150	150 (100%)	105 (70%)	135 (90%)
	1,250	1,140	1,120	1,145

Top tips. The figure of 1,250 above should equal the total units input in the reconciliation at the start of Step 1.

Step 2 Calculate cost per unit of output, losses and WIP

	Total $	Equivalent units	Cost per equivalent unit $
Material from process 2	4,902*	1,140	4.30
Added material	12,880	1,120	11.50
Conversion cost	9,160	1,145	8.00

*1,200 × $4.135 less scrap value of normal loss = $4,962 – (60 × $1) = $4,902

Step 3 Calculate the total cost of output, losses and WIP

	Opening WIP completed $	Fully worked units $	Abnormal loss $	Closing WIP $
Material from process 2 (at $4.30)	0	3,870	387	645.00
Added material (at $11.50)	287.50	10,350	1,035	1,207.50
Conversion cost (at $8)	160.00	7,200	720	1,080.00
	447.50	21,420	2,142	2,932.50

Step 4 Complete accounts

PROCESS 3 A/C – PERIOD 5

	Units	$		Units	$
Opening WIP	50	1,208	Normal loss		
Material from process 2	1,200	4,962	(scrap a/c)	60	60.00
Added materials		12,880	Abnormal loss a/c	90	2,142.00
Conversion cost		9,160	Output to process 4:		
			Opening WIP completed	50	1,655.50*
			Fully worked units	900	21,420.00
			Closing WIP	150	2,932.50
	1,250	28,210		1,250	28,210.00

* $1,208 (period 4 costs) + $447.50 (period 5 costs)

ABNORMAL LOSS A/C

	$		$
Process 3 a/c	2,142	Scrap a/c (90 × $1)	90
		Inc statement	2,052
	2,142		2,142

(b) **Step 1** Calculate equivalent units of production

	Total units	Equivalent units Process 2 material	Added material	Conversion cost
Good output (900 + 50)	950	950 (100%)	950 (100%)	950 (100%)
Normal loss	60	0	0	0
Abnormal loss	90	90 (100%)	90 (100%)	90 (100%)
Closing WIP	150	150 (100%)	105 (70%)	135 (90%)
	1,250	1,190	1,145	1,175

Step 2 Calculate cost per unit of output, losses and WIP

Calculation of total costs

	Process 2 material $	Added material $	Conversion cost $
Period 5 costs	4,902 (net)	12,880	9,160
Value of opening WIP	96	402	710
	4,998	13,282	9,870

Calculation of cost per equivalent unit

	Total $	Equivalent units	Cost per equivalent unit $
Material from process 2	4,998	1,190	4.20
Added material	13,282	1,145	11.60
Conversion cost	9,870	1,175	8.40
			24.20

Step 3 Calculate the total cost of output, losses and WIP

- Output to process 4 (opening WIP + units started and finished) = (900 + 50) × $24.20 = $22,990
- Abnormal loss = 90 × $24.20 = $2,178
- Closing WIP = (150 × $4.20) + (105 × $11.60) + (135 × $8.40) = $2,982

Step 4 Complete account

PROCESS 3 A/C – PERIOD 5

	Units	$		Units	$
Opening WIP	50	1,208	Normal loss		
Material from process 2	1,200	4,962	(scrap a/c)	60	60
Added materials		12,880	Abnormal loss a/c	90	2,178
Conversion cost		9,160	Output to process 4	950	22,990
			Closing WIP	150	2,982
	1,250	28,210		1,250	28,210

Chapter 9 – ABC Ltd

(a) **Process 1**

Step 1 **Determine output and losses**

Normal loss = 10% × 4,000 = 400

Total loss = 4,000 + 3,000 – 2,400 – 3,400 = 1,200

Therefore, abnormal loss = 800

	Equivalent kg Material costs	Conversion costs
Process 2	2,400	2,400
Abnormal loss	800	800
Closing WIP	3,400	1,360 *
	6,600	4,560

* 3,400 × 40%

Step 2 **Calculate cost per unit of output, losses and WIP**

$$\frac{\text{Costs incurred}}{\text{Equivalent units}} = \text{Cost per equivalent unit}$$

∴ Materials cost per equivalent unit $= \dfrac{\$4,400 + \$22,000}{6,600}$

$= \dfrac{\$26,400}{6,600}$

$= \$4$

∴ Conversion costs per equivalent unit $= \dfrac{\$3,744 + \$12,000 + \$18,000}{4,560}$

$= \dfrac{\$33,744}{4,560}$

$= \$7.40$

Step 3 **Calculate total cost of output, losses and WIP**

	Materials $	Conversion costs $	Total $
Transfers to process 2	9,600	17,760	27,360
Abnormal loss	3,200	5,920	9,120
Closing WIP	13,600	10,064	23,664
	26,400	33,744	60,144

Step 4 **Complete account**

PROCESS 1 ACCOUNT

	Kg	$		Kg	$
WIP materials	3,000	4,400	Process 2	2,400	27,360
WIP conversion costs	–	3,744	Normal loss	400	–
Materials	4,000	22,000	Abnormal loss	800	9,120
Labour	–	12,000	WIP materials	3,400	13,600
Overhead	–	18,000	WIP conversion costs	–	10,064
	7,000	60,144		7,000	60,144

Process 2

Step 1 Determine output and losses

Opening WIP + transfers from process 1 = finished goods + normal loss + abnormal loss/gain + closing stock

∴ 2,250 + 2,400 = 2,500 + (10% × 2,400) + abnormal loss/gain + 2,600

∴ Abnormal gain = 690 kg

	Equivalent kg	
	Process 1	Conversion costs
Finished goods	2,500	2,500
Abnormal gain	(690)	(690)
Closing WIP	2,600	1,040 *
	4,410	2,850

* 2,600 × 40%

Step 2 Calculate cost per unit of output, losses and WIP

$$\text{Process 1} = \frac{\$4,431 + \$27,360 - \$480^*}{4,410} = \$7.10$$

$$\text{Conversion costs} = \frac{\$5,250 + \$15,000 - \$22,500}{2,850} = \$15.00$$

* $2 × 240 units of normal loss (scrap value)

Step 3 Calculate total cost of output, losses and WIP

	Process 1	Conversion costs	Total
	$	$	$
Finished goods	17,750	37,500	55,250
Abnormal gain	4,899	10,350	15,249
Closing WIP	18,460	15,600	34,060
	41,109	63,450	104,559

Step 4 Complete account

PROCESS 2 ACCOUNT

	Kg	$		Kg	$
WIP Process 1	2,250	4,431	Finished goods	2,500	55,250
WIP conversion costs	–	5,250	Normal loss	240	480
Process 1	2,400	27,360	WIP Process 2	2,600	18,460
Labour	–	15,000	WIP conversion costs	–	15,600
Overhead	–	22,500			
Abnormal gain	690	15,249			
	5,340	89,790		5,340	89,790

Other workings

1

ABNORMAL LOSS ACCOUNT

	$		$
Balance b/f	1,400	Statement of profit or loss	10,520
Process 1	9,120		
	10,520		10,520

2   ABNORMAL GAIN ACCOUNT

	$		$
Scrap recovery lost (690 × $2)	1,380	Balance b/d	300
Statement of profit or loss	14,169	Process 2	15,249
	15,549		15,549

3   $(585,000 + 52,000)

4   Cost of sales for September = opening finished goods inventory + transfers of finished goods from Process 2 – closing finished goods inventory = $(65,000 + 55,250 – 60,000) = $60,250

5   Annual cost of sales = opening balance + balance for September
                        = $(442,500 + 60,250)
                        = $502,750

6   Overhead under or over absorbed = balance b/f + overheads charged to process 1 + overheads charged to process 2 – overheads incurred = $(250 + 18,000 + 22,500 – 54,000) = $13,250 under absorbed

ABC LTD STATEMENT OF PROFIT OR LOSS
FOR THE YEAR ENDED 30 SEPTEMBER 20X8

	$	$
Sales (W3)		637,000
Cost of sales (W5)		502,750
Gross profit		134,250
Under-absorbed overhead (W6)	13,250	
Abnormal loss (W1)	10,520	
Abnormal gain (W2)	(14,169)	
		9,601
Net profit		124,649

(b) (i) **Planning**

Joint cost **apportionments** are carried out on an **arbitrary basis**, often using output volume or sales value as the basis of apportionment. The resulting unit costs can **differ** widely depending on which apportionment basis is selected.

Managers using the resulting unit costs for **planning purposes** may **not arrive at correct cost projections** if they assume that they are relevant for any volume of output of each product.

(ii) **Control**

Cost control is achieved by **comparing actual costs** with a **standard** or **budget cost**. The budget costs must be a **realistic target** for the actual output which was achieved. This means that budgeted costs must be **flexed** to allow for changes in output volume, and then actual costs should be compared with these flexed costs.

The apportioned joint costs must therefore be **separated** into their **fixed** and **variable** elements so that the total budget cost can be correctly **flexed** to allow for changes in activity.

If costs are **correctly analysed** into their fixed and variable components then **apportioned joint costs** can be **used** for the **control** of total costs.

However, **no extra control information** is obtained by carrying out the joint cost apportionment since such an apportionment is purely **arbitrary**.

(iii) **Decision making**

Apportioned joint costs are of little use for decision making and in fact they can produce information which would lead to incorrect decisions.

Simply by changing the basis of cost apportionment it is possible to make an unprofitable product appear profitable, and *vice versa*.

Management should be encouraged to **concentrate attention** on the **incremental costs** over which they can exercise control. They can **only control the total amount of joint costs** and they may be misled by the product 'profits' or 'losses' which result from arbitrary apportionment of joint costs.

Chapter 10 – Job costing

This question tests candidates' ability to apply the techniques of job costing. It requires candidates to prepare journal entries and a profit and loss statement for jobs. The question also tests candidates' understanding of overhead costing especially in terms of how over- or under-absorbed overheads should be treated. (Syllabus reference 3.3)

(a) Journal entries

	Dr	Cr
	$'000	$'000
Materials control	400	
Cash		400
Work in Process Control	355	
Materials control		355
Manufacturing overheads control	50	
Materials control		50
Work in process control	65	
Manufacturing overhead control	45	
Wages payable control		110
Manufacturing overhead control	47	
Repairs payable		47
Work in process control (200% × $65,000)	130	
Manufacturing overhead control		130
Finished goods control	206	
WIP control		206
Bank	400	
Sales		400
Cost of goods sold	201	
Finished goods control		201
Manufacturing overhead control (under-absorbed overheads)**	12	
Cost of goods sold		12
Selling and Administration Exp	108	
Cash		108

** Under absorbed overhead was calculated as:

Actual overheads:

Indirect material	$50,000
Indirect labour	$45,000
Repairs	$47,000
	$142,000
Absorbed (200% of DL)	$130,000
Under	$12,000

(b) Statement of profit or loss

	$'000
Sales	400
Less cost of goods sold (201,000 + 12,000 under absorbed)	213
Gross profit	187
Less selling and administration	108
Operating profit	79

(c) Job costing vs. process costing

It would appear that a job costing system provides more accurate product costs because a separate cost is calculated for each job whereas with a process costing system the cost per unit is an average cost. On the other hand, a greater proportion of the costs are likely to be direct under process costing. With a job costing system, a large proportion of costs will be treated as overheads and the problem of apportioning and allocating overheads will result in inaccurate product costs. In this sense process costing might yield more accurate product costs. However, one problem with process costing is that there is a need to estimate the degree of completion of closing stocks of WIP in order to estimate equivalent units and cost per unit. If it is difficult to produce an accurate estimate of the degree of completion then the product costs will also be inaccurate. Therefore it depends on the circumstances – in some situations job costing product costs will be more accurate and in other situations process costing product costs may be more accurate.

ANSWERS TO END OF CHAPTER QUESTIONS

Chapter 11 – Utilities Company Ltd

This question tests candidates' ability to prepare cash budgets and to evaluate the liquidity positions of firms. It requires candidates to understand the differences in the treatment of cash and non-cash expenses. The evaluation of the cash flow position also requires candidates to understand the necessary measures to address a company's liquidity problems (Syllabus reference 3.5)

(a) Cash Budget

	December $	January $	February $	March $	April $
Sales					
25%	100,000	150,000	80,000	137,500	125,000
70%	350,000	280,000	420,000	224,000	385,000
3%	7,500	15,000	12,000	18,000	9,600
Total receipts	457,500	445,000	512,000	379,500	519,600
Less payments:					
Purchases	180,000	240,000	350,000	175,000	250,000
Motor car	40,000				
Salaries	45,000	50,000	40,000	60,000	55,000
Rent	60,000	40,000	55,000	62,500	70,000
Insurance	30,000	0	0	0	0
Advertising	130,000	145,000	80,000	100,000	75,000
Admin (exclude dep.)	9,000	9,000	9,000	9,000	9,000
Equipment	10,000	0	0	0	0
Total payments	504,000	484,000	534,000	406,500	459,000
Surplus/Deficit	–46,500	–39,000	–22,000	–27,000	60,600
Opening balance	50,000	3,500	–35,500	–57,500	–84,500
Closing balance	3,500	–35,500	–57,500	–84,500	–23,900

(b) Comments

Candidates should comment generally on the unhealthy cash position of the company. A good answer will include identifying the causes of the cash flow problems and suggesting ways to address the problem; such as offering discounts to induce early payments and negotiating with suppliers to take a longer credit. A possibility of paying other expenses in arrears and also determining alternative financing options for the machine could be considered. A good answer should include implications of any suggestions.

Chapter 12 – Standard costing

(a) What is standard costing?

The *CIMA Official Terminology* definition of standard costing is 'A control technique which compares standard costs and revenues with actual results to obtain variances which are used to stimulate improved performance'.

Setting standards for materials costs

Direct material prices will be estimated by the purchasing department from their existing knowledge.

- Purchase contracts already agreed
- Pricing discussions with regular suppliers
- Quotations and estimates from potential suppliers
- The forecast movement of prices in the market

- The availability of bulk purchase discounts
- Material quality required

Price inflation can cause difficulties in setting realistic standard prices. Suppose that a material costs $10 per kilogram at the moment, and during the course of the next 12 months, it is expected to go up in price by 20% to $12 per kilogram. **What standard price should be selected?**

- The **current price** of $10 per kilogram
- The **expected price** for the year, say, $11 per kilogram

Either price above would be possible, but neither would be entirely satisfactory.

Standard costing for materials is therefore more **difficult in times of inflation but it is still worthwhile**.

(i) Usage and efficiency variances will still be meaningful.

(ii) Inflation is measurable: there is no reason why its effects cannot be removed from the variances reported.

(iii) Standard costs can be revised, so long as this is not done too frequently.

(b) **Types of performance standard**

The setting of standards raises the problem of how demanding the standard should be. Should the standard represent a perfect performance or an easily attainable performance? The type of performance standard used can have behavioural implications. There are four types of standard.

(i) **Ideal** — These are based on **perfect operating conditions**: no wastage, no spoilage, no inefficiencies, no idle time, no breakdowns. Variances from ideal standards are useful for pinpointing areas where a close examination may result in large savings, but they are likely to have an **unfavourable motivational impact** because reported variances will always be adverse. Employees will often feel that the goals are **unattainable** and not work so hard.

(ii) **Attainable** — These are based on the hope that a standard amount of work will be carried out **efficiently**, machines properly operated or materials properly used. Some **allowance** is made for **wastage** and **inefficiencies**. If well-set they provide a useful psychological **incentive** by giving employees a **realistic**, but **challenging** target of efficiency. The consent and co-operation of employees involved in improving the standard are required.

(iii) **Current** — These are based on **current working conditions** (current wastage, current inefficiencies). The disadvantage of current standards is that they **do not attempt to improve** on **current** levels of **efficiency**.

(iv) **Basic** — These are kept **unaltered** over a **long period of time**, and may be **out of date**. They are used to show changes in efficiency or performance over a long period of time. Basic standards are perhaps the **least useful** and least common type of standard in use.

Ideal standards, attainable standards and current standards each have their supporters and it is by no means clear which of them is preferable.

(c) A **budget** is a **quantified monetary plan** for a future period, which managers will try to achieve. Its major function lies in communicating plans and co-ordinating activities within an organisation.

On the other hand, a **standard** is a carefully **predetermined quantity target** which can be achieved in certain conditions.

Budgets and standards are similar in the following ways.

(i) They both **involve looking to the future** and forecasting what is likely to happen given a certain set of circumstances.

(ii) They are both **used for control purposes**. A budget aids control by setting financial targets or limits for a forthcoming period. Actual achievements or expenditures are then compared with the budgets and action is taken to correct any variances where necessary. A standard also achieves control by comparison of actual results against a predetermined target.

As well as being similar, budgets and standards are interrelated. For example, a standard unit production cost can act as the basis for a production cost budget. The unit cost is multiplied by the budgeted activity level to arrive at the budgeted expenditure on production costs.

There are, however, important differences between budgets and standards.

Budgets

- Gives planned total aggregate costs for a function or cost centre
- Can be prepared for all functions, even where output cannot be measured
- Expressed in money terms

Standards

- Shows the until resource usage for a single task, for example the standard labour hours for a single unit of production
- Limited to situations where repetitive actions are performed and output can be measured
- Need not be expressed in money terms. For example, a standard rate of output does not need a financial value put on it

(d) **Uses of budgetary control**

A budgetary control system is concerned with **cost and revenue totals**, those totals representing **future expectations** of departments or the organisation as a whole. The major uses are as follows. A labour budget may therefore be set for a unit within a hospital or a fixed overhead budget may be set for the restaurant within a hotel.

(i) The totals are used as **yardsticks** against which actual performances are measured.

(ii) They also represent **expenditure allowances**. Management must maintain their expenditure within the allowance and can only exceed it if a case is made.

Uses of standard costing

Standard costing, on the other hand, represents **cost control** on a **units basis**, that is to say particular products or services. A labour standard may be set, therefore, for an operation in a hospital and a variable overhead standard may be set for each passenger/kilometre in a passenger transport organisation. The main use of standard costings are as follows.

(i) Standards are set as means of controlling activities.

(ii) Standards enable the principles of management by exception to be practised by highlighting variances that appear to be significant.

Why both methods should be used simultaneously

Standard costing and budgetary control should be used in conjunction with each other since together they can encompass the whole organisation. In fact, budgets and standards are **interrelated**. For example, a **standard labour operation cost** can act as the basis for the **budget of a unit** within a hospital. The **standard cost** is **multiplied** by the **budgeted activity level** to arrive at the **budgeted expenditure** on labour in the hospital unit.

It is well nigh impossible to set realistic budgets without considering the **operational level standards** and it makes little sense to plan or control at an operational level without planning and controlling at a department or organisation.

Chapter 13 – Sminko Ltd

This question examines a candidate's ability to calculate variances in sales, materials and labour; the production of standard and actual profit statements and reconciliation between the standard and actual profit. (Syllabus reference 3.5)

(a) Total sales variance (as a check)

Actual sales – Standard sales

(1,050 × $16) – (1,200 × $20) = 7,200 (Adv)

Sales price variance

Actual volume × (Actual price – Standard price)

1,050 × ($16 - $20) = 4,200 (Adv)

Sales volume variance

(Actual volume – Standard volume) × Standard price

(1,050 – 1,200 × $20 = 3,000 (Adv)

Direct material variance (as a check)

Actual material cost – Standard material cost

(350 kg × $9.40) – (380 kg/1,200 × 1,050 × $7.50) = 796.25 (Adv)

Material price variance

(Standard price per kg – Actual price per kg) × Actual kg

(7.50-9.40) × 350 = 665 (Adv)

Material usage variance

(Standard material used – Actual material used) × Standard price

[(380 kg/1,200 × 1,050) -350] × $7.50 = 131.25 (Adv)

Direct labour variance (as a check)

Actual labour cost – Standard labour cost

(900 hrs × $6.50) – (950 hrs/1,200 × 1,050) × $6.00 = 862.50 (Adv)

Labour rate variance

(Standard rate per hour – Actual rate per hour) × Actual hours worked

(6.00 – 6.50) × 900 = 450 (Adv)

Labour efficiency variance

(Standard hours – Actual hours) × Standard labour rate

[(950 hrs/1,200 × 1,050) – 900] × 6.00 = 412.50(Adv)

ANSWERS TO END OF CHAPTER QUESTIONS

(b) Standard Cost Operating Statement for September 20X8

			$	$
Standard Profit				8,019
Add/Less Variances				
Sales	–	Price	(4,200)	
	–	Volume	(3,000)	
Materials	–	Price	(665)	
	–	Usage	(131)	
Labour	–	Rate	(450)	
	–	Efficiency	(413)	
Overheads (8,500 – 9,700)			(1,200)	
Net Variances				(10,059)
Actual Loss				(2,040)

Working

Profit calculation for September 20X8.

	Standard $	Actual $
Sales (1,200 × 20) (1,050 × 16)	24,000	16,800
Less: Direct Materials (380 kg/1,200 × 1,050) × 750 (350 kg × $9.40)	2,494	3,290
Direct Labour (950 hrs/1,200 × 1,050) × $6.00 (900 × $6.50)	4,987	5,850
Overheads	8,500	9,700
Profit / (Loss)	8,019	(2,040)

(c) Sales – sold 150 fewer Gizmos, and at a price of $4 less per item.

Materials – Used 30kg less direct materials, but at $1.90 more per kg. The reduced materials usage may be due to the use of more expensive, but skilled labour.

Labour – Labour was more expensive, but fewer hours were worked, possibly due to more efficient or more skilled labour being used.

Courses of action – Investigate market for sales, what has changed? Are materials price increases permanent? Consider revising standards. Why has more expensive labour been used? Is this a permanent change that needs to be incorporated into the standard?

Chapter 15 – South-West Company Ltd

This question tests candidates' understanding of relevant costs and revenues in decision making. The question requires candidates to analyse an outsourcing decision and to discuss the importance of non-financial information in the outsourcing decision. (Syllabus reference 3.6)

(a) Analysis

Units		100,000	
		Make	Buy
Outside price	$40	$0	$4,000,000
Direct material	15	1,500,000	0
Other Variable Costs	22.50	2,250,000	0
Total variable costs		3,750,000	4,000,000
Direct departmental fixed cost		312,500	0
Total cost		4,062,500	4,000,000
Difference			62,500

Note. It is assumed that the depreciation and general fixed costs will be indifferent to the decision to make or buy hence they are irrelevant. Candidates are expected to generally comment on the results of their analysis. It appears from the analysis above that on financial grounds it is better to outsource the part than make it in-house. The result is however influenced by the treatment of the fixed overhead. Here we assume the general fixed overheads will not change and the direct departmental fixed overheads will not be incurred when production ceases. If we stop production we may sell the equipment used in making the component. This will be a cash inflow that will affect the decision.

(b) Discussion of factors

Candidates should identify relevant factors (both qualitative and quantitative) which could influence the decision.

(i) Quality of the outside supplies
(ii) Reliability of the outside supplier
(iii) Redundancy cost if production ceases
(iv) Image and reputation of the company if production ceases
(v) Technology in terms of the new machine

Chapter 16 – ABC and ABB

The answer may cover the following points:

Problems with ABC and ABB:

- Implementation is a time consuming and expensive process – identification of cost drivers, data collection, observation, interviews. Costs may outweigh benefits.

- Resistance to change by employees particularly if linked to cost reduction.

- Requires championing by a financial director.

- Difficulties in tracing overheads to products and services and therefore the accuracy of information for planning and control decisions might not increase.

- Techniques not always used to track value adding activities.

Overcoming problems:

- Ensure need – overheads form significant proportion of costs, new technology introduced affecting existing cost structure?

- Keep employees fully informed of reasons for, processes involved, involvement in implementation and succession planning for an ABC / ABB champion.

- Ensure clear reasons for adoption – attention directing information highlighting problem areas for analysis, managing customer centric product diversity, customer profitability analysis.

Exam Question Bank

EXAM QUESTION BANK

PART C1 QUESTIONS: THE ROLE AND NATURE OF MANAGEMENT ACCOUNTING

Questions 1.1 to 2.15 cover **Introduction to management accounting and the nature of costs**, the subjects of Chapter 1-2 of the Learning & Practice Workbook

1 Information for management

1.1 Which of the following is **not** an essential quality of good information?

    A   It should be relevant for its purposes
    B   It should be communicated to the right person
    C   It should be completely accurate
    D   It should be timely   **(2 marks)**

1.2 Which of the following statements about management accounts is/are true?

    (i)   They must be stated in purely monetary terms
    (ii)   Limited companies must, by law, prepare management accounts
    (iii)   They serve as a future planning tool and are not used as an historical record

    A   (i), (ii) and (iii)
    B   (i) and (ii)
    C   (ii) only
    D   None of the statements are correct   **(2 marks)**

1.3 A management control system is

    A   A possible course of action that might enable an organisation to achieve its objectives
    B   A collective term for the hardware and software used to drive a database system
    C   A set up that measures and corrects the performance of activities of subordinates in order to make sure that the objectives of an organisation are being met and their associated plans are being carried out
    D   A system that controls and maximises the profits of an organisation   **(2 marks)**

1.4 Which of the following statements are correct?

    (i)   Strategic information is mainly used by senior management in an organisation
    (ii)   Productivity measurements are examples of tactical information
    (iii)   Operational information is required frequently by its main users

    A   (i) and (ii) only
    B   (i) and (iii) only
    C   (ii) and (iii) only
    D   (i), (ii) and (iii)   **(2 marks)**

EXAM QUESTION BANK

1.5 Which of the following statements are correct?

A Forecasts will always provide a good source of data for historic costs

B Financial accounts provide the best source of data for future costs

C A good source of data for historic costs are the financial accounting records and the documents that back up these records

D It is a legal requirement to produce management accounts (2 marks)

1.6 Which of the following statements about management accounting is/are false?

(i) Reports relate to what happened in the past
(ii) Maybe made public
(iii) Gives up to date reports which can be used for controlling the business

A (i) and (ii) only
B (i) and (iii) only
C (ii) and (iii) only
D (i), (ii) and (iii) (2 marks)

1.7 Which of the following do management accountants provide information to management on?

(i) Costs of goods and services
(ii) Actual costs compared to expected costs
(iii) Expected profits and production plans

A (i) and (ii) only
B (i) and (iii) only
C (ii) and (iii) only
D (i), (ii) and (iii) (2 marks)

1.8 Which of the following is **not** a type of information?

A Strategic
B Relevant
C Operational
D Tactical (2 marks)

1.9 Choose the correct word to complete the 2 sentences below:

A .... (Data /Information) is the raw material for processing.

B .... (Data/Information) has already been process in such a way to make it meaningful to the person who receives it. (2 marks)

2 Cost classification and behaviour

2.1 Which one of the following would be classed as indirect labour?

A Machine operators in a company manufacturing washing machines
B A stores assistant in a factory store
C Plumbers in a construction company
D A consultant in a firm of management consultants (2 marks)

2.2 Variable costs are conventionally deemed to do which of the following?

 A   Be constant per unit of output
 B   Vary per unit of output as production volume changes
 C   Be constant in total when production volume changes
 D   Vary, in total, from period to period when production is constant

(2 marks)

2.3 The following is a graph of cost against level of activity

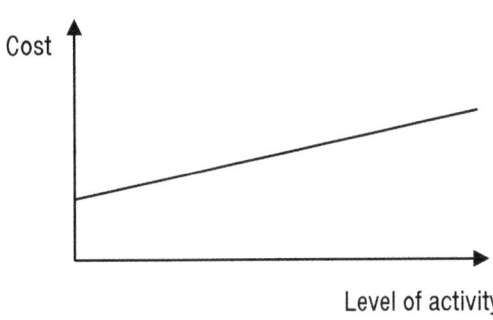

To which one of the following costs does the graph correspond?

 A   Electricity bills made up of a standing charge and a variable charge
 B   Bonus payment to employees when production reaches a certain level
 C   Salesman's commissions payable per unit up to a maximum amount of commission
 D   Bulk discounts on purchases, the discount being given on all units purchased **(2 marks)**

2.4 The following graphs depict various costs

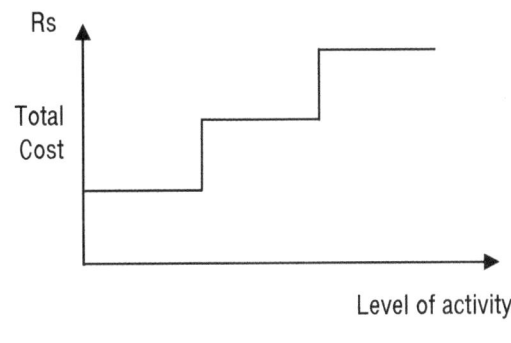

Graph 1

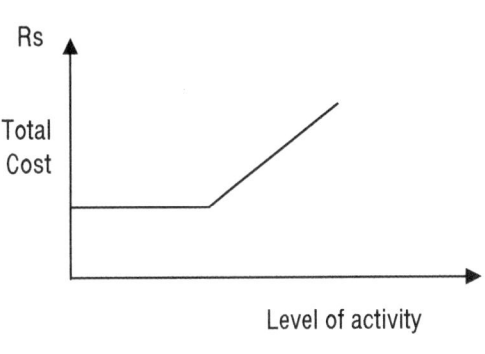

Graph 2

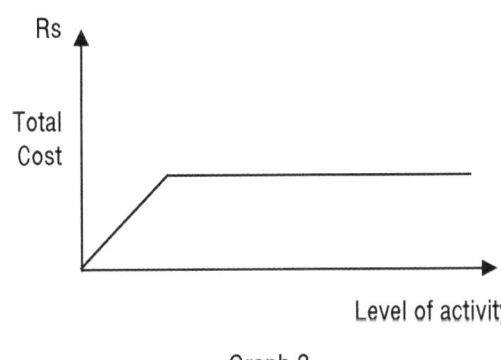

Graph 3

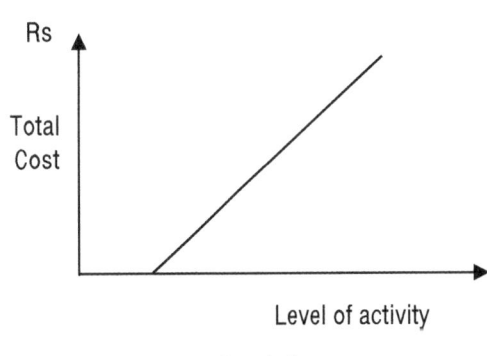

Graph 4

Which of the graphs shows supervisor salary costs, where one supervisor is needed for every five employees added to the staff.

- A Graph 1
- B Graph 2
- C Graph 3
- D Graph 4

(2 marks)

2.5 A firm has to pay a $100 per unit royalty to the inventor of a device which it manufactures and sells.

The royalty charge would be classified in the firm's accounts as a:

- A Selling expense
- B Direct expense
- C Production overhead
- D Administrative overhead

(2 marks)

2.6 Which of the following would be classed as indirect labour?

- A Assembly workers in a company manufacturing televisions
- B A stores assistant in a factory store
- C Plasterers in a construction company
- D An audit clerk in a firm of auditors

(2 marks)

2.7 A manufacturing firm is very busy and overtime is being worked.

The amount of overtime premium contained in direct wages would normally be classed as:

- A Part of prime cost
- B Factory overheads
- C Direct labour costs
- D Administrative overheads

(2 marks)

2.8 Which of the following items would most likely be treated as an indirect cost?

- A Wood used to make a chair
- B Metal used for the legs of a chair
- C Fabric to cover the seat of a chair
- D Staples to fix the fabric to the seat of a chair

(2 marks)

2.9 A company employs four supervisors to oversee the factory production of all its products. The salaries paid to these supervisors are:

- A A direct labour cost
- B A direct production expense
- C A production overhead
- D An administration overhead

(2 marks)

2.10 Which of the following best describes a controllable cost?

- A A cost which arises from a decision already taken, which cannot, in the short run, be changed.
- B A cost for which the behaviour pattern can be easily analysed to facilitate valid budgetary control comparisons.
- C A cost which can be influenced by its budget holder.
- D A specific cost of an activity or business which would be avoided if the activity or business did not exist.

(2 marks)

2.11 Which of the following items might be a suitable cost unit within the credit control department of a company?

- (i)   Stationery cost
- (ii) Customer account
- (iii) Cheque received and processed

- A Item (i) only
- B Item (ii) only
- C Item (iii) only
- D Items (ii) and (iii) only

(2 marks)

2.12 A company employs four supervisors to oversee the factory production of all its products. The salaries paid to these supervisors are:

- A A direct labour cost
- B A direct production expense
- C A production overhead
- D An administration overhead

(2 marks)

2.13 Fixed costs are conventionally deemed to be:

- A Constant per unit of output
- B Constant in total when production volume changes
- C Outside the control of management
- D Those unaffected by inflation

(2 marks)

2.14 A cost centre is:

- A A unit of product or service in relation to which costs are ascertained
- B An amount of expenditure attributable to an activity
- C A production or service location, function, activity or item of equipment for which costs are accumulated
- D A centre for which an individual budget is drawn up

(2 marks)

2.15 A cost .... is a unit of product, service or activity for which costs can be ascertained.

Fill in the missing word from the choices below:

- A object
- B centre
- C unit
- D pool

(2 marks)

2.16 Which of the following is an example of an environmental appraisal cost?

- A Choosing environmentally friendly suppliers
- B Decontaminating land
- C Recycling scrap
- D Conducting inspections (2 marks)

2.17 Which of the following would be classed as environmental external failure costs?

- (i) Cleaning up contaminated soil
- (ii) Government penalties and fines
- (iii) Training of employees

- A (i) and (ii) only
- B (i) and (iii) only
- C (ii) and (iii) only
- D (i), (ii) and (iii) (2 marks)

PART C2: COST IDENTIFICATION AND MEASURING COSTS FOR MANAGEMENT PURPOSES

Questions 3.1 to 7.14 cover **Types of costs and methods of costing** the subject of Chapters 3-7 of the Learning & Practice Workbook.

3 Material costs

3.1 In times of rising prices, the FIFO method of inventory valuation, when compared to the average cost method of inventory valuation, will usually result in which of the following?

- A A higher profit and a lower closing inventory value
- B A higher profit and a higher closing inventory value
- C A lower profit and a lower closing inventory value
- D A lower profit and a higher closing inventory value (2 marks)

3.2 During May 20X7, Bhavya's purchases were $126,500, and her sales were $150,000. Bhavya's gross profit is 20% of sales. The value of her inventory at 1 May 20X7 was $12,500.

What is the value of Bhavya's inventory at 31 May 20X7?

- A $ 6,000
- B $ 11,000
- C $ 14,000
- D $ 19,000 (2 marks)

3.3 Your organisation uses the cumulative weighted average cost method of valuing inventories (AVCO). During August 20X9, the following inventory details were recorded:

Opening balance	30 units valued at $ 200 each
5 August	Purchase of 50 units at $ 240 each
10 August	Issue of 40 units
18 August	Purchase of 60 units at $ 250 each
23 August	Issue of 25 units

Calculate the value of the inventory balance at 31 August 20X9.

A $18,000
B $19,000
C $14,000
D $19,500   (2 marks)

3.4 The following information is available from the inventory department concerning Material A. The company uses the AVCO method.

January 1	Balance	300kg	$25 per unit
January 2	Issue	250kg	
January 12	Receipt	400kg	$25.75 per unit
January 21	Issue	200kg	
January 29	Issue	75kg	

Calculate the cost of materials issues and the value of closing inventory at each of the dates above.

(2 marks)

3.5 SK sells bathroom fittings throughout the country in which it operates.

In order to obtain the best price, it has decided to purchase all its annual demand of 10,000 shower hinges from a single supplier. RR has offered to provide the required number of shower cabins each year under an exclusive long-term contract.

Demand for shower cabins is constant all year. The cost to SK of holding one shower cabin in inventory for one year is $4 plus 3% of the purchase price.

RR is located only a few miles from the SK main showroom. It supplies each shower cabin at $400 with a transport charge of $200 per delivery. It provides such a regular and prompt delivery service that SK believes it will not be necessary to hold any safety inventory (that is buffer inventory) if it uses RR as its supplier.

What is the optimal order size?

A   EOQ = 575
B   EOQ = 500
C   EOQ = 550
D   EOQ = 525   (2 marks)

3.6 JW sells kitchen fittings throughout the country in which it operates.

Demand for JW's liquid dispensers is 95,000 units per annum. Demand is evenly distributed throughout the year. The cost of placing an order is $15 and the cost of holding a unit of inventory for a year is $3.

Calculate how many orders of liquid dispensers JW should make in a year.

A   106
B   103
C   98
D   100 = 950   (2 marks)

3.7 OG sells door stoppers throughout the country in which it operates.

Demand for door stoppers is 2,500 packs per year, each pack contains four door stoppers. The door stoppers are purchased from a single supplier, and it costs $25 to place an order. The cost of holding a single door stopper in inventory for a year is 50c.

How many door stoppers should be ordered each time to minimise inventory costs (answer to the nearest 10).

A	EOQ = 1,000
B	EOQ = 1,050
C	EOQ = 1,075
D	EOQ = 1,025

(2 marks)

3.8 FLG Ltd wishes to minimise its inventory costs. Annual demand for a raw material costing $12 per unit is 60,000 units per year. Inventory management costs for this raw material are as follows:

Ordering cost: $ 6 per order
Holding cost: $ 0.5 per unit per year

The supplier of this raw material has offered a bulk purchase discount of 1% for orders of 10,000 units or more. If bulk purchase orders are made regularly, it is expected that annual holding cost for this raw material will increase to $2 per unit per year.

What is the total cost of inventory for the raw material when using the economic order quantity?

A	$ 720,600
B	$ 720,000
C	$ 750,000
D	$ 729,500

(2 marks)

3.9 Which of the following functions are fulfilled by a goods received note (GRN)?

(i) Provides information to update the stock records on receipt of goods
(ii) Provides information to check the quantity on the supplier's invoice
(iii) Provides information to check the price on the supplier's invoice

A	(i) and (ii) only
B	(i) and (iii) only
C	(ii) and (iii) only
D	All of them

(2 marks)

3.10 The following inventory movements have occurred so far this year:

Date		Units	Unit price $	Value $
1 Jan	Balance b/f	1,000	5.00	5,000
3 Mar	Issue	400		
4 Jun	Receipt	500	5.50	2,750
6 Jun	Receipt	500	6.00	3,000
9 Sept	Issue	700		

If the first-in, first-out method of pricing is used, what is the value of the issue on 9 September?

A	$ 3,500
B	$ 3,550
C	$ 3,950
D	$ 4,200

(2 marks)

3.11 There are 27,500 units of Part Number X35 on order with the suppliers and 16,250 units requisitioned not yet issued to production.

If the free inventory is 13,000 units, what is the physical stock?

A	1,750
B	3,250
C	24,250
D	29,250

(2 marks)

3.12 A domestic appliance retailer with multiple outlets stocks a popular toaster, known as the Autocrisp 2000, for which the following information is available:

Average sales   75 per day
Maximum sales   95 per day
Minimum sales   50 per day
Lead time   12-18 days
Reorder quantity 1,750

Based on the data above, what is the reorder level?

A   600 units
B   1,125 units
C   1,710 units
D   1,750 units   (2 marks)

3.13 A garden tools retailer with multiple outlets stocks a popular Garden Spade known as the DigDeep100, for which the following information is available:

Average sales   75 per day
Maximum sales   95 per day
Minimum sales   50 per day
Lead time   12-18 days
Reorder quantity 1,750
Reorder level   1,710

Based on the data above, what is the maximum inventory control level?

A   1,750 units
B   2,275 units
C   2,860 units
D   2,900 units   (2 marks)

3.14 The annual demand for a stock item is 2,500 units. The cost of placing an order is $ 80 and the cost of holding an item in stock for one year is $ 15. What is the economic order quantity, to the nearest unit?

A   31 units
B   115 units
C   163 units
D   26,667 units   (2 marks)

3.15 The following information relates to item 2362 X

Date		Units	Receipts Price per unit $	Value $	Units	Issues Price per unit $	Value $
1 June	Opening balance	100	5.00	500			
3 June	Receipts	300	4.80	1,440			
5 June	Issues				220		
12 June	Receipts	170	5.20	884			
24 June	Issues				300		

Using the cumulative weighted average price method of inventory valuation, the cost of the materials issued on 5 June was:

- A $ 1,056
- B $ 1,067
- C $ 1,078
- D $ 1,100

(2 marks)

3.16 The accounting entries for the return of unused direct material from production would be:

	Debit	Credit
A	Work in progress account	Stores control account
B	Stores control account	Work in progress account
C	Stores control account	Overhead control account
D	Overhead control account	Stores control account

3.17. A food retailer specialises in selling international food products at its store in a busy city. In addition to the cost of buying the food, it incurs the following costs:

- (i) Import duties
- (ii) Storage costs of keeping the food until it is sold
- (iii) Transport costs of bringing the food to the store
- (iv) Advertising costs

Which of the above costs should be included in the valuation of inventory according to IAS 2?

- A (i) only
- B (ii) and (iv)
- C (i) and (iii)
- D (ii) only
- E None of the above

(2 marks)

4 Labour costs

4.1 Which of the following would be classified as indirect labour?

- A Assembly workers in a company manufacturing televisions
- B A stores assistant in a factory store
- C Plasterers in a construction company
- D An audit clerk in a firm of auditors

(2 marks)

4.2 A job is budgeted to require 3,300 productive hours after incurring 25% idle time. If the total labour cost budgeted for the job is $36,300 what is the labour cost per hour?

- A $ 8.25
- B $8.80
- C $11.00
- D $14.67

(2 marks)

4.3 PR LTD manufactures a single product, M. Budgeted production output of product M during August is 200 units. Each unit of product M requires six labour hours for completion and PR LTD anticipates 20% idle time. Labour is paid at a rate of $7 per hour.

What would be the direct labour cost for August?

A $10,500
B $10,800
C $15,000
D $9,500 (2 marks)

4.4 The following data relate to work in the finishing department of a certain factory.

Normal working day　　　　　　　　　　　　　　　7 hours
Basic rate of pay per hour　　　　　　　　　　　　$5
Standard time allowed to produce 1 unit　　　　　4 minutes
Premium bonus payable at the basic rate　　　　60% of time saved

On a particular day one employee finishes 180 units. His gross pay for the day will be:

A $35
B $50
C $56
D $60 (2 marks)

4.5 An employee is paid on a piecework basis. The basis of the piecework scheme is as follows:

1 to 100 units   – $2.00 per unit
101 to 200 units   – $3.00 per unit
201 to 299 units   – $4.00 per unit

with only the additional units qualifying for the higher rates. Rejected units do not qualify for payment.

During a particular day, the employee produced 210 units of which 17 were rejected as faulty.

What did the employee earn for their day's work?

A $479
B $540
C $579
D $630 (2 marks)

4.6 Which of the following statements is/are true about group bonus schemes?

(i) Group bonus schemes are appropriate when increased output depends on a number of people all making extra effort

(ii) With a group bonus scheme, it is easier to award each individual's performance

(iii) Non-production employees can be rewarded as part of a group incentive scheme

A   (i) only
B   (i) and (ii) only
C   (i) and (iii) only
D   All of them (2 marks)

4.7 X LTD has recorded the following wages costs for direct production workers for November.

	$
Basic pay	70,800
Overtime premium	2,000
Holiday pay	500
Gross wages incurred	73,300

The overtime was not worked for any specific job.

The accounting entries for these wages' costs in the wages control account would be:

		Debit $	Credit $
A	Work in progress account	72,800	
	Overhead control account	500	
	Wages control account		73,300
B	Work in progress account	70,800	
	Overhead control account	2,500	
	Wages control account		73,300
C	Wages control account	73,300	
	Work in progress account		70,800
	Overhead control account		2,500
D	Wages control account	73,300	
	Work in progress account		72,800
	Overhead control account		500

(2 marks)

4.8 Akila works as a member of a three-person team in the assembly department of a factory. The team is rewarded by a group bonus scheme whereby the team leader receives 40 per cent of any bonus earned by the team, and the remaining bonus is shared evenly between Akila and the other team member. Details of output for one day are given below.

Hours worked by team	8 hours
Team production achieved	80 units
Standard time allowed to produce one unit	9 minutes
Group bonus payable at $60 per hour	70% of time saved

The bonus element of Jane's pay for this particular day will be:

A $50.40
B $72.00
C $100.80
D $168.00

(2 marks)

4.9 Job 198 requires 380 active labour hours to complete. It is expected that there will be five per cent idle time. The wage rate is $6 per hour. The labour cost of Job 198 is:

A $2,166
B $2,280
C $2,394
D $2,400

(2 marks)

4.10 A unit of product L requires 9 active labour hours for completion. The performance standard for product L allows for ten per cent of total labour time to be idle, due to machine downtime. The standard wage rate is $ 9 per hour. What is the standard labour cost per unit of product L?

    A $72.9
    B $81.0
    C $89.1
    D $90.0 (2 marks)

4.11 A manufacturing firm is very busy and overtime is being worked.

The amount of overtime premium contained in direct wages would normally be classed as:

    A   Part of prime cost
    B   Factory overheads
    C   Direct labour costs
    D   Administrative overheads (2 marks)

4.12 Kavith is paid $5.50 for every unit of product he produces but he has a guaranteed wage of $60 per eight-hour day. In a week he produces the following number of units:

Monday	12 units
Tuesday	14 units
Wednesday	9 units
Thursday	14 units
Friday	8 units

What does Kavith earn for the week?

    A $340.0
    B $329.5
    C $313.5
    D $300.0 (2 marks)

4.13 A company that manufactures electronic components has set a standard that in the standard labour hour 10 units will be manufactured. It has also set a budget of 8 hours per labourer.

Yesterday, one of the labourers worked for 9 hours He produced 85 units.

What are the capacity, efficiency and activity ratios for the labourer for yesterday?

	Efficiency	Capacity	Activity
A	94.4%	112.5%	106.25%
B	94.4%	106.25	112.5%
C	106.25%	94.4%	112.5%
D	106.25%	112.5%	94.4%

(2 marks)

4.14 Each labourer in a pot making plant is expected to work 8 hours per day and make 18 pots per hour.

Yesterday, one of the labourers worked for 9 hours. He produced 171 pots.

What was the productivity of the labourer?

    A   94.7%
    B   105.6%
    C   122.5%
    D   118.8% (2 marks)

EXAM QUESTION BANK

5 Overheads and absorption costing

5.1 Which of the following statements about overhead absorption rates are true?

(i) They are predetermined in advance for each period
(ii) They are used to charge overheads to products
(iii) They are based on actual data for each period
(iv) They are used to control overhead costs

A (i) and (ii) only
B (i), (ii) and (iv) only
C (ii), (iii) and (iv) only
D (iii) and (iv) only (2 marks)

5.2 A cost centre uses a direct labour hour rate to absorb overheads. Data for the latest period are as follows:

Budgeted overhead	$257,600
Actual overhead	$235,920
Actual direct labour hours	4,925
Overhead under absorbed	$9,370

How many direct labour hours were budgeted to be worked during the period?

A 4,925
B 5,378
C 5,600
D This cannot be calculated from the information provided (2 marks)

5.3 A call centre recovers overheads on the basis of the number of calls made. Budgeted overheads for the latest period were $1,125,300 but actual overhead expenditure amounted to $1,074,150.

During the period 68,200 calls were made and overhead was under recovered by $51,150. Calculate and identify the overhead absorption rate per call made.

A $25
B $20
C $15
D $14 (2 marks)

5.4 The following extract of information is available concerning the four cost centres of EG Ltd.

	Production cost centres			Service cost centre
	Machinery	Finishing	Packing	Canteen
Number of direct employees	7	6	2	–
Number of indirect employees	3	2	1	4
Overhead allocated and apportioned	$285,000	$183,000	$89,600	$84,000

The overhead cost of the canteen is to be re-apportioned to the production cost centres on the basis of the number of employees in each production cost centre. After the re-apportionment, the total overhead cost of the packing department, to the nearest $, will be:

A $12,000
B $99,680
C $100,800
D $101,600 (2 marks)

5.5 G Ltd has two production cost centres (K and L) and two service cost centres (stores and maintenance). It has been estimated that the service costs centres do work for each other and the production departments in the following proportions:

Stores	$140,000	Maintenance	$70,000
Production centre K	45%	Production centre K	50%
Production centre L	45%	Production centre L	45%
Maintenance	10%	Stores	5%

Calculate how much of the service department costs will end up in Production centre K after repeated distribution, to the nearest $100.

A $102,900
B $84,000
C $140,000
D $107,100

(2 marks)

5.6 A factory consists of two production cost centres (P and Q) and two service cost centres (X and Y). The total allocated and apportioned overhead for each is as follows:

P	Q	X	Y
$950,000	$820,000	$460,000	$300,000

It has been estimated that each service cost centre does work for the other cost centres in the following proportions:

	P	Q	X	Y
Percentage of service cost centre X to	40	40	–	20
Percentage of service cost centre Y to	30	60	10	–

Reapportionment of service cost centre costs is carried out using a method that fully recognises the reciprocal service arrangements in the factory,

Calculate the total overhead for production cost centre P.

A $1,270,000
B $1,160,000
C $1,260,000
D $1,070,000

(2 marks)

5.7 A private hospital has a budgeted annual overhead cost for cleaning of $1,250,000. There are 300 beds in the hospital and these are expected to be in use 95% of the year. The hospital uses a composite cost unit of occupied bed per night.

Calculate the overhead absorption rate for cleaning.

A $12.00
B $13.50
C $12.02
D $11.02

(2 marks)

5.8 Budgeted information relating to a department in JP Ltd for the next period is as follows.

Department	Production overhead $ '000	Direct material cost $ '000	Direct labour cost $ '000	Direct labour hours	Machine hours
1	27,000	67,500	13,500	2,700	45,000

Individual direct labour employees within each department earn differing rates of pay, according to their skills, grade and experience

What is the most appropriate production overhead absorption rate for department 1?

- A 40% of direct material cost
- B 200% of direct labour cost
- C $ 100 per direct labour hour
- D $ 600 per machine hour

(2 marks)

5.9 The following data is available for department X for the latest period.

Budgeted production overhead	$165,000
Actual production overhead	$ 65,000
Budgeted machine hours	60,000
Actual machine hours	55,000

Which of the following statements is correct?

- A No under or over-absorption of overhead occurred
- B Overhead was $13,750 under-absorbed
- C Overhead was $27,500 under-absorbed
- D Overhead was $27,500 over-absorbed

(2 marks)

5.10 A cost centre uses a direct labour hour rate to absorb overheads. Data for the latest period are as follows:

Budgeted overhead	$25,760
Actual overhead	$ 3,592
Actual direct labour hours	4,925
Overhead under absorbed	$937

How many direct labour hours were budgeted to be worked during the period?

- A 4,925
- B 5,378
- C 5,600
- D This cannot be calculated from the information provided

(2 marks)

5.11 Data for department Y for the latest period was as follows.

Budgeted direct labour hours	12,300
Actual direct labour hours	11,970
Production overhead absorption rate	$260 per direct labour hour
Production overhead under absorbed	$567,000

Calculate the actual production overhead incurred during the period.

- A $ 3,379,200
- B $ 7,952,000
- C $ 2,692,700
- D $ 3,679,200

(2 marks)

5.12 Over-absorbed overheads occur when:

    A   Absorbed overheads exceed actual overheads
    B   Absorbed overheads exceed budgeted overheads
    C   Actual overheads exceed absorbed overheads
    D   Actual overheads exceed budgeted overheads   (2 marks)

5.13 Which of the following are acceptable bases for absorbing production overheads?

    (i)   Direct labour hours
    (ii)   Machine hours
    (iii)   As a percentage of the prime cost
    (iv)   Per unit

    A   Method (i) and (ii) only
    B   Method (iii) and (iv) only
    C   Method (i), (ii), (iii) and (iv)
    D   Method (i), (ii) or (iii) only   (2 marks)

6 Absorption and marginal costing

6.1 A company manufactures and sells a single product. For this month the budgeted fixed production overheads are $48,000, budgeted production is 12,000 units and budgeted sales are 11,720 units.

The company currently uses absorption costing.

If the company used marginal costing principles instead of absorption costing for this month, what would be the effect on the budgeted profit?

    A $1,120 higher
    B $1,120 lower
    C $3,920 higher
    D $3,920 lower

6.2 A company's normal output is 1,000 units each period and budgeted fixed costs are incurred evenly throughout the year. The following production levels and associated production costs were recorded for two recent periods.

Period no.	Production (units)	Production costs $
6	1,210	3,394
9	990	3,086

In a period when production volume was 1,040 units and sales volume was 1,200 units a profit of $8,160 was reported using marginal costing.

Calculate the profit that would be reported for the period using an absorption costing system.

    A $ 7,888
    B $ 8,777
    C $ 9,888
    D $ 8,888   (2 marks)

6.3 A management accountant has calculated the following, based on budgeted production:

(i) Direct production costs per unit
(ii) Variable selling costs per unit
(iii) Variable production overheads per unit
(iv) Fixed overhead cost per unit

If the company uses marginal costing, which of the items above would be included in the value of inventory of finished goods?

A (i) and (ii) only
B (i) and (iii)
C (i), (ii) and (iii)
D (i), (ii), (iii) and (iv) (2 marks)

6.4 A manufacturing company has calculated its budgeted profit for next month for Product A as follows:

	$
Selling price (per unit)	70
Variable costs	(40)
Fixed production overheads	(10)
Profit per unit	20

Budgeted sales 1,000 units
Budgeted profit (20 × 1,000) $20,000

If production increases by 100 units and everything else is as per the budget, how much would profit increase by?

A $ 2,000
B $ 3,000
C $ 7,000
D It cannot be determined from the information above (2 marks)

6.5 The following statements have been made about marginal and absorption costing:

(i) The use of marginal costing for inventory valuation complies with IAS 2
(ii) Absorption costing may encourage managers to produce for inventory
(iii) Marginal costing is more useful for short term decision making.

Which of the above statements are correct?

A (iii) only
B (i) and (ii)
C (ii) and (iii)
D All of the statements are correct (2 marks)

6.6 Last month, a company made a marginal costing profit of $75,000. Opening inventory was 300 units and closing inventory is 500 units. Fixed production overheads are absorbed at the rate of $3 per unit.

What is the profit under absorption costing?

A $72,600
B $74,400
C $75,600
D $77,400 (2 marks)

6.7 A company produces and sells a single product for $15. Variable costs are $10 per unit and fixed costs are absorbed at the rate of $2 per unit based on a budgeted level of activity of 200,000 units.

How much profit is made under marginal costing if the company sells 220,000 units?

A $600,000
B $660,000
C $700,000
D $1,100,000 (2 marks)

6.8 When comparing the profits reported under absorption costing and marginal costing during a period when the level of inventory increased:

A Absorption costing profits will be higher and closing inventory valuations lower than those under marginal costing.

B Absorption costing profits will be higher and closing inventory valuations higher than those under marginal costing.

C Marginal costing profits will be higher and closing inventory valuations lower than those under absorption costing.

D Marginal costing profits will be higher and closing inventory valuations higher than those under absorption costing. (2 marks)

6.9 The following data is available for period 9.

Opening inventory 10,000 units
Closing inventory 8,000 units
Absorption costing profit $2,800,000

The profit for period 9 using marginal costing would be:

A $2,780,000
B $2,800,000
C $2,820,000
D Impossible to calculate without more information (2 marks)

6.10 A company had opening stock of 48,500 units and closing stock of 45,500 units. Profits based on marginal costing were $315,250 and on absorption costing were $288,250. What is the fixed overhead absorption rate per unit?

A $5.94
B $6.34
C $6.50
D $9.00 (2 marks)

7 Activity based costing

7.1 The following information is provided relating to two products, A and B:

	Product A	Product B	Total
Budgeted production (units)	2,500	5,000	7,500
Number of production runs	6	10	16
Number of inspections	4	4	8

Total set up costs $100,000
Total inspection costs $80,000

Using activity-based costing, what is the budgeted overhead cost per unit of Product B?

A $20.50
B $24.00
C $26.00
D $41.00

(2 marks)

7.2 A company which makes two products, Aye and Bee. It uses activity-based costing to absorb its overheads. One of the overheads is inspection costs and the cost driver for this is the number of inspections.

The following information has been provided:

Total inspection costs $260,000

	Aye	Bee
Budgeted production (units)	2,500	8,000
Units per batch	500	1,000

There is one inspection per bath.

What is the inspection cost per unit for product Bee?

A $20.00
B $28.10
C $34.70
D $40.00

(2 marks)

7.3 A machine needs to be set-up 400 times per month, at a total cost of $80,000. Product X is made in batches of 50, where each batch requires the machine to be set-up twice. Annual production of Product X is 5,000 units.

What are the set up costs per unit for Product X?

A $2
B $4
C $8
D $16

(2 marks)

7.4 The following statements have been made about activity-based costing (ABC):

(i) ABC requires a company to identify all activities that give rise to overheads.
(ii) The cost of implementing ABC may exceed the benefits for some businesses

Which of the above statements are true?

A (i) only
B (ii) only
C Neither (i) nor (ii)
D Both (i) and (ii) (2 marks)

7.5 Which of the following statements about activity-based costing is/are true?

(1) It is not relevant for service industry businesses
(2) It complies with IAS 2 inventory valuation

A 1 only
B 2 only
C Neither 1 nor 2
D Both 1 and 2 (2 marks)

7.6 A company has budgeted overheads for the next year as follows:

Production run set up costs
Machine running costs

Production is performed in batches. Before each batch, the machine must be setup. Machine running costs depend on the number of machine hours used.

In terms of hierarch if activities, what level is each of the two costs?

	Set up costs	Machine running costs
A	Batch level	Batch level
B	Batch level	Unit level
C	Unit level	Batch level
D	Unit level	Unit level

(2 marks)

7.7 The following statements have been made about activity-based costing (ABC):

(i) ABC does not eliminate the use of production volume as a means of apportioning costs.

(ii) If the cost of a product or service using both ABC and absorption costing is the same, there will be no benefit to be gained from adopting ABC

(iii) Judgement may be required in selecting the drivers for a particular activity.

Which of the above statements are true?

A (i) and (ii)
B (i) and (iii)
C (ii) and (iii)
D (i), (ii) and (iii) (2 marks)

7.8 The following statements have been made about Activity Based Costing (ABC):

(i) ABC is most useful in companies with a high level of overhead costs.
(ii) ABC is least useful in companies with a small number of products
(iii) ABC is only relevant for manufacturing companies.

Which of the above statements are true?

A (i) and (ii)
B (i) and (iii)
C (ii) and (iii)
D (i), (ii) and (iii)

7.9 One of the activities that a company performs is receiving materials. This involves checking the materials when they are delivered to the warehouse to ensure that they were ordered and are in acceptable condition.

What is likely to be the most appropriate cost driver for this activity if activity based costing is used?

A Value of materials
B Quantity of materials
C Time in storage
D Number of receipts

7.10 A company has introduced activity based costing. One of the activities it has analysed is the cost of ordering materials. The driver identified for this activity is the number of purchase orders. It is easy to increase or reduce the number of hours paid to staff in the purchasing department as many are on flexible contracts.

The factory manager has proposed the following steps to reduce order costs:

1 Increase the size of purchase orders.
2 Use a different driver of this activity.

Which of the above would be likely to reduce order costs?

A 1 only
B 2 only
C Neither 1 nor 2
D Both 1 and 2

7.11 The following criticisms have been made of traditional absorption costing:

(i) It often under allocates overhead costs to low volume products.
(ii) It assumes that overhead costs are volume related
(iii) It does not help managers to understand the underlying cause of many costs.

Which of the above criticisms are true?

A (i) and (ii)
B (i) and (iii)
C (ii) and (iii)
D (i), (ii) and (iii)

7.12 Product management is an example of what level of activity?

    A   Product level
    B   Batch level
    C   Product sustaining
    D   Facility sustaining

7.13 A company is introducing customer profitability analysis where overheads are apportioned to customers.

The budgeted distribution costs for the next year are:

	$
Haulage costs	2,000,000
Order processing	500,000

Haulage costs depend on the number of kilometres driven by the vehicles. It is estimated that next year this will be 1 million kilometres.

The number of orders is expected to be 800,000.

One customer placed 10 orders last month. The company made five trips to deliver these orders, covering a total distance of 750 km.

How much would be apportioned to this customer in respect of distribution costs?

    A $ 381.25
    B $1,000,00
    C $1,062.50
    D $ 1,625,00

7.14 The following statements have been made about activity-based costing (ABC):

(i) ABC may allow managers to get a more accurate knowledge of product profitability

(ii) Identifying the correct cost driver may be difficult as there may be more than one driver for some costs

(iii) ABC is not appropriate in services industries

Which of the above statements are correct?

    A   (i), (ii) and (iii)
    B   (i) and (ii)
    C   (ii) only
    D   None of the statements are correct

7.15 CT uses activity-based costing and manufactures three products called the MyWalk, MyRun and MySprint. The following information is available for 20X2:

	MyWalk	MyRun	MySprint
Budgeted production (units)	1,500	3,000	1,600
Units per batch	500	1,000	800
Number of environmental inspections per batch	3	8	7

The total cost for environmental inspections for 20X2 is expected to be $70,500.

What is the total environmental cost attributed to MyRun for 20X2 (to the nearest $)?

    A $1,500
    B $36,000
    C $120,000
    D $4,500

7.16 The following statements have been made about environmental costing:

(i) Environmental costing (eg using ABC) leads to more accurate pricing
(ii) Using an ABC system, environmental costs become cost drivers
(iii) Environmental overhead costs are easy to measure

Which of the above statements are correct?

A (i), (ii) and (iii)
B (i) and (ii)
C (ii) only
D None of the statements are correct

7.17 AB Co uses activity-based costing and manufactures two products called the Leaf and the Conker. The following information is available for quarter 1:

	Leaf	Conker	Total
Budgeted production (units)	20,000	30,000	50,000
Kg of hazardous waste per unit	2	4	160,000
Total pollution inspections (3 per 1,000 units produced)	60	90	150

The total cost for disposal of hazardous waste for quarter 1 is expected to be $40,000 and the total cost for pollution inspections is expected to be $15,000.

What is the total environmental cost attributed to Leaf for quarter 1 (to the nearest $)?

A $10,000
B $6,000
C $16,000
D $100.25

PART C3: INTRODUCTION TO COSTING SYSTEMS

Questions 8.1 to 10.14 cover **Planning & Control** the subject of Chapters 8-10 of the Learning & Practice Workbook.

8 Process costing

8.1 A company makes a single product, which passes through one process. Details of the process account for the period were as follows:

	$		
Material cost – 20,000kg	26,000	Output	18,800kg
Labour cost	12,000	Normal losses	5% of input
Production overhead cost	5,700		

There was no work-in-progress at the beginning or end of the period. Process losses have no value. The cost of the abnormal loss (to the nearest $) is

- A $437
- B $441
- C $460
- D $465

(2 marks)

8.2 A biscuit manufacturer uses process costing. The normal loss during the process is 10% and these can be sold to staff for $30 per kg. Last month there was no opening or closing work in progress.

Ingredients input	6,000kg @ $300 per kg
Labour hours	2,800 hours @ $50 per hour
Good output	5,600kg

Calculate the output value per unit for the month.

- A $348
- B $226
- C $258
- D $326

(2 marks)

8.3 A chemical process has a normal wastage of 10% of input. In a period, 2,500 kg of material were input and there was an abnormal loss of 75 kg.

What quantity of good production was achieved?

- A 2,175 kg
- B 2,250 kg
- C 2,325 kg
- D 2,425 kg

(2 marks)

8.4 A company manufactures Chemical X, in a single process. At the start of the month there was no work-in-progress. During the month 300 litres of raw material were input into the process at a total cost of $6,000. Conversion costs during the month amounted to $4,500. At the end of the month 250 litres of Chemical X were transferred to finished goods inventory. The remaining work-in-progress was 100% complete with respect to materials and 50% complete with respect to conversion costs. There were no losses in the process.

What are the equivalent units for closing work-in-progress at the end of the month?

	Material	Conversion costs
A	25 litres	25 litres
B	25 litres	50 litres
C	50 litres	25 litres
D	50 litres	50 litres

(2 marks)

8.5 A company manufactures a product using different processes. Last month, the following inputs and outputs related to Process 1:

Units input: 7,000
Units completed: 6,950
Opening WIP: 300 units 100% complete for materials and 70% complete for conversion costs.
Closing WIP: 350 units, 100% complete for materials and 30% complete for conversion costs.

The company uses the weighted average method of valuing inventory.

What were the equivalent units for conversion costs?

A 6,845
B 6,985
C 7,055
D 7,300

(2 marks)

8.6 A company manufactures a product using different processes. Last month, the following inputs and outputs related to Process 1:

Units input: 3,500
Units completed: 3,475
Opening WIP: 150 units 100% complete for materials and 70% complete for conversion costs.
Closing WIP: 175 units, 100% complete for materials and 30% complete for conversion costs.

The company uses the FIFO method of valuing inventory.

What were the equivalent units for conversion costs?

A 3,422.5
B 3,492.5
C 3,527.5
D 3,650.0

(2 marks)

8.7 A company uses process costing to value output. During the last month, the following information was recorded:

Output: 2,800 kg valued at $7.50 per kg
Normal loss 300 kg with a scrap value of $3 per kg
Actual loss 200 kg

What was the value of input?

A $22,600
B $21,900
C $21,600
D $21,150

(2 marks)

8.8 Which of the following best describes the term "equivalent units" when using the FIFO method?

A   The number of units started during the period, as the units started in the previous period have already been accounted for in that period.

B   The equivalent number of whole units produced during the period, taking into account the completion of opening work in progress and starting closing work in progress.

C   The number of units completed during the period, regardless of when they were started.

D   The equivalent number of whole units produced during the period, taking into account the work on starting closing work in progress but ignoring opening work in progress.

(2 marks)

8.9 The following information relates to a process for making a special chemical. During the last month, opening WIP was 200 units, which was 40% complete with respect to conversion costs. During the month, an additional 1,900 units were started. 1,800 units were finished during the month. There are no losses in the process. Closing work in progress was 50% complete with respect to conversion costs.

The value of conversion costs included in opening WIP was $7,000, and $93,500 of conversion costs were incurred during the month.

If the company uses a weighted average method what was the value per equivalent unit of conversion costs during the month?

A $44.52 per equivalent unit
B $50.00 per equivalent unit
C $51.54 per equivalent unit
D $51.94 per equivalent unit

(2 marks)

8.10 The following information relates to a process for making a special chemical. During the last month, opening WIP was 300 units, which was 30% complete with respect to conversion costs. During the month 1,900 units were started. There are no losses in the process. Closing work in progress was 200 units, which was 40% complete with respect to conversion costs.

The value of conversion costs included in opening WIP was $7,000, and $93,500 of conversion costs were incurred during the month.

If the company uses a FIFO method what was the value of conversion costs per equivalent unit?

A $46.98 per equivalent unit
B $48.32 per equivalent unit
C $50.00 per equivalent unit
D $50.50 per equivalent unit

(2 marks)

8.11 The following information relates to a process for making a special chemical. During the last month, opening WIP was 300 units, which was 40% complete with respect to conversion costs. During the month 1,900 units were started. There are no losses in the process. Closing work in progress was 150 units, which was 35% complete with respect to conversion costs.

The company has calculated that the conversion cost per equivalent unit was $50 per unit during the period.

What is the value of conversion costs included in closing WIP?

A $ 2,625
B $ 3,000
C $ 6,000
D $ 7,500

(2 marks)

8.12 The following information was recorded for process 1 for the last month:

Materials input: 2,000 units at $4.50 per unit

Conversion costs: $13,340
Normal loss: 5% of input
Actual loss: 150 units

There was no opening or closing inventory. Normal loss can be sold for a scrap value of $3 per unit.

What was the value of one unit of output?

A $11.80
B $11.60
C $11.20
D $11.00

(2 marks)

8.13   The following information was recorded for process 1 for the last month:

Materials input: 1,500 units at $4.00 per unit
Conversion costs: $12,000
Normal loss: 5% of input
Actual loss: 100 units

There was no opening or closing inventory. Lost units can be sold for a scrap value of $1 per unit.

What was the value of the abnormal loss?

A $25
B $289.5
C $314.5
D $315.79

(2 marks)

9 Process costing – joint products and by products

9.1 A company manufactures two joint products, P and R, in a common process. Data for June are as follows.

	$
Opening inventory	100,000
Direct materials added	1,000,000
Conversion costs	1,200,000
Closing inventory	300,000

	Production Units	Sales Units	Sales price $ per unit
P	4,000	5,000	500
R	6,000	5,000	1,000

If costs are apportioned between joint products on a sales value basis, what was the cost per unit of product R in June?

A $125
B $222
C $250
D $275

(2 marks)

9.2 Z Ltd manufactures three joint products (M, N and P) from the same common process, and can each be sold in their existing state, or processed further and then sold.

Product	Selling price after common process $/litre	Selling price after further processing $/litre	Further variable processing cost $/litre
M	6.25	8.40	1.75
N	5.20	6.45	0.95
P	6.80	7.45	0.85

Which of the three products should be processed further?

A   M only
B   M and N
C   N and P
D   All of the products

(2 marks)

9.3 PR Ltd manufactures two joint products, P and R, in a common process. Data for June are as follows.

	$
Opening inventory	100,000
Direct materials added	1,000,000
Conversion costs	1,200,000
Closing inventory	300,000

	Production Kgs	Sales Kgs	Sales price $ per Kg
P	4,000	5,000	500
R	6,000	5,000	1,000

EXAM QUESTION BANK

If costs are apportioned between joint products on a physical unit basis, what was the total cost of product P production in June?

    A $800,000
    B $880,000
    C $1,000,000
    D $1,200,000

(2 marks)

9.4 Which of the following statements is/are correct?

(i) A by-product is a product produced at the same time as other products which has a relatively low volume compared with the other products.

(ii) Since a by-product is a saleable item it should be separately costed in the process account, and should absorb some of the process costs.

(iii) Costs incurred prior to the point of separation are known as common or joint costs.

    A   (i) and (ii)
    B   (i) and (iii)
    C   (ii) and (iii)
    D   (iii) only

(2 marks)

9.5 EQ Ltd manufactures two joint products and one by-product in a single process. Data for November are as follows.

	$
Raw material input	216,000
Conversion costs	72,000

There were no stocks at the beginning or end of the period.

	Output Units	Sales price $. per unit
Joint product E	21,000	15
Joint product Q	18,000	10
By-product X	2,000	2

By-product sales revenue is credited to the process account. Joint costs are apportioned on a sales value basis. What were the full production costs of product Q in November (to the nearest $)?

    A $102,445
    B $103,273
    C $104,727
    D $180,727

(2 marks)

9.6 JW Ltd manufactures three joint products and one by-product from a single process.

Data for May are as follows:

Opening and closing stocks	Nil
Raw materials input	$180,000
Conversion costs	$50,000

Output

		Units	Sales price $ per unit
Joint product	L	3,000	32
	M	2,000	42
	N	4,000	38
By-product R		1,000	2

By-product sales revenue is credited to the sales account. Joint costs are apportioned on a sales value basis.

What were the full production costs of product M in May (to the nearest $)?

- A $57,687
- B $57,844
- C $58,193
- D $66,506

(2 marks)

10 Job, batch, service & contract costing

10.1 Which of the following costing methods is most likely to be used by a company involved in the manufacture of liquid soap?

- A Batch costing
- B Service costing
- C Job costing
- D Process costing

(2 marks)

10.2 Which of the following is a feature of job costing?

- A Production is carried out in accordance with the wishes of the customer
- B Associated with continuous production of large volumes of low-cost items
- C Establishes the cost of services rendered
- D Costs are charged over the units produced in the period

(2 marks)

10.3 State which of the following are characteristics of service costing.

- (i)   High levels of indirect costs as a proportion of total costs
- (ii) Use of composite cost units
- (iii) Use of equivalent units

- A (i) only
- B (i) and (ii) only
- C (ii) only
- D (ii) and (iii) only

(2 marks)

10.4 PA Ltd operates a job costing system. The company's standard net profit margin is 20 per cent of sales.

The estimated costs for job 173 are as follows.

Direct materials   5 metres @ $200 per metre
Direct labour   14 hours @ $88 per hour

Variable production overheads are recovered at the rate of $30 per direct labour hour.

Fixed production overheads for the year are budgeted to be $2,000,000 and are to be recovered on the basis of the total of 40,000 direct labour hours for the year.

Other overheads, in relation to selling, distribution and administration, are recovered at the rate of $800 per job.

What is the price to be quoted for job 173, to the nearest $?

- A $4,040
- B $4,240
- C $4,850
- D $5,050

(2 marks)

10.5 A firm makes special assemblies to customers' orders and uses job costing.

The data for a period are:

	Job number AA10 $	Job number BB15 $	Job number CC20 $
Opening WIP	26,800	42,790	0
Material added in period	17,275	0	18,500
Labour for period	14,500	3,500	24,600

The budgeted overheads for the period were $126,000 and are apportioned to jobs based on labour cost.

What overhead should be added to job number CC20 for the period?

- A $65,157
- B $69,290
- C $72,761
- D $126,000

(2 marks)

10.6 Didgit Ltd makes special widgets for customers' orders and uses job costing.

The data for a period are:

	Job number WID01 $	Job number WID02 $	Job number WID03 $
Opening WIP	26,800	42,790	0
Material added in period	17,275	0	18,500
Labour for period	14,500	3,500	24,600

The budgeted overheads for the period were $126,000. These are apportioned to jobs based on labour cost.

Job number WID02 was completed and delivered during the period and the firm wishes to earn 33.33% profit on sales.

What is the selling price of job number WID02?

- A $69,435
- B $75,505
- C $84,963
- D $258,435

(2 marks)

10.7 Wy NOT Ltd produces special assemblies to customers' orders and uses job costing.

The data for a period are:

	Job number YN12 $	Job number YN15 $	Job number YN20 $
Opening WIP	26,800	42,790	0
Material added in period	17,275	0	18,500
Labour for period	14,500	3,500	24,600

The budgeted overheads for the period were $126,000. Job number YN15 was completed during the period, but the other two jobs were still in progress at the end of the period.

What was the value of closing work-in-progress at the end of the period to the nearest $?

A $58,575
B $101,675
C $217,323
D $227,675 (2 marks)

10.8 What would be the most appropriate cost unit for a cake manufacturer?

Cost per:

A Cake
B Batch
C Kg
D Production run (2 marks)

10.9 Which of the following would be appropriate cost units for a passenger coach company?

(i) Vehicle cost per passenger-kilometre
(ii) Fuel cost for each vehicle per kilometre
(iii) Fixed cost per kilometre

A (i) only
B (i) and (ii) only
C (i) and (iii) only
D All of them (2 marks)

10.10 The following information is available for the Black Hotel for the latest thirty day period.

Number of rooms available per night	40
Percentage occupancy achieved	65%
Room servicing cost incurred	$39,000

What was the room servicing cost per occupied room-night for the period, to the nearest $?

A $32.50
B $50.00
C $97.50
D $150.00 (2 marks)

EXAM QUESTION BANK

10.11 Which of the following is NOT a characteristic of service costing?

    A   High levels of direct costs as a proportion of total costs
    B   Intangibility of output
    C   Use of composite cost units
    D   Can be used for internal services as well as external services   **(2 marks)**

10.12 Rushani Co manufactures ring binders which are embossed with the customer's own logo. A customer has ordered a batch of 300 binders. The following data illustrate the cost for a typical batch of 100 binders

	$'000
Direct materials	300
Direct wages	100
Machine set up	30
Design and artwork	150
	580

Direct employees are paid on a piecework basis.

Rushani Co absorbs production overhead at a rate of 20% of direct wages cost. Five per cent is added to the total production cost of each batch to allow for selling, distribution and administration overhead.

Rushani Co requires a profit margin of 25% of sales value.

Calculate the selling price for a batch of 300 binders.

    A $960,000
    B $2,016,000
    C $1,980,000
    D $2,200,000   **(2 marks)**

10.13 AL Ltd operates a job costing system. The company's standard net profit margin is 20% of sales value.

The estimated costs for job B124 are as follows.

| Direct materials | 3kg @ $50 per kg |
| Direct labour | 4 hours @ $90 per hour |

Production overheads are budgeted to be $2,400,000 for the period, to be recovered on the basis of a total of 30,000 labour hours.

Other overheads, related to selling, distribution and administration, are budgeted to be $1,500,000 for the period. They are to be recovered on the basis of the total budgeted production cost of $7,500,000 for the period.

What is the price to be quoted for job B124?

    A $1,245
    B $1,345
    C $1,145
    D $1,645   **(2 marks)**

10.14 The following statements relate to long term contracts:

(i) Levels of completion of the contract can be estimated using costs to date or work certified to date

(ii) Any anticipated losses should be taken as soon as they are expected

(iii) If the contract is half complete, it is expected that half the expected profit will always be taken

Which of the above are true?

A   (i) and (ii) only
B   (i) and (iii) only
C   (ii) and (iii) only
D   (i), (ii) and (iii)   **(2 marks)**

PART C4: Information for planning and performance management

Questions 11.1 to 13.21 cover **Information for planning and performance management, the subject of Chapters 11 to 13**

11 Budgeting

11.1 A flexible budget is a budget that:

- A Is changed during the budget period according to changed circumstances.
- B Is continuously updated by adding a further accounting period when the earliest accounting period has expired.
- C Results from the participation of budget holders.
- D Recognises different cost behaviour patterns and is designed to change as the volume of activity changes. **(2 marks)**

11.2 Which of the following statements is/are correct?

- I Fixed budgets are not useful for control purposes.
- II A prerequisite of flexible budgeting is a knowledge of cost behaviour patterns.
- III Budgetary control procedures are useful only to maintain control over an organisation's expenditure.

- A (I), (II) and (III)
- B (I) and (II) only
- C (II) and (III) only
- D (II) only **(2 marks)**

11.3 There are many behavioural implications of budgeting.

In this context, which of the following statements is true?

- A Additional pay for achieving budgets is always a good motivator.
- B It is generally easier for people to be motivated to achieve targets when they do not set the targets themselves.
- C Short-term planning in a budget can draw away from the longer-term consequences of decisions.
- D Budgets imposed using a top down approach are likely to be more realistic than participative budgets. **(2 marks)**

11.4 Which of the following is an adverse consequence of a participative ('bottom up') approach to budgeting?

- A In general they are unrealistic.
- B Managers may introduce budgetary slack.
- C Managers may become demotivated.
- D Specific resource requirements may be overlooked. **(2 marks)**

11.5 Which of the following statements about setting budget targets is/are correct?

(1) Setting 'ideal standards' as targets for achievement should motivate employees to perform to the best of their ability.

(2) Setting low standards as targets for achievement should motivate employees because they should usually achieve or exceed the target.

A 1 only is correct
B 2 only is correct
C Neither 1 nor 2 is correct
D Both 1 and 2 are correct (2 marks)

11.6 A company operates in export and import markets, and its costs and revenues are affected by movements in exchange rates, which are highly volatile. As a result, the company has great difficulty in establishing a budgeting system that is reliable for more than three months ahead.

Which of the following approaches to budgeting would be most appropriate for this company's situation?

A Flexible budgets
B Incremental budget
C Rolling budget
D Zero based budget (2 marks)

11.7 Which one of the following is **not** a common criticism of incremental budgeting?

A It assumes that all current activities and costs are still needed
B There is no requirement for managers to justify existing costs
C There is no incentive for managers to reduce costs
D There are no performance targets for managers (2 marks)

11.8 X Ltd manufactures specialist insulating products that are used in both residential and commercial buildings. The company is now preparing its budgets for the next four quarters. The following information has been identified for Product W:

Sales demand

Quarter 1	2,250 units
Quarter 2	2,050 units
Quarter 3	1,650 units
Quarter 4	2,050 units
Quarter 5	1,250 units

The company's inventory holding policy is that closing inventory of finished goods is equal to 30% of the following quarter's sales demand.

What is the total Production budget for the next four quarters in units?

A 7,000 units
B 7,700 units
C 7,900 units
D 8,000 units (2 marks)

11.9 BB Ltd, the produces three products X, Y and Z. For the coming accounting period budgets are to be prepared based on the following information:

Budgeted production

Product X 2,100
Product Y 4,200
Product Z 3,100

Budgeted usage of raw material RM1 (kg) per unit:

Product X	5
Product Y	3
Product Z	2
Cost per unit of material	$5

Raw materials inventory budget (kg)

	RM1
Opening	21,000
Closing	18,000

What is the budget for material purchases for the period?

A $26,300
B $131,500
C $146,500
D $161,500

(2 marks)

11.10 What is budgetary slack?

A The difference between the costs built into the budget and the costs actually incurred
B The difference between the minimum necessary costs and the costs actually incurred
C The difference between the minimum necessary costs and the costs built into the budget
D The difference between the flexible budget and the costs actually incurred

(2 marks)

11.11 Which of the following is unlikely to be contained with a budget manual?

A Organisational structures
B Objectives of the budgetary process
C Selling overhead budget
D Administrative details of budget preparation

(2 marks)

11.12 What does the statement 'sales is the principal budget factor' mean?

A The level of sales will determine the level of cash at the end of the period.
B The level of sales will determine the level of profit at the end of the period.
C The company's activities are limited by the level of sales it can achieve.
D Sales is the largest item in the budget.

(2 marks)

11.13 The following budget was prepared by F Ltd at the start of the accounting period:

	Original budget
Sales units	600
	$000
Sales revenue	54,000
Direct material	16,200
Direct labour	6,000
Variable overhead	3,000
Fixed overheard	15,000
Profit	13,800

If actual sales are 550 units, the flexed budgeted profit is:

- A $8,400,000
- B $11,400,000
- C $12,650,000
- D $13,800,000 (2 marks)

12 Standard costing

12.1 Which of the following best describes a basic standard?

- A A standard set at an ideal level, which makes no allowance for normal losses, waste and machine downtime.
- B A standard which assumes an efficient level of operation, but which includes allowances for factors such as normal loss, waste and machine downtime.
- C A standard which is kept unchanged over a period of time.
- D A standard which is based on current price levels. (2 marks)

12.2 What is an attainable standard?

- A A standard which includes no allowance for losses, waste and inefficiencies. It represents the level of performance which is attainable under perfect operating conditions.
- B A standard which includes some allowance for losses, waste and inefficiencies. It represents the level of performance which is attainable under efficient operating conditions.
- C A standard which is based on currently attainable operating conditions.
- D A standard which is kept unchanged, to show the trend in costs. (2 marks)

12.3 Which of the following statements is correct?

- A The operating standards set for production should be the most ideal possible.
- B The operating standards set for production should be the minimal level.
- C The operating standards set for production should be the attainable level.
- D The operating standards set for production should be the maximum level. (2 marks)

12.4 Which of the following would not be directly relevant to the determination of standard labour times per unit of output?

- A The type of performance standard to be used
- B The volume of output from the production budget
- C Technical specifications of the proposed production methods
- D The results of work study exercises

(2 marks)

12.5 CC PLC manufactures a carbonated drink, which is sold in 1 litre bottles. During the bottling process there is a 20% loss of liquid input due to spillage and evaporation. The standard usage of liquid per bottle is:

- A 0.80 litres
- B 1.00 litres
- C 1.20 litres
- D 1.25 litres

(2 marks)

12.6 Standard costing provides which of the following?

- (i)   Targets and measures of performance
- (ii) Information for budgeting
- (iii) Simplification of inventory control systems
- (iv) Actual future costs

- A (i), (ii) and (iii) only
- B (ii), (iii) and (iv) only
- C (i), (iii) and (iv) only
- D (i), (ii) and (iv) only

(2 marks)

12.7 A unit of product L requires 9 active labour hours for completion. The performance standard for product L allows for ten per cent of total labour time to be idle, due to machine downtime. The standard wage rate is $9 per hour. What is the standard labour cost per unit of product L?

- A $73.20
- B $81.00
- C $89.10
- D $90.00

(2 marks)

12.8 Which of the following criticisms of standard costing apply in all circumstances?

- (i)   Standard costing can only be used where all operations are repetitive and output is homogeneous.
- (ii) Standard costing systems cannot be used in environments which are prone to change. They assume stable conditions.
- (iii) Standard costing systems assume that performance to standard is acceptable. They do not encourage continuous improvement.

- A Criticism (i)
- B Criticism (ii)
- C Criticism (iii)
- D None of them

(2 marks)

13 Variance analysis

13.1 The fixed overhead volume variance is defined as:

A The difference between the budgeted value of the fixed overheads and the standard fixed overheads absorbed by actual production.

B The difference between the standard fixed overhead cost specified for the production achieved, and the actual fixed overhead cost incurred.

C The difference between budgeted and actual fixed overhead expenditure.

D The difference between the standard fixed overhead cost specified in the original budget and the same volume of fixed overheads, but at the actual prices incurred. (2 marks)

13.2 Which **one** of the following would **not** explain a favourable direct materials usage variance?

A Using a higher quality of materials than that specified in the standard.
B A reduction in materials wastage rates.
C An increase in suppliers' quality control checks.
D Achieving a lower output volume than budgeted. (2 marks)

13.3 A company operates a standard absorption costing system. The following fixed production overhead data are available for the latest period:

Budgeted Output   300,000 units
Budgeted Fixed Production Overhead $1,500,000
Actual Fixed Production Overhead $1,950,000
Fixed Production Overhead Total Variance $150,000 adverse

The actual level of production for the period was nearest to:

A 277,000 units
B 324,000 units
C 360,000 units
D 420,000 units (2 marks)

13.4 A company operates a standard absorption costing system. Details of budgeted and actual figures for February are given below.

	Budget	Actual
Production (units)	29,000	26,000
Direct labour hours per unit	3.0	2.8
Direct labour cost per hour	$10.0	$10.4

The labour rate variance for the period was:

A $ 34,800 A
B $ 34,800 F
C $ 29,120 A
D $ 31,200 A (2 marks)

13.5 A company operates a standard absorption costing system. Details of budgeted and actual figures for February are given below.

	Budget	Actual
Production (units)	29,000	26,000
Direct labour hours per unit	3.0	2.8
Direct labour cost per hour	$10	$10.4

The labour efficiency variance for the period was:

A $ 58,000 F
B $ 60,320 F
C $ 52,000 F
D $ 54,080 F   (2 marks)

13.6 AD Ltd manufactures and sells a single product, E, and uses a standard absorption costing system. Standard cost and selling price details for product E are as follows.

	$ per unit
Variable cost	80
Fixed cost	20
	100
Standard profit	50
Standard selling price	150

The sales volume variance reported for last period was $90,000 adverse.

AD Ltd is considering using standard marginal costing as the basis for variance reporting in future.

What would be the correct sales volume variance to be shown in a marginal costing operating statement for last period?

A $126,000 F
B $113,000 F
C $126,000 A
D $113,000 A   (2 marks)

13.7 The following details have been extracted from the company's accounting records for August.

	Budget	Actual
Output of RG	800 units	890 units
Materials	4,000 kg	4,375 kg
Cost per kg	$200	$216

Calculate the total materials cost variance for August.

A $55,000 F
B $66,000 F
C $50,000 A
D $55,000 A   (2 marks)

13.8 Once variances have been calculated, management must decide whether or not to investigate their causes.

Which factors that a company would need to consider before deciding whether to investigate a variance.

(i) Materiality
(ii) Responsibility
(iii) Cost
(iv) Controllability

A All of the above
B II and III
C III only
D I, II and IV   (2 marks)

13.9 A furniture company manufactures high quality dining room furniture that is sold to major retail stores.

Extracts from the budget for last year are given below:

	Tables
Sales quantity (units)	8,000
Average selling price	$2,200
Direct material cost per unit	$1,000
Direct labour cost per unit	$400
Variable overhead cost per unit	$40

Actual results for last year were as follows:

	Tables
Sales quantity (units)	7,200
Average selling price	$2,400
Direct material cost per unit	$1,100
Direct labour cost per unit	$450
Variable overhead cost per unit	$60

Required

Calculate the sales volume contribution variance

A $912,000 F
B $792,000 F
C $816,000 A
D $912,000 A   (2 marks)

13.10 SM Ltd manufactures a single product L, for which the standard material cost is as follows:

$ per unit
Material 14 kg × $30   420

During July, 800 units of L were manufactured, 12,000 kg of material were purchased for $336,000, of which 11,500 kg were issued to production.

SM Ltd values all stock at standard cost.

The material price and usage variances for July were:

	Price	Usage
A	$23,000 (F)	$9,000 (A)
B	$23,000 (F)	$3,000 (A)
C	$24,000 (F)	$9,000 (A)
D	$24,000 (F)	$8,400 (A)

(2 marks)

13.11 Nalin Ltd expected to produce 200 units of its product, the Bone, last week. In fact, 260 units were produced. The standard labour cost per unit was $70 (10 hours at a rate of $7 per hour). The actual labour cost was $18,600 and the labour force worked 2,200 hours although they were paid for 2,300 hours.

What is the direct labour rate variance for Nalin Ltd last week?

A $400 (A)
B $2,500 (F)
C $2,500 (A)
D $3,200 (A)

(2 marks)

13.12 Dharma Ltd expected to produce 200 units of its product, the Dragon, last week. In fact, 260 units were produced. The standard labour cost per unit was $70 (10 hours at a rate of $7 per hour). The actual labour cost was $18,600 and the labour force worked 2,200 hours although they were paid for 2,300 hours.

What is the direct labour efficiency variance for Dharma Ltd last week??

A $400 (A)
B $2,100 (F)
C $2,800 (A)
D $2,800 (F)

(2 marks)

13.13 Extracts from D Ltd's records from last period are as follows.

	Budget	Actual
Production	1,925 units	2,070 units
Variable production overhead cost	$115,500	$149,040
Labour hours worked	5,775	8,280

The variable production overhead variances for last period are:

	Expenditure	Efficiency
A	$16,560 (F)	$20,700 (A)
B	$16,560 (F)	$37,260 (A)
C	$16,560 (F)	$41,400 (A)
D	$33,540 (A)	$41,400 (A)

(2 marks)

13.14 SL Ltd has budgeted to make and sell 4,200 units of product X during the period.

The standard fixed overhead cost per unit is $40.

During the period covered by the budget, the actual results were as follows.

Production and sales 5,000 units
Fixed overhead incurred $175,000

The fixed overhead variances for the period were

	Fixed overhead expenditure variance	Fixed overhead volume variance
A	$7,000 (F)	$32,000 (F)
B	$7,000 (F)	$32,000 (A)
C	$7,000 (A)	$32,000 (F)
D	$7,000 (A)	$32,000 (A)

(2 marks)

13.15 A company manufactures a single product, and relevant data for December is as follows.

	Budget/standard	Actual
Production units	1,800	1,900
Labour hours	9,000	9,400
Fixed production overhead	$360,000	$394,800

The fixed production overhead capacity and efficiency variances for December are:

	Capacity	Efficiency
A	$16,000 (F)	$4,000 (F)
B	$16,000 (A)	$4,000 (A)
C	$16,000 (A)	$4,000 (F)
D	$16,000 (F)	$4,000 (A)

(2 marks)

13.16 Which of the following would help to explain a favourable direct material price variance?

(i) The standard price per unit of direct material was unrealistically high

(ii) Output quantity was greater than budgeted and it was possible to obtain bulk purchase discounts

(iii) The material purchased was of a higher quality than standard

A (i), (ii) and (iii)
B (i) and (ii) only
C (ii) and (iii) only
D (i) and (iii) only

(2 marks)

13.17 Which of the following would help to explain a favourable direct labour efficiency variance?

(i) Employees were of a lower skill level than specified in the standard

(ii) Better quality material was easier to process

(iii) Suggestions for improved working methods were implemented during the period

A (i), (ii) and (iii)
B (i) and (ii) only
C (ii) and (iii) only
D (i) and (iii) only

(2 marks)

13.18 Which of the following statements is correct?

A   An adverse direct material cost variance will always be a combination of an adverse material price variance and an adverse material usage variance

B   An adverse direct material cost variance will always be a combination of an adverse material price variance and a favourable material usage variance

C   An adverse direct material cost variance can be a combination of a favourable material price variance and a favourable material usage variance

D   An adverse direct material cost variance can be a combination of a favourable material price variance and an adverse material usage variance

(2 marks)

13.19 PQ Ltd currently uses a standard absorption costing system. The fixed overhead variances extracted from the operating statement for November are:

	$
Fixed production overhead expenditure variance	$58,000 adv
Fixed production overhead capacity variance	$42,000 fav
Fixed production overhead efficiency variance	$14,000 adv

PQ Ltd is considering using standard marginal costing as the basis for variance reporting in future. What variance for fixed production overhead would be shown in a marginal costing operating statement for November?

A   No variance would be shown for fixed production overhead
B   Expenditure variance: $58,000 adverse
C   Volume variance: $28,000 favourable
D   Total variance: $30,000 adverse

(2 marks)

13.20 Which of the following situations is most likely to result in a favourable selling price variance?

A   The sales director decided to change from the planned policy of market skimming pricing to one of market penetration pricing.

B   Fewer customers than expected took advantage of the early payment discounts offered.

C   Competitors charged lower prices than expected, therefore selling prices had to be reduced in order to compete effectively.

D   Demand for the product was higher than expected and prices could be raised without adverse effects on sales volumes.

(2 marks)

13.21 In a period 12,250 units were made and there was a favourable labour efficiency variance of $11,250. If 41,000 labour hours were worked and the standard wage rate was $6 per hour, how many standard hours (to two decimal places) were allowed per unit?

A   3.19
B   3.35
C   3.50
D   6.00

(2 marks)

PART C4 QUESTIONS: DECISION MAKING

Questions 14.1 to 16.05 cover **Decision Making** the subject of Chapters 14-16 of the Learning & Practice Workbook.

14 Cost-volume-profit analysis

14.1 The following information has been budgeted for next period:

Expected sales   10,000 units at $80 = $800,000
Variable cost $ 50 per unit
Fixed costs $ 210,000

Compute the breakeven point in units.

A   7,500 units
B   6,750 units
C   7,200 units
D   7,000 units

(2 marks)

14.2 Dandy Ltd makes and sells a product which has a variable cost of $ 30 and which sells for $40. Budgeted fixed costs are $70,000 and budgeted sales are 8,000 units.

Calculate the margin of safety.

A   900 units
B   1,000 units
C   1,100 units
D   1,200 units

(2 marks)

14.3 SG Ltd makes and sells a single product, for which variable costs are as follows.

	$
Direct materials	10
Direct labour	8
Variable production overhead	6
Total variable cost	24

The sales price is $ 30 per unit, and fixed costs per annum are $68,000. The company wishes to make a profit of $16,000 per annum.

Determine the sales in units required to achieve this profit.

A   13,000 units
B   14,000 units
C   15,000 units
D   16,000 units

(2 marks)

14.4 SLB wishes to sell 14,000 units of its product, which has a variable cost of $15 to make and sell.

Fixed costs are $47,000 and the required profit is $23,000.

Calculate the required sales price per unit.

A $22
B $18
C $20
D $24

(2 marks)

14.5 The following break-even chart shows total revenues, total costs and fixed costs:

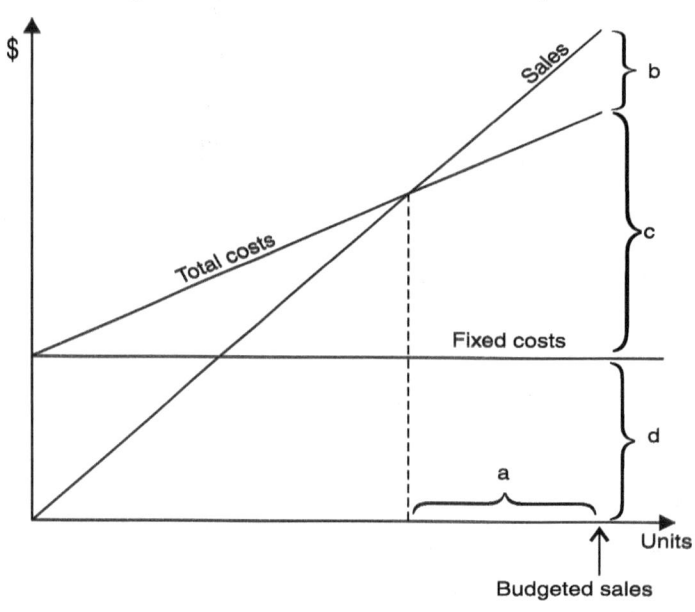

What is the value of contribution at budgeted sales?

A c
B b - d
C b + c
D b + d

(2 marks)

14.6 BGG manufactures and sells a single product. The profit statement for May is as follows.

	$
Sales value	80,000
Variable cost of sales	48,000
Contribution	32,000
Fixed costs	15,000
Profit	17,000

The management accountant has used the data for May to draw the following profit/volume chart.

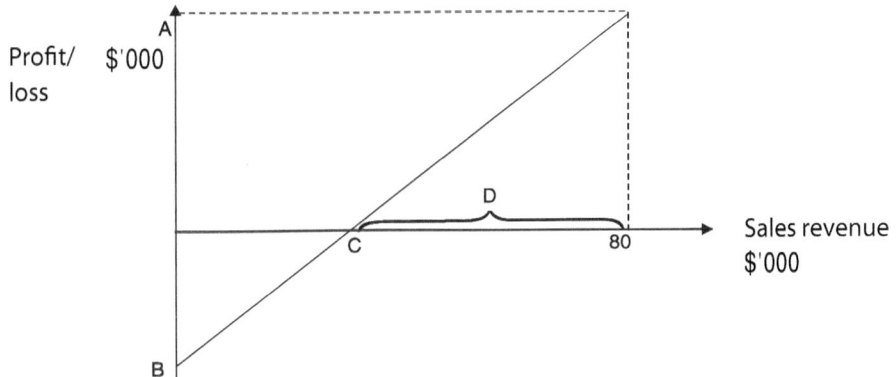

What is the value of the profit/ loss at point B?

A   A profit of $17,000
B   A loss of $17,000
C   A profit of $15,000
D   A loss of $15,000 (2 marks)

14.7 The accountant has prepared the following Profit volume chart.

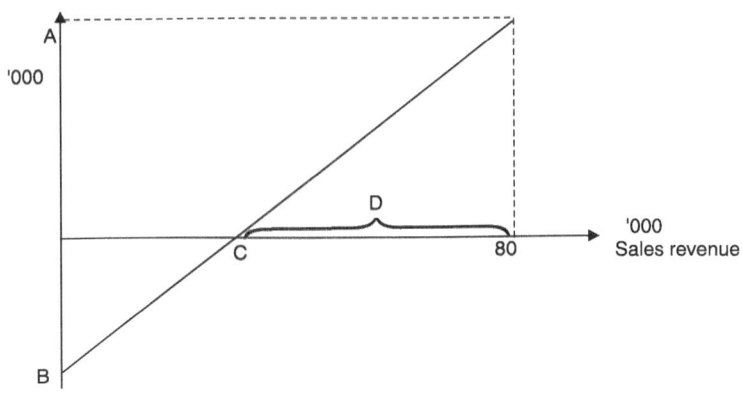

The term used to describe the distance D on the chart is:

A   Margin of safety
B   Breakeven point
C   Target profit
D   Contribution (2 marks)

14.8 BGG manufactures and sells a single product. The profit statement for May is as follows.

	$
Sales value	80,000
Variable cost of sales	48,000
Contribution	32,000
Fixed costs	15,000
Profit	17,000

The margin of safety for BGG's product is:

A   55% of budgeted sales
B   45% of budgeted sales
C   40% of budgeted sales
D   53% of budgeted sales (2 marks)

14.9 The following represents a profit/volume graph for an organisation:

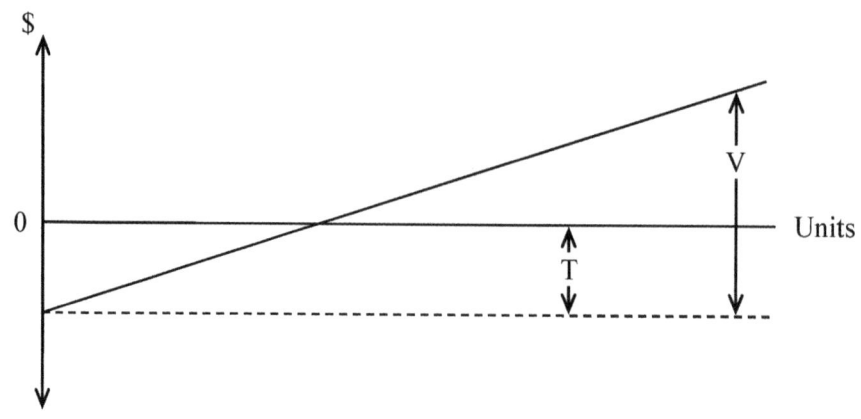

At the specific levels of activity indicated, what do the lines depicted as "T" and "V" represent?

	Line 'T'	Line 'V'
A	Loss	Profit
B	Total costs	Contribution
C	Total fixed costs	Revenue
D	Total fixed costs	Contribution

(2 marks)

14.10 A Co has reported the following in its recent management accounts:

	$
Sales	70,000
Variable costs	42,000
Fixed costs	15,000

What is A Co's break-even sales?

A $25,000
B $32,500
C $37,500
D $57,000

(2 marks)

14.11 B Co has produced the following budget:

	$
Sales	70,000
Variable costs	42,000
Profit	15,000

What is B Co's margin of safety?

A 46.4%
B 53.6%
C 87.6%
D 115.4%

(2 marks)

14.12 D Co has reported the following in its recent management accounts:

	$
Sales	90,000
Variable costs	63,000
Profit	12,000

Next year D Co wishes to make a profit of $20,000. What revenue would be required to achieve this?

- A $50,000
- B $98,000
- C $106,667
- D $116,667

(2 marks)

14.13 Which of the following is NOT an assumption of CVP analysis:

- A Variable cost per unit remains constant
- B Only one product is made
- C Fixed costs do not change
- D Sales prices are constant

(2 marks)

14.14 F Co has reported the following in its recent management accounts:

	$	
Sales	70,000	(10,000 units at $7 per unit)
Variable costs	42,000	
Fixed costs	15,000	

The sales manager has suggested increasing the selling price to $8 per unit. The managing directors is worried that increasing the price to $8 would reduce the level of sales. Fixed costs and variable costs per unit would remain unchanged.

How many units of the product would need to be sold at the new price of $8 to ensure that total profits remain unchanged?

- A 3,500 units
- B 5,652 units
- C 7,368 units
- D 8,750 units

(2 marks)

15 Relevant costing and decision making

15.1 The following details relate to three services provided by JHN Ltd.

	Service J	Service H	Service N
	$	$	$
Fee charged to customers	84	122	145
Unit service costs:			
Direct materials	12	23	22
Direct labour	15	20	25
Variable overhead	12	16	20
Fixed overhead	20	42	40

All three services use the same type of direct labour, which is paid $30 per hour.

The fixed overheads are general fixed overheads that have been absorbed on the basis of machine hours.

If direct labour is a scarce resource, the most and least profitable uses of it are:

	Most profitable	Least profitable
A	H	J
B	H	N
C	N	J
D	N	H

(2 marks)

15.2 A Ltd has three options for machine B. One of these options involves modifying it now at a cost of $7,200, which will mean that the company does not have to hire an alternative machine at a cost of $19,800. This modification would mean that machine B would have to be disposed of in one year's time at a cost of $4,000.

What is the relevant cost of this option?

A   A cost of $11,200
B   A cost of $7,200
C   A saving of $8,600
D   A saving of $12,000

(2 marks)

15.3 Company A has some inventory of materials which are no longer used in production. The materials could be used on a special contract, otherwise they will be disposed of.

What is the relevant cost of the materials for the contract?

A   Net realisable value
B   Replacement cost
C   Variable cost
D   Full cost

(2 marks)

15.4 BS Ltd has been asked to carry out a systems amendment for L Ltd. The amendment will require 400 programmer hours, and BS Ltd has only one programmer who is capable of doing the job.

The programmer is paid $100 per hour, including all employers contributions.

The programmer is scheduled to start work on a project for another customer, M Ltd, the revenue from which is $60,000 and non-salary direct costs are $15,000. This job will also take 400 hours. If the programmer is assigned to the L Ltd job, BS Ltd will have to hire an external programmer to carry out the M Ltd job at a cost of $80,000.

What is the relevant cost of the programmer's time for the systems amendment?

A $40,000
B $45,000
C $80,000
D $85,000

(2 marks)

15.5 Which of the following are non-relevant costs?

I   Avoidable costs
II   Opportunity costs
III   Notional costs
IV   Sunk costs

A   All of them
B   IV only
C   None of them
D   III and IV

(2 marks)

15.6 In the short-term decision-making context, which ONE of the following would be a relevant cost?

- A Specific development costs already incurred
- B The cost of special material which will be purchased
- C Depreciation on existing fixed assets
- D The original cost of raw materials currently in stock which will be used on the project

(2 marks)

15.7 Suits makes two products, the Trouser and the Jacket. Unit variable costs are as follows.

	Trouser $	Jacket $
Direct materials	1	3
Direct labour ($3 per hour)	6	3
Variable overhead	1	1
	8	7

The sales price per unit is $14 per Trouser and $11 per Jacket. During July the available direct labour is limited to 8,000 hours. Sales demand in July is expected to be as follows.

Trouser   3,000 units
Jacket   5,000 units

Fixed costs per month are $20,000 and that there is no opening inventory of finished goods or work in progress.

What is the contribution earned per unit of labour for Trousers.

- A $3.5
- B $. 2.9
- C $. 3.0
- D $. 3.25

(2 marks)

15.8 Which of the following is NOT an assumption typically made in relevant costing?

- A Cost behaviour patterns are known.
- B The amount of fixed costs, unit variable costs, sales prices and sales demand are known with certainty.
- C The objective of decision making in the short run is to maximise contribution.
- D There is no scarcity of resources.

(2 marks)

15.9 C Ltd is in the process of preparing a quotation for a special job for a customer. The job will require 700 units of material N. 400 units are already in stock at a book value of $50 per unit. The net realisable value per unit is $20. The replacement price per unit is $60. The material is in stock as the result of previous overbuying. No other use can be found for material N.

Required

Calculate the relevant cost of material N for this special job.

- A $26,000
- B $25,000
- C $26,500
- D $24,000

(2 marks)

15.10 H Co has just purchased a new machine costing $150,000 for a contract. It has an installation cost of $25,000 and is expected to have a scrap value of $10,000 in five years' time. The machine will be depreciated on a straight line basis over five years.

What is the relevant cost of the machine for the contract?

A $140,000
B $150,000
C $165,000
D $175,000

(2 marks)

15.11 A company produces three products which have the following details:

	A $	B $	C $
Direct labour (at $5 per hour)	40	25	30
Contribution per unit	35	25	48
Demand per month	4,000	5,000	2,000

Labour is limited to 35,000 hours per month.

What is the optimal production plan?

	A (units)	B (units)	C (units)
A	2,875	0	2,000
B	2,028	2,536	1,014
C	0	0	5,833
D	0	4,600	2,000

15.12 An electronics company uses three components in its products. The components are made in house, and information about the costs of making them is as follows:

	Exe $	Wye $	Zed $
Variable costs per unit	10	18	21
Labour hours per unit	1	4	3
Usage per month	10,000	2,500	3,000

There is a shortage of labour with only 19,000 hours available each month. The company can buy components externally. The cost of buying them is as follow:

	Exe	Wye	Zed
Variable costs per unit	15	26	30

Which of the products should be bought in?

A   Product Exe
B   Product Wye
C   Product Zed
D   None of the products

16 Modern approaches to management accounting

16.1 Which of the statements about activity based management is NOT correct?

- A The main purpose of activity based management is to achieve more accurate product costs.
- B Activity based management should lead to a reduction in costs in the longer run, while ensuring that customer needs are still met.
- C Activity based management is a process of continuous improvement rather than a one off change.
- D Employee empowerment is a key factor in a successful activity based management programme.

16.2 The following are modern developments in business management:

- (i) Activity based management
- (ii) Business process reengineering
- (iii) Total quality management

Which of the above include the aim of eliminating activities that do not add value to the customer?

- A (i) and (ii)
- B (i) and (iii)
- C (ii) and (iii)
- D (i), (ii) and (iii) **(2 marks)**

16.3 The processing time in a factory can be categorised under the following headings:

- (i) Production time
- (ii) Inspection time
- (iii) Transfer time

Which of the above time is considered to be value adding?

- A (i) only
- B (i) and (ii)
- C (i) and (iii)
- D All of the above **(2 marks)**

16.4 In activity-based costing, costs occur at different levels – unit level costs, batch costs, process level costs and organisational level costs.

Which of the following levels would equipment maintenance belong to?

- A Unit level
- B Batch level
- C Process level
- D Organisational level **(2 marks)**

16.5 Which of the following statements about the theory of constraints is NOT true?

- A It focuses on removing bottlenecks in production to improve throughput
- B Non-bottleneck resources should not be operated at full capacity
- C It can only be used in manufacturing organisations
- D It aims to reduce delays in meeting customer orders **(2 marks)**

16.6 A product must pass through three consecutive processes; Process 1, Process 2 then Process 3. The time taken per unit and the total hours available per week are as follows:

	Process 1	Process 2	Process 3
Hours per unit	2	4	3
Total hours available	150,000	200,000	120,000

Demand for the product is 45,000 units per week.

Which, if any, of the processes is the bottleneck?

A Process 1
B Process 2
C Process 3
D None of the above (2 marks)

16.7 The following statements have been made about the modern business world.

(i) Automation has led to much lower overheads as a portion of total production costs.

(ii) There is greater specialisation of production for customers meaning that standards are less easy to define.

(iii) Services businesses account for a larger volume of economic activity.

Which of the above statements is true?

A (i) and (ii)
B (i) and (iii)
C (ii) and (iii)
D All of the above (2 marks)

Exam Answer Bank

EXAM ANSWER BANK

PART C1: THE ROLE AND NATURE OF MANAGEMENT ACCOUNTING

1 Information for management

1.1 C Complete accuracy is not necessarily an essential quality of good information. It needs to be sufficiently accurate for its purpose, and often there is no need to go into unnecessary detail for pointless accuracy.

Relevance (option A) is an essential quality of good information. Busy managers should not be forced to waste their time reading pages of unnecessary information.

Communication of the information to the right person (option B) is essential. Individuals who are given the authority to do certain tasks must be given the information they need to do them.

The correct timing of information (option D) is essential. Information which is not available until after a decision is made will be useful only for comparisons and longer-term control and may serve no purpose even then. Information prepared too frequently can also be a waste of time and resources.

1.2 D Management accounts often incorporate non-monetary measures. Therefore statement (i) is incorrect.

There is no legal requirement to prepare management accounts. Therefore statement (ii) is incorrect.

Management accounts do serve as a future planning tool, but they are also useful as an historical record of performance. Therefore statement (iii) is incorrect.

1.3 C

1.4 D Statements (i), (ii) and (iii) are all correct.

1.5 C

1.6 A

1.7 D

1.8 B

1.9 (a) Data

(b) Information

2 Cost classification

2.1 B The stores assistant's wages cannot be charged directly to a product, therefore the stores assistant is part of the indirect labour force.

2.2 A By definition

2.3 A The depicted cost has a basic fixed element which is payable even at zero activity. A variable element is then added at a constant rate as activity increases.

2.4 A The cost described will increase in steps, remaining fixed at each step until another supervisor is required. Graph 1 depicts a step cost therefore the correct answer is A.

2.5	B	The royalty cost can be traced in full to the product, i.e. it has been incurred as a direct consequence of making the product. It is therefore a direct expense. Options A, C and D are all overheads or indirect costs which cannot be traced directly and in full to the product.
2.6	B	The wages paid to the stores assistant cannot be traced in full to a product or service, therefore this is an indirect labour cost.
		The assembly workers' wages can be traced in full to the televisions manufactured (option A), therefore this is a direct labour cost.
		The wages paid to plasterers in a construction company can be traced in full to the contract or building they are working on (option C). This is also a direct labour cost.
		The audit clerk's time can be traced to specific clients or jobs (option D) and would therefore be classified as a direct labour cost.
2.7	B	Overtime premium is always classed as factory overheads unless it is:
		• Worked at the specific request of a customer to get his order completed.
		• Worked regularly by a production department in the normal course of operations, in which case it is usually incorporated into the direct labour hourly rate.
2.8	D	Indirect costs are those which cannot be easily identified with a specific cost unit. Although the staples could probably be identified with a specific chair, the cost is likely to be relatively insignificant. The expense of tracing such costs does not usually justify the possible benefits from calculating more accurate direct costs. The cost of the staples would therefore be treated as an indirect cost, to be included as a part of the overhead absorption rate.
		Options A, B and C all represent significant costs which can be traced to a specific cost unit. Therefore, they are classified as direct costs.
2.9	C	The supervisors are engaged in the production activity, therefore option D can be eliminated. They supervise the production of all products, therefore their salaries are indirect costs because they cannot be specifically identified with a cost unit. This eliminates options A and B. The salaries are indirect production overhead costs, therefore option C is correct.
2.10	C	Controllable costs are items of expenditure which can be directly influenced by a given manager within a given time span.
		Option A describes a committed cost. A cost which can be easily analysed in terms of its cost behaviour (option B) would indeed be easier to monitor in terms of flexible budget comparisons, but this would not necessarily make it controllable. Option D describes an avoidable cost.
2.11	D	It would be appropriate to use the cost per customer account and the cost per cheque received and processed for control purposes. Therefore items (ii) and (iii) are suitable cost units.
		Stationery costs, item (i), is an expense of the department, therefore it is not a suitable cost unit.
2.12	C	The supervisors are engaged in the production activity, therefore option D can be eliminated. They supervise the production of all products, therefore their salaries are indirect costs because they cannot be specifically identified with a cost unit. This eliminates options A and B. The salaries are indirect production overhead costs, therefore option C is correct.

EXAM ANSWER BANK

2.13 B Within the relevant range, fixed costs are not affected by the level of activity, therefore option B is correct.

Option A describes a linear variable cost. Options C and D could apply to any type of cost, not just to fixed costs, so they are not the correct options.

2.14 C

2.15 A

2.16 D Conducting inspections is an appraisal cost because it is a cost associated with ensuring standards are met.

2.17 A Environmental external failure costs are costs arising when the business releases harmful waste into the environment. Cleaning up contaminated soil and government penalties and fines are therefore both examples of this, whereas staff training is a preventative measure so would be classified as an environmental prevention cost.

PART C2: COST IDENTIFICATION AND MEASURING COSTS FOR MANAGEMENT PURPOSES

3 Material costs

3.1   B   Lower-valued inventory has been used in production and higher-valued inventory remains on hand.

3.2   D

	$
Opening inventory	12,500
Purchases	126,500
Sales at cost price (150,000 × 80%)	(120,000)
Closing inventory	19,000

3.3   A

	Units	Unit cost $	Total $	Average $
Opening inventory	30	200	6000	
5 August purchase	50	240	12,000	
	80		18,000	225
10 August issue	(40)	225	(9,000)	
	40		9,000	
18 August purchase	60	250	15,000	
	100		24,000	240
23 August issue	(25)	240	(6,000)	
	75		18,000	

3.4   AVCO

<table>
<tr><th colspan="8">Inventory Record Card</th></tr>
<tr><th></th><th colspan="3">Purchases</th><th colspan="3">Requisitions</th><th colspan="2">Balance</th></tr>
<tr><th>Date</th><th>Quantity</th><th>Cost</th><th>Total cost</th><th>Quantity</th><th>Cost</th><th>Total cost</th><th>Quantity</th><th>Total cost</th></tr>
<tr><td></td><td>(kg)</td><td>$</td><td>$</td><td></td><td>$</td><td>$</td><td></td><td>$</td></tr>
<tr><td>1 Jan</td><td></td><td></td><td></td><td></td><td></td><td></td><td>300</td><td>7,500</td></tr>
<tr><td>2 Jan</td><td></td><td></td><td></td><td>250</td><td>25.00</td><td>6,250</td><td>50</td><td>1,250</td></tr>
<tr><td>12 Jan</td><td>400</td><td>25.75</td><td>10,300</td><td></td><td></td><td></td><td>450</td><td>11,550</td></tr>
<tr><td>21 Jan</td><td></td><td></td><td></td><td>200</td><td>25.67</td><td>5,134</td><td>250</td><td>6,416</td></tr>
<tr><td>29 Jan</td><td></td><td></td><td></td><td>75</td><td>25.67</td><td>1,925</td><td>175</td><td>4,491</td></tr>
</table>

3.5 B

Optimal order size = 500 units

$$EOQ = \sqrt{\frac{2 \times \text{order cost} \times \text{demand}}{\text{holding cost}}}$$

$$EOQ = \sqrt{\frac{2 \times 200 \times 10{,}000}{4 + (3\% \times \$400)}}$$

EOQ = 500

3.6 C

$$\sqrt{\frac{2 \times 15 \times 95{,}000}{3}} \times \sqrt{950{,}000} \times 975$$

No. of orders = 95,000/975 = 98 orders

3.7 A

$$EOQ = \sqrt{\frac{(2 \times 25 \times 10{,}000)}{0.50}}$$

$$= 1{,}000$$

3.8 A

$$EOQ = \sqrt{\frac{2 \times \text{demand (units)} \times \text{ordering cost}}{\text{holding cost}}}$$

$$= \sqrt{\frac{2 \times 60{,}000 \times 6}{0.5}}$$

$$= \sqrt{1{,}440{,}000}$$

$$= 1{,}200 \text{ units}$$

Number of orders per year = 60,000/1,200 = 50 orders

Annual ordering cost = 50 × $6 = $ 300

Average inventory held = 1,200/2 = 600 units

Annual holding cost = 600 × 0.5 = $300

Inventory cost = 60,000 × $12 = $720,000

Total cost of inventory using EOQ = 720,000 + 300 + 300 = **$720,600**

3.9 A Among other things, the GRN is used to update the inventory records and to check that the quantity invoiced by the supplier was actually received. The GRN does not usually contain price information. Therefore, the correct answer is A.

3.10 B Using FIFO, the issue on 9 September would consist of the remaining 600 units from the opening balance (40 units were issued on 3 March) plus 100 units from the batch received on 4 June.

	$
600 units × $5	3,000
100 units × $5.50	550
	3,550

If you selected **option A** you used the opening stock rate of $5 for all the units issued: you did not notice that 400 of these units had already been issued on 3 March.

If you selected **option C** you ignored the opening stock and based your calculations only on the receipts during the year.

Option D is incorrect because it values all the issues at the latest price paid, $6 per unit.

3.11 A Free inventory balance = units in stock + units on order from suppliers − units requisitioned not yet issued to production

13,000 = units in stock + 27,500 − 16,250

∴ Units in stock = 13,000 − 27,500 + 16,250

= 1,750

Option B is simply the difference between the units outstanding on customers' orders and the free stock balance.

If you selected **option C** you have interchanged stock on order and the outstanding orders.
If you selected **option D** you have simply added the free stock to the units outstanding on existing orders.

3.12 C Reorder level = maximum usage × maximum lead time

= 95 × 18

= 1,710 units

If you selected **option A** you have used the minimum figures for usage and lead time.
Option B uses the average figures and **option D** is simply the reorder quantity.

3.13 C Maximum level = reorder level + reorder quantity − (minimum usage × minimum lead time)

= 1,710 + 1,750 − (50 × 12) = 2,860 units

If you selected options A, C or D you have used the correct formula, but used the incorrect reorder level as calculated in the previous question.

3.14 C $EOQ = \sqrt{\dfrac{2C_oD}{C_h}} = \sqrt{\dfrac{2 \times \$80 \times 2,500}{\$15}} = 163$

If you selected **option A** you have interchanged Co and Ch.

If you selected **option B**, you have omitted the 2.

If you selected **option D** you forgot to take the square root.

3.15 B

Date	Received	Issued	Balance	Total Stock value $	Unit cost
1 June			100	500	5.00
3 June	300			1,440	4.80
			400	1,940	4.85 *
5 June		220		(1,067)	4.85
			180	873	4.85
12 June	170			884	5.20
			350	1,757	5.02 *
24 June		300		(1,506)	5.02
Closing stock			50	251	5.02

EXAM ANSWER BANK

* A new weighted average price is calculated every time there are receipts into inventory.

From the above records, it can be seen that the cost of material issued on 5 June was $ 1,067. Therefore, the correct answer is B.

If you selected **option A** you used a unit rate of $ 4.80, ie the price of the latest goods received, rather than the average price of $ 4.85.

If you selected **option C** you used a simple average price of $ 4.90, rather than a weighted average price.

If you selected **option D** you used a unit rate of $ 5, ie the price of the oldest items in stock.

3.16   B   The entries for the return of direct material to stores are the **reverse** of those made when the material is first issued to production. **The work in progress account** is credited to 'remove' the cost of the material from the production costs. The **stores account is debited** to increase the value of stock. Therefore, the correct answer is B.

If you selected **option A** you identified the correct accounts, but **your entries were reversed**.

Option C represents the entries for the return of indirect materials to stores. **Option D** represents the entries for the issue of indirect materials from stores.

3.17   C   IAS 2 states that imports and costs of transport of the goods to the current location should be included in the costs of inventory.

Storage costs are specifically excluded from inventory unless it is necessary to store a product for a long period as part of the production process.

Sales costs are also excluded from inventory.

4 Labour costs

4.1   B   The others are direct labour

4.2   A   3,300 hours represent 75% of the total time for the job. Therefore, the total time must be 3,300 ÷ 0.75 = 4,400 hours.

Labour cost per hour = $\dfrac{36,300}{4,400}$ = 8.25

4.3   A

	Hours
Active hours required for production = 200 × 6 hours =	1,200
Allowance for idle time (20% of total time = 25% of active time)	300
Total hours to be paid for	1,500
× $ 7 per hour	
Direct labour cost budget	$ 10,500

4.4   B

	Hours
Standard time for 180 units (× 4/60)	12
Actual time taken	7
Time saved	5

		$
Basic pay 7 hours × $5		35
Bonus: 60% × 5 hours saved × $5 per hour		15
		50

Option A is the basic daily pay, without consideration of any bonus. If you selected option C, you simply added 60 per cent to the basic daily pay, so you have misunderstood how to calculate the bonus.

Option D is based on the standard time allowance for 180 units, without considering the basic pay for the seven-hour day.

4.5 A Number of units qualifying for payment = 210 – 17
= 193

Piecework payment to be made:

	$
First 100 units @ $2	200
Last 93 units @ $3	279
	479

Option B is not correct because it includes payment for the 17 rejected units. If you selected option C you calculated the correct number of units qualifying for payment, but you evaluated all of them at the higher rate of $3 per unit. Option D is incorrect because it includes the 17 rejected units and evaluates them all at the higher rate of $3 per unit.

4.6 C Group bonus schemes are useful to reward performance when production is integrated so that all members of the group must work harder to increase output, for example in production line manufacture. **Statement (i)** is therefore true.

Group bonus schemes are not effective in linking the reward to a particular individual's performance. Even if one individual makes a supreme effort, this can be negated by poor performance from other members of the group. Therefore **statement (ii)** is not true.

Non-production employees can be included in a group incentive scheme, for example when all employees in a management accounting department must work harder to produce prompt budgetary control reports. **Statement (iii)** is therefore true, and the correct option is C.

4.7 C Overtime premium and holiday pay would be booked to overhead control accounts. Therefore, only the basic pay of $70,800 is booked to the work in progress account. B is wrong because the WIP account has been credited. The account is debited to the WIP account in the wages control account (and debited to the WIP account in production).

4.8 A

	Hours
Standard time for 80 units (× 9/60)	12
Actual time taken	8
Time saved	4

Group bonus: 70% × 4 hours saved × $60 per hour = $68

Akila's share of bonus = 50% × ($168 × 60%)
= $50.40

If you selected **option B** you took all of the time saved as the bonus hours, instead of only 70 per cent. **Option C** is the bonus payable to Akila and her team-mate combined. If you selected **option D,** you have calculated the group bonus correctly but have not taken the final step to calculate Jane's share of the bonus.

4.9 D

	Hours
Active hours required	380
Add idle time (5/95)	20
Total hours to be paid	400 @ $6 per hour
Total labour cost	$2,400

If you selected option A you reduced the active hours by five per cent. However, the hours to be paid must be **greater than** the active hours, therefore the idle hours must be added. If you selected option B you made no allowance for the idle hours, which must also be paid for. If you selected option C you added five per cent to the active hours but note that the idle time is quoted as a **percentage of the total time to be paid for.**

4.10 D   Standard labour cost per unit = 9 hours $\times \dfrac{100}{90} \times \$9 = \$90$

You should have been able to eliminate **option A** because it is less than the basic labour cost of $81 for 9 hours of work. Similar reasoning also eliminates **option B**. If you selected **option C** you simply added 10% to the 9 active hours to determine a standard time allowance of 9.9 hours per unit. However, the idle time allowance is given as 10% of the total labour time.

4.11 B   Overtime premium is always classed as factory overheads unless it is:

- Worked at the specific request of a customer to get his order completed.

- Worked regularly by a production department in the normal course of operations, in which case it is usually incorporated into the direct labour hourly rate.

4.12 A

Monday	12 units × $ 5.5 = $66
Tuesday	14 units × $ 5.5 = $77
Wednesday	9 units × $ 5.5 = $9.5 – therefore paid $60
Thursday	14 units × $ 5.5 = $77
Friday	8 units × $ 5.5 = $44 therefore paid $60

Total = 66 + 77 + 60 + 77 + 60 = $340

4.13 A

Efficiency ratio = $\dfrac{\text{Standard hours for actual output}}{\text{Actual hours worked}} = \dfrac{8.5}{9} = 94.4\%$

Capacity ratio = $\dfrac{\text{Actual hours worked}}{\text{Budgeted hours}} = \dfrac{9}{8} = 112.5\%$

Activity ratio = $\dfrac{\text{Standard hours for actual output}}{\text{Budgeted hours}} = \dfrac{8.5}{8} = 106.25\%$

4.14 B   171 pots should take 9.5 hours
171 pots did take 9 hours

$\Rightarrow$ productivity = 9.5/9 = 105.6%

5 Overheads and absorption costing

5.1 A Overhead absorption rates are determined in advance for each period, usually based on budgeted data. Therefore statement (i) is correct and statement (iii) is incorrect. Overhead absorption rates are used in the final stage of overhead analysis, to absorb overheads into product costs. Therefore statement (ii) is correct. Statement (iv) is not correct because overheads are controlled using budgets and other management information. Therefore, the correct answer is A.

5.2 C

		$
Actual overhead incurred		235,920
Overhead under absorbed		(9,370)
Overhead absorbed during period		226,550
Overhead absorption rate per direct labour hour	=	226,550/4,925
	=	$46
Number of direct labour hours budgeted	=	257,600/$46
	=	5,600

5.3 C

	$
Actual overhead incurred	1,074,150
Overhead under recovered	(51,150)
Total overhead recovered by 68,200 calls made	1,023,000

Overhead absorption rate per call made = $1,023,000/68,200
= $15

5.4 D Number of employees in packing department = 2 direct + 1 indirect = 3
Number of employees in all production departments = 15 direct + 6 indirect = 21

Packing department overhead

Canteen cost apportioned to packing department	=	3/21 × 84,000
	=	$12,000
Original overhead allocated and apportioned	=	$89,600
Total overhead after apportionment of canteen costs	=	$ 101,600

5.5 D

	Production centre K $	Production centre L $	Stores $	Maintenance $
Overhead costs			140,000	70,000
First stores apportionment	63,000	63,000	(140,000)	14,000
			0	84,000
First maintenance apportionment	42,000	37,800	4,200	(84,000)
			4,200	0
Second stores apportionment	1,890	1,890	(4,200)	420
			0	420
Second maintenance apportionment	210	189	21	(420)
			21	0
Third stores apportionment (approx)	10	11	(21)	0
	107,110	102,890		
To the nearest hundred	107,100	102,900		

5.6 A

	Production centre P $	Production centre Q $	X $	Y $
Overhead costs	950,000	820,000	460,000	300,000
First X apportionment	184,000	184,000	(460,000)	92,000
			0	392,000
First Y apportionment	117,600	235,200	39,200	(392,000)
			39,200	0
Second X apportionment	15,680	15,680	(39,200)	7,840
			0	7,840
Second Y apportionment	2,350	4,710	780	(7,840)
			780	0
Third X apportionment	310	310	(780)	160
			0	160
Third Y apportionment (approx)	60	100	0	(160)
	1,270,000	1,260,000	0	0

5.7 C

Budgeted number of occupied beds per night = 300 beds × 365 × 95%

= 104,025 occupied bed nights

Overhead absorption rate for cleaning = $ 1,250,000/104,025 = $ 12.02

5.8 D

Department 1 appears to undertake primarily machine-based work, therefore a machine-hour rate would be most appropriate.

$$\frac{27,000,000}{45,000} = \$ 600 \text{ per machine hour}$$

Therefore, the correct answer is D.

5.9 B

Production overhead absorption rate	= $165,000/60,000
	= $2.75 per machine hour
Production overhead absorbed	= $2.75 × 55,000 hours
	= $151,250
Production overhead incurred	= $165,000
Production overhead under absorbed	= $13,750

5.10 C

	$
Actual overhead incurred	23,592
Overhead under absorbed	(937)
Overhead absorbed during period	22,655
Overhead absorption rate per direct labour hour	= 22,655/4,925
	= $4.60
Number of direct labour hours budgeted	= 5,760/$4.60
	= 5,600

	$
Production overhead absorbed (11,970 hours × $ 260)	3,112,200
Production overhead under absorbed	567,000
Production overhead incurred	3,679,200

5.12 A **Description B** could lead to under-absorbed overheads if actual overheads far exceeded both budgeted overheads and the overhead absorbed. **Description C** could lead to under-absorbed overheads if overhead absorbed does not increase in line with actual overhead incurred.

5.13 C All of the methods are acceptable bases for absorbing production overheads. However, the percentage of prime cost has serious limitations and the rate per unit can only be used if all cost units are identical.

6 Absorption and marginal costing

6.1 B Sales < production by 280 units

Marginal costing profit would be lower by 280 × (48,000 ÷ 12,000) = $1,120

6.2 A Using the high two method to determine the period fixed costs:

Production (units)	Production costs
	Rs
1,210	3,394
990	3,086
220	308

Variable cost per unit = 308/220 = $ 1.40

Fixed cost = $ 3,394 – (1,210 × $ 1.40) = $1,700

Overhead absorption rate = $1,700/1,000 units
= $1.70 per unit

Difference in reported profit = change in inventory units × $1.70
= (1,200 – 1,040) × $1.70
= $ 272

The absorption costing profit will be lower than the marginal costing profit because the number of units in inventory reduced during the period.

Absorption costing profit = $ 8,160 – $ 272 = $ 7,888

6.3 B Marginal costing means that only variable costs are included in the valuation of cost per unit. (iv) is therefore excluded.

Selling costs are never included in inventory valuation, since inventory valuation should include only the costs incurred in getting the inventory to the state it is in at the reporting date – so selling costs would be a future cost.

6.4 B Contribution per unit = 70 – 40 = $30

Therefore, increase in profits = 100 units ×30 = $3,000

Answer B is obtained by multiplying profit per unit by the additional 100 units. This is incorrect, as the calculation of profit per unit includes fixed costs. However, fixed costs do not change as output changes.

Answer C is obtained by assuming that revenues will increase but costs will not. This is wrong. As output increases, variable costs per unit increase.

6.5 C IAS 2 requires production overheads to be included in the valuation of inventory, so marginal costing does not comply with IAS 2. Statement (i) is therefore incorrect.

Closing inventory includes a share of overheads. The higher the value of closing inventory, the less will be the cost of overheads charged to the cost of sales in the current accounting period, so managers may be encouraged to produce more inventory to carry forward a higher amount of overheads into the following period. (ii) is therefore correct.

Marginal costing, being the variable cost per unit, allows managers to see easily how costs will change as production changes, and changes in contribution indicate how much profits will change by. (iii) is therefore correct.

6.6 C

	$
Marginal costing profits	75,000
Add: fixed overheads in closing inventory	1,500
Less: fixed overheads in opening inventory	(900)
Absorption costing profit	75,600

6.7 C

	$
Contribution (15 – 10) × 220,000	1,100,000
Less: Fixed costs (2 ×200,000)	(400,000)
Profit	700,000

6.8 B Closing inventory valuation under absorption costing will always be higher than under marginal costing because of the absorption of fixed overheads into closing inventory values.

The profit under absorption costing will be greater because the fixed overhead being carried forward in closing inventory is greater than the fixed overhead being written off in opening inventory.

6.9 D We know that the profit using marginal costing would be higher than the absorption costing profit, because stocks are decreasing. However, we cannot calculate the value of the difference without the fixed overhead absorption rate per unit.

Difference in profit = 2,000 units stock reduction × fixed overhead absorption rate per unit

6.10 D Decrease in inventory levels = 48,500 – 45,500 = 3,000 units

Difference in profits = $315,250 – $288,250 = $27,000

The difference in profits is due to the reduction in inventory

Fixed overhead per unit = $\dfrac{27,000}{3,000}$ = $9 per unit

If you selected one of the other options you attempted various divisions of all the data available in the question!

7 Activity based costing

7.1 A Set-up costs per production run = $100,000/16 = $6,250
Cost per inspection = $80,000/8 = $10,000

Overhead costs of product B:

	$
Set-up costs (10 × $6,250)	62,500
Inspection costs (4 × $10,000)	40,000
	102,500

Overhead cost per unit = $102,500/5,000 units = $20.50

EXAM ANSWER BANK

7.2   A

	Aye	Bee	Total
Production volume	2,500	8,000	
Units per batch	500	1,000	
Total batches	5	8	13

⇒ Cost per batch = 260,000/ 13 = $20,000.
Apportioned to Bee = 8 × 20,000 = 160,000
Cost per unit = 160,000/ 8,000 = $20.00 per unit.

7.3   C   Cost driver rate = $80,000 ÷ 400 = $200 per set up
Number of batches of Product X = 5,000 units/ 50 = 100 batches.
Each batch requires 2 setups ⇒ 200 setups in total for product X
⇒ total set up costs apportioned to product X = 200 × $200 =$40,000.
Setup per unit = 40,000 ÷ 5,000 units = $8 per unit.

7.4   B   (ii) only

It would be unfeasible for most companies to identify all activities. Instead they identify the major categories of activity. (i) is therefore untrue.

The costs of implementing ABC are high – for businesses with a limited product range, the benefits may not be sufficient to justify these costs.

7.5   B   ABC can be used in service industries as well as manufacturing, so (1) is not true. Activity based costing would comply with IAS 2 as it includes all costs of production including overhead costs.

7.6   B   Setup costs are incurred each time a "batch" of products is made. They are therefore batch level costs. Machine costs depend on machine hours, which depends on the number of units of products made. This is therefore a unit level cost.

7.7   B   (i) This statement is true. While some cost drivers are not volume based, some are, so the use of ABC does not eliminate the use of production volume.

(ii) is not true. ABC provides insights into cost behaviour so even if the cost per unit is the same, management will benefit from understanding the causes of the costs.

(iii) is true. For some activities there may be several possible drivers, but only one can be chosen for each activity.

7.8   B   ABC is possibly more useful in service industries because costs are less dependent on volume. (1) is not true. ABC does produce more accurate product costs due to the fact that costs are apportioned based on the real caused (the drivers) that cause them.

7.9   D   The cost of the receiving department is most likely driven by the number of receipts.

A and B are bases that may be used under traditional absorption costing. However, the value of the material and the volume used does not directly increase the costs of the receiving department. Storage of materials is an activity that takes place after the receipt, so is not part of the cost of receiving.

7.10 A   Increasing the order size would reduce the number of orders as there would be a smaller number of bigger orders. This would save the time of the staff in the order department, so saving labour costs.

Changing the driver would not have any impact on the cost.

7.11 D All of these are criticisms of traditional absorption costing.

(i) Where products are produced in smaller volumes, they often use proportionately more overheads – for example, a machine set up will still have to be performed even for a small number of products.

(ii) Overhead absorption uses bases such as labour hours or machine hours to apportion costs to products. These are volume based.

(iii) Absorption costing does not try to understand the root causes of the overheads.

7.12 C Product sustaining activities are activities undertaken to develop or sustain a product. They depend on the number of products, not the number of units of a product.

7.13 C Cost per unit of driver for the two activities is as follows:

Haulage: $2 per kilometre ($2 million ÷ 1 million)
Order processing (500,000 ÷ 800,000) $0.625
⇒ cost for the customer:
Haulage   1,500
Order processing   6.25 (10 × 0.625)
Total cost: 1,062.5

7.14 B The first two items are true. ABC provides more accurate product costs. Some costs may have more than one potential driver (e.g. IT costs may depend on the number of users, or the number of transactions etc.)

Activity based costing is appropriate in service industries where a high portion of costs are overhead costs.

7.15 B Total number of environmental inspections = [(1,500/500) × 3] + [(3,000/1,000) × 8] + [(1,600/800) × 7] = 9 + 24 + 14 = 47

Cost per inspection = $70,500 / 47 = $1,500

Cost attributed to MyRun = $1,500 × 24 inspections = $36,000

7.16 B Identifying environmental costs associated with individual products or services leads to more accurate costs and therefore more accurate pricing.

A problem with traditional costing methods is that they fail to analyse environmental costs and the costs are often hidden within overhead costs. They are therefore not necessarily easy to measure. One solution to this is to use activity-based costing where the environmental costs become cost drivers.

7.17 $16,000

Cost per kg of hazardous waste disposed of = $40,000 / 160,000 kg = $0.25 per kg.
Cost attributed to Leaf = $0.25 × 2 × 20,000 = $10,000.
Cost per inspection = $15,000 / 150 = $100 per inspection.
Cost attributed to Leaf = $100 × 60 = $6,000.
Total cost attributed to Leaf = $10,000 + $6,000 = $16,000.

PART C3: PART C3: INTRODUCTION TO COSTING SYSTEMS

8 Process costing

8.1 C The value of the abnormal loss for the period is $460

	kg
Input	20,000
Normal loss (5% × 20,000 kg)	(1,000)
Abnormal loss	(200)
Output	18,800

$$\text{Cost per kg} = \frac{\text{Input costs - scarp value of normal loss}}{\text{Expected output}}$$

$$= \frac{26,000 + 12,000 + 19,000 - \text{nil}}{20,000 - 1,000}$$

$$= \frac{43,700}{19,000} = \$2.30$$

Value of abnormal loss = 200 × $2.30 = $460

8.2 D $326

Actual output	5,600
Normal loss (10% × 6,000)	600
Abnormal gain	(200)
Input	6,000

$$\text{Cost per unit} = \frac{\text{Cost of input less scrap value of normal loss}}{\text{Expected units}}$$

$$= \frac{1,800,000 + 140,000 - (6,000 \times \$30)}{6,000 \times 90\%}$$

$$= 1,760,000/5,400$$

$$= \$326 \text{ per unit}$$

8.3 A Good production = input − normal loss − abnormal loss

$$= (2,500 - (2,500 \times 10\%) - 75) \text{ kg}$$
$$= 2,500 - 250 - 75$$
$$= \underline{2,175} \text{ kg}$$

8.4 C Work in progress = 300 litres input − 250 litres to finished goods
= 50 litres

Equivalent litres for each cost element are as follows.

	Material		Conversion costs	
	%	Equiv. litres	%	Equiv. litres
50 litres in progress	100	50	50	25

8.5	C	Completed output	6,950
		Work on closing WIP	105 (350 units × 30%)
			7,055

8.6	A	Completion of opening WIP	45.0 (150 units × 0.3)
		Goods started & finished	3,325.0 (3,500 – 175)
		Work on closing WIP	52.5 (175 units ×30%)
			3,422.5

8.7   D

Expected output:
Actual output	2,800
Add actual loss	200
Units input	3,000
Less normal loss	300
Expected output	2,700

$$\text{Value of output} = \frac{\text{Inputs} - \text{scrap value of normal loss}}{\text{Expected output}} = \$7.50$$

$$\Rightarrow \frac{\text{Inputs} - (300 \times 3)}{2,700} = 7.5, \Rightarrow \text{Inputs} - 900 = 20,250 \Rightarrow \text{Inputs} = 21,150.$$

8.8   B   Item C describes the weighted average method. Items A and D are not appropriate under either method.

8.9   C   Flow of units: Open WIP + Goods started = Closing WIP + Goods completed

200 + 1,900 = 1,800 + 300 (balancing figure)

Since the weighted average method is used, the costs included in opening WIP are added to the production costs incurred during the period. In the calculation of completed units, 100% pf goods that were completed during the period are included in the statement of completed units:

Goods completed	1,800	
+ closing WIP	150	(300 units 50% complete)
Total equivalent units	1,950	

	$
Total costs: b/f in opening WIP	7,000
Incurred during the month	93,500
Total costs	100,500

$$\Rightarrow \text{cost per equivalent unit} = \frac{100,500}{1,950} = \$51.54.$$

Answer A – this ignores the work done on closing WIP.
Answer B is the valuation that would be obtained using FIFO
Answer D – is incorrect. It did not multiply the closing WIP by the degree of completion.

8.10   A   Flow of units: Open WIP + Goods started = Closing WIP + Goods completed

300 + 1,900 = 2,000 (balancing fig) + 200

Goods started & finished = 1,900 – 200 – 1,700,

Statement of equivalent units:

Completion of opening WIP	210	(300 * 70%)
Good started and finished	1,700	
Start closing WIP	80	(200 * 40%)
Total equivalent units	1,990	

The FIFO method does not include the value of opening WIP

$$\Rightarrow \text{Cost per equivalent unit} = \frac{93,500}{1,990} = \$46.98$$

If you chose answer B, you used the weighted average method, not FIFO.

If you chose answer C, you may have wrongly calculated that completion of opening WIP was 30%, not 70% of 300 units.

If you chose answer D you may have included the cost of opening inventory in the calculation of cost per equivalent unit. This should only be done for the weighted average method.

8.11 A Closing work in progress was 150 units, 35% complete with respect to conversion costs, giving 52.5 equivalent units. The value is therefore $2,625 (52.5 ×50).

8.12 B $\text{Cost per unit} = \frac{\text{Inputs} - \text{scrap value of normal loss}}{\text{Expected output}}$

Normal loss = 5% × 2,000 = 100 ⇒ expected output = 1,900 units
Scrap value of normal loss = 100 × 3 = 300

$$\Rightarrow \text{value of one unit of output} = \frac{(2,000 \times 4.50) + 13,340 - 300}{1,900} = \$11.60$$

8.13 B Normal loss = 5% × 1,500 = 75 ⇒ expected output = 1,425 units

Abnormal loss = 100 − 75 = 25 units. Abnormal loss is valued at full cost per unit minus scrap value.

$$\text{Full cost per unit} = \frac{\text{Inputs} - \text{scrap value of normal loss}}{\text{Expected output}} = \frac{(1,500 \times 4.0) + 12,000 - 75}{1,425} = \$12.58$$

⇒ Value of abnormal loss = (25 × 12.58) − (25 × 1) = 289.5

9 Process costing – joint products and by products

9.1 C Total production inventory

	$
Opening inventory	100,000
Direct materials added	1,000,000
Conversion costs	1,200,000
	2,300,000
Less closing inventory	300,000
Total production cost	2,000,000

EXAM ANSWER BANK

	Production Units		Sales value $000		Apportioned cost $'000
P	4,000	(× $.500)	2,000	($2,000,000 × 2/8)	500
R	6,000	(× $1,000)	6,000	($2,000,000 × 6/8)	1,500
			8,000		2,000

Product R cost per unit = $1,500,000/6,000 = $250 per unit.

9.2 B

Product	Extra revenue from further processing per litre	Further variable processing costs/ litre	Further process? (if extra revenue > further costs)
M	2.15 (8.40 – 6.25)	1.75	Yes
N	1.25 (6.45 – 5.20)	0.95	Yes
P	0.65 (7.45 – 6.80)	0.85	No

9.3 A

	$
Opening inventory	100,000
Direct materials added	1,000,000
Conversion costs	1,200,000
	2,300,000
Less closing inventory	300,000
Total production cost	2,000,000

	Production Units		Apportioned cost $
P	4,000	($2,000,000 × 4/10)	800,000
R	6,000	($2,000,000 × 6/10)	1,200,000
	10,000		2,000,000

If you selected **option B** you made no adjustment for inventories when calculating the total costs.

If you selected **option C** you apportioned the production costs on the basis of the units sold. **Option D** is the total cost of product R.

9.4 D Statement (i) is incorrect because the value of the product described could be relatively high even though the output volume is relatively low. This product would then be classified as a joint product.

Statement (ii) is incorrect. Since a by-product is not important as a saleable item, it is not separately costed and does not absorb any process costs.

Statement (iii) is correct. These common or joint costs are allocated or apportioned to the joint products.

9.5 B Net process costs

	$
Raw material input	216,000
Conversion costs	72,000
Less by-product revenue	(4,000)
Net process cost	284,000

	Production Units		Sales value $		Apportioned cost $
E	21,000	(× $15)	315,000	($284,000 × 315/495)	180,727
Q	18,000	(× $10)	180,000	($284,000 × 180/495)	103,273
			495,000		284,000

If you selected **option A** you apportioned some of the net process costs to the by-product. **Option C** makes no allowance for the credit of the by-product revenue to the process account, and **option D** is the production cost of product E.

9.6   C   No costs are apportioned to the by-product. The by-product revenue is credited to the sales account, and so does not affect the process costs. Total process costs are therefor $230,000 (180,000 + 50,000).

	Units		Sales value $		Apportioned cost $
L	3,000	(× $32)	96,000	($230,000 × 96/332)	66,506
M	2,000	(× $42)	84,000	($230,000 × 84/332)	58,193
N	4,000	(× $38)	152,000	($230,000 × 152/332)	105,301
			332,000		230,000

If you selected **option A** you credited the by-product sales revenue to the process account, but the question states that by-product revenue is credited to the sales account.

If you selected **option B** you apportioned some of the process costs to the by-product. **Option D** is the production cost for product L.

10 Job, batch, service & contract costing

10.1   D   Process costing is a costing method used where it is not possible to identify separate units of production, or jobs, usually because of the continuous nature of the production process. The manufacture of liquid soap is a continuous production process.

10.2   A   Job costing is a costing method applied where work is undertaken to customers' special requirements. Option B describes process costing, C describes service costing and D describes absorption costing.

10.3   B   In service costing it is difficult to identify many attributable direct costs. Many costs must be shared over several cost units, therefore characteristic (i) does apply. Composite cost units such as tonne-mile or room-night are often used, therefore characteristic (ii) does apply. Equivalent units are more often used in costing for tangible products, therefore characteristic (iii) does not apply, and the correct answer is B.

10.4   D

	$
Direct materials (5 × $200)	1,000
Direct labour (14 × $80)	1,120
Variable overhead (14 × $30)	420
Fixed overhead (14 × $50*)	700
Other overhead	800
Total cost of job 173	4040
Profit margin (× 20/80)	1010
Selling price	5050

EXAM ANSWER BANK

*Fixed production overhead absorption rate $= \dfrac{\$2,000,000}{40,000}$

$= \$50$ per direct labour hour

Option A is the total cost, but a profit margin should be added to this to determine the selling price. If you selected option B you added only $50 for fixed production overhead: but this is the hourly rate, which must be multiplied by the number of direct labour hours. If you selected option C you calculated 20 per cent of cost to determine the profit: but the data states that profit is calculated as 20 per cent of the sales value.

10.5 C The most logical basis for absorbing the overhead job costs is to use a percentage of direct labour cost.

Overhead $= \dfrac{24,600}{14,500 + 3,500 + 24,600} \times 126,000$

$= \dfrac{24,600}{42,600} \times 126,000$

$= 72,761$

If you selected option A you used the materials cost as the basis for overhead absorption. This would not be equitable because job number BB15 incurred no material cost and would therefore absorb no overhead. Option B is based on the prime cost of each job (material plus labour) and therefore suffers from the same disadvantage as option A. Option D is the total overhead for the period, but some of this cost should be charged to the other two jobs.

10.6 C

	Job WID02 $
Opening WIP	42,790
Labour for period	3,500
Overheads ($\dfrac{3,500}{42,600} \times 126,000$)	10,352
Total costs	56,642
Profit (33.33% on sales $\Rightarrow$ 50% on costs)	28,321
	$84,963

If you selected option A you forgot to add on overhead cost. If you selected option B you calculated the profit as 33.33 % on cost, instead of 33.33% on sales. If you selected option D you charged all of the overhead to job WID02, but some of the overhead should be charged to the other two jobs.

10.7 C

Job number	WIP $
YN12 (26,800 + 17,275 + 14,500) + ($\dfrac{14,500}{42,600} \times 126,000$)	101,462
YN20 (18,500 + 24,600) + ($\dfrac{24,600}{42,600}$ 126,000)	115,861
	217,323

Option A is the direct cost of job YN12, with no addition for overhead. Option B is the direct cost of both jobs in progress, but with no addition for overhead. Option D is the result of charging all of the overhead to the jobs in progress, but some of the overhead must be absorbed by the completed job YN15.

EXAM ANSWER BANK

10.8 B Cost per cake would be very small and therefore not an appropriate cost unit. The most appropriate cost unit would be cost per batch.

10.9 B The vehicle cost per passenger-kilometre (i) is appropriate for cost control purposes because it combines the distance travelled and the number of passengers carried, both of which affect cost.

The fuel cost for each vehicle per kilometre (ii) can be useful for control purposes because it focuses on a particular aspect of the cost of operating each vehicle.

The fixed cost per kilometre (iii) is not particularly useful for control purposes because it varies with the number of kilometres travelled.

10.10 B Number of occupied room-nights = 40 rooms × 30 nights × 65% = 780

Room servicing cost per occupied room-night = $\dfrac{39,000}{780}$ = $50

Option A is the cost per available room-night. This makes no allowance for the 65% occupancy achieved. If you selected option C you simply divided $39,000 by 40 rooms. This does not account for the number of nights in the period, nor the percentage occupancy achieved. If you selected option D you calculated the cost per occupied room, rather than the cost per occupied room-night.

10.11 A For most services it is difficult to identify many attributable direct costs. A high level of indirect costs must be shared over several cost units, therefore option A is not a characteristic of service costing.

Many services are intangible, for example an accountancy practice offers an intangible service, therefore option B is a characteristic of service costing.

Composite cost units such as tonne-kilometre or room-night are often used, therefore characteristic C does apply. Service costing can also be used to establish a cost for an internal service such as a maintenance department which does work for other departments. Therefore, option D is a characteristic of service costing.

10.12 B Since wages are paid on a piecework basis they are a variable cost which will increase in line with the number of binders. The machine set-up cost and design costs are fixed costs for each batch which will not be affected by the number of binders in the batch.

For a batch of 300 binders:

	$'000
Direct materials (3 × 300)	900
Direct wages (3 × 100)	300
Machine set up	30
Design and artwork	150
Production overhead (300 × 20%)	60
Total production cost	1,440
Selling, distribution and administration overhead (+ 5%)	72
Total cost	1,512
Profit (25% margin = 33% of cost)	504
Selling price for a batch of 300	2,016

10.13 A The price to be quoted for job B124 is $1,245

Production overhead absorption rate = $2,400,000/30,000 = $80 per labour hour

Other overhead absorption rate = ($1,500,000/$7,500,000) × 100% = 20% of total production cost

Job B124
Direct materials (3 kg × $50)	150
Direct labour (4 hours × $90)	360
Production overhead (4 hours × $80)	320
Total production cost	830
Other overhead (20% × $830)	166
Total cost	996
Profit margin: 20% of sales (× 20/80)	249
Price to be quoted	1,245

10.14 A (i) is correct. Any prudent method of estimating the extent of completion can be used.

(ii) is correct - in the interests of prudence, losses should be recognised on long term contracts as soon as it is realised that the loss will be made.

(iii) is not true. If the contract is between 35% and 85% complete, then a factor of the profit earned to date will be taken (e.g. 2/3 or ¾) So if the contract is 50% complete, then 50% × 2/3 of the profit (or 50% × ¾) of the profit would be taken.

Part C4: Information for planning and performance management

11 Budgeting

11.1 D Recognises different cost behaviour patterns and is designed to change as the volume of activity changes.

A flexible budget is designed to change as the volume of activity changes.

11.2 D (II) only.

(I) While flexed budgets may be more useful for control than fixed budgets, fixed budgets are still useful. So (I) is not true.

(III) Budgets have may uses other than control – such as planning, coordination etc. So (III) is not true.

11.3 C

A: Additional pay is not always a good motivator. Research has shown that it may motivate managers and employees in the short term, but that the effect soon wears off.

B: People are more likely to accept targets if they have had some participation in setting them.

C: Participative budgets are likely to be more realistic as managers know the real situation in their department than central management.

11.4 B A participative approach to budgeting means that managers have some participation in preparing their own budgets rather than having budgets imposed on them.

A: Budgets are usually more realistic when a participative approach is used, since managers know their department better than senior management.

B: A risk of participation is that managers may be tempted to make their budgets easy by adding slack – that is, overstating expenses or understating revenue. This reduces the value of the budget so is an adverse consequence.

C: Generally managers are more motivated if they participate in preparing their budget.

D: As with A, managers know their own department best, so are less likely to overlook resource requirements.

11.5 C There is likely to be a demotivating effect where an ideal standard of performance is set, because adverse efficiency variances will always be reported. It is important that adverse variances are not used to lay blame if targets have been set with the aim of motivation.

A low standard of efficiency is also demotivating, because there is no sense of achievement in attaining the required standards. Managers and employees will often outperform the standard or target when in fact they could have performed even better if they had been sufficiently motivated.

11.6 C Rolling budgets are useful where there is uncertainty in the external environment that means that budgets become outdated very quickly. Rolling budgets are updated on a regular basis.

EXAM ANSWER BANK

11.7 D There are usually performance targets in a budget, but with incremental budgeting these are often not challenging. There is no incentive with incremental budgeting for managers to reduce costs; on the contrary, there is an incentive for managers to make sure that they spend up to their budget limit in order to retain the spending in next year's budget.

11.8 B Production budget in units = **7,700 Units**

	Q1	Q2	Q3	Q4	Total
Budgeted sales	2,250	2,050	1,650	2,050	8,000
Closing inventories (30% of next quarter's sales)	615	495	615	375	375
Opening inventory	(675)	(615)	(495)	(615)	(675)
(Decrease)/increase in inventory	(60)	(120)	120	(240)	(300)
Production	2,190	1,930	1,770	1,810	7,700

11.9 B

	$
Usage:	
Product Y (2,100 units × 5)	10,500
Product Y (4,200 × 3)	12,600
Product Z (3,100 × 2)	6,200
Usage (kgs)	29,300
Add: Closing inventory	18,000
Less: Opening inventory	(21,000)
Material purchases (kgs)	26,300
Cost per kg)	5
Material purchases ($)	131,500

11.10 C

11.11 C Budget manuals contain instructions and objectives rather than the budgets themselves.

11.12 C The **principal budget factor** is the factor that limits the activities of an organisation.

Although cash and profit are affected by the level of sales (options A and B), sales is not the only factor that determines the level of cash and profit.

11.13 B The correct answer is: $ 11,400,000.

	Original budget	Per unit	Flexed amount
Sales units	600		550
	$ 000		$ 000
Sales revenue	54,000	90	49,500
Direct material	16,200	27	14,850
Direct labour	6,000	10	5,500
Variable overhead	3,000	5	2,750
Fixed overhead	15,000	N/A	15,000
Profit	13,800		11,400

Alternatively, you could calculate the contribution per unit: 90 – 27 – 10 – 5 = $48.

Total flexed contribution: $ 48 × 550 =	26,400
Less fixed costs	(15,000)
Flexed profit	11,400

12 Standard costing

12.1 C A basic standard is one which is kept unaltered over a long period of time and may be out of date. They are used to show changes in efficiency or performance over a long period of time.

12.2 B An attainable standard assumes efficient levels of operation, but includes allowances for normal loss, waste and machine downtime.

Option A describes an ideal standard.
Option C describes a current standard.
Option D describes a basic standard.

12.3 C It is generally accepted that the use of attainable standards has the optimum motivational impact on employees. Some allowance is made for unavoidable wastage and inefficiencies, but the attainable level can be reached if production is carried out efficiently.

Option A and option D are not correct because employees may feel that the goals are unattainable and will not work so hard.

Option B is not correct because standards set at a minimal level will not provide employees with any incentive to work harder.

12.4 B The volume of output would influence the total number of labour hours required, but it would not be directly relevant to the standard labour time per unit.

The type of performance standard (option A) would be relevant. For example, if an ideal standard is used there would be no extra time allowed for inefficiencies. Options C and D would be relevant because they would provide information about the tasks to be performed and the time that those tasks should take.

12.5 D Required liquid input = 1 litre $\times \frac{100}{80}$ = 1.25 litres

If you selected option A you deducted 20 per cent from the required output, instead of adding extra to allow for losses, whereas option B makes no allowance for losses.

Option C simply adds an extra 20 per cent to the completed output, but the wastage is 20 per cent of the liquid input, not 20 per cent of output.

12.6 A Standard costing provides targets for achievement, and yardsticks against which actual performance can be monitored (item (i)). It also provides the unit cost information for evaluating the volume figures contained in a budget (item (ii)). Inventory control systems are simplified with standard costing. Once the variances have been eliminated, all inventory units are valued at standard price (item (iii)).

Item (iv) is incorrect because standard costs are an estimate of what will happen in the future, and a unit cost target that the organisation is aiming to achieve.

12.7 D Standard labour cost per unit = 9 hours $\times \frac{100}{90} \times \$9 = \$10$

You should have been able to eliminate option A because it is less than the basic labour cost of $81 for 9 hours of work. Similar reasoning also eliminates option B. If you selected option C you simply added 10% to the 9 active hours to determine a standard time allowance of 9.9 hours per unit. However the idle time allowance is given as 10% of the total labour time.

EXAM ANSWER BANK

12.8   D   None of the criticisms apply in all circumstances.

Criticism (i) has some validity but even where output is not standardised it may be possible to identify a number of standard components and activities whose costs may be controlled effectively by the use of standard costs.

Criticism (ii) also has some validity but the use of information technology means that standards can be updated rapidly and more frequently, so that they may be useful for the purposes of control by comparison.

Criticism (iii) can also be addressed in some circumstances. The use of ideal standards and more demanding performance levels can combine the benefits of continuous improvement and standard costing control.

13 Variance analysis

13.1   A

13.2   D   The direct materials usage variance compares the standard material usage for the actual production with the actual material used. This means that the budgeted output volume is not relevant because it is not included in the calculation of the variance.

13.3   C   360,000 units

Fixed overhead total variance

	$'000
Fixed overhead incurred	1,950
Fixed overhead absorbed (1,500/300 × actual production)	X
	150 (A)

So X = 1,950,000 – 150,000 = 1,800,000

∴ 1,500,000/300,000 × actual production = 1,800,000

∴ actual production = 360,000 units

13.4   C   Actual hours = 26,000 × 2.8 = 72,800

	$
72,800 hours should have cost (× $10)	728,000
But did cost	757,120
	29,120 (A)

13.5   C

26,000 units should have taken (× 3 hours)	78,000 hours
But did take (26,000 × 2.8)	72,800 hours
Variance in hours	5,200 (F)
× standard cost per hour	× $10
	$ 52,000 (F)

13.6   C   Sales volume variance in units was $90,000/50 = 1800 units.

The sales volume variance in a marginal costing system is valued at standard contribution per unit, rather than standard profit per unit.

Contribution per unit of E = $150 – $80 = $70

Sales volume variance in terms of contribution = 1,800 × $70 = $126,000

13.7 D   Total material cost variance

	$
890 units should have cost (890 × $200 × 5kg)	890,000
But did cost ($216 × 4,375kg)	945,000
	55,000(A)

13.8 D   **Materiality**

Small variations in a single period are bound to occur and are unlikely to be significant. Obtaining an 'explanation' is likely to be time-consuming and irritating for the manager concerned. The explanation will often be 'chance', which is not, in any case, particularly helpful. For such variations further investigation is not worthwhile.

Controllability

Controllability must also influence the decision whether to investigate further. If there is a general worldwide price increase in the price of an important raw material there is nothing that can be done internally to control the effect of this. For example, if a central decision is made to award all employees a 10% increase in salary, staff costs in division A will increase by this amount and the variance is not controllable by division A's manager. Uncontrollable variances call for a change in the plan, not an investigation into the past.

Cost

The likely cost of an investigation needs to be weighed against the cost to the organisation of allowing the variance to continue in future periods.

13.9 A

Contribution

	Tables
	$
Sales price	2,200
Materials	(1,000)
Labour	(400)
Variable o/head	(40)
Contribution	760

Sales quantity contribution variance

	Actual sales Std mix	Standard sales Std mix	Difference in units	× Std contribution	Variance Rs'000
Tables	9,200	8,000	1,200 (F)	× $760	$912 (F)

13.10 C   Since stocks are valued at standard cost, the material price variance is based on the materials purchased.

	$
12,000 kg material purchased should cost (× $30)	360,000
but did cost	336,000
Material price variance	24,000 (F)

800 units manufactured should use (× 14 kg)	11,200 kg
but did use	11,500 kg
Usage variance in kg	300 kg (A)
× standard price per kg	× $30
Usage variance in £	$9,000 (A)

If you selected option A or B you based your calculation of the material price variance on the material actually used, and if you selected option B you forgot to evaluate the usage variance in kg at the standard price per kg. If you selected option D you evaluated the usage variance at the actual price per kg, rather than the standard price per kg.

13.11 C

	$
2,300 hours should have cost (× $7)	16,100
but did cost	18,600
Rate variance	2,500 (A)

Option A is the total direct labour cost variance. If you selected option B you calculated the correct money value of the variance but you misinterpreted its direction. If you selected option D you based your calculation on the 2,200 hours worked, but 2,300 hours were paid for and these hours should be the basis for the calculation of the rate variance.

13.12 D

260 units should have taken (× 10 hrs)	2,600 hrs
but took (active hours)	2,200 hrs
Efficiency variance in hours	400 hrs (F)
× standard rate per hour	× $7
Efficiency variance in £	$2,800 (F)

Option A is the total direct labour cost variance. If you selected option B you based your calculations on the 2,300 hours paid for; but efficiency measures should be based on the active hours only, ie 2,200 hours.

If you selected option C you calculated the correct money value of the variance but you misinterpreted its direction.

13.13 C   Standard variable production overhead cost per hour

= $115,500 ÷ 5,775 = $20

	$
8,280 hours of variable production overhead should cost (× $20)	165,600
but did cost	149,040
Variable production overhead expenditure variance	16,560 (F)

Standard time allowed for one unit = 5,775 hours ÷ 1,925 units = 3 hours

2,070 units should take (× 3 hours)	6,210 hours
but did take	8,280 hours
Efficiency variance in hours	2,070 hours (A)
× standard variable production overhead cost per hour	× $20
Variable production overhead efficiency variance	$41,400 (A)

If you selected option A you calculated the correct efficiency variance in hours but you omitted to evaluate it at the standard variable overhead cost per hour. If you selected option B you evaluated the efficiency variance at the actual variable overhead rate per hour, instead of at the standard rate per hour. If you selected option D you calculated the expenditure variance as the difference between the budget and actual expenditure. However, this does not compare like with like. The actual expenditure should be compared with the expected expenditure for the number of hours actually worked.

13.14 C   Fixed overhead expenditure variance

	$
Budgeted fixed overhead expenditure (4,200 units × $40 per unit)	168,000
Actual fixed overhead expenditure	175,000
Fixed overhead expenditure variance	7,000 (A)

The variance is adverse because the actual expenditure was higher than the amount budgeted.

Fixed overhead volume variance

	$
Actual production at standard rate (5,000 × $40 per unit)	200,000
Budgeted production at standard rate (4,200 × $40 per unit)	168,000
Fixed overhead volume variance	32,000 (F)

The variance is favourable because the actual volume of output was greater than the budgeted volume of output.

If you selected an incorrect option you misinterpreted the direction of one or both of the variances.

13.15 A Capacity variance

Budgeted hours of work	9,000 hours
Actual hours of work	9,400 hours
Capacity variance in hours	400 hours (F)
× standard fixed overhead absorption rate per hour *	× $40
Fixed production overhead capacity variance	$16,000 (F)

* $360,000/9,000 = $40 per hour

If you selected option B or C you performed the calculations correctly but misinterpreted the variance as adverse. Since the labour force worked 400 hours longer than budgeted, there is the potential for output to be 400 standard hours (or 80 units of production) higher than budgeted and hence the variance is favourable.

Efficiency variance

1,900 units of product should take (× 9,000/1,800 hrs)	9,500 hours
but did take	9,400 hours
Efficiency variance in hours	100 hours (F)
× standard fixed overhead absorption rate per hour *	× $40
Fixed production overhead efficiency variance in $	$4,000 (F)

* $360,000/9,000 = $40 per hour

If you selected option B or D you performed the calculations correctly but misinterpreted the variance as adverse. Time was saved compared to the standard time allowed for 1,900 units and so the efficiency variance is favourable.

13.16 B Statement (i) is consistent with a favourable material price variance. If the standard is high then actual prices are likely to be below the standard.

Statement (ii) is consistent with a favourable material price variance. Bulk purchase discounts would not have been allowed at the same level in the standard, because purchases were greater than expected.

Statement (iii) is not consistent with a favourable material price variance. Higher quality material is likely to cost more than standard, resulting in an adverse material price variance.

13.17 C Statement (i) is not consistent with a favourable labour efficiency variance. Employees of a lower skill level are likely to work less efficiently, resulting in an adverse efficiency variance.

Statement (ii) is consistent with a favourable labour efficiency variance. Time would be saved in processing if the material was easier to process.

Statement (iii) is consistent with a favourable labour efficiency variance. Time would be saved in processing if working methods were improved.

Therefore the correct answer is C.

13.18 D Direct material cost variance = material price variance + material usage variance

The adverse material usage variance could be larger than the favourable material price variance. The total of the two variances would therefore represent a net result of an adverse total direct material cost variance.

The situation in option A would sometimes arise, but not always, because of the possibility of the situation described in option D.

Option B could sometimes be correct, depending on the magnitude of each of the variances. However it will not always be correct as stated in the wording.

Option C is incorrect because the sum of the two favourable variances would always be a larger favourable variance.

13.19 B The only fixed overhead variance in a marginal costing statement is the fixed overhead expenditure variance. This is the difference between budgeted and actual overhead expenditure, calculated in the same way as for an absorption costing system.

There is no volume variance with marginal costing, because under or over absorption due to volume changes cannot arise.

13.20 D Raising prices in response to higher demand would result in a favourable selling price variance.

Market penetration pricing (option A) is a policy of low prices. This would result in an adverse selling price variance, if the original planned policy had been one of market skimming pricing, which nvolves charging high prices.

Early payment discounts (option B) are financial accounting items which do not affect the recorded selling price.

Reducing selling prices (option C) is more likely to result in an adverse selling price variance.

13.21 C Let x = the number of hours 12,250 units should have taken

12,250 units should have taken	x hrs
but did take	41,000 hrs
Labour efficiency variance (in hrs)	x – 41,000 hrs

Labour efficiency variance (in $) = $11,250 (F)

$$\therefore \text{Labour efficiency variance (in hrs)} = \frac{11,250}{6}$$

= 1875 (F)

∴ 1,875 hrs = (x – 41,000) hrs
∴ standard hours for 12,250 units = 41,000 + 1,875
= 42,875 hrs

$$\therefore \text{Standard hours per unit} = \frac{42,875 \text{ hrs}}{12,250 \text{ units}}$$

= 3.50 hrs

If you selected option A you treated the efficiency variance as adverse. Option B is the actual hours taken per unit and option D is the figure for the standard wage rate per hour.

PART C4: DECISION MAKING

14 Cost-volume-profit analysis

14.1 D The contribution per unit is $(80 – 50) = $30

Contribution required to break even = fixed costs = $210,000

Breakeven point (BEP) = 210,000 ÷ $30

= 7,000 units

14.2 B Breakeven point = $\dfrac{\text{Total fixed costs}}{\text{Contribution per unit}}$ = 7,000 units

Margin of safety = 8,000 – 7,000 units = 1,000 units

14.3 B Required contribution = fixed costs + profit

= $68,000 + $16,000 = $84,000

Required sales = $\dfrac{\text{Required contribution}}{\text{Contribution per unit}} = \dfrac{84{,}000}{6}$ = 14,000 units

14.4 C Sales price per unit

Required contribution = fixed costs plus profit

= $47,000 + $23,000

= $70,000

Required sales = 14,000 units

	$
Required contribution per unit sold (70,000/14,000)	5
Variable cost per unit	15
Required sales price per unit	20

14.5 D On the chart: b = total sales – total costs = total profit.

d = total fixed costs.

Contribution = profit + fixed costs, ⇒ = b + d.

Note: total costs = c + d. Fixed costs = d ⇒ c = total variable costs.

14.6 D At point B, revenue = zero, therefore contribution = zero. At this point, the company would make a loss equal to the fixed cost.

14.7 A The term used to describe the distance D on the chart is the margin of safety. (This is the difference between the sales revenue budgeted or achieved, and the revenue required to break even.)

14.8 D Margin of safety = budgeted sales – break even sales

C/S ratio = Budgeted contribution/ budgeted sales = 32,000/80,000 = 0.4

Break even sales = $\dfrac{\text{Fixed costs}}{\text{C/S ratio}} = \dfrac{15{,}000}{0.4}$ = 37,500

Margin of safety = 80,000 – 37,500 = 42,500. This is 53.125% of budgeted sales.

14.9 D   Contribution = profit + fixed cost. For line V, the part above the 0 line represents the profits made, and the part below the 0 line and the dashed line represents fixed costs, so the sum of these is the contribution.

14.10 C   Break even sales = $\dfrac{\text{Fixed costs}}{\text{C/S ratio}}$

Contribution = 70,000 – 42,000 = 28,000 ⇒ C/S ratio = $\dfrac{28,000}{70,000}$ = 0.4

Break even sales = $\dfrac{15,000}{0.4}$ = $37,500

14.11 B   Margin of safety = $\dfrac{\text{Budgeted sales} - \text{Break even sales}}{\text{Budgeted sales}} \times 100$

Break even sales = $\dfrac{\text{Fixed costs}}{\text{C/S ratio}}$

Fixed costs = contribution – profit = 70,000 – 42,000 – 15,000 = 13,000

Contribution = 70,000 – 42,000 = 28,000 ⇒ C/S ratio = $\dfrac{28,000}{70,000}$ = 0.4

Break even revenue = $\dfrac{13,000}{0.4}$ = $32,500

⇒ margin of safety = $\dfrac{70,000 - 32,500}{70,000}$ = 53.6%

14.12 D   Revenue required to achieve a profit = $\dfrac{\text{Profit required} + \text{Fixed cost}}{\text{C/S ratio}}$

Contribution = 90,000 – 63,000 = 27,000

Fixed cost = contribution – profit = 27,000 – 12,000 = 15,000

C/S ratio = 27/90 = 0.3

⇒ revenue required = $\dfrac{20,000 + 15,000}{0.3}$ = $116,667

14.13 B   Break even analysis can be used where more than one product is made. However, in this case, it is necessary to assume that the product mix is constant.

14.14 C   In order to ensure profits remain unchanged, contribution needs to remain unchanged.

Existing contribution = 70,000 – 42,000 = 28,000.

Variable costs per unit = 42,000 ÷ 10,000 = $4.20 per unit.

At new price of $8, contribution per unit would be $3.80 per unit

⇒ in order to ensure that total contribution remains the same, required sales volume = $\dfrac{28,000}{3.80}$ = 7,368 units

15 Relevant costing and decision making

15.1 A

	Service J	Service H	Service N
Contribution per unit	$45	$63	$78
Labour hours required per unit	1/2	2/3	5/6
Contribution per labour hour	$90	$94.50	$93.60
Ranking	3	1	2

15.2 C Modification = $7,200, hire costs avoided = $(19,800) and disposal costs = $4,000 and so the relevant cost is a saving of $8,600.

15.3 A Their net realisable value will, of course, depend on the manner in which they are to be disposed. It might be scrap value less any disposal costs or, if they could be sold for an alternative use once work has been carried out on them, the net realisable value will be selling price less the costs of the further work.

Option B is incorrect because replacement cost is not an appropriate relevant cost, as the units are no longer required.

Option C is incorrect because variable cost is only relevant in certain circumstances (if net realisable value is the same as variable cost).

Option D is incorrect because full cost includes absorbed fixed overheads, which are not relevant.

15.4 B If the in-house programmer is taken away from the M LLC project, the relevant cost would be:

	$
Lost revenue on M LLC	60,000
Less; additional costs on M LLC	(15,000)
Lost contribution on M LLC	45,000

Note. The salary costs of the programmer would be incurred regardless so have not been taken into account.

Taking the in-house programmer away from M LLC is less than hiring an external programmer for $80,000 so the external programmer would not be hired.

15.5 D (I) is incorrect because this term is used to describe a cost that will differ under some or all of the decision options.

II is incorrect because relevant costs can be expressed as opportunity costs.

Notional cost (III) is a hypothetical accounting cost used to reflect the benefit from the use of something for which no actual cash expense is incurred.

Sunk cost (IV) is a term used to describe a cost that has already been incurred or committed and which is therefore not relevant to subsequent decisions.

15.6 B The cost of special material which will be purchased is a relevant cost in a short-term decision-making context.

Costs already incurred are not relevant as whatever decision is taken, those costs cannot be recovered. A is not therefore a relevant cost.

Relevant costs do not include costs that would be incurred anyway, such as depreciation so C is not relevant. This is an example of a committed cost.

For materials, the original cost is never relevant (D). Either the replacement cost, if the materials are in regular use, or the opportunity cost (usually the scrap value) if they are not.

15.7 C

	Trouser
	$000
Sales price	14
Variable cost	8
Unit contribution	6
Labour hours per unit	2 hrs
Contribution per labour hour	3

15.8 D This is not an assumption in relevant costing.

15.9 A 400 of the units required are already in stock. They have no other use and if not used for this job, they could be sold. The opportunity cost of using these 400 units is therefore the sales revenue forgone. The remaining 300 units would have to be purchased. The relevant cost is therefore (400 × $20) + (300 × $60) = $26,000.

15.10 C

Cost of acquisition	$150,000
Cost of installation	$25,000
Less expected scrap proceeds	($10,000)
Relevant cost	$165,000

15.11 D

	A	B	C
	$	$	$
Contribution per unit	35	25	48
Labour hours per unit (cost ÷5)	8	5	6
Contribution per labour hour	4.375	5	8
Ranking	3	2	1

Production plan – 35,000 hours

	Hours
Produce 2,000 units C	12,000
Produce 4,600 units B	23,000 (to use the remaining 23,000 hours)
Produce 0 units of A	0

16 Modern approaches to management accounting

16.1 A This describes the purpose of activity based costing, not activity based management. Activity based management has a much broader purpose than costing – it aims to take the principles of activity based costing and apply them to managing the organisation more profitably.

B is correct. By eliminating activities that do not add value, and increasing the efficiency of activities that do, costs should be reduced without reducing the quality of products or services provided to customers.

C is correct. ABM is a continuous process.

D is correct. Employees will become involved in helping to identify the activities and drivers that is a necessary part of ABM.

16.2 D All three include the aim of eliminating activities that do not add value.

Activity based management involves managing the activities that an organisation performs, and reducing the cost of these, or eliminating those activities that are not adding any value.

Business process reengineering involves redesigning business processes to eliminate those processes that do not add any value.

Total quality management is a focus on providing what customers want and continuous improvement. In particular, eliminating defects.

16.3 A Only production time is spent doing something that the customer values.

While inspection time is important to ensure the products are of the right quality, it is the production of quality items, not the inspection, that the customers value.

Transfer time is time spent moving goods around the factory. It adds no value to customers.

16.4 C Process level. It supports a particular product or process, rather than a specific batch or specific unit of production.

16.5 C The theory of constraints can be used in any organisation where there is a sequence of steps that are followed – this could include service or manufacturing industries. All other statements are correct.

16.6 C

	Process 1	Process 2	Process 3
Total hours available	150,000	200,000	120,000
Hours per unit	2	4	3
Maximum weekly output	75,000	50,000	40,000

Process 3 has the lowest output per week of 40,000 units. Since this is less than demand of 45,000 units, it represents a bottleneck.

16.7 C Statement (i) is incorrect. Greater automation has increased the value of overhead costs.

Statements (ii) and (iii) are correct.

Exam Question Bank

EXAM QUESTION BANK

1   Which one of the following would be classified as indirect cost in a mobile phone manufacturing company?

   A   Wages of assembly workers on the production line
       These are direct costs

   B   Cost of mobile phone screens
       Direct costs

   C   Salary of factory supervisor
       This is the only indirect cost and correct answer

   D   Cost of speakers used in a phone
       Direct costs

2   For a manufacturing company the monthly direct materials cost is £20,000, direct labour cost is £40,000. The direct expenses are £25,000, production overheads are £10,000 while other overheads are £5,000. What is the prime cost for this company?

   A   £85,000

       Prime cost = Direct materials + Direct labour + Direct expenses. Therefore, (DM, 20,000 + DL, 40,000 + DE, 25,000)

   B   £95,000

       (20,000 + 40,000 + 25,000 + 10,000)

   C   £70,000

       (20,000 + 40,000 + 10,000)

   D   £60,000

       (20,000 + 40,000)

3   Which of the following best describes fixed costs?

   A   Constant per unit
       True for variable cost

   B   They are unaffected by inflation
       All costs are affected by inflation

   C   They are unaffected by management decisions
       Management decision would affect fixed costs

   D   Remain constant over wide ranges of activity
       This is the definition of fixed costs

4   When items of materials have reached their re-order point which of the following documents is initiated?

   A   Purchase order

   A document sent by the purchasing department to a supplier requesting that items listed are supplied.

   B   Purchase requisition

   A document issued by the stores department of a manufacturing organisation to the purchase department, requesting that inventories of an item are re-ordered.

   C   Goods received note

   A document prepared by the receiving section of the stores department when goods are delivered.

   D   Purchase invoice

   A commercial document presented to a buyer by a seller for payment within a stated period that indicates what has been purchased, in what amount and for what price.

5   A document sent by the purchasing department to a supplier requesting that items listed are supplied is called:

   A   Purchase order

   A document sent by the purchasing department to a supplier requesting that items listed are supplied

   B   Purchase invoice

   A commercial document presented to a buyer by a seller for payment within a stated period that indicates what has been purchased, in what amount and for what price.

   C   Sales invoice

   A sales invoice is a document that a company uses to communicate to clients about the sums that are due in exchange for goods that have been sold.

   D   Purchase requisition

   A document issued by the stores department for a manufacturing organisation to the purchase department, requesting that inventories of an item are re-ordered.

6   Which inventory costing method assigns the most recent costs incurred to closing inventory?

   A   LIFO

   This method assigns the oldest cost to closing inventory as it is assumed that items bought last were sold first.

   B   Average cost method

   This method assigns the average cost

   C   FIFO

   This assigns the most recent cost as the items bought first are assumed to have been sold first

   D   Standard cost method

   There is no method called standard cost method

7   A quality control supervisor is paid $11.20 per hour and has a normal working week of 37 hours. Overtime is paid at the basic rate plus 50 per cent. If in week 12, the supervisor worked 45 hours, the overtime premium paid would be?

Overtime premium

Basic rate		11.2
Premium	50%	5.6
Hours worked		45
Working week		37
Addition hours worked	(45 -37)	8
b. Correct answer 5.6 * 8		44.8
c. 11.2 * 8		89.6
d. 37 * 5.6		207.2
a. 5.6 + (11.2)* 8		134.4

8   An employee whose wages are regarded as direct cost is paid £11 per hour. The employee is contracted to work 40 hours per week and is entitled to 5 weeks paid holiday per year. The company's working year is 52 weeks. Calculate the inflated hourly rate after taking into account the holiday pay.

Base rate	11
Working week	40
Holiday entitlement (weeks)	5
Holiday Pay/week (11 * 40)	440
Holiday pay per year (440 × 5)	2200
Option (C) Hourly rate after Holiday pay (11 + 1.17)	12.17
Hours per year	1880
Weeks per year (excluding holiday)	47
Holiday pay per hour (2200/1880)	1.17
Option a) (this is the original rate)	11
Option b) 47 *11/52	9.94
Option d) 47 * (11+1.17)/52	10.04

9   The budgeted labour hours are 11,500 and budgeted overheads are £184,000. At the year end the actual labour hours worked are 7,520 while the actual overheads are £162,500. Calculate the amount of the overhead under-/over-absorbed.

   A   42,180   Under-absorbed

   184,000/11,500 = 16 overhead absorption rate

   Absorbed = 16 × 7,520 =120320 – actual (162500)

   B   42,180   Over absorbed

   Not correct as the actual are more than the absorbed

   C   63,680   Under-absorbed

   184,000 - 120320

   D   86,004   Over absorbed

   162,500/7520 = 21.60 (absorption rate)

   21.60 × 11500 = 248500 - 162500

EXAM QUESTION BANK

10   Urban Construction Ltd makes one product using a single process. Details of the process account for 2020 are:

	$
Materials cost-30,000 kg	60,000
Labour cost	24,000
Production overheads	11,400
Output	37,600
Normal losses	5%
Units produced	40,000

There was no work in progress at the beginning or end of 2020. Process losses are considered to have no value. What is the cost of the abnormal loss (to the nearest $)?

A $1068

[(60,000 + 24,000 + 11,400)/37,600)*0.95] = 2.67

(40,000 − 2000) − 37,600)* 2.67

B $1004

[(60,000 + 24,000 + 11,400)/40,000)*0.95]= 2.51

(40,000 − 2000) − 37,600)* 2.51

C $954

[(60,000 + 24,000 + 11,400)/40,000)]= 2.385

(40,000 − 2000) − 37,600)* 2.385

D $1015

[(60,000 + 24,000 + 11,400)/37,600)]= 2.537

(40,000 − 2000) − 37,600)* 2.537

11   A company manufactures a product using three processes, A, B & C. Process B had no opening inventory and 7,500 units of raw materials were transferred in from Process A at £3.50 per unit. Additional materials at £2.50 per unit were added in Process B. The labour and overheads costs are £7.50 per completed unit and £3 per unit incomplete. It is assumed that materials are fully complete in Process B. If 6,230 units were transferred to Process C, what is the value of closing inventory in Process B?

Opening inventory	0
Input	7500
Completed	6230
Per Unit Cost Input	3.5
Material	2.5
Labour & Overhead (Completed)	7.5
Labour & Overhead (Incomplete)	3
Closing inventory (6500 − 6230)	1270
Cost	
Material (3.5 + 2.5)	6
Labour & overheads	3

504

	Option a Value of closing inventory(1270*6+1270 *3)(a)	£11,430
	Option b (1270 * 3.5 + 1270* 3)	£8,255
	Option c (1270 * 7.5 + 1270*6)	£17,145
	Option d (6230*6 + 6230*3)	£56,070

- A £11,430
- B £8,255
- C £17,145
- D £56,070

12 A company manufactures office furniture. In March 2020 it produced a batch of 100 tables. The direct materials cost for this batch was $2,500, production overhead costs were $3,900 and direct labour cost was $4,200. Calculate the conversion cost per table.

A 64

3900/100 + 2500/100

B 106

4200/100 + 3900/100 + 2500/100

C 81

Conversion cost = Direct labour + production overheads
= 4200/100 + 3900/100

D 67

2500/100 + 4200/100

13 Alpha Ltd operates a process to jointly produce two products Beta and Gamma. Information (in units) relating to the two products for January 20X0 is as follows:

Product	Sales	Opening inventory	Closing inventory
Beta	3,500	200	500
Gamma	5,500	600	600

Joint production costs in January 20X0 were $130,000. Alpha Ltd apportion joint production costs on the basis of the number of units produced for a product. What were the joint production costs (nearest of $) apportioned to Product Beta for January 20X0?

A 52,317

Units produced = Beta = 3500 -200 = 3300
Gamma = 5500 – 600 = 4900
130,000 × 3300/(3300+ 4900)

B 51,485

Units produced = Beta = 3500 +500 = 4000
Gamma = 5500 – 600 = 6100
130,000 × 4000/(6100+ 4000)

C 47,816

Units produced = Beta = 3500 -300 = 3200
Gamma = 5500 – 0 = 5500
130,000 × 3200/(3200 + 5500)

D 53,118

Units produced = Beta = 3500 -200 + 500 = 3800
Gamma = 5500 – 600 + 600 = 5500
130,000 × 3800/(3800 + 5500) = 53118

14 A cost driver that is based on the number of times an activity is performed is known as:

A   Volume based cost driver

Assigning indirect costs that assume that a product's consumption of overheads is directly determined to the volume of units produced

B   Transaction driver

An activity cost driver that is based on the number of times that an activity is performed

C   Duration driver

An activity cost driver that is based on the amount of times required to perform an activity

D   Batch driver

An activity cost driver that is based on every time a batch of a product is produced

15 The budgeted production for Star Ltd is 20,000 units of a particular product. It requires 14,000 machine hours per year. However, the practical capacity for machine hours is 12,000 hours and 10,000 labour hours. The estimated manufacturing overhead cost for the year is $840,000. The cost driver rate per machine hour is:

A   60 (840,000/14,000)
B   42 (840,000/20,000)
C   70 (840,000/12,000)
D   84 (840,000/10,000)

16 For a high volume product in a traditional costing system which apportions overhead costs on the basis of volume will lead to:

A   The product being over-costed

This is because the cost driver is associated with the volume produced

B   The product being under-costed

Higher volume leads to higher cost being apportioned rather than lower

C   Neither over-costed nor under-costed

This is not correct as the cost driver is associated with the volume produced and it is a high volume product.

D   None of the above

17 A cost difference between a master budget cost and a flexible budget cost is called:

   A   Budget variance.

   A budget variance is the difference between the budgeted amount of expense or revenue, and the actual amount

   B   Spending variance.

   The variance that arises because of the difference in the budgeted and actual spending

   C   Flexible budget variance.

   This is the difference between flexible budget and actual output

   D   Planning variance.

   By definition, planning variance is equal to the difference between master budget and flexible budget.

18 A company manufactures a product, which requires 9kg of raw materials. The budgeted data relating to the next period is as follows:

	Units
Sales	17,000
Opening inventory of finished goods	6,000
Closing inventory of finished goods	5,000

	kg
Opening inventory of raw materials	35,000
Closing inventory of raw materials	15,000

What is the budgeted raw material purchases for next period (in kg)?

	Units
Sales	17,000
Opening inventory of finished goods	6,000
Closing inventory of finished goods	5,000
	kg
Opening inventory of raw materials	35,000
Closing inventory of raw materials	15,000
Raw material per product	9
Total required (17,000 × 9)	153,000
Budgeted production (17,000 + 5,000 – 6,000)	16,000
Correct answer (a) (16,000 × 9) + 15,000 – 35,000	**124,000**
b: (17,000 × 9)	153,000
c: (17,000 × 9) + 15,000 – 35,000	133,000
d: (16,000 × 9)	144,000

A   124,000
B   153,000
C   133,000
D   144,000

19 The budgeted materials cost for 20X0 for company X is £135,000 for the production of 30,000 units of product R. Each unit of product R requires 2kg of materials and the standard cost of materials is £2.5 per kg. To produce 33,000 units of product R, 57,000kg of materials were used which cost £145,500.

Calculate the materials price variance and indicate whether it is favourable or adverse.

33,000 units should have used	66,000
Actual used	57,000
Quantity variance (66,000 – 57,000)* 2.5	22,500

57,000 kgs @ £2.5 of material should have cost	£142,500
Actual cost	£145,500

Price variance (option d) (145,500 –142,500) 3,000 Adverse

A   3,000 F

Actual is more than budgeted so cannot be favourable

B   9,000 F

22,500/2.5

C   9,000 A

22,500/2.5

D   3,000 A

20 Root Ltd produces and sells cricket bats. The budgets sales and cost information for Root Ltd is given below:

Sales (1,000 bats @ $500 per bat)	$500,000
Variable cost	$200,000
Fixed cost	$60,000

How many cricket bats must be sold by Root Ltd in order for it to break even?

A   300

60,000/200

B   200

BEP = 60,000/(500 – 200)

C   260

(60,000 + 200,000)/1,000

D   400

200,000/500

21 A company manufactures and sells one product and it wishes to make a profit of $250,000 in 20X1. The selling price per unit is $30 and the variable cost per unit is $7.5. Total fixed costs are $75,000.

How many units (nearest whole number) need to be sold to achieve the target profit?

A   14,444

Target profit = 75,000 + 250,000/(30 – 7.5)

B   433,333

75,000 + 250,000/0.75 (contribution margin ratio) this is sales in value required.

C   3,333

75,000 /(30 – 7.5)

D   10,833

75,000 + 250,000/(30)

22 Stokes Ltd requires 50kg of raw material P for a contract it is evaluating. It has 30kg of material P in the warehouse which was purchased two months ago. Since then the purchase price of material P has risen by 10% to £22 per kg. Material P is used regularly by Stokes Ltd in normal production.

Calculate the total relevant cost of raw material P for the contract.

A   1,040 (30 × 20 + 20 × 22)
B   1,000 (50 × 20)
C   1,100 (22 × 50)
D   1,060 (30 × 22 + 20 × 20)

23 A company has purchased machinery at the cost of $1,000,000 three years ago. The useful life of this machinery is expected to be 5 years. This machinery can now be replaced at the cost of $1,100,000. The machinery currently makes a contribution of $20,000 per year but if used to manufacture another product it will generate a contribution of $25,000 per year. The sunk cost in respect of this machinery is:

A $600,000

This is the depreciation for the three years and is irrelevant cost. It is a notional cost and does not affect the cash flows

B $1,000,000

This cost has been incurred i.e. sunk cost

C $400,000

This is the unused value of the asset

D $1,100,000

Replacement cost

EXAM QUESTION BANK

24 For a company the following cost information is relevant for a product:

Time period	Output	Cost
Period 1	3,000	8,500
Period 2	4,500	15,000

Using the high-low technique, calculate the variable cost per unit (to the nearest two decimal points.

Option a (15,000 – 8,500)/ (4,500 – 3,000)	4.33
Option b 8,500/3,000	2.83
Option c 15,000/4,500	3.33
Option d (15,000 + 8,500)/ (4,500 + 3,000)	3.13

A 4.33
B 2.83
C 3.33
D 3.13

25 A company manufactures three products X, Y and Z. The following information is relevant for 20X0:

	X	Y	Z
Maximum demand (units)	3,000	6,500	4,000
	Per unit	Per unit	Per unit
Selling price	£38	£32	£25
Variable costs:			
Raw materials (£1 per kg)	4	2	3
Direct labour (£11 per unit)	12	9	18

The company predicts that it will have a shortage of raw materials and will not be able to produce all of the units demanded by the market. In what order should the materials be allocated to the three products if the company wants to maximise its profit?

	X	Y	Z
Maximum demand (units)	3,000	6,500	4,000
	Per unit	Per unit	Per unit
Selling price	£38	£32	£25
Variable costs:			
Raw materials (£1 per kg)	4	2	3
Direct labour (£11 per unit)	12	9	18
Contribution	22	21	4
Contribution per kg of materials	5.5	10.5	1.33
Ranking	2	1	3

	1st	2nd	3rd
A	Z	X	Y
B	X	Y	Z
C	Y	X	Z
D	Y	Z	X

26 Which one of the following costs are conventionally deemed to be constant per unit of output?

    A   Fixed costs
    B   Variable costs
    C   Mixed costs (semi-variable costs)
    D   Step fixed costs (semi-fixed costs)

27 Obtaining data about actual results and comparing it with the expected outcomes happens at which of following stages of planning, control and decision-making process?

    A   Control
    B   Planning
    C   Identifying objectives
    D   Searching for alternative courses of action

28 Which of the following is a characteristic of a revenue centre?

    A   The manager is accountable for costs and revenues
    B   The manager is accountable for profits only
    C   The manager is accountable for investments
    D   The manager is accountable for revenues only

29 A manager has 1,325 units of Part X135 in inventory. There are also 3,400 units of this part on order from a supplier. 437 units of Part X135 have been requisitioned but not yet issued. Calculate the free inventory balance.

    A   4,288
    B   1,325
    C   888
    D   4,725

30 Company ABC Ltd maintains the following information for Part PS398 which is used in the production of a number of different products:

Average usage	250	Per day
Minimum usage	90	Per day
Maximum usage	380	Per day
Minimum lead time for replenishment	8	Days
Maximum lead time for replenishment	12	Days
Re-order quantity	4,300	
Re-order level	4,200	

    Based on the above information what is maximum inventory?

    A   5,400
    B   3,940
    C   7,780
    D   5,500

31 Under IAS 2, which of the following inventory costing methods are not permitted?

   A   Average cost
   B   LIFO
   C   FIFO
   D   Periodic weighted average

32 Ping Ltd has planned to make 35,000 standard units of product PL123 during a budget period. In this period Ping Ltd has budgeted for 120,000 labour hours and each unit will take 3 hours to be completed.

   Actual output during the period was, 37,000 units which took 129,000 hours to make.

   Calculate the efficiency ratio (round to the nearest whole number)?

   A   108%
   B   93%
   C   81%
   D   86%

33 A direct-machine hour basis to allocate overheads is appropriate in which of the following manufacturing environments?

   A   Labour-intensive
   B   Machine-intensive
   C   When all units produced take the same amount of time
   D   Just-in-time

34 ALG Ltd manufactures laptop bags, Product XZ378. The following budgeted information is available for Product XZ378:

	$
Selling price	100
Direct material	25
Direct labour	15
Units produced and sold	10,000
Total number of purchase requisitions	2,500
Total number of set ups	400
Number of purchase requisitions for XZ378	1,200
Number of set ups for XZ378	240

   Overheads

Purchases	1,400,000
Machine set ups	1,200,000

   Calculate the budgeted cost per unit for Product XZ378 using activity-based costing.

   A   179.20
   B   164.20
   C   154.20
   D   40.00

35 ML2 Ltd uses process costing to value its output and all materials are considered input at the start of the process to manufacture product P321. The following information relates to the process for one quarter.

	Units
Input	7,500
Opening stock	364
Losses	5%
Closing stock	740

Calculate the output from the process if actual losses were the same as normally expected in the process?

A 7,864
B 8,604
C 7,124
D 6,749

35 Java Ltd makes one product using a single process. Details of the process account for 2021 are:

	$
Materials cost-24,000 kg	72,000
Labour cost	32,500
Production overheads	17,600
Output	42,000
Normal losses	3%
Units	56,000
Total cost	122,100

Taking into account the normal losses, calculate the per unit cost.

A 2.18
B 2.25
C 2.90
D 2.99

37 Cai Ltd uses FIFO method of process costing. At the end of a weak, the following information was available for process Delta:

	Units
Opening WIP	2,500
Closing WIP	1,300
Transferred to next process	4,375

Calculate the number of units started and completed during the period.

A 5,575
B 6,875
C 3,075
D 5,675

38 Beyond budgeting approach to budgeting in contemporary organisations calls for:

    A   Activity based budgeting
    B   Fixed budgeting
    C   Zero-based budgeting
    D   Abandoning budgeting altogether

39 Zabaleta Ltd produces products, X321 and Y456 from a joint process. Both products can be sold individually after completion. For the month of September 2020 there were no opening inventories or work in process. The following data is available for September 2020:

	$		
Total joint production costs	336,000		
Product	Production units	Sales units	Selling price per unit
Y451	14,000	10,000	15
X321	15,000	10,000	10

Using the sales value method of apportioning joint production costs, calculate the value of the closing inventory of product X321 for September 2020.

    A   46,570
    B   81,667
    C   57,931
    D   40,000

40 A cost driver that assumes that a product's consumption of overheads is directly determined by the volume of units produced is known as:

    A   Transaction driver
    B   Duration driver
    C   Batch driver
    D   Volume based cost driver

41 Smith Ltd is a car manufacturing company. As part of its manufacturing process, it uses a type of computer chips in the manufacturing of all its cars. However, there are shortages of computer chips in the international market at the moment, making production as the limiting budgetary factor for Smith Ltd. To prepare their budget for 2023 the company expects sales demand to be 50,000 cars but they can only acquire computer chips for the manufacturing of 35,000 cars.

Which of the following budgets should be prepared first by Smith Ltd for 2023:

    A   Sales budget
    B   Machine hours budget
    C   Production budget
    D   Labour hours budget

42 Woakes Ltd is a manufacturing company which uses standard costing. The budgeted material cost is $175,000 for the production of 35,000 units per month. Each unit produced is budgeted to use 2.5 kgs of material. The standard cost of material is $3.50 per kg.

Actual materials in the month cost $195,000 for 43,000 units and 103,000 kgs were purchased and used.

What was the favourable material usage variance?

A $8,000
B $15,750
C $11,250
D $4,500

43 A favourable labour efficiency variance could indicate which of the following?

A Motivated employees producing output more quickly
B Lost time in excess of standard allowed
C Lack of training
D Equipment used and the working conditions are of lower quality

44 Hamilton Ltd manufactures safety gear for racing car drivers. The wages budget for 2020 was based on a standard time of 72 minutes per helmet and a standard wage rate of $17.60 per hour.

At the end of the budget period, the following information was reported:

Number of helmets produced   61,000
Labour rate variance (adverse) $ 5,600
Labour efficiency variance   Nil

Calculate the actual wage rate.

A $17.60
B $10.89
C $17.52
D $17.68

45 A company manufactures two products X and Y. The company currently uses full cost pricing and wishes to make a profit of 25% on full production costs. Overheads are absorbed on the basis of direct labour hours. Product Y is labour intensive as compared to product X. Currently, the price of product X is $218.60 and product Y is $238.50. The company has recently carried out an analysis of its production support activities and found out that its fixed costs actually vary in accordance with non-volume related activities such as, set ups, materials handling and inspection. The company has also established that product X uses most of these non-volume related activities.

If the company moves to activity-based pricing, which one of the following will happen:

A Price of product Y will increase
B Price of product X will increase
C Prices of both products will be unchanged
D Price of product X will decrease

46 Whitty Manufacturing produces thermometers which it sells for $24 each. The contribution to sales ratio for each thermometer is 30%. The company's monthly break-even point is sales of $30,000.

Calculate the profit in Week 30 when 1,700 thermometers are sold.

A $3,240
B $7,560
C $8,568
D $1,190

47 Xi Manufacturing Ltd manufactures laptop screens. The skilled employees are paid $20 per hour. All of the skilled labour is fully employed manufacturing a special type of touch screens. The following data is available:

	$ per unit	$ per unit
Selling price		215
Less		
Variable costs:		
Skilled labour	100	
Others	25	
		(125)
		90

Xi Manufacturing Ltd is evaluating a contract for producing anti-glare touch screens which require 450 skilled labour hours to complete. Skilled labour is in short supply and no other supplies are available at the moment.

Calculate the total relevant skilled labour cost of the contract.

A $9,000
B $17,100
C $40,500
D $29,250

48 ABC Ltd manufactures two products, Alpha and Beta. The sales demand and the standard unit selling prices and costs for 2022 are estimated as follows:

	Alpha	Beta
Maximum demand	6,500	8,500
Selling price	28	22
Variable costs:		
Raw materials ($2 per kg)	6	10
Direct labour ($15 per hour)	30	45
Machine hours ($1 per hour)	2	3

If supplies are restricted to 63,000 kgs of raw material, 37,000 hours of direct labour and 27,000 hours of machine time.

The limiting factor would be:

A   Machine hours
B   Raw materials
C   Both machine hours and labour hours
D   Direct labour hours

49 In activity-based management approach, the costs that are caused by the production of a single product or delivery of a single unit of service are classified as:

   A   Batch level costs
   B   Product/process level costs
   C   Unit level costs
   D   Organisation/facility costs

50 Rooney Ltd manufactures footballs which it sells to amateur football clubs. The variable cost per football is £18. The company's total weekly fixed costs are £17,000 and the contribution to sales ratio is 40%.

   This week Rooney Ltd plans to manufacture and sell 4,500 footballs. What is the margin of safety for Rooney Ltd (in number of units)?

   A   3,083
   B   1,417
   C   2,700
   D   1,800

51 Conversion cost is:

   A   All costs incurred in the production of a product
   B   The sum of direct labour and manufacturing overheads
   C   The material cost of a product
   D   All direct manufacturing costs

52 Superleague Ltd manufactures footballs. Its weekly direct materials cost is $6,000, direct labour cost is $18,000. The direct expenses are $15,000, production overheads are $8,000 while other overheads are $3,000. What is the prime cost for this company?

   A $39,000
   B $47,000
   C $32,000
   D $24,000

53 Which inventory costing method assigns the oldest costs to the cost of goods sold?

   A   LIFO
   B   Average cost method
   C   Standard cost method
   D   FIFO

54 Alpha manufactures office chairs. The safety inventory level of raw materials is 2,000 pieces of wood. The reorder quantity is 14,000. The current market demand is 10,000 chairs per month. Calculate the average inventory.

   A   9,000
   B   16,000
   C   12,000
   D   8,000

EXAM QUESTION BANK

55 Secure Lock Ltd manufacture door handles. It maintains the following information for Part SL138 which is used in the production of a number of various types of door handles:

Average usage	550	Per day
Minimum usage	120	Per day
Maximum usage	800	Per day
Minimum lead time for replenishment	4	Days
Maximum lead time for replenishment	7	Days
Re-order quantity	5,000	
Re-order level	8,000	

Based on the above information what is the minimum level of inventory?

    A   12,520
    B   6,280
    C   4,97
    D   7,400

56 Beta Ltd produces T-shirt and pays its employees $10 per piecework hour. In a 37-hour week employee John Simpson produces the following output for Week 13:

Product	Units Produced	Piecework time allowed per unit
T-Shirt M	4	3 hours
T-Shirt W	6	7 hours

Calculate John Simpson's pay for Week 13.

    A $370
    B $540
    C $420
    D $470

57 An employee produces 32 units of product A in an 8-hour working day. In a 5-day working week the employee worked for 40 hours and produced 128 units of product A. The decrease in output is caused only by idle time. Calculate the idle time ratio (round your answer to the nearest whole number).

    A   25%
    B   27%
    C   80%
    D   20%

58 JK Ltd is a machine intensive manufacturing company. It uses machine hours to allocate its manufacturing overheads to products. The budgeted machine hours for June 20X2 are 16,000 and budgeted overheads are £80,000. At the end of the month the actual machine hours worked are 10,400 while the actual overheads are £62,400. Calculate the amount of the overhead under-/over-absorbed?

    A   £42,180 Over-absorbed
    B   £10,400 Under-absorbed
    C   £28,000 Under-absorbed
    D   £10,400 Over-absorbed

59 An activity cost driver that is based on the amount of time required to perform an activity is known as:

   A   Duration driver
   B   Volume based cost driver
   C   Transaction driver
   D   Batch driver

60 Tech Ltd manufactures burglar alarms for customers' orders. It has three production departments Designing, Manufacturing and Assembly, which have overhead absorption rates per labour hour. Tech Ltd has received an order from a commercial customer to manufacture an alarm system. Direct cost and absorption rates for this job are as follows:

	AlarmC123
Direct material	$450
Direct labour hours	
Designing	40
Manufacturing	16
Assembly	10
Absorption rate per labour hour	
Designing	$9
Manufacturing	$7
Assembly	$4

Labour rate per hour	Designing	Manufacturing	Assembly
	$20	$14	$11

Calculate the total cost for job AlarmC123.

   A $2,096
   B $1,410
   C $962
   D $1,316

61 NetworkRoad is a construction company. One of its contracts RD345NW commenced on 1 February 20X2. NetworkRoad has the following data for this contract:

Contract price	$4,000,000.
Value certified	$3,000,000.
Cash received	$800,000.
Costs incurred	$2,000,000.
Cost of work certified	$1,800,000.

Calculate the profit to date for this contract (round your answer to the nearest whole number).

   A $391,111
   B $177,778
   C $355,556
   D $213,333

62 XYZ manufacturing makes one product using a single process. Details of the process account for 2022 are:

	$
Materials cost-32,000 kg	128,000
Labour cost	54,000
Production overheads	28,000
Output units	64,000
Normal losses	8%
Units produced	90,000

There was no work in progress at the beginning or end of 2022. Process losses are considered to have no value. What is the cost of the abnormal loss (round your answer to the nearest whole number)?

- A $67,052
- B $47,681
- C $43,867
- D $61,688

63 AlphaVac Ltd manufactures two types of vaccines, AVac1 and AVac2. It operates a process to jointly produce two products AVac1 & AVac2. Information (in units) relating to the two vaccines for December 20X2 is as follows:

Product	Sales	Opening inventory	Closing Inventory
AVac1	18,500	4,000	1,800
AVac2	34,600	10,000	6,000

Joint production costs in December 20X2 were $460,000. AlphaVac Ltd apportions joint production costs on the basis of the number of units produced for a product. What were the joint production costs (nearest of $) apportioned to AVac2 in December 20X2?

- A $170,588
- B $153,333
- C $300,128
- D $158,561

64 McCullumB Ltd manufactures badminton equipment. The output of the manufacturing process consists of two joint products, ReckL and ReckS and a by-product SD. ReckS could go through a further process to make it more appealing to customers and increase its sales value. To assist the production manager of McCullumB Ltd in making the decision whether to carry out further processing, which one of the following is relevant for the decision whether or not to further process ReckS?

- A The share of the total cost that has already been allocated to ReckS
- B The sales value of ReckL
- C The sales value of product SD
- D Further processing cost for ReckS and the increase in the sales value that will result from further processing

65 The budgeted production for Moon Ltd is 52,500 units of product PXLM. It requires 16,500 machine and 24,000 labour hours per year. The estimated manufacturing overhead costs for the year is $264,000. However, the practical capacity for labour hours is 22,000 hours. The cost driver rate per labour hour is:

A 16
B 5
C 11
D 12

66 Klusener Ltd manufactures washing machines. The production manager is preparing the production budget for June 20X2. The opening stock of product WM305 is 7,500 units and the company normally maintains a closing stock of 3,000 units. The sales quantity expected for June 20X2 is 15,000 units.

Calculate the quantity to be produced in June 20X2.

A 4,500 units
B 25,500 units
C 10,500 units
D 19,500 units

67 Manne is the production manager of division SW in a company which has 3 other divisions. Manne receives monthly information that compares actual and budgeted expenditures as well as revenues for division SW. From division SW products are transferred to distribution centres prior to being dispatched to customers. The selling prices are set by Manne but decisions involving capital expenditures at SW are taken at the head office of the company.

Which of the following describes Manne's role in division SW?

A An investment centre manager
B A profit centre manager
C A cost centre manager
D A revenue centre manager

68 Malan Ltd manufactures cardboard boxes and uses standard costing. The budgeted material cost is $16,000 for the production of 32,000 boxes per month. Each box produced is budgeted to use 1 kgs of material. The standard cost of material is $2 per kg.

Actual materials in the month cost $24,000 for 18,000 cardboard boxes while 46,000 kgs were purchased and used.

What was the material price variance?

A $68,000 Adverse
B $68,000 Favourable
C $56,000 Favourable
D $28,000 Adverse

69 A favourable material price variance accompanied by an adverse materials usage variance could indicate which of the following?

A Low quality materials purchased at lower prices
B Efficient use of materials
C Purchase of good quality materials at higher prices
D Equipment used and the working conditions are of good quality

70 ComfyFoot produces shoes. The budgeted sales and cost information for ComfyFoot is given below:

Sales (20,000 pairs @ $50 per pair) $1,000,000
Variable cost $600,000
Fixed cost $96,000

How many pairs of shoes must be sold by ComfyFoot in order for it, to break even?

A   3,200
B   20,000
C   12,000
D   4,800

71 Yonghua Ltd manufactures binoculars. Budgeted information for September 20X2 is given below:

Selling price per unit   £65
Variable cost per unit   £25
Fixed production costs   £180,000
Fixed selling and administrative costs £120,000
Sales   24,000 units

Calculate the margin of safety as a percentage of sales (round your answer to the nearest whole number).

A   31%
B   69%
C   62%
D   220%

72 SmartTablets Ltd requires 300kg of raw material ST11W to fulfil a customer order for 300 tablets. It has 40kg of material ST11W in the warehouse which were purchased three months ago. Since then the purchase price of material ST11W has risen by 25% to $40 per kg. Material ST11W is used regularly by SmartTablets Ltd in normal production. If the material is not used for this order it will be used for another product that will make a contribution of $2 per kg of ST11W.

Calculate the total relevant cost of raw material ST11W for the order under consideration.

A   12,600
B   20,800
C   9,600
D   9,920

73 A company that has purchased manufacturing equipment at the cost of $750,000 five years ago. The useful life of this equipment is expected to be 12 years. When the equipment was purchased the company also paid $48,000 for maintenance and servicing for 12 years. This machinery can now be replaced at the cost of $1,200,000. The machinery currently makes a contribution of $430,000 per year but if used to manufacture another product it will generate a contribution of $500,000 per year.

The sunk cost in respect of this machinery is:

A $312,500
B $798,000
C $437,500
D $1,200,000

74 LMN Ltd manufactures a single product. The production and cost data for the last three months is given below:

Month	Production units	Total cost $
1	1,300	80,000
2	1,100	56,000
3	1,800	90,000

The variable cost per unit is unchanged if the production is below 2,200 units per month. However, if production goes above 1,400 units per month, the fixed costs increase by $8,000.

Calculate the total cost if 1,200 units are produced in a month.

A $78,000
B $80,000
C $82,000
D $70,000

75 A commercial document presented to a buyer by a seller for payment within a stated period that indicates what has been purchased, in what amount and for what price is called:

A Purchase order
B Sales invoice
C Purchase invoice
D Purchase requisition

76 Tactical management accounting information is used by:

A Senior managers
B Middle managers
C Front-line managers
D Operational employees

77 Which one of the following costs are fixed but only within certain levels of activity?

A Step fixed costs (semi-fixed costs)
B Variable costs
C Mixed costs (semi-variable costs)
D Fixed costs

78 Which inventory costing method assigns the oldest costs to the closing inventory?

A Average cost method
B Standard cost method
C FIFO
D LIFO

79 An employee is paid $13.20 per hour and has a normal working week of 40 hours. Overtime is paid at the basic rate plus 50 per cent. If in week 6, the employee worked 48 hours, the overtime premium paid would be (round your answer to 2 decimals):

A $52.80
B $105.60
C $264.00
D $158.40

80 A commercial document presented to a buyer by a seller for payment within a stated period that indicates what has been purchased, in what amount and for what price is called:

    A   Purchase order
    B   Purchase requisition
    C   Purchase invoice
    D   Goods received note

81 LMN Ltd manufactures 1,500 components at an even rate during a year. Each order placed with the supplier is for 500 components, which is the economic order quantity. LMN Ltd holds a buffer inventory of 300 components. The annual cost of holding one component of inventory is $5.

What is the total annual cost of holding inventory of the component?

    A $4,000
    B $2,750
    C $2,500
    D $7,500

82 A system that converts a production schedule into a listing of the materials and components required to meet that schedule, so that adequate stock levels are maintained and items are available when needed, is referred to as:

    A   Economic Order Quantity (EOQ)
    B   Two-bin system
    C   Just-in-time (JIT)
    D   Material requirements planning (MRP)

83 Alpha manufactures toy cars. In January 2023 it produced a batch of 1,000 toy cars. The direct materials cost for this batch was $3,300, production overhead costs were $2,400 and direct labour cost was $7,200.

Calculate the conversion cost per toy car.

    A $5.70
    B $9.60
    C $12.90
    D $10.50

84 Finny Ltd operates a job costing system. The company absorbs overheads at the rate of $6.00 per machine hour. Finny Ltd is preparing a quote for a potential customer for job number FIN202. The company's policy is to add a mark-up of 40% to the production cost when preparing price estimates. Job FIN202 will have the following requirements:

Direct materials	$13,450
Direct labour	$18,750
Machine hours	350

Calculate the price that should be provided in the quotation.

    A $47,180
    B $45,080
    C $54,880
    D $34,300

85 The budgeted production for Discovery Ltd is 30,000 units of ProductD3. The budgeted machine hours are 8,000 and budgeted labour hours are 16,000 hours per year. The actual machine hours were 20,000 hours and 10,000 labour hours. The estimated manufacturing overhead cost for the year is $640,000.

Calculate the overhead absorption rate per labour hour.

A $40
B $80
C $32
D $64

86 Cai Processing Ltd manufactures crayons and uses process costing to value its materials used in manufacturing. All materials are input at the start of the process. The following information relates to the process for one week:

Input	8,000
Opening Stock	1,500
Normal Losses	10%
Closing stock	1,200
Actual losses	800

How many good units were output from the process if actual losses were 800 units?

A   7,700
B   6,930
C   7,200
D   7,500

87 Wang Ltd manufactures a single product WJ. In January 2022 the opening inventory for WJ was 14,400 units and closing inventory was 18,100 units. The profit based on marginal costing was $60,350 and profit using absorption costing was $70,450. Calculate the fixed overhead absorption rate per unit (round your answer to two decimal points).

A $4.89
B $2.73
C $3.89
D $3.33

88 A cost difference between flexible budget and actual results is called:

A   Budget variance
B   Spending variance
C   Flexible budget variance
D   Planning variance

89 Zhang Ltd uses marginal costing and generated a profit of $73,500 in 2022. The opening inventory was 9,535 units and the closing inventory was 7,350 units. Zhang Ltd uses machine hours to absorb overheads and the overhead absorption rate is $5.

Calculate the profit using absorption costing.

A $84,425
B $75,685
C $62,575
D $71,315

EXAM QUESTION BANK

90 In an Activity Based Costing (ABC) system, overhead costs driven by the number of batches would be an example of:

A Product level activities
B Product sustaining activities
C Facility sustaining activities
D Batch level activities

91 XYZ Ltd manufactures a single pet food product. The product requires 5kg of raw materials. The budgeted data relating to the next period is as follows:

	Units
Sales	25,000
Opening inventory of finished goods	7,500
Closing inventory of finished goods	3,000
	kg
Opening inventory of raw materials	44,000
Closing inventory of raw materials	8,000

Prepare the raw material purchase budget for next period (in kg).

A 125,000
B 89,000
C 102,500
D 66,500

92 Jia Ltd uses standard costing. The details for March 2023 were as follows:

Budgeted output	25,000	Units
Budgeted labour hours	100,000	Hours
Budgeted labour cost	$900,000	
Actual output	20,000	Units
Actual labour hours paid	102,000	Hours
Productive labour hours	96,000	Hours
Actual labour cost	$1,020,000	

Calculate the labour efficiency variance.

A $220,000 Favourable
B $160,000 Adverse
C $160,000 Favourable
D $220,000 Adverse

EXAM QUESTION BANK

93 Conway plc uses standard costing. The following data is available for April 2022:

	Budget	Actual
Output and sales (units)	11,300	16,000
Selling price per unit	$15	$14
Variable cost per unit	$8	$8

The sales price variance for April 2022 was:

A $16,000 Favourable
B $16,000 Adverse
C $65,800 Favourable
D $70,500 Adverse

94 In a standard costing system which of the following standards is based on perfect operating conditions:

A Attainable standards
B Ideal standards
C Current standards
D Basic standards

95 HaydonM is a manufacturing company which produces ironing boards. As part of its manufacturing process, it uses a special type of machine for welding. However, there are shortages of electricity due to which machine hours are restricted to 1,000 hours per month. The sales demand is 5,000 ironing boards but the machine hours will only allow the manufacturing of 4,000 ironing boards. Labour hours are available to manufacture 4,100 ironing boards.

Which of the following is a limiting factor?

A Machine hours
B Sales demand
C Production capacity
D Labour hours

96 Cook Ltd is a manufacturer of kettles. The variable cost per kettle is $28. The company's total weekly fixed costs are $46,000 and the contribution to sales ratio is 30%.

Cook Ltd plans to manufacture and sell 5,500 kettles.

Calculate the break-even point in revenue (round your answer to whole number).

A $3,833
B $107,333
C $66,000
D $153,333

97 LingTV assembles TVs. The price per TV is $700 and the variable cost is $300. Fixed costs for 2022 were $450,000. LingTV wants to make a minimum profit of $150,000.

Calculate the number of TVs required to be sold to achieve the target profit (round your answer to whole number).

A 1,125
B 1,500
C 857
D 1,050,000

98 Buttler plc is evaluating a sales order. The sales order requires 2,500kg of raw material KL23. The company currently has 1,300kg of material KL23, which was purchased at $20 per kg. Due to supply chain issues, the price of material KL23 has increased by 50% since it was last purchased by Buttler plc. Material KL23 is used regularly by the company in production.

Calculate the total relevant cost of raw material KL23 for the sales order under consideration.

- A $75,000
- B $62,000
- C $50,000
- D $63,000

99 KLM Ltd bought an asset for $140,000 five years ago. The machine can be used for another five years and it is expected to generate future revenues of $50,000. The scrap value of the machine is $15,000. If KLM Ltd were to replace the machine with another one in the same condition, it would cost the company $40,000.

What is the deprival value of the machine for KLM Ltd?

- A $140,000
- B $40,000
- C $70,000
- D $50,000

100 Oasis Ltd manufactures three products Basic, Intermediate and Premium. The following information is relevant for 2023:

	Basic	Intermediate	Premium
Maximum demand (units)	6,000	12,000	3,000
	Per unit	Per unit	Per unit
Selling price	$44	$58	$96
Variable costs:			
Raw materials ($2 per kg)	8	12	16
Direct labour ($12 per unit)	12	18	24

The company predicts that for 2024, labour hours, which is used by all three products, will be restricted to 84,000 hours.

In what order should the labour hours be allocated to the three products, if Oasis Ltd wants to maximise its profit?

	1st	2nd	3rd
A	Premium	Basic	Intermediate
B	Basic	Premium	Intermediate
C	Intermediate	Premium	Basic
D	Premium	Intermediate	Basic

101 Which of the following is an example of a strategic planning decision?

- A Setting sales targets for the upcoming month
- B Determining the optimal product pricing strategy
- C Allocating overhead costs to different departments
- D Monitoring the budget variance for a specific project

102 Which of the following is the first step in the decision-making process?

    A   Identifying the problem or opportunity
    B   Evaluating alternatives
    C   Implementing the decision
    D   Monitoring and reviewing the decision

103 Which of the following statements best describes variable costs?

    A   Costs that remain constant regardless of the level of activity
    B   Costs that increase in steps as the level of activity changes
    C   Costs that cannot be easily traced to specific cost objects
    D   Costs that fluctuate in direct proportion to the level of activity

104 Gardens Ltd manufactures garden furniture and it has 4,250 garden tables outstanding for existing customers' orders. Garden Ltd has 2,950 tables in inventory and the free inventory of tables is 7,250 units. Calculate the units on order.

    A   8,550
    B   7,200
    C   14,450
    D   11,500

105 Which of the following is the correct sequence of steps in the procurement ordering procedure?

    A   Purchase requisition, purchase order, purchase invoice
    B   Purchase invoice, purchase requisition, purchase order
    C   Purchase order, purchase requisition, purchase invoice
    D   Purchase requisition, purchase invoice, purchase order

106 For company ALM the cost of holding one item of inventory is $45. The cost of ordering 500 items is $2,500 and the total demand is 15,000 units.

Calculate the Economic Order Quantity (EOQ) for ALM.

    A   577
    B   520
    C   367
    D   212

107 Marsh Ltd's stock purchases for Week 30 in 2022 were as follows:

Day	Price per unit ($)	Units purchased
1	4	60
2	6	120
3	7	160
4	8	200
5	9	250

Assuming there was no stock at the beginning of the week and 630 units were issued to production.

Using first in, first out (FIFO) method of inventory valuation, calculate the value of closing stock for Marsh Ltd.:

A 640
B 1,200
C 1,280
D 1,440

108 Boland Manufacturing Ltd incurred the following costs in April 2023. Direct materials cost is £65,000, direct labour cost is £90,000. In April 2023, the direct expenses are £43,000, production overheads are £27,000 while other overheads are £13,000.

What is the prime cost for Boland Manufacturing Ltd?

A £211,000
B £198,000
C £168,000
D £155,000

109 An employee whose wages are regarded as direct cost is paid £14 per hour. The employee is contracted to work 37 hours per week and is entitled to 4 weeks paid holiday per year. The company's working year is 50 weeks. Calculate the inflated hourly rate after taking into account the holiday pay (round your answer to two decimal places).

A 15.22
B 14.00
C 12.88
D 12.96

110 DN Ltd specialises in manufacturing door numbers. DN Ltd has three in-house departments, Designing, Manufacturing and Assembly. In all of the three departments use labour hours to absorb overheads. Direct cost and absorption rates for job DNH23 are as follows:

	DNH23
Direct material	650
Direct labour hours	
Designing	5
Manufacturing	4
Assembly	2
Absorption rate per labour hour	
Designing	$10
Manufacturing	$6
Assembly	$5

Labour rate	Designing	Manufacturing	Assembly
	$13	$10	$9

Calculate the total cost for job DNH23.

A $857
B $723
C $734
D $805

111 Alpha is a building construction company which is working on a project that commenced on 1 February 2020. Alpha has the following data for this contract:

Contract price	$6,000,000
Value certified	$7,000,000
Cash received	$900,000
Costs incurred	$4,000,000
Cost of work certified	$1,900,000

Calculate the profit to date for this contract (round your answer to the nearest whole number).

A $351,429
B $257,143
C $171,429
D $437,143

112 HG Ltd manufactures various sports equipment and it operates a job costing system. The company absorbs overheads at the rate of $10.00 per labour hour. HG Ltd is preparing a quote for a potential customer. HG Ltd.'s policy is to add a mark-up of 60% to the cost when preparing price estimates. The following information is relevant for this job:

Direct materials	$14,750
Machine hours	$28,500
Direct labour hours	600

Calculate the price that should be provided in the quotation.

A $75,200
B $69,200
C $78,800
D $49,250

113 NEOM manufactures uPVC windows and doors. The budgeted production for NEOM is 7,500 units of product GP23. The budgeted machine hours are 16,000 and budgeted labour hours are 32,000 hours per year. The actual for machine hours 40,000 hours and 20,000 labour hours. The estimated manufacturing overhead cost for the year is $1,280,000.

Calculate the overhead absorption rate per labour hour.

A $40
B $80
C $32
D $64

EXAM QUESTION BANK

114 Ping Ltd produces two types of fruit shoots STRA1 and RASB1. It operates a process to jointly produce two products STRA1 & RASB1. Information (in units) relating to the two products for December 20X2 is as follows:

Product	Sales	Opening inventory	Closing Inventory
STRA1	20,500	8,000	2,500
RASB1	36,800	12,000	5,000

Joint production costs in March 2023 were $840,000. Ping Ltd apportions joint production costs on the basis of the number of units produced for a product. What were the joint production costs (nearest of $) apportioned to STRA1 in March 2023.

A $281,501
B $298,148
C $281,250
D $558,750

115 Bayes Ltd manufactures a single product and the budgeted production for 2023 is 24,000 units of product BAY1. BAY1 requires 12,000 machine and 8,000 labour hours per year. The estimated manufacturing overhead costs for the year is $240,000. However, the practical capacity for labour hours is 5,000 hours and for machine, it is, 10,000 hours.

The cost driver rate per machine hour is:

A $30
B $20
C $10
D $24

116 Cummins Ltd manufactures office chairs. In the first quarter of 2023 the sales expected are 24,000 units. It is the company's policy to maintain a closing stock level of 1,500 units. The opening stock at the beginning of the first quarter was, 3,500 units.

Calculate the quantity to be produced in the first quarter of 2023.

A 29,000
B 22,500
C 22,000
D 26,000

117 In budgetary control, the difference between a master budget cost and a flexible budget cost is called:

A Budget variance
B Spending variance
C Planning variance
D Flexible budget variance

118 The marginal costing profit for Ping Ltd in 2023 is $84,300. The opening inventory was 11,300 and the closing inventory was 3,400. Ping Ltd uses direct labour hours to absorb overheads and the overhead absorption rate is $9 per labour hour.

Calculate the difference in profit between absorption costing and marginal costing.

A $53,700
B $92,200
C $71,100
D $76,400

119 In an Activity Based Costing (ABC) system, an activity cost driver that is based on the number of times that an activity is performed is known as:

   A   Batch driver
   B   Volume based cost driver
   C   Duration driver
   D   Transaction driver

120 Jerry Ltd produces a single soft drink product. The soft drink is sold in a pack of 6 bottles. Each batch requires 6 kg of sugar. The budgeted data relating to the next period is as follows:

	Units
Sales	50,000
Opening inventory of finished goods	15,000
Closing inventory of finished goods	6,000
	kg
Opening inventory of raw materials	88,000
Closing inventory of raw materials	16,000

   Prepare the raw material purchase budget for sugar for the next period (in kg).

   A   300,000
   B   228,000
   C   246,000
   D   174,000

121 The budgeted materials cost for 2022 for company LMN is $270,000 for the production of 60,000 units of product Alpa1. Each unit of product Alpha1 requires 4kg of materials and the standard cost of materials is $5 per kg. To produce 66,000 units of product Alpha1, 114,000kg of materials were used which cost $290,000.

   Calculate the materials price variance and indicate whether it is favourable or adverse.

   A $150,000 Favourable
   B $150,000 Adverse
   C $280,000 Favourable
   D $280,000 Adverse

122 Tong Ltd is a book publisher. The budgets sales and cost information for Tong Ltd is given below:

Sales (20,000 books @ $25 each)	$500,000
Variable cost	$120,000
Fixed cost	$240,000

   How many books must be sold by Tong Ltd in order for it to break even? (Round your answer to whole number).

   A   40,000
   B   12,632
   C   9,600
   D   20,000

123 In a standard costing system, as standard which assumes that it should be attainable under efficient operating is referred to as:

A Attainable standards
B Ideal standards
C Current standards
D Basic standards

124 Ali Ltd manufactures bicycle parts and the budgeted information for January 2023 is given below:

Selling price per unit	$130
Variable cost per unit	$50
Fixed production costs	$360,000
Fixed selling and administrative costs	$240,000
Sales (units)	48,000
Target profit	$120,000

Calculate the margin of safety in units.

A 55,500
B 40,500
C 72,000
D 120,000

125 Travis plc has purchased a manufacturing equipment at the cost of $750,000 five years ago. The useful life of this equipment is expected to be 20 years. When the equipment was purchased Travis plc also paid $96,000 for maintenance and servicing for 15 years. This machinery can now be replaced at the cost of $1,600,000. The machinery currently makes a contribution of $860,000 per year but if used to manufacture another product it will generate a contribution of $1,000,000 per year.

The opportunity cost in respect of the manufacturing equipment is:

A $1,600,000
B $1,000,000
C $860,000
D $846,000

Exam Answer Bank

EXAM ANSWERS BANK

1	C	The distractors, options a, b & d are incorrect because all of them represent direct costs
2	A	The distractors, options b, c & d use wrong workings.
3	D	The distractors, options a, b & c provide wrong definition for fixed costs.
4	B	The distractors, options a, c & d provide definition for other documents.
5	A	The distractors, options b, c & d provide definition for other documents.
6	C	The distractors, options a, b & d are not true in the case of FIFO.
7	B	The distractors, options a, c & d use wrong workings.
8	C	The distractors, options a, b & d use wrong workings A company uses labour hours to allocate its manufacturing overheads to products.
9	A	The distractors, options b, c & d use wrong workings.
10	B	The distractors, options a, c & d use wrong workings.
11	A	The distractors, options b, c & d use wrong workings.
12	C	The distractors, options a, b & d use wrong workings.
13	D	The distractors, options a, b & c use wrong workings
14	B	The distractors, options a, c & d provide definitions of other drivers.
15	C	The distractors, options a, b & d use wrong drivers to calculate the rate.
16	A	The distractors, options b, c & d provide incorrect explanations.
17	D	The distractors, options a, b & c provide definitions of other types of variances.
18	A	The distractors, options b, c & d use wrong workings.
19	D	The distractors, options a, b & c use wrong workings.
20	B	The distractors, options a, c & d use wrong workings.
21	A	The distractors, options b, c & d use wrong workings.
22	C	The distractors, options a, b & d use wrong workings.
23	B	The distractors, options a, c & d do not meet the criteria of sunk cost.
24	A	The distractors, options b, c & d use wrong workings.
25	C	The distractors, options a, b & d incorrectly rank the products.

26 B **Distractors**

The distractors, options a, c & d are incorrect because they have fixed costs included in them. Fixed costs decrease proportionally with the level of activity and will not remain constant per unit of output.

C1: LO 9

27 A **Distractors**

Options b, c & d are incorrect, as they are part of the planning stage in the decision-making process.

C1: LO 8

28	D	**Distractors**	

Options a, b & c provide wrong definition for profit and investment centre.

C1: LO 9

29 A Free inventory balance = Materials in inventory (1,325) + materials on order (3,400) − materials requisitioned (437) = 4,288.

Distractors

Options b, c & d provide use wrong formulae to calculate the balance. They inaccurately account for material requisitioned.

C2: LO 10

30 C Maximum Inventory (7,780) = re-order level (4,200) + re-order quantity (4,300) − (minimum usage (90) * minimum lead time (8))

Distractors

Options a, b & d use wrong formulae to calculate the maximum inventory. They inaccurately use maximum usage and average use in the calculation.

C2: LO 10

31 B **Distractors**

Options, a, c & d are permitted for inventory valuation under IAS 2.

C2: LO 9

32 D Efficiency ratio = ((37,000 * 3)/129,000) ×100 = 86%

Distractors

Options a, b & c use wrong formulae to calculate efficiency ratio. They inaccurately use budgeted hours and standard units in calculation.

C2: LO 10

33 B **Distractors**

Options a, c and d are not appropriate environments to use direct-machine hours as the basis to allocate overheads.

C2: LO 10

34 A Cost per unit:

Direct cost (25+15)	40
Overheads/Purchases allocated ((1,400,000/2,500)*1,200))/10,000	67.20
Overheads/Set ups allocated ((1,200,000/400)*240))/10,000	72.00
Total cost per unit (40+67.20+72.00)	179.20

Distractors

Options b, c and d use wrong working to calculate the cost per unit. They use inaccurate drivers for overhead calculations.

C3: LO 10

35 D

	Units
Opening stock	364
Input	7,500
	7,864
Closing stock	(740)
Normal losses (7,500 * 5%)	(375)
Output	6,749

Distractors

Options a, b and c use wrong working to calculate the cost per unit. The treatment of closing stock is inaccurate.

C3: LO 10

36 B Unit cost = ((72,000+32,500+17,600))/56,000)/(1-.03)=2.25

Distractors

Options a, c & d use wrong workings. The incorporation of normal losses in the calculation is inaccurate.

C3: LO 10

37 C Opening WIP (2,500) + Units introduced (4,375)- Closing (1,300)= 5,575 -2,500 = 3,075

Distractors

Options a, b & d use wrong workings. The treatment of opening and closing stock is inaccurate.

C3: LO 10

38 D **Distractors**

Options a, b & c do not define the beyond budgeting concept.

C5: LO 11

39 A

Sales value of production:
Y451	210,000
X321	150,000
	42
Amount apportioned to product X321 (336,000 × 0.42)	40,
	141,120
%of X321 in closing inventory	33%
X321's production in inventory	46,570

Distractors

Options b, c & d use wrong workings. The options use amount apportioned and closing inventory inaccurately in the calculations.

C3: LO 9

40	D	Assigning indirect costs that assume that a product's consumption of overheads is directly determined by the volume of units produced

Distractors

Options a, b & c provide definitions of other drivers. i.e. transaction, duration and batch drivers.

C4: LO 11

41	C	Budget for the limiting factor is produced first. Production is the limiting budgetary factor in this scenario.

Distractors

Options a, b and d are incorrect as the limiting factor budget is the first to be prepared.

C4: LO 11

42	B	43,000 units should have used (43,000 *2.5) 107,500 kg of material but the actual is 103,000 kg. variance = (107,500 – 103,000) * $3.5 = $15,750

Distractors

Options b, c & d use wrong workings. They inaccurately ignore using standard cost in the calculation.

C4: LO 11

43	A	**Distractors**

Options a, b and d are incorrect as they are not the factors which could lead to increased labour efficiency.

C4: LO 11

44	D	(61,000 helmets should have cost = 61,000 * 1.2*17.60 = $1,288,320, Actual cost = $1,288,320 plus adverse labour variance $5,600) = $1,293,920. Therefore, the actual wage rate = $1,293,920/(61,000 * 1.2) = $17.68

Distractors

Options a, b & c use wrong workings. The use of standard time in these and actual production is inaccurate.

C4: LO 11

45	B	This is because more of the non-volume related activities costs will be allocated to product X, increasing its cost and therefore the price.

Distractors

Options a, c & d are incorrect, as they will not necessarily lead to a higher cost for Product X.

C5: LO 11

46	A	(Break-even point in units =$30,000/24 = 1,250 thermometers Contribution per unit = $24 *0.30 = $7.2 Profit when 1,700 units are sold = (1,700 -1,250)*7.2 = $3,240.

Distractors

Options b, c & d use wrong workings. The use of BEP is incorrect in these calculations.

C5: LO 11

EXAM ANSWERS BANK

| 47 | B | The relevant cost of the skilled labour is the hourly wage rate is $20 plus the lost contribution of $18 per hour ($90/5) giving $38 per hour. Therefore, the total relevant labour cost of the contract is: $38*450 = $17,100 |

Distractors

Options a, c & d use wrong workings as not all relevant costs are included in the calculations.

C5: LO 11

| 48 | D | |

	Alpha	Beta	Total
Maximum demand	6,500	8,500	
Material in kgs	19,500	42,500	62,000
Labour hours	13,000	25,500	38,500
Machine hours	9,750	17,000	26,750

The total labour hours requirement to meet the demand is 38,500 hours which is more than the maximum available i.e. 27,000 hours. For both Machine hours and Direct material, enough capacity is available to meet the demand. Therefore, option 'D' is the correct answer.

Distractors

Options a, b & c are not correct choices as they incorrectly apply the limiting factor concept.

C5: LO 11

| 49 | C | It is the definition of unit level costs. |

Distractors

Options a, b & d are not caused by product level changes.

C5: LO 11

| 50 | A | The selling price per unit is =18/0.6 = £30
Contribution per unit = £30*.4 = 12
Break even point = 17,000/12 = 1,417 units
Margin of safety = 4,500 – 1,417 = 3,083 |

Distractors

Options b, c & d use wrong workings in terms of BEP and contribution

C5: LO 11

| 51 | B | **Distractors** |

The distractors, options a, c & d are incorrect because these do not define conversion costs.

C1: LO 8.

| 52 | A | Prime cost = Direct materials + Direct labour + Direct expenses. |

Therefore, prime cost is: $39,000 [6,000 + 18,000 + 15,000].

Distractors

Options b, c & d are incorrect, as they use incorrect workings to calculate prime cost. These wrong answers include overheads in the calculations.

C1: LO 8.

53	D	FIFO assigns the oldest cost as the items bought first are assumed to have been sold first.

Distractors

Options a, b & c show wrong as they don't assign the oldest cost to the cost of goods sold.

C2: LO 9.

54	A	Average inventory = Safety inventory + ((1/2)*reorder quantity).

Average inventory = 2,000 + (0.5*14,000) = 9,000.

Distractors

Options b, c & d use wrong formulae to calculate average inventory.

C2: LO 10.

55	C	Minimum level of Inventory (4,975) = re-order level (8,000) – (average usage (550)* average lead time (5.5)).

Distractors

Options a, b & d use wrong formulae to calculate the minimum level of inventory. They inaccurately use minimum usage and average use in the calculation.

C2: LO 10.

56	B	Weekly pay = piecework hours*rate of pay

$= (4 \times 3 + 6 \times 7) \times 10 = \$540$.

Distractors

Options, a, c & d use wrong numbers to calculate the pay. Option a = 37*10, c = 7*6*10, d = (37 + 3 + 7)*10

C2: LO 9.

57	D	Idle time ratio = (idle hours/total hours) × 100.

Based on normal production rate the employee should have produced 160 (5 × 32) units of product A but they only produced 128 units i.e. 32 units less than the normal expected. Therefore, the employee remained idle for 8 hours as the normal production rate is 32 units in an 8 hour-working day. Therefore, idle time ratio = (8/40)*100 = 20%.

Distractors

Options a, b & c use wrong formulae to calculate idle time. Option a = 32/128*100, c = 128/160*100.

C2: LO 10.

58	B	80,000/16,000 = 5 overhead absorption rate.

Overheard Under-absorbed = 5 × 10,400 = 52,000 – actual (62,400) = £10,400.

Distractors

Options a, c and d use wrong workings to calculate the under-absorbed overhead. Option a = 52,000 – 10,400, c = 80,000 – 52,000, d, correct calculation but wrong understanding.

C2: LO 10.

EXAM ANSWERS BANK

| 59 | A | An activity cost driver that is based on the amount of time required to perform an activity is known as duration driver in the activity-based costing system. |

Distractors

Options b, c and d do not provide the correct definition for a duration activity cost driver.

C5: LO 11.

| 60 | A | Total cost = 450 + (40*9 + 16*7 + 10*4) + (40*20 + 16*14 + 10*11) = $2,096. |

Distractors

Options b, c and d use wrong working to calculate the cost per unit. c = 450 + (40*20 + 16*10), c = 450 + (40*9 + 16*7 + 10*4), d = 450 + (40*9 + 20) + 16*(7 + 14) + 10*(20 + 11)

C3: LO 10.

| 61 | D | Profit to date = 2/3 × notional profit (3,000,000 – 1,800,000) × 800,000 (cash received)/ 3,000,000 (value of work certified). |

Distractors

Options a, b and c use wrong working to calculate the profit to date. Option a = **2/3 × (4,000,000 – 1,800,000) × 800,000/3,000,000, b = 2/3 × (3,000,000 – 2,000,000) × 800,000/3,000,000, c =2/3 × (4,000,000 – 2,000,000) × 800,000/3,000,000**

C3: LO 10.

| 62 | B | [(128,000 + 54,000 + 28,000)/(90,000*0.92)] = 2.53623188. |

Normal losses value = 90,000 × 8% = 7,200.

Abnormal losses value = (90,000 – 7,200) – 64,000)*2.53623188 = $47,681.

Distractors

Options a, c & d use wrong workings. The incorporation of normal losses in the calculation is inaccurate.

C3: LO 10.

| 63 | C | Units produced = AVac1 = 18,500 – 4,000 + 1,800 = 16,300. |

AVac2 = 34,600 – 10,000 + 6,000 = 30,600.

Costs apportioned to AVac2 = 460,000 × 30,600/(16,300 + 30,600) = $300,128.

Distractors

Options a, b & d use wrong workings. The treatment of opening and closing stock is inaccurate.

C3: LO 10.

| 64 | D | As only this option represents the relevant variables for the decision. |

Distractors

Options a, b & c do not outline the relevant costs and revenues for the given scenario.

C3: LO 10.

EXAM ANSWERS BANK

65 D 264,000/22,000 = 12

Distractors

Options a, b & c use wrong bases to calculate the cost driver rate.

C4: LO 11.

66 C 15,000 – 7,500 + 3,000 = 10,500.

Distractors.

Options a, b and d are incorrect as they use wrong formulae to calculate production budget. Option a = 7,500 – 3000, b = **15,000 + 7,500 + 3,000, d = 15,000 + 7,500 – 3000**

C4: LO 11.

67 B As the given scenario highlights the key attributes of a profit centre.

Distractors

Options a, c & d do not apply to this situation as they define other types of responsibility centres.

C4: LO 11.

68 B 46,000 units should have cost (46,000*2) 92,000 but the actual cost is 24,000. Variance = (92,000 – 24,000) = $68,000 Favourable

Distractors

Options b, c & d use wrong workings. Option b uses correct calculations but wrong application and understanding, c = (46,000 – 18,000)*2, d = 46,000 – 18,000

C4: LO 11.

69 A Purchasing lower quality material at a lower price will lead to favourable price variance but more material will be used, which leads to an adverse usage variance.

Distractors

Options b, c and d are incorrect as they are not the factors which could lead to favourable price as well as adverse usage variance.

C4: LO 11.

70 D BEP = 96,000/(50 – 30) = 4,800. Variable cost = 600,000/20,000 = 30

Distractors

Options a, b & c use wrong workings. Options a = 96,000/30, b = 100,000/50, c = 600,000/50

C5: LO 11.

71 B

Budgeted contribution per unit	£40.00
BEP (180,000 + 120,000)/40	7,500
Margin of safety in units (24,000 – 7,500)	16,500
Margin of safety in % (16,500/24,000)	69%

Distractors

Options a, c & d are incorrect, as they use wrong workings to calculate the margin of safety. Option a = 24,000/7,500, c = 65/70, d = 7,500/16,500

C5: LO 11.

72	A	Relevant cost = 300 × 40 + 2*300 = 12,600.

Distractors

Options b, c & d include irrelevant costs in the calculations. i.e. the cost for items already in stock and old price

C5: LO 11.

73	B	The original purchase price and the service charges paid represent sunk cost.

Distractors

Options a, c & d use wrong workings as not all relevant costs are included in the calculations.

C5: LO 11.

74	D	Since the variable costs are constant in the given product ranges, fixed costs at the highest and lowest activity can be compared to derive the variable cost per unit. i.e. 10,000/500 = 20. Total fixed costs at 1,800 = 90,000 – 36,000 = 54,000. Total cost at 1,200 units = 54,000 – 8,000 + 1,200*20.

Distractors

Options a, b & c are not correct choices as they use incorrect workings. Option a = 90,000 – (1800 – 1200)*20, b = 1200*20 + 56000, c = 80,000 + (1200 – 1100)*20

C5: LO 11.

75	C	A commercial document presented to a buyer by a seller for payment within a stated period that indicates what has been purchased, in what amount and for what price.

Distractors

Options a, b & d do not provide the correct definition for a purchase invoice.

C2: LO 9.

76	B	Anthony's management hierarchy states that middle managers use tactical management accounting information.

Distractors

The distractors, options a), c) & d) are incorrect because according to Anthony's management hierarchy, senior managers use strategic information and front-line managers and employees use operational information.

C1: LO 8.

77	A	As step fixed costs are fixed but only within certain levels of activity.

Distractors

The distractors, options b), c) & d) do not provide the correct definition for step fixed costs.

C1: LO 8.

78	D	FIFO assigns the oldest cost as the items bought first are assumed to have been sold first.

Distractors

Options a) is incorrect as it assigns the average cost to the closing inventory, b) Standard costing is not used in inventory valuation c) FIFO assigns the newest (most recent) cost to the closing inventory and the oldest cost to the cost of sales.

C2: LO 9.

| 79 | A | Overtime premium = (48-40) *[(13.20) *0.50)]. |

Distractors

Options b), c) & d) use wrong workings: b (13.20*8), c (13.2*.50) *40, d [(48-40) *(13.20 + (13.2)*.5)].

C2: LO 10.

| 80 | C | As purchase invoice is a commercial document presented to a buyer by a seller for payment within a stated period that indicates what has been purchased, in what amount and for what price. |

Distractors

Options a), b) & d) do not define a purchase invoice.

C2: LO 10.

| 81 | B | Annual holding cost= Buffer inventory (300 + (EOQ (500/2)) * $5 = 550 * 5 = $2,750. |

Distractors

Options a), c) & d) use wrong numbers to calculate the total holding costs: a = (300 + (500)) * $5, c = 500* $5, d = 1,500 *$5.

C2: LO 10.

| 82 | D | This option provides the accurate definition for MRP as outlined by CIMA. |

Distractors

Options a), b) & c) refer to other management accounting concepts.

C2: LO 10.

| 83 | B | $9.60: (7,200/1000 + 2,400/1000) = $9.6. |

Distractors

Options a), c) and d) use wrong workings to calculate the conversion cost. a.5.70 (2400/1000 + 3300/1000, c 12.90, (7200/1000 + 3300/1000 + 2400/1000), d.10.50 (3300/1000 + 7200/1000).

C2: LO 9.

| 84 | A | |

	$
Direct materials	13,450
Direct labour	18,750
Prime cost	32,200
Production overheads	2,100
Mark-up	12,880
Estimated Price	$47,180

Distractors

Options b), c) and d) use wrong workings. b (32,200 + 32,2008*40%), c (32,200 + 2,100)*60% + 32,200 + 2,100), d(32,200 + 2,100).

C5: LO 10.

EXAM ANSWERS BANK

85 A Overhead absorption rate = 640000/16,000.

Distractors

Options b), c) and d) use wrong working to calculate the cost per unit. b (640,000/8,000), c (640,000/20000), d (640,000/10,000).

C3: LO 10.

86 D 7,500.

Opening Stock	1,500
Input	8,000
	9,500
Closing stock	(1200)
Actual Losses	(800)
	7,500

Distractors

Options a), b) and c) use wrong working to calculate the output. a) = 8,000 + 1,200 – 1500 = 7,700, b) = 7,700 – (7,700*10%), c) = 8,000 – (8,000*10%).

C3: LO 10.

87 B Movement in inventory (units)= 18,100 – 14,400 = 3,700. Difference in profit = ($70,450 - $60,350) = $10,100. 10,100/3,700 =$ 2.73.

Distractors

Options a, c & d use wrong workings. a) = 18,700/3,700, c) = 14,400/3,700, d) = 60,350/18,100.

C3: LO 10.

88 C As flexible budget variance is the difference between flexible budget and actual output.

Distractors

Options a, budget variance is the difference between the budgeted amount of expense or revenue, and the actual cost, b Spending variance is the difference between the actual amount of a particular expense and the expected (or budgeted) amount of an expense d, a planning is the difference between the original flexed budget and the revised flexed budget.

C3: LO 11.

89 C Difference in profits = (9,535 – 7,350) * $5 = $10,925.

Therefore, absorption costing profit = $73,500 – 10,925 = $62,575

Distractors

Options a, b & d use wrong workings. a (73,500 + 19,925), b ((9,535 – 7,350)+ $73,500), d (73,500 –(9,535 – 7,350).

C3: LO 10.

90 D As only this option correctly identifies batch related costs.

Distractors

Options a, b & c outline other types of activities In ABC hierarchy.

C4: LO 10.

EXAM ANSWERS BANK

91   D

Raw material per product	5
Total required (25,000 × 5)	125,000
Budgeted production (25000 + 3000 -7,500)	20,500
Correct answer (20,500× 5 + 8000 - 44000	66,500

Distractors.

Options a), b) & c) use wrong bases to calculate the cost driver rate.

Option a (25,000 × 5)	125,000
Option b (25,000 × 5) + 8000 - 44000	89,000
Option 3 (20,500 × 5)	102,500

C4: LO 11.

92   C   (20,000*4)- 96,000]*$10.

Distractors

Options a, b and d are incorrect. a & d (use labour hours paid rather than productive labour hours. b, shows wrong application).

C4: LO 11.

93   B   (16,000 × 15) – (16,000× 14).

Distractors

Options a), c) & d) are not correct. Option a shows wrong application, option c) and d) inaccurately use actual price and quantity respectively in calculations.

C4: LO 11.

94   B   As ideal standards are based on perfect operating conditions.

Distractors

Options b), c) & d) do not provide the definition for ideal standards.

C4: LO 11.

95   A   As machine hours is the limiting budgetary factor in this scenario.

Distractors

The distractors, options b), c) and d) are not limiting factors.

C5: LO 11.

96   D   BEP revenue = 46,000/0.3

Distractors

Options a), b) & c) use wrong workings. a is BEP in units, b (3,833 × 28), c (12 (CM)* 5,500).

C5: LO 11.

EXAM ANSWERS BANK

97 B Sales required to = (450,000+150,000)/0.5714)= 1,050,000/700.

Distractors

Options a), c) & d) are incorrect, as they use wrong workings to calculate the required number of units, a (450,000/400), c (450,000+150,000)/700, d is the sales value required.

C5: LO 11.

98 A Relevant cost = a. $75,000 (2,500 x 30) as the only relevant cost is the current price i.e. 20*1.5.

Distractors

Options b), c) & d) include irrelevant costs in the calculations. b) $62,000 (1,300 x 20 + 1,200 × 30), c) $50,000 (2,500 × 20), d) $63,000 (1,300 × 30 + 20 × 1,200).

C5: LO 11.

99 B $40,000 (lower of the replacement cost and future revenues (higher of NRV and expected revenues).

Distractors

Options a), c) & d) do not provide the accurate definition of deprival value of an asset.

C5: LO 11.

100 A

	Basic	Intermediate	Premium
Maximum demand (units)	6000	12000	3000
	Per unit	Per unit	Per unit
Selling price	$44	$58	$96
Variable costs:			
Raw materials ($2 per kg)	8	12	16
Direct labour ($12 per unit)	12	18	24
Labour hours used	1	1.5	2
Labour hours available	84,000		
Contribution	$24.0	28.00	$56.0
Contribution per labour hour	$24.0	$18.7	$28.0
Ranking	2	3	1

Distractors

Options B C & D do not rank the production on the basis of contribution made per labour hour.

C2: LO 11.

EXAM ANSWERS BANK

101 B Determining the optimal product pricing strategy, is the correct answer because it aligns with the definition of a strategic planning decision. Strategic planning decisions involve long-term considerations and determining the overall direction and positioning of the organization.

Distractors

A Setting sales targets does not specifically relate to strategic planning decisions. It is more closely associated with operational planning.

C This option is more related to the allocation of costs and budgeting within departments, rather than strategic planning decisions.

D Monitoring budget variance is part of the control process and does not directly involve strategic planning decisions.

C1: LO 8.

102 A It is the stage where a problem or an opportunity is identified, and there is a recognition that a decision needs to be made to address the situation.

Distractors

B This step involves generating and assessing various alternatives or options to address the identified problem or opportunity. It includes considering different courses of action and evaluating their potential outcomes.

C This step involves putting the chosen alternative into action. It includes planning and executing the necessary steps to implement the decision effectively.

D This step involves tracking the implementation of the decision and evaluating its outcomes. It includes assessing whether the decision achieved the desired results and making any necessary adjustments or improvements.

C1: LO 8.

103 D Variable costs vary in direct proportion to the level of activity. As the activity level increases, variable costs increase, and as the activity level decreases, variable costs decrease.

Distractors

A This describes fixed costs rather than variable costs. Fixed costs do not change with changes in the level of activity.

B This describes stepped costs. Stepped costs are fixed over a specific range of activity levels and then increase in a step-like manner when the activity level exceeds certain thresholds.

C This describes indirect costs or common costs rather than variable costs. Variable costs can be directly attributed to specific cost objects or activities.

C2: LO 8.

104 A Free Inventory balance = units in inventory + units on order − units ordered, but not yet issued.

Units on order = Free inventory (7,250) + units ordered (4,250) − units in inventory (2,950)
Units on order =8550

Distractors

B = 4,250 + 2,950 = 7,200:
C = 7,250 + 4,250 + 2,950 = 14,450
D = 4,250 + 7,250 = 11,500

C2: LO 10.

EXAM ANSWERS BANK

105 C The procurement process usually begins with a purchase order, which is a legally binding document issued by the buyer to the supplier. The purchase requisition comes after the purchase order and serves as the initial request for goods or services. Finally, the purchase invoice is received from the supplier to request payment for the provided goods or services.

Distractors

A, B and D do not describe the correct procurement ordering procedure.

C2: LO 9.

106 B $$EOQ = \sqrt{\frac{2DC_o}{C_{Ho}}}$$

$$= \sqrt{\frac{2 \times 15,000 \times 45}{5}}$$

Distractors

$$A = \sqrt{\frac{2 \times 15,000 \times 500}{45}}$$

$$C = \sqrt{\frac{15,000 \times 45}{5}}$$

$$D = \sqrt{\frac{2 \times 2,500 \times 45}{5}}$$

C2: LO 10.

107 D Closing stock value = (790−630) * $9.

Distractors

A = (790−630) *60.
B = (790−630) *7.50.
C = (790−630) *200.

C2: LO 10.

108 B (65,000 + 90,000 + 43,000) = £198,000.

Distractors

A = 65,000 + 90,000 + 43,000 + 13,000,
C = 65,000 + 90,000 + 13,000 12.90,
D = 65,000 + 90,000.

C2: LO 9.

109 A

Base rate	14
Hours in a working week	37
Holiday entitlement (weeks)	4
Holiday pay per week (37*14)	518
Holiday pay per year (4* 518)	2,072
Hours per year (37*46)	1,702
Weeks per year (excluding holiday)	46
Holiday pay per hour (2072/1702	1.22
Total working weeks in a year	50
Hourly rate after holiday pay (14+1.22)	15.22

Distractors

B = it's the base rate £14.
C = (14*46/50.
D = (14 *46 + 4)/50.

C5: LO 10.

110   A   Total cost = 650 + (5*10 + 4*6 + 2*5) + (5*13 + 4*10 + 2*9) = $857.

Distractors

B = 650 + (5*13 + 8).
C = 650 + (5*10 + 4*6 + 2*5),
D = 650 + (5*10 + 13) + 4*(10 + 6) + 2*(5 + 9).

C3: LO 10.

111   D   Profit to date = 2/3 × notional profit (7,000,000 – 1,900,000) × 900,000 (cash received)/7,000,000(value of work certified).

Distractors

A = 2/3 × (6,000,000 – 1,900,000) × 900,000 /7,000,000.
B = 2/3 × (7,000,000 – 4,000,000) × 900,000 /7,000,000.
C = 2/3 × (6,000,000 – 4,000,000) × 900,000 /7,000,000.

C3: LO 10.

112   A

	$
Direct materials	14,750
Machine hours	28,500
Prime cost	43,250
Production overheads	6,000
Mark-up	25,950
Estimated Price	$75,200

Distractors

B = (43,250 + 43,250*60%),
C = (43,250 +6,000)*60% + 43,250 + 6,000),
D = (43,250 + 6000).

C3: LO 10.

113   A   Overhead absorption rate = 1,280,000/32,000.

Distractors

B = (1,280,000/16,000),
C = (1,280,000/40000),
D = (1,280,000/20,000).

C3: LO 10.

EXAM ANSWERS BANK

114 C Units produced = STRA1 = 20,500 − 8,000 + 2,500 = 15,000.
RASB1 = 36,800 −12,000 + 5,000 = 29,800.
Costs apportioned to STRA1= 840,000 × 15,000/(15,000+ 29,800) = $281,250.

Distractors

A = Units produced = STRA1 = 20,500 − 8,000 = 12,500
RASB1 = 36,800 −12,000 = 24,800
840,000 × 12,500/(12,500+ 24,800) = $281,501.

B = Options a= Units produced = STRA1 = 20,500 +2,500 = 22,500
RASB1 = 36,800 +5,000 = 41,800
840,000 × 22,500/(22,500+ 41,800) = $298,148.

D = Units produced = STRA1 = 20,500 − 8,000 + 2,500 = 15,000
RASB1 = 36,800 −12,000 + 5,000 = 29,800

Costs apportioned to STRA1= 840,000× 29,800/(15,000+ 29,800) = $558,750.

C3: LO 10.

115 D =240,000/10,000.

Distractors

A = 240,000/8,000.
B = 240,000/12,000.
C = 240,000/24,000.

C4: LO 11.

116 C 24,000 − 3,500 + 1,500 = 22,000.

Distractors.

A = 24,000 + 3,500 + 1,500,
B = 24,000 - 1,500,
D = 24,000 + 3,500 - 1,500.

C4: LO 11.

117 C A planning variance is the difference between the original flexed budget and the revised flexed budget

Distractors

A Budget variance is the difference between the budgeted amount of expense or revenue, and the actual cost,

B Spending variance is the difference between the actual amount of a particular expense and the expected (or budgeted) amount of an expense,

D Flexible budget variance is the difference between flexible budget and actual output.

C4: LO 11.

118 C Difference in profits = (11,300 − 3,400) * $9 = $71,100.

Distractors
A, B and D use wrong workings.
A (84,300 − (3,400)*9,
B (11,300 − 3,400) + 84,300,
D 84,300 − (11,300 − 3,400) .

C3: LO 11.

119 D   An activity cost driver that is based on the number of times that an activity is performed.

Distractors

A   Batch driver is an activity cost driver that is based on every time a batch of a product is produced.

B   Volume-based cost driver is determined to the volume of units produced.

C   An activity cost driver that is based on the amount of times required to perform an activity.

C4: LO 11.

120 D

Raw material per product	6
Total required (50,000× 6)	300,000
Budgeted production (50000 + 6000 -15000)	41000

Correct answer (41,000 × 6) + 16000- 88000 = 174,000

Distractors

A	= (50,000 × 6)	300,000
B	= (50,000 × 6) – 88000 +16000	228,000
C	= (41,000 × 6)	246,000

C4: LO 11.

121 C

114,000 kgs of material should have cost	
(114,000 × 5)	$570,000
Actual cost	$290,000
	$280,000 (Favourable)

Distractors

A and B =

66,000 units should have used	264000
Actual used	114000
Quantity variance	$750,000 favourable

D   Actual spent on materials is less than the budgeted so it's not adverse.

C4: LO 11.

122 B   = 240,000/(25-6(w1).
W1= 120,000/20,000

Distractors

A   240,000/6
C   =240,000/25
D   =500,000/25

C5: LO 11.

EXAM ANSWERS BANK

123 A Attainable standards are based on the assumption that standard costs should be attainable under efficient operating conditions.

Distractors

B As ideal standards are based on perfect operating conditions.

C These are based on current working conditions.

D Basic Standards are the unaltered standards which are used over for a longer period of time and do not reflect current conditions.

C4: LO 11.

124 B BEP = (360,000+240,000)/(130-50)
Margin of safety = 48,000-7,500

Distractors

A = 48,000 + 7,500,
C = 120,000 – 48,000.
D = 360,000 – 240,000.

C5: LO 11.

125 B The potential contribution foregone is the opportunity cost.

Distractors

A = replacement cost,
C = current contribution.
D = 750,000 +96,000.

C5: LO 11.

EXAM ANSWERS BANK

Mock exam 1
questions and answers

MOCK EXAM 1 QUESTIONS

1. What type of information is primarily internal, detailed, and produced frequently and regularly?

    A   Strategic information
    B   Tactical information
    C   Operational
    D   Tactical and operational

2. The following expenses are incurred by a manufacturing company:

    (i)   Employment costs of production supervisors
    (ii)   Rent of the factory
    (iii)   Salaries of the accounting staff

    Which of the above items are production overheads?

    A   (i) and (ii)
    B   (i) and (iii)
    C   (ii) and (iii)
    D   (i), (ii) and (iii)

3. A company operates a process costing system. Last month, opening WIP consisted of 200 units that were 30% complete. 3,000 units were started during the month. Closing WIP was 250 units that were 40% complete.

    The company uses a FIFO method of valuing work in progress. What were equivalent units of production during the period?

    A   2,910
    B   2,990
    C   3,000
    D   3,050

4. A budgeting process that requires managers to ignore previous year's budgets and start by identifying and justifying all activities or items on expenditure in the budget is described as:

    A   Incremental budgeting
    B   Rolling budgets
    C   Continuous budgeting
    D   Zero based budgeting

5. Aye Company is considering a proposed one-off contract. This will require 1,000 kg of Material D. Aye Company does not use Material D in its other activities but does have 400kg in the warehouse left over from another contract. This had cost $7.50 per kg. If not used in the contract, the material could be sold to company Bee, who would pay $5.00 per kg. The current market price of Material D is $9.00 per kg.

    What is the relevant cost of the material needed for the project?

    A $7,400
    B $7,500
    C $8,400
    D $9,000

6 At the end of last month, an electronics company reported a favourable labour efficiency variance of $2,000, representing 5% of the budgeted labour cost for the month.

Which of the following is unlikely to be a reason for the variance?

A The standard time per unit was increased at the start of the month because of complaints that it had been unachievable.

B A major service of the machines in the previous month meant that budgeted machine breakdowns, which had been allowed for in the standard, did not occur.

C Workers were offered a bonus related to efficiency gains.

D A lower grade of labour was used which meant the wage rate was below the standard.

7 Which of the following best describes a by-product?

A A product produced at the same time as other products which has a relatively low volume compared with the other products.

B A product produced at the same time as other products which requires further processing before it can be sold.

C A product produced at the same time as other products which has a relatively low sales value compared with the other products

D A product that has been spoiled during production so cannot be sold for its expected purpose.

8 Which of the following statements are true when comparing the profits reported under absorption costing and marginal costing during a period when the level of inventory increased?

A Absorption costing profits will be higher and closing inventory valuations lower than those under marginal costing.

B Absorption costing profits will be higher and closing inventory valuations higher than those under marginal costing.

C Marginal costing profits will be higher and closing inventory valuations lower than those under absorption costing.

D Marginal costing profits will be higher and closing inventory valuations higher than those under absorption costing.

9 Department X uses absorption costing and absorbs production overheads on the basis of machine hours. Information for the latest period was as follows:

Budgeted production overhead $245,000
Actual production overhead $250,000
Budgeted machine hours 70,000
Actual machine hours 75,000

Which of the following statements is correct?

A Overhead was $5,000 under absorbed
B Overhead was $5,000 over absorbed
C Overhead was $12,500 over absorbed
D Overhead was $17,500 over absorbed

10 The management accountant has drafted the following break even chart:

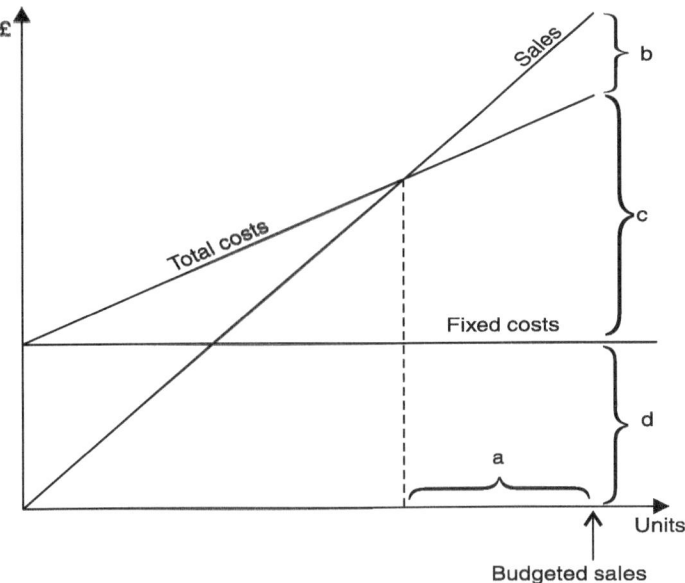

At the budgeted level of sales, which letters represent the value of profit achieved and the value of variable costs?

	Profit	Variable Cost
A	b	c
B	b	d
C	a	c
D	a	d

11 Which of the following documents is matched with the purchase invoice before payment to ensure that only goods that were actually received are paid for?

A Purchase order
B Purchase requisition form
C Delivery note
D Good received note

12 Which of the following remuneration schemes is least likely to incentivise staff to work more efficiently?

A A day rate system
B A high day rate system
C An individual bonus scheme based on work done
D A piecemeal work system

13 A consultant has made the following statements about introducing Activity-Based Costing (ABC) in a small manufacturing company:

(i)   ABC helps managers to understand better the underlying cost behaviour and this can be used to control costs more effectively.

(ii) The benefits of introducing ABC will always exceed the costs, particularly for small companies.

(iii) ABC can lead to more accurate costing of products which can lead to better decision making

Which of the statements are correct?

- A (i) and (ii)
- B (i) and (iii)
- C (ii) and (iii)
- D (i), (ii) and (iii)

14 The standard material cost of producing 1 unit of product Cee is 0.5kg of material X at $7 per kg.

During the last month 21,000 units of Cee were produced using 10,000 kg of material X. 12,000 kg of material X were purchased for $90,000. Inventories are valued at standard cost.

What was the material price variance?

- A An adverse variance of $1,000
- B An adverse variance of $5,000
- C An adverse variance of $5,250
- D An adverse variance of $6,000

15 Which of the statements about Activity Based Management is NOT correct?

- A The main purpose of Activity Based Management is to achieve more accurate product costs.
- B Activity Based Management should lead to a reduction in costs in the longer run, while ensuring that customer needs are still met.
- C Activity Based Management is a process of continuous improvement rather than a one off change.
- D Employee empowerment is a key factor in a successful Activity Based Management programme.

16 A company makes one product, the Dee. Budgeted fixed costs are $4,500 per month. Budgeted sales and production are 12,000 units of Dee per month.

Last month, due to a machine breakdown, only 11,000 units of Dee were produced and only 10,000 units were sold. Fixed costs were $5,000. The marginal costing profit for the month was $35,000.

What would be the absorption costing profit?

- A $34,625
- B $35,375
- C $34,454
- D $36,250

17 A manufacturing company uses a very labour intensive production process. Production is based around teams of five workers. One supervisor is employed per every 10 workers. The supervisor does not perform any production, but manages the workers, and earns a fixed salary. Recently a new supervisor was recruited because due to growth in demand for the company's products, it has recruited an additional 10 workers.

What type of cost is the supervisor's salary?

- A Direct production cost
- B Indirect variable production cost
- C Indirect stepped production cost
- D Stepped administrative overhead

18 A process produces normal losses which can be sold for a small amount of scrap value. What is the correct way of calculating the value per unit of good output?

   A   Total value of inputs ÷ expected output
   B   Total value of inputs ÷ actual output
   C   (Total value of inputs − scrap value of normal loss) ÷ expected output
   D   (Total value of inputs − scrap value of all losses) ÷ actual output

19 Which one of the following is NOT a characteristic of a service?

   A   Simultaneity
   B   Homogeneity
   C   Intangibility
   D   Perishability

20 A company manufactures and sells one product at a price of $50 per unit. Monthly fixed costs are $10,000. The accountant has calculated that the break-even point is 500 units per month.

   What is the contribution to sales (C/S) ratio for the product?

   A   0.3
   B   0.4
   C   0.6
   D   Cannot be determined from the information above

21 A company uses 20,000 kg of Material A per year. The cost of 1 kg is $10. Costs of holding Material A in the warehouse are estimated to be $3 per kilo per annum. Each time an order is placed, the company incurs costs of $2 per order for clerical time.

   What quantity should of Material A should be ordered each time an order is placed in order to minimise total order costs + holding costs?

   A   89 units
   B   115 units
   C   163 units
   D   245 units

22 A company produced the following fixed budget at the start of the month based on the assumption that it would produce and sell 9,000 units of product Aye.

	$
Revenue	135,000
Variable costs	(90,000)
Fixed costs	(15,000)
Profit	30,000

   Fixed costs do not increase unless production reaches 15,000 units per month.

   How much profit would be shown in a flexible budget prepared for 10,000 units?

   A $30,000
   B $33,333
   C $35,000
   D $45,000

MOCK EXAM 1 QUESTIONS

23 The following statements have been made about the modern business world:

(i)   Business must focus more on quality in a competitive environment.

(ii) Service industries have become much more important.

(iii) The environment within which businesses operate is much more dynamic and managers must respond quickly to changes.

Which of the above statements suggest that traditional budgetary control is out of date in the modern business world??

A (i) and (ii)
B (i) and (iii)
C (ii) and (iii)
D (i), (ii) and (iii)

24 A building company has won a special contract and wishes to know what the relevant cost of doing the work would be.

The manager has identified the following costs:

(i) An apportionment of 30% of the central overheads of the building company.

(ii) Costs of preparing the bid for the contract. These were incurred before the contract was won.

Which of the above costs are relevant?

A (i) only
B (ii) only
C (i) and (ii)
D Neither (i) nor (ii)

25 The following costs have been incurred by a factory:

	$
Rent & rates	40,000
Machine maintenance	15,000
Machine insurance	10,000

The expenses need to be apportioned to the two production departments in the factory. The following information has been obtained:

	Dept 1	Dept 2
NBV of machines $000	25	70
Floor area	30 m²	50 m²
Machine hours	1,000	1,500

What is the total value of the overheads apportioned to department 2?

A $23,632
B $24,375
C $40,625
D $41,368

MOCK EXAM 1 ANSWERS

1 C Strategic information is generally high level (not detailed) and may be external or internal. Tactical information is more detailed than strategic information but not produced frequently.

2 A Salaries of accounting staff are treated as administrative overheads not production overheads. Supervisors and rent of the factory are production overheads.

3 B 1. Establish the flow of units to find out how many units were completed:

Opening WIP + Goods started = Goods completed + Closing WIP
200 + 3,000 = 2,950 (bal.fig.) + 250
Goods started & finished = 3,000 – 250 = 2,750

2. Statement of equivalent units:

Completion of opening WIP (200 × 70%)	140
Goods started & finished	2,750
Start closing WIP (250 × 40%)	100
Equivalent units	2,990

4 D Zero based budgets.

Incremental budgets start with the previous year's budgets and add increments or changes to these. Rolling budgets and continuous budgeting are the same thing, and relate to budgets that are continually updated (e.g. at the end of each month).

5 A The material in the warehouse is not used in other activities so if not used in the contract would be sold to Bee for $5.00 per unit. This is an opportunity cost, so is the relevant cost for the first 400kg.

The remaining 600kg needed would have to be acquired from the market, so the current market price of $9.00 per Kg would be relevant.

Relevant cost is therefore $7,400 (400kg × $5) + (600kg × $9)

6 D Using a lower grade of labour would be expected to lead to an adverse efficiency variance because the workers would be slower.

If the standard had been revised, it may have become too easy, which could lead to a favourable efficiency variance just for working at a normal rate.

If an allowance for idle time during machine breakdowns is included in the standard, then there would be a favourable labour efficiency variance if the breakdowns did not occur.

7 C The distinguishing feature of by-products is their low sales value relative to the other main products that are produced by the process.

Joint products may require further processing, but that does not make them by-products (answer B).

8 B Closing inventory valuation under absorption costing will always be higher than under marginal costing because fixed overheads are included in the closing inventory values.

The profit under absorption costing will be greater because the fixed overhead being carried forward in closing inventory is greater than the fixed overhead being brought forward in opening inventory.

9 C Budgeted absorption rate: $245,000/ 70,000 = 3.50 per machine hour.

Actual overhead	250,000	
Less absorbed	262,500	(75,000 × $3.50)
Over absorption	$12,500	

MOCK EXAM 1 ANSWERS

10   A   Profit is the difference between sales and total costs, represented by b at the budgeted level of sales.

Variable costs = total costs less fixed costs, and this is represented by c at the budgeted level of sales.

d represents the value of fixed costs and a is the margin of safety being the difference between budgeted sales and break-even sales.

11   D   The good received note (GRN) is issued by the receiving department in the warehouse, and shows details of the goods actually received. When the purchase invoice arrives, the accounting department check the invoice against the goods received note to ensure that they are only paying for goods that have been received.

A delivery note is issued by the supplier, and is a control for the supplier rather than the receiver of the goods.

12   A   A day rate system means staff get paid by the hour, regardless of how much they produce. This does not incentivise them to work more efficiently as they will be paid regardless of how much they achieve.

A high day rate system is where employees are paid a higher rate per hour than the standard day rate system, but are expected to achieve higher production. This higher rate ought to incentivise staff to some extent.

The individual bonus scheme would motivate employees to work harder if they can achieve higher remuneration.

A piecemeal work system is where staff are paid per unit of production. If they are not efficient, they produce less and therefore earn less.

13   B   Identifying the drivers of costs helps managers understand what causes costs to change. In traditional costing, the assumption was that costs are vary with the level of output, but ABC recognises that this is not always the case. (i) is therefore true.

The costs of introducing ABC can be high, and the benefits may not exceed the costs, particularly for small companies with a limited range of products, where the additional information provided by ABC would not provide much benefit. (ii) is therefore incorrect.

By costing products based on identifying the drivers of those costs, product costs will be more accurate than under traditional costing. This will indeed lead to better decisions, such as knowing what the true profit per unit of a product is, which may lead to changes in product mixes.

14   D   Since inventory is valued at standard cost, the materials price variance will be based on the quantity purchased, not the quantity used.

	$	
12,000 kg should have cost	84,000	(12,000 × $7)
But did cost	90,000	
Price variance	6,000	adv.

Answer B is based on the materials used in production so is wrong.

Answer C is based on the standard quantity of materials – this is wrong because price variances are based on actual purchases rather than standard use.

Answer D assumes that a variance is only recognised on the materials transferred to closing inventory.

MOCK EXAM 1 ANSWERS

15 A This describes the purpose of Activity Based Costing, not Activity Based Management (ABM). ABM has a much broader purpose than costing – it aims to take the principles of Activity Based Costing and apply them to managing the organisation more profitably.

B is correct. By eliminating activities that do not add value, and increasing the efficiency of activities that do, costs should be reduced without reducing the quality of products or services provided to customers.

C is correct. ABM is a continuous process.

D is correct. Employees will become involved in helping to identify the activities and drivers that is a necessary part of ABM.

16 B The difference in profits between absorption and marginal costing will be due to fixed costs included in inventory. Inventory has increased by 1,000 units (Production of 11,000 less sales of 10,000) so under absorption costing, 1,000 units worth of fixed overhead will be transferred to the next period via closing inventory.

Fixed overhead per unit, based on budget = 4,500/12,000 = 0.375 per unit

Marginal costing profit:	35,000
Add fixed overheads in increased inventory	375 (0.375 × 1,000)
Absorption costing profit	35,375

Answer A is wrong because the fixed overhead in the inventory change has been deducted from marginal costing profit.

Answer C is based on a revised standard profit per unit of $39,545 based on contribution of $40 per unit less actual fixed cost divided by actual production. This is wrong as inventory valuation should be based on a normal level of production.

Answer D has calculated a standard profit per unit by taking the contribution per unit of $40 and subtracting the fixed cost per unit of $0.375 giving $36.25. This was multiplied by 10,000 units. This is incorrect because it does not take into account the under absorption of fixed costs due to the reduced level of activity and the higher level of fixed costs.

17 C The supervisor supports the production workers, so their cost is a production cost rather than an administrative one. Since their work is that of supervision, it is not possible to trace their salary costs to specific units of output, so it is not a direct cost. The supervisor is on a fixed salary – however, as output increases beyond a certain point, additional supervisors will have to be recruited, so the cost increases in steps as output increases. It is therefore an example of a stepped production overhead.

18 C The expected scrap value of normal losses reduces the production costs of the good input.

19 B Homogeneity means all products are identical. It is often a feature of mass production, but not a characteristic of services. Services tend to be heterogeneous which means that each time a service is produced, the standard varies slightly, because services are provided by people and therefore prone to human factors.

20 B At break-even point, total contribution = fixed costs

⇒ if sales are 500 units, contribution = 10,000

⇒ contribution per unit = $20 (10,000/ 500)

The contribution sales ratio = $20/$50 = 0.4.

21 C Using the economic order quantity model $\sqrt{\frac{2C_oD}{C_h}}$

Where C_o = cost of placing an order
C_h = cost of holding 1 unit in inventory for a period (e.g. 1 year)
D = demand (or usage) per period

Applying the formula gives: EOQ = $\sqrt{\frac{2 \times 2 \times 20{,}000}{3}}$ = 163 units.

22 C The flexible budget would be:

	$	
Revenue	150,000	(10,000/ 9,000) ×135,000
Variable costs	(100,000)	(10,000/ 9,000) ×90,000
Fixed costs	(15,000)	(no change)
Profit	35,000	

23 B (i) The traditional approach to budgetary control did not concentrate on quality and non-financial aspects of performance. It focussed on cost control. Therefore this would suggest that traditional budgeting is out of date where organisations focus on quality.

(ii) The growth in services businesses does not make traditional budgeting less relevant. Service businesses must also budget.

(iii) Traditional budgetary control has been criticised for representing a "command and control" culture where local management are not given autonomy to make their own decisions. This would stop them reacting quickly to changes in the environment. If the environment is more dynamic it follows that traditional budgetary control is less relevant.

24 D Central overheads of the building company would be incurred regardless of whether the contract goes ahead and are not incremental to the decision. They are not therefore relevant.

The costs of preparing the bid have already been incurred so are "sunk costs". They are therefore not relevant.

25 D

	Basis	Dept. 1	Dept. 2
Rent & rates	Floor area	15,000	25,000
Maintenance	Machine hours	6,000	9,000
Machine insurance	NBV of machines	2,632	7,368
Total costs		23,632	41,368

Mock exam 2
questions and answers

MOCK EXAM 2 QUESTIONS

1. PH Ltd produces a single product and currently uses absorption costing for its internal management accounting reports. The fixed production overhead absorption rate is $34 per unit. Opening inventories for the year were 100 units and closing inventories were 180 units. The company's management accountant is considering a switch to marginal costing as the inventory valuation basis.

    If marginal costing were used, the marginal costing profit for the year, compared with the profit calculated by absorption costing, would be:

    A $ 2,720 lower
    B $ 2,720 higher
    C $ 3,400 lower
    D $400 higher

2. AL Ltd operates a job costing system. The company's standard net profit margin is 20% of sales value.

    The estimated costs for job B124 are as follows.

    Direct materials   3kg @ $5 per kg
    Direct labour   4 hours @ $9 per hour

    Production overheads are budgeted to be $240,000 for the period, to be recovered on the basis of a total of 30,000 labour hours.

    Other overheads, related to selling, distribution and administration, are budgeted to be $150,000 for the period. They are to be recovered on the basis of the total budgeted production cost of $ 750,000 for the period.

    Calculate the price to be quoted for job B124.

    A $124.50
    B $134.50
    C $114.50
    D $164.50

3. The following statements have been made about management accounts and financial statements.

    (i)   Financial statements are principally prepared for external stakeholders while management accounts are for internal management.

    (ii) Financial statements provide more detailed analysis of costs than management accounts.

    (iii) Financial statements are mainly historic while management accounts may contain both historic information and future plans and forecasts.

    Which of the above statements are correct?

    A   (i) and (ii)
    B   (i) and (iii)
    C   (ii) and (iii)
    D   All of the above

4   The monthly electricity bill includes a fixed service charge and a charge for usage based on the number of kilowatt hours used during the month at a standard rate per kilowatt hour.

   This type of cost is best described as:

   A   A variable cost
   B   A semi-variable cost
   C   A stepped cost
   D   A hybrid cost

5   A manufacturing company uses absorption costing. Budgeted fixed costs are $28,000 per month and these are absorbed on a labour hour basis. Budgeted production is 1,400 units per month. Standard labour time per unit is 2 hours.

   During the last month, 1,500 units were produced using 3,100 hours. Actual fixed costs were $27,000.

   What were the fixed overhead volume capacity and fixed overhead volume efficiency variances?

	Capacity	Efficiency
A	$2,000 adverse	$871 favourable
B	$2,000 favourable	$1,000 adverse
C	$3,000 adverse	$871 adverse
D	$3,000 favourable	$1,000 adverse

6   In order to ensure that the labourers are productive, a company has set a target that each worker should produce 100 units of output per hour. The standard working day is 8 hours and there are 10 workers in the department. The factory is open five days per week.

   Last week total labour hours worked was 450 hours. Output achieved was 42,500.

   What was the labour activity ratio for the company?

   A   106.25%
   B   88.9%
   C   112.5%
   D   106.25%

7   One two main products. and one by-product are produced by a process. The by-product generates a small amount of income. The following statements have been made about the correct way to account for the by product:

   (i)   A share of the process costs should be apportioned to the by-product using the same method for apportioning costs to the main products.

   (ii) A by product is a product which has a small relative value compared to the other joint costs.

   (iii) The most common way of accounting for by products is to deduct the net realisable value of the by-product from the production costs of the main products.

   A   (i) and (ii)
   B   (i) and (iii)
   C   (ii) and (iii)
   D   All of the above

8   Which of the following statements about "top down" budgeting is NOT correct

    A   The top down budgeting process is quicker and more efficient than using bottom up budgeting.

    B   Top down budgets achieve greater coordination of the different departments than bottom up budgeting.

    C   Top down budgeting is more likely to motivate proactive departmental managers than bottom up.

    D   Top down budgets are more likely to be consistent with the organisation's overall objectives than bottom up.

9   A company makes one product with a contribution sales ratio of 0.6. Total fixed costs are $12,000 per month. The company enjoys a margin of safety of 20%. What is the budgeted sales revenue?

    A $20,000
    B $24,000
    C $25,000
    D $30,000

10 A company is considering accepting a special one-off contract. If the contract goes ahead, it will require labour to be taken away from regular work, since no additional labourers with the appropriate skills are available.

    How is the relevant cost of the labour for the special contract calculated?

    A   The direct cost of the labour
    B   The lost contribution on lost production of regular work.
    C   The direct cost of the labour plus the lost contribution on lost production of regular work
    D   The direct cost of labour plus the lost revenue on lost production of regular work.

11 What is meant by an inventory reorder level?

    A   It is the quantity that is ordered each time an order is placed
    B   It is a minimum level of inventory set to avoid delays to production
    C   It is a department that places orders again if the supplier has not delivered
    D   It is the inventory level at which an order is placed for new inventory

12 A manufacturing company absorbs fixed overheads at a rate of $15 per labour hour. Budgeted fixed overheads are $120,000 per month. Last month the actual fixed overhead was $115,000 and 7,500 labour hours were worked. What was the under/ over absorption of overheads last month?

    A $2,500 under absorption
    B $5,000 under absorption
    C $7,500 under absorption
    D $2,500 over absorption

13 A company uses process costing and values inventory using the FIFO method. Last month, opening inventory was 400 units each 40% complete with respect to conversion costs. 2,000 units were started. Closing WIP was 200 units each 30% complete.

How many equivalent units of production with respect to conversion costs, were performed during the month?

A   1,980 units
B   2,020 unit
C   2,100 units
D   2,200 units

14 The following statements have been made about standard costing:

(i)   Standard costing is most useful in industries where there is repetitive work
(ii) Standard costing is not used for inventory valuation
(iii) Standard costing is a control device

Which of the above statements are true?

A   (i) and (ii)
B   (i) and (iii)
C   (ii) and (iii)
D   All of the above

15 Which of the following statements about the economic order quantity is NOT correct?

A   If the costs of placing an order increase, the economic order quantity will increase.
B   If the costs of holding inventory increase, the economic order quantity will increase.
C   At the economic order quantity, the total holding costs = the total order costs for the period.
D   The model does not take into account any bulk discounts that may be available.

16 The following diagram shows how one of the factory costs varies as output increases.

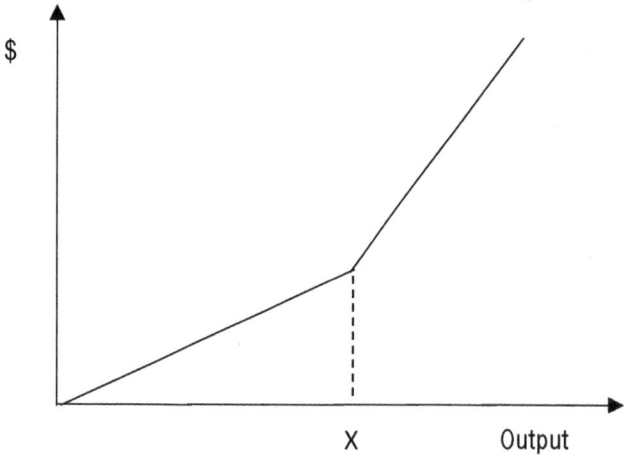

Which of the following costs is consistent with the diagram above?

A   One of the materials used in production, where the supplier gives a discount if the level of production exceeds X.

B   The salaries of supervisors, who are on fixed salaries, but if production exceeds X then an additional supervisor would be hired.

C   The wages of factory workers who are paid an hourly rate, but would be paid an overtime premium if output exceeds X.

D   Energy costs where there is a fixed service charge and a variable cost based on use.

17 A hospital has started to use Activity Based Costing (ABC) to calculate the cost of each patient that visits the hospital. It has identified the following activities along with the total costs for last year:

Activity	Total cost	Driver
Surgery	$120 million	Time in theatre
Nursing costs	$50 million	Length of stay
Cleaning operating theatres	$2 million	Number of operations

The number of units of driver last year was as follows:

Time in theatre	60,000 hours
Length of stay	125,000 patient nights
Number of operations	40,000

Last year, Bob had an operation to remove an appendix. The operation took one hour. Bob spent two nights in hospital after the operation.

What was the total cost of Bob's operation and hospital stay?

A $800
B $2,400
C $2,450
D $2,850

18 The most recent month's variance analysis identified a large materials price variance.

Which of the following would NOT cause an adverse materials price variance?

A   A sudden shortage of raw materials due to an increase in demand made market prices of the material increase.

B   A machine breakdown occurred which led to some material being wasted.

C   The normal supplier of the material went bankrupt and an alternative supplier, who charged a less favourable price was found.

D   The old purchasing manager left the company, and the new purchasing manager is not a good negotiator.

19 The management accountant has drawn the following profit volume chart, where A is the budgeted revenue.

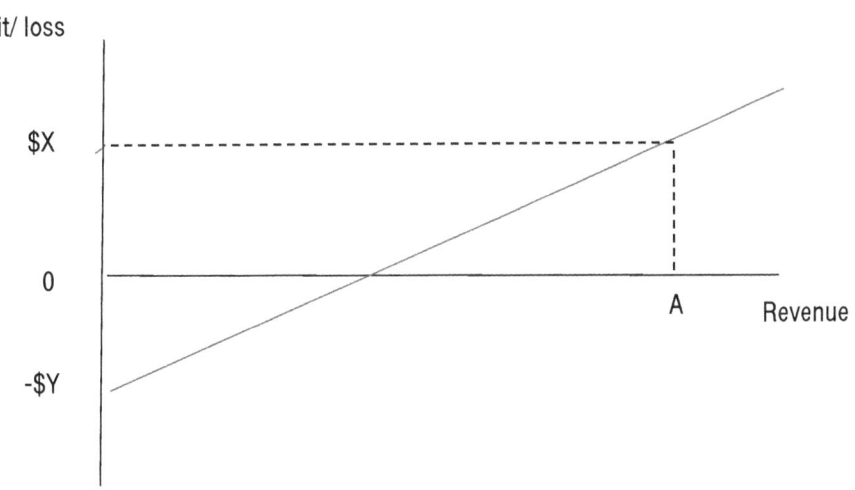

What is the value of contribution at budgeted revenue?

- A $X
- B $X + $Y
- C $X – $Y
- D $Y

20 Activity-Based Management (ABM) describes core activities, secondary activities and discretionary activities. Which of the following statements is true about secondary activities?

- A They support core activities so should be retained even though they do not add value themselves.
- B They support core activities but should not be retained as they do not add value themselves.
- C They are activities that relate to failures in an organisation.
- D They are activities that do not support the main objectives of the organisation.

21 Information about three products that are made by a company are as follows:

	Product 1 $	Product 2 $	Product 3 $
Selling price	35	50	60
Materials cost per unit	10	15	20
Labour and variable overheads	15	22	25
Contribution per unit	10	13	15

The material cost for all three products relates to material A, which costs $5 per kilo. Material A is in limited supply, and there is not enough available to meet demand for all three products.

In order to maximise profits, in what order should the products be ranked when preparing the production plan?

	1	2	3
A	1st	2nd	3rd
B	3rd	2nd	1st
C	2nd	1st	3rd
D	3rd	1st	2nd

22 The following statements have been made about marginal costing:

(i)   Marginal cost includes only direct costs.
(ii) Marginal cost does not comply with IAS 2 inventory valuation.
(iii) Marginal cost is better for short term decision making.

Which of the above statements are correct?

- A (i) and (ii)
- B (i) and (iii)
- C (ii) and (iii)
- D All of the above

23 A budget is prepared at the start of the year. At the end of the year, before comparing the actual results against the budget, the budget is recalculated so that the budgeted quantities are the same as the actual quantities, but the costs per unit are as per the original budget.

This method of budgeting is referred to as what?

- A Rolling budgeting
- B Incremental budgeting
- C Zero based budgeting
- D Flexible budgeting

24 The standard cost card for a new product is as follows:

	$
Selling price	90
Variable costs	60
Fixed costs per unit	20
Profit per unit	10

The company uses absorption costing and budgeted sales per month are 10,000 units.

Last month, actual sales were 9,000 units at a selling price of $95.

What was the sales volume variance?

- A $90,000 adverse
- B $30,000 adverse
- C $10,000 adverse
- D $5,000 adverse

25 What does the term "prime cost" mean?

- A The direct costs of production
- B The lowest cost achieved during the year
- C Total variable costs
- D Total production costs

MOCK EXAM 2 QUESTIONS

MOCK EXAM 2 ANSWERS

1   A   If marginal costing is used to value inventory instead of absorption costing, the difference in profits will be equal to the change in inventory volume multiplied by the fixed production overhead absorption rate = 80 units × $ 34 = $ 2,720

Since closing inventory is higher than opening inventory, the marginal costing profit will be lower that the absorption costing profit (so **option B** is incorrect). This is because the marginal costing profit does not 'benefit' from the increase in the amount of fixed production overhead taken to inventory (rather than to the income statement).

If you selected **options C or D,** you based the difference on 100 units of opening inventory.

2   A   The price to be quoted for job B124 is $124.50

	$
Materials	15 (3 kg ×5)
Labour	36 (4 hours × 9)
Production overhead	32 (4 hours × 8) (W1)
Total production cost	83
Other overheads	16.60 (W2)
Total cost	99.60
Profit	24.90 (99.60 × 20/80)
Quoted price	124.50

Workings:

(W1) Production overhead absorption rate = 240,000/30,000 = $8 per labour hour

(W2) Other overhead absorption rate =150,000/ 750,000 × 100% = 20% of total production costs

3   B   (i) is correct.

(ii) is not correct. The detail in most financial statements is limited to the requirements of appropriate accounting regulations, which do not require much detailed analysis of costs. Much of management accounting is concerned with controlling costs so more detailed information about product costs is provided.

(iii) is correct since financial statements report performance for the past period, whereas management accounts will be concerned with the past and present.

4   B   A semi variable cost is made up of both a fixed element and a variable element.

5   D

Standard fixed overhead absorption rate = 28,000 ÷ (1,400 × 2) = $10 per labour hour.

Fixed overhead volume efficiency variance

1,500 units of should take (× 2 hrs)	3,000 hrs
but did take	3,100 hrs
Fixed overhead volume efficiency variance in hours	100 hrs (A)
× standard fixed overhead absorption rate per hour	× 10
Fixed overhead volume efficiency variance in $	$1,000 (A)

MOCK EXAM 2 ANSWERS

Fixed overhead volume capacity variance

The volume capacity variance is the difference between the budgeted hours of work and the actual active hours of work

Budgeted hours of work (1,400 × 2)	2,800 hrs
Actual hours of work	3,100 hrs
Fixed overhead volume capacity variance	300 hrs (F)
× standard fixed overhead absorption rate per hour	× 10
Fixed overhead volume capacity variance in $	$3,000 (F)

6 A

$$\text{Activity ratio} = \frac{\text{Standard hours for actual output}}{\text{Budgeted hours}} = \frac{425}{400} = 106.25\%$$

C is the capacity ratio, which is calculated as $\dfrac{\text{Standard hours for actual output}}{\text{Actual hours worked}}$

7 C (i) is incorrect. In a joint process, product costs are not apportioned to the by product. The other 2 items are true.

8 C Proactive managers may become demotivated if they are not allowed to participate in preparing their departmental budgets.

9 C $\text{Break even revenue} = \dfrac{\text{Fixed costs}}{\text{C/S ratio}} = \dfrac{12,000}{0.6} = \$20,000$

Since the company enjoys a margin of safety of 20%, then the break-even revenue is 80% of the budgeted sales

⇒ Budgeted sales = $25,000 (20,000 ÷ 80%)

10 C The lost contribution on lost production of regular work is an opportunity cost that must be taken into consideration.

11 D A reorder level is a level of inventory that is set so that when inventory reaches that level, a new order is placed, to ensure that the delivery arrives before the inventory runs out.

A describes the order quantity.

B is buffer inventory.

12 A

	$	
Actual fixed overheads	115,000	
Absorbed into production	112,500	(7,500 × 15)
Under absorption	2,500	

13 C Flow of units: Opening WIP + Goods started = goods completed + closing WIP

400 + 2,000 = 2,200 (bal. fig) + 200

Equivalent units:

Completion of opening WIP: (60% × 400)	240
Goods started and finished (2,000 – 200)	1,800
Closing WIP (30% × 200)	60
	2,100

MOCK EXAM 2 ANSWERS

14 B (i) Standard costing is most useful in industries where the work is repetitive, as the standard is more relevant. In industries where each job is different, it can be difficult to define a standard, as there is no standard product.

(ii) Standard costs can be used for inventory valuation, meaning this statement is incorrect.

(iii) A standard cost is a control device, whereby actual costs are compared to the standard, and any resulting variances are investigated.

15 B If the costs of holding inventory increase, then larger orders become expensive due to the higher inventory levels. The order quantity would fall.

It can be shown mathematically that the total of the holding costs plus order costs is minimised at the point where they are both equal.

16 C The gradient of the line represents the cost per unit. Initially the gradient is not as steep, but becomes steeper after X, which means the cost per unit increases after X. This is consistent with C, where an overtime premium is paid if production increases beyond X.

17 D Cost per unit of driver:

Surgery: $2,000 per hour ($120 million ÷ 60,000 hours)

Nursing costs: $400 per night ($50 million ÷ 125,000)

Operating theatre cleaning: $50 per operation ($2 million÷40,000)

Cost of Bob's visit:

	$
1 hour of surgery	2,000
2 nights nursing	800
Operating theatre cleaning	50
Total cost	2,850

18 B A machine breakdown may affect the material usage, but not the price paid, so would have no impact on the price variance. All the other items may explain an increase in the price paid for the materials and would lead to an adverse price variance.

19 B The level of profit at X is shown as being $X. Fixed cost is equal to $Y, as this is the value of the loss that is made when revenue is zero. Contribution = Profit + Fixed cost, therefore $X + $Y.

20 A Secondary activities support core activities. They should be retained because without them, the core activities would not function.

21 A Since material A is in short supply, the products should be ranked according to which produces the highest contribution per kg of material A:

	Product 1	Product 2	Product 3
	$	$	$
Contribution per unit	10	13	15
Kgs of material A per unit	2	3	4
Contribution per unit of A	5	4.33	3.75
⇒ ranking	1st	2nd	3rd

MOCK EXAM 2 ANSWERS

22 C The marginal cost of a product includes all variable costs, including variable overheads, which are not direct costs. (i) is therefore incorrect.

(ii) is correct. IAS 2 states that all production costs should be included in inventory valuation, so that included fixed as well as variable.

(ii) is correct. Marginal cost allows managers to see how much costs will increase by if output increases.

23 D Flexible budgeting. The aim is to make the budget comparable with the actual results.

24 C Sales volume variance

	Units
Actual sales	9,000
Budgeted sales	10,000
Variance (units)	1,000
X standard profit per unit	$10
Volume variance (adverse)	$10,000

25 A This is the definition of prime costs.

Index

Note. **Key Terms** and their page references are given in **bold**.

ABC, 150
ABC method of stores control, 64
ABM, 367
Abnormal gain, 171
Abnormal loss, 171, 172
Absorption base, 121
Absorption costing, 108, 152
Absorption costing and marginal costing compared, 139
Absorption costing versus ABC, 152
Absorption of overheads, 119
Activity analysis, 369
Activity based analysis, 364
Activity based approaches, 364
Activity based budgeting (ABB), 373
Activity based costing (ABC), 150, 365
Activity based management (ABM), 367, 368
Activity ratio, 88
Administration overhead, 28
Administration overheads, 129
Allocation, 110
Attainable standards, 273, 285
Attendance record, 97
Attributable fixed costs, 346
Automation, 87
AVCO (cumulative weighted average pricing), 70
Average cost, 70
Average inventory, 60
Avoidable cost, 344
Avoidable costs, 33, 344

Balancing transactions, 152
Basic standards, 273, 285
Basis of apportionment, 113
Batch, 226
Batch costing, 226
Batch processing, 18
Bill of materials, 219
Bin cards, 55
Blanket absorption rates, 122
Blanket overhead absorption rate, 122
Bonus schemes, 91
Bonus/incentive schemes, 91
Bottom up (participatory budget), 274
Bottom up budgeting, 274
Breakeven analysis, 324
Breakeven arithmetic, 326
Breakeven charts, 331
Breakeven point, 324, 326, **339**
Budget, 256
Budget bias, 276

Budget committee, 259
Budget manual, 258
Budget period, 258
Budget preparation, 259
Budgetary planning, 256
Budgetary slack, 275
Business Process Re-engineering, 364
By-product, 202, 209
   rolling, 277

C/S (Contribution/sales) ratio, 324
Capacity ratio, 88
Cellular manufacturing, 18
Change transactions, 152
Characteristics of services, 228
Clock card, 97
Common costs, 203
Computerised inventory control systems, 53
Computers, 272
Continuous improvement, 372
Continuous stocktaking, 56
Contract accounts, 235
Contract costs, 235
Contribution, 136
Contribution breakeven charts, 335
Contribution charts, 331, 335
Contribution to sales (C/S) ratio, 324
Control, 9
Controllable cost, 33, 345
Core activity, 370
Core/primary activities, 370
Corporate planning, 8
Cost accounting department, 101
Cost accounts, 14
Cost behaviour, 36
Cost behaviour and budgeting, 36
Cost behaviour and cost control, 36
Cost behaviour and decision making, 36
Cost behaviour and levels of activity, 36
Cost behaviour assumptions, 41
Cost behaviour patterns, 37
Cost behaviour principles, 36
Cost centres, 33
Cost driver, 151, 154
Cost driver analysis, 371
Cost formulas, 75
Cost management, 159
Cost object, 33, 34
Cost per service unit, 229
Cost plus pricing, 221
Cost pool, 151
Cost pools, 151

INDEX

Cost reduction, 368
Cost unit, 34
Cost units, 33, 34
Costing methods, 218
Costs of conversion, 74
Costs of purchase, 74
Cost-volume-profit (CVP) analysis, 324
Creative budgets, 276
Credit note, 52
Cumulative weighted average pricing, 70
Current standards, 273, 285
Curvilinear, 39
Curvilinear variable costs, 39
Customer profitability analysis (CPA), 159
Customer profitability analysis (CPA), 159
CVP analysis, 324

Daily time sheets, 98
Data, **4**, **123**, **129**
Day-rate system, 89
Decision making, 10
Decision-making problems, 351
Dedicated cell layout, 18
Delivery note, 52
Departmental absorption rates, 122
Deprival value of an asset, 350
Deteriorating inventory, 57
Differential costs, 344
Direct cost, 26
Direct costs, 26
Direct expenses, 28
Direct labour, 27
Direct labour budget, 262
Direct labour cost variances, 294
Direct labour efficiency variance, 295
Direct labour rate variance, 294
Direct labour rates, 286
Direct labour total variance, 294
Direct material, 26
Direct material cost variances, 292
Direct material price variance, 292
Direct material prices, 286
Direct material total variance, 292
Direct material usage variance, 292
Direct wages, 27
Discontinuance problems, 356
Discretionary activities, 370
Discretionary costs, 33
Distribution overhead, 29, 129
Diversionary activities, 370
Diversionary/discretionary activities, 370
Dysfunctional decision making, 276, 277

Economic Order Quantity (EOQ), 61, 62
Effectiveness, 11
Efficiency, 11
Efficiency ratio, 88
Empire building, 276
Employee empowerment, 17
Employee share ownership plan, 94
Equivalent units, 183
Expenses, 26

Facility-sustaining activities, 157
Factory overhead, 28
FIFO, 66
FIFO (first in, first out), 66, **67**, 75, 188
Financial accounts, 13
Financial information, 6
Fixed budget, 266, **267**
Fixed cost, 31, **32**, **37**, 346
Fixed costs, 37
Fixed overhead expenditure variance, 298, **299**
Fixed overhead total variance, 299
Fixed overhead variances, 299
Fixed overhead volume capacity variance, 299
Fixed overhead volume efficiency variance, 299
Fixed overhead volume variance, 298, **299**
Fixed production overhead variances, 297
Flexible budget, 266, **267**
Forecast, 261
Free inventory, 55
Function costing, 227
Functional costs, 30

Goal congruence, 276
Goods received note (GRN), 52
Group bonus scheme, 93
Guaranteed minimum wage, 90

Hierarchy of activities, 157
High day-rate system, 92
Holding costs, 58

IAS 2 Inventories, 73
Ideal standards, 273, 285
Idle time, 100
Idle time ratio, 102
Imposed budget, 274
Imposed style of budgeting, 274
Incentive schemes, 91
Incentive schemes involving shares, 94
Incremental costs, 344

586

INDEX

Indirect cost, 26
Indirect expenses, 28
Indirect materials, 28
Indirect wages, 28
Individual bonus scheme, 93
Information, 4
Innovation, 17
Interdependence between variances, 305
International Accounting Standard 2 (IAS 2), 110
Inventories, 73
Inventory codes, 56
Inventory control, 50, 59
Inventory control levels, 58, 59
Inventory control systems, 53
Inventory costs, 58
Inventory discrepancies, 57
Inventory valuation, 65
Inventory valuation and profitability, 77
Investment centre, 35
Investment centres, 35

Job, 218
Job card, 218
Job cost cards, 219
Job cost information, 219
Job cost sheet, 218
Job costing, 218
Job costing and computerisation, 221
Job costing for internal services, 224
Job time, 98
Jobbing industries, 18
Joint costs, 202
Joint products, 202
Joint products and common costs, 203
Joint products in process accounts, 206
Just-in-time, 64
Just-in-time (JIT), 64
Just-in-time production, 64
Just-in-time purchasing, 64
Just-in-time systems, 64

Key budget factor, 260

Labour, 26
Labour activity, 86
Labour budget, 262
Last in, first out, 66, 69
Ledger entries relating to overheads, 127
LIFO, 69
LIFO (last in, first out), 66, 69
Limiting budget factor, 260
Limiting factor, 351

Logistical transactions, 152
Long-term planning, 8, 258
Long-term strategic planning, 8
Losses in process costing, 171
Losses on incomplete contracts, 244
Losses with a disposal cost, 182
Losses with scrap value, 177

Make or buy decisions, 354
Management accounts, 13
Management control, 11
Management control system, 12
Margin of safety, 325
Marginal and absorption costing compared, 139
Marginal cost, 136
Marginal costing, 136, 139
Marginal costing and absorption costing compared, 139
Marginal costing operating statement, 311
Marginal costing principles, 137
Mass production, 18
Material purchases budget, 264
Material requirements planning (MRP), 65
Materials, 26
Materials codes, 56
Materials requisition note, 53
Materials returned note, 53
Materials returns, 53
Materials transfer note, 53
Materials transfers, 53
Materials variances and opening and closing stock, 294
Maximum level, 59
Minimum level, 59
Mixed cost, 40
Modern business environment, 16

Negotiated style of budgeting, 276
Net realisable value, 73, 76
Non-financial information, 6
Non-linear variable costs, 39
Non-manufacturing overheads, 128
Non-production overheads, 266
Non-relevant variable costs, 346
Non-value-added, 369
Normal loss, 171

Objective, 7
Objectives of organisations, 7
Obsolete inventory, 57
Operating statement, 307
Operation card, 99
Operational control, 11, 372

Opportunity costs, 344
Optimum production plan, 352
Order cycling method of stores control, 63
Ordering costs, 58
Ordering materials, 50
Over and under absorption of overheads, 124
Over-absorption, 124
Overhead, 26, 108
Overhead absorption, 119, 121
Overhead absorption rate, 122, 128, **129**, 286, 298
Overhead allocation, 110
Overhead apportionment, 111, 112
Overhead recovery, 119
Overheads, 108
Overtime, 27
Overtime premium, 89

P/V (profit/volume) chart, 335
P/V ratio (profit/volume), 324
Padding the budget, 275
Pareto (80/20) distribution, 64
Participation, 274
Participatory budget, 274
Performance evaluation, 372
Performance standards, 285
Period costs, 32
Periodic stocktaking, 56
Periodic weighted average, 72
Perpetual inventory, 57
Personnel department, 96
Piecework, 90
Piecework scheme, 89
Piecework ticket, 99
Planning, 7, 258
Predetermined overhead absorption rate, 120
Presentation of information to management, 15
Pricing and ABC, 160
Primary activity, 370
Principal budget factor, 260
Process accounts, 170
Process costing, 170
Process costing and closing work in progress, 183
Process costing and losses, 171
Process costing and opening work in progress, 188
Process costing framework, 171
Process improvement, 368
Procurement costs, 58
Product life cycle, 17
Product mix decisions, 351
Production and productivity, 86
Production and related budgets, 261
Production budget, 261, 262

Production overhead, 28
Production planning department, 97
Production volume (P/V) ratio, 88
Productivity, 86
Productivity ratio, 88
Product-sustaining activities, 157
Profit centres, 34
Profit sharing scheme, 93
Profit/volume (P/V) chart, 335
Profit/volume (P/V) ratio, 324
Profits on contracts, 238
Profit-sharing schemes, 93
Progress payments, 238
Progress payments and retentions, 238
Prudence, 242
Purchase invoice, 52
Purchase order, 51
Purchase requisition, 51

Quality transactions, 152
Quotations, 51

R N Anthony, 10
Receiving materials, 50
Reciprocal (repeated distribution) method of apportionment, 115
Recording labour costs, 96
Rectification costs, 221
Relative sales value method, 204
Relevant cost of labour, 348
Relevant cost of materials, 346
Relevant costs, 344
Remuneration methods, 89
Remuneration systems, 89
Reorder level, 59
Reorder quantity, 60
Reports, 15
Responsibility accounting, 257
Responsibility centres, 33, 35
Retail method, 74
Retention monies, 238
Revenue centres, 35

Salaried labour, 100
Sales budget, 261
Sales variances, 306
Sales variances – significance, 307
Sales volume profit variance, 306
Scrap, 177
Secondary activity, 370
Selling and distribution overheads, 129, 130
Selling overhead, 29, 129
Selling price variance, 306

INDEX

Semi-fixed cost, 40
Semi-variable cost, 40
Separate absorption rates, 123
Service cost analysis, 229
Service cost analysis in service industry situations, 232
Service costing, 227
  unit cost measures, 228
Setting standards, 285
Share option scheme, 94
Shift premium, 89
Short-term tactical planning, 8
Shutdown problems, 356
Signing-in book, 97
Slow-moving inventories, 57
Split off point, 202
Standard cost, 74, 282
Standard cost card, 284
Standard costing, 272, 282, **284**
Standard hour, 262
Standard hour, 262
Standard hour of production, 86
Standard operation sheet, 287
Standard product specification, 287
Standard resource requirements, 287
Step cost, 38
Stockout costs, 58
Storage of raw materials, 54
Stores ledger accounts, 55
Stores requisition, 53
Strategic information, 12
Strategic planning, 11
Strategy, 7
Strategy and organisational structure, 8
Sunk cost, 345

Tactical information, 12
Target profit, 327
The changing business environment, 16
The inventory count (stocktake), 56
The reciprocal (algebraic) method of apportionment, 116
The wages control account, 102
Time work, 89
Timekeeping department, 97
Top down, 274
Total value-chain analysis, 17
Transactions analysis, 152
Transfers and returns of materials, 53
Two-bin system of stores control, 63

Unavoidable costs, 33
Uncontrollable costs, **33**, 345
Under-/over-absorbed overhead account, 127
Under-absorption, 124

Value-added, 94, 369
Value-added incentive schemes, 94
Variable cost, 31, **32**, **38**, 346
Variable overhead total variance, 296
Variable production overhead efficiency variance, 297
Variable production overhead expenditure variance, 296
Variable production overhead variances, 296
Variance, **292**, 292, 306
Variances, 292
Variances – interdependence, 305
Variances – significance, 304
Variances and operating statements, 307
Variances in a standard marginal costing system, 310

Wages department, 101
Weekly time sheets, 98
Weighted average cost, 75
Weighted average cost method, 193
Weighted average price, 70
WIP and FIFO, 188